The Art & Science of Java

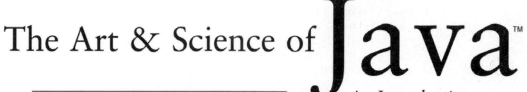

*An Introduction
to Computer Science*

ERIC S. ROBERTS
Stanford University

PEARSON

Addison
Wesley

Boston San Francisco New York
London Toronto Sydney Tokyo Singapore Madrid
Mexico City Munich Paris Cape Town Hong Kong Montreal

Publisher	Greg Tobin
Executive Editor	Michael Hirsch
Assistant Editor	Lindsey Triebel
Associate Managing Editor	Jeffrey Holcomb
Senior Production Supervisor	Marilyn Lloyd
Cover Designer	Joyce Cosentino Wells
Photo Researcher	Beth Anderson
Senior Marketing Manager	Michelle Brown
Marketing Assistant	Sarah Milmore
Senior Technical Art Specialist	Joe Vetere
Senior Manufacturing Buyer	Carol Melville
Developmental Editor	Lauren Rusk

Photo credits:
Cover image (lion at New York Public Library): © Rudy Sulgan/Corbis
Pages 23 and 249 (Grace Hopper and Herman Hollerith): Bettmanm/Corbis
Page 57 (George Boole): The Image Works
Page 95 (Dennis Ritchie): Bell Labs
Page 133 (David Parnas): Photo supplied by David Parnas
Page 177 (Kristen Nygaard and Ole-Johan Dahl): Universitat Klagenfurt
Page 221 (Jay Forrester): © The Mitre Corporation, used by permission
Page 295 (Ivan Sutherland): Photo supplied by Ivan Sutherland
Page 349 (Alan Kay): Audio Engineering Society, Inc.
Page 409 (Dan Bricklin and Bob Frankston): Stichting History of Computing
Page 461 (C. A. R. Hoare): University of Koblenz, Germany
Page 545 (Anita Borg): Anita Borg Institute for Women in Computing

Library of Congress Cataloging-in-Publication Data is available upon request.

Reproduced by Addison-Wesley from camera-ready copy supplied by the author.

ISBN-13: 978-0-311-48612-7

ISBN-10: 0-321-48612-9

1 2 3 4 5 6 7 8 9 10—CRS—10 09 08 07

Dedicated to the memory of Anita Borg (1949–2003)
for her tireless efforts to bring the excitement
of computing to a wider audience.

To the Student

Welcome! By picking up this book, you have taken a step into the world of computer science—a field of study that has grown from almost nothing half a century ago to one of the most vibrant and active disciplines of our time.

Over that time, the computer has opened up extraordinary possibilities in almost every area of human endeavor. Business leaders today are able to manage global enterprises on an unprecedented scale because computers enable them to transfer data anywhere in a fraction of a second. Scientists can now solve problems that were beyond their reach in the days before computers made the necessary calculations possible. The World Wide Web puts a vast amount of information at your fingertips and lies at the foundation of a vibrant industry that did not exist a decade ago. Filmmakers can use computer technology to create animated features that would have been unthinkable in Walt Disney's time. Modern computation has revolutionized many fields, enabling biologists to sequence the human genome, economists to model international markets, and literary scholars to assess whether an unattributed Elizabethan manuscript might have been penned by Shakespeare.

Computing is a profoundly empowering technology. The computing industry continues to grow, with more jobs available today than at the height of the Internet boom of the 1990s. But the advances we have seen up to now are small compared to what we will experience in this century. Those of you who are students today will soon inherit the responsibility of guiding that progress. No matter what field you choose, understanding how to use computing effectively will be of enormous value.

Like most skills that are worth knowing, learning how computers work and how to control their enormous power takes time. You will not understand it all at once. You must start somewhere. Twenty-five centuries ago, the Chinese philosopher Lao-tzu observed that the longest journey begins with a single step. This book can be your beginning.

For many of you, however, the first step can be the hardest to take. Many students find computers overwhelming and imagine that computer science is beyond their reach. Learning the basics of programming, however, does not require advanced mathematics or a detailed understanding of electronics. What matters in programming is whether you can progress from the statement of a problem to its solution. To do so, you must be able to think logically. You must have the necessary discipline to express your logic in a form that the computer can understand. Perhaps most importantly, you must be able to see the task through to its completion without getting discouraged by difficulties and setbacks. If you stick with the process, you will discover that reaching the solution is so exhilarating that it more than makes up for any frustrations you encounter along the way.

I wish you a pleasant journey along that road.

Eric Roberts
Stanford University
January 2007

To the Instructor

This text is intended for use in the first programming course in a typical college or university curriculum. It covers the material in a traditional CS1 course, as defined in the *Curriculum '78* report prepared by the Association for Computing Machinery (ACM). It also includes the full set of topics specified for the $CS101_O$ or $CS111_O$ courses in the computer science volume of the more recent *Computing Curriculum 2001* report.

The Art and Science of Java uses a similar approach to that of my 1995 textbook, *The Art and Science of C*. Each of these texts uses libraries to make programming less complex and consequently more accessible to the novice. In the C-based version, those libraries proved to be extremely successful with students, not only at Stanford, but at many other institutions as well. This book uses the ACM Java Libraries to achieve the same goals.

In the years since its initial release in 1995, the Java programming language has become increasingly important as an instructional language, to the point that it is now something of a standard in introductory computing courses. On the positive side, Java offers many advantages over earlier teaching languages, primarily by making it possible for students to write highly interactive programs that capture their interest and imagination. At the same time, Java is far more sophisticated than languages that have traditionally filled the role of teaching languages, such as BASIC and Pascal. The complexity that accompanies Java's sophistication can be a significant barrier to both teachers and students as they try to understand the structure of the language.

To address the problems that introductory instructors encountered using Java, in 2004 the ACM established the Java Task Force and gave it the following charge:

> To review the Java language, APIs, and tools from the perspective of introductory computing education and to develop a stable collection of pedagogical resources that will make it easier to teach Java to first-year computing students without having those students overwhelmed by its complexity.

Over the next two years, the Java Task Force developed a new set of libraries intended to support the use of Java at the introductory level. After releasing two preliminary drafts to obtain community feedback, the Java Task Force published its final report in the summer of 2006. The ACM Java Libraries described in that report are available on the following web site:

`http://jtf.acm.org/`

In addition to the ACM Java Libraries themselves, the web site contains a large collection of demo programs, a tutorial guide, an extensive discussion of the rationale behind the design of the various packages, and an executive summary that identifies the following as the greatest strengths of the libraries. The ACM Java Libraries provide

- *A simple object-oriented model for programs.* The **Program** class defined in the **acm.program** package offers an easy-to-use model for writing simple programs. In addition to hiding the static **main** method, the **Program** class and its standard subclasses provide a highly intuitive example of object-oriented class hierarchies.
- *A model for input and output that treats traditional console I/O and dialog I/O symmetrically.* The **acm.io** package defines the classes **IOConsole** and **IODialog** that share a common interface for all input/output operations. This design addresses Java's lack of a simple input mechanism in a way that emphasizes the value of interface-based design.
- *An extensive library of graphical objects.* The **acm.graphics** package implements a simple but extremely powerful model for creating graphical pictures based on the metaphor of a felt board in which students construct graphical objects of various types and place them on a canvas. This design emphasizes the use of objects and frees the student from having to respond explicitly to repaint requests.
- *A minimal set of new classes to support development of graphical user interfaces.* The **acm.gui** package includes a small set of classes to bring Java's extensive GUI-development resources within the reach of novice programmers.
- *Backward compatibility for applets.* Unlike most Java code today, programs developed using the ACM Java Libraries can typically be executed as applets even on older web browsers. This flexibility makes these libraries an ideal foundation for web-based teaching tools and lecture demonstrations.

Given the enormous number of classes and methods that are available in Java's own libraries, it is inevitable that a book of this sort will leave out some particular feature of Java. It is impossible to cover everything and still produce a book that is accessible to the average student. In terms of the choice of topics, this book seeks to offer a coherent presentation that teaches the fundamentals of computer science rather than to cover everything there is to know about Java. In many ways, the guiding principle for the choice of topics in this book comes from the following observation from Antoine de Saint-Exupéry in his 1942 memoire *Pilote de Guerre* (later quoted by Tony Hoare in his 1980 Turing Award lecture):

> Perfection is attained, not when there is nothing left to add, but when there is nothing left to take away.

While this book certainly makes no claims to perfection, it would probably have been better to leave more topics out than to put more topics in.

Although the book covers topics in an order that has proven successful here at Stanford, you may want to vary the order of presentation to suit your audience and the goals of your course. The following notes provide an overview of the chapters and indicate some of the more important dependencies.

Chapter 1 traces the history of computing and describes the programming process. The chapter requires no programming *per se* but provides the contextual background for the rest of the text.

I have designed Chapter 2 for students with little or no computing background. This chapter is conceptual in its approach and focuses on developing a holistic understanding of object-oriented programming rather than on the details of the Java language. When new students are faced with detailed rules of syntax and structure, they concentrate on learning the rules instead of the underlying concepts, which are vastly more important at this stage. If your students already know some programming, you can probably move quickly through this material.

Chapters 3, 4, and 5 offer relatively traditional introductions to expressions, statements, and methods so that students understand these basic concepts.

Chapters 6 and 7 then go on to introduce the fundamentals of objects and classes. Chapter 6 provides the high-level view, focusing on how to use objects and classes rather than on their underlying structure. Chapter 7 then turns to the low-level details involved of how objects are represented in memory. Although Chapter 7 is not absolutely required, students who can picture the internal structure of an object are much more likely to understand the essential concept of a reference.

The next three chapters introduce particular classes from either Java's standard libraries or the ACM packages. Chapter 8 covers the `String` class, which is presumably an important topic in any introductory course. Chapter 9 describes the `acm.graphics` package in detail, which makes it possible for students to write far more exciting programs. Parts of the `acm.graphics` package are included in earlier chapters, and it is certainly possible to cover only some of the topics in Chapter 9. Chapter 10 offers a similar overview of event-driven programming. The first several sections in Chapter 10 focus on mouse and keyboard events; the remaining sections provide an introduction to graphical user interfaces (GUIs) and the standard interactor classes from `javax.swing`. This second part of the chapter is valuable if you want to have students design GUI-based programs, but it is not necessary to understand subsequent chapters.

Chapters 11 and 12 address the idea of arrays, but do so from different perspectives. Chapter 11 introduces both the built-in array type and the `ArrayList` utility class from the `java.util` package. Both of these topics seem essential to any Java-based introductory course. Chapter 12 focuses on algorithms for searching and sorting arrays. The chapter also includes a brief discussion of computational complexity that will help students understand the importance of algorithmic design.

Chapter 13 describes the Java Collections Framework, which is perhaps more often presented in a second programming course. However, because Java takes care of so many of the underlying details, it is actually quite reasonable to teach introductory students how to *use* these classes, even if they can't understand their implementation. The only essential class from the Java Collections Framework is `ArrayList`, which has already appeared in Chapter 11.

Chapter 14 includes four important topics that sometimes appear in a first programming course: recursion, concurrency, networking, and programming patterns. At Stanford, which is on the quarter system, we teach these topics in the second course. If you decide to teach recursion in the first course, I strongly recommend that you do so early enough to allow students time to assimilate the material. One possibility is to discuss recursive functions immediately after Chapter 5 and recursive algorithms at the end of Chapter 12.

Supplemental Resources

For students

The following items are available to all readers of this book at the Addison-Wesley web site (**http://www.aw.com/cssupport/**):

- Source code files for each example program in the book
- Full-color PDF versions of sample runs
- Answers to review questions

For instructors

The following items are available to qualified instructors from Addison-Wesley's Instructor Resource Center (**http://www.aw.com/irc/**):

- Source code files for each example program in the book
- Full-color PDF versions of sample runs
- Answers to review questions
- Solutions to programming exercises
- Applet-based lecture slides that include animations of the program examples

For adopters of the ACM Java Libraries

The Association for Computing Machinery maintains an extensive web site on the ACM Java Libraries developed by the Java Task Force (**http://jtf.acm.org/**). That site includes the following resources:

- An executive summary outlining the purpose of the ACM Java Libraries
- Downloadable copies of ACM libraries in both source and compiled form
- An extensive demo gallery including source code for the examples
- An introductory tutorial to using the ACM libraries
- A comprehensive discussion of the rationale behind the design

Acknowledgments

Writing a textbook is never the work of a single individual. In putting this book together, I have been extremely fortunate to have the help of many talented and dedicated people. I particularly want to thank my colleagues on the ACM Java Task Force—Kim Bruce, James H. Cross II, Robb Cutler, Scott Grissom, Karl Klee, Susan Rodger, Fran Trees, Ian Utting, and Frank Yellin—for their hard work on the project, as well as the National Science Foundation, the ACM Education Board, and the SIGCSE Special Projects Fund for their financial support. I also want to thank everyone who responded to the Java Task Force's call for proposals in 2004: Alyce Brady, Kim Bruce, Pam Cutter, Ken Lambert, Robert McCartney, Dave Musicant, Martin Osborne, Nick Parlante, Viera Proulx, Richard Rasala, Juris Reinfelds, Dean Sanders, Kathryn Sanders, Ruth Ungar, and Andries van Dam. As the design document for the Java Task Force makes clear, these suggestions were of enormous value even if the task force did not adopt the designs in their original form.

Here at Stanford, thanks are due to many people. In many ways, the people who have shaped the book as much as anyone have been my students, who have had to learn the material from a series of preliminary drafts over the last year and a half. For one thing, the students in Stanford's introductory course have certainly risen to the challenge of using a new approach to the material and have demonstrated beyond my expectations how much students can accomplish using the ACM Java Libraries. For another, my students have proven to be vigilant readers of the various drafts, never hesitating to point out opportunities for improvement. I also want to thank the entire team of undergraduate teaching assistants, who have had to explain to students all the concepts I left out of the earlier versions.

I want to express my gratitude to my editor, Michael Hirsch, and the other members of the team at Addison-Wesley for their support on this book as well as its predecessor.

As always, the greatest thanks are due to my wife Lauren Rusk, who has again worked her magic as my developmental editor. Lauren's expertise has added considerable clarity and polish to the text. As I said in the preface to my 1995 book, without her, nothing would ever come out as well as it should.

Contents

CHAPTER 1

Introduction

[The Analytical Engine offers] a new, a vast, and a powerful language . . . for the purposes of mankind.

—Augusta Ada Byron, Lady Lovelace, 1843

Augusta Ada Byron, Lady Lovelace (1815–1852)

Augusta Ada Byron, the daughter of English poet Lord Byron, was encouraged to pursue her interests in science and mathematics at a time when few women were allowed to study those subjects. At the age of 17, Ada met Charles Babbage, a prominent English scientist who devoted his life to designing machines for carrying out mathematical computations—machines whose construction he was never able to complete. Ada was firmly convinced of the potential of Babbage's Analytical Engine and wrote extensive notes on its design, along with several complex mathematical programs that have led many people to characterize her as the first programmer. In 1980, the U.S. Department of Defense named the programming language Ada in her honor.

Given our vantage point at the beginning of the 21st century, it is hard to believe that computers did not even exist in 1940. They are everywhere today, and it is popular wisdom, at least among headline writers, to say that we live in the computer age.

1.1 A brief history of computing

In a certain sense, computing has been around since ancient times. Much of early mathematics was devoted to solving computational problems of practical importance, such as monitoring the number of animals in a herd, calculating the area of a plot of land, or recording a commercial transaction. These activities required people to develop new computational techniques and, in some cases, to invent machines to help in the process of calculation. For example, the abacus, a simple counting device consisting of beads that slide along rods, has been used in Asia for thousands of years, possibly since 2000 BCE.

Throughout most of its history, computing has progressed relatively slowly. In 1623, a German scientist named Wilhelm Schickard invented the first known mechanical calculator, capable of performing simple arithmetical computations automatically. Although Schickard's device was lost to history through the ravages of the Thirty Years' War (1618–1648), the French philosopher Blaise Pascal used similar techniques to construct a mechanical adding machine in the 1640s, a copy of which remains on display in the Conservatoire des Arts et Métiers in Paris. In 1673, the German mathematician Gottfried Leibniz developed a considerably more sophisticated device, capable of multiplication and division as well as addition and subtraction. All these devices were purely mechanical and contained no engines or other source of power. The operator entered numbers by setting metal wheels to a particular position; the act of turning those wheels set other parts of the machine in motion and changed the output display.

During the Industrial Revolution, the rapid growth in technology made it possible to consider new approaches to mechanical computation. The steam engine already provided the power needed to run factories and railroads. In that context, it was reasonable to ask whether one could use steam engines to drive more sophisticated computing machines, machines that would be capable of carrying out significant calculations under their own power. Before progress could be made, however, someone had to ask that question and set out to find an answer. The necessary spark of insight came from a British mathematician named Charles Babbage, who is one of the most interesting figures in the history of computing.

During his lifetime, Babbage designed two different computing machines, which he called the Difference Engine and the Analytical Engine; each represented a considerable advance over the calculating machines available at the time. The tragedy of his life is that he was unable to complete either of these projects. The Difference Engine, which he designed to produce tables of mathematical functions, was eventually built by a Swedish inventor in 1854—30 years after its original design. The Analytical Engine, Babbage's lifelong dream, remained incomplete when Babbage died in 1871. Even so, its design contained many of the essential features found in modern computers. Most importantly, Babbage conceived of the Analytical Engine as a general-purpose machine, capable of performing many different functions depending upon how it was *programmed*. In Babbage's design, the operation of the Analytical Engine was controlled by a pattern of holes punched on a card that the machine could read. By changing the pattern of holes, one could change the behavior of the machine so that it performed a different set of calculations.

Much of what we know of Babbage's work comes from the writings of Augusta Ada Byron, the daughter of the poet Lord Byron and his wife Annabella. More than most of her contemporaries, Ada appreciated the potential of the Analytical Engine and became its champion. She designed several sophisticated programs for the machine, thereby becoming the first programmer. In the 1970s, the U.S. Department of Defense named its own programming language Ada in honor of her contribution.

Some aspects of Babbage's design did influence the later history of computation, such as the use of punched cards to control a process—an idea that had first been introduced by the French inventor Joseph Marie Jacquard as part of a device—which soon became known as the Jacquard loom—to automate the process of weaving fabric. In 1890, Herman Hollerith used punched cards to automate data tabulation for the U.S. Census. To market this technology, Hollerith went on to found a company that later became the International Business Machines (IBM) corporation, which dominated the computer industry for most of the twentieth century.

Babbage's vision of a programmable computer did not become reality until the 1940s, when the advent of electronics made it possible to move beyond the mechanical devices that had dominated computing up to that time. A prototype of the first electronic computer was assembled in late 1939 by John Atanasoff and his student Clifford Barry at Iowa State College. They completed a full-scale implementation containing 300 vacuum tubes in May 1942. The computer was capable of solving small systems of linear equations. With some design modifications, the Atanasoff-Barry computer could have performed more intricate calculations, but work on the project was interrupted by World War II.

The first large-scale electronic computer was the ENIAC, an acronym for *Electronic Numerical Integrator and Computer*. Completed in 1946 under the direction of J. Presper Eckert and John Mauchly at the Moore School of the University of Pennsylvania, the ENIAC contained more than 18,000 vacuum tubes and occupied a 30- by 50-foot room. The ENIAC was programmed by plugging wires into a pegboard-like device called a **patch panel**. By connecting different sockets on the patch panel with wires, the operators could control ENIAC's behavior. This type of programming required an intimate knowledge of the internal workings of the machine and proved to be much more difficult than the inventors of the ENIAC had imagined.

Perhaps the greatest breakthrough in modern computing occurred in 1946, when John von Neumann at the Institute for Advanced Study in Princeton proposed that programs and data could be represented in a similar way and stored in the same internal memory. This concept, which simplifies the programming process enormously, is the basis of almost all modern computers. Because of this aspect of their design, modern computers are said to use **von Neumann architecture.**

Since the completion of ENIAC and the development of von Neumann's stored-programming concept, computing has evolved at a furious pace. New systems and concepts have been introduced in such rapid succession that it would be pointless to list them all. Most historians divide the development of modern computers into the following four generations, based on the underlying technology.

- *First generation.* The first generation of electronic computers used vacuum tubes as the basis for their internal circuitry. This period of computing begins with the Atanasoff-Barry prototype in 1939.
- *Second generation.* The invention of the transistor in 1947 ushered in a new generation of computers. Transistors are semiconducting devices that perform the same functions as vacuum tubes but are much smaller and require a fraction of the electrical power. The first computer to use transistors was the IBM 7090, introduced in 1958.
- *Third generation.* Even though transistors are tiny in comparison to vacuum tubes, a computer containing 100,000 or 1,000,000 individual transistors requires a large amount of space. The third generation of computing was enabled by the development in 1959 of the **integrated circuit** or **chip,** a small wafer of silicon that has been photographically imprinted to contain a large number of transistors connected together. The first computer to use integrated circuits in its construction was the IBM 360, which appeared in 1964.
- *Fourth generation.* The fourth generation of computing began in 1975, when the technology for building integrated circuits made it possible to put the entire processing unit of a computer on a single chip of silicon. The fabrication technology is called **large-scale integration.** Computer processors that consist of a single chip are called **microprocessors** and are used in most computers today.

The early machines of the first and second generations are historically important as the antecedents of modern computers, but they would hardly be useful today. They were the dinosaurs of computer science: gigantic, lumbering beasts with small mental capacities, soon to become extinct. The late Robert Noyce, one of the inventors of the integrated circuit and founder of Intel Corporation, observed that, compared to the ENIAC, the typical modern computer chip "is twenty times faster, has a larger memory, is thousands of times more reliable, consumes the power of a light bulb rather than that of a locomotive, occupies 1/30,000 the volume, and costs 1/10,000 as much." Computers have certainly come of age.

1.2 What is computer science?

Growing up in the modern world has probably given you some idea of what a computer is. This text, however, is less concerned with computers as physical devices than with computer science. At first glance, the words *computer* and *science* seem an incongruous pair. In its classical usage, *science* refers to the study of natural phenomena; when people talk about *biological science* or *physical science*, we understand and feel comfortable with that usage. Computer science doesn't seem the same sort of thing. The fact that computers are human-made artifacts makes us reticent to classify the study of computers as a science. After all, modern technology has also produced cars, but we don't talk about "car science." Instead, we refer to "automotive engineering" or "automobile technology." Why should computers be any different?

To answer this question, it is important to recognize that the computer itself is only part of the story. The physical machine that you can buy today at your local computer store is an example of computer **hardware.** It is tangible. You can pick it up, take it home, and put it on your desk. If need be, you could use it as a doorstop, albeit a rather expensive one. But if there were nothing there besides the hardware, if a machine came to you exactly as it rolled off the assembly line, serving as a doorstop would be one of the few jobs it could do. A modern computer is a general-purpose machine, with the potential to perform a wide variety of tasks. To fulfill that potential, however, the computer must be **programmed.** The act of programming a computer consists of providing it with a set of instructions—a **program**—that specifies all the steps necessary to solve the problem to which it is assigned. These programs are generically known as **software,** and it is the software, together with the hardware, that makes computation possible.

In contrast to hardware, software is an abstract, intangible entity. It is a sequence of simple steps and operations, stated in a precise language that the hardware can interpret. When we talk about computer science, we are concerned primarily with the domain of computer software and, more importantly, with the even more abstract domain of problem solving. Problem solving turns out to be a highly challenging activity that requires creativity, skill, and discipline. For the most part, computer science is best thought of as the science of problem solving in which the solutions happen to involve a computer.

This is not to say that the computer itself is unimportant. Before computers, people could solve only relatively simple computational problems. Over the last 50 years, the existence of computers has made it possible to solve increasingly difficult and sophisticated problems in a timely and cost-effective way. Moreover, as the underlying technology improves, it becomes possible to solve ever more complex problems. As the problems to solve become more complex, however, so does the task of finding effective solution strategies. The science of problem solving has thus been forced to advance along with the technology of computing.

1.3 A brief tour of computer hardware

The flexibility that computers offer to solve complex problems comes from the fact that computers are controlled by software that can be redesigned for each individual application. Given that software embodies the problem-solving strategies that are the essence of computer science, this text focuses almost exclusively on the software side of computation. Even so, it is important to spend some time in this chapter talking about the structure of computer hardware at a very general level of detail. The reason is simple: programming is a learn-by-doing discipline. You will not become a programmer just by reading this book, even if you solve all the exercises on paper. Learning to program is hands-on work that requires you to work with a computer.

In order to use a computer, you need to become acquainted with its hardware. You have to know how to turn the computer on, how to use the keyboard to type in a program, and how to execute that program once you've written it. Unfortunately, the steps you must follow in order to perform these operations differ significantly from one computer system to another. As someone who is writing a general textbook, I cannot tell you how your own particular system works and must instead concentrate on general principles that are common to any computer you might be using. As you read this section, you should look at the computer you have and see how the general discussion applies to that machine.

Most computer systems today consist of the components shown in Figure 1-1. Each of the components in the diagram is connected by a communication channel called a **bus,** which allows data to flow between the separate units. The individual components are described in the sections that follow.

The CPU

The **central processing unit** or **CPU** is the "brain" of the computer. It performs the actual computation and coordinates the activity of the entire computer. The actions of the CPU are determined by a program consisting of a sequence of coded instructions stored in the memory system. One instruction, for example, might direct the computer to add a pair of numbers. Another might make a character appear on the computer screen. By executing the appropriate sequence of simple instructions, the CPU can perform complex tasks.

In a modern computer, the CPU consists of an **integrated circuit**—a tiny chip of silicon that has been imprinted with millions of microscopic transistors connected to form larger circuits capable of carrying out simple arithmetic and logical operations.

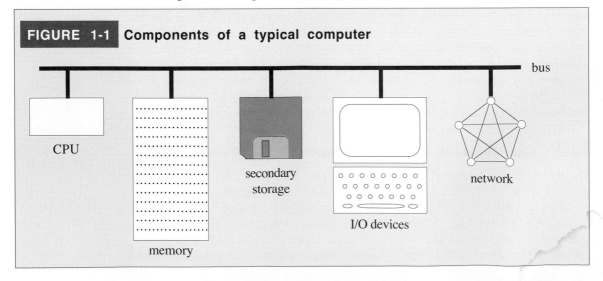

FIGURE 1-1 **Components of a typical computer**

Memory

When a computer executes a program, it must have some way to store both the program itself and the data involved in the computation. In general, any piece of computer hardware capable of storing and retrieving information is a storage device. The storage devices that are used while a program is actively running constitute its **primary storage,** which is more often called its **memory.** Since John von Neumann first suggested the idea in 1946, computers have used the same memory to store both the individual instructions that compose the program and the data used during computation.

Memory systems are engineered to be very efficient so that they can provide the CPU with extremely fast access to their contents. In today's computers, memory is usually built out of a special integrated-circuit chip called a **RAM,** which stands for *random-access memory*. Random-access memory allows the program to use the contents of any memory cell at any time.

Secondary storage

Although computers usually keep active data in memory whenever a program is running, most primary storage devices have the disadvantage that they function only when the computer is turned on. When you turn off your computer, any information that was stored in primary memory is lost. To store permanent data, you need to use a storage device that does not require electrical power to maintain its information. Such devices constitute **secondary storage.**

There are many kinds of secondary storage devices used in computers today. Almost any machine you might buy contains a hard disk capable of storing a considerable amount of information that persists even if you turn off the computer. When you compose and edit a program, you typically do so on the hard disk. If you want to move the program to another computer or make a backup copy for safekeeping, you can copy the program to a more portable medium, which might be a floppy disk, a writable CD, or a memory stick.

Input/output devices

For the computer to be useful, it must have some way to communicate with users in the outside world. Computer input usually consists of characters typed on a keyboard. Output from the computer typically appears on the computer screen or on a printer. Collectively, hardware devices that perform input and output operations are called **I/O devices.**

I/O devices vary significantly from one machine to another. Beyond the standard alphabetic keys, computer keyboards have different arrangements and even use different names for some of the important keys. For example, the key used to indicate the end of a line is labeled Return on some keyboards and Enter on others. On some computer systems, you make changes to a program by using special **function keys** on the top or side of the keyboard that provide simple editing operations. On other systems, you can accomplish the same task by using a hand-held pointing device called a **mouse** to select program text that you wish to change.

In either case, the computer keeps track of the current typing position, which is usually indicated on the screen by a flashing line or rectangle called the **cursor**.

Network

The final component in Figure 1-1 is the star-shaped symbol labeled **network.** This portion of the diagram indicates a connection to the constellation of other computers that are connected together as part of the **Internet,** which is the vast collection of computers throughout the world that are connected together by communication lines that allow them to share data and programs. In many ways, the network is simply part of the I/O structure, but it is useful to keep in mind that input and output operations for modern computers are not limited to the local machine but extend out into that much larger universe enabled by the Internet. Considering the network is particularly important when learning about Java because Java's success as a programming language was closely linked to the rise of networking, as discussed later in this chapter.

1.4 Algorithms

Now that you have a sense of the structure of a computer system, let's turn to computer science. Because computer science is the discipline of solving problems with the assistance of a computer, you need to understand a concept that is fundamental to both computer science and the abstract discipline of problem solving—the concept of an **algorithm.** The word *algorithm* comes to us from the name of the ninth-century Persian mathematician Abu Ja'far Mohammed ibn Mûsâ al-Khowârizmî, who wrote a treatise on mathematics entitled *Kitab al jabr w'al-muqabala,* whose title gave rise to the English word *algebra*. Informally, you can think of an algorithm as a strategy for solving a problem. To appreciate how computer scientists use the term, however, it is necessary to formalize that intuitive understanding and tighten up the definition.

To be considered an algorithm, a solution technique must fulfill three basic requirements. First of all, an algorithm must be presented in an unambiguous form that makes it clear to the reader precisely what steps are involved. Second, the steps within an algorithm must be effective, in the sense that it is possible to carry them out in practice. For example, a technique that includes the operation "multiply r by the exact value of π" is not effective, since it is not possible to compute the exact value of π. Third, an algorithm must not run on forever but must deliver its answer in a finite amount of time. In summary, an algorithm must be

1. *Clearly and unambiguously defined.*
2. *Effective,* in the sense that its steps are executable.
3. *Finite,* in the sense that it terminates after a bounded number of steps.

These properties will turn out to be especially important later on when you begin to work with complex algorithms. For the moment, it is sufficient to think of algorithms as abstract solution strategies—strategies that will eventually become the core of the programs you write.

As you will soon discover, algorithms—like the problems they are intended to solve—vary significantly in complexity. Some problems are so simple that an appropriate algorithm springs immediately to mind, and you can write the programs to solve such problems without too much trouble. As the problems become more complex, however, the algorithms needed to solve them begin to require more thought. In most cases, several different algorithms can be used to solve a particular problem, and you need to consider a variety of potential solution techniques before writing the final program.

1.5 Stages in the programming process

Solving a problem by computer consists of two conceptually distinct steps. First, you need to develop an algorithm, or choose an existing one, that solves the problem. This part of the process is called **algorithmic design.** The second step is to express that algorithm as a computer program in a programming language. This process is called **coding.**

As you begin to learn about programming, the process of coding—translating your algorithm into a functioning program—will seem to be the more difficult phase of the process. Since as a new programmer you will begin with simple problems that tend to have simple solutions, the algorithmic design phase will not seem particularly challenging. The coding, however, may at times seem difficult and arbitrary because the language and its rules are unfamiliar. I hope it is reassuring to say that coding will rapidly become easier as you learn more about the programming process. At the same time, algorithmic design will get harder as the problems you are asked to solve increase in complexity.

When new algorithms are introduced in this text, they will usually be expressed initially in English. Although it is often less precise than one would like, English is a reasonable language in which to express solution strategies as long as the communication is entirely between people who speak English. Obviously, if you wanted to present your algorithm to someone who spoke only Russian, English would no longer be an appropriate choice. English is likewise an inappropriate choice for presenting an algorithm to a computer. Although computer scientists have been working on this problem for decades, getting a computer to understand English or Russian or any other human language continues to lie beyond the boundaries of current technology. To enable a computer to interpret your algorithm, you need to translate it into a programming language. There are many programming languages, including Fortran, BASIC, Pascal, Lisp, C, C++, and a host of others. In this text, you will learn how to use the programming language Java—a language developed by Sun Microsystems in 1995 that has since become something of a standard both for industry and for computer science courses.

Creating and editing programs

Before you can run a program on most computer systems, it is necessary to enter the text of the program and store it in a **file,** which is the generic name for any collection of information stored in the computer's secondary storage. Every file must have a name, which is usually divided into two parts separated by a period, as in **MyProgram.java**. When you create a file, you decide on the **root name,** which is the part of the name preceding the period, to tell yourself what the file contains. The portion of the filename following the period indicates what the file is used for and is called the **extension.** Certain extensions have preassigned meanings. For example, the extension **.java** indicates a program file written in the Java language. A file containing program text is called a **source file.**

The general process of entering or changing the contents of a file is called **editing** that file. Because the editing process differs significantly for different computer systems, it is not possible to describe the process in a way that applies to every type of hardware. When you work on a particular computer system, you will need to learn how to create new files and edit existing ones. You can find this information in the manual or online documentation for the programming environment you are using.

The compilation process

Once you have created your source file, the next step in the process is to translate your program into a form the computer can understand. Languages like Java, C, and C++ are examples of what computer scientists call **higher-level languages.** Such languages are designed to make it easier for human programmers to express algorithms without having to understand in detail exactly how the underlying hardware will execute those algorithms. Higher-level languages are also typically independent of the particular characteristics that differentiate individual machine architectures. Internally, however, each computer system understands a low-level language that is specific to that type of hardware, which is called its **machine language.** For example, the Apple Macintosh and a Windows-based computer use different underlying machine languages, even though both of them can execute programs written in a higher-level language.

To make it possible for a program written in a higher-level language to run on different computer systems, there are two basic strategies. The classical approach is to use a program called a **compiler** to translate the programs that you write into the low-level machine language appropriate to the computer on which the program will run. With this strategy, computers based on different hardware architectures require different translators. For example, if you are writing C programs for a Macintosh, you need to run a compiler that translates C into the machine language for the Macintosh. If you want to run the same program on a Windows-based computer, you need to use a different compiler because the underlying hardware uses a different machine language.

The second approach is to translate the program into an **intermediate language** that is independent of the underlying architecture. For any given machine architecture, these intermediate-language programs run are executed by an **interpreter** that implements the intermediate language on that machine. For example, if the intermediate-language program contains an instruction to add two numbers, the interpreter accomplishes that task by executing whatever instructions are required to perform that addition on the underlying hardware. In contrast to a compiler, however, an interpreter does not actually produce a machine-language instruction to perform the specific addition operation specified by the original program. What happens instead is that the interpreter simulates the addition operation by executing instructions that have the same effect.

Modern Java systems use a hybrid strategy that combines the functions of a compiler and an interpreter. In the initial compilation phase, Java translates your programs into a common intermediate language that is independent of the underlying hardware. That intermediate language is then interpreted by a program called the **Java Virtual Machine** (or JVM for short), which executes the intermediate language for that machine. The program that runs the Java Virtual Machine often compiles pieces of the intermediate code into the underlying machine language. As a result, Java can often achieve a level of efficiency that is unattainable with traditional interpreters.

In classical compiler-based systems, the compiler translates the source file you've written into a second file called an **object file** that contains the corresponding instructions for that computer system. This object file is then combined together with other object files, typically including predefined object files called **libraries** that contain the machine-language instructions for various common operations. Together, these combined files produce a single **executable file** that can be run on the system. The process of combining all the individual object files into an executable file is called **linking.** Figure 1-2 illustrates the entire compilation process.

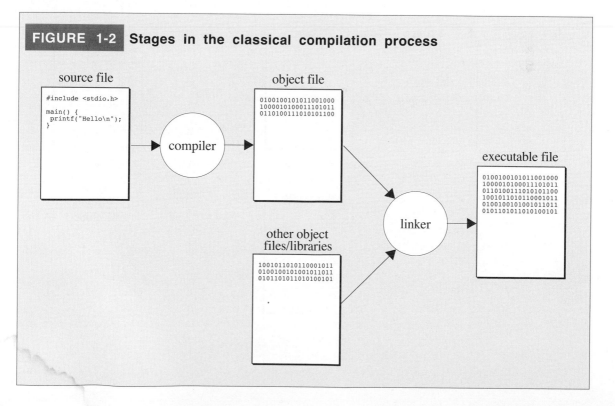

FIGURE 1-2 **Stages in the classical compilation process**

In Java, the process is slightly more elaborate. As noted earlier in this section, Java produces intermediate code that it stores in files called **class files.** Those class files are then combined with other class files and libraries to produce a complete version of the intermediate program with everything it needs linked together. The usual format for that version of the program is a compressed collection of individual files called a **JAR archive.** That archive file is then interpreted by the Java Virtual Machine in such a way that the output appears on your computer. This process is illustrated in Figure 1-3.

Programming errors and debugging

Besides translation, compilers perform another important function. Like human languages, programming languages have their own vocabulary and their own **syntax,** which is the set of grammatical rules that governs how you can combine the various parts of the language. These syntactic rules make it possible to determine that certain statements are properly constructed and that others are not. In English, for example, it is not correct to say "we goes" because the subject and verb do not agree in number. Programming languages each have their own syntax, which determines how the elements of a program can be put together in that language.

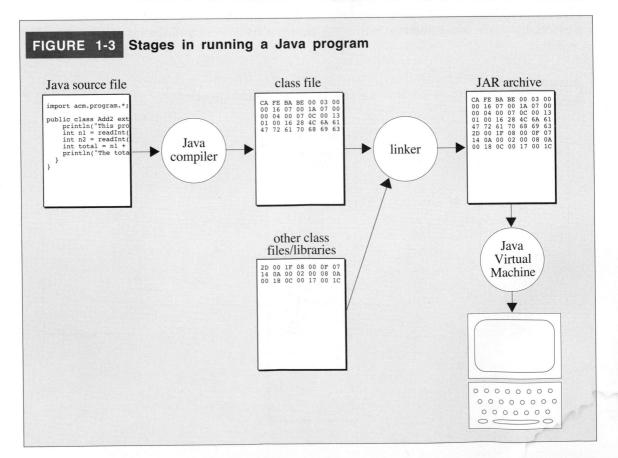

FIGURE 1-3 **Stages in running a Java program**

When you compile a program, the compiler first checks to see whether your program is syntactically correct. If you have violated the syntactic rules, the compiler displays an error message. Errors that result from breaking these rules are called **syntax errors.** Whenever you get a message from the compiler indicating a syntax error, you must go back and edit the program to correct it.

Although syntax errors can be frustrating, particularly for new programmers, they will not be your biggest source of frustration. More often than not, if a program you write fails to operate correctly, the problem is not syntactic but logical. In many cases, your perfectly legal program somehow comes up with incorrect answers or fails to produce answers at all. You look at the program and discover that you have made a mistake in the logic of the program—the type of mistake programmers call a **bug.** The process of finding and correcting such mistakes, called **debugging,** is an important part of programming.

Bugs can be extremely insidious and frustrating. You will be absolutely certain that your algorithm is correct, and then discover that it fails to handle some case you had previously overlooked. Or perhaps you will recognize that some section of your program needs further work, only to forget that fact later on. Or you might make a mistake that seems so silly you cannot believe anyone could possibly have blundered so badly.

Relax. You're in excellent company. Even the best programmers have shared this experience. The truth is that all programmers make logic errors. In particular, *you* will make logic errors. Algorithms are tricky things, and you will often discover that you haven't really gotten it right.

In many respects, discovering your own fallibility is an important rite of passage as a programmer. Describing his experiences of the early 1960s, the pioneering computer scientist Maurice Wilkes wrote:

> Somehow, at the Moore School and afterwards, one had always assumed there would be no particular difficulty in getting programs right. I can remember the exact instant in time at which it dawned on me that a great part of my future life would be spent in finding mistakes in my own programs.

What differentiates good programmers from the rest of their colleagues is not that they manage to avoid bugs altogether but that they take pains to minimize the number of bugs that persist in the finished code. When you design an algorithm and translate it into a syntactically legal program, it is critical to understand that your job is not finished. Almost certainly, your program has a bug in it somewhere. Your job as a programmer is to find that bug and fix it. Once that is done, you should find the next bug and fix that. Always be skeptical of your own programs and test them as thoroughly as you can.

Software maintenance

One of the more surprising aspects of software development is that programs require maintenance. In fact, studies of software development indicate that, for most programs, paying programmers to maintain the software after it has been released constitutes between 80 and 90 percent of the total cost. In the context of software, however, it is a little hard to imagine precisely what maintenance means. At first hearing, the idea sounds rather bizarre. If you think in terms of a car or a bridge, maintenance occurs when something has broken—some of the metal has rusted away, a piece of some mechanical linkage has worn out from overuse, or something has gotten smashed up in an accident. None of these situations apply to software. The code itself doesn't rust. Using the same program over and over again does not in any way diminish its functioning. Accidental misuse can certainly have dangerous consequences but does not usually damage the program itself; even if it does, the program can often be restored from a backup copy. What does maintenance mean in such an environment?

Software requires maintenance for two principal reasons. First, even after considerable testing and, in some cases, years of field use, bugs can still survive in the original code. Then, when some unanticipated situation arises, the bug, previously dormant, causes the program to fail. Thus, debugging is an essential part of program maintenance. It is not, however, the most important part. Far more consequential, especially in terms of how much it contributes to the overall cost of program maintenance, is what might be called **feature enhancement.** Programs are written to be used; they perform, usually faster and less expensively than other methods, a task that the customer needs done. At the same time, the programs probably don't do everything the customer wants. After working with a program for a while, the customer decides it would be wonderful if the program also did something else, or did something differently, or presented its data in a more useful way, or ran a little faster, or had an expanded capacity, or just had a few more simple but attractive features (often called **bells and whistles** in the trade). Since software is extremely flexible, suppliers have the option of responding to such requests. In either case—whether one wants to repair a bug or add a feature—someone has to go in, look at the program, figure out what's going on, make the necessary changes, verify that those changes work, and then release a new version. This process is difficult, time-consuming, expensive, and prone to error.

Part of the reason program maintenance is so difficult is that most programmers do not write their programs for the long haul. To them it seems sufficient to get the program working and then move on to something else. The discipline of writing programs so that they can be understood and maintained by others is called **software engineering**. In this text, you are encouraged to write programs that demonstrate good engineering style.

As you write your programs, try to imagine how someone else might feel if called upon to look at them two years later. Would your program make sense? Would the program itself indicate to the new reader what you were trying to do? Would it be easy to change? Or would it seem obscure and convoluted? If you put yourself in the place of the future maintainer (and as a new programmer in most companies, you will probably be given that role), it will help you to appreciate why good style is critical.

Many novice programmers are disturbed to learn that there is no precise set of rules you can follow to ensure good programming style. Good software engineering is not a cookbook sort of process. Instead it is a skill blended with more than a little bit of artistry. Practice is critical. One learns to write good programs by writing them, and by reading others, much as one learns to be a novelist. Good programming requires discipline—the discipline not to cut corners or to forget, in the rush to complete a project, about that future maintainer. And good programming style requires developing an aesthetic sense—a sense of what it means for a program to be readable and well presented.

1.6 Java and the object-oriented paradigm

As noted earlier in this chapter, this text uses the programming language Java to illustrate the more general concepts of programming and computer science. But why Java? The answer lies primarily in the way that Java encourages programmers to think about the programming process.

Over the last decade, computer science and programming have gone through something of a revolution. Like most revolutions—whether political upheavals or the conceptual restructurings that Thomas Kuhn describes in his 1962 book *The Structure of Scientific Revolutions*—this change has been driven by the emergence of an idea that challenges an existing theoretical framework, or **paradigm.** Initially, the two viewpoints compete. For a while, the old order maintains its dominance. Over time, however, the strength and popularity of the new idea grows, until it begins to displace the older idea in what Kuhn calls a **paradigm shift.** In the programming world today, the old order is represented by the **procedural paradigm,** in which programs consist of a collection of procedures and functions that operate on data. The challenger is the **object-oriented paradigm,** in which programs are viewed instead as a collection of "objects," for which the data and the associated operations are encapsulated into integrated units. Most traditional languages, including Fortran, Pascal, and C, embody the procedural paradigm. The best-known representatives of the object-oriented paradigm are Smalltalk, C++, and Java.

Although object-oriented languages are gaining popularity at the expense of procedural ones, it would be a mistake to regard the object-oriented and procedural paradigms as mutually exclusive. Programming paradigms are not so much competitive as they are complementary. The object-oriented and the procedural paradigm—along with other important paradigms such as the functional programming style embodied in LISP and Scheme—all have important applications in practice. Even within the context of a single application, you are likely to find a use for more than one approach. As a programmer, you must master many different paradigms, so that you can use the conceptual model that is most appropriate to the task at hand. In this book, you will get a solid introduction to the object-oriented paradigm but will learn a few things about the procedural paradigm as well.

The history of object-oriented programming

The idea of object-oriented programming is not really all that new. The first object-oriented language was SIMULA, a language for coding simulations, designed in the early 1960s by the Scandinavian computer scientists Ole-Johan Dahl, Björn

Myhrhaug, and Kristen Nygaard. With a design that was far ahead of its time, SIMULA anticipated many of the concepts that later became commonplace in programming, including the concept of abstract data types and much of the modern object-oriented paradigm. In fact, most of the terminology used to describe object-oriented systems comes from the original reports on the initial version of SIMULA and its successor, SIMULA 67.

For many years, however, SIMULA mostly just sat on the shelf. Few people paid much attention to it, and the only place you were likely to hear about it would be in a course on programming language design. The first object-oriented language to gain any significant level of recognition within the computing profession was Smalltalk, which was developed at the Xerox Palo Alto Research Center (more commonly known as Xerox PARC) in the late 1970s. The purpose of Smalltalk, which is described in the book *Smalltalk-80: The Language and Its Implementation* by Adele Goldberg and David Robson, was to make programming accessible to a wider audience. As such, Smalltalk was part of a larger effort at Xerox PARC that gave rise to much of the modern user-interface technology that is now standard on personal computers.

Despite many attractive features and a highly interactive user environment that simplifies the programming process, Smalltalk never achieved much commercial success. The profession as a whole took an interest in object-oriented programming only when the central ideas were incorporated into variants of the programming language C, which had become an industry standard. Although there were several parallel efforts to design an object-oriented language based on C, the most successful such language was C++, designed in the early 1980s by Bjarne Stroustrup at AT&T Bell Laboratories. By making it possible to integrate object-oriented techniques with existing C code, C++ enabled large communities of programmers to adopt the object-oriented paradigm in a gradual, evolutionary way.

The Java programming language

The most recent chapter in the history of object-oriented programming is the development of Java by a team of programmers at Sun Microsystems led by James Gosling. In 1991, when Sun initiated the project that would eventually create Java, the goal was to design a language suitable for programming the microprocessors embedded in consumer electronic devices. Had this goal remained the focus of the project, it is unlikely that Java would have caught on to the extent that it has. As is often the case in computing, the direction of the Java project changed during its developmental phase in response to changing conditions in the industry. The key factor leading to the change in focus was the phenomenal growth in the Internet that occurred in the early 1990s, particularly in the form of the **World Wide Web,** an ever-expanding collection of interconnected resources contributed by computer users all over the world. When interest in the Web skyrocketed in 1993, Sun redesigned Java as a tool for writing highly interactive, Web-based applications. That decision proved extremely well-timed. Since the announcement of the language in May 1995, Java has generated unprecedented excitement in both the academic and commercial computing communities. In the process, object-oriented programming has become firmly established as a central paradigm in the computing industry.

To get a sense of the strengths of Java, it is useful to look at Figure 1-4, which contains excerpts from a now-classic paper on the initial Java design written in 1996 by James Gosling and Henry McGilton. In that paper, the authors describe Java with a long series of adjectives: simple, object-oriented, familiar, robust, secure, architecture-neutral, portable, high-performance, interpreted, threaded, and dynamic. The discussion in Figure 1-4 will provide you with a sense as to what these buzzwords mean, and you will come to appreciate the importance of these features even more as you learn more about Java and computer science.

1.7 Java and the World Wide Web

In many ways, Java's initial success as a language was tied to the excitement surrounding computer networks in the early 1990s. Computer networks had at that time been around for more than 20 years, ever since the first four nodes in the ARPANET—the forerunner of today's Internet—came on line in 1969. What drove the enormous boom in Internet technology throughout the 1990s was not so much the network itself as the invention of the World Wide Web, which allows users to move from one document to another by clicking on interactive links.

Documents that contain interactive links are called **hypertext**—a term coined in 1965 by Ted Nelson, who proposed the creation of an integrated collection of documents that has much in common with today's World Wide Web. The fundamental concepts, however, are even older; the first Presidential Science Advisor, Vannevar Bush, proposed a similar idea in 1945. This idea of a distributed hypertext system, however, was not successfully put into practice until 1989, when Tim Berners-Lee of CERN, the European Particle Physics Laboratory in Geneva, proposed creating a repository that he called the World Wide Web. In 1991, implementers at CERN completed the first **browser,** a program that displays Web documents in a way that makes it easy for users to follow the internal links to other parts of the Web.

After news of the CERN work spread to other researchers in the physics community, more groups began to create browsers. Of these, the most successful was Mosaic, which was developed at the National Center for Supercomputing Applications (NCSA) in Champaign, Illinois. After the appearance of the Mosaic browser in 1993, interest in the Web exploded. The number of computer systems implementing World Wide Web repositories grew from approximately 500 in 1993 to over 35,000,000 in 2003. The enthusiasm for the Web in the Internet community has also sparked considerable commercial interest, leading to the formation of several new companies and the release of commercial Web browsers like Apple's Safari, Netscape's Navigator, and Microsoft's Internet Explorer.

The number of documents available on the World Wide Web has grown rapidly because Internet users can easily create new documents and add them to the Web. If you want to add a new document to the Web, all you have to do is create a file on a system equipped with a program called a **Web server** that gives external users access to the files on that system. The individual files exported by the server are

---

| FIGURE 1-4 | **Insights from Java's developers on language design** |

DESIGN GOALS OF THE JAVA™ PROGRAMMING LANGUAGE

The design requirements of the Java™ programming language are driven by the nature of the computing environments in which software must be deployed.

The massive growth of the Internet and the World Wide Web leads us to a completely new way of looking at development and distribution of software. To live in the world of electronic commerce and distribution, Java technology must enable the development of secure, high performance, and highly robust applications on multiple platforms in heterogeneous, distributed networks.

Operating on multiple platforms in heterogeneous networks invalidates the traditional schemes of binary distribution, release, upgrade, patch, and so on. To survive in this jungle, the Java programming language must be architecture neutral, portable, and dynamically adaptable.

The system that emerged to meet these needs is simple, so it can be easily programmed by most developers; familiar, so that current developers can easily learn the Java programming language; object oriented, to take advantage of modern software development methodologies and to fit into distributed client-server applications; multithreaded, for high performance in applications that need to perform multiple concurrent activities, such as multimedia; and interpreted, for maximum portability and dynamic capabilities.

Together, the above requirements comprise quite a collection of buzzwords, so let's examine some of them and their respective benefits before going on.

Simple, Object Oriented, and Familiar

Primary characteristics of the Java programming language include a simple language that can be programmed without extensive programmer training while being attuned to current software practices. The fundamental concepts of Java technology are grasped quickly; programmers can be productive from the very beginning.

The Java programming language is designed to be object oriented from the ground up. Object technology has finally found its way into the programming mainstream after a gestation period of thirty years. The needs of distributed, client-server based systems coincide with the encapsulated, message-passing paradigms of object-based software. To function within increasingly complex, network-based environments, programming systems must adopt object-oriented concepts. Java technology provides a clean and efficient object-based development platform.

Programmers using the Java programming language can access existing libraries of tested objects that provide functionality ranging from basic data types through I/O and network interfaces to graphical user interface toolkits. These libraries can be extended to provide new behavior.

Even though C++ was rejected as an implementation language, keeping the Java programming language looking like C++ as far as possible results in it being a familiar language, while removing the unnecessary complexities of C++. Having the Java programming language retain many of the object-oriented features and the "look and feel" of C++ means that programmers can migrate easily to the Java platform and be productive quickly.

Robust and Secure

The Java programming language is designed for creating highly reliable software. It provides extensive compile-time checking, followed by a second level of run-time checking. Language features guide programmers towards reliable programming habits.

The memory management model is extremely simple: objects are created with a new operator. There are no explicit programmer-defined pointer data types, no pointer arithmetic, and automatic garbage collection. This simple memory management model eliminates entire classes of programming errors that bedevil C and C++ programmers. You can develop Java code with confidence that the system will find many errors quickly and that major problems won't lay dormant until after your production code has shipped.

Java technology is designed to operate in distributed environments, which means that security is of paramount importance. With security features designed into the language and run-time system, Java technology lets you construct applications that can't be invaded from outside. In the network environment, applications written in the Java programming language are secure from intrusion by unauthorized code attempting to get behind the scenes and create viruses or invade file systems.

☞

Architecture Neutral and Portable

Java technology is designed to support applications that will be deployed into heterogeneous network environments. In such environments, applications must be capable of executing on a variety of hardware architectures. Within this variety of hardware platforms, applications must execute atop a variety of operating systems and interoperate with multiple programming language interfaces. To accommodate the diversity of operating environments, the Java Compiler™ product generates bytecodes—an architecture neutral intermediate format designed to transport code efficiently to multiple hardware and software platforms. The interpreted nature of Java technology solves both the binary distribution problem and the version problem; the same Java programming language byte codes will run on any platform.

Architecture neutrality is just one part of a truly portable system. Java technology takes portability a stage further by being strict in its definition of the basic language. Java technology puts a stake in the ground and specifies the sizes of its basic data types and the behavior of its arithmetic operators. Your programs are the same on every platform—there are no data type incompatibilities across hardware and software architectures.

The architecture-neutral and portable language platform of Java technology is known as the Java virtual machine. It's the specification of an abstract machine for which Java programming language compilers can generate code. Specific implementations of the Java virtual machine for specific hardware and software platforms then provide the concrete realization of the virtual machine. The Java virtual machine is based primarily on the POSIX interface specification—an industry-standard definition of a portable system interface. Implementing the Java virtual machine on new architectures is a relatively straightforward task as long as the target platform meets basic requirements such as support for multithreading.

High Performance

Performance is always a consideration. The Java platform achieves superior performance by adopting a scheme by which the interpreter can run at full speed without needing to check the run-time environment. The automatic garbage collector runs as a low-priority background thread, ensuring a high probability that memory is available when required, leading to better performance. Applications requiring large amounts of compute power can be designed such that compute-intensive sections can be rewritten in native machine code as required and interfaced with the Java platform. In general, users perceive that interactive applications respond quickly even though they're interpreted.

Interpreted, Threaded, and Dynamic

The Java interpreter can execute Java bytecodes directly on any machine to which the interpreter and run-time system have been ported. In an interpreted platform such as Java technology-based system, the link phase of a program is simple, incremental, and lightweight. You benefit from much faster development cycles—prototyping, experimentation, and rapid development are the normal case, versus the traditional heavyweight compile, link, and test cycles.

Modern network-based applications, such as the HotJava™ Browser for the World Wide Web, typically need to do several things at the same time. A user working with HotJava Browser can run several animations concurrently while downloading an image and scrolling the page. Java technology's multithreading capability provides the means to build applications with many concurrent threads of activity. Multithreading thus results in a high degree of interactivity for the end user.

The Java platform supports multithreading at the language level with the addition of sophisticated synchronization primitives: the language library provides the Thread class, and the run-time system provides monitor and condition lock primitives. At the library level, moreover, Java technology's high-level system libraries have been written to be thread safe: the functionality provided by the libraries is available without conflict to multiple concurrent threads of execution.

While the Java Compiler is strict in its compile-time static checking, the language and run-time system are dynamic in their linking stages. Classes are linked only as needed. New code modules can be linked in on demand from a variety of sources, even from sources across a network. In the case of the HotJava Browser and similar applications, interactive executable code can be loaded from anywhere, which enables transparent updating of applications. The result is on-line services that constantly evolve; they can remain innovative and fresh, draw more customers, and spur the growth of electronic commerce on the Internet.

—White Paper: The Java Language Environment
James Gosling and Henry McGilton, May 1996

called **Web pages.** Web pages are usually written in a language called **HTML,** which is short for *Hypertext Markup Language.* HTML documents consist of text along with formatting information and links to other pages elsewhere on the Web. Each page is identified by a **uniform resource locator,** or **URL,** which makes it possible for Web browsers to find this page in the sea of existing pages. URLs for the World Wide Web begin with the prefix `http://`, which is followed by a description of the Internet path needed to reach the desired page.

One of the particularly interesting aspects of Java is that the virtual machine is not always running on the same machine that houses the programs. One of Java's design goals was to make the language work well over a network. A particularly interesting consequence of this design goal is that Java supports the creation of **applets,** which are programs that run in the context of a network browser. The process of running an applet is described in Figure 1-5.

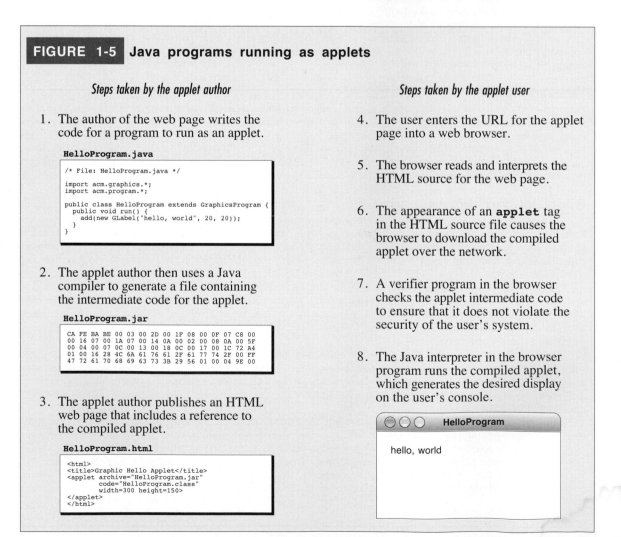

FIGURE 1-5 **Java programs running as applets**

Steps taken by the applet author

1. The author of the web page writes the code for a program to run as an applet.

   HelloProgram.java
   ```
   /* File: HelloProgram.java */

   import acm.graphics.*;
   import acm.program.*;

   public class HelloProgram extends GraphicsProgram {
      public void run() {
         add(new GLabel("hello, world", 20, 20));
      }
   }
   ```

2. The applet author then uses a Java compiler to generate a file containing the intermediate code for the applet.

   HelloProgram.jar
   ```
   CA FE BA BE 00 03 00 2D 00 1F 08 00 0F 07 C8 00
   00 16 07 00 1A 07 00 14 0A 00 02 00 08 0A 00 5F
   00 04 00 07 0C 00 13 00 18 0C 00 17 00 1C 72 A4
   01 00 16 28 4C 6A 61 76 61 2F 61 77 74 2F 00 FF
   47 72 61 70 68 69 63 73 3B 29 56 01 00 04 9E 00
   ```

3. The applet author publishes an HTML web page that includes a reference to the compiled applet.

   HelloProgram.html
   ```
   <html>
   <title>Graphic Hello Applet</title>
   <applet archive="HelloProgram.jar"
           code="HelloProgram.class"
           width=300 height=150>
   </applet>
   </html>
   ```

Steps taken by the applet user

4. The user enters the URL for the applet page into a web browser.

5. The browser reads and interprets the HTML source for the web page.

6. The appearance of an **applet** tag in the HTML source file causes the browser to download the compiled applet over the network.

7. A verifier program in the browser checks the applet intermediate code to ensure that it does not violate the security of the user's system.

8. The Java interpreter in the browser program runs the compiled applet, which generates the desired display on the user's console.

   HelloProgram

   hello, world

Summary

The purpose of this chapter is to set the stage for learning about computer science and programming, a process that you will begin in earnest in Chapter 2. In this chapter, you have focused on what the programming process involves and how it relates to the larger domain of computer science.

The important points introduced in this chapter include:

- The physical components of a computer system—the parts you can see and touch—constitute *hardware*. Before computer hardware is useful, however, you must specify a sequence of instructions, or *program*, that tells the hardware what to do. Such programs are called *software*.
- Computer science is not so much the science of computers as it is the science of solving problems using computers.
- Strategies for solving problems on a computer are known as *algorithms*. To be an algorithm, the strategy must be clearly and unambiguously defined, effective, and finite.
- Programs are typically written using a *higher-level language* designed to be understood by human readers.
- There are two principal strategies for executing a program written in a higher-level language: *compilation* and *interpretation*. A *compiler* translates a program into the machine language of a specific computer system, thereby allowing the program to run directly on the hardware of that computer. An *interpreter* simulates that process by reading through the program structure and executing the necessary operations as it goes.
- Java uses a hybrid strategy for program execution: a Java compiler translates a program into an *intermediate language* that is then interpreted. The intermediate language acts as the machine language for a hypothetical computer called the *Java Virtual Machine*.
- Programming languages have a set of *syntax rules* that determine whether a program is properly constructed. The compiler checks your program against these syntax rules and reports a *syntax error* whenever the rules are violated.
- The most serious type of programming error is one that is syntactically correct but that nonetheless causes the program to produce incorrect results or no results at all. This type of error, a mistake in logic that prevents your program from correctly solving a problem, is called a *bug*. The process of finding and fixing bugs is called *debugging*.
- Most programs must be updated periodically to correct bugs or to respond to changes in the demands of the application. This process is called *software maintenance*. Designing a program so that it is easier to maintain is an essential part of *software engineering*.
- This text uses the programming language Java to illustrate the programming process. The primary feature that sets Java apart from most of its predecessor languages is the fact that it is an *object-oriented language,* which means that it encapsulates data and any associated operations into conceptually unified entities called *objects*.

- Java was designed during the "Internet boom" of the 1990s and is designed to work well in a networked environment. In particular, Java makes it possible to run programs in the context of a web browser. Programs that run in this way are called *applets*.

Review questions

1. Even though neither of Babbage's machines were ever completed, the design of his Analytical Engine nonetheless introduced a new idea that remains central to modern computing. What was the important feature that distinguished the Analytical Engine from the earlier Difference Engine?

2. Who is generally regarded as the first programmer?

3. What concept lies at the heart of von Neumann architecture?

4. What is the difference between hardware and software?

5. Traditional science is concerned with abstract theories or the nature of the universe—not human-made artifacts. What abstract concept forms the core of computer science?

6. What are the three criteria an algorithm must satisfy?

7. What is the distinction between algorithmic design and coding? Which of these activities is usually harder?

8. What is meant by the term *higher-level language?* What higher-level language is used as the basis of this text?

9. How does an interpreter differ from a compiler?

10. What is the relationship between a source file and an object file? As a programmer, which of these files do you work with directly?

11. What is the difference between a syntax error and a bug?

12. True or false: Good programmers never introduce bugs into their programs.

13. True or false: The major expense of writing a program comes from the development of that program; once the program is put into practice, programming costs are negligible.

14. What is meant by the term *software maintenance?*

15. Why is it important to apply good software engineering principles when you write your programs?

16. What is the fundamental difference between the object-oriented and procedural paradigms?

17. What steps are involved in running an applet under the control of a web browser? In what ways does running a Java applet differ from running a Java application?

CHAPTER 2
Programming by Example

Example is always more efficacious than precept.
—Samuel Johnson, *Rasselas*, 1759

Grace Murray Hopper (1906–1992)

Grace Murray Hopper studied mathematics and physics at Vassar College and went on to earn her Ph.D. in mathematics at Yale. During the Second World War, Hopper joined the United States Navy and was posted to the Bureau of Ordinance Computation at Harvard University, where she worked with computing pioneer Howard Aiken. Hopper became one of the first programmers of the Mark I digital computer, which was one of the first machines capable of performing complex calculations. Hopper made several contributions to computing in its early years and was one of the major contributors to the development of the language COBOL, which continues to have widespread use in business programming applications. In 1985, Hopper became the first woman promoted to the rank of admiral. During her life, Grace Murray Hopper served as the most visible example of a successful woman in computer science. In recognition of that contribution, there is now a biennial Celebration of Women in Computing, named in her honor.

The purpose of this book is to teach you the fundamentals of programming. Along the way, you will become quite familiar with a particular programming language called Java, but the details of that language are not the main point. Programming is the science of solving problems by computer, and most of what you learn from this text will be independent of the specific details of Java. Even so, you will have to master many of those details eventually so that your programs can take maximum advantage of the tools that Java provides.

From your position as a new student of programming, the need to understand both the abstract concepts of programming and the concrete details of a specific programming language leads to a dilemma: there is no obvious place to start. To learn about programming, you need to write some fairly complex programs. To write those programs in Java, you must know enough about the language to use the appropriate tools. But if you spend all your energy learning about Java, you will probably not learn as much as you should about more general programming issues. Moreover, Java was designed for experts and not for beginning programmers. There are many details that just get in the way if you try to master Java without first understanding something about programming.

Because it's important for you to get a feel for what programming is before you master its intricacies, this chapter begins by presenting a few simple programs in their entirety. When you look at these programs, try to understand what is happening in them generally without being concerned about details just yet. You can learn about those details in Chapters 3 and 4. The main purpose of this chapter is to help build your intuition about programming and problem solving, which is far more important in the long run.

▇▇ 2.1 The "Hello world" program

Java is part of a collection of languages that grew out of C, one of the most successful programming languages in the history of the field. In the book that has served as C's defining document, *The C Programming Language* by Brian Kernighan and Dennis Ritchie, the authors offer the following advice on the first page of Chapter 1.

> The only way to learn a new programming language is by writing programs in it. The first program to write is the same for all languages:
>
> *Print the words*
> **hello, world**
>
> This is the big hurdle; to leap over it you have to be able to create the program text somewhere, compile it successfully, load it, run it, and find out where the output went. With these mechanical details mastered, everything else is comparatively easy.

That advice was followed by the four-line text of the "hello world" program, which became part of the heritage shared by all C programmers. Java is, of course, different from C, but the underlying advice is still sound: the first program you write should be as simple as possible to ensure that you can master the mechanics of the programming process.

At the same time, it is important to remember that this is now the 21st century, and the programs that were appropriate to the early 1970s are not the same ones we would use today. The mechanical teletypes and consoles—primitive character-based display screens connected with a keyboard—that were available then have been replaced by more sophisticated hardware, and the ability to print a series of words is no longer quite as exciting as it once was. Today, that output would more likely be directed to a graphical window on the screen. Fortunately, the Java program that does precisely that is still very simple. The Java version of the "hello world" program appears in Figure 2-1.

As Figure 2-1 indicates, **HelloProgram** is divided into three separate sections: a *program comment*, a list of *imports*, and the *main class*. Although its structure is extremely simple, **HelloProgram** is typical of the programs you will see in the next few chapters, and you can use it as a model of how Java programs should be organized.

Comments

The first section of **HelloProgram** is an English-language **comment**, which is simply program text that the compiler ignores. In Java, comments come in two forms. The first consists of text enclosed between the markers /* and */, even if that text continues for several lines. The second—which I don't use in this book—is introduced by the symbol // and continues up to the end of the line. In **HelloProgram**, the comment begins with the /* on the first line and ends with the */ seven lines later.

Comments are written for human beings, not for the computer. They are intended to convey information about the program to other programmers. When the

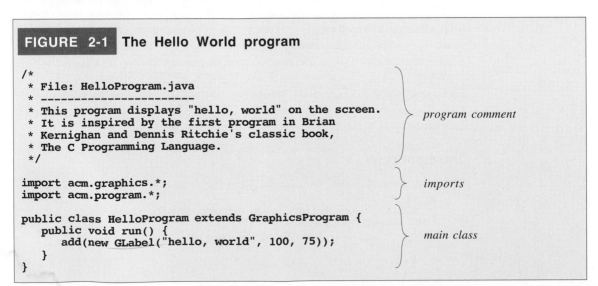

FIGURE 2-1 The Hello World program

```
/*
 * File: HelloProgram.java
 * ----------------------
 * This program displays "hello, world" on the screen.       program comment
 * It is inspired by the first program in Brian
 * Kernighan and Dennis Ritchie's classic book,
 * The C Programming Language.
 */

import acm.graphics.*;                                        imports
import acm.program.*;

public class HelloProgram extends GraphicsProgram {
   public void run() {                                        main class
      add(new GLabel("hello, world", 100, 75));
   }
}
```

Java compiler translates a program into a form that can be executed by the machine, it ignores the comments entirely.

In this book, every program begins with a special comment called the **program comment** that describes the operation of the program as a whole. That comment includes the name of the program file and a sentence or two that describe the operation of the program. In this case, the program comment also provides credit for the original idea of the program. Comments might also describe any particularly intricate parts of the program, indicate who might use it, offer suggestions on how to change the program's behavior, or provide any additional information that other programmers might want to know about the program. For one as simple as **HelloProgram**, extensive comments are usually not necessary. As your programs become more complicated, however, you will discover that including useful comments along with the code is one of the best ways to make those programs understandable to someone else—or to figure out what you yourself intended if you return to a program after not looking at it for a while.

Imports

The second section of **HelloProgram** consists of the lines

```
import acm.graphics.*;
import acm.program.*;
```

These lines indicate that the program uses two library packages. A **library package** is a collection of tools written by other programmers that perform specific operations. The libraries used by **HelloProgram** are a graphics library and a program library, each of which come from a collection of packages produced by the Association for Computing Machinery (ACM). The asterisk at the end of the package name is used to indicate that all components from the relevant package should be imported. Every program in this book will import at least the **acm.program** package, and any programs that use graphics will import **acm.graphics**, which means that most of your programs will also need to include these lines immediately after the program comment. Some programs will use additional packages as well and must contain an **import** line for each one.

When you write your own programs, you can use the tools provided by these packages, which saves you the trouble of writing them yourself. Libraries are critical to programming, and you will quickly come to depend on several important packages as you begin to write more sophisticated programs.

The main class

The last section of the **HelloProgram.java** file consists of the lines

```
public class HelloProgram extends GraphicsProgram {
   public void run() {
      add(new GLabel("hello, world", 100, 75));
   }
}
```

These five lines are your first example of a class definition in Java. A **class** is the primary unit into which Java programs are divided and constitutes a template for the creation of individual objects. That definition is admittedly relatively vague at this point and will be refined in the section entitled "Classes and objects" later in this chapter.

To make sense of this program definition, it is useful to break it down hierarchically. A class definition—like many other structures in Java—consists of two parts: a **header line** that defines certain essential characteristics of the Java definition as a whole and a **body** that fills in the details. When you are reading through a program definition, it often helps to think about the header line and the body independently. The following, for example, is a schematic diagram of the **HelloProgram** class in which the body of the class has been replaced by a box:

```
public class HelloProgram extends GraphicsProgram {
```
┌──┐
│   *body of the class definition*   │
└──┘
```
}
```

When you adopt this perspective on the **HelloProgram** class, you can focus on the header line. Once you understand the header line, you can then look inside the body to figure out the details.

In a class definition, the header line provides important information about the characteristics of the class. The first word in the header line of the **HelloProgram** class is **public**, which indicates that other programs can have access to this class. All programs are defined as public classes because some other application—which is either a web browser or the programming environment you're using to test your programs—has to be able to start those programs up. The second word in the header line is **class**, which tells Java that this line is the beginning of a class definition. The words **public**, **class**, and **extends** later in the header line all have a specific meaning in Java. Such words are called **keywords.**

The **extends** keyword in this header line indicates that **HelloProgram** is a subclass of **GraphicsProgram**, which is one of the program types defined in the **acm.program** package. The specific capabilities of the **GraphicsProgram** class are presented in overview form in section 2.6 and then defined in detail in Chapter 9. For the moment, it is sufficient to understand that **HelloProgram** is a **GraphicsProgram** and can therefore do any of the things that **GraphicsProgram** can do, the details of which you will discover later.

The body of the class definition for **HelloProgram** contains a single definition, which looks like this:

```
public void run() {
   add(new GLabel("hello, world", 100, 75));
}
```

This definition is an example of a Java **method**, which is simply a sequence of program steps that have been collected together and given a name. The name of this method, as given on its own header line, is **run**. The steps that the method performs are listed between the curly braces and are called **statements.** Collectively, the statements constitute the body of the method. The method **run** shown in the **HelloProgram.java** example has only one statement, but it is common for methods to contain several statements that are performed sequentially, beginning with the first statement and continuing through the last statement in the body.

The method **run** plays a special role in programs that use the **acm.program** package. Whenever you run a Java program, the computer executes the statements enclosed in the body of the **run** method for the main class. In **HelloProgram**, the body of **run** consists of the single statement

```
add(new GLabel("hello, world", 100, 75));
```

This statement uses two facilities from the library packages. The first is the **GLabel** class, which comes from **acm.graphics**. The part of the line that reads

```
new GLabel("hello, world", 100, 75)
```

is an example of a Java expression called a **constructor,** which is used to create new objects. In this case, the constructor creates a new **GLabel** object containing the text **"hello, world"** that begins at a point whose *x* and *y* coordinates are 100 and 75. (At this point, you don't yet know exactly what those coordinates mean, but you shouldn't let that stop you from getting a general sense of the program. The Java coordinate model will be introduced in the section on "The **GRect** class " later in this chapter.) The statement as a whole is

add(│ *newly generated label* │ **);**

which takes the new **GLabel** and adds it to the list of objects that are currently part of the display. The result is that the program produces the following image in a graphics window:

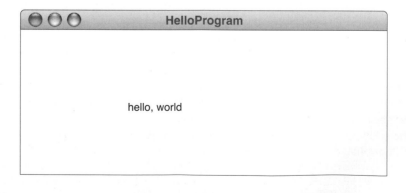

2.2 Perspectives on the programming process

The point of this chapter is not to understand the details of how Java works, but rather to get a good overall perception—what psychologists often call a **gestalt**—of a few simple programs. You could figure out a great deal about Java simply by typing the **HelloProgram.java** file into the computer and experimenting with it, which is in fact the first exercise at the end of this chapter. It would be easy, for example, to change the text displayed by the program from **"hello, world"** to something more interesting. You could put that text at a different position in the graphics window by changing the numbers 100 and 75 to something else. In the process, you would discover some of the interesting peculiarities of the Java coordinate system, such as the fact that the origin is in the upper left corner instead of the lower left corner as it is in traditional geometry. Thus, if you change the *y* coordinate from 75 to 100, the **GLabel** moves *downward* on the screen. You might also develop an intuitive sense of the units used to express these coordinate values, even before you knew precisely why these units were chosen. All you would need to do would be to try a few different values and see how things moved on the screen. And there would be nothing to stop you from putting more than one **GLabel** into the same graphics window. If you wanted to include a second **GLabel** in a different part of the window, you could simply add a line to the program that looked pretty much like the first one, although it would presumably specify a different text string and a different set of *x* and *y* coordinates.

The important thing to remember is that you can discover an enormous amount through experimentation. As Brian Kernighan and Dennis Ritchie assert, "the only way to learn a new programming language is by writing programs in it." And the more programs you write and the more you play around with those programs, the more you will learn about how programming works.

At some point, of course, you will need to learn about the details of Java statements so that you can understand how each statement works. Making a detailed analysis, however, is not the only useful way to think about a program. Sometimes it helps to stand back and look at a program as a whole. The analytical, step-by-step examination of a program is an example of a *reductionistic* approach. If you look at a program from a more global perspective—as a complete entity whose operation as a whole is of primary concern—you are adopting a more *holistic* perspective that allows you to see the program in a different light.

Reductionism is the philosophical principle that the whole of an object can best be understood by understanding the parts that make it up. Its antithesis is **holism**, which recognizes that the whole is often more than the sum of its parts. As you learn how to write programs, you must learn to see the process from each of these perspectives. If you concentrate only on the big picture, you will end up not understanding the tools you need for solving problems. However, if you focus exclusively on details, you will invariably miss the forest for the trees.

When you are first learning about programming, the best approach is usually to alternate between these two perspectives. Taking the holistic view helps sharpen your intuition about the programming process and enables you to stand back from a program and say, "I understand what this program does." On the other hand, to practice writing programs, you have to adopt enough of the reductionistic perspective to know how those programs are put together.

▓▓ 2.3 A program to add two numbers

Learning to program by example is easier if you have a variety of examples. Figure 2-2 shows a different kind of program that asks the user to enter two integers (which is simply the mathematical term for whole numbers without fractional parts), adds those integers together, and then displays the sum.

The program in Figure 2-2 introduces several programming concepts that are not part of **HelloProgram**. First, **Add2Integers** is a different kind of program, as indicated by its header line:

`public class Add2Integers extends ConsoleProgram`

This program extends **ConsoleProgram** instead of **GraphicsProgram**, which means that it has access to a different set of facilities. The **ConsoleProgram** class supports user interaction in a traditional text-based style. A **ConsoleProgram** can request keyboard input from the user and display information back in a window on the computer screen; for historical reasons, this keyboard/display combination is called a **console**. The interaction with a **ConsoleProgram** is illustrated in the following diagram, which shows what you might see if you ran the **Add2Integers** program:

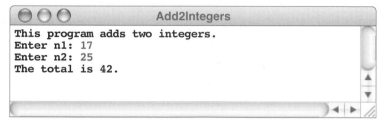

```
This program adds two integers.
Enter n1: 17
Enter n2: 25
The total is 42.
```

FIGURE 2-2	**Program to add two integers**

```java
/*
 * File: Add2Integers.java
 * --------------------------
 * This program adds two integers and prints their sum.
 */

import acm.program.*;

public class Add2Integers extends ConsoleProgram {

   public void run() {
      println("This program adds two integers.");
      int n1 = readInt("Enter n1: ");
      int n2 = readInt("Enter n2: ");
      int total = n1 + n2;
      println("The total is " + total + ".");
   }

}
```

Diagrams of this sort that show the output that a program produces are called **sample runs.** Although it is impossible to see in the black-and-white printing used in this book, the input that the user types appears in blue on the screen.

If you took a holistic look at this program, you could almost certainly determine what the program was supposed to do even before you understood the details of the individual statements. If nothing else, the program comment and the first line of the **run** method are dead giveaways. But even without those signposts, most beginning programmers would have little trouble understanding the function of the code. Programs are typically easier to read than they are to write. Moreover, just as it is easier to write a novel after having read a number of them, you will find that it is easier to write good programs if you take the time to read several well-designed programs and learn to emulate their structure and style. The meaning of a particular statement—much like that of unfamiliar words in a novel—often becomes clear from the context. Before going on to the detailed explanations in the next few paragraphs, try looking at each line of **Add2Integers** and see how much sense you can make of it on your own.

The first line in the **run** method is

```
println("This program adds two integers.");
```

The **println** method—which is a contraction of *print line*—is used to display information on the window displayed by the **ConsoleProgram**. The value in parentheses tells the **println** method what it should display. Such values are called **arguments.** The double quotes surrounding the text

```
This program adds two integers.
```

do not appear in the output but are used by Java to indicate that the characters between the quotation marks are an instance of text data called a **string,** which is discussed in detail in Chapter 8. The effect of the **println** method is to display the argument string and then to return to the beginning of the next line. Thus, if you make several **println** calls in succession, each string in the output will appear on a separate line.

In creating a line of output for the user, it is sometimes convenient to print the line in pieces. The **ConsoleProgram** class offers a method called **print**, which is the same as **println** except that it doesn't move to the next line. The **print** method lets you print part of a line and subsequently finish it with a call to **println**. Because the concatenation operator described later in this section also makes it easy to combine several values on a line, the **print** method rarely appears in this book.

The purpose of the first line in this program is not to tell other programmers what the program does; that function is accomplished by the program comments at the beginning of the file. The first call to **println** exists to tell the user what the program does. Most people who use computers today are not programmers, and it wouldn't be reasonable to expect those users to look at the code for a program to determine what it did. The program itself has to make its purpose clear.

The next line of the **run** method looks like this:

```
int n1 = readInt("Enter n1: ");
```

At a holistic level, the intent of the line is reasonably clear, given that everything you can see suggests that it must be reading the first integer value. If you adopt a reductionistic perspective, however, this line of code introduces several new concepts. Of these, the most important is that of a **variable,** which is easiest to think of as a placeholder for some piece of data whose value is unknown when the program is written. When you write a program to add two integers, you don't yet know what integers the user will want to add. The user will enter those integers when the program runs. So that you can refer to these as-yet-unspecified values in your program, you create a variable to hold each value you need to remember, give it a name, and then use its name whenever you want to refer to the value it contains. Variable names are usually chosen so that programmers who read the program in the future can easily tell how each variable is used. In the **Add2Integers** program, the variables **n1** and **n2** represent the integers to be added, and the variable **total** represents the sum.

When you introduce a new variable in Java, you must **declare** that variable. To do so, you need to supply a **declaration,** a line of code that specifies the name of the variable and tells the compiler what type of data that variable will contain. In Java, the type used to store integer data is called **int**. A declaration of the form

> **int n1 =** | *value* | **;**

introduces a new integer variable called **n1** whose value is given by whatever expression appears in the box labeled *value*. In this case, that expression is

> **readInt("Enter n1: ")**

Like the **println** example from the first line, this expression invokes the **readInt** method in **ConsoleProgram**. The **readInt** method begins by displaying its argument on the screen so that the user knows what to do next. A strings of this sort that tells the user what to enter is generally called a **prompt**. Unlike **println**, however, the **readInt** method does not return to the beginning of the next line but waits after the prompt for the user to type an integer. When the user has finished typing the integer and presses the RETURN or ENTER key, that integer is then passed back to the **run** method as the result of the **readInt** method. In programming terminology, we say that **readInt returns** the value the user typed.

When tracing through the operation of a program on paper, programmers often use box diagrams to indicate the values assigned to variables. If you look at the sample run earlier in this section, you will see that the user entered the value 17 in response to the first input request. Thus, to illustrate that the assignment statement has stored the value 17 in the variable **n1**, you draw a box, name the box **n1**, and then indicate its value by writing a 17 inside the box, as follows:

The third line in the run method is almost exactly the same as the second; it reads a value for the variable **n2**. If the user entered 25 in response to the prompt, you could update your box diagram to show the new variable, as follows:

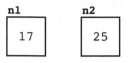

The next line in the **run** method is

```
int total = n1 + n2;
```

This statement declares the variable **total** and assigns it the value to the right of the equal sign, which is

```
n1 + n2
```

This piece of the code is an example of an essential programming construct called an *expression,* which represents the result of computation. The structure of expressions is defined more formally in Chapter 3, but it is often easy to understand what Java expressions mean because many of them look very much like expressions in traditional mathematics.

In the **Add2Integers** program, the goal is to add the values stored in the variables **n1** and **n2**. To do so, you use the **+** operator, which you've understood since elementary-school arithmetic. Calculating the sum, however, is not enough. You also need to store the sum in a variable so that you can refer to it later. The statement

```
int total = n1 + n2;
```

combines each of these operations. It computes the sum of the variables **n1** and **n2** and then introduces the variable **total** to hold that value.

The final statement in the **run** method is

```
println("The total is " + total + ".");
```

which accomplishes the task of displaying the computed result. For the most part, this statement looks like the first statement in the program, which is also a call to the **println** method. This time, however, there's a new twist. Instead of taking a single string argument, this statement passes to **println** the argument value

```
"The total is " + total + "."
```

As in the **n1 + n2** expression from the previous statement, this expression uses the **+** operator to combine individual values. In this statement, at least some of the values to which **+** is applied are strings rather than the numeric values for which addition is traditional defined. In Java, applying the **+** operator to string data reinterprets that operator to mean adding the strings together end to end to combine their characters. This operation is called **concatenation.** If there are any parts of the expression that are not strings, Java converts them into their standard string representation before applying the concatenation operator. The effect of this last **println** statement is to display the value of **total** after concatenating it with the strings that tell the user what the output value represents. You can see the effect of this statement in the sample run.

Although **Add2Integers** is set up to work only with integers, Java is capable of working with many other types of data as well. You could, for example, change this program so that it added two real numbers simply by changing the types of the variables and the names of the input methods, as shown in Figure 2-3.

In most programming languages, numbers that include a decimal fraction are called **floating-point numbers,** which are used to approximate real numbers in mathematics. The most common type of floating-point number in Java is the type **double**, which is short for *double-precision floating-point*. If you need to store floating-point values in a program, you must declare variables of type **double**, just as you previously had to declare variables of type **int** to write **Add2Integers**. The only other change in the program is that it requests input from the user by calling **readDouble** instead of **readInt**. The basic pattern of the program is unchanged.

2.4 Programming idioms and patterns

Recognizing that programs often follow specific patterns that you can adapt to new applications is an essential step in learning to program. In the preceding section, it didn't require any deep insight to change the **Add2Integers** program into **Add2Doubles**; all you needed to do was change a few words here and there to indicate that the program should use the type **double** rather than the type **int**. You could just as easily have gone on to create an **Add3Doubles** program by adding the line

---

FIGURE 2-3 **Program to add two double-precision numbers**

```
/*
 * File: Add2Doubles.java
 * ------------------------
 * This program adds two double-precision floating-point numbers
 * and prints their sum.
 */

import acm.program.*;

public class Add2Doubles extends ConsoleProgram {

   public void run() {
      println("This program adds two numbers.");
      double n1 = readDouble("Enter n1: ");
      double n2 = readDouble("Enter n2: ");
      double total = n1 + n2;
      println("The total is " + total + ".");
   }

}
```

```
double n3 = readDouble("Enter n3: ");
```

and then changing the calculation of **total** to read

```
double total = n1 + n2 + n3;
```

If you look at these lines in a reductionistic way, there is actually quite a bit going on. To understand these lines in detail, you need to know various things about the **readDouble** method and the way Java performs computation. If you instead think about the statements holistically, none of those details are essential. It works just fine to use the statements as idiomatic patterns that perform a particular operation. For example, if you want to read a floating-point value that the user enters, all you need to remember is that the following pattern always works:

```
double variable = readDouble("prompt");
```

The only things you have to fill in are the name of the variable and the prompt string that you want the user to see. That pattern therefore serves as a template for any operation that requires reading a floating-point value from the user. The pattern for reading an integer value is almost the same:

```
int variable = readInt("prompt");
```

Once you know these patterns, you don't need to remember the details.

Patterns of this sort have been important tools through human history. Before the invention of writing, history and religion passed from generation to generation as part of oral tradition. *The Iliad* and *The Odyssey* of Homer, the Vedic literature of India, the Old Norse mythologies, the sermons and songs that kept African traditions alive through centuries of slavery—all are examples of oral tradition. These works are characterized by the patterned repetition of phrases, which make it easier for singers, preachers, and storytellers to remember them. The repeated patterns provide memory cues that make it possible to remember and make variations on a long and complicated story.

Taken in their entirety, the rules of Java and the many additional features provided by the Java libraries form a long and complicated story with so many details that it is nearly impossible to remember them all. Even so, as you write your programs, you will notice that many formulaic structures come up repeatedly, as do the formulas of oral tradition. If you learn to recognize these formulas and think of them as conceptual units, you will soon discover that there is less to remember about programming in Java than you might have thought. In programming, such formulas are called **idioms** or **programming patterns.** To write programs effectively, you must learn how to apply these programming patterns to the task at hand. Eventually, you should be able to do so without devoting any conscious attention to the process. A general idea will come into your mind as part of a solution strategy, and you will automatically translate that idea into the appropriate pattern as you compose the program.

2.5 Classes and objects

Before continuing on to the details of expressions and statements in Chapters 3 and 4, it is important to introduce one more high-level concept illustrated by the examples in this chapter. The programs you've seen—**HelloProgram**, **Add2Integers**, and **Add2Doubles**—are each defined as Java *classes*. These classes, moreover, are defined as extensions of existing classes supplied by the **acm.program** package: **HelloProgram** is an extension of **GraphicsProgram**, and the other two are extensions of **ConsoleProgram**. Whenever you define a new class as an extension of an existing one, the new class is said to be a **subclass** of the original. Thus, **HelloProgram** is a subclass of **GraphicsProgram**. Symmetrically, **GraphicsProgram** is a **superclass** of **HelloProgram**.

The concept of a class is one of the most important ideas in Java. At its essence, a **class** is an extensible template that specifies the structure of a particular style of object. Each object is an **instance** of a particular class, which can, in turn, serve as a template for many different objects. If you want to create objects in Java, you must first define the class to which those objects belong and then construct individual objects that are instances of that class.

An **object** is a conceptually integrated entity that encapsulates both *state* and *behavior*. The **state** of an object consists of a set of attributes that pertain to that object and might change over time. For example, an object might be characterized by its location in space, its color, its name, and a host of other properties. The **behavior** of an object refers to the ways in which that object responds to events in its world or to requests generated by other objects. In the language of object-oriented programming, the generic word for anything that triggers a particular behavior in an object is called a **message.** In Java, sending a message corresponds to calling a method associated with the object to which that message is directed, which makes it possible to think of messages and method calls as different names for the same idea.

Class hierarchies

Classes in Java form hierarchies. These hierarchies are similar in structure to many more familiar classification structures such as the organization of the biological world originally developed by the Swedish botanist Carl Linnaeus in the eighteenth century. Portions of this hierarchy are shown in the diagram in Figure 2-4. At the top of the chart is the universal category of all living things. That category is subdivided into several kingdoms, which are in turn broken down by phylum, class, order, family, genus, and species. In the classification tree shown in Figure 2-4, the last two levels—the genus and the species, which together constitute the formal biological name for a particular type of living thing—are *Iridomyrmex purpureus,* which is the name for a type of red ant. The individual red ants in the world correspond to the objects in a programming language. Thus, each of the individuals

is an instance of the species *purpureus*. By virtue of the hierarchy, however, that individual is also an instance of the genus *Iridomyrmex*, the class *Insecta*, and the phylum *Arthropoda*. It is similarly, of course, both an animal and a living thing. Moreover, each red ant has the characteristics that pertain to each of its ancestor categories. For example, red ants have six legs, which is one of the defining characteristics of the class *Insecta*.

The biological metaphor illustrates one of the fundamental properties of classes in Java. Any instance of a particular class is also an instance of every one of its superclasses. Thus, any instance of **HelloProgram** is, by definition, also an instance of **GraphicsProgram**. Moreover, each instance of **HelloProgram**

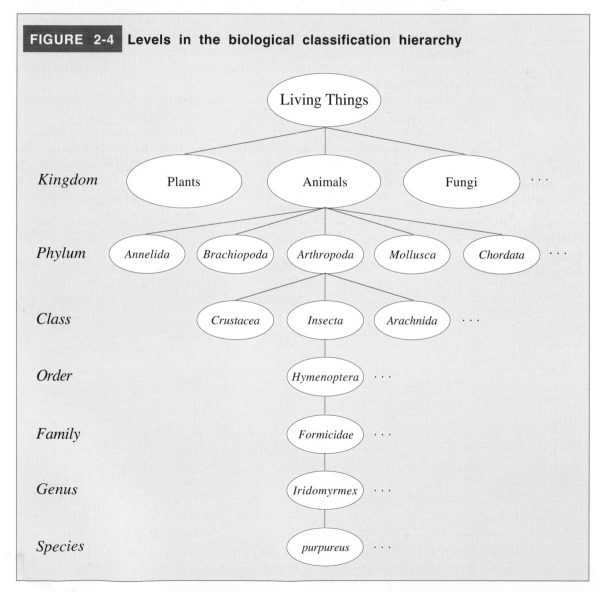

FIGURE 2-4 **Levels in the biological classification hierarchy**

automatically acquires the public behavior of **GraphicsProgram**. This property of taking on the behavior of your superclasses is called **inheritance**.

The **Program** class hierarchy

The classes defined by the **acm.program** form a hierarchy with a little more structure and complexity than you have seen up to this point. That hierarchy appears in Figure 2-5. Each of the classes you have seen—**GraphicsProgram** and **ConsoleProgram**—is a subclass of a higher-level class called **Program**. The **Program** class is a subclass of the **JApplet** class, which is itself a specialized subclass of the standard Java class called **Applet**. The diagram shows that every instance of a program you design, such as the instance of **HelloProgram** shown in Figure 2-1, is simultaneously a **GraphicsProgram**, a **Program**, a **JApplet**, and an **Applet**. The fact that your program is an applet means that you can run it on a web browser, which is a property that all **Applet**s share, along with all **Program**s and **GraphicsProgram**s, through inheritance.

Figure 2-5 also shows that there is another **Program** subclass besides the two you have already seen. The **DialogProgram** subclass turns out to be quite similar in its overall organization to **ConsoleProgram**. In particular, it shares exactly the same set of methods, which are in fact all specified by the **Program** class. The difference is that these methods have a different interpretation. In a **ConsoleProgram**, method calls to **println** and **readInt** specify user interaction under the control of the text-based window that every **ConsoleProgram** displays. In a **DialogProgram**, calls to these same methods specify user interaction through interactive dialog boxes that

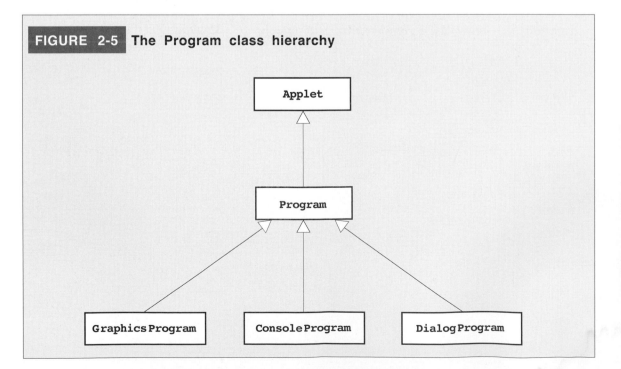

FIGURE 2-5 **The Program class hierarchy**

pop up as the program runs. If you were to change the class header line shown in Figure 2-2 so that it read

```
public class Add2Integers extends DialogProgram {
```

the program would still add two numbers, but the style of interaction would be quite different. Running this new version of the program produces the series of dialog boxes shown in Figure 2-6.

The classes **ConsoleProgram** and **DialogProgram** each define their own version of **println** and **readInt** so that they operate in the style appropriate to that class. Redefining an existing method so that it behaves differently from the implementation defined by its superclass is called **overriding** that method.

2.6 Graphical programs

As you will discover in the next several chapters, the **ConsoleProgram** class provides a useful framework for illustrating new programming concepts. In most cases, it is easier to illustrate these concepts in a **ConsoleProgram** than it would be in a **GraphicsProgram** because programs that use graphics tend to be more complex than their console-based counterparts. On the other hand, graphical programs are typically more exciting than console programs. For many students, the fact that

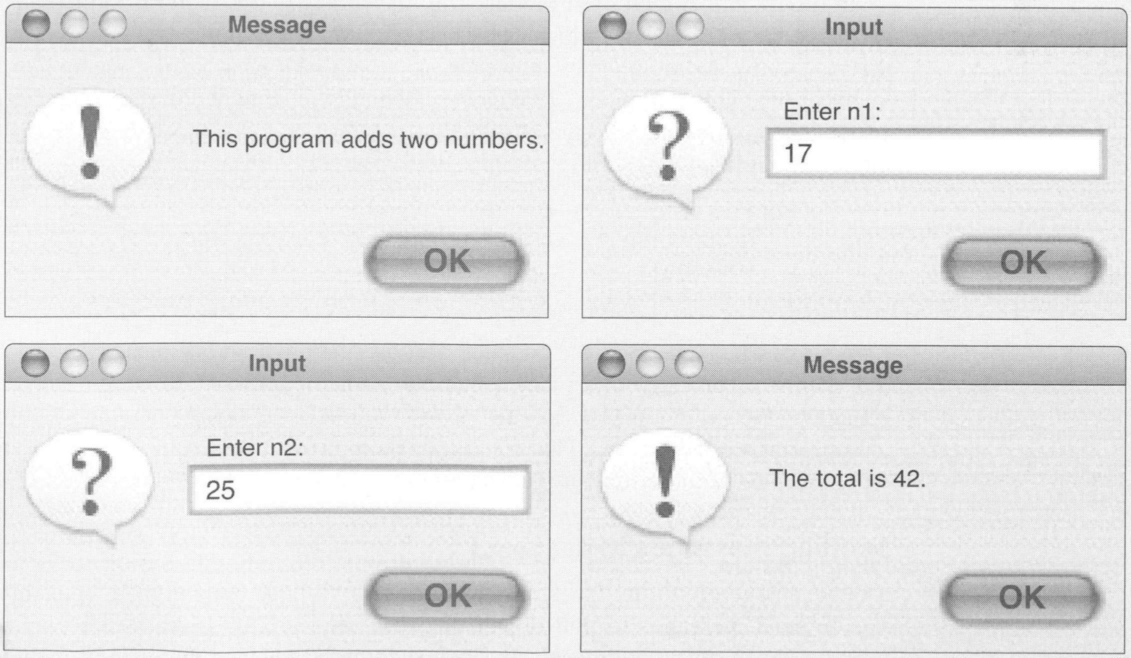

FIGURE 2-6   Dialog boxes that appear when running dialog version of Add2Integers

graphical programs seem more interesting and fun more than makes up for any additional complexity they involve.

Fortunately, it is possible to take a holistic approach to the **GraphicsProgram** class as well. Just as you can write a simple **ConsoleProgram** without mastering the underlying details, you can start creating **GraphicsProgram**s as soon as you learn a few simple concepts. The rest of this chapter teaches you to write simple **GraphicsProgram**s by example, so that you can start building interesting applications even before you get to the detailed discussion of the **acm.graphics** package in Chapter 9.

The **HelloProgram** example revisited

As a first step toward understanding the structure of a **GraphicsProgram**, it makes sense to look a little more closely at the **HelloProgram** example from Figure 2-1. The **run** method for this program looks like this:

```
public void run() {
    add(new GLabel("hello, world", 100, 75));
}
```

From the discussion in section 2.1, you already have some insight into how to interpret the call to **add** that constitutes the body of this method. In particular, you know that **GLabel** is a class defined in the **acm.graphics** package that makes it possible to display text strings in a graphics window. You also know that the keyword **new** causes the program to construct a new object of this class, which is initialized to display the string **"hello, world"** at location (100, 75).

In this example, the object produced by the **GLabel** constructor is immediately passed to the **add** method, which causes it to appear in the graphics window. Now that you know about variables, however, you can make what at first seems like a minor change in the program. That change is simply to store the **GLabel** object in a variable before passing it to the **add** method. After you make this change, the **run** method looks like this:

```
public void run() {
    GLabel msg = new GLabel("hello, world", 100, 75);
    add(msg);
}
```

In terms of what appears in the graphics window, the program operates exactly as it did before. The only difference is in the implementation: the **GLabel** object containing the string **"hello, world"** is now stored in the variable **msg** in addition to appearing on the screen. That change—as simple as it is—makes it possible to write much more interesting programs.

Sending messages to **GObject**s

The advantage of storing the **GLabel** object in a variable is that doing so enables you to send messages to that object, because the variable gives you a way to indicate which object you mean. In Java, such messages take the form of method calls that specify the object to which the message is directed, which is called the **receiver.** The general syntactic pattern for a method call with an explicit receiver is

> *receiver* . *name* (*arguments*)

where *receiver* is the object to which the message is being sent, *name* is the name of the method that responds to that particular message, and *arguments* is a list—possibly empty—of values that gives the receiver whatever additional information is necessary to respond appropriately.

In the **acm.graphics** packages, you can use such messages to change the appearance of the graphical objects displayed in the graphics window. As an example, one of the things you might like to change about the appearance of the display produced by **HelloProgram** is the size of the lettering. The original version of the program displays **"hello, world"** in letters that are tiny in comparison to the size of the screen. To make the output more visually striking, you might want to send a message to the **GLabel** asking it to make the displayed text bigger.

In Java, the way to change the size and appearance of a label is to change the *font* in which that label appears. In all likelihood, you are already familiar with fonts from other computer applications and have an intuitive sense that fonts determine the style in which characters appear. More formally, a **font** is an encoding that maps characters into images that appear on the screen. Java fonts are composed of three components: a **family name** (which might be something like Times or Helvetica, but is preferably one of the standard family names defined later in this section), a **style** (bold or italic, for example), and a **point size** (an integer indicating the size of the characters using the standard printer's unit of a **point,** which is equal to 1 / 72 of an inch).

You can change the font of a **GLabel** by sending it a **setFont** message that specifies the new family name, style, and point size in the form of a string. For example, you could specify a 24-point Helvetica font by changing the **run** method, as follows:

```
public void run() {
   GLabel msg = new GLabel("hello, world", 100, 75);
   msg.setFont("Helvetica-24");
   add(msg);
}
```

The line

```
msg.setFont("Helvetica-24");
```

provides a simple example of the syntax Java uses to send a message to an object. In this case, the receiver is the **GLabel** object stored in the variable **msg**, the name of the method that implements that message is **setFont**, and the argument consists of the string **"Helvetica-24"**. As you would expect, the **GLabel** object responds to the message by changing its font to Helvetica with a point size of 24.

After you make this change to **HelloProgram**, the display looks like this:

Much more readable, but perhaps not any more exciting.

As you probably know from using your word processor, it can be fun to experiment with different fonts. On my laptop, for example, there is a font called Lucida Blackletter that produces a stylized script reminiscent of the style of illuminated manuscripts of medieval times. Thus, if I were to change the **setFont** call in this program to

```
msg.setFont("Lucida Blackletter-28");
```

I would see the output

which is certainly fancier than the previous display. The problem with being so fancy, however, is that other people who run this program might not see the same output. The output appears in this form only if the Lucida Blackletter font is available on the computer they happen to be using. On a machine that doesn't have Lucida Blackletter in its font list, Java will substitute a default font that will in all likelihood have a completely different appearance.

If you're interested in writing portable programs that run on many different computers, it is best to avoid such unconventional fonts. In fact, if you want your programs to be as portable as possible, it is best to stick with the following font family names:

Serif   A traditional newspaper-style font in which the characters have short lines at the top and bottom, called **serifs,** that lead the eye to read words as single units. The most common example of a serif font is Times.

`SansSerif`	A simpler, unadorned font style lacking serifs, of which the most common example is Helvetica.
`Monospaced`	A typewriter-style font in which all characters have the same width. The most common monospaced font is `Courier`.
`Dialog`	A system-dependent font used for output text in dialog boxes.
`DialogInput`	A system-dependent font for user input in dialog boxes.

The remaining chapters in this book use only these generic font names.

What else might you want to change? To generate an even fancier display, you might want to change the color of the text by sending a `setColor` message to the `GLabel`. Although you can work with a wide variety of colors in Java, the `Color` class defines a set of standard colors that is sufficient for most purposes. These predefined colors have the following names:

```
Color.BLACK          Color.RED           Color.BLUE
Color.DARK_GRAY      Color.YELLOW        Color.MAGENTA
Color.GRAY           Color.GREEN         Color.ORANGE
Color.LIGHT_GRAY     Color.CYAN          Color.PINK
Color.WHITE
```

You could, for example, change the color of the `GLabel` to red by adding one more line to the `run` method, as follows:

```
public void run() {
    GLabel msg = new GLabel("hello, world", 100, 75);
    msg.setFont("Helvetica-24");
    msg.setColor(Color.RED);
    add(msg);
}
```

The `Color` class that defines the standard color names is defined in a package called `java.awt`. This package implements the **Abstract Windowing Toolkit** (or **AWT**, for short) that is the foundation of Java's own graphics libraries. Thus, if you want to use any of these color names in one of your programs, you must import that package by including the line

```
import java.awt.*;
```

at the beginning of your program.

The `GObject` class hierarchy

The `GLabel` class is only one of several classes defined by the `acm.graphics` package. A small portion of the `acm.graphics` hierarchy appears in Figure 2-7. The top of the diagram is occupied by the `GObject` class, which represents the general class of graphical objects that can be displayed in a graphics window. The next level of the hierarchy consists of four `GObject` subclasses, each of which represents a specific type of graphical object that you might want to display. You have already seen the `GLabel` class, which is used to display text strings. The

GRect, **GOval**, and **GLine** classes are used to display rectangles, ovals, and straight lines, respectively.

Like the classes in the **Program** hierarchy in Figure 2-5, the classes in Figure 2-7 offer a useful illustration of subclassing and inheritance. Any behavior that is common to every graphical object is defined at the **GObject** level, from which it is automatically inherited by each of the subclasses. For example, because all graphical objects can be colored, the **setColor** method is defined as part of the high-level definition of **GObject**. The program at the end of the preceding section was able to use **setColor** to change the color of the **GLabel** because **GLabel** inherits the **setColor** method from its superclass. By contrast, the **setFont** method is defined only for the **GLabel** class. Fonts, after all, make sense only for structures that involve characters. Because it would be meaningless to set the font of a rectangle, oval, or line, the **setFont** method is defined only for the **GLabel** class.

Figure 2-8 includes a few useful methods for the **GLabel**, **GRect**, **GOval**, and **GLine** classes. Although each of these classes includes methods beyond the ones listed here, this set should be enough to get you started, particularly if you have a few sample programs to use as models.

The GRect class

The **GRect** class is used to represent a rectangular box that can be displayed in a graphics window. As with any of the **GObject** subclasses, the process of putting a **GRect** object on the screen consists of the following steps:

1. Use the **GRect** constructor to generate a new instance of the **GRect** class. In most cases, you will need to store this object in a variable so that you can refer to it later.
2. Send the object any messages that are necessary to make sure it appears correctly on the display. For a **GRect** object, the most useful methods are **setColor**, which you already know from the earlier **GLabel** examples, and **setFilled**, which determines whether the rectangle should appear as a solid-color box or just the exterior outline.

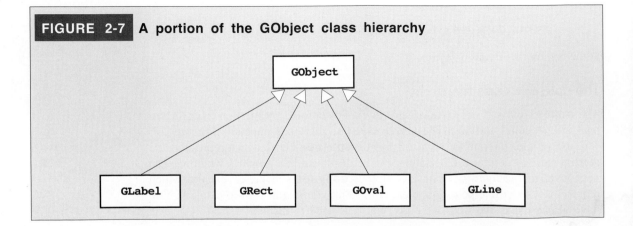

FIGURE 2-7 **A portion of the GObject class hierarchy**

FIGURE 2-8 Useful methods to get you started with the acm.graphics package

Constructors

new GLabel(*string*, *x*, *y*)
  Creates a new **GLabel** object containing the specified string that begins at the point (*x*, *y*).

new GRect(*x*, *y*, *width*, *height*)
  Creates a new **GRect** object with the specified dimensions whose upper left corner is at (*x*, *y*).

new GOval(*x*, *y*, *width*, *height*)
  Creates a new **GOval** object whose size is set to fit inside the **GRect** with the same arguments.

new GLine(x_1, y_1, x_2, y_2)
  Creates a new **GLine** object connecting the points (x_1, y_1) and (x_2, y_2).

Methods common to all graphical objects

object.**setColor**(*color*)
  Sets the color of the object to *color*, which is ordinarily a color name from **java.awt**.

object.**setLocation**(*x*, *y*)
  Changes the location of the object to the point (*x*, *y*).

object.**move**(*dx*, *dy*)
  Moves the object by adding *dx* to its *x* coordinate and *dy* to its *y* coordinate.

Methods available for GRect and GOval only

object.**setFilled**(*fill*)
  Sets whether this object is filled (**true** means filled, **false** means outlined).

object.**setFillColor**(*color*)
  Sets the color used to fill the interior of the object, which may be different from the border.

Methods available for GLabel only

label.**setFont**(*string*)
  Sets the font for *label* as indicated by *string*, which gives the family name, style, and point size.

---

3. Use the **add** method in the **GraphicsProgram** class to add the new rectangle to the set of graphical objects displayed in the graphics window.

Figure 2-9 contains a simple program called **GRectExample** that produces the following output:

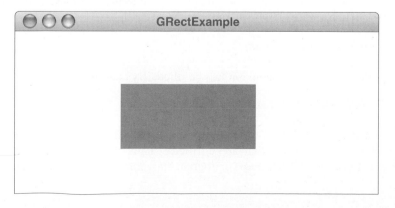

FIGURE 2-9   **Program to display a red rectangle**

```
/*
 * File: GRectExample.java
 * --------------------------
 * This program creates a new GRect object, sets it to be filled,
 * colors it red, and then displays it on the screen.  The GRect
 * is 125 pixels wide by 60 pixels high, with its upper left
 * corner at the point (100, 50).
 */

import acm.graphics.*;
import acm.program.*;
import java.awt.*;

public class GRectExample extends GraphicsProgram {

   public void run() {
      GRect rect = new GRect(100, 50, 125, 60);
      rect.setFilled(true);
      rect.setColor(Color.RED);
      add(rect);
   }

}
```

If you look through the statements in the **run** method, you can almost certainly follow the logic of the program even if some of the details remain fuzzy. In four statements, the **run** method creates a new **GRect** instance, sets it to be filled, colors it red, and then adds it to the graphics window.

There are, however, a couple of details about the code that warrant further explanation. First, the argument to the **setFilled** method is listed in Figure 2-8 as having one of two values: **true** or **false**. These values are instances of an extremely important Java type called **boolean** that you will learn more about in Chapter 3. For the moment, however, it is sufficient to think of these two values in terms of their conventional English interpretation. Calling

```
rect.setFilled(true);
```

indicates that the rectangle should in fact be filled. By contrast, calling

```
rect.setFilled(false);
```

indicates that it should not be, which leaves only the outline. By default, the **GRect** constructor creates objects that are unfilled. Thus, if you were to leave this statement out of the **GRectExample** program altogether, the output would look like this:

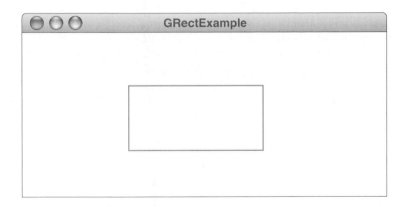

The second aspect of the program that deserves additional discussion is the
GRect constructor. As it stands, the arguments to the constructor—the numbers
100, 50, 125, and 60—might seem a little baffling, particularly if they weren't
explained in the program comments. To understand what these arguments mean,
you have to know what values the constructor expects. As you become more
familiar with Java, you will eventually learn how to figure out what each argument
means by looking at the definition or, better yet, the online documentation for the
class. In this case, you can find the documentation you need in Figure 2-8, which
tells you that the parameters to the **GRect** constructor are, in order from left to right,
the *x* coordinate of the object's location, the corresponding *y* coordinate, the width
of the object, and its height.

So far, so good. Knowing what each of the arguments to the **GRect** constructor
signifies offers some insight into how the rectangle will appear on the screen, but
you also need to understand more about how Java interprets the values of those
arguments. In particular, you need to know the following facts about Java's
coordinate system:

- In Java, the location $(0, 0)$ is at the upper left corner of the graphics window.
  This point is called the **origin.** Accordingly, the location given for a
  graphical object usually specifies the coordinates of its upper left corner.
- In contrast to the traditional Cartesian coordinate system, values for the *y*
  coordinate increase as you move *downward.* Values for the *x* coordinate
  increase from left to right, as usual.
- Coordinates and distances are expressed in units corresponding to the
  individual dots that make up the display, which are called **pixels.**

Thus, the constructor call

```
new GRect(100, 50, 125, 60)
```

specifies a rectangle whose upper left corner is 100 pixels to the right and 50 pixels
down from the upper left corner of the graphics window. The size of the rectangle
is specified by the two remaining parameters: this rectangle is 125 pixel units wide
and 60 pixels high. The geometry of this rectangle in relation to its window is
illustrated graphically in Figure 2-10.

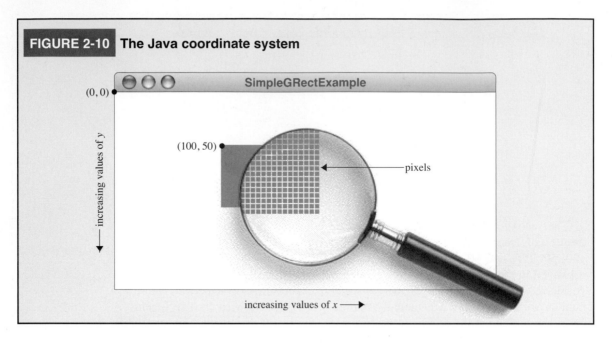

FIGURE 2-10 The Java coordinate system

The GOval class

As its name suggests, the **GOval** class is used to display an oval-shaped figure in a graphics window. Structurally, the **GOval** class is similar to the **GRect** class: the constructors for the two classes take the same arguments, and the two classes respond to the same set of methods. The difference is that the two classes generate a different figure on the screen. The **GRect** class displays a rectangle whose location and size are determined by the argument values *x, y, width,* and *height.* The **GOval** class displays the oval whose edges just touch the boundaries of that rectangle.

The relationship between the **GRect** and the **GOval** classes is most easily illustrated by example. The **GRectPlusGOval** program in Figure 2-11 takes the code from the earlier **GRectExample** program and extends it by adding a **GOval** with the same coordinates and dimensions. The resulting output looks like this:

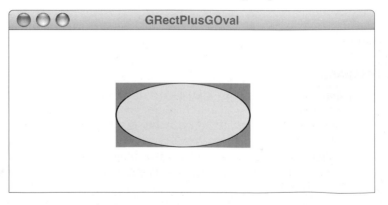

| FIGURE 2-11 | **Program to display a red rectangle and a green oval** |

```
/*
 * File: GRectPlusGOval.java
 * --------------------------
 * This program creates a GRect and a GOval using  the same
 * parameters.  The GRect is colored red; the GOval is outlined
 * in black but filled in green.  The example illustrates that
 * the GOval fills the boundary set by the enclosing rectangle.
 */

import acm.graphics.*;
import acm.program.*;
import java.awt.*;

public class GRectPlusGOval extends GraphicsProgram {

    public void run() {
        GRect rect = new GRect(100, 50, 125, 60);
        rect.setFilled(true);
        rect.setColor(Color.RED);
        add(rect);
        GOval oval = new GOval(100, 50, 125, 60);
        oval.setFilled(true);
        oval.setFillColor(Color.GREEN);
        add(oval);
    }

}
```

There are two important things to notice in this example. First, the green **GOval** extends so that its edges—which are outlined in black because the program changes only the fill color of the **GOval**—touch the boundary of the rectangle. Second, the **GOval**, which was added after the **GRect**, hides the portions of the rectangle that lie underneath the boundary of the oval. If you were to add these figures in the opposite order, all you would see is the **GRect**, because the entire **GOval** would be underneath the boundaries of the **GRect**.

The GLine class

In many ways, the **GLine** class is the simplest of the **GObject** subclasses included in the class diagram in Figure 2-7. The **GLine** constructor takes four arguments, which are the x and y coordinates of the two endpoints. Because it doesn't make sense to fill a line or set its font, the **GLine** class doesn't include methods like **setFilled** or **setFont**. Of the methods you've seen, the only one that applies to a **GLine** instance is **setColor**, which changes the color of the line.

Figure 2-12 presents a program called **TicTacToeBoard**, which draws the #-shaped pattern of lines used to play the game of Tic-Tac-Toe:

| FIGURE 2-12 | **Program to display a Tic-Tac-Toe board** |

```
/*
 * File: TicTacToeBoard.java
 * ---------------------------
 * This program draws a Tic-Tac-Toe board as an illustration
 * of the GLine class.  This version uses explicit coordinate
 * values which makes the program difficult to extend or
 * maintain.  In Chapter 3, you will learn how to use constants
 * and expressions to calculate these coordinate values.
 */

import acm.graphics.*;
import acm.program.*;

public class TicTacToeBoard extends GraphicsProgram {

   public void run() {
      add(new GLine(30, 60, 120, 60));
      add(new GLine(30, 90, 120, 90));
      add(new GLine(60, 30, 60, 120));
      add(new GLine(90, 30, 90, 120));
   }

}
```

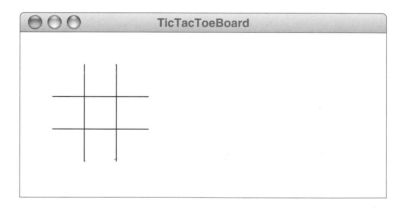

The **run** method for this program simply adds four **GLine** objects to the picture. The first connects the points (30, 60) and (120, 60), the second connects (30, 90) and (120, 90), and so on. The first two lines have the same y coordinate and are therefore horizontal; the last two have the same x coordinate and are therefore vertical.

The problem with this program is that the coordinate values are all specified explicitly. Using explicit coordinate values makes the program harder to write, harder to read, and harder to maintain. How would you figure out, for example, that the endpoints of the first horizontal line should be (30, 60) and (120, 60)? The easiest way would be to draw the picture you want to produce on a piece of graph paper and then use a ruler to measure the coordinates and dimension values. All that is tedious and subject to error. What you would really like to do is compute these values from a smaller set of parameters that collectively define the dimensions of the figure as a whole. In the case of the Tic-Tac-Toe board, for example, you know that the horizontal lines should divide the vertical lines into thirds, and vice versa. Thus, you could calculate the coordinates of the crossing points simply by dividing the size of the figure by three. To do so, however, you would need to understand how to specify such calculations using Java *expressions,* which you will learn about in the next chapter.

Summary

In this chapter, you have had the opportunity to look at several complete Java programs to get an idea of their general structure and how they work. The details of those programs have been deferred to later chapters; at this point, your principal objective has been to focus on the programming process itself by adopting a holistic view. Even so, by building on the programming examples provided so far, you should be ready at this point to write simple programs that involve only the following operations:

- Reading in numeric values entered by the user by calling the methods **readInt** and **readDouble**. In a **ConsoleProgram**, the user enters the data in a text-based window created by the program; in a **DialogProgram**, the user enters the data in an interactive dialog box.
- Displaying information to the user by calling the **println** method.
- Generating graphical programs by creating instances of the **GRect**, **GOval**, **GLine**, and **GLabel** classes.

Important points about programming introduced in this chapter are:

- Well-written programs contain *comments* that explain in English what the program is doing.
- Most programs use *packages* that provide tools the programmer need not recreate from scratch. The programs in this chapter use two packages: **acm.program** and **acm.graphics**. Subsequent chapters introduce additional packages.
- You gain access to packages by including an **import** line for that package at the top of the program.
- The Java programs in this book usually consist of a class definition that extends one of the classes in the **acm.program** package. That class is called the *main class*.
- Every main class contains a method called **run**. When the program is executed, the statements in the body of **run** are executed in order.
- A *class* acts as a template for creating *objects* that represent individual *instances* of the class. One class can give rise to many objects that are instances of that class. Each object, however, is an instance of a particular class.

- New instances are created by specifying the keyword **new** followed by a call to a *constructor* for that class.
- Classes form hierarchies that reflect the **extends** relationship. If class **A** extends class **B**, then **A** is a *subclass* of **B** and **B** is a *superclass* of **A.**
- Subclasses *inherit* the behavior of their superclass.
- The **Program** class in **acm.program** has three defined subclasses: **GraphicsProgram**, **ConsoleProgram**, and **DialogProgram**.
- The **GObject** class in **acm.graphics** has many useful subclasses. Although you won't have a chance to see the details until Chapter 9, you can use the **GLabel**, **GRect**, **GOval**, and **GLine** classes to create simple pictures.
- In object-oriented languages like Java, the standard way to affect the state of an object is to send it a message. Such messages are implemented using method calls and are written in the following form:

  receiver **.** *name* **(** *arguments* **)**

- All **GObject** subclasses respond to the **setColor** method, which changes the color in which the object is displayed. Because this behavior is shared by every subclass, it can be defined at the level of the **GObject** class.
- Several of the **GObject** subclasses define methods that apply specifically to that subclass. The **GLabel** class, for example, defines the method **setFont**, which changes the font in which the label appears. The **GRect** and **GOval** classes define the method **setFilled**, which determines whether the shape is filled in a solid color or displayed as an outline.
- Java uses a coordinate system in which the *origin* is in the upper left corner of the graphics window and in which the values of the *y* coordinate increase as you move downward. All coordinates and distances are expressed in terms of *pixels*, which are the individual dots that fill the surface of the screen.

Review questions

1. What is the purpose of the comments shown at the beginning of each program in this chapter?

2. What is the role of a library package?

3. What is the name of the method that is executed when a Java program starts up under the control of the **acm.program** package?

4. To what does the word *argument* refer in programming? What purpose do arguments serve?

5. Describe the function of the **println** method. What is the significance of the letters **ln** at the end of its name?

6. What is the purpose of the **readInt** method? How would you use it in a program?

7. This chapter describes two uses for the **+** operator in Java programs. What are they, and how does Java determine which interpretation to use?

8. Describe the difference between the philosophical terms *holism* and *reductionism*. Why are these concepts important to programming?

9. What is the difference between a *class* and an *object?*

10. Define the terms *subclass, superclass,* and *inheritance*.

11. What Java keyword is associated with the use of a constructor?

12. What is the difference between a **ConsoleProgram** and a **DialogProgram**?

13. True or false: The process of sending a message to a Java object is usually implemented by calling a method in that object.

14. In Java, how do you specify the object to which a message is directed?

15. What are the four **GObject** subclasses described in this chapter?

16. Which of these subclasses respond to the method **setFilled**? Which respond to the method **setFont**?

17. In Chapter 9, you will learn about several additional **GObject** subclasses beyond the four listed here. Will these classes respond to the method **setColor**?

18. In what ways does Java's coordinate system differ from the traditional Cartesian coordinate system?

Programming exercises

1. Type in the **HelloProgram.java** program exactly as it appears in this chapter and get it working. Change the message so that it reads "I love Java" instead. Add your name as a signature to the lower right corner.

2. The following program was written without comments or instructions to the user, except for a couple of input prompts:

```
import acm.program.*;

public class MyProgram extends ConsoleProgram {
    public void run() {
        double b = readDouble("Enter b: ");
        double h = readDouble("Enter h: ");
        double a = (b * h) / 2;
        println("a = " + a);
    }
}
```

Read through the program and figure out what it is doing. What result is it calculating? Rewrite this program so it is easier to understand, both for the user and for the programmer who must modify the program in the future.

3. Extend the **Add2Integers** program shown in Figure 2-2 so that it adds three integers instead.

4. Write a **GraphicsProgram** that generates the following simple picture of a house with a peaked roof, two windows, and a door with a circular doorknob:

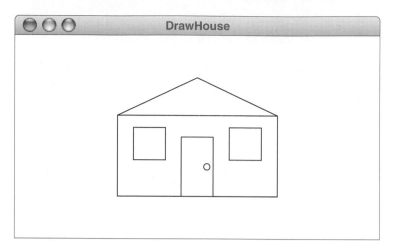

As with each of the graphical exercises in this chapter, you should choose coordinate values for your programs that produce a reasonable approximation of the diagram shown. In Chapter 3, you will learn how to compute coordinate values so that, for example, the house is centered in the window, the door is centered in the house frame, and the windows are centered horizontally between the door and the side walls.

5. Write a **GraphicsProgram** that draws the following picture of a robot face:

The eyes are orange, the nose is black, and the mouth is white. The face is filled in gray but outlined in black.

6. Write a **GraphicsProgram** that draws the following picture of an archery target, which also happens to be the logo of a large discount chain:

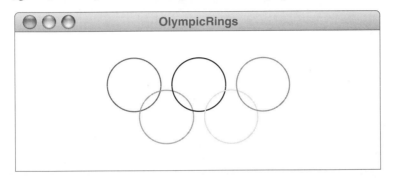

Both the outer and inner circles should be colored red.

7. Write a **GraphicsProgram** that draws the five interlocking rings (blue, yellow, black, green, and red) that form the symbol of the Olympic Games:

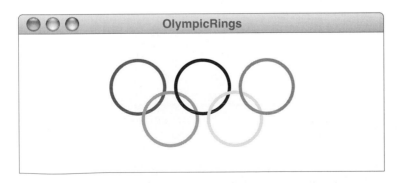

8. On most output devices, the Olympic Games logo from the preceding exercise doesn't show up all that well because the yellow circle (and to a lesser extent the green one) tends to disappear against the white background of the window. Part of the problem is that the outlines that Java draws for the **GOval** class are only one pixel wide, which doesn't show up well when drawn in lighter colors. It would be easier to see the rings if the borders were three pixels wide, like this:

Making this change would be easy if the **GOval** class included a method to set the width of the border, but, alas, it does not. Think about the problem for a bit and see whether you can come up with a strategy for creating the three-pixel-wide display using only the tools you currently have.

9. Write a **GraphicsProgram** that draws a picture of a rainbow that looks something like this:

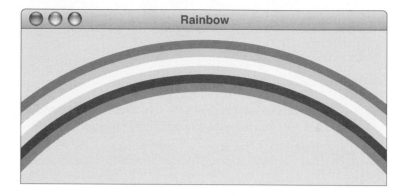

Starting at the top, the six stripes in the rainbow are red, orange, yellow, green, blue, and magenta, respectively; cyan makes a lovely color for the sky.

At first glance, it might seem as if this problem requires you to draw arcs. As it turns out, you can create the stripes in the rainbow using only circles, although seeing how this is possible forces you to think outside the box—in a literal as well as a figurative sense. The common center for each circle is some distance below the bottom of the window, and the diameters of the circles are wider than the screen. The **GraphicsProgram** shows only the part of the figure that actually appears in the window. This process of reducing a picture to the visible area is called **clipping.**

CHAPTER 3
Expressions

"What's twice eleven?" I said to Pooh.
("Twice what?" said Pooh to Me.)
"I think it ought to be twenty-two."
"Just what I think myself," said Pooh.
　　　　　　　　—*A. A. Milne, Now We Are Six*, 1927

George Boole (1815-1864)

Even though he was largely self-taught and never earned a formal university degree, George Boole achieved sufficient prominence to be appointed Professor of Mathematics at Queen's College in County Cork, Ireland, and to be elected as a Fellow of the Royal Society. His most influential work was an 1854 book entitled *An Investigation into the Laws of Thought, on Which are Founded the Mathematical Theories of Logic and Probabilities.* That book introduced a system of logic that has come to be known as *Boolean algebra* and which serves as the foundation for the **boolean** data type described in this chapter.

In Chapter 2, you had the opportunity to see a couple of simple programs— **Add2Integers** and **Add2Doubles**—that perform arithmetic manipulation. The idea in Chapter 2 was for you to get a sense of what that type of program looks like. In this chapter, your goal is to learn the underlying rules that allow you to write Java programs that specify computation. In doing so, you will combine a reductionistic understanding of the details with a holistic understanding of the program as a whole.

In each of those programs, the actual computation is specified by the appearance in the code of

```
n1 + n2
```

which indicates, naturally enough, that the computer should add the values stored in the variables **n1** and **n2**. This combination of variables and the **+** operator is an example of an **expression,** which is the symbolic representation in a programming language of the sequence of operations necessary to produce a desired result. To make programming easier for humans, these expressions tend to have a syntactic form that mirrors as closely as possible the representation used in traditional mathematical formulae. Indeed, the name of the programming language FORTRAN, which was the first language to include expression syntax, is a contraction of the words *formula translation,* because that aspect of the language was widely seen as its principal advantage over machine-language programming.

As in most languages, an **expression** in Java is composed of *terms* and *operators*. A **term**, such as **n1** or **n2** in the expressions from Chapter 2, represents a single data value. An **operator**, such as the **+** sign, is a character (or sometimes a short sequence of characters) that indicates a computational operation. In an expression, a term must be one of the following:

- *A constant*. An explicit data value that appears as part of the program is called a **constant**. Numbers such as 0 or 3.14159 are examples of constants.
- *A variable*. Variables serve as placeholders for data that can change during the execution of a program.
- *A method call*. Values are often generated by calling other methods, possibly from library packages, that return data values to the original expression. In the **Add2Integers** program, for example, the method **readInt** is used to read in each of the input values; the method call **readInt** is therefore an example of a term. Method calls are discussed in more detail in Chapter 5.
- *An expression in parentheses*. Parentheses may be used to indicate grouping within an expression, much as they are in mathematics. From the compiler's point of view, the subexpression in parentheses becomes a term, which is then treated as a unit.

When a program runs, the process of carrying out each of the specified operations in an expression is called **evaluation**. When the computer evaluates a Java expression, it applies each operator to the values represented by the surrounding terms. After all the operators have been evaluated, what remains is a single data value that represents the result of the computation. For example, given the expression

```
n1 + n2
```

the evaluation process consists of taking the values in the variables **n1** and **n2** and adding them together, and the result of the evaluation is whatever that sum happens to be.

3.1 Primitive data types

Before turning to the details of expression formation, it is useful to take a quick survey of the types of data that expressions can manipulate. In much of this text, you will work primarily with data objects that are representatives of a class. Those objects and classes represent the defining characteristic of the object-oriented paradigm on which Java is based. Expressions, however, tend to work with simpler types of data that, at least in Java, fall outside the object hierarchy. These data types, which are all defined as part of the language, are the **primitive data types** from which more complex objects are built.

To be useful in a wide variety of applications, programs must be able to store many different types of data. As you saw in Chapter 2, it is possible to write programs like **Add2Integers** that work with whole numbers but also programs like **Add2Doubles** in which numbers have fractional parts, such as 1.5 or 3.1415926. When you use a word-processing program, the individual data values are characters, which are then assembled into larger units such as words, sentences, and paragraphs. As your programs get more complicated, you will begin to work with large collections of information structured in a variety of ways. All these different classes of information constitute **data**.

Whenever you work with some piece of data—which might be an integer or a number with a fractional part or a character—the Java compiler needs to know its **data type**. Holistically speaking, a data type is defined by two properties: a set of values, or domain, and a set of operations. The **domain** is simply the set of values that are elements of that type. For example, the domain of the type **int** includes all integers ($\ldots -2, -1, 0, 1, 2 \ldots$) up to the limits defined by the Java language. For character data, the domain is the set of symbols that appear on the keyboard or that can be displayed on the terminal screen. The **set of operations** comprises the tools you have to manipulate values of that type. For example, given two integers, you might multiply them together or divide one by another. Given text data, on the other hand, it is hard to imagine what an operation like multiplication might mean. You would instead expect to use operations such as comparing two words to see if they are in alphabetical order or displaying a message on the screen. Thus, the operations must be appropriate to the elements of the domain, and the two components together—the domain and the operations—define the data type.

Java defines eight primitive data types, which appear in Figure 3-1. The first four types—**byte**, **short**, **int**, and **long**—represent integers with different

FIGURE 3-1	Primitive types in Java	

Type	Domain	Common operations
byte	8-bit integers in the range −128 to 127	*The arithmetic operators:* + add * multiply − subtract / divide % remainder
short	16-bit integers in the range −32768 to 32767	
int	32-bit integers in the range −2147483648 to 2147483647	*The relational operators:* == equal != not equal < less than <= less or equal > greater than >= greater or equal
long	64-bit integers in the range −9223372036854775808 to 9223372036854775807	
float	32-bit floating-point numbers in the range $\pm 1.4 \times 10^{-45}$ to $\pm 3.4028235 \times 10^{38}$	*The arithmetic operators except* % *The relational operators*
double	64-bit floating-point numbers in the range $\pm 4.39 \times 10^{-322}$ to $\pm 1.7976931348623157 \times 10^{308}$	
char	16-bit characters encoded using Unicode	*The relational operators*
boolean	the values **true** and **false**	*The logical operators:* && and || or ! not

maximum and minimum values that reflect the capacity of the memory cells in which they are stored. The next two—**float** and **double**—represent floating-point numbers, again with different dynamic ranges. Except in those rare cases in which a library method requires the use of one of the other types, this text will use **int** and **double** as its standard numeric types. The type **char** is used to represent character data and is covered in Chapter 8. The type **boolean**—which you encountered briefly in Chapter 2—is so important to programming that it merits an entire section of its own later in this chapter.

In addition to the primitive data types listed in Figure 3-1, it is often useful to think of the Java type **String** as if it were a primitive type, even though it is actually a class defined in the package **java.lang**. One reason for treating it as primitive is that the **String** class is built into the Java language in much the same ways that the primitive types are. For example, Java specifies a special syntax for string constants, just as it does for **int** or **double** or **boolean**. But a more important reason for regarding **String** as a primitive type is that doing so helps you think about strings in a more holistic way. As you will discover in Chapter 8, the **String** class defines a large number of methods that perform a variety of useful operations. Although understanding the details of those methods and how to use them will become important at some point, you can usually get away with imagining that string values are pretty much like integer values except that the two types have different domains. Just as you can declare a variable to be of type **int** and assign it an integer value, you can declare a variable to be of type **String** and assign it a string value. It is only when you need to use the methods provided by the **String** class that it makes any difference whether **String** is a class or a primitive type.

3.2 Constants and variables

The two simplest types of terms in an expression are constants and variables. Constants appear when you need to use an explicit value that doesn't change over the course of the program. Variables are placeholders for data that can change during execution. The sections that follow show you how to write constants and variables, and detail the rules that Java imposes on their specification.

Constants

When you write a formula in mathematics, some symbols in the formula typically represent unknown values while other symbols represent constants whose values are known. Consider, for example, the mathematical formula for computing the circumference (C) of a circle given its radius (r):

$$C = 2\pi r$$

To translate this formula into a expression, you would use variables to record the radius and circumference. These variables change depending on the data. The values 2 and π, however, are constants—explicit values that never change. The value 2 is an integer constant, and the value π is a real-number constant, which would be represented in a program by a floating-point approximation, such as 3.14159265358979323846. Because constants are an important building block for constructing expressions, it is important to be able to write constant values for each of the basic data types.

- *Integer constants.* To write an integer constant as part of a program or as input data, you simply write the digits that make up the number. If the integer is negative, you write a minus sign before the number, just as in mathematics. Commas are never used. Thus, the value one million must be written as 1000000 and not as 1,000,000.

- *Floating-point constants.* In Java, floating-point constants are written with a decimal point. Thus, if **2.0** appears in a program, the number is represented internally as a floating-point value; if the programmer had written **2**, this value would be an integer. Floating-point values can also be written in a special programmer's style of scientific notation, in which the value is represented as a floating-point number multiplied by a integral power of 10. To write a number using this style, you write a floating-point number in standard notation, followed immediately by the letter **E** and an integer exponent, optionally preceded by a **+** or **–** sign. For example, the speed of light in meters per second is approximately

  $$2.9979 \times 10^{8}$$

  which can be written in Java as

  2.9979E+8

  where the **E** stands for the words *times 10 to the power*.

- *Boolean constants*. There are only two constants of type **boolean**, which are represented by the Java keywords **true** and **false**.

Character constants also exist and are described in Chapter 8.

There is, however, one additional form of constant that you need to know about, even though it is not a primitive type:

- *String constants*. You write a string constant in Java by enclosing the characters that comprise the string in double quotation marks. For example, the very first example of data used in this text was the string

  ```
  "hello, world"
  ```

  in the **HelloProgram** example from Chapter 2. This string consists of the characters shown between the quotation marks, including the letters, the comma, and the space. The quotation marks are not part of the string but serve only to mark its beginning and end. There are several additional rules for writing string constants that allow you to include special characters (such as quotation marks) within the string. These rules are described in detail in Chapter 8.

Variables

A **variable** is a placeholder for a value and has three important attributes: a *name*, a *value*, and a *type*. To understand the relationship of these attributes, it is easiest to think of a variable as a box with a label attached to the outside. The name of the variable appears on the label and is used to tell the different boxes apart. If you have three boxes (or variables), you can refer to a particular one using its name. The value of the variable corresponds to the contents of the box. The name on the label of the box is fixed, but you can change the value as often as you like. The type of the variable indicates what kind of data value can be stored in the box. For example, if you have a box designed to hold a value of type **int**, you cannot put a value of type **String** into that box.

Names in Java—for variables as well as for other sorts of things such as classes and methods—are called **identifiers.** Identifiers must be constructed according to the following rules:

1. Identifiers must start with a letter or the underscore character (_). In Java, uppercase and lowercase letters appearing in an identifier are considered to be different, so the names **ABC**, **Abc**, and **abc** are three separate identifiers.

2. All other characters in an identifier must be letters, digits, or the underscore. No spaces or other special characters are permitted. Identifiers can be of any length.

3. Identifiers must not be one of the following **reserved words**, which are names that Java defines for a specific purpose:

abstract	else	interface	super
boolean	extends	long	switch
break	false	native	synchronized
byte	final	new	this
case	finally	null	throw
catch	float	package	throws
char	for	private	transient
class	goto	protected	true
const	if	public	try
continue	implements	return	void
default	import	short	volatile
do	instanceof	static	while
double	int	strictfp	

In addition, good programming style requires two more rules, as follows:

4. Identifiers should make obvious to the reader the purpose of the variable, class, or method. Although friends' names, expletives, and the like may be legal according to the other rules, they do absolutely nothing to improve the readability of your programs.

5. Identifiers should match the case conventions that have become standard in Java. In particular, variable names should begin with a lowercase letter, and class names with an uppercase letter. Thus, **n1** is appropriate as the name of a variable, and **HelloProgram** is appropriate as the name of a class. Each additional English word appearing in the name is typically capitalized to improve readability, as in the variable name **numberOfStudents**. Names that are used as constants, which are discussed in the section entitled "Named constants" later in this chapter, use only uppercase letters and separate words with underscores, as in **PLANCKS_CONSTANT**.

Declarations

As noted in the discussion of the **Add2Integers** program in Chapter 2, you must explicitly specify the data type of each variable when you introduce it into a program. This process is known as declaring the variable. The syntax for declaring a variable is shown in the box on the right. The line

> *type identifier* = *expression*;

is an example of a **syntax template.** The words in italics

Syntax for declarations

> *type identifier* = *expression*;

where:
> *type* is the type of the variable
> *identifier* is the name of the variable
> *expression* specifies the initial value

---

represent items you can fill in with anything that fits the specification of that template. In writing an assignment statement, for example, you can declare variables of any type, use any identifier to the left of the equal sign, and supply any expression on the right. The boldface items in the template—in this case the equal sign and the semicolon—are fixed. Thus, in order to write a declaration, you start with the type name, followed by the variable name, an equal sign, an expression, and a semicolon, in that order.

Whenever new syntactic constructs are introduced in this text, they will be accompanied by a **syntax box** that defines their structure, such as the one at the beginning of this section that details the structure of a declaration. Syntax boxes contain a capsule summary of the grammatical rules for Java and serve as a handy reference.

Variables can be declared in several different parts of the program. The variables you have seen up to this point have all been declared inside the body of a method. (So far, that method has always been **run**, but it is legal to declare variables in any method.) Variables declared inside a method are called **local variables** because they are available only to that method and not to any other parts of the code. You can, however, declare variables within the definition of a class but outside of any method. Variables defined at this level are called **instance variables,** or **ivars** for short, and are stored as part of each object. Instance variables must be used with a certain amount of caution, and it is probably best to avoid them until you have a chance to learn a bit more about the structure of classes in Chapter 6.

In addition to local and instance variables, Java supports a third style of variable declaration called **class variables,** which, as their name suggests, are defined at the level of the class rather than of a specific method or object. Class variables are declared in much the same way that instance variables are; the only difference is that class variables include the keyword **static** as part of the declaration. Class variables must also be used with care, but they are precisely the right tool for introducing names for constants, as discussed in the next section.

Named constants

As you write your programs, you will find that you often use the same constant many times in a program. If, for example, you are performing geometrical calculations that involve circles, the constant π comes up frequently. Moreover, if those calculations require high precision, you might actually need all the digits that fit into a value of type **double**, which means you would be working with the value 3.14159265358979323846. Writing that constant over and over again is tedious at best, and likely to introduce errors if you type it in by hand each time instead of cutting and pasting the value. It would be better if you could give this constant a name and then refer to it by that name everywhere in the program. You could, of course, simply declare it as a local variable by writing

```
double pi = 3.14159265358979323846;
```

but you would then be able to use it only within the method in which it was defined. A better strategy is to declare it as a class variable like this:

```
private static final double PI = 3.14159265358979323846;
```

The keywords at the beginning of this declaration each provide some information about the nature of the declaration. The **private** keyword indicates that this constant can be used only within the class that defines it. It often makes more sense to declare constants to be **public**, but good programming practice suggests that you should keep all declarations private unless there is a compelling reason to do otherwise. The **static** keyword indicates that this declaration introduces a class variable rather than an instance variable. The **final** keyword declares that the value will not change after the variable is initialized, thereby ensuring that the value remains constant. It would not be appropriate, after all, to change the value of π (despite the fact that a bill was introduced in 1897 into the Indiana State Legislature attempting to do just that). The rest of the declaration consists of the type, the name, and the value, as before. The only difference is that the name is written entirely in uppercase to be consistent with Java's naming scheme.

   Using named constants offers several advantages. First, descriptive constant names usually make the program easier to read. More importantly, using constants can dramatically simplify the problem of maintaining the code for a program as it evolves. This process is considered in more detail in the section entitled "Designing for change" later in this chapter.

3.3 Operators and operands

In an expression, the actual computational steps are indicated by symbolic operators that connect the individual terms. The simplest operators to define are those used for arithmetic expressions, which use the standard operators from arithmetic. The arithmetic operators that apply to all numeric data types are:

+	Addition
−	Subtraction (or negation, if written with no value to its left)
*	Multiplication
/	Division

Each of these operators forms a new expression by connecting two smaller expressions, one to the left and one to right of the operator. These subsidiary expressions (or **subexpressions**) to which the operator is applied are called the **operands** for that operator. For example, in the expression

        x + 3

the operands for the **+** operator are the subexpressions **x** and **3**. Operands are often individual terms, but they can also be more complicated expressions. For example, in the expression

        (2 * x) + (3 * y)

the operands to **+** are the subexpressions **(2 * x)** and **(3 * y)**.

   As in conventional mathematics, the operator **−** can be used in two forms. When it is positioned between two operands, it indicates subtraction, as in **x − y**. When used with no operand to its left, it indicates negation, so **−x** denotes the negative of whatever value **x** has. When used in this way, the **−** operator is called a **unary operator** because it applies to a single operand. The other operators (including **−**

when it denotes subtraction) are called **binary operators** because they apply to a pair of operands.

These operators make it possible to write programs that compute much more interesting and useful results than the **Add2Doubles** program, given that you now have subtraction, multiplication, and division in your repertoire. Having this larger collection of operators makes it possible, for example, to write a program that converts a length given in inches to its metric counterpart in centimeters. All you really need to know is that 1 inch equals 2.54 centimeters; you can construct the rest of the program just by adapting lines from the **Add2Doubles** example from Chapter 2 and putting them back together in the appropriate way. Figure 3-2 shows the final result.

Combining integers and floating-point numbers

In Java, values of type **int** and **double** can be freely combined. If you use a binary operator with two values of type **int**, the result is of type **int**. If either or both operands are of type **double**, however, the result is always of type **double**. Thus, the value of the expression

      `n + 1`

is of type **int**, if the variable **n** is declared as type **int**. On the other hand, the expression

      `n + 1.5`

FIGURE 3-2   **Program to convert inches to centimeters**

```
/*
 * File: InchesToCentimeters.java
 * ----------------------------------
 * This program converts inches to centimeters.
 */

import acm.program.*;

public class InchesToCentimeters extends ConsoleProgram {

   public void run() {
      println("This program converts inches to centimeters.");
      double inches = readDouble("Enter value in inches: ");
      double cm = inches * CENTIMETERS_PER_INCH;
      println(inches + "in = " + cm + "cm");
   }

/* Private constants */
   private static final double CENTIMETERS_PER_INCH = 2.54;

}
```

is always of type **double**. This convention ensures that the result of the computation is as accurate as possible. In the case of the expression **n + 1.5**, for example, there would be no way to represent the .5 if the result were computed using integer arithmetic.

Integer division and the remainder operator

As noted in the preceding section, applying an arithmetic operator to integer operands always produces an integer result. This fact leads to an interesting situation with respect to division. If you write an expression like

```
9 / 4
```

Java's rules specify that the result of this operation must be an integer, because both operands are of type **int**. When the program evaluates this expression, it divides 9 by 4 and throws away any remainder. Thus, the value of the expression is 2, not 2.25. If you want to compute the mathematically correct result, at least one of the operands must be a floating-point number. For example, the three expressions

```
9.0 / 4
9 / 4.0
9.0 / 4.0
```

each produce the floating-point value 2.25. The remainder is thrown away only if both operands are of type **int**.

There is an additional arithmetic operator that computes a remainder, which is indicated in Java by the percent sign (**%**). The **%** operator requires that both operands be of type **int**. It returns the remainder when the first operand is divided by the second. For example, the value of

```
9 % 4
```

is 1, since 4 goes into 9 twice, with 1 left over. The following are some other examples of the **%** operator:

```
0 % 4   =   0                19 % 4   =   3
1 % 4   =   1                20 % 4   =   0
4 % 4   =   0              2001 % 4   =   1
```

The **/** and **%** operators turn out to be extremely useful in a wide variety of programming applications. The **%** operator, for example, is often used to test whether one number is divisible by another. For example, to determine whether an integer **n** is divisible by 3, you just check whether the result of the expression **n % 3** is 0.

As a side note, it is not always easy to understand what happens when one or both of the operands to **%** are negative. Java does define the result in such cases, but the definition was developed to be consistent with the way machine architectures work, which is unfortunately different from what mathematicians would like. To obviate any confusion, this text will avoid using % with negative operands, and it probably makes sense to adopt the same convention in your own code.

Precedence

If an expression has more than one operator, the order in which those operators are applied becomes an important issue. In Java, you can always specify the order by putting parentheses around individual subexpressions, just as you would in traditional mathematics. For example, the parentheses in the expression

```
(2 * x) + (3 * y)
```

indicate that Java should perform each of the multiplication operations before the addition. But what happens if the parentheses are missing? Suppose that the expression is simply

```
2 * x + 3 * y
```

How does the Java compiler decide the order in which to apply the individual operations?

In Java, as in most programming languages, that decision is dictated by a set of ordering rules designed to conform to standard mathematical usage. They are called **rules of precedence**. For arithmetic expressions, the rules are:

1. The Java compiler first applies any unary minus operators (a minus sign with no operand to its left).
2. The compiler then applies the multiplicative operators (*, /, and %). If two of these operators apply to the same operand, the leftmost one is performed first.
3. It then applies the additive operators (+ and -). Once again, if two operators at this level of precedence apply to the same operand, Java starts with the leftmost one.

Thus, in the expression

```
2 * x + 3 * y
```

the multiplication operations are performed first, even when the parentheses are missing. Using parentheses may make the order clearer, but in this case their use is not required because the intended order of operations matches the precedence assumptions of traditional mathematics. If you instead want the addition to be performed first, you must indicate that fact explicitly by using parentheses, as in

```
2 * (x + 3) * y
```

The rules of precedence apply only when two operators "compete" for a single operand. For instance, in the expression

```
2 * x + 3 * y
```

the operators $*$ and $+$ compete for the operand **x**. The rules of precedence dictate that the $*$ is performed first because multiplication has higher precedence than addition. Similarly, looking at the two operators next to the value 3, you can again determine that the $*$ is performed first, for precisely the same reason. In cases in which operators do not actually compete for the same operand, as is the case with the two multiplication operations in this expression, Java performs the computation in left-to-right order. Thus, Java will multiply **x** by 2 before multiplying **y** by 3.

Precedence rules can make a significant difference in the outcome of expression evaluation. Consider, for example, the expression

```
10 - 5 - 2
```

Because Java's precedence rules dictate that the leftmost $-$ be performed first, the computation is carried out as if the expression had been written

```
(10 - 5) - 2
```

which yields the value 3. If you want the subtractions performed in the other order, you must use explicit parentheses:

```
10 - (5 - 2)
```

In this case, the result is 7.

There are many situations in which parentheses are required to achieve the desired result. For example, suppose that, instead of adding two floating-point numbers the way **Add2Doubles** does, you want them averaged instead. The program is almost the same, as shown in Figure 3-3.

FIGURE 3-3 **Program to average two double-precision numbers**

```
/*
 * File: Average2Doubles.java
 * ------------------------------
 * This program averages two double-precision floating-point numbers.
 */

import acm.program.*;

public class Average2Doubles extends ConsoleProgram {

   public void run() {
      println("This program averages two numbers.");
      double n1 = readDouble("Enter n1: ");
      double n2 = readDouble("Enter n2: ");
      double average = (n1 + n2) / 2;
      println("The average is " + average + ".");
   }

}
```

Note that the parentheses are necessary in the statement

```
double average = (n1 + n2) / 2;
```

to ensure that the addition is performed before the division. If the parentheses were missing, Java's precedence rules would dictate that the division be performed first, and the result would be the mathematical expression

$$n1 + \frac{n2}{2}$$

instead of the intended

$$\frac{n1 + n2}{2}$$

Applying rules of precedence

To illustrate precedence rules in action, let's consider the expression

```
8 * (7 - 6 + 5) % (4 + 3 / 2) - 1
```

Put yourself in the place of the computer. How would you go about evaluating this expression?

Your first step is to evaluate the parenthesized subexpressions, which happens in left-to-right order. To compute the value of **(7 - 6 + 5)**, you subtract 6 from 7 to get 1, and then add 5 to get 6. Thus, after evaluating the first subexpression, you are left with

```
8 *  6  % (4 + 3 / 2) - 1
```

where the box indicates that the value is the result of a previously evaluated subexpression.

You can then go on to evaluate the second parenthesized subexpression. Here, you must do the division first, since division and multiplication take precedence over addition. Thus, your first step is to divide 3 by 2, which results in the value 1 (remember that integer division throws away the remainder). You then add the 4 and 1 to get 5. At this point, you are left with the following expression:

```
8 *  6  %  5  - 1
```

At this point in the calculation, Java's precedence rules dictate that you perform the multiplication and remainder operations, in that order, before the subtraction: 6 times 8 is 48, and the remainder of 48 divided by 5 is 3. Your last step is to subtract 1, leaving 2 as the value of the complete expression.

Type conversion

You have already learned that it is possible to combine values of different numeric types within a Java program. When you do so, Java handles the situation by using **automatic type conversion**, a process in which the compiler converts values of one type into values of another compatible type as an implicit part of the computation. For example, whenever you combine an integer and a floating-point value using an arithmetic operator, Java automatically converts the integer into the mathematically equivalent **double** before applying the operation. Thus, if you write the expression

```
1 + 2.3
```

Java converts the integer 1 into the floating-point number 1.0 before adding the two values together.

In Java, automatic type conversions also occur whenever a variable is assigned a value of a more restrictive type. For example, if you write the declaration

```
double total = 0;
```

Java converts the integer 0 into a **double** before assigning it to the variable **total**. Some programming languages (and some programmers) insist on writing this statement as

```
double total = 0.0;
```

In terms of its effect, this statement has the same meaning as the earlier one. On the other hand, the values 0 and 0.0 mean different things to mathematicians. Writing the value 0 indicates that the value is precisely 0, because integers are exact. When 0.0 appears in a statistical or mathematical context, however, the usual interpretation is that it represents a number close to zero, but one whose accuracy is known only to one significant digit after the decimal point. To avoid such ambiguity, this text uses integers to indicate exactness, even in floating-point contexts.

It is, however, illegal in Java to use a value of type **double** as the initial value of a variable of type **int**. You can get around this restriction by using a syntactic construct called a **type cast**, which consists of the desired type in parentheses followed by the value you wish to convert. Thus, if you write the declaration

```
int n = (int) 1.9999;
```

Java will convert 1.9999 to an integer before assigning it as the initial value of **n**. You may, however, be surprised to learn that the integer it chooses is 1 rather than 2. Converting a value from floating-point to integer representation—which happens both with type casts and in integer division—simply throws away any fraction. That form of conversion is called **truncation.**

As an example of how truncation is useful, suppose that you have been asked to write a program that translates a metric distance in centimeters back into English units—the inverse of the **InchesToCentimeters.java** program in Figure 3-2. If all you need is the number of inches, the body of the program will look pretty much the same as before; the only difference in the computation is that you divide by **CENTIMETERS_PER_INCH** instead of multiplying.

Suppose, however, that your employer wants you to display the answer not simply as the total number of inches, but as an integral number of feet plus the number of leftover inches. To compute the whole number of feet, you can divide the total number of inches by 12 and throw away any remainder. To calculate the number of inches left over, you can multiply the number of feet by 12 and subtract that quantity from the total number of inches. The entire program is shown in Figure 3-4.

The declaration

```
int feet = (int) (totalInches / INCHES_PER_FOOT);
```

throws away the remainder because the operator **(int)** casts the result into an **int**. The parentheses surrounding **(totalInches / INCHES_PER_FOOT)** are necessary in this expression because the type-cast operator has very high precedence. If you were to leave these parentheses out, Java would convert **totalInches** to an integer first and then divide the result by **INCHES_PER_FOOT**.

There are also cases in which you need to specify a type conversion even though the rules for automatic conversion do not apply. Suppose, for example, you have

---

FIGURE 3-4 **Program to convert centimeters into feet and inches**

```
/*
 * File: CentimetersToFeetAndInches.java
 * ------------------------------------------
 * This program converts centimeters to an integral number of feet
 * and any remaining inches.
 */

import acm.program.*;

public class CentimetersToFeetAndInches extends ConsoleProgram {

   public void run() {
      println("This program converts centimeters to feet and inches.");
      double cm = readDouble("Enter value in centimeters: ");
      double totalInches = cm / CENTIMETERS_PER_INCH;
      int feet = (int) (totalInches / INCHES_PER_FOOT);
      double inches = totalInches - INCHES_PER_FOOT * feet;
      println(cm + "cm = " + feet + "ft + " + inches + "in");
   }

/* Private constants */
   private static final int INCHES_PER_FOOT = 12;
   private static final double CENTIMETERS_PER_INCH = 2.54;

}
```

declared two integer variables, **num** and **den**, and you want to compute their mathematical quotient (including the fraction) and assign the result to a newly declared **double** variable named **quotient**. You can't simply write

```
double quotient = num / den;
```

because both **num** and **den** are integers. When the division operator is applied to two integers, it throws away the fraction. To avoid this problem, you have to convert at least one of the values to **double** before the division is performed. You could, for example, convert the denominator of the fraction by writing

```
double quotient = num / (double) den;
```

Since the denominator is now of type **double**, the division is carried out using floating-point arithmetic and the fraction is retained. Equivalently, you could convert the numerator by writing

```
double quotient = (double) num / den;
```

This statement has the same effect, but only because the precedence of a type cast is higher than that of division, which means that the type conversion happens first.

3.4 Assignment statements

In Java, you can assign values to variables in either of two ways. In the programs you have seen so far, the value of each variable has been set as part of its declaration. More sophisticated programs, however, often change the value of variables after the initial declaration, since one of the central advantages of variables is that their values can change over the lifetime of a program. To assign a new value to a variable, you need to use an **assignment statement,** as described in the syntax box shown on the right. The syntax is clearly very close to that used in declarations; the only difference is that the name of the type is missing.

> **Syntax for assignment statements**
>
> > *variable* **=** *expression***;**
>
> where:
> > *variable* is the variable you wish to set
> > *expression* specifies the new value

As noted in Chapter 2, drawing box diagrams can help you visualize the role of variables in a program. Whenever you declare a local variable as part of a method definition, you can draw a new box to hold its value and label the box with the variable name. For example, suppose that a method introduces three new variables—two of type **int** with the names **n1** and **n2**, and one of type **String** with the name **msg**—using the following declarations:

```
int n1 = 17;
int n2 = 0;
String msg = "Hello";
```

You can represent the variables in that method graphically by drawing a box for each variable, as follows.

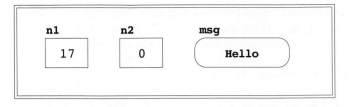

In this text, the double-line border surrounding all the variables is used to indicate that those variables are defined within the same method. In programming, a collection of variables associated with a particular invocation of a method is called a **stack frame,** for reasons that will be described in Chapter 7. I have also chosen to draw the box for the **String** variable with a different size and shape to emphasize that it holds values of a different type.

Assignment statements change the value of variables in the current stack frame. Thus, if your program executes the statement

    n2 = 25;

you can represent this assignment in the diagram by writing 25 inside the box named **n2**:

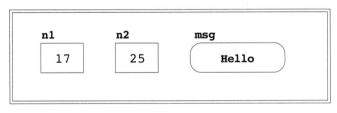

Similarly, you can indicate the effect of the statement

    msg = "Welcome";

as follows:

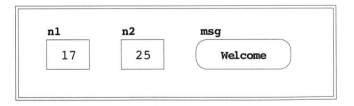

Again, it is important to keep in mind that a variable can only hold a value of the appropriate type. If, for instance, you were to write the statement

    msg = 173;

in your program, the Java compiler would mark this statement as an error because the variable **msg** has been declared as a **String**.

The most important property illustrated by the diagram is that each variable holds precisely one value. Once you have assigned a value to a variable, the variable maintains that value until you assign it a new one. The value of one variable does not disappear if you assign its value to another variable. Thus the assignment

      n2 = n1;

changes **n2** but leaves **n1** undisturbed:

Assigning a new value to a variable erases its previous contents. Thus, the statement

      msg = "Aloha!";

changes the picture to

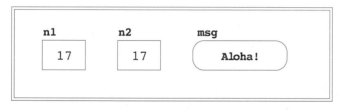

The previous value of the variable **msg** is lost.

It is particularly important to recognize that assignment is an active operation and not a mathematical statement of equality. The mathematical equation

$$x = x + 1$$

is nonsensical. There are no values of x for which x is equal to $x + 1$. The corresponding assignment statement

      x = x + 1;

has a perfectly legitimate—and extraordinarily useful—meaning. As in any assignment statement, the value of the expression on the right of the equal sign is stored in the variable appearing on the left. The effect of this statement, therefore, is to replace the value of **x** with one more than its previous value or, in other words, to add 1 to **x**. This construct is so common in programming that Java defines a special idiom for this purpose, as described in the following section.

Shorthand assignment operators

As you begin to gain more familiarity with programming, you will discover that certain types of assignment statements come up frequently in practice. Although you will certainly see many assignment statements in which the result of the expression is assigned to a variable that plays no role in the calculation, many assignment statements have the effect of changing the value of an existing variable. You will find, for example, that you often need to change a variable by adding something to its current value, subtracting something from it, or performing some similar operation. For example, if you were writing a program to balance your checkbook, you might expect to use following assignment statement:

```
balance = balance + deposit;
```

This statement adds the value in the variable **deposit** to the current value of the variable **balance**, leaving the result in **balance**. In more colloquial English, the effect of this statement can be summarized as "add **deposit** to **balance**."

However, even though the statement

```
balance = balance + deposit;
```

has the desired effect, it is not a statement that a Java programmer would usually write. Statements that perform some operation on a variable and then store the result back in that same variable occur so frequently in programming that the designers of C—from which Java's expression structure is derived—included an idiomatic shorthand for it. For any binary operator *op*, the statement

> *variable* = *variable* *op* *expression*;

can be replaced by

> *variable* *op*= *expression*;

The combination of an operator with the = used for assignment form is called a **shorthand assignment operator**.

Using the shorthand assignment operator for addition, the more common form of the statement

```
balance = balance + deposit;
```

is therefore

```
balance += deposit;
```

which means, in English, "add **deposit** to **balance**."

Because this same shorthand applies to any binary operator in Java, you can subtract the value of **surcharge** from **balance** by writing

```
balance -= surcharge;
```

or divide the value of **x** by 10 using

```
x /= 10;
```

or double the value of **salary** by using

```
salary *= 2;
```

The increment and decrement operators

Beyond the shorthand assignment operators, Java offers a further level of abbreviation for two particularly common programming operations—adding or subtracting 1 from a variable. Adding 1 to a variable is called **incrementing** that variable; subtracting 1 is called **decrementing** that variable. To indicate these operations in an extremely compact form, Java provides the operators **++** and **−−**. For example, the statement

```
x++;
```

has the same ultimate effect as

```
x += 1;
```

which is itself short for

```
x = x + 1;
```

Similarly,

```
y--;
```

has the same effect as

```
y -= 1;
```

or

```
y = y - 1;
```

The **++** and **−−** operators occur all the time in Java programs and are actually more complex in their operation than this presentation suggests. The form shown here, however, is sufficient for you to understand how these operators are used in the statement forms introduced in Chapter 4.

3.5 Boolean expressions

In the course of solving a problem, it is often necessary to have your program test a particular condition that affects the subsequent behavior of the program. If a particular condition is true, you want your program to take one action; if that condition is false, you want it to do something else. In Java, you can express conditions of this sort by constructing expressions whose values are either true or false. Such expressions are called **Boolean expressions,** after the mathematician George Boole, who developed an algebraic approach for working with this type of data. In Java, Boolean values are represented using the primitive type `boolean`, which has a domain consisting of only two values: `true` and `false`. Java defines several operators that work with `boolean` values. These operators fall into two major classes—relational operators and logical operators—which are discussed in the next two sections.

Relational operators

The **relational operators** are used to compare two values. Java defines six relational operators, which fall into two precedence classes. The operators that test the ordering relationship between two quantities are

`>`	Greater than	`>=`	Greater than or equal to
`<`	Less than	`<=`	Less than or equal to

These operators appear in the precedence hierarchy below the arithmetic operators, and are in turn followed by the operators

`==`	Equal	`!=`	Not equal

which test for equality and inequality.

When you write programs that test for equality, be very careful to use the `==` operator, which is composed of two equal signs. A single equal sign is the assignment operator. Since the double equal sign is not part of standard mathematics, replacing it with a single equal sign is a particularly common mistake. Fortunately, the Java compiler usually catches the error when it compiles your program, because the assignment is usually illegal in the context in which it appears.

The relational operators can only be used to compare **atomic data** values—data values that are not built up from smaller component parts. For example, integers, floating-point numbers, Boolean values, and characters constitute atomic data because they cannot be decomposed into smaller pieces. Strings, on the other hand, are not atomic because they are composed of individual characters. Thus, you can use relational operators to compare two values of the types `int`, `double`, `char`, or even `boolean` itself, but you cannot use them to compare two values of type `String`. You will learn how to compare strings in Chapter 8.

Logical operators

In addition to the relational operators, which take atomic values of any type and produce Boolean results, Java defines three operators that take Boolean operands and combine them to form other Boolean values:

`!`	Logical not (`true` if the following operand is `false`)
`&&`	Logical and (`true` if both operands are `true`)
`||`	Logical or (`true` if either or both operands are `true`)

These operators are called **logical operators** and are listed in decreasing order of precedence.

The operators &&, | |, and ! closely resemble the English words *and*, *or*, and *not*. Even so, it is important to remember that English can be somewhat imprecise when it comes to logic. To avoid that imprecision, it is often helpful to think of these operators in a more formal, mathematical way. Logicians define these operators using **truth tables**, which show how the value of a Boolean expression changes as the values of its operands change. For example, the truth table for the && operator, given Boolean values p and q, is

p	q	p && q
false	false	false
false	true	false
true	false	false
true	true	true

The last column of the table indicates the value of the Boolean expression p && q given the individual values of the Boolean variables p and q shown in the first two columns. Thus, the first line in the truth table shows that when p is **false** and q is **false**, the value of the expression p && q is also **false**.

The truth table for | | is

p	q	p || q
false	false	false
false	true	true
true	false	true
true	true	true

Even though the | | operator corresponds to the English word *or*, it does not indicate *one or the other*, as it often does in English, but instead indicates *either or both*, which is its mathematical meaning.

The ! operator has the following simple truth table:

p	!p
false	true
true	false

If you need to determine how a more complex logical expression operates, you can break it down into these primitive operations and build up a truth table for the individual pieces of the expression.

In most cases, logical expressions are not so complicated that you need a truth table to figure them out. The only common case that seems to cause confusion is when the ! or != operator comes up in conjunction with && or | |. When English speakers talk about situations that are not true (as is the case when you work with the ! and != operators), a statement whose meaning is clear to human listeners is often at odds with mathematical logic. Whenever you find that you need to express a condition involving the word *not*, you should use extra care to avoid errors.

As an example, suppose you wanted to express the idea "x is not equal to either 2 or 3" as part of a program. Just reading from the English version of this

COMMON PITFALLS

Be careful when using the && and | | operators with relational tests that involve the ! and != operators. English can be somewhat fuzzy in its approach to logic; programming requires you to be precise.

conditional test, new programmers are very likely to code this expression as follows:

```
x != 2 || x != 3
```

This book uses the bug symbol, as above, to mark sections of code that contain deliberate errors. In this case, the problem is that an informal English translation of the code does not correspond to its interpretation in Java. If you look at this conditional test from a mathematical point of view, you can see that the expression is **true** if either (a) **x** is not equal to 2 or (b) **x** is not equal to 3. No matter what value **x** has, one of the statements must be **true**, since, if **x** is 2, it cannot also be equal to 3, and vice versa. To fix this problem, you need to refine your understanding of the English expression so that it states the condition more precisely. That is, you want the condition to be **true** whenever "it is not the case that either **x** is 2 or **x** is 3." You could translate this expression directly to Java by writing

```
!(x == 2 || x == 3)
```

but the resulting expression is a bit ungainly. The question you really want to ask is whether *both* of the following conditions are **true**:

- **x** is not equal to 2, *and*
- **x** is not equal to 3.

If you think about the question in this form, you can write the test as

```
x != 2 && x != 3
```

This simplification is a specific illustration of the following more general relationship from mathematical logic:

$$!(p \ || \ q) \quad \textit{is equivalent to} \quad !p \ \&\& \ !q$$

for any logical expressions p and q. This transformation rule and its symmetric counterpart

$$!(p \ \&\& \ q) \quad \textit{is equivalent to} \quad !p \ || \ !q$$

are called **De Morgan's laws**. Forgetting to apply these rules and relying instead on the English style of logic is a common source of programming errors.

Another common mistake comes from forgetting to use the appropriate logical connective when combining several relational tests. In mathematics, one often sees an expression of the form

$$0 < x < 10$$

While this expression makes sense in mathematics, it is not meaningful in Java. In order to test whether the variable **x** is both greater than 0 and less than 10, you need to indicate both conditions explicitly, as follows:

```
0 < x && x < 10
```

Short-circuit evaluation

Java interprets the **&&** and **||** operators in a way that differs from the interpretation used in many other programming languages. In the programming language Pascal, for example, evaluating these operators (which are written as AND and OR) requires evaluating both halves of the condition, even when the result can be determined halfway through the process. The designers of Java took a different approach that is often more convenient for programmers.

Whenever a Java program evaluates any expression of the form

$$exp_1 \ \&\& \ exp_2$$

or

$$exp_1 \ || \ exp_2$$

the individual subexpressions are always evaluated from left to right, and evaluation ends as soon as the answer can be determined. For example, if exp_1 is **false** in the expression involving **&&**, there is no need to evaluate exp_2 since the final answer will always be **false**. Similarly, in the example using **||**, there is no need to evaluate the second operand if the first operand is **true**. This style of evaluation, which stops as soon as the answer is known, is called **short-circuit evaluation.**

A primary advantage of short-circuit evaluation is that it allows one condition to control the execution of a second one. In many situations, the second part of a compound condition is meaningful only if the first part comes out a certain way. For example, suppose you want to express the combined condition that (1) the value of the integer **x** is nonzero and (2) **x** divides evenly into **y**. You can express this conditional test in Java as

```
(x != 0) && (y % x == 0)
```

because the expression **y % x** is evaluated only if x is nonzero. The corresponding expression in Pascal fails to generate the desired result, because both parts of the Pascal condition will always be evaluated. Thus, if **x** is 0, a Pascal program containing this expression will end up dividing by 0 even though it appears to have a conditional test to check for that case. Conditions that protect against evaluation errors in subsequent parts of a compound condition, such as the conditional test

```
(x != 0)
```

in the preceding example, are called **guards**.

Flags

Variables of type **boolean** are called **flags**. For example, if you declare a Boolean variable using the declaration

```
boolean done = false;
```

the variable **done** becomes a flag, which is initially set to **false**. You can the use that variable to record whether or not you are finished with some phase of the operation. You can assign new values to flags just as you can to any other variable. For example, you can set the value of **done** to **true** by writing

```
done = true;
```

More importantly, you can assign any expression that has a Boolean value to a Boolean variable. For example, suppose the logic of your program indicates that you are finished with some phase of the operation as soon as the value of the variable **itemsRemaining** becomes 0. To set **done** to the appropriate value, you can simply write

```
done = (itemsRemaining == 0);
```

The parentheses in this expression are not necessary but are often used to emphasize the fact that you are assigning the result of a conditional test to a variable. The statement above says, "Calculate the value of (**itemsRemaining == 0**), which will be either **true** or **false**, and store that result in the variable **done**."

An example of Boolean calculation

Even though it isn't possible to use Boolean expressions in a program until you learn the statement forms introduced in Chapter 4, it is useful to look at a practical example of Boolean computation. Suppose that you are writing a program that works with dates and needs to be able to determine whether a given year in history is a leap year. Although we tend to think of leap years as occuring once every four years, astronomical realities are not quite so tidy. Because it takes about a quarter of a day more than 365 days for the earth to complete its annual orbital circuit around the sun, adding an extra day once every four years does help to keep the calendar in sync with the sun, but it is still off by a slight amount. To ensure that the beginning of the year does not slowly drift through the seasons, the rule used for leap years needs to be more complicated. Leap years come every four years, except for years ending in 00, which are leap years only if they are divisible by 400. Thus, 1900 was not a leap year even though 1900 is divisible by 4. The year 2000, on the other hand, was a leap year because 2000 is divisible by 400. Thus, for any leap year, one of the following conditions must hold:

- The year is divisible by 4 but not divisible by 100, *or*
- The year is divisible by 400.

Although this rule seems more complicated than the simplified one-year-in-every-four approach that works most of the time, it is easy to code the correct rule in

Java as a Boolean expression. If the year is contained in the variable **y**, the following expression evaluates to **true** or **false** depending on whether that year is or is not a leap year:

$$((y \text{ \% } 4 == 0) \text{ \&\& } (y \text{ \% } 100 != 0)) \text{ } || \text{ } (y \text{ \% } 400 == 0)$$

Although none of the parentheses in this expression are actually required given Java's rules of precedence, using parentheses can make long Boolean expressions easier to read. If you take the result of this expression and store it in a flag called **isLeapYear**, you can then test the flag at other points in the program to determine whether the **isLeapYear** condition is true.

3.6 Designing for change

For the most part, the programs you have seen so far are simple enough that issues of programming style don't seem to have much import. At this level of sophistication, most programs are easy enough to understand whether or not you include good comments, choose appropriate variable names, or use named constants in place of explicit numeric values. It is, however, precisely when programs are this simple that it is most important to develop your software engineering skills. If you wait until your programs become so complex that good programming style is essential, you won't have honed your strategies for reducing that complexity. If, however, you develop good software habits early, the leap to more complicated programs will become far easier to make.

One of the most important aspects of good software engineering is designing your programs so that they are easy to change. As noted in the section on "Software maintenance" in Chapter 1, software systems tend to change significantly over their lifetimes. The cost of making those changes—which typically is much greater than the cost of producing the software in the first place—can be reduced substantially if you recognize up front that changes will inevitably occur and do as much as you can to support that evolutionary process. You can't, of course, know in advance exactly what all the changes will be, but you can nonetheless simplify the work of future maintainers by observing a few simple principles of software design.

The importance of readability

The most important principle to observe is that programs must be written in a way that makes them easy to read. As a new programmer struggling with the syntactic details of an unfamiliar language, you may find yourself focusing much of your energy on the problem of getting the Java compiler to accept your program without issuing all sorts of error messages. That part of the problem, however, is in some sense the easy part. If you want others to be able to maintain your code in the years to come, you have to design it to be readable by human beings, and not just by the compiler.

In the chapters that follow, you will learn many simple strategies that substantially improve the readability of your programs. As an example, you may already have noticed that the statements that form the body of each method are indented several spaces beyond the indentation level of the method header. That simple convention—which will become all the more critical once you start using the compound statement forms in Chapter 4—makes it possible to see at a glance what lines are included in the body of each syntactic unit. Another strategy that this chapter has already emphasized is to use meaningful names for your variables, methods, and classes. Even something as simple as putting a space on each side of an operator can dramatically enhance the readability of a program.

These strategies, however, are simply means toward the greater end of making your programs understandable to human readers. The important thing is that you keep those readers in mind as you write your program and think about whether what you've written would make sense to someone encountering it for the first time. When you design a program, you know what you want it to do. The critical question is whether your code conveys that intent to your reader. Particularly if you've taken care to observe the simple stylistic rules of proper indentation and well-chosen names, it is sometimes the case that the code itself is sufficient to express what you had in mind. But if you are doing anything at all complicated or unusual, it is helpful to document that aspect of your design in a comment for the benefit of future readers.

Using named constants to support program maintenance

Several of the programs in this chapter have used named constants to make the resulting programs easier to read. The **CentimetersToFeetAndInches** program in Figure 3-4, for example, included the following constant definition:

```
private static final int INCHES_PER_FOOT = 12;
```

Using the name **INCHES_PER_FOOT** in a program enhances readability because it tells the reader what the constant means. If you happened to see the number 12 in a program, you wouldn't have any idea what it signified. It might equally well be the number of items in a dozen, the number of hours on a clock, or the number of months in a year. Giving the constant a descriptive name eliminates this ambiguity.

Beyond enhancing readability, named constants have another important role in supporting software evolution. In all likelihood, the number of inches in a foot is not likely to change any time soon. That value is truly a constant in the literal as well as the programming sense. By contrast, many constants in a program specify things that might change as the program evolves, even though they will be constant for a particular version of that program.

The importance of this principle is easiest to illustrate by historical example. Imagine for the moment that you are a programmer in the late 1960s working on the initial design of the **ARPANET,** which was the first large-scale computer network and the ancestor of today's Internet. Because resource constraints were quite serious at that time, you would probably need to impose a limit—as the actual designers of the ARPANET did in 1969—on the number of computers (which were called *hosts* in the ARPANET days) that could be connected. In the early years of the ARPANET, that limit was 127 hosts. If Java had existed in those days, you might have declared a constant that looked like this:

```
private static final int MAXIMUM_NUMBER_OF_HOSTS = 127;
```

At some later point, however, the explosive growth of networking would force you to raise this bound. That process would be relatively easy if you used named constants in your programs. To raise the limit on the number of hosts to 1023, it might well be sufficient to change this declaration so that it read

```
private static final int MAXIMUM_NUMBER_OF_HOSTS = 1023;
```

If you adopted this approach and used **MAXIMUM_NUMBER_OF_HOSTS** everywhere in your program in which you needed to refer to that maximum value, then making this simple change would automatically propagate to every part of the program in which this name was used.

Note that the situation would be entirely different if you had used the numeric constant 127 instead. In that case, you would need to search through the entire program and change all instances of 127 used for this purpose to the larger value. Some instances of 127 might well refer to other things than the limit on the number of hosts, and it would be just as important not to change any of those values. In the likely event that you made a mistake, you would have a very hard time tracking down the bug.

Using named constants to support program development

The advantage of using named constants to simplify the maintenance process is not limited to the kind of change that occurs over the long-term evolution of a program. Giving names to constants is also valuable in the development process, particularly when you need to do some experimentation to figure out what values a particular constant should have. This situation is extremely common in graphical programs, where you often want to adjust the sizes and locations of particular objects to achieve the optimal aesthetic effect.

To get a better sense of how using named constants can support the development of graphical programs, it helps to take another look at the **GRectPlusGOval** program from Chapter 2. That program superimposes a green oval on top of a red rectangle to demonstrate the geometry of the **GOval** class, as follows:

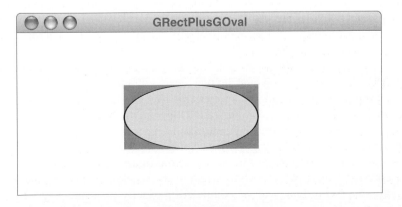

The **run** method that produces this figure looks like this:

```
public void run() {
   GRect rect = new GRect(100, 50, 125, 60);
   rect.setFilled(true);
   rect.setColor(Color.RED);
   add(rect);
   GOval oval = new GOval(100, 50, 125, 60);
   oval.setFilled(true);
   oval.setFillColor(Color.GREEN);
   add(oval);
}
```

As you refine your sense of programming aesthetics through practice, you will quickly become suspicious of programs written in this way. The indication that something is amiss is that the calls to the **GRect** and **GOval** constructors use explicit numeric values, which is typically a sign of poor programming style. Part of the problem concerns the readability of the program. The numbers 100, 50, 125, and 60 give you no hint as to what those values signify. If you were to give those values descriptive names like **RECT_X**, **RECT_Y**, **RECT_WIDTH**, and **RECT_HEIGHT**, your readers would have less trouble figuring out what those values meant.

There is, however, a more significant stylistic problem in the **GRectPlusGOval** example. To make its point that a **GOval** fits precisely inside the corresponding **GRect**, it doesn't matter what the values of the arguments are; what matters is that the arguments are the same in each case. Thus, what you really want to do is to define constants with names such as **FIGURE_X**, **FIGURE_Y**, **FIGURE_WIDTH**, and **FIGURE_HEIGHT** and then use those constant names in both the **GRect** and **GOval** constructors. That way, all you have to do to change the dimensions or location of the diagram is edit the definition of the appropriate named constants. The change is made in one place, but the effect of that change propagates to every point in the program at which those named constants appear.

When I look at the output produced by the **GRectPlusGOval** program, my first aesthetic reaction is that the figure should be a little taller. If I rewrote the program as suggested in the preceding paragraph, I could play around with **FIGURE_HEIGHT** until I hit upon a value that seemed satisfactory, which seems to be somewhere around 75. My second aesthetic reaction is that the figure really ought to be centered in the window, instead of slightly off to the left. Although I could try to correct the positioning by experimenting with different values for **FIGURE_X** and **FIGURE_Y**, it is unlikely that I would get things precisely right. A better strategy is to calculate what these values have to be in order to achieve the desired effect, which is that the rectangle and oval are both centered in the window.

To accomplish this goal, it is necessary to know how big the window is. Fortunately, getting that information is easy because the **GraphicsProgram** class includes two methods—**getWidth** and **getHeight**—that return the dimensions of the graphics window. Knowing these dimensions makes it easy to calculate the x and y coordinates of the upper left corner of the figure. The x coordinate of that upper corner, for example, is half the width of the window minus half the width of the figure; the y coordinate can be computed in exactly the same way. Thus, you can compute the coordinates of the upper left corner for both the **GRect** and the **GOval** by using the lines

```
double x = (getWidth() - FIGURE_WIDTH) / 2;
double y = (getHeight() - FIGURE_HEIGHT) / 2;
```

Note that the variables **x** and **y** will automatically get the correct values even if you change the value of the **FIGURE_WIDTH** and **FIGURE_HEIGHT** constants or change the size of the window. Figure 3-5 shows the complete program incorporating these changes.

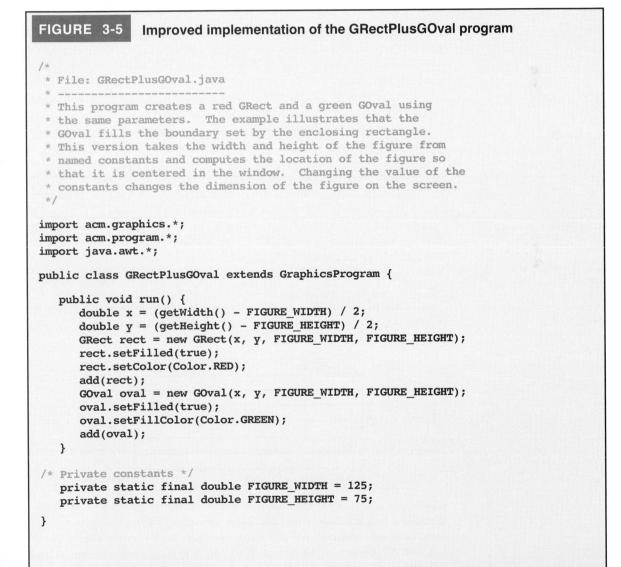

FIGURE 3-5   Improved implementation of the GRectPlusGOval program

```
/*
 * File: GRectPlusGOval.java
 * ----------------------------
 * This program creates a red GRect and a green GOval using
 * the same parameters.  The example illustrates that the
 * GOval fills the boundary set by the enclosing rectangle.
 * This version takes the width and height of the figure from
 * named constants and computes the location of the figure so
 * that it is centered in the window.  Changing the value of the
 * constants changes the dimension of the figure on the screen.
 */

import acm.graphics.*;
import acm.program.*;
import java.awt.*;

public class GRectPlusGOval extends GraphicsProgram {

    public void run() {
        double x = (getWidth() - FIGURE_WIDTH) / 2;
        double y = (getHeight() - FIGURE_HEIGHT) / 2;
        GRect rect = new GRect(x, y, FIGURE_WIDTH, FIGURE_HEIGHT);
        rect.setFilled(true);
        rect.setColor(Color.RED);
        add(rect);
        GOval oval = new GOval(x, y, FIGURE_WIDTH, FIGURE_HEIGHT);
        oval.setFilled(true);
        oval.setFillColor(Color.GREEN);
        add(oval);
    }

/* Private constants */
    private static final double FIGURE_WIDTH = 125;
    private static final double FIGURE_HEIGHT = 75;

}
```

Summary

In this chapter, you have had the opportunity to learn about Java expressions and how to use them in programs. Important points introduced in the chapter include:

- Data values come in many different types, each of which is defined by a *domain* and a *set of operations*.
- *Constants* are used to specify values that do not change within a program.
- *Variables* have three attributes: a name, a type, and a value. All variables used in a Java program must be *declared* using a line of the form

  type identifier = *expression*;

  which establishes the name, type, and initial value of the variable.
- You can use *class variables* to create *named constants*. Declarations of named constants appear outside of any method and include the keywords **static** and **final**.
- Expressions consist of individual *terms* connected by *operators*. The subexpressions to which an operator applies are called its *operands*.
- When you apply an arithmetic operator to two operands of type **int**, the result is also of type **int**. If either or both operands are of type **double**, so is the result.
- If you apply the **/** operator to two integers, the result is the integer obtained by dividing the first operand by the second and then throwing the remainder away. The remainder can be obtained by using the **%** operator.
- Automatic conversion between numeric types occurs when values of different types appear in an arithmetic expression or when you assign a value to a variable with a more general type.
- You can specify explicit conversion between numeric types by using a *type cast*.
- The order of operations in an expression is determined by *rules of precedence*. The operators introduced so far fall into the following precedence classes:

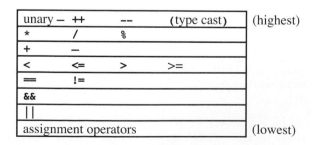

unary –	++	––	(type cast)	(highest)
*	/	%		
+	–			
<	<=	>	>=	
==	!=			
&&				
||				
assignment operators				(lowest)

Except for assignment, Java applies binary operators in left-to-right order whenever two operators from the same precedence class compete for the same operand. (Assignment and unary operators are evaluated from right to left, but this book uses no examples in which it is necessary to understand this rule.)

- You can change the value of variables through the use of *assignment statements*. Each variable can hold only one value at a time; when you assign a new value to a variable, any previous value is lost.
- Java includes an abbreviated form of the assignment statement in which the statement

    variable op= expression;

acts as a shorthand for the longer expression

    variable = variable op expression;

- Java includes special operators `++` and `--`, which specify adding and subtracting 1 from a variable, respectively.
- Java defines a data type called **boolean** that is used to represent Boolean data. The type **boolean** has only two values: **true** and **false**.
- You can generate Boolean values using the *relational operators* (`<`, `<=`, `>`, `>=`, `==`, and `!=`), and you can combine Boolean values using the *logical operators* (`&&`, `||`, and `!`).
- The logical operators `&&` and `||` are evaluated in left-to-right order in such a way that the evaluation stops as soon as the program can determine the result. This behavior is called *short-circuit evaluation*.
- Named constants are particularly useful in writing programs that are easy to change.

Review questions

1. What are the two attributes that define a data type?

2. Identify which of the following are legal constants in Java. For the ones that are legal, indicate whether they are integers or floating-point constants.

    a) `42`   g) `1,000,000`
    b) `-17`   h) `3.1415926`
    c) `2+3`   i) `123456789`
    d) `-2.3`   j) `0.000001`
    e) `20`   k) `1.1E+11`
    f) `2.0`   l) `1.1X+11`

3. Rewrite the following floating-point constants in Java's form for scientific notation:

    a) 6.02252×10^{23}
    b) 29979250000.0
    c) 0.00000000529167
    d) 3.1415926535

    (By the way, each of these constants represents an approximation of an important value from chemistry, physics, or mathematics: (a) Avogadro's number, (b) the speed of light in centimeters per second, (c) the Bohr radius in centimeters, and (d) the mathematical constant π. In the case of π, there is no advantage in using the scientific notation form, but it is nonetheless possible and you should know how to do so.)

4. Indicate which of the following are legal variable names in Java:

   a) `x`
   b) `formula1`
   c) `average_rainfall`
   d) `%correct`
   e) `short`
   f) `tiny`
   g) `total output`
   h) `aReasonablyLongVariableName`
   i) `12MonthTotal`
   j) `marginal-cost`
   k) `b4hand`
   l) `_stk_depth`

5. Indicate the values and types of the following expressions:

   a) `2 + 3`
   b) `19 / 5`
   c) `19.0 / 5`
   d) `3 * 6.0`
   e) `19 % 5`
   f) `2 % 7`

6. What is the difference between the unary minus operator and the binary subtraction operator?

7. By applying the appropriate precedence rules, calculate the result of each of the following expressions:

   a) `6 + 5 / 4 - 3`
   b) `2 + 2 * (2 * 2 - 2) % 2 / 2`
   c) `10 + 9 * ((8 + 7) % 6) + 5 * 4 % 3 * 2 + 1`
   d) `1 + 2 + (3 + 4) * ((5 * 6 % 7 * 8) - 9) - 10`

8. If the variable **k** is declared to be of type **int**, what value does **k** contain after the program executes the assignment statement

   ```
   k = (int) 3.14159;
   ```

   What value would **k** contain after the assignment statement

   ```
   k = (int) 2.71828;
   ```

9. In Java, how do you specify conversion between numeric types?

10. What idiom would you use to multiply the value of the variable **cellCount** by 2?

11. What is the most common way in Java to write a statement that has the same effect as the statement

    ```
    x = x + 1;
    ```

12. What are the two values of the data type **boolean**?

13. What happens when a programmer tries to use the mathematical symbol for equality in a conditional expression?

14. How would you write a Boolean expression to test whether the value of the integer variable **n** was in the range 0 to 9, inclusive?

15. Describe in English what the following conditional expression means:

> (x != 4) || (x != 17)

For what values of **x** is this condition **true**?

16. What does the term *short-circuit evaluation* mean?

17. Describe in your own words how the use of named constants makes programs easier to change over time.

Programming exercises

1. Extend the **InchesToCentimeters** program given in Figure 3-2 so that it reads in two input values: the number of feet, followed on a separate line by the number of inches. Here is a sample run of the program:

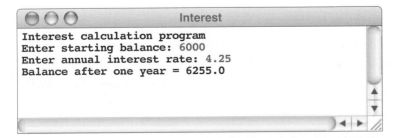

2. Write a program that reads in two numbers: an account balance and an annual interest rate expressed as a percentage. Your program should then display the new balance after a year. There are no deposits or withdrawals—just the interest payment. Your program should be able to reproduce the following sample run:

```
            ◯◯◯                    Interest
        Interest calculation program
        Enter starting balance: 6000
        Enter annual interest rate: 4.25
        Balance after one year = 6255.0
```

3. Extend the program you wrote in Exercise 2 so that it also displays the balance after two years have elapsed, as shown in the following sample run:

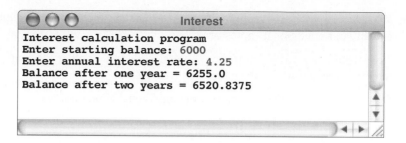

Note that the interest used in this example is compounded annually, which means the interest from the first year is added to the bank balance and is therefore itself subject to interest in the second year. In the first year, the $6,000 earns 4.25% interest, or $255. In the second year, the account earns 4.25% interest on the entire $6,255.

4. Write a program that asks the user for the radius of a circle and then computes the area of that circle (*A*) using the formula

$$A = \pi r^2$$

Note that there is no "raise to a power" operator in Java. Given the arithmetic operators you know Java has, how can you write an expression that achieves the desired result?

5. Write a program that reads in a temperature in degrees Fahrenheit and returns the corresponding temperature in degrees Celsius. The conversion formula is

$$C = \frac{5}{9}(F - 32)$$

The following is a sample run of the program:

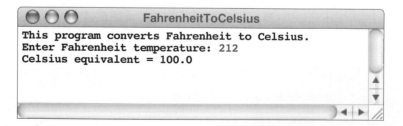

If you write this program carelessly, the answer always comes out 0. What bug causes this behavior?

6. In Norton Juster's children's book *The Phantom Tollbooth*, the Mathemagician gives Milo the following problem to solve:

$$4 + 9 - 2 * 16 + 1 / 3 * 6 - 67 + 8 * 2 - 3 + 26 -$$
$$1 / 34 + 3 / 7 + 2 - 5$$

According to Milo's calculations, which are corroborated by the Mathemagician, this expression "all works out to zero." If you do the calculation, however, the expression comes out to zero only if you start at the beginning and apply all the operators in strict left-to-right order. What would the answer be if the Mathemagician's expression were evaluated using Java's precedence rules? Write a program to verify your calculation.

7. Write a program that converts a metric weight in kilograms to the corresponding English weight in pounds and ounces. The conversion factors you need are

> 1 kilogram = 2.2 pounds
> 1 pound = 16 ounces

8. Write a program that computes the average of four integers.

9. There's an old nursery rhyme that goes like this:

> As I was going to St. Ives,
> I met a man with seven wives,
> Each wife had seven sacks,
> Each sack had seven cats,
> Each cat had seven kits:
> Kits, cats, sacks, and wives,
> How many were going to St. Ives?

The last line turns out to be a trick question: only the speaker is going *to* St. Ives; everyone else is presumably heading in the opposite direction. Suppose, however, that you want to find out how many representatives of the assembled multitude—kits, cats, sacks, and wives—were coming *from* St. Ives. Write a Java program to calculate and display this result. Try to make your program follow the structure of the problem so that anyone reading your program would understand what value it is calculating.

10. The **TicTacToeBoard** program shown in Figure 2-12 generates the following output:

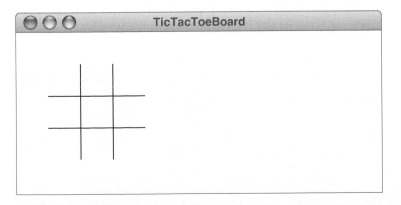

The program, however, uses poor programming style because the coordinates for each of the lines are specified explicitly in the code. Rewrite this program so that it centers the board in the window and uses a single constant called **BOARD_SIZE** to define the height and width of the figure.

11. Exercise 4 in Chapter 2 asks you to write a graphics program that produces a diagram of a simple frame house. If you wanted to make the **DrawHouse** program easy to change, what named constants should you define to provide the necessary flexibility? Rewrite the program so that it uses these named constants rather than explicit coordinate values.

CHAPTER 4

Statement Forms

The statements was interesting but tough.
— Mark Twain, *Adventures of Huckleberry Finn*, 1884

Dennis Ritchie

As a young research scientist at Bell Labs, Dennis Ritchie created the C programming language in 1970 to simplify the development of the Unix operating system that he developed jointly with Ken Thompson. Both Unix and C have had enormous impact on the field of computing. C, in particular, provided the foundation from which many of today's most important programming languages, including Java, got their start. Ritchie's design of C's statement structure has been carried over into Java in almost exactly its original form. Ritchie and Thompson jointly received the ACM Turing Award—the computing profession's highest honor, named after the pioneering British computer scientist Alan Turing—in 1983.

In Chapter 2, you saw several examples of Java programs that extend the **Program** hierarchy. Such programs operate by executing the statements contained within the body of a method called **run**. This chapter covers the different statement types available in Java and, in the process, extends the set of tools you have for solving problems.

▌ 4.1 Statement types in Java

Statements in Java fall into three major categories:

1. *Simple statements,* which perform some action
2. *Compound statements,* which combine other statements into a sequence of operations
3. *Control statements,* which affect the way other statements are executed

You have already seen a variety of simple statements in Java, such as assignments and calls to the **println** method. And even though you didn't know the term, you have also worked with compound statements since your very first programs because the body of each **run** method is a compound statement. Control statements, however, are new and will take up most of this chapter. Before introducing those control statements in detail, this chapter begins by looking at each category of statement at a more abstract level.

Simple statements

In the programs in Chapters 2 and 3, you saw simple statements used to accomplish a variety of tasks. For example, the very first program in the text contained a **run** method consisting of the following simple statement:

```
add(new GLabel("hello, world", 100, 75));
```

Similarly, you have been introduced to assignment statements, such as the shorthand form

```
balance += deposit;
```

and statements that display information, such as

```
println("The total is " + total + ".");
```

Syntax for simple statements

A simple statement consists of an expression followed by a semicolon.

Informally, it makes sense to think of these statement types as separate tools and to use them idiomatically. If you need to read an integer, it helps enormously to remember that there is an idiom in Chapter 2 that does just that. All you have to do is write it down. If you think about statements more formally, however, you will discover that they share a unified structure that makes it easy for the Java compiler to recognize a legal statement in a program. In Java, all simple statements—regardless of their function—have the syntactic form shown in the box on the right. The template for a simple statement is therefore simply

> *expression***;**

Adding the semicolon after the expression turns the expression into a legal statement.

Even though any expression followed by a semicolon is a *legal* statement in Java, it is not true that every such combination represents a *useful* statement. To be useful, a statement must have some discernible effect. The statement

```
n1 + n2;
```

consists of the expression **n1 + n2** followed by a semicolon and is therefore a legal statement. It is, however, an entirely useless one because nothing is ever done with the answer; the statement adds the variables **n1** and **n2** together and then throws the result away. Simple statements in Java are typically assignments (including the shorthand assignments and increment/decrement operators) or calls to methods, such as **println**, that perform some useful operation.

It is easy to see that program lines such as

```
println("The total is " + total + ".");
```

are legal statements because they fit the template for simple statements. In the definition of *expression* given in Chapter 2, method calls are legal expressions, so the method call part of the above line—everything except the semicolon—is a legal expression. Putting the semicolon at the end of the line turns that expression into a simple statement.

But what about assignments? If a line like

```
total = 0;
```

is to fit the template for simple statements, it must be the case that

```
total = 0
```

is itself an expression.

In Java, the equal sign used for assignment is simply a binary operator, just like **+** or **/**. The **=** operator takes two operands, one on the left and one on the right. For our present purposes, the left operand must be a variable name. When Java executes the assignment operator, it does so by evaluating the expression on the right-hand side and then storing the resulting value in the variable that appears on the left-hand side. Because the equal sign used for assignment is an operator,

```
total = 0
```

is indeed an expression, and the line

```
total = 0;
```

is therefore a simple statement.

Compound statements

Simple statements allow programmers to specify actions. Except for the **HelloProgram** example in Chapter 2, however, every program you have seen so far requires more than one simple statement to do the job. For most programs, the solution strategy requires a coordinated action consisting of several sequential steps. The **Add2Integers** program in Chapter 2, for example, has to first get one number, then get a second, then add the two together, and finally display the result. Translating this sequence of actions into actual program steps requires the use of several individual statements that all become part of the main program body.

To specify that a sequence of statements is part of a coherent unit, you can assemble the statements into a **compound statement**—also called a **block**—which is a collection of statements and declarations enclosed in curly braces, as follows:

```
{
    statement₁
    statement₂
    statement₃
      . . .
    statementₙ
}
```

Any of these statements can be replaced by a declaration, and it is probably easiest to think of declarations as simply another form of statement. Moreover, whenever the notation *statement* appears in a syntax template or an idiomatic pattern, you can substitute for it either a single statement or a compound statement.

The statements in the interior of a block are usually indented relative to the enclosing context. The compiler ignores the indentation, but the visual effect is helpful to the human reader, because it makes the structure of the program jump out at you from the format of the page. Empirical research has shown that using either three or four spaces at each new level makes the program structure easiest to see; the programs in this text use four spaces for each new level. Indentation is critical to good programming, so you should make sure to develop a consistent indentation style in your programs.

Control statements

In the absence of any directives to the contrary, the individual statements that appear inside a block are executed one at a time in the order in which they appear. For most applications, however, this strictly top-to-bottom ordering is not sufficient. Solution strategies for real-world problems tend to involve such operations as repeating a set of steps or choosing between alternative sets of actions. Statements that affect the way in which other statements are executed are called **control statements.**

Control statements in Java fall into two basic classes:

1. *Conditionals.* In solving problems, you will often need to choose between two or more independent paths in a program, depending on the result of some conditional test. For example, you might be asked to write a program that

behaves one way if a certain value is negative and a different way otherwise. The type of control statement needed to make decisions is called a **conditional**. In Java, there are two conditional statement forms: the `if` statement and the `switch` statement.

2. *Iteration*. Particularly as you start to work with problems that involve more than a few data items, your programs will often need to repeat an operation a specified number of times or as long as a certain condition holds. In programming, such repetition is called **iteration,** and the portion of code that repeats is called a **loop.** In Java, the control statements used as the basis for iteration are the `while` statement and the `for` statement.

Each control statement in Java consists of two parts: the **control line,** which specifies the nature of the repetition or condition, and the **body,** which consists of the statements that are affected by the control line. In the case of conditional statements, the body may be divided into separate parts, where one set of statements is executed in certain cases and another set of statements is executed in others.

The body of each control statement consists of a statement, which is typically a block. The control line—no matter whether it specifies repetition or conditional execution—applies to the entire body. The body, moreover, may contain control statements, which in turn contain other statements. When a control statement is used within the body of another control statement, those statements are said to be **nested**. The ability to nest control statements, one inside another, is one of the most important characteristics of modern programming languages.

4.2 Control statements and problem solving

Before looking at the details of Java's control statements, it is useful to take a step back and think holistically about the role that control statements play in the programming process. Students in my introductory courses often believe that there must be some rule that determines when they need to use the various control statements that Java provides. That's not how programming works. Control statements are tools for solving problems. Before you can determine what control statement makes sense in a particular context, you have to give serious thought to the problem you are trying to solve and the strategy you have chosen to solve it. You write the code for a program *after* you have decided how to solve the underlying problem. There is nothing automatic about the programming process.

Although students are often disappointed to learn that there are no magic rules that turn a problem statement into a working program, that fact is what makes programming such a valuable skill. If it *were* possible to carry out the programming process according to some well-defined algorithm, it would then be straightforward to automate the entire process and eliminate altogether the need for human programmers. Programming requires an enormous amount of ingenuity and creativity. The essence of programming consists of solving problems, many of which are extremely complex and challenging. Solving such problems is what makes computer programming hard; it is also what makes programming interesting and fun.

Generalizing the `Add2Integers` program

The programs you have seen so far in this book were chosen to illustrate how simple programs are written rather than to give you experience in solving problems. Now, so you can experience the excitement that comes from the problem-solving side of programming, it is time to take up some more interesting problems. Although the **Add2Integers** program in Chapter 2 is not in itself anything to write home about, it can serve as a foundation for more interesting examples. If you wanted to make the program useful in practice, the first thing you would do is generalize the program so that it could add more than two numbers. Most people are perfectly capable of adding two integers together with reasonable speed and accuracy. For a job that simple, a computer isn't necessary. But what if you needed to add ten integers, or a thousand integers, or a million? At that point, the advantages of a computer become more clear.

But how would you go about changing the **Add2Integers** program so that it could add integers on a larger scale? If you wanted to add four integers, you could simply add a few lines to the **run** method, as follows:

```
public void run() {
   println("This program adds four integers.");
   int n1 = readInt("Enter n1: ");
   int n2 = readInt("Enter n2: ");
   int n3 = readInt("Enter n3: ");
   int n4 = readInt("Enter n4: ");
   int total = n1 + n2 + n3 + n4;
   println("The total is " + total + ".");
}
```

While this approach is suitable for adding four integers, it would quickly become tedious if you tried to apply the same strategy for ten integers, let alone a thousand or a million.

Suppose that you wanted to write the program for adding ten integers in a way that did not require the declaration of ten variables. Let's think about the problem for a minute. Imagine that you are adding up ten numbers—without a computer— and that someone starts calling those numbers out to you: 7, 4, 6, and so on. What would you do? You could write down the numbers and then add them at the end. This strategy is analogous to the one used in the **Add2Integers** program. It's effective, but it won't win any prizes for speed or cleverness. Alternatively, you could add the numbers as you go: 7 plus 4 is 11, 11 plus 6 is 17, and so on. If you adopt this strategy, you don't have to keep track of each individual number, just the current total. When you hear the last number, you're all set to announce the answer.

The fact that you don't have to remember each individual number should help answer the question of how to add ten integers without declaring ten variables. With this new strategy, you should be able to write a new **Add10Integers** program using only two variables: one for each number as it comes in (**value**) and one for the sum of the numbers so far (**total**). Each time you read a new number into **value**, you simply add it to **total**, which keeps track of the running total. Once you've done so, you can go back and reuse **value** to hold the next number, which is treated in precisely the same way.

This insight should enable you to begin the task of coding a program that uses the new strategy. For each input value, you know that you must execute the following steps:

1. Request an integer value from the user and store it in the variable **value.**
2. Add **value** to the running sum stored in the variable **total**.

You already know how to code the first step; it is a perfect example of the read-an-integer-from-the-user pattern that you saw in Chapter 2 and that has the following general form:

```
int variable = readInt(prompt);
```

You also know how to code the second step. Adding **value** to **total** is an instance of the shorthand assignment pattern introduced in Chapter 3. To add **value** to **total**, the idiom is

```
total += value;
```

The two patterns—one for reading in an integer and one for adding that integer to a running total—give you everything you need to code the operations that must occur for each input value in the **Add10Integers** program. For each of the 10 input values, the program must execute the following statements:

```
int value = readInt(" ? ");
total += value;
```

At this point, all you need to do is find some way to make the program execute this set of statements 10 times.

The repeat-N-times pattern

Later in this chapter, you will learn about the **for** statement and how to use it in a variety of applications. In Java, the **for** statement turns out to be extremely flexible and powerful—much more so than in most languages. While that flexibility and power is often useful for experienced programmers, my experience suggests that the vast majority of **for** loops fit a much simpler pattern whose only function is to repeat a block of code a predetermined number of times. You can use that pattern as a programming idiom along the lines suggested in Chapter 2, even before you understand the details of the **for** statement itself.

The **repeat-N-times pattern** has the following form:

```
for (int i = 0; i < N; i++) {
    statements to be repeated
}
```

In this pattern, the value N indicates the number of repetitions you want. For example, if you replace N with 5, the statements enclosed within the braces will be executed five times. To use this pattern in the **Add10Integers** program, you need to replace *N* by 10. The statements enclosed in the braces are the statements that (1) read an integer into **value** and (2) add that value to **total**. If you make these substitutions in the paradigm, you get the following code:

```
for (int i = 0; i < 10; i++) {
   int value = readInt(" ? ");
   total += value;
}
```

At this point, you are almost set to write the complete **Add10Integers** program, but there is still a minor wrinkle to iron out. The variable **value** is declared as an integer as part of the pattern for reading in an integer from the user. The variable **total**, however, is not yet declared. For this loop to work properly, **total** must be declared outside the loop and given an initial value of 0. Thus, before the **for** loop, you need to include the declaration

```
int total = 0;
```

to make sure that this variable can serve its function as a running total. Setting a variable to its proper starting value is called **initialization**. In many languages, failure to initialize variables is a common source of bugs. Java, however, is pretty good about checking for uninitialized variables and letting you know that initialization is needed.

This final piece of the puzzle is all you need to complete the **Add10Integers** program. The **run** method you would need looks like this:

```
public void run() {
   println("This program adds ten integers.");
   int total = 0;
   for (int i = 0; i < 10; i++) {
      int value = readInt(" ? ");
      total += value;
   }
   println("The total is " + total + ".");
}
```

This program, however, is not engineered as well as one would like. You won't always be in the position of adding exactly ten integers, and it should be easy to change your code so that it can add a different number of integers. As things stand, you would have to go into the guts of the code and change both the initial message and the limit in the **for** loop. A better approach is to introduce a named constant as described in Chapter 3. If you chose to call this constant **N_VALUES**, you would come up with a program that looked something like the **AddNIntegers** program in Figure 4-1.

The read-until-sentinel pattern

Even after you have specified the number of values as a named constant, the **AddNIntegers** program is unlikely to meet the needs of any significant number of users in its present form. The most serious problem with the current version of the

---

FIGURE 4-1 **Program to add a predefined number of integers**

```java
/*
 * File: AddNIntegers.java
 * --------------------------
 * This program adds a predefined number of integers and
 * then prints the sum at the end.  To change the number
 * of integers, change the definition of N_VALUES.
 */

import acm.program.*;

public class AddNIntegers extends ConsoleProgram {

    public void run() {
        println("This program adds " + N_VALUES + " integers.");
        int total = 0;
        for (int i = 0; i < N_VALUES; i++) {
            int value = readInt(" ? ");
            total += value;
        }
        println("The total is " + total + ".");
    }

/* Specifies the number of values */
    private static final int N_VALUES = 10;

}
```

---

program is that updating the program so that it adds a different number of integers requires an explicit change in the program and a recompilation. What you really need is a more general program that can add any input values in such a way that the number of values does not have to be specified in advance. From the user's point of view, having to count the numbers in advance makes the program seem cumbersome. If you were using such a program, what you would like to do is just enter the numbers until you finished your list. At that point, you'd want to be able to tell the program that you had run out of numbers.

A common approach to solving this problem is to define a special input value and let the user enter that value to signal the end of the input list. A special value used to terminate a loop is called a **sentinel**. The choice of an appropriate value to use as a sentinel depends on the nature of the input data. The value chosen as a sentinel should not be a legitimate data value; that is, it should not be a value that the user would ever need to enter as normal data. For example, when adding a list of integers, the value 0 is an appropriate sentinel. Although choosing 0 as a sentinel means that you can't enter 0 as a data value, anyone using a program to add a list of values can simply ignore any 0 values in the data because they won't affect the final total. The situation would be different if you were writing a program to average exam scores. Averaging in a 0 score does change the result, and some students have been known to get 0 scores from time to time. In this situation, 0 is a legitimate data value. To allow the user of the program to enter 0 as a score, it is necessary to choose a different sentinel value that does not represent an actual score. Because it is typically impossible to get a negative score on most exams, it would probably make sense to choose a value like –1 as the sentinel for that application.

To extend **AddNIntegers** into a new **AddIntegerList** program, the only change you need to make is in the loop structure. The **for** loop, which is most commonly used to execute a set of operations a predetermined number of times, is no longer appropriate. You need a new pattern that reads data until the user enters the sentinel that signals the end of the input. That pattern is the **read-until-sentinel pattern** and has the following form:

```
while (true) {
    prompt user and read in a value
    if (value == sentinel) break;
    rest of body
}
```

This new pattern for a sentinel-based loop enables you to complete the **AddIntegerList** program, which is shown in Figure 4-2.

FIGURE 4-2   **Program to add a list of integers where the end is marked by a sentinel**

```java
/*
 * File: AddIntegerList.java
 * ----------------------------
 * This program reads integers one per line until the
 * user enters a special sentinel value to signal the
 * end of the input.  At that point, the program
 * prints the sum of the numbers entered so far.
 */

import acm.program.*;

public class AddIntegerList extends ConsoleProgram {

    public void run() {
        println("This program adds a list of integers.");
        println("Enter values, one per line, using " + SENTINEL);
        println("to signal the end of the list.");
        int total = 0;
        while (true) {
            int value = readInt(" ? ");
            if (value == SENTINEL) break;
            total += value;
        }
        println("The total is " + total + ".");
    }

/* Specifies the value of the sentinel */
    private static final int SENTINEL = 0;

}
```

Later in this chapter, you will learn the details of the control statements out of which the read-until-sentinel pattern is formed. Even before you understand the details, you will find the pattern very useful. As you learn more about programming, however, you will discover that even expert programmers often use code that they don't understand in detail. In fact, one of the marks of an expert programmer is being able to use a library or a piece of code *without* understanding all the underlying details. As programs become more complex, the ability to use tools you understand only at the holistic level is an increasingly important skill.

4.3 The if statement

The simplest way to express conditional execution in Java is by using the **if** statement, which comes in two forms:

> **if** (*condition*) *statement*

> **if** (*condition*) *statement₁* **else** *statement₂*

The *condition* component of this template is a Boolean expression, as defined in Chapter 3. In the simple form of the **if** statement, Java executes *statement* only if the specified condition evaluates to **true**. If that condition is **false**, Java skips the body of the **if** statement entirely. In the form that includes the **else** keyword, Java executes *statement₁* if the condition is **true** and *statement₂* if the condition is **false**. In both forms of the **if** statement, the code that Java executes when the conditional expression is **true** is called the **then clause.** In the **if-else** form, the code executed when the condition is **false** is called the **else clause.**

The decision as to whether to use a simple **if** statement or the **if-else** form depends entirely on how your solution strategy operates. You use the simple **if** statement form when your solution strategy calls for a set of statements to be executed only if a particular condition applies. You use the **if-else** form for situations in which the program must choose between two independent sets of actions based on the result of a test. You can often make this decision based on how you would describe the problem in English. If that description contains the word *otherwise* or some similar word, there is a good chance that you'll need the **if-else** form. If the English description conveys no such notion, then the simple **if** statement is probably sufficient.

The use of the **if** statement is illustrated by the **LeapYear** program in Figure 4-3, which uses the Boolean expression developed in Chapter 3 to determine whether a given year is a leap year. The version of the program shown in the figure requires the **if-else** form because the program needs to print one message if the specified year is a leap year and a different message otherwise. If the problem were instead structured so that a message were printed only in leap years, you would use the simple **if** form instead, as follows:

```
if (isLeapYear) {
   println(year + " is a leap year.");
}
```

FIGURE 4-3 **Program to determine whether a year is a leap year**

```
/*
 * File: LeapYear.java
 * ---------------------
 * This program reads in a year and determines whether it is a
 * leap year.  A year is a leap year if it is divisible by four,
 * unless it is divisible by 100.  Years divisible by 100 are
 * leap years only if divisible by 400.
 */

import acm.program.*;

public class LeapYear extends ConsoleProgram {
   public void run() {
      println("This program checks for leap years.");
      int year = readInt("Enter year: ");
      boolean isLeapYear = ((year % 4 == 0) && (year % 100 != 0))
                         || (year % 400 == 0);
      if (isLeapYear) {
         println(year + " is a leap year.");
      } else {
         println(year + " is not a leap year.");
      }
   }
}
```

The fact that the **else** clause is optional in the **if** statement sometimes creates an ambiguity, which is called the **dangling-else problem**. If you write several **if** statements nested one within another, some of which have **else** clauses and some of which don't, it can be difficult to tell which **else** goes with which **if**. When faced with this situation, the Java compiler follows the simple rule that each **else** clause is paired with the most recent **if** statement that does not already have an **else** clause. While this rule is simple for the compiler, it can be hard for human readers to recognize quickly where each **else** clause belongs. By adopting a more disciplined programming style than Java requires, it is possible to get rid of dangling-else ambiguities.

This book eliminates the dangling-else problem by adopting the blocking rule expressed in the syntax box to the left. As a result, the **if** statement appears only in one of the following four forms:

> **The if/else blocking rule**
>
> *type identifier* = *expression*;
>
> where:
> *type* is the type of the variable
> *identifier* is the name of the variable
> *expression* specifies the initial value

1. A single-line **if** statement used for extremely short conditions
2. A multiline **if** statement in which the statements are enclosed in a block
3. An **if-else** statement that *always* uses blocks to enclose the statements controlled by the **if** statement, even if they consist of a single statement
4. A *cascading* **if** statement, used for expressing a series of conditional tests

The sections that follow discuss each of these forms in more detail.

Single-line `if` statements

The simple one-line format shown in the syntax box to the right is used only for those `if` statements in which there is no `else` clause and in which the body is a single statement short enough to fit on the same line as the `if`. In this type of situation, using braces and extending the `if` statement from one to three lines would make the program longer and more difficult to read.

Multiline `if` statements

Whenever the body of an `if` statement consists of a compound statement or a simple statement that is too long for a single line, that code should enclosed in a block, as shown in the syntax box. In this form, the code inside the block is executed if the condition is `true`. If the condition is `false`, the program takes no action at all and continues with the statement following the `if`.

The `if-else` statement

To avoid the dangling-else problem, the bodies of `if` statements that have `else` clauses are always enclosed within blocks, as shown in the syntax box to the right. Technically, the curly braces that surround the block are necessary only if there is more than one statement governed by that condition. However, by systematically using those braces, you can minimize the possibility of confusion and make your programs easier to maintain.

Cascading `if` statements

The final syntax box for the `if` statement illustrates an important special case that is useful for applications in which the number of possible cases is larger than two. The characteristic form is that the `else` part of a condition consists of yet another test to check for an alternative condition. Such statements are called **cascading if statements** and may involve any number of `else if` lines. For example, the program `SignTest` in Figure 4-4 uses the cascading `if` statement to report whether a number is positive, zero, or negative. Note that there is no need to check explicitly for the `n < 0` condition. If the program reaches that last `else` clause, there is no other possibility, since the earlier tests have eliminated the positive and zero cases.

Syntax for single-line `if` statements

```
if (condition) statement;
```

where:
   condition is a Boolean expression
   statement is a single statement to be
      executed if *condition* is `true`

Syntax for multiline `if` statements

```
if (condition) {
    statements;
}
```

where:
   condition is a Boolean expression
   statements is a block of statements to be
      executed if the condition is `true`

Syntax for `if-else` statements

```
if (condition) {
    statementsT
} else {
    statementsF
}
```

where:
   condition is a Boolean expression
   statements$_T$ is a block of statements to
      be executed if *condition* is `true`
   statements$_F$ is a block of statements to
      be executed if *condition* is `false`

Syntax for cascading `if` statements

```
if (condition1) {
    statements1
} else if (condition2) {
    statements2
} else if (condition3) {
    statements3
      . . .
} else {
    statementsnone
}
```

where:
   each *condition$_i$* is a Boolean expression
   each *statements$_i$* is a block of statements
      to be executed if *condition$_i$* is `true`
   statements$_{none}$ is a block of statements to
      be executed if no condition is `true`

FIGURE 4-4   **Program to classify an integer according to its sign**

```
/*
 * File: SignTest.java
 * ---------------------
 * This program reads in an integer and classifies it as negative,
 * zero, or positive depending on its sign.
 */

import acm.program.*;

public class SignTest extends ConsoleProgram {
   public void run() {
      println("This program classifies an integer by its sign.");
      int n = readInt("Enter n: ");
      if (n > 0) {
         println("That number is positive.");
      } else if (n == 0) {
         println("That number is zero.");
      } else {
         println("That number is negative.");
      }
   }
}
```

In many situations, it makes more sense to use the **switch** statement to choose among a set of independent cases than to adopt the cascading **if** form. The **switch** statement is described in section 4.4.

The ?: operator

The Java programming language provides another, more compact mechanism for expressing conditional execution that can be extremely useful in certain situations: the **?:** operator. (This operator is referred to as *question-mark colon*, even though the two characters do not actually appear adjacent to each other.) Unlike any other operator in Java, **?:** is written in two parts and requires three operands. The general form of the operation is

condition **?** *expression₁* **:** *expression₂*

When Java encounters the **?:** operator, it first evaluates the condition. If the condition turns out to be **true**, *expression₁* is evaluated and used as the value of the entire expression; if the condition is **false**, the value is the result of evaluating *expression₂*. The **?:** operator is therefore a shorthand form of the **if** statement

```
if (condition) {
   value = expression₁;
} else {
   value = expression₂;
}
```

where the value of the `?:` expression as a whole is whatever would have been stored in **value** in the expanded, `if`-statement form.

For example, you can use the `?:` operator to assign to **max** either the value of **x** or the value of **y**, whichever is greater, as follows:

```
max = (x > y) ? x : y;
```

The parentheses around the condition are not technically required, but many Java programmers tend to include them in this context to enhance the readability of the code.

One of the most common situations in which the `?:` operator makes sense is in calls to **println** where the output you want differs slightly depending on some condition. For example, suppose you are writing a program that counts the number of some item and that, after doing all the counting, stores the number of items in the variable **nItems**. How would you report this value to the user? The obvious way is just to call **println** using a statement like

```
println(nItems + " items found.");
```

But if you are a grammatical purist, you might be a little chagrined to read the output

when **nItems** happens to have the value 1. You could, however, correct the English by enclosing the **println** line in the following `if` statement:

```
if (nItems == 1) {
   println(nItems + " item found.");
} else {
   println(nItems + " items found.");
}
```

The only problem is that this solution strategy requires a five-line statement to express a relatively simple idea. As an alternative, you could use the `?:` operator as follows:

```
println(nItems + " item" + (nItems == 1 ? "" : "s")
                 + " found.");
```

The string `"item"` in the output would then be followed by the empty string if **nItems** is equal to one and the string `"s"` otherwise. Note that the parentheses are necessary around the expression

```
(nItems == 1 ? "" : "s")
```

The `?:` operator has relatively low precedence with respect to `+`, which means that Java would try to do the concatenation first.

Although the `?:` operator is extremely useful in certain contexts, it is easy to overuse it. The problem arises if you embed an essential part of the decision-making structure inside a `?:` operator, because the code for that decision becomes much harder to find. On the other hand, if using `?:` makes it possible to handle a small detail without writing a complicated `if` statement, this operator can simplify the program structure considerably.

■ 4.4 The `switch` statement

The `if` statement is ideal for applications in which the program logic calls for a two-way decision point: some condition is either `true` or `false`, and the program acts accordingly. Some applications, however, call for more complicated decision structures involving more than two choices, where those choices can be divided into a set of mutually exclusive cases: in one case, the program should do x; in another case, it should do y; in a third, it should do z; and so forth. In many applications, the most appropriate statement to use for such situations is the `switch` statement, which is outlined in the syntax box on the left.

The header line of the `switch` statement is

$$\texttt{switch } (e)$$

where e is an expression that evaluates to an integer (or, as you will see in Chapter 8, any value that behaves like an integer, such as a character). In the context of the `switch` statement, this expression is called the **control expression**. The body of the `switch` statement is divided into individual groups of statements introduced with one of two keywords: `case` or `default`. A `case` line and all the statements that follow it up to the next instance of either of these keywords are called a **case clause**; the `default` line and its associated statements are called the **default clause**. For example, in the template shown in the syntax box, the range of statements

```
case c₁:
    statements₁
    break;
```

constitutes the first `case` clause.

> **Syntax for the `switch` statement**
>
> ```
> switch (e) {
>     case c₁:
>         statements₁
>         break;
>     case c₂:
>         statements₂
>         break;
>     ... more case clauses ...
>     default:
>         statementsdef
>         break;
> }
> ```
>
> where:
> e is the control expression, which is used to choose what statements are executed
> each c_i is a constant value
> each $statements_i$ is a sequence of statements to be executed if c_i is equal to e
> $statements_{def}$ is a sequence of statements to be executed if none of the c_i values match the expression e

When the program executes a `switch` statement, the control expression e is evaluated and compared against the values c_1, c_2, and so forth, each of which must be a constant. If one of the constants matches the value of the control expression, the statements in the associated `case` clause are executed. When the program reaches the **break** statement at the end of the clause, the operations specified by that clause are complete, and the program continues with the statement following the entire **switch** statement. If none of the case constants match the value of the control expression, the statements in the **default** clause are executed.

The template shown in the syntax box deliberately suggests that the **break** statements are a required part of the syntax. I encourage you to think of the **switch** syntax in precisely that form. Java is defined so that if the **break** statement is missing, the program starts executing statements from the next clause after it finishes the selected one. While this design can be useful in some cases, it tends to cause more problems than it solves. To reinforce the importance of remembering to include the **break** statement, every **case** clause in this text ends with an explicit **break** statement (or sometimes with a **return** statement, as discussed in Chapter 5).

The one exception to this rule is that multiple **case** lines specifying different constants can appear together, one after another, before the same statement group. For example, a **switch** statement might include the following code:

```
case 1:
case 2:
    statements
    break;
```

which indicates that the specified statements should be executed if the **select** expression is either 1 or 2. The Java compiler treats this construction as two **case** clauses, the first of which is empty. Because the empty clause contains no **break** statement, a program that selects that path simply continues on with the second clause. From a conceptual point of view, however, you are probably better off thinking of this construction as a single **case** clause that represents two possibilities.

The **default** clause is optional in the **switch** statement. If none of the cases match and there is no **default** clause, the program simply continues on with the next statement after the **switch** statement without taking any action at all. To avoid the possibility that the program might ignore an unexpected case, it is good programming practice to include a **default** clause in every **switch** statement unless you are certain you have enumerated all the possibilities.

Because the **switch** statement can be rather long, programs are easier to read if the **case** clauses themselves are short. If there is room to do so, it also helps to put the **case** identifier, the statements forming the body of the clause, and the **break** statement all together on the same line. This style is illustrated in the **CardRank** program in Figure 4-5, which shows an example of a **switch** statement that might prove useful in writing a program to play a card game. In this game, the cards in each suit are represented by the numbers 1 to 13. Displaying the number of the card is fine for the cards between 2 and 10, but this style of output is not very satisfying for the values 1, 11, 12, and 13, which should properly be represented using the names Ace, Jack, Queen, and King. The **CardRank** program uses the **switch** statement to display the correct symbol for each card.

The fact that the **switch** statement can only be used to choose between cases identified by an integer (or integer-like) constant does place some restrictions on its use. You will encounter situations in which you want to use a string value to

COMMON PITFALLS

It is good programming practice to include a **break** statement at the end of every **case** clause within a **switch** statement. Doing so will help you avoid programming errors that can be extremely difficult to find. It is also good practice to include a **default** clause unless you are sure you have covered all the cases.

FIGURE 4-5 **Program to convert an integer to its rank as a playing card**

```
/*
 * File: CardRank.java
 * ---------------------
 * This program reads in an integer between 1 and 13 and
 * prints the appropriate symbol for a playing card
 * of that rank.
 */

import acm.program.*;

public class CardRank extends ConsoleProgram {

   public void run() {
      println("This program converts integers to card ranks.");
      int n = readInt("Enter an integer between 1 and 13: ");
      switch (n) {
         case  1: println("Ace"); break;
         case 11: println("Jack"); break;
         case 12: println("Queen"); break;
         case 13: println("King"); break;
         default: println(n); break;
      }
   }
}
```

---

choose among a variety of cases or in which the values you want to use as **case** indicators are not constants. Since you cannot use the **switch** statement in such situations, you will instead need to rely on cascading **if** statements. On the other hand, using a **switch** statement when it is possible to do so can make your programs both more readable and more efficient.

4.5 The `while` statement

The simplest iterative construct is the **while** statement, which repeatedly executes a simple statement or block until the conditional expression becomes **false**. The template for the **while** statement appears in the syntax box on the left. As with the **if** statement, the Java compiler allows you to eliminate the curly braces surrounding the body if the body consists of a single statement. However, to improve readability, I always enclose the body in braces.

The entire statement, including both the **while** control line itself and the statements enclosed within the body, constitutes a **while loop**. When the program executes a **while** statement, it first evaluates the conditional expression to see if it is **true** or **false**. If the condition is **false**, the loop **terminates** and the program continues with the next statement after the entire loop. If the condition is **true**, the entire body is executed, after which

---

Syntax for the `while` statement

```
while (condition) {
   statements
}
```

where:
condition is the conditional test used to determine whether the loop should continue for another cycle
statements are the statements to be repeated

the program goes back to the top to check the condition again. A single pass through the statements in the body constitutes a **cycle** of the loop.

There are two important principles to observe about the operation of a **while** loop:

1. The conditional test is performed before every cycle of the loop, including the first. If the test is **false** initially, the body of the loop is not executed at all.
2. The conditional test is performed only at the *beginning* of a loop cycle. If that condition happens to become **false** at some point during the loop, the program doesn't notice that fact until it has executed a complete cycle. At that point, the program evaluates the test condition again. If it is still **false**, the loop terminates.

Using the while loop

Learning how to use the **while** loop effectively usually requires looking at several examples in which the **while** loop comes up naturally in the solution strategy. As an example, suppose that you have been asked to write a program called **DigitSum** that adds up the digits in a positive integer. Thus, given the input 1729, a sample run for the program might look like this:

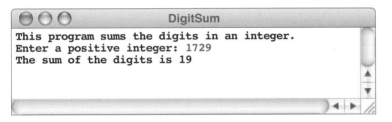

The value 19 comes from adding the digits in the input number: $1 + 7 + 2 + 9 = 19$. How would you go about writing such a program?

When you read the discussion of the **AddNIntegers** program from Figure 4-1 earlier in this chapter, you learned how to keep a running total. To solve the **DigitSum** problem, you need to declare a variable for the sum, initialize it to 0, add in each digit, and finally display the sum at the end. That much of the structure, with the rest of the problem left written in English, is shown below:

```
public void run() {
    println("This program sums the digits in an integer.");
    int n = readInt("Enter a positive integer: ");
    int dsum = 0;
    For each digit in the number, add that digit to dsum.
    println("The sum of the digits is " + dsum);
}
```

The sentence

> *For each digit in the number, add that digit to* **dsum**.

clearly specifies a loop structure of some sort, since there is an operation that needs to be repeated for each digit in the number. If it were easy to determine how many digits a number contained, you might choose to use a **for** loop and count up to the number of digits. Unfortunately, finding out how many digits there are in an integer is just as hard as adding them up in the first place. The best way to write this program is just to keep adding in digits until you discover that you have added the last one. Loops that run until some condition occurs are most often coded using the **while** statement.

The essence of this problem lies in determining how to break up a number into its component digits. The crucial insight is that the arithmetic operators **/** and **%** are sufficient to accomplish the task. The last digit of an integer **n** is simply the remainder left over when **n** is divided by 10, which is the result of the expression **n % 10**. The rest of the number—the integer that consists of all digits *except* the last one—is given by **n / 10**. For example, if **n** has the value 1729, you can use the **/** and **%** operators to break that number into two parts, 172 and 9, as shown in the following diagram:

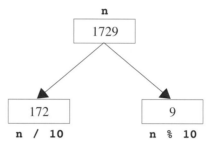

Thus, in order to add up the digits in the number, all you need to do is add the value **n % 10** to the variable **dsum** on each cycle of the loop and then divide the number **n** by 10. The next cycle will add in the second-to-last digit from the original number, and so on, until the entire number has been processed in this way.

But how do you know when to stop? Eventually, as you divide **n** by 10 in each cycle, you will reach the point at which **n** becomes 0. At that point, you've processed all the digits in the number and can exit from the loop. In other words, as long as the value of **n** is greater than 0, you should keep going. Thus, the **while** loop needed for the problem is

```
while (n > 0) {
   dsum += n % 10;
   n /= 10;
}
```

The entire **DigitSum** program appears in Figure 4-6.

Infinite loops

When you use a **while** loop in a program, it is important to make sure that the condition used to control the loop will eventually become **false**, so that the loop can exit. If the condition in the **while** control line always evaluates to **true**, the

---

FIGURE 4-6   **Program to sum the digits in an integer**

```
/*
 * File: DigitSum.java
 * ---------------------
 * This program sums the digits in a positive integer.
 * The program depends on the fact that the last digit of
 * an integer n is given by n % 10 and the number consisting
 * of all but the last digit is given by the expression n / 10.
 */

import acm.program.*;

public class DigitSum extends ConsoleProgram {

   public void run() {
      println("This program sums the digits in an integer.");
      int n = readInt("Enter a positive integer: ");
      int dsum = 0;
      while (n > 0) {
         dsum += n % 10;
         n /= 10;
      }
      println("The sum of the digits is " + dsum);
   }

}
```

---

computer will keep executing cycle after cycle without stopping. This situation is called an **infinite loop**.

As an example, suppose that you had carelessly written the **while** loop in the **DigitSum** program with a **>=** operator in the control line instead of the correct **>** operator, as shown below:

```
while (n >= 0) {
   dsum += n % 10;
   n /= 10;
}
```

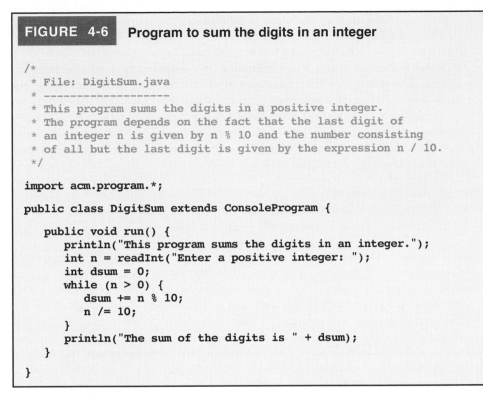

> **COMMON PITFALLS**
>
> Think carefully about the conditional expression you use in a **while** loop so that you can be sure the loop will eventually exit. A loop that never finishes is called an *infinite loop*.

The loop no longer stops when **n** is reduced to 0, as it does in the correctly coded example. Instead, the computer keeps executing the body over and over and over again, with **n** equal to 0 every time.

To stop an infinite loop, you must type a special command sequence on the keyboard to interrupt the program and forcibly cause it to quit. This command sequence differs from machine to machine, and you should be sure to learn what command to use on your own computer.

Solving the loop-and-a-half problem

The **while** loop is designed for situations in which there is some test condition that can be applied at the beginning of a repeated operation, before any of the statements in the body of the loop are executed. If the problem you are trying to solve fits this structure, the `while` loop is the perfect tool. Unfortunately, many programming problems do not fit easily into the standard `while` loop template. Instead of allowing a convenient test at the beginning of the operation, some problems are structured in such a way that the test you would like to write to determine whether the loop is complete falls most naturally somewhere in the middle of the loop.

Consider for example, the problem of reading input data until a sentinel value appears, which is discussed in the section on the read-until-sentinel pattern earlier in this chapter. When expressed in English, the structure of the sentinel-based loop consists of repeating the following steps:

1. Read in a value.
2. If the value is equal to the sentinel, exit from the loop.
3. Perform whatever processing is required for that value.

Unfortunately, there is no test you can perform at the very beginning of the loop to determine whether the loop is finished. The termination condition for the loop is reached when the input value is equal to the sentinel; in order to check this condition, the program must have first read in some value. If the program has not yet read in a value, the termination condition doesn't make sense. Before the program can make any meaningful test, it must have executed the part of the loop that reads in the input value. When a loop contains some operations that must be performed before testing for completion, it represents an instance of what programmers call the **loop-and-a-half problem**.

One way to solve the loop-and-a-half problem in Java is to use the `break` statement, which, in addition to its use in the `switch` statement, has the effect of immediately terminating the innermost enclosing loop. By using `break`, it is possible to code the loop structure for the sentinel problem in a form that follows the natural structure of the problem:

```
while (true) {
    prompt user and read in a value
    if (value == sentinel) break;
    process the data value
}
```

The initial line

```
while (true)
```

needs some explanation. The `while` loop is defined so that it continues until the condition in parentheses becomes `false`. The symbol `true` is a constant, so it can never become `false`. Thus, as far as the `while` statement itself is concerned, the loop will never terminate. The only way this program can exit from the loop is by executing the `break` statement inside it.

It is possible to code this sort of loop without using the `while (true)` control line or the `break` statement. To do so, however, you must change the order of operations within the loop and request input data in two places: once before the loop begins and then again inside the loop body. When structured in this way, the template for the sentinel-based loop is

> *prompt user and read in the first value*
> **while** (*value* != *sentinel*) {
>   *process the data value*
>   *prompt user and read in a new value*
> }

Figure 4-7 shows how this template can be used to implement the **AddIntegerList** program presented in Figure 4-2 without using a **break** statement.

Unfortunately, there are two drawbacks to using this strategy. First, the order of operations in the loop is not what most people would expect. In any English explanation of the solution strategy, the first step is to get a number and the second is to add it to the total. The **while** loop template used in Figure 4-7 reverses the order of the statements within the loop and makes the program more difficult to follow. The second problem is that this template requires two copies of the statements that read in a number. Duplication of code presents a serious maintenance problem because subsequent edits to one set of statements might not be

---

FIGURE 4-7   **Rewrite of AddIntegerList without a break statement**

```java
/*
 * File: AddIntegerList.java
 * --------------------------------
 * This program reads integers one per line until the
 * user enters a special sentinel value to signal the
 * end of the input.  At that point, the program
 * prints the sum of the numbers entered so far.
 */

import acm.program.*;

public class AddIntegerList extends ConsoleProgram {

   public void run() {
      println("This program adds a list of integers.");
      println("Enter values, one per line, using " + SENTINEL);
      println("to signal the end of the list.");
      int total = 0;
      int value = readInt(" ? ");
      while (value != SENTINEL) {
         total += value;
         value = readInt(" ? ");
      }
      println("The total is " + total + ".");
   }

/* Specifies the value of the sentinel */
   private static final int SENTINEL = 0;

}
```

made in the other. Empirical studies have shown that students who learn to solve the loop-and-a-half problem using the **break** statement are far more likely to write correct programs than those who don't.

▰▰ 4.6 The `for` statement

One of the most important control statements in Java is the **for** statement, which is most often used in situations in which you want to repeat an operation a particular number of times. The general form of the **for** statement is shown in the syntax box to the left.

Syntax for the `for` statement

> **for** (*init*; *test*; *step*) {
>   *statements*
> }

where:
>   *init* is a declaration that initializes the loop index variable
>   *test* is a conditional test used to determine whether the loop should continue, just as in the **while** statement
>   *step* is an expression used to prepare for the next loop cycle
>   *statements* are the statements to be repeated

The operation of the **for** loop is determined by the three italicized expressions on the **for** control line: *init*, *test*, and *step*. The *init* expression indicates how the **for** loop should be initialized, usually by declaring an index variable and setting its initial value. For example, if you write

```
for (int i = 0; . . .
```

the loop will begin by declaring the index variable **i** and setting it to 0. If the loop begins

```
for (int i = -7; . . .
```

the variable **i** will start as **-7**, and so on.

The *test* expression is a conditional test written exactly like the test in a **while** statement. As long as the test expression is **true**, the loop continues. Thus, in the loop that has served as our canonical example up to now

```
for (int i = 0; i < n; i++)
```

the loop begins with **i** equal to 0 and continues as long as **i** is less than **n**, which turns out to represent a total of **n** cycles, with **i** taking on the values 0, 1, 2, and so forth, up to the final value **n − 1**. The loop

```
for (int i = 1; i <= n; i++)
```

begins with **i** equal to 1 and continues as long as **i** is less than or equal to **n**. This loop also runs for **n** cycles, with **i** taking on the values 1, 2, and so forth, up to **n**.

The *step* expression indicates how the value of the index variable changes from cycle to cycle. The most common form of step specification is to increment the index variable using the **++** operator, but this is not the only possibility. For example, one can count backward by using the **--** operator, or count by twos by using **+= 2** instead of **++**.

As an illustration of counting in the reverse direction, the **Countdown** program in Figure 4-8 counts down from 10 to 0. When you execute the **Countdown** program, it generates the following sample run:

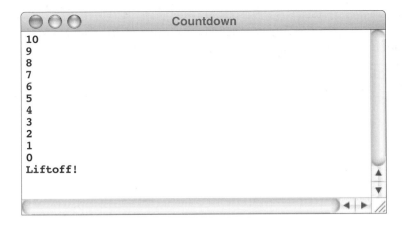

The **Countdown** program demonstrates that any variable can be used as an index variable. In this case, the variable is called **t**, presumably because that is the traditional variable for a rocket countdown, as in the phrase "T minus 10 seconds and counting." In any case, the index variable must be declared at the beginning of the program, just like any other variable.

The expressions *init*, *test*, and *step* are each optional, but the semicolons must appear. If *init* is missing, no initialization is performed. If *test* is missing, it is assumed to be **true**. If *step* is missing, no action occurs between loop cycles. Thus the control line

```
for (;;)
```

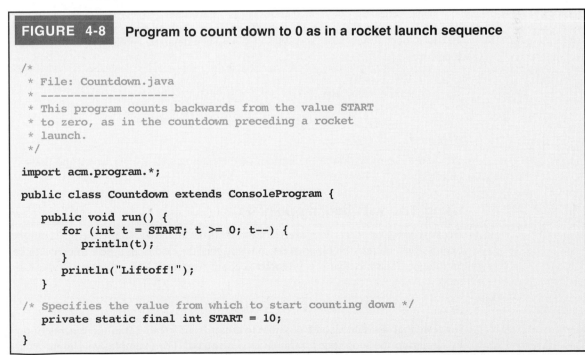

FIGURE 4-8   **Program to count down to 0 as in a rocket launch sequence**

```java
/*
 * File: Countdown.java
 * -----------------------
 * This program counts backwards from the value START
 * to zero, as in the countdown preceding a rocket
 * launch.
 */

import acm.program.*;

public class Countdown extends ConsoleProgram {

   public void run() {
      for (int t = START; t >= 0; t--) {
         println(t);
      }
      println("Liftoff!");
   }

/* Specifies the value from which to start counting down */
   private static final int START = 10;

}
```

is identical in operation to

```
while (true)
```

The relationship between `for` and `while`

As it happens, the **for** statement

```
for (init; test; step) {
    statements;
}
```

is identical in operation to the **while** statement

```
init;
while (test) {
    statements;
    step;
}
```

Even though you can easily rewrite the **for** statement using **while**, there are considerable advantages to using the **for** statement whenever it is possible to do so. With a **for** statement, all the information you need to understand exactly which cycles will be executed is contained in the header line of the statement. For example, whenever you see the statement

```
for (int i = 0; i < 10; i++) {
    ... body ...
}
```

in a program, you know that the statements in the body of the loop will be executed 10 times, once for each of the values of **i** between 0 and 9. In the equivalent **while** loop form

```
int i = 0;
while (i < 10) {
    ... body ...
    i++;
}
```

the increment operation at the bottom of the loop can easily get lost if the body is large.

Using `for` with floating-point data

Because the *init*, *test*, and *step* components of the **for** loop can be arbitrary expressions, there is no obvious reason why the loop index in a **for** loop has to be an integer. The fact that it is possible to count from 0 to 10 by twos using the **for** loop

```
for (int i = 0; i <= 10; i += 2) . . .
```

suggests that it might also be possible to count from 1.0 to 2.0 in increments of 0.1 by declaring the loop index variable as a **double**. For example, you might try to display the values in this range by writing

```
for (double x = 1.0; x <= 2.0; x += 0.1) {
   println(x);
}
```

However, if you run this program in Java, you don't get a list that begins 1.0, 1.1, 1.2, and so on up to 2.0, but instead see the following output:

```
ForLoopWithDoubles
1.0
1.1
1.2000000000000002
1.3000000000000003
1.4000000000000004
1.5000000000000004
1.6000000000000005
1.7000000000000006
1.8000000000000007
1.9000000000000008
```

There are a lot of seemingly extraneous digits and there is nothing even close to the value 2.0.

The problem is that floating-point numbers are not exact. The value 0.1 is very close to the mathematical fraction $\frac{1}{10}$ but is not precisely equal to it. As 0.1 is successively added to the index variable x, the inaccuracy can accumulate to the point that, when x is tested against 2.0 to determine whether the loop is finished, its value may be 2.000000001 or something similar, which is not less than or equal to 2.0. The condition in the **for** loop is therefore not satisfied, and the loop terminates after running for what seems to be one too few cycles. The best way to fix this problem is to restrict yourself to using integers as index variables in **for** loops. Because integers are exact, the problem never arises.

The same warning about comparing floating-point numbers for equality applies in many other contexts besides the **for** loop. Numbers that seem as if they should be exactly equal may not be, given the limitations on the accuracy of floating-point numbers.

> **COMMON PITFALLS**
>
> Be careful when testing floating-point numbers for equality. Because floating-point numbers are only approximations, they do not behave in the same way as real numbers in mathematics. In general, it is best to avoid using a floating-point variable as a **for** loop index.

Nested **for** statements

In many applications, you will discover that you need to write one **for** loop inside another so that the statements in the innermost loop are executed for every possible combination of values of the **for** loop indices. This situation often comes up in graphical applications in which you have to repeat some operation in both the x and y directions. Consider, for example, how you might write a program to generate a checkerboard pattern that looks like this:

The checkerboard consists of eight horizontal rows and eight vertical columns. To create the individual squares, you need a pair of nested **for** loops: an outer loop that runs through each of the rows and an inner loop that runs through each of the columns. The code inside the inner **for** loop will be executed once for every row and column, for a total of 64 individual squares.

A program to draw this checkerboard appears in Figure 4-9. It is worth taking some time to go through the code, paying particular attention to the following details:

- The program is designed so that you can easily change the dimensions of the checkerboard by changing the definition of the named constants **N_ROWS** and **N_COLUMNS**.
- The checkerboard is arranged so that its left edge is aligned against the left side of the graphics window. The size of the individual squares is calculated so that the checkerboard fills the available vertical space. This means that the size of each square must be the height of the window divided by the number of rows.
- The first statements inside the inner **for** loop compute the coordinates for the current square from the calculated square size and the **for** loop indices **i** and **j**.
- The decision to fill the square is made by checking whether the sum of its row number and column number is even or odd. White squares are the ones for which this sum is even; black squares are the ones for which this sum is odd. Note, however, that you don't need to include an **if** statement in the code to test this condition. All you need to do is call the **setFilled** method with the appropriate Boolean value.

Simple graphical animation

The **Checkerboard** program in the preceding section makes it clear that **for** loops can be just as useful in graphical programs as they are in console-based programs. In the **Checkerboard** example, the **for** loops make it easier to construct the diagram

FIGURE 4-9	Program to draw a checkerboard

```
/*
 * File: Checkerboard.java
 * ---------------------------
 * This program draws a checkerboard.  The dimensions of the
 * checkerboard are specified by the constants N_ROWS and
 * N_COLUMNS, and the size of the squares is chosen so
 * that the checkerboard fills the available vertical space.
 */

import acm.graphics.*;
import acm.program.*;

public class Checkerboard extends GraphicsProgram {

    public void run() {
        double sqSize = (double) getHeight() / N_ROWS;
        for (int i = 0; i < N_ROWS; i++) {
            for (int j = 0; j < N_COLUMNS; j++) {
                double x = j * sqSize;
                double y = i * sqSize;
                GRect sq = new GRect(x, y, sqSize, sqSize);
                sq.setFilled((i + j) % 2 != 0);
                add(sq);
            }
        }
    }

/* Private constants */
    private static final int N_ROWS = 8;
    private static final int N_COLUMNS = 8;

}
```

by making it possible to repeat the same code for each of the eight rows and eight columns. As with all the other **GraphicsProgram** examples you have seen so far, the image generated by the program is fixed. Once you've drawn the checkerboard, it just sits there passively on the screen. If you want to write programs that are a bit more exciting, it is important to move graphical objects around on the screen or have them change their size and color. In computer graphics, the process of updating a displayed image so that it changes over time is called **animation.**

The easiest way to animate graphical programs is to include a loop that makes a small change to the graphical objects on the screen and then suspends the program for a short time interval. A simple example of this style of graphics is illustrated by the program in Figure 4-10, which moves a square diagonally across the screen from its initial location in the upper left corner to its final location in the lower right. The operation of the program is illustrated by the following sample run, which shows the initial position of the square in gray and uses an arrow to indicate its approximate trajectory:

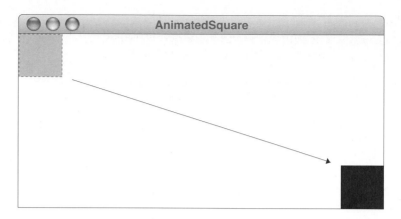

The first three lines of the **run** method in Figure 4-10 create the square, set it to be filled, and then add it to the display at the upper left corner. The remaining lines in the **run** method are responsible for moving the square to its final position in a sequence of time steps in which the square moves by a small amount. In this

---

FIGURE 4-10   **Program to move a square diagonally across the screen**

```
/*
 * File: AnimatedSquare.java
 * --------------------------------
 * This program animates a square so that it moves from the
 * upper left corner of the window to the lower right corner.
 */

import acm.graphics.*;
import acm.program.*;

public class AnimatedSquare extends GraphicsProgram {

   public void run() {
      GRect square = new GRect(0, 0, SQUARE_SIZE, SQUARE_SIZE);
      square.setFilled(true);
      add(square);
      double dx = (getWidth() - SQUARE_SIZE) / N_STEPS;
      double dy = (getHeight() - SQUARE_SIZE) / N_STEPS;
      for (int i = 0; i < N_STEPS; i++) {
         square.move(dx, dy);
         pause(PAUSE_TIME);
      }
   }

/* Private constants */
   private static final int N_STEPS = 1000;
   private static final int PAUSE_TIME = 20;
   private static final double SQUARE_SIZE = 50;
}
```

implementation, the named constant **N_STEPS** specifies the number of time steps. To determine how far the square must move in each time step, you need to divide the total distance it traverses by the number of steps. The lines

```
double dx = (getWidth() - SQUARE_SIZE) / N_STEPS;
double dy = (getHeight() - SQUARE_SIZE) / N_STEPS;
```

perform this calculation in each dimension. By shifting the location of the square by **dx** and **dy** in the horizontal and vertical dimensions on each cycle, the program ensures that the square reaches its desired position in the lower right at the end of the run.

The animation itself is implemented by the **for** loop at the end of the **run** method, which cycles through each of the time steps, as follows:

```
for (int i = 0; i < N_STEPS; i++) {
   square.move(dx, dy);
   pause(PAUSE_TIME);
}
```

In each of the time steps, the program calls

```
square.move(dx, dy);
```

which adjusts the location of the square by the appropriate distance in each dimension. The second line of the **for** loop is

```
pause(PAUSE_TIME);
```

which causes the program to suspend its operation for the specified number of milliseconds. Using a pause time of 20 milliseconds means that the display will be updated 50 times a second, which is well below the threshold at which the eye perceives motion as continuous. The call to **pause** in the **AnimatedSquare** program is necessary to achieve the effect of animation. Computers today run so quickly that the square would instantly jump to the lower right corner if you didn't slow things down enough to bring the operation back to human speed.

You can change the speed of an animation in either of two ways. First, you can change the number of time steps required to move an object over a particular distance. For example, if you changed the number of time steps from 1000 to 250, the square would appear to move twice as fast because the **dx** and the **dy** values would be four times as large. At some point, however, the values of **dx** and **dy** may become so large that the motion appears jerky. The second approach is to change the delay time. Intuitively, it seems as if you could double the speed of the display by halving the delay time on each cycle, although that strategy also has limits in practice. The delay that a program experiences when it calls **pause** is not guaranteed to be precise. Moreover, there is always some overhead associated with pausing a program, and it is impossible to run the animation with a cycle time that is less than the overhead. Thus, there is always some point at which reducing the value of **PAUSE_TIME** in this example will no longer have any noticeable effect.

Summary

In Chapter 2, you looked at the process of programming from a holistic perspective. Along the way, you learned about several control statements in an informal way. In this chapter, you were able to investigate how those statements work in more detail.

The important points introduced in this chapter include:

- *Simple statements* consist of an expression followed by a semicolon.
- The = used to specify assignment is an operator in Java. Assignments are therefore legal expressions, which makes it possible to write *embedded* and *multiple assignments*.
- Individual statements can be collected into *compound statements*, more commonly called *blocks*.
- Control statements fall into two classes: *conditional* and *iterative*.
- The **if** statement specifies conditional execution when a section of code should be executed only in certain cases or when the program needs to choose between two alternate paths.
- The **switch** statement specifies conditional execution when a problem has the following structure: in case 1, do this; in case 2, do that; and so forth.
- The **while** statement specifies repetition that occurs as long as some condition is met.
- The **for** statement specifies repetition in which some action is needed on each cycle in order to update the value of an index variable.
- You can animate a graphical image by updating it slightly on each cycle of a loop and then calling **pause** to delay the program for a short interval.

Review questions

1. Is the construction

        17;

   a legal statement in Java? Is it useful?

2. What is a *block?* What important fact about blocks is conveyed by the term *compound statement*, which is another name for the same concept?

3. What are the two classes of control statements?

4. What does it mean to say that two control statements are *nested?*

5. What are the four different formats of the **if** statement used in this text?

6. Describe in English the general operation of the **switch** statement.

7. Suppose the body of a **while** loop contains a statement that, when executed, causes the condition for that **while** loop to become **false**. Does the loop terminate immediately at that point or does it complete the current cycle?

8. Why is it important for the **DigitSum** program in Figure 4-6 to specify that the integer is positive?

9. What is the *loop-and-a-half problem*? What two strategies are presented in the text for solving it?

10. What is the purpose of each of the three expressions that appear in the control line of a **for** statement?

11. What **for** loop control line would you use in each of the following situations:

    a) Counting from 1 to 100.
    b) Counting by sevens starting at 0 until the number has more than two digits.
    c) Counting backward by twos from 100 to 0.

12. Why is it best to avoid using a floating-point variable as the index variable in a **for** loop?

13. Describe in your own words the strategy this chapter uses to implement simple animations.

14. What is the purpose of the call to **pause** in the **AnimatedSquare** program in Figure 4-10? What would happen if you removed the call to **pause**?

Programming exercises

1. As a way to pass the time on long bus trips, young people growing up in the United States have been known to sing the following rather repetitive song:

   > 99 bottles of beer on the wall.
   > 99 bottles of beer.
   > You take one down, pass it around.
   > 98 bottles of beer on the wall.
   >
   > 98 bottles of beer on the wall. . . .

   Anyway, you get the idea. Write a Java program to generate the lyrics to this song. In testing your program, it would make sense to use some constant other than 99 as the initial number of bottles.

2. While we're on the subject of silly songs, another old standby is "This Old Man," for which the first verse is

   > This old man, he played 1.
   > He played knick-knack on my thumb.
   > With a knick-knack, paddy-whack,
   > Give your dog a bone.
   > This old man came rolling home.

   Each subsequent verse is the same, except for the number and the rhyming word at the end of the second line, which get replaced as follows:

2—shoe	5—hive	8—pate
3—knee	6—sticks	9—spine
4—door	7—heaven	10—shin

Write a program to display all 10 verses of this song.

3. Write a program that reads in a positive integer *N* and then calculates and displays the sum of the first *N* odd integers. For example, if *N* is 4, your program should display the value 16, which is 1 + 3 + 5 + 7.

4. *Why is everything either at sixes or at sevens?*
    — Gilbert and Sullivan, *H.M.S. Pinafore,* 1878

    Write a program that displays the integers between 1 and 100 that are divisible by either 6 or 7 but not both.

5. Using the **AddIntegerList** program from Figure 4-2 as a model, write a program called **AverageList** that reads in a list of integers representing exam scores and then prints out the average. Because some unprepared student might actually get a score of 0, your program should use –1 as the sentinel to mark the end of the input.

6. Rewrite the **DigitSum** program given in Figure 4-6 so that instead of adding the digits in the number, it generates the number that has the same digits in the reverse order, as illustrated by this sample run:

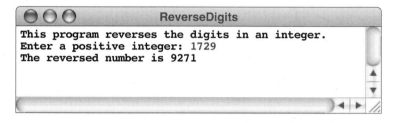

The idea in this exercise is not to take the integer apart character by character, which you will not learn how to do until Chapter 8. Instead, you need to use arithmetic to compute the reversed integer as you go. In this example, the new integer will be 9 after the first cycle of the loop, 92 after the second, 927 after the third, and 9271 after the fourth.

7. The **digital root** of an integer *n* is defined as the result of summing the digits repeatedly until only a single digit remains. For example, the digital root of 1729 can be calculated using the following steps:

Step 1:	1 + 7 + 2 + 9	→	19
Step 2:	1 + 9	→	10
Step 3:	1 + 0	→	1

    Because the total at the end of step 3 is the single digit 1, that value is the digital root.

    Rewrite the **DigitSum** program shown in Figure 4-6 so that it calculates the digital root of the input value.

8. Rewrite the **Countdown** program given in Figure 4-8 so that it uses a **while** loop instead of a **for** loop.

9. In mathematics, there is a famous sequence of numbers called the Fibonacci sequence after the thirteenth-century Italian mathematician Leonardo Fibonacci. The first two terms in this sequence are 0 and 1, and every subsequent term is the sum of the preceding two. Thus the first several terms in the Fibonacci sequence are as follows:

$$
\begin{aligned}
F_0 &= 0 \\
F_1 &= 1 \\
F_2 &= 1 \quad (0 + 1) \\
F_3 &= 2 \quad (1 + 1) \\
F_4 &= 3 \quad (1 + 2) \\
F_5 &= 5 \quad (2 + 3) \\
F_6 &= 8 \quad (3 + 5)
\end{aligned}
$$

Write a program to display the values in this sequence from F_0 through F_{15}.

10. Modify the program in the preceding exercise so that instead of specifying the index of the final term, the program displays those terms in the Fibonacci sequence that are smaller than 10,000.

11. Write a **GraphicsProgram** subclass that draws a pyramid consisting of bricks arranged in horizontal rows, so that the number of bricks in each row decreases by one as you move up the pyramid, as shown in the following sample run:

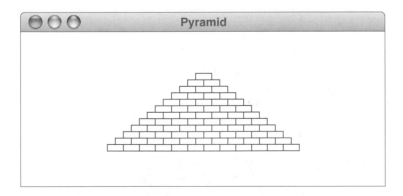

The pyramid should be centered in the window and should use named constants for the following parameters:

BRICK_WIDTH	The width of each brick
BRICK_HEIGHT	The height of each brick
BRICKS_IN_BASE	The number of bricks in the base

12. Write a **ConsoleProgram** that reads in a list of integers, one per line, until the user enters a sentinel value of 0 (which you should be able to change easily to some other value). When the sentinel is read, your program should display the largest value in the list, as illustrated in this sample run:

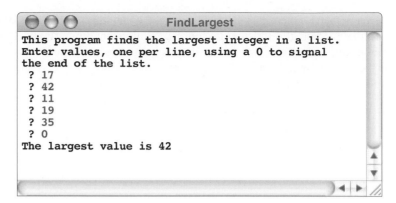

13. Extend the program from the preceding exercise so that it finds both the largest and the second largest values in the list, as shown in the following sample run:

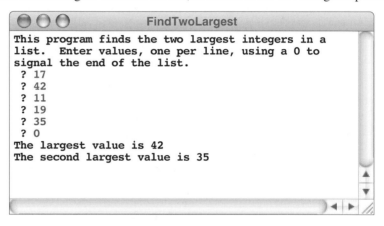

14. Enhance the **Checkerboard** program so that it centers the checkerboard horizontally and draws the set of red and black checkers corresponding to the initial state of the game, which looks like this:

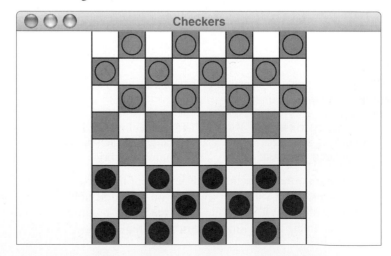

The other change in this program is that the color of the dark squares has been changed from black to gray so that the black checkers are not lost against the background.

15. Using the **AnimatedSquare** program as a model, write an animated **BouncingBall** program that bounces a ball inside the boundaries of the graphics window. Your program should begin by placing a **GOval** in the center of the window to represent the ball. On each time step, your program should shift the position of the ball by **dx** and **dy** pixels, where both **dx** and **dy** initially have the value 1. Whenever the leading edge of the ball touches one of the boundaries of the window, your program should make the ball bounce by negating the value of **dx** or **dy**, as appropriate. For example, if the ball hits the bottom wall of the window, your program should bounce the ball vertically by negating the value of **dy**. Your program should therefore begin with the ball tracing out a path that looks like this, where the gray circle represents the original position of the ball and the arrow indicates where the ball has moved:

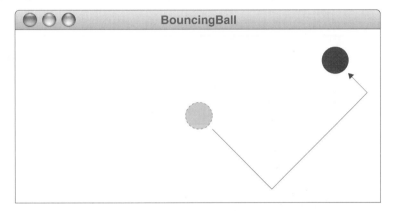

Don't worry about figuring out how to get the program to stop. For this exercise, you should simply use a

```
while (true)
```

loop so that the program just keeps bouncing the ball until you exit the program.

16. In New York's Times Square, you can get the news of the day by watching headlines on large display screens that show a single line of text. The headline initially begins to appear at the right edge of the screen and then moves quickly from right to left. Your job in this exercise is to write a **GraphicsProgram** that simulates this type of headline display by moving a **GLabel** across the screen.

Suppose, for example, that you want to use your program to display the famous *Chicago Tribune* headline from when the paper incorrectly called the result of the 1948 presidential election:

DEWEY DEFEATS TRUMAN

Your program should create a **GLabel** containing the headline and then position it so that the entire text of the label is clipped beyond the right edge of the screen. Your program should then execute an animation loop that moves the **GLabel** a few pixels to the left on each time step. After a few time steps, the display will show the first letter of the headline, as follows:

The headline continues to scroll across the screen, so that a few seconds later the entire first word is visible:

As the label continues to scroll, these letters will disappear off the left edge of the screen as new letters appear on the right. Thus, at some point, the text that is visible on the screen will include the later characters in the headline, like this:

The text will continue to scroll toward the left until the entire **GLabel** disappears from view.

CHAPTER 5

Methods

With method and logic one can accomplish anything.

—Agatha Christie, *Poirot Investigates,* 1924

David Parnas

David Parnas is Professor of Software Engineering at the University of Limerick in Ireland, where he directs the Software Quality Research Laboratory, and has also taught at universities in Germany, Canada, and the United States. His most influential contribution to software engineering is his groundbreaking 1972 paper entitled "On the criteria to be used in decomposing systems into modules," which provided much of the foundation for the strategy of decomposition described in this chapter. Professor Parnas also attracted considerable public attention in 1985 when he resigned from a Department of Defense panel investigating the software requirements of the proposed Strategic Defense Initiative—more commonly known as "Star Wars"—on the grounds that the requirements of the system were impossible to achieve. For his courageous stand in bringing these problems to light, Parnas received the 1987 Norbert Wiener Award from Computer Professionals for Social Responsibility.

This chapter examines in more detail the concept of a method, which was first introduced in Chapter 2. A method is a set of statements that have been collected together and given a name. Because methods allow the programmer to invoke the entire set of operations using a single name, programs become much shorter and much simpler. Without methods, programs would become unmanageable as they increased in size and sophistication.

In order to appreciate how methods reduce the complexity of programs, you need to understand the concept in two ways. From the reductionistic perspective, you need to understand how methods work in an operational sense so you can predict their behavior. At the same time, you must be able to take a step backward and look at methods holistically, so that you can also understand why they are important and how to use them effectively.

■■■ 5.1 A quick overview of methods

You have been working with methods ever since Chapter 2. Before turning to the details of how methods work, it helps to review the basic terminology for methods that was introduced in that chapter. First of all, a **method** consists of a set of statements that have been collected together and given a name. The act of executing the set of statements associated with a method is known as **calling** that method. To indicate a method call in Java, you write the name of the method, followed by a list of expressions enclosed in parentheses. These expressions, which are called **arguments,** allow the caller to pass information to the method.

As an example, consider the first line from the **Add2Integers** program that appeared as Figure 2-2, which looks like this:

```
println("This program adds two integers.");
```

This statement represents a call to the **println** method, which prints a line of information on the console. To make any sense of that idea, however, the **println** method has to know what information to display. Here, that information is provided through the argument, which consists of the string

```
"This program adds two integers."
```

Once called, a method takes the data supplied as arguments, does its work, and then returns to the point in the program at which the call was made. Remembering what the calling program was doing and being able to get back precisely to that point is one of the defining characteristics of the method-calling mechanism. The operation of going back to the calling program is called **returning** from the method. As part of the return operation, methods can also send results back to the calling program, as illustrated by the **readInt** method in the now-familiar declaration

```
int n1 = readInt("Enter n1: ");
```

After the **readInt** method performs its task of reading in an integer from the user, it passes that integer back to the calling program as the value of the call. This operation is called **returning a value.**

Methods as mechanisms for hiding complexity

When the **Add2Integers** program first appears in Chapter 2, the text describes the function of the **println** method in very simple terms: it takes the string you have provided as an argument and makes it appear on the console that is supplied as part of every **ConsoleProgram**. The chapter, however, is silent on the question of how **println** accomplishes that operation. The details of the underlying implementation remain largely a mystery, which to a certain extent makes the operation of **println** seem like magic.

In J. K. Rowling's *Harry Potter and the Chamber of Secrets,* Arthur Weasley warns that you should "never trust anything that can think for itself if you can't see where it keeps its brain." While that may be sage advice in the wizarding world, programmers must often accept things on faith. You did not write **println** and indeed would have no way of doing so at this point in your study of programming. It would be extremely difficult even to understand how it works. Even so, there is nothing to stop you from using it effectively.

In fact, one of the great advantages of methods is that you can use them without having to understand the complexity underneath. Methods provide a way of hiding lower-level implementation details so that the caller need not be bothered by them. In computer science, this technique is called **information hiding.** The fundamental idea, which was championed by David Parnas in the early 1970s, is that the complexity of programming systems is best managed by making sure that details are visible only at those levels of the program at which they are relevant. For example, only the programmers who implement **println** and make sure that it works need to know the intricate details of its operation. Programmers who merely use **println** can remain blissfully unaware of the underlying mechanism.

Methods as tools for programmers rather than users

Students who are just beginning their study of programming sometimes have difficulty understanding the distinction between methods and programs. To some extent, both programs and methods have the effect of collecting a sequence of statements and giving it a single name. If you look at the **Add2Integers** program, it acts as if it is a shorthand for the set of steps contained in its **run** method.

It is, however, important to keep the two concepts distinct. The principal difference between a method and a program lies in who or what makes use of it. When, as a user, you sit down in front of your computer and start up an application, you are running a program that performs some action on your behalf. Thus, programs are invoked by and serve the needs of an external *user*. Methods, on the other hand, provide a mechanism by which a *program* can invoke a set of previously defined operations on its behalf. The operation of a method is thus internal to the program domain.

A similar confusion often arises between the arguments and program input on the one hand, and return values and program output on the other. It is easy to see input data entered using **readInt** as analogous to values passed as arguments. Both, after all, represent a way of passing data into some piece of a program. Despite that conceptual similarity, it is critically important to make a sharp

---

COMMON PITFALLS

Be careful to differentiate in your mind the ideas of input and output in the program domain and the related concepts of arguments and results in the method domain. Input and output refer to communication between a *program* and its *user*. Arguments and results represent communication between a *method* and its *caller*.

distinction between input operations, such as **readInt**, and the use of arguments in the method domain. A method like **readInt** provides a mechanism for getting input from the *user*. When **readInt** needs an input value, whoever is sitting in front of the terminal must physically enter that value on the keyboard. Arguments to a method, on the other hand, provide a means for a method to receive input from its caller, which is simply another part of the program. Data passed in the form of arguments may have been entered by the user at an earlier point in the program, but could just as easily have been calculated as part of the program operation. You should also be careful to differentiate the use of output operations, such as **println**, from the technique of returning a result. When you use **println**, the output appears on the console. When a method returns a result, that information goes back to its caller, which is free to use it in whatever way makes sense for the program. New programmers have a tendency to use input/output operations within methods when the logic of the situation calls for using arguments and results.

Method calls as expressions

In Chapter 3, method calls were listed as one of the categories of Java expressions. As you try to understand how methods fit into the overall Java framework, it will often be helpful to remember that a method call is simply an expression and can be used in any context in which an expression can appear. Moreover, the arguments to a method are also expressions, which can themselves contain method calls or any other operations that would be legal in an expression.

To illustrate that methods and their arguments are expressions, it is useful to introduce several standard methods from the **Math** class, which are listed in Figure 5-1. As you can see from the list of available methods, the **Math** class includes many of the standard mathematical functions you learned in high-school algebra and trigonometry. For example, the **Math** class includes the method **sqrt** for taking the square root of its argument, as well as **sin** and **cos** for trigonometric sines and cosines. Each of these methods takes a **double** as an argument and returns a result, also of type **double**. You can use these methods in simple statements, such as

```
double root3 = Math.sqrt(3.0);
```

or in more complicated ones. For example, you can compute the distance from the origin to the point (x, y) using the standard distance formula for points in a plane:

$$distance = \sqrt{x^2 + y^2}$$

In Java, this formula corresponds to the statement

```
double distance = Math.sqrt(x * x + y * y);
```

The methods listed in Figure 5-1 are defined as part of the **Math** class, which is available to all Java programs as part of the standard package **java.lang**. Unlike most methods in Java, however, the methods in the **Math** class are not associated with an object but instead are part of the class as a whole. Such methods are called **static methods.** When you call a static method, Java requires you to specify the

---

FIGURE 5-1 Selected methods from the Math class

`Math.abs(x)`   Returns the absolute value of **x**, which can be of any numeric type.
`Math.min(x, y)`   Returns the smaller of **x** and **y**.
`Math.max(x, y)`   Returns the larger of **x** and **y**.
`Math.sqrt(x)`   Returns the square root of the value **x**.
`Math.log(x)`   Returns the natural logarithm of **x**, which uses the mathematical constant *e* as its base.
`Math.exp(x)`   Returns the inverse logarithm of **x**, which is e^x.
`Math.pow(x, y)`   Returns the value **x** raised to the **y** power.
`Math.sin(theta)`   Returns the trigonometric sine of the angle **theta**, which is measured in radians.
`Math.cos(theta)`   Returns the cosine of the angle **theta**.
`Math.tan(theta)`   Returns the tangent of the angle **theta**.
`Math.asin(x)`   Returns the angle whose sine is **x**.
`Math.acos(x)`   Returns the angle whose cosine is **x**.
`Math.atan(x)`   Returns the angle whose tangent is **x**.
`Math.toRadians(degrees)`   Converts an angle from degrees to radians.
`Math.toDegrees(radians)`   Converts an angle from radians to degrees.

name of the class along with the method name. Thus, the static `sqrt` method in the `Math` class must be written as `Math.sqrt` whenever it is called.

Method calls as messages

Static methods of the sort provided by the `Math` class are something of an anachronism in languages like Java, throwbacks to a style of programming that existed before object-oriented programming arrived on the scene. Object-oriented languages use methods in a different way than traditional languages do, mostly because the object-oriented paradigm depends on a different conceptual model of the underlying process. Once you understand that conceptual model, the structure of method calls in Java and the terminology used to describe it will make a great deal of intuitive sense.

In the object-oriented world, objects communicate by sending information and requests from one object to another. Collectively, these transmissions among objects are called **messages.** The act of sending a message corresponds to having one object invoke a method that belongs to a different object. For consistency with the conceptual model of sending messages, the object that initiates the method is called the **sender,** and the object that is the target of that transmission is called the **receiver.** In Java, the sender identifies the receiver by making a call in the following form:

receiver **.** *name* **(** *arguments* **)**

You have already seen this style of method call, which you have used since Chapter 2 to send messages to graphical objects.

Except for a few calls to static methods that always include an explicit class name, the method calls you have seen in this book have all had a receiver, even if that receiver has not been explicitly specified. If you call a method without specifying a receiver, then Java assumes that the sending and receiving objects are the same. That interpretation makes it possible to think about calls like

println(*value* **)**

without abandoning the conceptual model of sending and receiving message. If a line of this form appears in a program, you can interpret that line as sending a message requesting an action—specifically, to display the value on an output device—associated with the method name **println**. Since no explicit receiver is included in the call, the target of that message is the program itself. Fortunately, the program is able to respond appropriately to that message because the method **println** is defined as part of the **Program** class. Every subclass of **Program** inherits this method, which means that those subclasses can invoke the operation using the simplified method call. If you wanted to make the receiver explicit—as some instructors do—you could use the Java keyword **this**, which refers to the current object, as follows:

this.println(*value* **)**

5.2 Writing your own methods

Most of the methods you have seen so far have been defined as part of some library package. Library methods are certainly useful, but they are by no means sufficient to solve complex programming problems. When you are faced with a large problem, you will need to develop your own methods as a way of controlling the complexity of the code. Breaking a program up into methods makes it possible for you to look at the different parts of the program in smaller units that are individually much simpler to understand. Writing your own methods is also a way to provide yourself with tools that don't happen to be part of an existing library package.

As an example, suppose that you have been assigned the task of writing a program that generates a conversion table from the Celsius scale used in most countries to the Fahrenheit scale used in the United States. You will probably want to define a simple conversion method that you can then use in other parts of the program. The computation is relatively easy, because the process of converting one temperature scale to another is simply a matter of applying the formula

$$F = \frac{9}{5} C + 32$$

The format of a method definition

To define a new method in Java, you begin by writing its header, as specified in the syntax box on the right. Until you start defining your own classes, the distinction between public and private methods doesn't mean a great deal. Even so, since it is usually best to keep things private if possible, you should declare any method used only within a single class as **private**. The *type* element in the pattern represents the type of value the method returns; if the method doesn't need to return a value, the *type* element should be specified as **void**. The *name* element indicates the name of the method, which can be any identifier formed according to the rules given in Chapter 2. Most importantly, the name should make it easy for anyone reading the program to determine what the method does. The code inside the parentheses, which is labeled *parameters* in this pattern, specifies what arguments the method requires. The parameter list has the same form as variable declarations except that no initial value is assigned. Methods that take more than one argument separate these declarations with commas.

In this example, you are writing a method that converts from Celsius to Fahrenheit. The header line therefore looks like this:

```
private double celsiusToFahrenheit(double c)
```

The header line is then followed by the **method body,** which is always a block and therefore consists of statements enclosed in curly braces. The statements in the block may include variable declarations such as the ones that have appeared in most of the program examples so far.

Syntax for a method header

> *visibility type name* (*parameters*)

where:
> *visibility* is typically **public** or **private**
> *type* is the type of value returned, or
>   **void** if the method returns no value
> *name* is the name of the method
> *parameters* is a list of parameter
>   declarations

The `return` statement

If a method returns a result, the statements in the method body must include at least one **return** statement, which specifies the value to be returned. The paradigmatic form for the **return** statement is shown in the syntax box to the right.

In most cases, the **return** statement includes an expression that indicates the value of the result, although that expression is omitted if the method does not return a value. When it is used in the

> *return expression;*

Syntax for the `return` statement

> **return** *expression*;

where:
> *expression* is the value to be returned.

If the method has no result, the syntax is

> **return**;

form, the **return** statement causes the method to return the indicated value immediately. As such, the **return** statement encompasses both of the following English ideas: "I'm done now" and "Here is the answer." In some programming languages, such as Pascal and Fortran, indicating that the execution of a method is complete and specifying its result are separate operations. If you have had experience with such languages, it may take some time to get used to the **return** statement in Java.

The **return** statement completes the list of tools you need to write the implementation of the **celsiusToFahrenheit** method:

```
private double celsiusToFahrenheit(double c) {
   return 9.0 / 5.0 * c + 32;
}
```

To create the table of temperature conversions, you need to create a **ConsoleProgram** subclass whose **run** method calls **celsiusToFahrenheit** for each entry in the table. The complete program is shown in Figure 5-2.

FIGURE 5-2　**Program to generate a temperature-conversion table**

```
/*
 * File: TemperatureConversionTable.java
 * ---------------------------------------------
 * This program creates a table of Celsius to Fahrenheit
 * equivalents using a function to perform the conversion.
 */

import acm.program.*;

public class TemperatureConversionTable extends ConsoleProgram {

   public void run() {
      println("Celsius to Fahrenheit table.");
      for (int c = LOWER_LIMIT; c <= UPPER_LIMIT; c += STEP_SIZE) {
         int f = (int) celsiusToFahrenheit(c);
         println(c + "C = " + f + "F");
      }
   }

/* Returns the Fahrenheit equivalent of the Celsius temperature c. */
   private double celsiusToFahrenheit(double c) {
      return 9.0 / 5.0 * c + 32;
   }

/* Private constants */
   private static final int LOWER_LIMIT = 0;
   private static final int UPPER_LIMIT = 100;
   private static final int STEP_SIZE = 5;

}
```

Methods involving internal control structures

Methods are not usually as simple as `celsiusToFahrenheit`. In many cases, calculating a method requires making some tests or writing a loop. Such details add to the complexity of the implementation but do not change its basic form. For example, the `abs` method in the `Math` class computes the absolute value of its argument, which for now you can assume is an integer. But suppose for a moment that the method did not exist. How would you write its implementation? The definition of absolute value indicates that if the argument is negative, the method should return its negation, which is a positive number. If the argument is positive or zero, the method should simply return the argument value unchanged. Thus, you can implement the `abs` method as follows:

```
private int abs(int n) {
    if (n < 0) {
        return -n;
    } else {
        return n;
    }
}
```

As this implementation shows, a `return` statement can occur anywhere in the method body, and may appear more than once.

Similarly, you could define a method `min` to return the smaller of two floating-point arguments as follows:

```
private double min(double x, double y) {
    if (x < y) {
        return x;
    } else {
        return y;
    }
}
```

The control structure used within a method can be much more complex than the preceding examples. Suppose that you want to define a method called `factorial` that takes an integer **n** and returns the product of the integers between 1 and **n**. The first several factorials are shown in the following list:

`factorial(0)`	`=`	`1`		*(by definition)*
`factorial(1)`	`=`	`1`	`=`	`1`
`factorial(2)`	`=`	`2`	`=`	`1 × 2`
`factorial(3)`	`=`	`6`	`=`	`1 × 2 × 3`
`factorial(4)`	`=`	`24`	`=`	`1 × 2 × 3 × 4`
`factorial(5)`	`=`	`120`	`=`	`1 × 2 × 3 × 4 × 5`
`factorial(6)`	`=`	`720`	`=`	`1 × 2 × 3 × 4 × 5 × 6`
`factorial(7)`	`=`	`5050`	`=`	`1 × 2 × 3 × 4 × 5 × 6 × 7`

Factorials are usually designated in mathematics with an exclamation point, as in $n!$, and have extensive applications in statistics, combinatorial mathematics, and computer science. A method to compute factorials is a useful tool for solving problems in those domains. The `factorial` method takes an integer and returns an integer, so its header line looks like this:

```
private int factorial(int n)
```

Implementing `factorial`, however, requires some work. As a programming problem, the task of computing a factorial is similar in many respects to adding a list of numbers. In the `AddList` program from Chapter 4, a variable called `total` is declared to keep track of the running total. At the beginning of the program, `total` is initialized to 0. As each new value comes in, it is added to `total` so that `total` continues to reflect the sum of the numbers entered so far. For the current problem, the situation is much the same, except that you have to keep track of a product rather than a sum. To do so, you can:

1. Declare a variable called `result`.
2. Initialize it to 1.
3. Multiply it by each of the integers between 1 and `n`.
4. Return the final value of `result` as the result of the method.

To cycle through each of the integers required in step 3, you need a `for` loop, which begins at 1 and continues until it reaches `n`. The `for` loop requires an index variable, for which the traditional choice of `i` seems quite appropriate. The variable `result` holds the running product, and `i` holds the index.

The implementation of `factorial` is short enough to present all at once without explaining the details step by step:

```
private int factorial(int n) {
   int result = 1;
   for (int i = 1; i <= n; i++) {
      result *= i;
   }
   return result;
}
```

Methods that return nonnumeric values

The examples of methods presented so far in this chapter all return numeric results, but that is by no means necessary. Methods in Java can return values of any data type. For example, if you were writing a program to work with dates, it might be useful to have a method to convert a numeric month between 1 and 12 into a `String` indicating the corresponding month name between January and December. While numeric values are often easier to work with internally, the output display is usually more readable with traditional English names. To solve this problem, you could define the method `monthName` as follows:

```
private String monthName(int month) {
    switch (month) {
        case  1: return ("January");
        case  2: return ("February");
        case  3: return ("March");
        case  4: return ("April");
        case  5: return ("May");
        case  6: return ("June");
        case  7: return ("July");
        case  8: return ("August");
        case  9: return ("September");
        case 10: return ("October");
        case 11: return ("November");
        case 12: return ("December");
        default: return ("Illegal month");
    }
}
```

To use this method, you would call **monthName** from some other part of the program and then use **println** to display the result. For example, if the integer variables **month**, **day**, and **year** contained the values 7, 20, and 1969 (the date of the Apollo 11 landing on the moon), the statement

```
println(monthName(month) + " " + day + ", " + year);
```

would generate the output

```
┌──────────────────────────────────────────────┐
│  ◯ ◯ ◯          MonthName                     │
├──────────────────────────────────────────────┤
│  July 20, 1969                              ▲ │
│                                             ▓ │
│                                             ▲ │
│                                             ▼ │
│  ◄ ▶                                          │
└──────────────────────────────────────────────┘
```

In the **switch** statement within the **monthName** method, the **return** statements in each **case** clause automatically exit from the entire method and make an explicit **break** statement unnecessary. As indicated in the section on the **switch** statement in Chapter 4, you can avoid a lot of pain in the debugging process if you make sure that every **case** clause ends with either a **break** or a **return** statement.

Given that strings are so integral to Java that they seem more like primitive types than objects, it is useful to see methods that return other kinds of objects as well, such as the graphical objects introduced in Chapter 2. Consider, for example, the following method, which creates a circular **GOval** centered at the point (**x**, **y**) with a radius of **r** pixels, filled with the color specified by **color**:

```
private GOval createFilledCircle(double x, double y,
                                 double r, Color color) {
    GOval circle = new GOval(x - r, y - r, 2 * r, 2 * r);
    circle.setColor(color);
    circle.setFilled(true);
    return circle;
}
```

The **DrawStoplight** program in Figure 5-3 shows how this method can be used to draw a conventional stoplight with red, yellow, and green lamps that looks like this:

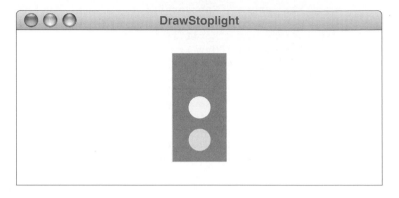

Using the **createFilledCircle** method simplifies the code because the program can create each of the lamps simply by calling that method with the appropriate arguments. Defining a method that contains this common code saves having to rewrite the same set of steps for each of the red, yellow, and green lamps.

Predicate methods

The examples in the preceding section illustrate that methods can return values of different data types. The method **factorial**, for example, returns a value of type **int**, and the method **monthName** returns a value of type **String**. Although methods in Java can return values of any type, there is one result type that deserves special attention—the data type **boolean**, which was introduced in Chapter 4. Methods that return values of type **boolean** are called **predicate methods** and play an important role in modern programming.

As you will recall, there are only two values of type **boolean**: **true** and **false**. Thus a predicate method—no matter how many arguments it takes or how complicated its internal processing may be—must eventually return one of these two values. The process of calling a predicate method is therefore analogous to asking a yes/no question and getting an answer.

As an example, the following method definition answers the question "is **n** an even number?" for a particular integer **n** supplied by the caller as an argument:

```
private boolean isEven(int n) {
   return (n % 2 == 0);
}
```

A number is even if there is no remainder when that number is divided by two. If **n** is even, the expression

```
n % 2 == 0
```

therefore has the value **true**, which is returned as the result of the **isEven** method. If **n** is odd, the method returns **false**. Because **isEven** returns a Boolean result,

---

FIGURE 5-3   Program to draw a stoplight using the createFilledCircle method

```java
/*
 * File: DrawStoplight.java
 * ---------------------------
 * This program draws a traditional stoplight with a red, yellow,
 * and green light in a gray rectangular frame.
 */

import acm.graphics.*;
import acm.program.*;
import java.awt.*;

public class DrawStoplight extends GraphicsProgram {

    public void run() {
        double cx = getWidth() / 2;
        double cy = getHeight() / 2;
        double fx = cx - FRAME_WIDTH / 2;
        double fy = cy - FRAME_HEIGHT / 2;
        double dy = FRAME_HEIGHT / 4 + LAMP_RADIUS / 2;
        GRect frame = new GRect(fx, fy, FRAME_WIDTH, FRAME_HEIGHT);
        frame.setFilled(true);
        frame.setColor(Color.GRAY);
        add(frame);
        add(createFilledCircle(cx, cy - dy, LAMP_RADIUS, Color.RED));
        add(createFilledCircle(cx, cy, LAMP_RADIUS, Color.YELLOW));
        add(createFilledCircle(cx, cy + dy, LAMP_RADIUS, Color.GREEN));
    }

/*
 * Creates a circular GOval object centered at (x, y) with radius r.
 * The GOval is set to be filled and colored in the specified color.
 */
    private GOval createFilledCircle(double x, double y,
                                     double r, Color color) {
        GOval circle = new GOval(x - r, y - r, 2 * r, 2 * r);
        circle.setColor(color);
        circle.setFilled(true);
        return circle;
    }

/* Private constants */
    private static final double FRAME_WIDTH = 50;
    private static final double FRAME_HEIGHT = 100;
    private static final double LAMP_RADIUS = 10;
}
```

you can use it directly in a conditional context. For example, the following **for** loop uses **isEven** to list all the even numbers between 1 and 100:

```
for (int i = 1; i <= 100; i++) {
   if (isEven(i)) println(i);
}
```

The **for** loop runs through each number, and the **if** statement asks the simple question "is this number even?" If it is, **println** displays it on the screen; if not, nothing happens.

The standard class definitions in Java often include predicate methods. One particularly important example is the **equals** method, which is defined in the universal class **Object** and can therefore be applied to any object. The **equals** method asks whether one object has the same value as another. By contrast, the **==** operator asks whether its operands are precisely the same object, which is not ordinarily as useful.

The distinction between **equals** and **==** is easiest to illustrate with respect to strings. Suppose, for example, that your program contains the following statement to ask the user a simple yes-or-no question:

```
String answer = readLine("Would you like instructions? ");
```

Once the user has entered a response, the program needs to determine whether that answer is **"yes"** or **"no"** or perhaps some other string entirely. The following approach doesn't work:

```
if (answer == "yes") . . .
```

The value read in from the user may well be a string object composed of the characters **'y'**, **'e'**, and **'s'** but it will not be the *same* object as the constant string **"yes"** that appears in the program. What you need to ask instead is whether the two strings contain the same sequence of characters, which is precisely what the **equals** method does. Thus, the statement you need to write is

```
if (answer.equals("yes")) . . .
```

Note that this statement uses the receiver syntax and can therefore be interpreted as sending an **equals** message to the **answer** object and then having it send back the result of the comparison.

As another example of a predicate method, you could write one that tested whether a given year is a leap year, as follows:

```
private boolean isLeapYear(int year) {
   return ( ((year % 4 == 0) && (year % 100 != 0))
            || (year % 400 == 0) );
}
```

You encountered the Boolean expression to determine whether **year** is a leap year in Chapter 4. Putting this expression in a method allows you to simplify the process of checking for leap years in different parts of the program. Once the method is defined, other parts of the program can simply use statements of the form:

```
if (isLeapYear(year)) . . .
```

5.3 Mechanics of the method-calling process

So far in this chapter, you have looked at methods mostly from a holistic perspective. Thinking about methods in this way helps you understand how they are used and what they provide as a programming resource. To develop confidence that the methods you write will work as they should, however, you also need to develop an understanding of how methods operate internally.

As a first step toward understanding the mechanics of methods, consider the program shown in Figure 5-4, which includes both the **factorial** method presented earlier in this chapter and a main program that displays a factorial table. The **FactorialTable** program is easy to understand if you look at it as two separate pieces. The main program simply counts from **LOWER_LIMIT** to **UPPER_LIMIT**. On each cycle, it calls **factorial** on the index **i** and then displays the result. By this point, you are accustomed to using the name **i** to indicate an otherwise unremarkable index variable used to count cycles in a **for** loop. No surprises here. The **factorial** method is likewise straightforward. There is a little more going on than in the main program, but not much more. You can easily understand what this method is doing. In particular, you should recognize that **n** is the number whose factorial we're computing, that **result** holds the accumulating product on each cycle, and that **i** is once again an unremarkable index variable used to track the progress of the **for** loop. Thus, each piece of the program makes sense on its own.

For many students, confusion begins to creep in only when they look at the program in its entirety. If you try to comprehend the program as a whole without first learning how to think about methods, you are likely to encounter a variety of conceptual problems. First, there are two variables named **i**, one in the main program and one in the **factorial** method. Each variable is used as a loop index, but the two variables will usually have different values. Second, there are parts of the program in which two different names are used to refer to the same value. In the **run** method, the number whose factorial you are calculating is stored in the loop index **i**. In the **factorial** method, that same value is called **n**. Thus, in the program as a whole, you have variables with the same name holding different values, and values with the same meaning stored in variables with different names.

This apparent instability in terms of the association of names and values seems certain to generate confusion. In fact, it has precisely the opposite effect. Freeing the programmer from maintaining fixed associations between names and values makes it possible to develop programs in independent pieces. As programs grow, there is no way you can comprehend them as a whole. Your only hope of making sense of a large program is to break it down into independent pieces, each of which is simple enough to understand on its own. In the **FactorialTable** program, the

---

FIGURE 5-4 **Program to generate a table of factorials**

```
/*
 * File: FactorialTable.java
 * ---------------------------
 * This file generates a table of factorials.
 */

import acm.program.*;

public class FactorialTable extends ConsoleProgram {

   public void run() {
      for (int i = LOWER_LIMIT; i <= UPPER_LIMIT; i++) {
         println(i + "! = " + factorial(i));
      }
   }

/*
 * Returns the factorial of n, which is defined as the
 * product of all integers from 1 up to n.
 */
   private int factorial(int n) {
      int result = 1;
      for (int i = 1; i <= n; i++) {
         result *= i;
      }
      return result;
   }

/* Private constants */
   private static final int LOWER_LIMIT = 0;
   private static final int UPPER_LIMIT = 10;

}
```

---

problem of generating a list of factorials is separated into two pieces—the **run** method and the **factorial** method—each of which is easy to understand on its own.

Parameter passing

To understand how the two pieces of the **FactorialTable** program work together, you will find it helpful to develop a sense of how Java keeps track of the different names and values. That it manages to do so is important for us as programmers and enables us to think about the individual methods separately. How does Java take account of the facts that the same name may be used for different values and that a single conceptual value may be represented by different names? To understand the answer to this question, it helps to make a semantic distinction between argument values in the caller and the variables used to hold those values in the context of a method. The arguments in the method call may be arbitrary expressions. The variables that appear in the corresponding positions in the method header serve as placeholders for these values and are called **formal parameters.**

Whenever you call a method, the runtime system that executes the program on the Java Virtual Machine takes the following steps:

1. It computes the value of each argument in the context of the calling method. Because the arguments are expressions, this computation can involve operators and other method calls, all of which must be evaluated before the new method is called.
2. It copies the value of each argument expression into the corresponding formal parameter variable. If there is more than one argument, the runtime system copies the arguments into the parameters in order; the first argument is copied to the first parameter, and so forth. If necessary, the runtime system performs automatic type conversions between the argument values and the formal parameters as in an assignment statement. For example, if you pass a value of type **int** to a method where the parameter is declared as a **double**, the runtime system converts the integer into the equivalent floating-point value before copying that value into the parameter variable.
3. It evaluates the statements in the method body until a **return** statement appears.
4. It evaluates the expression associated with the **return** statement and, if necessary, converts it to the result type specified for the method.
5. It continues to execute the code in the calling method from where it left off, substituting the returned value in place of the call.

Every call to a method results in the creation of a separate set of variables. To give yourself a better sense of that process, you will probably find it useful to draw box diagrams that show the values of each variable, along the lines of the various examples in Chapter 2. For programs that are subdivided into separate methods, you need to draw a new set of variable boxes each time one method calls another. For each method, you need a separate box for each variable that method declares, including the formal parameters. These variables are meaningful only within the method that declares them and are therefore called **local variables**.

For example, when you trace the execution of the **FactorialTable** example, you first need to create space for the variables in the method **run**. The method **run** declares only one variable—the loop index **i**—allowing you to represent the variables for **run** as follows:

The double lines around the variable boxes are used to enclose all the variables associated with a particular method call. This collection of variables is called the **frame**—or, for reasons that will quickly become apparent, the **stack frame**—for that method.

When you trace the execution of a program on your own, it is useful to represent each stack frame on an index card so that you can keep track of several frames at the same time. Whenever the program calls a new method, you need to create a new index card and place it on top of the index cards that currently exist. When that method returns, you can discard its index card, revealing the card that was previously on top of the stack. As you will discover in Chapter 7, the variables in a stack frame are stored in a physically contiguous section of memory, which means that the concept of a frame is not simply an abstract notion.

Let's assume that `LOWER_LIMIT` is defined to be 0, as it was in the program listing. In this case, on the first cycle through the `for` loop, `i` has the value 0. As before, you can represent this condition in the frame by noting the value inside the box for that variable.

run

```
i

  0
```

The main program then calls `println` and, as part of evaluating the arguments to `println`, computes the result of the expression

```
factorial(i)
```

To represent the computer's actions in the frame diagram, you begin by looking up the value of `i` in the current frame, where you discover that the value is 0. You must then create a new frame for `factorial`, for which the value 0 is the first (and only) argument. The `factorial` method has three variables: the formal parameter `n` and the local variables `result` and `i`. Your frame for `factorial` therefore needs three variable cells:

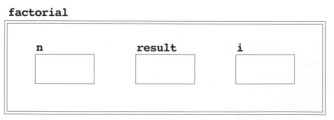

factorial

```
n            result        i
```

At this point in the program execution, the Java runtime system initializes the formal parameter `n` to the value of the corresponding argument, which was 0. The contents of the frame then look like this:

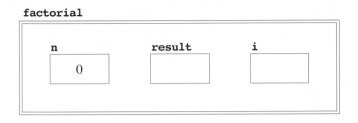

When you create the frame for **factorial**, the frame for **run** does not go away entirely. That frame remains in suspension until the operation of **factorial** is complete. To indicate this situation in the conceptual model, you simply put the index card for each new frame on top of the card for the previous one, thereby covering it up. For example, when you call the method **factorial**, the index card representing the **factorial** frame goes on top of the frame for **run**.

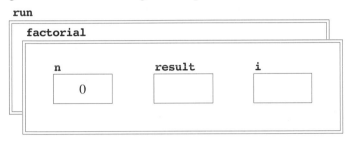

As the diagram shows, the entire set of frames forms a stack with the most recent frame on top. The frame for **run** is still there; you just can't see any of it as long as the method **factorial** is active. In particular, the name **i** no longer refers to the variable declared in **run** but to the variable named **i** in **factorial**.

As soon as the Java runtime system has initialized the formal parameters, it executes the body of **factorial** by running through each of its steps in the current frame. The variable **result** is initialized to 1, and the program reaches the **for** loop. In the **for** loop, the variable **i** is initialized to 1, but since the value is already larger than **n**, the body of the **for** loop is not executed at all. Thus, when the program reaches the **return** statement, the frame looks like this:

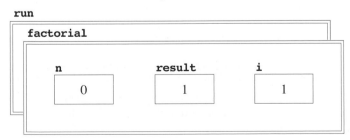

When **factorial** returns, the value of **result** is passed back to the caller as the result of the method. Returning from a method also discards its stack frame, exposing once again the variables in **run**:

The result, 1, is then passed to the `println` method. The `println` method goes through the same process; the details of that operation, however, are hidden from you because you don't know how `println` works internally. Eventually, `println` displays the value 1 on the screen and then returns, after which the method `run` goes on to execute the next `for` loop cycle.

Calling methods from within other methods

Much of the power of methods comes from the fact that once you have defined a method, you can use it not only in the context of a main program, but also as a tool to implement other, more sophisticated methods. You can then call these methods from other methods, creating an arbitrarily complex hierarchy.

To illustrate the idea of multiple levels of methods, let's suppose that you have a group of **n** distinct objects on a table in front of you. From that group of objects, you would like to select **k** objects. How might you write a method that would tell you how many different ways there are to select **k** objects out of the original collection of size **n**?

To make the problem more concrete, imagine that the objects on the table are five U.S. coins: a penny, a nickel, a dime, a quarter, and a half-dollar. Your task is to determine how many different ways there are to take, for example, two coins from the table. You could take the penny and the nickel, the penny and the dime, the nickel and the quarter, or any of several other combinations. If you list all the possibilities, you discover that there are 10 different combinations, as follows:

penny + nickel	nickel + quarter
penny + dime	nickel + half-dollar
penny + quarter	dime + quarter
penny + half-dollar	dime + half-dollar
nickel + dime	quarter + half-dollar

In this example, **n** is 5 and **k** is 2. The essence of the problem is finding a way to compute the number of ways to choose **k** objects from a set of **n** objects as a function of the values **n** and **k**. That function comes up frequently in probability and statistics and is called the **combinations function,** which is often written in mathematics as

$$\binom{n}{k}$$

or, in functional notation, as

$$C(n, k)$$

As it turns out, the combinations function has a simple definition in terms of factorials:

$$C(n, k) \quad = \quad \frac{n!}{k! \times (n{-}k)!}$$

For example, you can verify that $C(5, 2)$ is indeed 10 by working out the mathematics step by step:

$$C(5, 2) \quad = \quad \frac{5!}{2! \times 3!}$$

$$= \quad \frac{120}{2 \times 6}$$

$$= \quad 10$$

If you want to implement this method in Java, it would probably be best to use a longer name than the single letter C used in mathematics. As a general rule, method names used in this text tend to be longer and more expressive than local variable names. Unlike local variable names, method calls often appear in parts of the program that are far removed from the point at which those methods are defined. Since the definition may be hard to locate in a large program, it is best to choose a method name that conveys enough information about the method so that the reader does not need to look up the definition. Local variables, on the other hand, are used only within the body of a single method, which makes it easier to keep track of what they mean. In the interest of having the name of the combinations method make sense immediately when anyone looks at it, we will use the name **combinations** as the method name, rather than the letter **C**.

To implement the **combinations** method using the definition based on factorials, you can take advantage of the fact that you already have an implementation of **factorial**. Given that you can call **factorial** in the implementation, the body of the **combinations** method is a straightforward translation of its mathematical definition:

```
private int combinations(int n, int k) {
   return factorial(n) / (factorial(k) * factorial(n - k));
}
```

You can then write a simple main program to test the **combinations** method, as follows:

```
public void run() {
   int n = readInt("Enter number of objects in the set (n): ");
   int k = readInt("Enter number to be chosen (k): ");
   println("C(" + n + ", " + k + ") = " + combinations(n, k));
}
```

The complete program, `Combinations.java`, is shown in Figure 5-5. The following sample run shows one possible execution of the program:

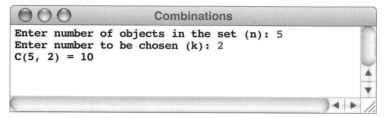

FIGURE 5-5 Program to compute the combinations function C(n, k)

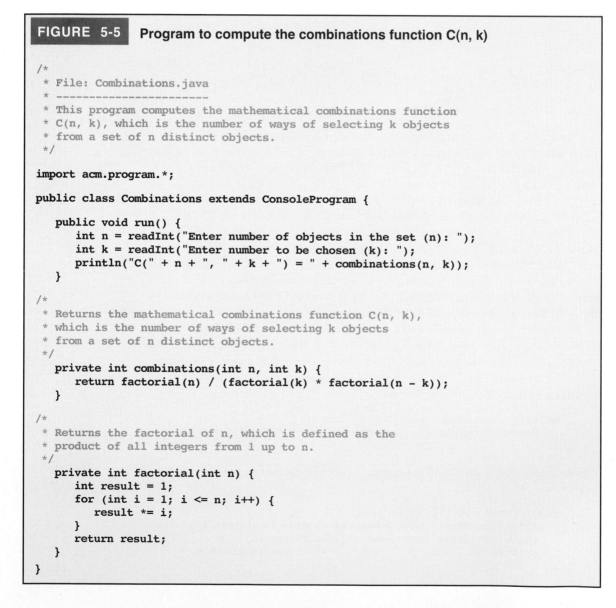

```
/*
 * File: Combinations.java
 * -------------------------
 * This program computes the mathematical combinations function
 * C(n, k), which is the number of ways of selecting k objects
 * from a set of n distinct objects.
 */

import acm.program.*;

public class Combinations extends ConsoleProgram {

    public void run() {
        int n = readInt("Enter number of objects in the set (n): ");
        int k = readInt("Enter number to be chosen (k): ");
        println("C(" + n + ", " + k + ") = " + combinations(n, k));
    }

/*
 * Returns the mathematical combinations function C(n, k),
 * which is the number of ways of selecting k objects
 * from a set of n distinct objects.
 */
    private int combinations(int n, int k) {
        return factorial(n) / (factorial(k) * factorial(n - k));
    }

/*
 * Returns the factorial of n, which is defined as the
 * product of all integers from 1 up to n.
 */
    private int factorial(int n) {
        int result = 1;
        for (int i = 1; i <= n; i++) {
            result *= i;
        }
        return result;
    }
}
```

What happens inside the computer when this program runs? Just as in the factorial example, the runtime system creates a frame for the method **run**, which now declares two variables, **n** and **k**. After the user enters the two values and the program reaches the **println** statement, the variables in the frame have the following values:

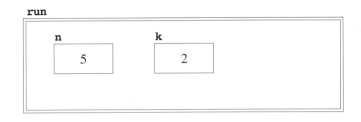

To execute the **println** statement, the computer must evaluate the call to the **combinations** method, which results in the creation of a new frame that overlays the previous one:

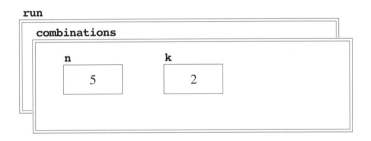

In this example, which has more method calls than the factorial example, each new frame must record precisely what the program was doing before it made the call. Here, for example, the call to **combinations** comes from the last line in **run**, as indicated by the tag R_1 in the program text that follows:

```
public void run() {
    int n = readInt("Enter number of objects in the set (n): ");
    int k = readInt("Enter number to be chosen (k): ");
    println("C(" + n + ", " + k + ") = " + combinations(n, k));
}
```

R_1

When the computer executes a new method call, it keeps track of where execution should continue in the calling program once the call is completed. The point at which execution should continue, called the **return address,** is represented in these diagrams with a circled tag. To keep track of where you are in the execution of the program, you need to record in the frame diagram the point from which the call was made, like this:

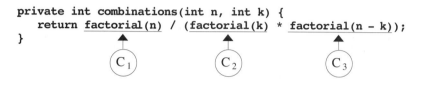

Once the new frame has been created, the program begins to execute the body of the **combinations** method, which is reprinted with each call to **factorial** noted with a tag as follows:

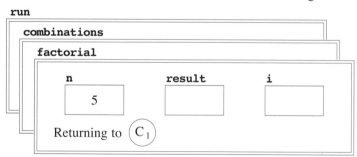

To execute this statement, the computer must make the three indicated calls to the method **factorial**. According to the rules specified by Java, the compiler must make these calls in left-to-right order. The first call requests the computer to calculate **factorial(n)** and results in the creation of the following frame:

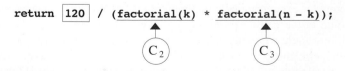

The **factorial** method runs through its operation just as it did before and returns the value 120 to the point in its caller indicated by the tag C_1. The frame for the **factorial** method disappears, and you are left in the frame for **combinations**, ready to go on to the next phase of the computation. You can illustrate the current state of things by going back and filling in the returned value in place of the original call like this:

```
return  120  / (factorial(k) * factorial(n - k));
                       ▲                  ▲
                      C₂                 C₃
```

The box around 120 in the diagram indicates that the enclosed value is not part of the program but the result of a previous computation.

From this point, the computer goes on to evaluate the second call to **factorial**, where the argument is **k**. Since **k** has the value 2, this call causes the following frame to be created:

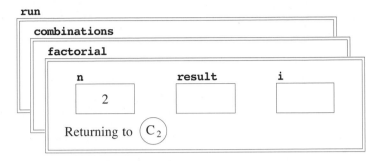

Once again, the **factorial** method completes its operation without making further calls, and the method returns to point C_2 with the value of 2!, which is 2. Inserting this value into the expression that records the result so far shows the computation in the following state:

There is now only one more call to make, which begins by evaluating the argument expression **n - k**. Given the values of **n** and **k** in the **combinations** frame, the argument expression has the value 3, which leads to the creation of another frame:

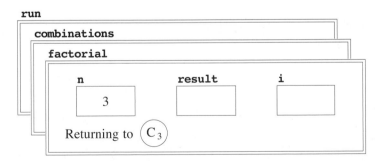

From this point, **factorial** calculates the value of 3! and returns the value 6 to position C_3 in the caller, which results in the following position:

$$\texttt{return } \boxed{120} \texttt{ / (} \boxed{2} \texttt{ * } \boxed{6} \texttt{);}$$

The **combinations** method now has all the values it needs to calculate the result, which is 10. To find out what to do with this result, you need to consult the **combinations** frame, which is once again the top frame on the stack:

```
run
   combinations
        n                    k
        [  5  ]              [  2  ]

        Returning to  (R₁)
```

The frame indicates that the program should take the return value and substitute it in place of the call at R_1 in the method **run**. If you substitute 10 for the call to **combinations** in the **println** statement, you get the following state:

```
println("C(" + n + ", " + k + ") = " + [ 10 ] );
```

Given this result, **println** can happily generate the desired output.

This exercise of going through all the internal details is intended to help you understand the method-calling mechanism in Java. You might find it helpful to trace through your own programs once or twice at this level of detail, but you should not make a habit of it. Instead, you should learn to think about methods more informally and try to develop an intuitive sense of how they work. When a program calls a method, the method performs its operation and the program then continues from the point at which the call was made. If the method returns a result, the calling program is free to use that result in subsequent computation. As a programmer, you need to get to the point where you feel comfortable thinking about the process without worrying about the details. The computer, after all, is taking care of them for you.

5.4 Decomposition

One of the most important challenges you will face as a programmer is finding ways to reduce the conceptual complexity of your programs. Large programs are typically very difficult to understand as a whole. The only way to keep such programs within the limits of human comprehension is to break them up into simpler, more manageable pieces. This process is called **decomposition.**

Decomposition is a fundamental strategy that applies at several levels of the programming process. In Java, large systems are broken up first into packages, which are then decomposed into classes, which themselves contain a set of methods. You will begin to learn how decomposition applies at those more abstract levels in Chapter 6. At the method level, decomposition is the process of breaking large tasks down into simpler subtasks that together complete the task as a whole. Those subtasks may themselves require further decomposition, which creates a hierarchy of subtasks of the sort illustrated in Figure 5-6. In that diagram—which presents only the general structure of a typical solution and offers no details about the problem itself—the complete task is decomposed into three primary subtasks. The second of those subtasks is then divided further into two subtasks at an even lower

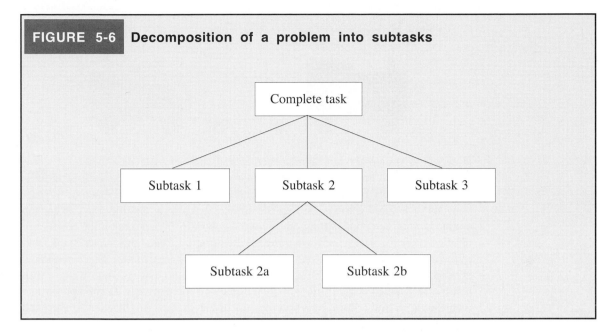

FIGURE 5-6   **Decomposition of a problem into subtasks**

level of detail. Depending on the complexity of the actual problem, the subdivision may require more subtasks or more levels of decomposition.

Learning how to find the most useful decomposition requires considerable practice. If you define the individual subtasks appropriately, each one will have conceptual integrity as a unit and make the program as a whole much simpler to understand. If you choose the subtasks inappropriately, your decomposition can end up getting in the way. Although this chapter offers some useful guidelines, there are no hard-and-fast rules for selecting a particular decomposition; you will learn how to apply this process through experience.

Stepwise refinement

When you are trying to find an effective decomposition strategy, the best approach is to start at the highest levels of abstraction and work your way downward to the details. You begin by thinking about the program as a whole. Assuming that the program is large enough to require decomposition, your next step is to divide the entire problem into its major components. Once you figure out what the major subtasks are, you can then repeat the process to decompose any of the subtasks that are themselves too large to solve in a few lines of code. At the end of this process, you will be left with a set of individual tasks, each of which is simple enough to be implemented as a single method. This process is called **top-down design,** or **stepwise refinement**.

The best way to understand the process of stepwise refinement is to work through a simple example. Suppose that you wanted to write a `GraphicsProgram` that created the following picture of a three-car train consisting of a black engine, a green boxcar, and a red caboose:

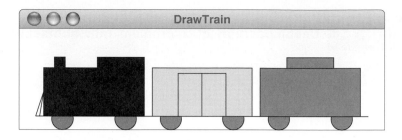

How would you go about designing such a program?

There are two important things to notice about this picture. The first is that it is composed entirely of shapes that you already know how to draw. Each of the cars consists of a filled **GRect**, as does the smokestack on the engine, the cab for the engineer, and the cupola sitting on top of the caboose. The doors on the boxcar are unfilled **GRect**s. The wheels are **GOval**s filled in gray. The cowcatcher at the front of the engine and the connectors between the train cars are **GLine**s. Since you know how to create the components of the picture, you could start off and write a **run** method that added each of the graphical objects to the canvas with the appropriate location, size, and color. Before doing so, however, you might want to stop and think about possible strategies for simplifying the problem.

The second important thing to notice about the train picture is that, even though the diagram is more complicated than any of the graphical examples so far in this book, it subdivides easily into smaller pieces. The task of drawing this particular train decomposes naturally into three subtasks: drawing an engine, drawing a boxcar, and drawing a caboose. Thus, if you want to write your **run** method in a way that exploits the power of decomposition, you should subdivide it into three methods—**drawEngine**, **drawBoxcar**, and **drawCaboose**—each of which is responsible for drawing that type of car. This division of responsibility is illustrated in the following diagram:

Decomposing the program into methods has several advantages. For one thing, this kind of subdivision makes the program easier to write by allowing you to focus on one part of the problem at a time. While writing **drawEngine**, for example, you can ignore the details of **drawBoxcar** and **drawCaboose**. Perhaps more importantly, such decomposition makes the program much easier to read, thereby reducing substantially the conceptual complexity for programmers who may need to modify the code in the future. For one thing, the method names make it clear what is going on in each part of the code. If you had instead combined all the individual steps necessary to create the picture into a single method, readers would have a much harder time figuring out which lines of code contributed to particular parts of the picture. Finally, decomposition often supplies you with tools that you can reuse. In this simple train diagram, there is only one boxcar. In the real world, a freight train with only one boxcar would almost certainly run at a loss. To be economical, a single engine should pull many such cars. Having a **drawBoxcar** method allows you to draw as many boxcars as you need.

Specifying parameters

At this point, you know that it makes sense to decompose the problem of drawing a train into methods that draw each type of car. The next step in the process is to determine how those methods get the information they need to draw the picture correctly. In order to draw a picture of the sort shown in the sample run, each of the methods needs various pieces of information. For example, the **drawBoxcar** method needs to know the dimensions of the boxcar, what color it should be, and where to place it on the canvas so that it correctly links up with the other cars.

There are two strategies you can use to provide such information to a method. One is to pass information from the caller in the form of arguments. The other is to include that information explicitly as part of the program, typically by defining a named constant that has the appropriate value. Adding more arguments provides more flexibility but often makes it harder to understand how the method works. Whenever you call a method, you have to know what each of its arguments means. If drawing a boxcar requires you to specify the color of the boxcar, its location on the canvas, the size of the car itself, the size of the doors, and the radius of the wheels, you will probably have trouble keeping all those details straight. On the other hand, if you instead choose to define each of these parameters as a named constant, you can draw a boxcar only in one color, in one size, and in one place.

To avoid the problems of each extreme, you need to strike a balance between these two strategies. As a general rule, it makes sense to apply the following guidelines in making that decision:

- Use arguments whenever individual callers are likely to supply different values for that parameter.
- Use named constants whenever callers are likely to be satisfied with a value you've chosen.

In the case of the train diagram, the caller is probably not interested in controlling the radius of the wheels. That value should therefore be specified as a named constant. At the other end of the spectrum, callers will certainly need to indicate where on the canvas a particular car should be placed. That information must therefore be conveyed through arguments, presumably in the form of an x and a y location on the canvas. Other values, such as the size and color of the car, fall somewhere in the middle of these extremes. Allowing the caller to specify these values provides additional flexibility but increases the conceptual complexity of the call. For the purposes of this example, it is probably sufficient to make the following assumptions:

- All the cars are the same size.
- Engines are always black.
- Cabooses are always red.
- Boxcars come in many colors.

These assumptions imply that the only arguments for **drawEngine** and **drawCaboose** are the location at which to place the car. The **drawBoxcar** method needs that same information along with the color of the car. The method headers for these three methods will therefore look like this:

```
private void drawEngine(double x, double y)
private void drawBoxcar(double x, double y, Color color)
private void drawCaboose(double x, double y)
```

The rest of the information necessary to create the picture can be specified using named constants. For the train diagram shown in the sample run, these constants have the values shown in Figure 5-7.

FIGURE 5-7 **Named constants that control the parameters of the train diagram**

```
/* Dimensions of the frame of a train car */
   private static final double CAR_WIDTH = 75;
   private static final double CAR_HEIGHT = 36;

/* Distance from the bottom of a train car to the track below it */
   private static final double CAR_BASELINE = 10;

/* Width of the connector, which overlaps between successive cars */
   private static final double CONNECTOR = 6;

/* Radius of the wheels on each car */
   private static final double WHEEL_RADIUS = 8;

/* Distance from the edge of the frame to the center of the wheel */
   private static final double WHEEL_INSET = 16;

/* Dimensions of the cab on the engine */
   private static final double CAB_WIDTH = 35;
   private static final double CAB_HEIGHT = 8;

/* Dimensions of the smokestack and its distance from the front */
   private static final double SMOKESTACK_WIDTH = 8;
   private static final double SMOKESTACK_HEIGHT = 8;
   private static final double SMOKESTACK_INSET = 8;

/* Dimensions of the door panels on the boxcar */
   private static final double DOOR_WIDTH = 18;
   private static final double DOOR_HEIGHT = 32;

/* Dimensions of the cupola on the caboose */
   private static final double CUPOLA_WIDTH = 35;
   private static final double CUPOLA_HEIGHT = 8;
```

As the header lines indicate, the **drawEngine**, **drawBoxcar**, and **drawCaboose** methods take an **x** and a **y** parameter to indicate the location of the car on the canvas. Callers that use these methods need to know what those coordinates mean in terms of where the car is drawn relative to the point (**x**, **y**). There are many possible interpretations, and part of your job as programmer is to choose an appropriate design. One possibility is to adopt the convention used by the **acm.graphics** package and define the point (**x**, **y**) to be the upper left corner of a car. In the absence of a compelling reason to the contrary, choosing a model that matches the existing library packages is a good idea. In this case, however, there may indeed be a compelling reason. The location of the upper left corner of a train car depends on how tall the car is. In this example, the engine and the caboose have graphical figures on their top side that make them taller than the boxcar. Thus, to calculate the *y* coordinate of the top of a car, you would need to know the type of car. On the other hand, it is easy to calculate the *y* coordinate of the bottom of the car because all the cars are sitting on a track. Because all cars have a common baseline, it makes sense to let the **x** parameter indicate the left edge of the connector that extends from the car and to let the **y** parameter indicate the level of the track. This interpretation is therefore similar to the one that the **acm.graphics** package uses for the **GLabel** class. Because each letter rests on a horizontal baseline, the *y* coordinate in the **GLabel** class indicates the position of the baseline.

Designing from the top down

Now that you have decided on the method headers for the **drawEngine**, **drawBoxcar**, and **drawCaboose** methods, it might seem as if the logical next step would be to go ahead and implement them. Although doing so is indeed an option, it is usually better to complete the code at each level of decomposition before moving on to the next. By doing so, you can convince yourself that you have chosen the right decomposition. If you have left out a subtask or failed to include enough flexibility in the arguments to the methods, you will discover the problem when you try to code the highest level of the program. The principle of top-down design suggests that you should start with the **run** method and then work your way down toward the details.

The decomposition of the problem into subsidiary methods makes the **run** method reasonably straightforward. You know that the body of the **run** method will include calls to **drawEngine**, **drawBoxcar**, and **drawCaboose**. The only remaining issue is figuring out what values to supply for the coordinates in each call. If you look at picture in the sample run, you will see that the train is resting on the bottom of the canvas. The *y* coordinate of the track is therefore equal to the *y* coordinate of the bottom of the canvas; because Java coordinate values increase as you move downward, the *y* coordinate of the bottom of the canvas is simply the height of the canvas, which you can get by calling the **getHeight** method. Finding the *x* coordinate of each car requires a little more calculation. In this example, the entire train is centered in the window. Thus, calculating the *x* coordinate for the engine requires figuring out how long the entire train is and then subtracting half that length from the coordinates of the center of the canvas. Each subsequent car begins at a point whose *x* coordinate is shifted rightward by the width of a car and the width of its connector. Expressing these calculations in Java gives rise to the following **run** method:

```
public void run() {
    double trainWidth = 3 * CAR_WIDTH + 4 * CONNECTOR;
    double x = (getWidth() - trainWidth) / 2;
    double y = getHeight();
    double dx = CAR_WIDTH + CONNECTOR;
    drawEngine(x, y);
    drawBoxcar(x + dx, y, Color.GREEN);
    drawCaboose(x + 2 * dx, y);
}
```

Looking for common features

Now that the **run** method is out of the way, you can turn your attention to the methods that draw the individual cars. Although one is often tempted to run to the keyboard and start typing in code, there is an enormous advantage in taking the time to think about the problem. When you choose a decomposition, one of the things you should look for is subtasks that come up in more than one part of the problem. To see how that strategy might apply in the current problem, it's worth taking another look at the three different types of cars:

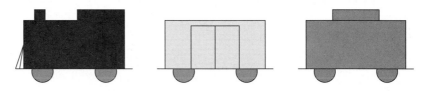

If you look carefully at the diagrams of these three cars, you will see that they share a number of common features. The wheels are the same, as are the connectors that link the car to its neighbors. In fact, the body of the car itself is the same except for the color. Each type of car, therefore, shares a common framework that looks like this:

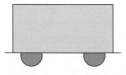

If you color the gray part of this picture with the appropriate color, you can use it as the foundation for any of the three car types. For the engine, you need to add a smokestack, a cab, and a cowcatcher. For the boxcar, you need to add doors. For the caboose, you need to add a cupola. In each case, most of the work of drawing the car can be shared by defining a method that draws the basic framework of the car. That method—which itself decomposes into a method that draws each of the wheels—looks like this:

```
private void drawCarFrame(double x, double y, Color color) {
    double x0 = x + CONNECTOR;
    double y0 = y - CAR_BASELINE;
    double top = y0 - CAR_HEIGHT;
    add(new GLine(x, y0, x + CAR_WIDTH + 2 * CONNECTOR, y0));
    drawWheel(x0 + WHEEL_INSET, y - WHEEL_RADIUS);
    drawWheel(x0 + CAR_WIDTH - WHEEL_INSET, y - WHEEL_RADIUS);
    GRect r = new GRect(x0, top, CAR_WIDTH, CAR_HEIGHT);
    r.setFilled(true);
    r.setFillColor(color);
    add(r);
}

private void drawWheel(double x, double y) {
    double r = WHEEL_RADIUS;
    GOval wheel = new GOval(x - r, y - r, 2 * r, 2 * r);
    wheel.setFilled(true);
    wheel.setFillColor(Color.GRAY);
    add(wheel);
}
```

Completing the decomposition

Once you have a tool for creating the framework of an individual car, you can
complete the **drawTrain** program by filling in the definitions of the **drawEngine**,
drawBoxcar, and **drawCaboose** methods. Some of the methods are easy enough to
code without further decomposition. Here, for example, is an implementation of
drawBoxcar that draws the background frame and then adds the two door panels:

```
private void drawBoxcar(double x, double y, Color color) {
    drawCarFrame(x, y, color);
    double xRight = x + CONNECTOR + CAR_WIDTH / 2;
    double xLeft = xRight - DOOR_WIDTH;
    double yDoor = y - CAR_BASELINE - DOOR_HEIGHT;
    add(new GRect(xLeft, yDoor, DOOR_WIDTH, DOOR_HEIGHT));
    add(new GRect(xRight, yDoor, DOOR_WIDTH, DOOR_HEIGHT));
}
```

You might, however, choose to decompose some of these methods further. For
example, you could decide to break up the diagram of the train engine into its
component parts and then code **drawEngine** like this:

```
private void drawEngine(double x, double y) {
    drawCarFrame(x, y, Color.BLACK);
    drawSmokestack(x, y);
    drawCab(x, y);
    drawCowcatcher(x, y);
}
```

Private methods that tackle smaller parts of a problem, such as **drawSmokestack**,
drawCab, and **drawCowcatcher** in this example, are often called **helper methods.**

If you adopt this decomposition strategy, you will have to write implementations
for these helper methods along with the as-yet-unimplemented **drawCaboose**.
You'll have a chance to finish the decomposition in exercise 8.

While stepwise refinement is a critically important skill, object-oriented languages offer another approach to simplifying a problem. Instead of dividing a program into methods that implement successively simpler subtasks, you can usually accomplish the same goal by defining a hierarchy of classes that reflects the same decomposition strategy. When you are programming in Java, that strategy usually has distinct advantages. In Chapter 9, you'll have a chance to reimplement the **DrawTrain** program by defining a class hierarchy in which each of the specific car types—engines, boxcars, and cabooses—is a subclass of a more general class that encompasses each of the individual types.

5.5 Algorithmic methods

In addition to their role as a tool for managing complex programs, methods are important to programming because they provide a basis for the implementation of algorithms, which were introduced briefly in Chapter 1. An algorithm is an abstract strategy; writing a method is the conventional way to express that algorithm in the context of a programming language. Thus, when you want to implement an algorithm as part of a program, you typically write a method—which may in turn call other methods to handle part of its work—to carry out that algorithm.

Although you have seen several algorithms implemented in the context of the sample programs, you have not had a chance to focus on the nature of the algorithmic process itself. Most of the programming problems you have seen so far are simple enough that the appropriate solution technique springs immediately to mind. As problems become more complex, however, their solutions require more thought, and you will need to consider more than one strategy before writing the final program.

As an illustration of how algorithmic strategies take shape, the sections that follow consider two solutions to a problem from classical mathematics, which is to find the greatest common divisor of two integers. Given two integers x and y, the **greatest common divisor** (or **gcd** for short) is the largest integer that divides evenly into both. For example, the gcd of 49 and 35 is 7, the gcd of 6 and 18 is 6, and the gcd of 32 and 33 is 1.

Suppose that you have been asked to write a method that accepts the integers x and y as input and returns their greatest common divisor. From the caller's point of view, what you want is a method **gcd(x, y)** that takes two integers as arguments and returns another integer that is their greatest common divisor. The header line for this method is therefore

```
public int gcd(int x, int y)
```

How might you go about designing an algorithm to perform this calculation?

The "brute force" approach

In many ways, the most obvious approach to calculating the gcd is simply to try every possibility. To start, you simply "guess" that **gcd(x, y)** is the smaller of **x** and **y**, because any larger value could not possibly divide evenly into a smaller number. You then proceed by dividing **x** and **y** by your guess and seeing if it divides evenly into both. If it does, you have the answer; if not, you subtract 1 from your guess and try again. A strategy that tries every possibility is often called a **brute force approach.**

The brute-force approach to calculating the **gcd** function looks like this in Java:

```
public int gcd(int x, int y) {
    int guess = Math.min(x, y);
    while (x % guess != 0 || y % guess != 0) {
        guess--;
    }
    return guess;
}
```

Before you decide that this implementation is in fact a valid algorithm for computing the **gcd** function, you need to ask yourself several questions about the code. Will the brute-force implementation of **gcd** always give the correct answer? Will it always terminate, or might the method continue forever?

To see that the program gives the correct answer, you need to look at the condition in the **while** loop

```
x % guess != 0 || y % guess != 0
```

As always, the **while** condition indicates under what circumstances the loop will continue. To find out what condition causes the loop to terminate, you have to negate the **while** condition. Negating a condition involving **&&** or **||** can be tricky unless you remember how to apply De Morgan's law, which was introduced in the section on "Logical operators" in Chapter 4. De Morgan's law indicates that the following condition must hold when the **while** loop exits:

```
x % guess == 0 && y % guess == 0
```

From this condition, you can see immediately that the final value of **guess** is certainly a common divisor. To recognize that it is in fact the greatest common divisor, you have to think about the strategy embodied in the **while** loop. The critical factor to notice in the strategy is that the program counts *backward* through all the possibilities. The greatest common divisor can never be larger than **x** (or **y**, for that matter), and the brute-force search therefore begins with that value. If the program ever gets out of the **while** loop, it must have already tried each value between **x** and the current value of **guess**. Thus, if there were a larger value that divided evenly into both **x** and **y**, the program would already have found it in an earlier iteration of the **while** loop.

To recognize that the method terminates, the key insight is that the value of **guess** must eventually reach 1, even if no larger common divisor is found. At this point, the **while** loop will surely terminate, because 1 will divide evenly into both **x** and **y**, no matter what values those variables have.

Euclid's algorithm

Brute force is not, however, the only effective strategy. Although brute-force algorithms have their place in other contexts, they are a poor choice for the **gcd** function if you are concerned about efficiency. For example, if you call the method with the integers 1,000,005 and 1,000,000, the brute-force algorithm will run through the body of the **while** loop almost a million times before it comes up with 5—an answer that you can easily determine just by thinking about the two numbers.

What you need to find is an algorithm that is guaranteed to terminate with the correct answer but that requires fewer steps than the brute-force approach. This is where cleverness and a clear understanding of the problem pay off. Fortunately, the necessary creative insight has already been supplied by the Greek mathematician Euclid, whose *Elements* (book 7, proposition II) contains an elegant solution to this problem. In modern English, Euclid's algorithm can be described as follows:

1. Divide **x** by **y** and compute the remainder; call that remainder **r**.
2. If **r** is zero, the procedure is complete, and the answer is **y**.
3. If **r** is not zero, set **x** equal to the old value of **y**, set **y** equal to **r**, and repeat the entire process.

You can easily translate this algorithmic description into the following Java code:

```java
int gcd(int x, int y) {
    int r = x % y;
    while (r != 0) {
        x = y;
        y = r;
        r = x % y;
    }
    return y;
}
```

This implementation of the **gcd** method also correctly finds the greatest common divisor of two integers. It differs from the brute-force implementation in two respects. On the one hand, it computes the result much more quickly. On the other, it is more difficult to prove correct.

Defending the correctness of Euclid's algorithm

Although a formal proof of correctness for Euclid's algorithm is beyond the scope of this book, you can easily get a feel for how the algorithm works by adopting the mental model of mathematics the Greeks used. In Greek mathematics, geometry held center stage, and numbers were thought of as distances. For example, when Euclid set out to find the greatest common divisor of two whole numbers, such as 55 and 15, he framed the problem as one of finding the longest measuring stick that could be used to mark off each of the two distances involved. Thus, you can visualize the specific problem by starting out with two sticks, one 55 units long and one 15 units long, as follows:

The problem is to find a new measuring stick that you can lay end to end on top of each of these sticks so that it precisely covers each of the distances **x** and **y**.

Euclid's algorithm begins by marking off the large stick in units of the shorter one:

Unless the smaller number is an exact divisor of the larger one, there is some remainder, as indicated by the shaded section of the upper stick. In this case, 15 goes into 55 three times with 10 left over, which means that the shaded region is 10 units long. The fundamental insight that Euclid had is that the greatest common divisor for the original two distances must also be the greatest common divisor of the length of the shorter stick and the distance represented by the shaded region in the diagram.

Given this observation, you can solve the original problem by reducing it to a simpler problem involving smaller numbers. Here, the new numbers are 15 and 10, and you can find their greatest common divisor by reapplying Euclid's algorithm. You start by representing the new values, **x´** and **y´**, as measuring sticks of the appropriate length. You then mark off the larger stick in units of the smaller one.

Once again, this process results in a leftover region, which this time has length 5. If you then repeat the process one more time, you discover that the shaded region of length 5 is itself the common divisor of **x´** and **y´** and, therefore, by Euclid's proposition, of the original numbers **x** and **y**. That this new value is indeed a common divisor of the original numbers is demonstrated by the following diagram:

Euclid supplies a complete proof of his proposition in the *Elements*. If you are intrigued by how mathematicians thought about such problems almost 2500 years ago, you may find it interesting to look up the original source.

Comparing the efficiency of the two algorithms

To illustrate the difference in efficiency of the two algorithmic strategies for computing the greatest common divisor, let's consider once again the integers 1,000,005 and 1,000,000. To find the greatest common divisor of these two integers, the brute-force algorithm requires a million steps; Euclid's algorithm requires only two. At the beginning of Euclid's algorithm, x is 1000005, y is 1000000, and r is set to 5 during the first cycle of the loop. Since the value of r is not 0, the program sets x to 1000000, sets y to 5, and starts again. On the second cycle, the new value of r is 0, so the program exits from the **while** loop and reports that the answer is 5.

The two strategies for computing greatest common divisors presented in this chapter offer a clear demonstration that the choice of algorithm can have a profound effect on the efficiency of the solution. If you continue your study of computer science, you will learn how to quantify such differences in performance along with several general approaches for improving algorithmic efficiency.

Summary

In this chapter, you learned about *methods*, which enable you to refer to an entire set of operations with a single name. More importantly, by allowing the programmer to ignore the internal details and concentrate only on the effect of a method as a whole, methods provide a critical tool for reducing the conceptual complexity of programs.

The important points introduced in this chapter include:

- A *method* consists of a set of program statements that have been collected together and given a name. Other parts of the program can then *call* that method, possibly passing it information in the form of *arguments* and receiving a result *returned* by that method.
- A method that returns a value must have a **return** statement that specifies the result. Methods may return values of any type.
- In object-oriented languages like Java, method calls are used to represent the process of sending a *message* from one object to another. When you use a method call to send a message, you need to specify the receiver as part of the method call, like this:

    receiver **.** *name* (*arguments*)

- Methods that return Boolean values are called *predicate methods*. Because you can use the result of such methods to specify a condition in an **if** or **while** statement, predicate methods play an important role in programming.
- Within the body of a method, variables that act as placeholders for the argument values are called *formal parameters*.
- Variables declared with a method are local to that method and cannot be used outside of it. Internally, all the variables declared within a method, including the parameters, are stored together in a *stack frame*.
- When a method returns, it continues from precisely the point at which the call was made. The computer refers to this point as the *return address*.

- Methods are a powerful tool for reducing the complexity of programs because they allow you to *decompose* large tasks into smaller, more manageable subtasks.
- In most cases, it makes sense to decompose a program by starting at the level of the problem as a whole and then working your way downward to the details. This strategy is called *top-down design* or *stepwise refinement*.
- Because methods tie together a collection of statements so as to have a specific effect, methods provide the standard framework for expressing algorithms in Java.
- There are often many different algorithms for solving a particular problem. Choosing the algorithm that best fits the application is an important part of your task as a programmer.

Review questions

1. Explain in your own words the difference between a method and a program.

2. Define the following terms as they apply to methods: *call*, *argument*, *return*.

3. What is the difference between passing information to a method by using arguments and reading input data using methods like **readInt**? When would each action be appropriate?

4. How do you specify the result of a method in Java?

5. Can there be more than one **return** statement in the body of a method?

6. How do you indicate that you want to apply a method to another object?

7. Why has it been unnecessary to specify receivers in the programs presented in the earlier chapters?

8. Why was it unnecessary to include a **break** statement at the end of each **case** clause in the **monthName** method presented in this chapter?

9. What is a predicate method?

10. How do you tell whether two strings contain the same characters?

11. What is the relationship between arguments and formal parameters?

12. Variables declared within a method are called *local variables*. What is the significance of the word *local* in this context?

13. What does the term *return address* mean?

14. Explain in your own words the process of *stepwise refinement*.

15. What is a brute-force algorithm?

16. Use Euclid's algorithm to compute the greatest common divisor of 7735 and 4185. What values does the local variable **r** take on during the calculation?

17. In the examples of Euclid's algorithm to calculate **gcd(x, y)** that appear in this chapter, **x** is always larger than **y**. What happens if **x** is smaller than **y**?

Programming exercises

1. In high-school algebra, you learned that the standard quadratic equation

    $$ax^2 + bx + c = 0$$

    has two solutions given by the formula

    $$x = \frac{-b \pm \sqrt{b^2 - 4ac}}{2a}$$

    The first solution is obtained by using + in place of $\pm$; the second is obtained by using – in place of $\pm$.

    Write a Java program that accepts values for **a**, **b**, and **c**, and then calculates the two solutions. If the quantity under the square root sign is negative, the equation has no real solutions, and your program should display a message to that effect. You may assume that the value for **a** is nonzero. Your program should be able to duplicate the following sample run:

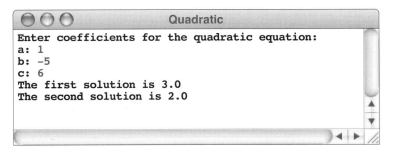

```
Quadratic
Enter coefficients for the quadratic equation:
a: 1
b: -5
c: 6
The first solution is 3.0
The second solution is 2.0
```

2. The Fibonacci sequence, in which each new term is the sum of the preceding two, was introduced in Chapter 4, exercise 9. Rewrite the program requested in that exercise, changing the implementation so that your program calls a method **fibonacci(n)** to calculate the nth Fibonacci number. In terms of the number of mathematical calculations required, is your new implementation more or less efficient that the one you used in Chapter 4?

3. Write a method **raiseIntToPower** that takes two integers, **n** and **k**, and returns n^k. Use your method to display a table of values of 2^k for all values of **k** from 0 to 10.

4. Write a method **countDigits(n)** that returns the number of digits in the integer **n**, which you may assume is positive. Design a main program to test your method. For hints about how to write this program, you might want to look back at the **DigitSum** program in Figure 4-6.

5. Rewrite the **Target** program given in Chapter 2, exercise 5 so that it uses the **createFilledCircle** method that appears in Figure 5-3. In addition, change the program so that the target is always centered in the window and so that the number and dimensions of the circles are controlled by the following named constants:

```
    private static final int N_CIRCLES = 5;
    private static final double OUTER_RADIUS = 75;
    private static final double INNER_RADIUS = 10;
```

Given those values, the program should generate the following display:

6. Rewrite the **DrawStoplight** program shown in Figure 5-3 so that it also includes a private method **createFilledRect** that creates a filled **GRect** object in much the same way that **createFilledCircle** creates a filled **GOval**. Part of the problem is working out what parameters the **createFilledRect** method needs to take.

7. Write a predicate method **askYesNoQuestion(prompt)** that prints the string **prompt** as a question for the user and then waits for a response. If the user enters the string **"yes"**, the **askYesNoQuestion** method should return **true**; if the user enters **"no"**, the method should return false. If the user enters anything else, **askYesNoQuestion** should remind the user that it is seeking a yes-or-no answer and then repeat the question. For example, if the program includes the statement

```
    if (askYesNoQuestion("Would you like instructions? "))
```

the interaction with the user might look like this:

8. Complete the implementation of the **DrawTrain** program by supplying the missing methods (**drawSmokestack**, **drawCab**, **drawCowcatcher**, and **drawCaboose**).

9. Write a **GraphicsProgram** that draws a line drawing of the house shown in the following diagram:

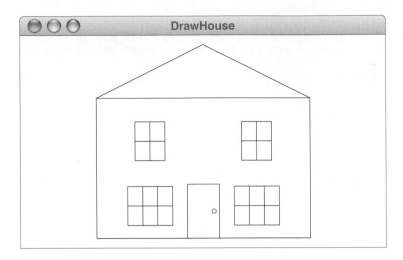

Make sure that you use stepwise refinement to decompose this figure into useful pieces.

10. If you think that the house in the preceding exercise seems a bit mundane, you might instead want to draw a diagram of the House of Usher, which Edgar Allan Poe describes as follows:

> With the first glimpse of the building, a sense of insufferable gloom pervaded my spirit. . . . I looked upon the scene before me—upon the mere house, and the simple landscape features of the domain—upon the bleak walls—upon the vacant eye-like windows . . . upon a few white trunks of decayed trees—with an utter depression of soul.

From Poe's description, you might imagine a house and grounds that look something like this:

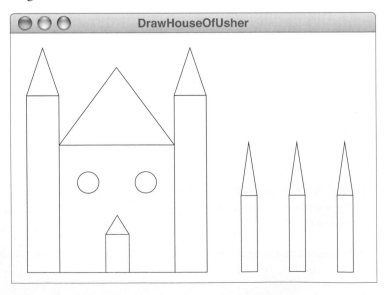

The figure on the left is the house with its "vacant eye-like windows" and the three figures on the right are a stylized rendition of the "few white trunks of decayed trees."

Write a `GraphicsProgram` that draws the figure shown in this sample run. Make sure that you break the program down by stepwise refinement, that you look for repeated elements in the diagram, and that you use named constants to specify the dimensions of the various figures that make up the scene.

11. An integer greater than 1 is said to be **prime** if it has no divisors other than itself and one. The number 17, for example, is prime, because it has no factors other than 1 and 17. The number 91, however, is not prime because it is divisible by 7 and 13. Write a predicate method `isPrime(n)` that returns **true** if the integer **n** is prime, and **false** otherwise. As an initial strategy, implement `isPrime` using a brute-force algorithm that simply tests every possible divisor. Once you have that version working, try to come up with improvements to your algorithm that increase its efficiency without sacrificing its correctness.

12. Greek mathematicians took a special interest in numbers that are equal to the sum of their proper divisors (a proper divisor of *n* is any divisor less than *n* itself). They called such numbers **perfect numbers.** For example, 6 is a perfect number because it is the sum of 1, 2, and 3, which are the integers less than 6 that divide evenly into 6. Similarly, 28 is a perfect number because it is the sum of 1, 2, 4, 7, and 14.

Write a predicate method `isPerfect(n)` that returns **true** if the integer **n** is perfect, and **false** otherwise. Test your implementation by writing a main program that uses the `isPerfect` method to check for perfect numbers in the range 1 to 9999 by testing each number in turn. Whenever it identifies a perfect number, your program should display that number on the screen. The first two lines of output should be 6 and 28. Your program should find two other perfect numbers in that range as well.

13. Although Euclid's algorithm and the problem of finding perfect numbers from the preceding exercise are both drawn from the domain of mathematics, the Greeks were fascinated with algorithms of other kinds as well. In Greek mythology, for example, Theseus of Athens escapes from the Minotaur's labyrinth by taking in a ball of string, unwinding it as he goes along, and then following the path of string back to the exit. Theseus's strategy represents an algorithm for escaping from a maze, but it is not the only algorithm he could have used to solve this problem. For example, if a maze has no internal loops, you can escape by keeping your right hand against a wall at all times. This algorithm is called the **right-hand rule.**

For example, imagine that Theseus is lost in the maze shown at the top of the next page. In this diagram, Theseus's position marked by the Greek letter theta (Θ).

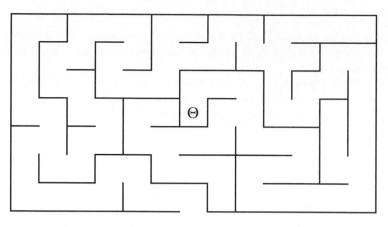

To get out, Theseus walks along the path shown by the dotted line in the next diagram, which he can do without taking his right hand off the wall.

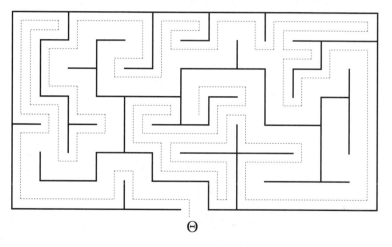

   Suppose you have been asked to write a program for a robot to escape from a maze. Assume that you have access to a class named **MazeRunningRobot** that implements the following methods:

```
void moveForward()      /* Move forward one square  */
void turnRight()        /* Turn right without moving */
void turnLeft()         /* Turn left without moving */
boolean isBlocked()     /* True if facing a wall    */
boolean isOutside()     /* True if outside the maze */
```

Use these methods to write an algorithmic method

```
private void solveMaze(MazeRunningRobot robot)
```

that gets the robot out of the maze using the right-hand rule.

CHAPTER 6
Objects and Classes

To beautify life is to give it an object.
—José Martí, *On Oscar Wilde*, 1882

Kristen Nygaard (1926-2002)

Ole-Johan Dahl (1931-2002)

Norwegian computer scientists Kristen Nygaard and Ole-Johan Dahl developed the central ideas of object-oriented programming more than 40 years ago as part of their work on the programming language SIMULA. Early versions of SIMULA appeared in the early 1960s, but the stable version of the language that brought these concepts to the attention of the world appeared in 1967. The initial work on SIMULA was carried out at the Norwegian Computing Center, a state-funded research laboratory in Norway focusing on developing better software-engineering techniques. Both later joined the faculty at the University of Oslo. Although their work took several decades to become established in the industry, interest in object-oriented techniques has grown considerably in the last two decades, particularly after the release of modern object-oriented languages like C++ and Java. For their contributions, Nygaard and Dahl received both the 2001 Turing Award from the Association for Computing Machinery and the John von Neumann Medal for the same year from the Institute of Electrical and Electronic Engineers.

After starting off with a holistic look at programs in Chapter 2, the three most recent chapters have taken a reductionistic tack, teaching you how to use the fundamental building blocks of programming—expressions, statements, and methods—starting from the ground up. In a way, this chapter extends that progression by looking at objects and classes, which form the next level in the hierarchical structure of the Java language. On the other hand, objects and classes are the primary tools for thinking about programs in a high-level, abstract way. In its emphasis on that high-level perspective, this chapter represents a return to the holistic viewpoint of Chapter 2. The chapter begins with an example that illustrates the use of an existing class that is important in its own right—the `RandomGenerator` class in the `acm.util` package. The rest of the chapter then turns to the question of how to implement your own classes in a Java application.

Although being able to adopt a holistic perspective about classes and objects is essential to using them effectively, that perspective is usually not sufficient for understanding how objects behave in practice. For most students, it is also important to develop a mental model of objects that allows you to visualize how they are represented inside the machine. To avoid cluttering the high-level vision with too much detail, this book defers those issues of internal representation to Chapter 7.

6.1 Using the `RandomGenerator` class

Until now, every program in this text has behaved **deterministically,** which means that its actions are predictable with any given set of input values. The behavior of such programs is repeatable. If the program produces a particular result when you run it today, it will produce the same result tomorrow.

In some programming applications, such as games or simulations, however, it is important that the behavior of your programs not be so predictable: a computer game that always had the same outcome would be boring. In order to build a program that behaves randomly, you need some mechanism for representing a random process, such as flipping a coin or tossing a die. Programs that simulate such random events are called **nondeterministic** programs.

Partly because early computers were used primarily for numerical applications, the idea of generating randomness using a computer is often expressed in terms of being able to generate a **random number** in a particular range. From a theoretical perspective, a number is random if there is no way to determine in advance what value it will have among a set of equally probable outcomes. For example, rolling a die generates a random number between 1 and 6. If the die is fair, there is no way to predict which number will come up. The six possible values are equally likely.

Although the idea of a random number makes intuitive sense, it is a difficult notion to represent inside a computer. Computers operate by following a sequence of instructions in memory and therefore function in a deterministic mode. If a number is generated by a deterministic process, any user should be able to work through that same set of rules and anticipate the computer's response. This situation seems paradoxical. How is it possible for a computer to generate unpredictable results by following a deterministic set of rules?

Pseudorandom numbers

In almost all cases, computer programmers today sidestep this paradox by giving up on the notion of true randomness. Java programs that use random numbers in fact compute those numbers using a deterministic procedure. Although doing so means that a user could, in theory, follow the same set of rules and anticipate the computer's response, the strategy works in practice because no one actually bothers to perform those calculations. In most practical applications, it doesn't matter whether the numbers *are* random; all that matters is that the numbers *appear* to be random. For numbers to appear random, they should (1) behave like random numbers from a statistical point of view and (2) be sufficiently difficult to predict in advance that users won't bother. "Random" numbers generated by an algorithmic process inside a computer are formally referred to as **pseudorandom numbers** to underscore the fact that no truly random activity is involved. Informally, however, it is easier to call them **random numbers,** despite the fact that this is not entirely accurate.

The techniques for generating random numbers tend to be simple in terms of their computational requirements but highly sophisticated in terms of their mathematical underpinnings. Stanford Professor Don Knuth, author of a landmark series of books entitled *The Art of Computer Programming,* devotes well over 100 pages to the question of how one might code a random number generator to make the output appear as random as possible. The details of that mathematical analysis are well beyond the scope of an introductory text. Fortunately, almost no programmers ever have to write the code to generate random numbers. That code has already been developed by someone who has studied the necessary mathematics and waded through all the complex practical and theoretical issues necessary to make it work. Most programmers are interested only in *using* random numbers and have no interest in the details of how they are calculated. For those programmers, it is sufficient to think of the random number generator as a black box. You ask it for a random value, and out pops the next one.

The idea of thinking of parts of your programs as black boxes is fundamental to the concept of object-oriented programming. To generate random numbers, you need a random number generator, which can be illustrated by the following box:

RandomGenerator
instance

In the Java domain, this black box constitutes an object. Its class is **RandomGenerator**, which is defined in the **acm.util** package. As the label indicates, the box is a particular instance of the **RandomGenerator** class. When you want to generate a random value, you do so by sending a message to the object, which can be represented pictorially as follows:

Give me the next random number  **RandomGenerator**
instance

The random generator object then replies with the next random number, computed by some algorithmic process, the details of which are hidden inside the black box. For example, given a request for a random number, the random generator object might give the following reply:

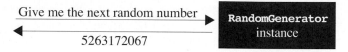

As is usually the case in object-oriented programming, the message takes the form of a method call. The reply is simply the value that method returns. As you will learn in the next section, the random generator object responds to several different methods, depending on the type of random value your application needs.

Using the `RandomGenerator` class

The most important public methods in the **RandomGenerator** class are listed in Figure 6-1. For the most part, these methods are easy to understand. The only method that requires much explanation is the static **getInstance** method, which returns an new instance of the **RandomGenerator** class. The important thing to remember is that a **RandomGenerator** is not itself a random value but rather an object that generates random values. Although typically you will want to generate many different random values in the course of a program, you only need to have one generator. Moreover, because you will probably want to use that generator in several methods within your program, it is easiest to declare it as an instance variable, as follows:

FIGURE 6-1   **Useful methods in the RandomGenerator class**

`static RandomGenerator getInstance()`
Returns an instance of the **RandomGenerator** class, which is shared throughout the program.
`int nextInt(int n)`
Returns a random integer chosen from the **n** values in the range 0 to **n** - 1, inclusive.
`int nextInt(int low, int high)`
Returns a random integer in the range **low** to **high**, inclusive.
`double nextDouble()`
Returns a random double d in the range $0 \le d < 1$; a range excluding one end is called **half-open.**
`double nextDouble(double low, double high)`
Returns a random double d in the half-open range **low** $\le d <$ **high**.
`boolean nextBoolean()`
Returns a **boolean** that is **true** roughly 50 percent of the time.
`boolean nextBoolean(double p)`
Returns a **boolean** that is **true** with probability **p**, which must be between 0 and 1.
`Color nextColor()`
Returns a random Java color.
`void setSeed(long seed)`
Sets a "seed" to indicate a starting point for the pseudorandom sequence.

```
private RandomGenerator rgen = RandomGenerator.getInstance();
```

That line both declares and initializes the variable **rgen** as a source of random values for the program as a whole.

Once you've declared and initialized the **rgen** variable, you can then use the other methods in **RandomGenerator** to generate the next random value of the appropriate type. Which method you select depends on the application. If you wanted a random integer in a specific range, for example, you could use the two-argument version of **nextInt**. Thus, you could simulate rolling a standard six-sided die by writing

```
int die = rgen.nextInt(1, 6);
```

If you wanted to generate a random real number between –1.0 and +1.0, you would call

```
double r = rgen.nextDouble(-1.0, +1.0);
```

If you wanted to simulate the toss of a coin, you could use **nextBoolean**:

```
String coinFlip = rgen.nextBoolean() ? "Heads" : "Tails";
```

The program in Figure 6-2 illustrates the use of the **RandomGenerator** class in the context of a complete application. This program simulates the casino game of Craps, which is played as follows. You start by rolling two six-sided dice and looking at the total. The game then breaks down into the following cases based on that first roll:

- Your first roll is a 2, 3, or 12. Rolling these numbers on your first roll is called *craps* and means that you lose.
- Your first roll is a 7 or an 11. When either of these numbers comes up on your first roll, it is called a *natural,* and you win.
- Your first roll is one of the other numbers (4, 5, 6, 8, 9, or 10). In this case, the number you rolled is called your *point*, and you continue to roll the dice until either (a) you roll your point a second time, in which case you win, or (b) you roll a 7, in which case you lose. If you roll any other number—including 2, 3, 11, and 12, which are no longer treated specially—you just keep on rolling until your point or a 7 appears.

The program in Figure 6-2 is a straightforward translation of the English rules into Java code. The sample runs in Figure 6-3 illustrate each of the possible outcomes.

The **Craps.java** program offers a general programming pattern for working with random numbers. As always, you declare and initialize the random number generator using the line

```
private RandomGenerator rgen = RandomGenerator.getInstance();
```

near the end of the program. Once you have that generator, you can then use it in the **rollDice** method to create a succession of random values, as follows:

FIGURE 6-2   Program to play the casino game of Craps

```java
/*
 * File: Craps.java
 * ------------------
 * This program plays the casino game of Craps.  At the beginning of the game,
 * the player rolls a pair of dice and computes the total.  If the total is 2,
 * 3, or 12 (called "craps"), the player loses.  If the total is 7 or 11
 * (called a "natural"), the player wins.  If the total is any other number,
 * that number becomes the "point."  From here, the player keeps rolling the
 * dice until (a) the point comes up again, in which case the player wins or
 * (b) a 7 appears, in which case the player loses.  The numbers 2, 3, 11,
 * and 12 no longer have special significance after the first roll.
 */

import acm.program.*;
import acm.util.*;

public class Craps extends ConsoleProgram {

    public void run() {
        int total = rollTwoDice();
        if (total == 7 || total == 11) {
            println("That's a natural.  You win.");
        } else if (total == 2 || total == 3 || total == 12) {
            println("That's craps.  You lose.");
        } else {
            int point = total;
            println("Your point is " + point + ".");
            while (true) {
                total = rollTwoDice();
                if (total == point) {
                    println("You made your point.  You win.");
                    break;
                } else if (total == 7) {
                    println("That's a 7.  You lose.");
                    break;
                }
            }
        }
    }

/* Rolls two dice and returns their sum. */
    private int rollTwoDice() {
        int d1 = rgen.nextInt(1, 6);
        int d2 = rgen.nextInt(1, 6);
        int total = d1 + d2;
        println("Rolling dice: " + d1 + " + " + d2 + " = " + total);
        return total;
    }

/* Create an instance variable for the random number generator */
    private RandomGenerator rgen = RandomGenerator.getInstance();

}
```

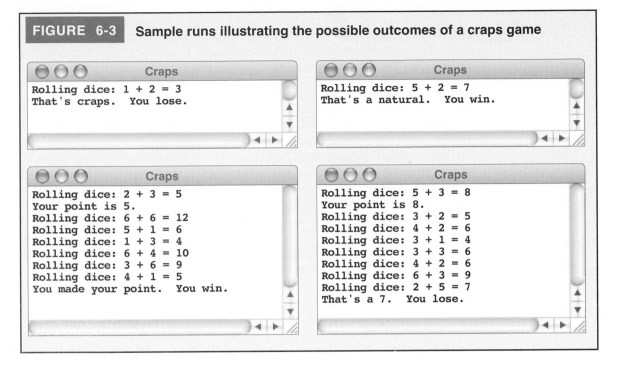

FIGURE 6-3   Sample runs illustrating the possible outcomes of a craps game

```
Rolling dice: 1 + 2 = 3
That's craps.  You lose.
```

```
Rolling dice: 5 + 2 = 7
That's a natural.  You win.
```

```
Rolling dice: 2 + 3 = 5
Your point is 5.
Rolling dice: 6 + 6 = 12
Rolling dice: 5 + 1 = 6
Rolling dice: 1 + 3 = 4
Rolling dice: 6 + 4 = 10
Rolling dice: 3 + 6 = 9
Rolling dice: 4 + 1 = 5
You made your point.  You win.
```

```
Rolling dice: 5 + 3 = 8
Your point is 8.
Rolling dice: 3 + 2 = 5
Rolling dice: 4 + 2 = 6
Rolling dice: 3 + 1 = 4
Rolling dice: 3 + 3 = 6
Rolling dice: 4 + 2 = 6
Rolling dice: 6 + 3 = 9
Rolling dice: 2 + 5 = 7
That's a 7.  You lose.
```

```
int d1 = rgen.nextInt(1, 6);
int d2 = rgen.nextInt(1, 6);
```

Each of these declarations uses the random generator **rgen** to obtain a new random integer between 1 and 6, inclusive.

The role of the random number seed

Most of the methods shown in Figure 6-1 for the **RandomGenerator** class return random values of a particular type, which might be integers, double-precision numbers, Boolean values chosen with a particular probability, or even random colors for use in graphical programs. Besides **getInstance**, the other method that does not fit into this framework is the **setSeed** method at the very end of the list. To understand what this method does, it is necessary to think a little more concretely about what goes on inside the black box that represents the random number generator.

   Given that an object was defined in Chapter 2 as a conceptually integrated entity that encapsulates both behavior and state, understanding how the random generator object works involves thinking about both those aspects. First, the behavior of the object is defined by the messages to which it responds. Second, the random generator object must also maintain internal state so that it can generate a new random value each time one of its methods is called. The typical pseudorandom number generator is implemented so that it produces a sequence of seemingly random values from a given starting point. That starting point is called the **seed.** Each time you call one of the methods that generates a random value, the generator takes the current seed, applies a mathematical function to generate the next value in the random sequence, and then stores the result back in the memory reserved for the seed. The method then converts the new seed to the specific type and range of values appropriate to the method call. For example, if you call

```
rgen.nextInt(1, 6);
```

the method converts the current random seed from its internal value as a **long** into an **int** in the range between 1 and 6, inclusive.

Since each call to the random number generator updates the seed, any series of calls to the methods in that generator will produce a sequence of different random values. If you don't know the starting point for that sequence, the pattern of random numbers will be impossible to predict. By default, Java sets the initial seed to the time registered on the internal system clock. As a result, the sequence of values will seem to shift each time you run the program. You can, however, use the **setSeed** method to give the random sequence a specific starting point. If you do that at the beginning of your program, the so-called random values will be the same each time.

On the face of it, the idea that it might be useful for a program to generate the same random sequence each time seems a bit crazy. If you're trying to play a computer game, the last thing you want is to have it behave in exactly the same way each time. Such a game would be entirely predictable and would quickly become boring. Even so, there is a very important reason why one might want—at least on a temporary basis—to set a specific random seed even in the context of a computer game, which is simply that deterministic programs are generally much easier to debug.

To illustrate this principle, suppose you have just written a program to play an intricate game, such as Monopoly. As is always the case with newly written programs, the odds are good that your program has a few bugs. In a complex program, bugs can be relatively obscure, in the sense that they only occur in rare situations. Suppose you've been playing the game and find that the program starts behaving in a bizarre way, but that you weren't alert enough to pay attention to all the relevant symptoms. You would like to run the program again and watch more carefully this time.

If your program is running in a nondeterministic way, however, a second run of the program will behave differently from the first. Bugs that showed up the first time may not occur on the second pass. In general, it is extremely difficult to reproduce the conditions that cause a program to fail if the program is behaving in a random fashion. If, on the other hand, your program can be made to operate deterministically, it will do the same thing each time it runs. This behavior makes it possible for you to recreate a problem, which is just what you need during the debugging phase.

Making it possible to force deterministic behavior during debugging is the primary reason that the **RandomGenerator** class includes the **setSeed** method. For example, if during the debugging phase of your program development, you include a call

```
rgen.setSeed(1);
```

at the beginning of your program, that program will replay the same set of values every time it is run. If you set the seed to something else, the program will step through a different sequence of random values but will still behave deterministically. Before you ship your Monopoly program to the world, you will of course want to remove this statement, but it can be a enormous help when you're trying to get things to work.

6.2 The javadoc **documentation system**

The method summary of the **RandomGenerator** class presented in Figure 6-1 is sufficient for many applications but does not represent a complete description of the class. For one thing, the **RandomGenerator** class also includes a few specialized methods that novices are unlikely to use but that may be important for more sophisticated users. For another, the descriptions given in Figure 6-1 are limited to the method header and a one-sentence summary. If you needed more detail about one of these methods, you would have to look elsewhere for that information. In the early years of computing before the development of modern object-oriented languages, the ultimate source for such additional information would have been the code that implemented the **RandomGenerator** class. Looking at that code, however, is not an attractive prospect. If you are interested only in using the facilities of a class, you are unlikely to care about how that class is actually implemented. The code brings that implementation to the fore where its plethora of details can easily get in the way of discovering what you really need to know. There has to be a better way.

Before discussing the approach Java has adopted to separate the general documentation from the details of the underlying implementation, it is useful to introduce two terms that express the difference in perspective between programmers who implement a class and those who use it. Naturally enough, a programmer who implements a class is called an **implementor.** Because the word *user* refers to someone who runs a program rather than someone who writes part of one, computer scientists have adopted the term **client** to refer to a programmer who makes use of the facilities provided by an implementor. As a client, you don't need to know the details of how a class works but do need to know what public methods it contains. As an implementor, your job is to hide as many details of the implementation from the client as possible, releasing only the information that clients absolutely need.

In the Java world, clients are not expected to look at the code to understand how to use a particular class. What clients usually do instead is consult the web-based documentation for a class, which is produced automatically by a tool called **javadoc.** The **javadoc** system, which is provided as part of the standard Java Development Kit from Sun, reads through the code for a package and creates documentation for each of the classes it contains.

Figure 6-4 shows the **javadoc** page for the **RandomGenerator** class. As you can see, many of the words in the **javadoc** descriptions are **hyperlinks** that take you to other pages or to specific entries on this page. These hyperlinks, which are produced automatically by the **javadoc** system, make it much easier to negotiate the documentation.

FIGURE 6-4 The javadoc page for RandomGenerator

Overview Package **Student** Complete Tree Index Help
PREV CLASS NEXT CLASS   FRAMES NO FRAMES
SUMMARY: FIELD | CONSTR | METHOD   DETAIL: FIELD | CONSTR | METHOD

---

acm.util
Class RandomGenerator

java.lang.Object
  |
  +--java.util.Random
        |
        +--acm.util.RandomGenerator

`public class RandomGenerator extends Random`

This class implements a simple random number generator that allows clients to generate pseudorandom integers, doubles, booleans, and colors. To use it, the first step is to declare an instance variable to hold the random generator as follows:

```
private RandomGenerator rgen = RandomGenerator.getInstance();
```

By default, this `RandomGenerator` object is initialized to begin at an unpredictable point in a pseudorandom sequence. During debugging, it is often useful to set the internal seed for the random generator explicitly so that it always returns the same sequence. To do so, you need to invoke the setSeed method.

The `RandomGenerator` object returned by `getInstance` is shared across all classes in an application. Using this shared instance of the generator is preferable to allocating new instances of `RandomGenerator`. If you create several random generators in succession, they will typically generate the same sequence of values.

Constructor Summary

RandomGenerator()	
	Creates a new random generator.

Method Summary

RandomGenerator	getInstance()
	This method returns a `RandomGenerator` instance that can be shared among several classes.
boolean	nextBoolean(double p)
	Returns a random `boolean` value with the specified probability.
Color	nextColor()
	Returns a random opaque Color whose components are chosen uniformly in the 0-255 range.
double	nextDouble(double low, double high)
	Returns the next random real number in the specified range.
int	nextInt(int low, int high)
	Returns the next random integer in the specified range.

Inherited Method Summary

boolean	nextBoolean()
	Returns a random boolean that is true 50 percent of the time.
double	nextDouble()
	Returns a random double d in the range $0 \leq d < 1$.
int	nextInt(int n)
	Returns a random integer k in the range $0 \leq k < n$.
void	setSeed(long seed)
	Sets a new starting point for the random generator sequence.

FIGURE 6-4   The javadoc page for RandomGenerator (continued)

Constructor Detail

`public RandomGenerator()`

> Creates a new random generator. Most clients will not use the constructor directly but will instead call `getInstance` to obtain a `RandomGenerator` object that is shared by all classes in the application.
>
> **Usage:**   `RandomGenerator rgen = new RandomGenerator();`

Method Detail

`public static RandomGenerator getInstance()`

> This method returns a `RandomGenerator` instance that can be shared among several classes.
>
> **Usage:**   `RandomGenerator rgen = RandomGenerator.getInstance();`
> **Returns:**   A shared `RandomGenerator` object

`public boolean nextBoolean(double p)`

> Returns a random `boolean` value with the specified probability. You can use this method to simulate an event that occurs with a particular probability. For example, you could simulate the result of tossing a coin like this:
>
> `String coinFlip = rgen.nextBoolean(0.5) ? "HEADS" : "TAILS";`
>
> **Usage:**   `if (rgen.nextBoolean(p)) . . .`
> **Parameter:** `p` A value between 0 (impossible) and 1 (certain) indicating the probability
> **Returns:**   The value `true` with probability `p`

`public Color nextColor()`

> Returns a random opaque `Color` whose components are chosen uniformly in the 0-255 range.
>
> **Usage:**   `Color color = rgen.newColor()`
> **Returns:**   A random opaque `Color`

`public double nextDouble(double low, double high)`

> Returns the next random real number in the specified range. The resulting value is always at least `low` but always strictly less than `high`. You can use this method to generate continuous random values. For example, you can set the variables `x` and `y` to specify a random point inside the unit square as follows:
>
> `double x = rgen.nextDouble(0.0, 1.0);`
> `double y = rgen.nextDouble(0.0, 1.0);`
>
> **Usage:**   `double d = rgen.nextDouble(low, high)`
> **Parameters:** `low` The low end of the range
>   `high` The high end of the range
> **Returns:**   A random `double` value d in the range $low \le d < high$

`public int nextInt(int low, int high)`

> Returns the next random integer in the specified range. For example, you can generate the roll of a six-sided die by calling
>
> `rgen.nextInt(1, 6);`
>
> or a random decimal digit by calling
>
> `rgen.nextInt(0, 9);`
>
> **Usage:**   `int k = rgen.nextInt(low, high)`
> **Parameters:** `low` The low end of the range
>   `high` The high end of the range
> **Returns:**   The next random `int` between `low` and `high`, inclusive

If you look at the beginning of the **javadoc** description in Figure 6-4, you will discover that the **RandomGenerator** class in the **acm.util** package is a subclass of the **Random** class in **java.util**. Like any subclass, **RandomGenerator** inherits the methods of its superclass. The method summary in Figure 6-4 makes this inheritance explicit. Although some methods, such as **nextColor**, are defined by the **RandomGenerator** class itself, other methods, such as the simple version of **nextBoolean** that returns **true** 50 percent of the time, are inherited from **Random**. For the most part, it doesn't matter at all which of these two classes actually implements a particular method. All that matters to you as a client of **RandomGenerator** is that you have ready access to the complete set of methods.

The **Random** and **RandomGenerator** classes illustrate a common situation in object-oriented programming in which a class provides some but not all of the functionality you need. Defining a subclass allows you to extend those capabilities because the new class inherits the methods of the old one. You can then repeat the process so that a class inherits behavior from an entire chain of superclasses. Because each new class builds on the framework provided by its predecessors, such hierarchies are referred to as **layered abstractions.**

6.3 Defining your own classes

At least to a certain extent, the prospect of defining your own classes in Java should not be a particularly daunting prospect. You have, after all, been defining your own classes ever since Chapter 2. Every program is a class definition that extends one of the **Program** subclasses, which means that you have seen enough examples to get a sense of the basic structure of class definitions. The purpose of this section and the examples in the sections that follow is to fill in the details about how class definitions in Java work.

The structure of a class definition

Syntax for a public class definition

```
public class name extends super {
    class body
}
```

where:
   name is the name of the new class
   super is the name of the superclass
   class body is a sequence of definitions
      that typically includes constructors,
      methods, named constants, and
      instance variables

The syntactic structure of a class definition is shown in the box on the left. In Java, every class that is available for use by clients—as opposed to being defined only within the context of a package—must be marked with the keyword **public**. Each public class definition, moreover, should be in a separate source file called *name*.**java** where *name* is the name of the new class.

The **extends** specification indicates the superclass from which the class extends. This specification is optional; if it is missing, the new class becomes a direct subclass of the built-in **Object** class, which is the root of Java's class hierarchy. If you start with any class and follow the chain that begins with its superclass and continues through the succession of superclasses, those chains always end at the **Object** class. Thus, every Java class is—directly or indirectly—a subclass of **Object**. Moreover, any object in Java is therefore an instance of the **Object** class.

The body of the class consists of a sequence of definitions of various kinds, which are collectively called **entries.** In the classes you have seen so far, these definitions have been limited to methods and named constants. In addition, classes often contain **constructors,** which specify how to create new instances of the class, and **instance variables,** which maintain the state of the objects. Constructors are defined the same way as methods, with two exceptions: (1) the name of the constructor is always the same as that of the class, and (2) a constructor does not specify a result type. Instance variable declarations look much like any other variable declaration except that they appear at the top level of a class rather than inside a method definition. Instance variables are defined in much the same way as variable definitions in a method except that they occur at the level of the class as a whole.

Controlling the visibility of entries

The entries in a class definition are typically marked with a keyword to indicate what classes have access to those entries. In Java, you can use one of three keywords to control access to the individual entries within a class:

- `public`—Visible to every class in the program
- `private`—Visible only within the class that defines it
- `protected`—Visible only to subclasses and classes in the same package

There is also a fourth option, which is to omit this keyword entirely. Entries written without this keyword are called **package-private** and are visible only to classes in the same package, but not to subclasses in other packages.

Although protected and package-private entries have their uses, the examples in this book use only the `public` and `private` options. Entries that are designated as `public` are said to be **exported.** As a general rule, you should designate entries as `private` unless there is a compelling reason for exporting them.

Encapsulation

One of the most important functions of a class is to combine related pieces of data into a single unit. When you work with data in the real world, individual data values typically tend to combine in ways that form larger conceptual structures. As a simple example, the x and y coordinate values you use to refer to coordinate positions in the `acm.graphics` package rarely appear independently. In almost all cases, you end up supplying both an x and a y value at the same time. Conceptually, the two values together represent a *point* in the graphical space. As you will discover in Chapter 9, the `acm.graphics` package includes a class called `GPoint`, which combines an x and a y coordinate into a structure that you can then manipulate as a single unit. You can, for example, determine the location of any graphical object by calling `getLocation`, which returns a `GPoint` object. Working with that `GPoint` is often much more convenient than manipulating two separate variables, one for each coordinate.

Combining several data values into a single object is part of the process that computer scientists refer to as **encapsulation.** Metaphorically, the process of aggregating data in this way is similar to putting objects into a capsule. The objects are still present inside the capsule, but you can now work with the collection as a whole. In the real world, for example, you could take the capsule and ship it to someone half a world away, who could then unpack the capsule to recover the contents. In the programming domain, the situation is similar in that you can combine individual data values into a new encapsulated object and then pass that object to a method as a single value. If necessary, the method can open up the object to recover the original data values, but it can also work with the encapsulated object as a whole.

The word *encapsulation,* however, has an additional implication in computer science, just as it does in English. Although combining data values into an integrated unit is an essential part of the process, the idea of encapsulation also suggests that the contents are protected in some way. Just as a space capsule protects its occupants from the dangers of outer space, a well-designed encapsulated object generally protects its elements from the dangers of undisciplined access by other parts of the program. The examples in the remainder of this chapter highlight this aspect of the encapsulation process along with the more general issues of how to write class definitions in Java.

6.4 Representing student information

To get a sense of how class definitions work, the best approach is to look at an example. Imagine that the administrative computing department at your university has asked you to implement a new Java-based system to keep track of which students are able to graduate. A central element of that implementation is a class called **Student**, which keeps track of the information necessary to make that determination. Although an actual implementation of a **Student** class would almost certainly contain more detail, you have been asked to include only the following pieces of data:

- The name of the student
- The student's six-digit ID number
- The number of credits the student has earned (which at this university may need to include digits after the decimal point to account for half- and quarter-credit courses)
- A flag indicating whether the student has paid all university fees

Students are eligible to graduate only if they have earned the requisite number of credits and have no outstanding bills.

Declaring instance variables

As you begin to design the structure of the **Student** class, one of the first questions to answer is what instance variables you need to store the state of each object. According to the specifications in the introduction to this section, each **Student** object must contain four pieces of information. You can, moreover, represent each of these data values using Java's predefined types. You can use a **String** to represent the student's name, an **int** for the ID number, a **double** for the number of credits, and a **boolean** to indicate whether all the bills have been paid. Thus, you can keep track of the state of a **Student** object using four instance variables, as follows:

```
private String studentName;
private int studentID;
private double creditsEarned;
private boolean paidUp;
```

These declarations are similar to the declarations of local variables except in two respects. First, they appear at a different point in the file. Local variables are defined in the body of a method and can be used only within that method. Instance variables are defined outside of any method and can be used by any method defined within the class. Second, instance variable declarations typically include a keyword to indicate the extent to which that variable is visible to methods in other classes. Although Java offers the four visibility options described in the section on "Controlling the visibility of entries" earlier in this chapter, there are significant advantages in declaring all instance variables using the keyword **private**. The primary reason for doing so grows out of the fact that encapsulation is as much a strategy for protecting data as it is for aggregating it. By disallowing access to the internal instance variables, the designers of a class can protect its integrity. As an example, it would be dangerous to allow clients of the **Student** class to change the student name and ID number independently. In most universities, students keep the same ID number throughout their entire time at that institution. If other parts of the overall record-keeping system are able to give a new ID to an existing student, the integrity of the stored information becomes more difficult to maintain. Designating these instance variables as private makes it impossible for other classes in the system to change these values without relying on the methods provided by the designers of the **Student** class.

In fact, the advantages of private instance variables are so compelling that all instance variables in this book—and indeed all instance variables used in the implementation of the ACM libraries—are marked using the keyword **private**. Although public instance variables have occasional uses, you will develop better programming habits if you try to maintain the convention of using only private instance variables.

> **COMMON PITFALLS**
>
> When you declare instance variables in a class, it is almost always best to declare those variables as **private**. Restricting instance variables to the methods of the class in which they appear reduces the chance that the information becomes compromised.

Completing the class definition

Instance variables, however, represent only one part of the class definition. As noted in the section on "Defining your own classes" earlier in this chapter, class definitions typically contain constructors, methods, and named constant definitions along with the declaration of instance variables. A complete definition of the **Student** class, which contains at least one example of each of these entry types, appears in Figure 6-5.

| FIGURE 6-5 | Definition of a student information class |

```java
/**
 * The Student class keeps track of the following pieces of data
 * about a student: the student's name, ID number, the number of
 * credits the student has earned toward graduation, and whether
 * the student is paid up with respect to university bills.
 * All of this information is entirely private to the class.
 * Clients can obtain this information only by using the various
 * methods defined by the class.
 */

public class Student {

/**
 * Creates a new Student object with the specified name and ID.
 * @param name The student's name as a String
 * @param id The student's ID number as an int
 */
    public Student(String name, int id) {
        studentName = name;
        studentID = id;
    }

/**
 * Gets the name of this student.
 * @return The name of this student
 */
    public String getName() {
        return studentName;
    }

/**
 * Gets the ID number of this student.
 * @return The ID number of this student
 */
    public int getID() {
        return studentID;
    }

/**
 * Sets the number of credits earned.
 * @param credits The new number of credits earned
 */
    public void setCredits(double credits) {
        creditsEarned = credits;
    }
```

[handwritten annotation pointing to constructor line: "Constructor: • name of class used as constructor name • does'nt specify return type • initializes object. • called when object is created"]

FIGURE 6-5	**Definition of a student information class** (continued)

```java
/**
 * Gets the number of credits earned.
 * @return The number of credits this student has earned
 */
   public double getCredits() {
      return creditsEarned;
   }

/**
 * Sets whether the student is paid up.
 * @param flag The value true or false indicating paid-up status
 */
   public void setPaidUp(boolean flag) {
      paidUp = flag;
   }

/**
 * Returns whether the student is paid up.
 * @return Whether the student is paid up
 */
   public boolean isPaidUp() {
      return paidUp;
   }

/**
 * Creates a string identifying this student.
 * @return The string used to display this student
 */
   public String toString() {
      return studentName + " (#" + studentID + ")";
   }

/* Public constants */

/** The number of credits required for graduation */
   public static final double CREDITS_TO_GRADUATE = 32.0;

/* Private instance variables */

   private String studentName;   /* The student's name          */
   private int studentID;        /* The student's ID number     */
   private double creditsEarned; /* The number of credits earned */
   private boolean paidUp;       /* Whether student is paid up   */

}
```

If you consider only the size of Figure 6-5, you can easily get the idea that the **Student** class—which is, after all, the first programming example to take up more than a page—is somehow more complicated than the examples you have seen in the earlier chapters. Nothing could be further from the truth. If you read through the code more closely, you will discover that the constructor is only two lines long and that the body of every other method contains just a single line. The bulk of the space is taken up by comments. Worse still, the text of those comments seems incredibly repetitive. The comments for the method **isPaidUp**, for example, read like this:

```
/**
 * Returns whether the student is paid up.
 * @return Whether the student is paid up
 */
```

Surely, one would think, the first line is enough to get the point across.

Writing javadoc comments

In fact, the code in Figure 6-5 exemplifies a coding style that is extremely useful in Java development. Although the change is subtle, you may have noticed that the comments for the public methods and constants in the **Student** class begin with the characters **/**** instead of the more conventional **/*** used to mark comments. Such comments are intended not only for the human reader, but also for the **javadoc** documentation system described earlier in this chapter. The Java compiler ignores the comment text, just as it always does. If, however, you run this program through the **javadoc** application that comes with the standard Java tools, it will automatically create a web page that describes the class along the lines shown in Figure 6-4. The **javadoc** application reads the comments and the code together to create a standardized description of a class.

The summary section of the **javadoc** entry for a method shows the header line for the method along with the first sentence in the comment. The detail section of the **javadoc** entry also shows the header line along with the full text of the comment. In addition, the detail section includes a description of each parameter that the method accepts and the result it produces. These descriptions are taken from the **@param** and **@result** tags that appear in the **javadoc** comment. It is useful to get in the habit of including these tags as you write your code, both because doing so makes it easier to generate the automatic documentation and because these markers provide useful information to readers of your code.

Writing the constructor

The constructor for the **Student** class looks like this:

```
public Student(String name, int id) {
   studentName = name;
   studentID = id;
}
```

As noted in the section on "Defining your own classes" earlier in the chapter, the constructor has the same form as a method definition except that it lacks a result type. Clients invoke the constructor by writing the keyword **new**, the name of the class, and a list of arguments that match the parameter list. Thus, another part of the program could create a student entry using a declaration like this:

```
Student topStudent = new Student("Hermione Granger", 314159);
```

This statement declares a variable named **topStudent** and assigns it the result of invoking the **Student** constructor with the specified arguments. The constructor creates a new **Student** object and assigns the parameter values to the instance variables **studentName** and **studentID** respectively. Thus, the **studentName** instance variable is assigned the string **"Hermione Granger"**, and the **studentID** variable gets the value 314159. The remaining instance variables are assigned default values appropriate to their type. The **creditsEarned** variable is initialized to zero, and the **paidUp** variable is initialized to **false**.

In this implementation of the **Student** constructor, the identifier names used for the parameters and the instance variables are different. Some Java programmers prefer to use the same identifier names, because both the parameter name and instance variable name refer to the same value. It is not possible, however, to code the constructor as

```
public Student(String studentName, int studentID)
   studentName = studentName;
   studentID = studentID;
}
```

When the Java compiler translates this code, it will interpret both sides of each assignment statement as a parameter name. Thus, the code for this incorrect version of the constructor will simply take the value of the **studentName** variable and assign it to that variable itself. If you want to use the same names for both a parameter and an instance variable, you need some way to differentiate the two. In Java, the easiest way to make this distinction is to use the keyword **this**, which refers to the current object. You can therefore correct the buggy implementation of the constructor by changing it to

```
public Student(String studentName, int studentID)
   this.studentName = studentName;
   this.studentID = studentID;
}
```

After making this change, the Java compiler can tell that the variables on the left side of the assignment statements are the instance variables belonging to this object.

The only problem with the strategy of using the same name for parameters and instance variables is that some Java compilers issue a warning message whenever a parameter name matches the name of an instance variable. To avoid triggering such warnings, the code in this text and in the ACM libraries always uses distinct names in this situation.

Getters and setters

Most of the methods in the **Student** class are used either to retrieve the value of an instance variable or to change it to a different value. For example, you can get the name of the student stored in the variable **topStudent** by calling

```
String name = topStudent.getName();
```

or set the number of credits for **topStudent** to 97 by calling

```
topStudent.setCredits(97);
```

Methods whose only function is to retrieve the value of an instance variable or to assign it some new value are called **getters** and **setters,** respectively. (In formal writing about Java, such methods tend to be called *accessor* and *mutator* methods, but far fewer people will have any idea what you mean if you use these fancy-sounding terms.) By convention, getters begin with the prefix **get**, and setters begin with the prefix **set**, as illustrated by the examples in the implementation of the **Student** class. The only exception to this naming convention, which also appears in the example, is for getters that return a value of type **boolean**, which were defined in Chapter 5 as *predicate methods*. For methods that retrieve a Boolean value, the getter conventionally begins with the prefix **is**. Thus, even though you would set the flag showing that **topStudent** was paid up by calling

```
topStudent.setPaidUp(true);
```

the code that tests that condition would call something like

```
if (topStudent.isPaidUp()) . . .
```

Boolean values, after all, are used to represent the answer to yes-or-no questions, and the naming convention makes the program extremely easy to read.

It is important to note that the implementation of the **Student** class does not include setters for either the student name or the student ID. These values are set only by the constructor and cannot be changed thereafter. This design makes it impossible to break the association between the name of a student and that student's ID number, which is not supposed to change.

The **toString** method

The only method in the implementation of the **Student** class that is not a getter or a setter is the **toString** method, which has the responsibility of converting the value of an object into a string that human readers can understand. The **toString** method has a special role in Java. Whenever Java needs to convert an object into a string—which occurs most often in expressions that use the **+** operator to signify concatenation—it does so by calling the object's **toString** method. For example (assuming that the variable **topStudent** is still initialized to represent Hermione Granger as it was earlier in the chapter), executing the line

```
    println("Top student = " + topStudent);
```

would produce the following output:

```
┌─────────────────────────────────────────────────┐
│  ⊖ ⊙ ⊖              StudentToString              │
├─────────────────────────────────────────────────┤
│  Top student = Hermione Granger (#314159)      ▲ │
│                                                ▲ │
│                                                ▼ │
│  ◀ ▶                                           // │
└─────────────────────────────────────────────────┘
```

Had you left out the implementation of the **toString** method, Java would instead use the default definition of the **toString** method from the **Object** class. The result in that case would be something like

```
┌─────────────────────────────────────────────────┐
│  ⊖ ⊙ ⊖              StudentToString              │
├─────────────────────────────────────────────────┤
│  Top student = Student@1758942                 ▲ │
│                                                ▲ │
│                                                ▼ │
│  ◀ ▶                                           // │
└─────────────────────────────────────────────────┘
```

which is rather less informative. The string of digits in the output—which might differ from computer to computer—has nothing to do with Hermione's student ID number but is instead an internal code through which Java can identify the object.

Supplying a definition for **toString** in the **Student** class means that this new definition takes precedence over the original definition in the **Object** class. In object-oriented programming, that process is called **overriding.** The mechanics of overriding methods are discussed in more detail in the section entitled "Rules for inherited methods" later in this chapter.

Defining named constants in a class

Many classes export definitions of named constants along with other entry types. Because named constants cannot be changed by clients, there is little danger in making them public. Doing so means that clients of the exporting class can use that constant in their own code. To do so, the client writes the class name, a dot, and the name of the constant.

One easily appreciated example of an exported constant is **PI**, which is defined as follows in the **Math** class in **java.lang**:

```
public static final double PI = 3.14159265358979323846;
```

Because this definition is marked as **public**, every class has access to the mathematical value of π by writing **Math.PI**. Other examples that you have seen include the constants in the **Color** class, such as **Color.GREEN** and **Color.MAGENTA**, which have objects as their values rather than primitive types.

The definition of the **Student** class exports a named constant that specifies the number of credits a student needs to graduate:

```
public static final double CREDITS_TO_GRADUATE = 32.0;
```

As with any named constant, including this definition offers two advantages. First, the code that uses it tends to be easier to read, assuming that the name of the constant is chosen so that its meaning is self-explanatory. Second, that code becomes easier to maintain, because it is possible to change the number of credits required for graduation in a single place within the program.

Using the Student class

Although it is difficult to write interesting applications involving **Student** objects until you know how to represent an entire list of students, it is still possible to see how a client programmer might write a method that makes use of the **Student** class. The following method takes a **Student** object and determines whether that student meets the conditions for graduation:

```
private boolean isEligibleToGraduate(Student student) {
    return student.getCredits() >= Student.CREDITS_TO_GRADUATE
            && student.isPaidUp();
}
```

6.5 Rational numbers

Although the **Student** class defined in the preceding section illustrates the basic mechanics of classes, developing a solid understanding of the topic requires you to consider a more sophisticated example. To get a sense of the importance of the specific example, imagine yourself back in elementary school facing the problem of adding the following fractions:

$$\frac{1}{2} + \frac{1}{3} + \frac{1}{6} = 1$$

Basic arithmetic—or even a little intuition—makes it clear that the mathematically exact answer is 1, but that answer might be difficult to obtain using double-precision arithmetic on a computer. Consider, for example, the following **run** method:

```
public void run() {
    double sum = 1.0/2.0 + 1.0/3.0 + 1.0/6.0;
    println("1.0/2.0 + 1.0/3.0 + 1.0/6.0 = " + sum);
}
```

If you executed a Java program containing this **run** method, you would get the following output:

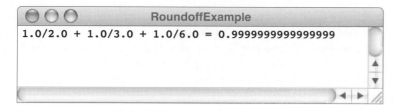

Although the result of 0.9999999999999999 is certainly close enough for practical purposes, your elementary school teacher would surely suspect that you used a calculating device if you gave this answer in class.

The problem is that the memory cells used to store numbers inside a computer have a limited storage capacity, which in turn restricts the precision they can offer. Within the limits of double-precision arithmetic, the sum of one-half plus one-third plus one-sixth is 0.9999999999999999, even though such an answer is not mathematically satisfying. To get an exact answer you need to move out of the realm of double-precision numbers and into the domain of **rational numbers,** which are those values that can be represented as the quotient of two integers. Rational numbers are well understood as a mathematical concept and have their own arithmetic rules, which are summarized in Figure 6-6. Unfortunately, Java does not include rational numbers among its predefined types. To use rational arithmetic in Java, you have to define a new class to represent them.

If you were able to define a **Rational** class, you could use it in Java programs to perform mathematically precise calculations. For example, the following **run** method would perform the fraction calculation used in the earlier examples:

```java
public void run() {
   Rational a = new Rational(1, 2);
   Rational b = new Rational(1, 3);
   Rational c = new Rational(1, 6);
   Rational sum = a.add(b).add(c);
   println(a + " + " + b + " + " + c + " = " + sum);
}
```

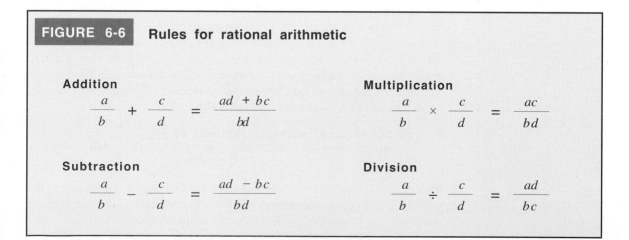

FIGURE 6-6   Rules for rational arithmetic

Addition

$$\frac{a}{b} + \frac{c}{d} = \frac{ad + bc}{bd}$$

Multiplication

$$\frac{a}{b} \times \frac{c}{d} = \frac{ac}{bd}$$

Subtraction

$$\frac{a}{b} - \frac{c}{d} = \frac{ad - bc}{bd}$$

Division

$$\frac{a}{b} \div \frac{c}{d} = \frac{ad}{bc}$$

The code declares three variables—**a**, **b**, and **c**—and initializes them to the rational values corresponding to the fractions in the calculation. The next line then declares the variable **sum** and initializes it to the sum of **a**, **b**, and **c**. The only possible source of confusion in this line is that addition for the **Rational** class must be expressed using the **add** method because the **+** operator is defined only for the primitive types. The last line then prints the three values and their sum. The output of this program—assuming that the **Rational** class operates as it should—looks like this:

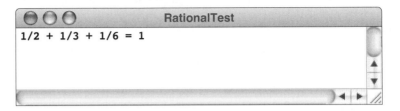

Figure 6-7 shows a scaled-down implementation of a **Rational** class that implements the four basic arithmetic operations: addition, subtraction, multiplication, and division. Much of the class definition is straightforward, but the code does illustrate several new features, as follows:

- *Multiple constructors.* The **Rational** class in Figure 6-7 defines three different constructors. Calling **new Rational()** creates a new rational number whose value is 0, which is represented internally as the fraction 0 / 1. Calling **new Rational(***n***)** creates a new rational number equal to the integer *n*, which is simply the fraction *n* / 1. Finally, calling **new Rational(***x***,** *y***)** creates a new rational number equal to the fraction *x* / *y*. Java can tell which constructor to call by looking at the arguments provided by the client. Constructors and methods that have multiple argument forms under the same name are said to be **overloaded.**

- *New uses for the keyword **this**.* As you know from the discussion of the **Student** class earlier in this chapter, Java defines the keyword **this** to mean the current object. This **Rational** class uses the keyword **this** in two new ways. The first appears in the constructors, which use **this** to delegate the creation of this object to another version of the constructor with a different set of arguments. The second appears in the methods that perform arithmetic, where **this** is used to emphasize that the **num** and **den** instance variables are the ones in the current rational number. Consider, for example, the definition of the **multiply** method, which looks like this:

```
public Rational multiply(Rational r) {
    return new Rational(this.num * r.num, this.den * r.den);
}
```

This method generates a new **Rational** value whose numerator is the product of this object's numerator and **r**'s numerator and whose denominator is likewise the product of the denominators of these same two objects.

FIGURE 6-7 Definition of a class to represent rational numbers

```java
/**
 * The Rational class is used to represent rational numbers, which
 * are defined to be the quotient of two integers.
 */
public class Rational {

/** Creates a new Rational initialized to zero. */
   public Rational() {
      this(0);
   }

/**
 * Creates a new Rational from the integer argument.
 * @param n The initial value
 */
   public Rational(int n) {
      this(n, 1);
   }

/**
 * Creates a new Rational with the value x / y.
 * @param x The numerator of the rational number
 * @param y The denominator of the rational number
 */
   public Rational(int x, int y) {
      int g = gcd(Math.abs(x), Math.abs(y));
      num = x / g;
      den = Math.abs(y) / g;
      if (y < 0) num = -num;
   }

/**
 * Adds the rational number r to this one and returns the sum.
 * @param r The rational number to be added
 * @return The sum of the current number and r
 */
   public Rational add(Rational r) {
      return new Rational(this.num * r.den + r.num * this.den,
                          this.den * r.den);
   }

/**
 * Subtracts the rational number r from this one.
 * @param r The rational number to be subtracted
 * @return The result of subtracting r from the current number
 */
   public Rational subtract(Rational r) {
      return new Rational(this.num * r.den - r.num * this.den,
                          this.den * r.den);
   }
```

FIGURE 6-7   **Definition of a class to represent rational numbers** (continued)

```java
/**
 * Multiplies this number by the rational number r.
 * @param r The rational number used as a multiplier
 * @return The result of multiplying the current number by r
 */
   public Rational multiply(Rational r) {
      return new Rational(this.num * r.num, this.den * r.den);
   }

/**
 * Divides this number by the rational number r.
 * @param r The rational number used as a divisor
 * @return The result of dividing the current number by r
 */
   public Rational divide(Rational r) {
      return new Rational(this.num * r.den, this.den * r.num);
   }

/**
 * Creates a string representation of this rational number.
 * @return The string representation of this rational number
 */
   public String toString() {
      if (den == 1) {
         return "" + num;
      } else {
         return num + "/" + den;
      }
   }

/**
 * Calculates the greatest common divisor using Euclid's algorithm.
 * @param x First integer
 * @param y Second integer
 * @return The greatest common divisor of x and y
 */
   private int gcd(int x, int y) {
      int r = x % y;
      while (r != 0) {
         x = y;
         y = r;
         r = x % y;
      }
      return y;
   }

/* Private instance variables */
   private int num;    /* The numerator of this Rational   */
   private int den;    /* The denominator of this Rational */

}
```

- *Public and private methods together in one class.* The public methods in the **Rational** class are those that clients of the class will need to call. These include the constructors, the methods that implement the arithmetic operators, and the **toString** method described in the preceding point. This class, however, also includes a private method used in its own implementation that does not need to be exported to clients. That method is the **gcd** function from Chapter 5 that implements Euclid's algorithm and is used here to reduce the fraction to lowest terms. As a general rule, you should mark methods as **private** whenever you can.

- *Converting an integer to a string.* The implementation of the **toString** method converts the value of a **Rational** number to a string in one of two ways. In most cases, it creates a string by concatenating the numerator and denominator with a slash between them by evaluating the expression

      num + "/" + den

  In the special case that the denominator is 1, the **Rational** number is really an integer, and the **toString** method leaves out the slash and the denominator. It would not, however, be possible simply to return the value of **num** because that is an **int** rather than a **String**. Although there are other ways to convert an integer to a string, most Java programmers adopt the shorthand form

      "" + num

  which concatenates the value of **num** with a string that contains no characters at all.

The **Rational** class provides even more evidence in support of keeping instance variables private. While it might be useful to some clients to be able to obtain the numerator and denominator of a rational number **r** by selecting the **r.num** and **r.den** variables within the object, making these variables public compromises the integrity of the class. The implementation of the **Rational** class ensures that the following properties are maintained:

1. The denominator of the rational number is always positive. If the denominator is negative, the constructor transfers the sign to the numerator by negating that value.

2. The fraction represented by the numerator and denominator is always reduced to lowest terms by dividing both parts of the fraction by their greatest common divisor. This design decision ensures that rational numbers are always displayed in their simplest form.

Properties that are guaranteed to be true throughout a body of code are called **invariants.** Maintaining these invariants is possible only if the class can guard against clients that accidentally or maliciously undermine them. If the instance variables were public, any client could violate the first invariant of rational number **r** by setting **r.den** to 0 or violate the second invariant in any number of ways.

The implementation of the **Rational** class in Figure 6-7 actually goes even further to preserve the invariants of the class. Declaring the instance variables as private ensures that clients cannot assign new values to them in an assignment statement. If you look carefully at the methods—as opposed to the constructors—in the **Rational** class, you will discover that none of them ever assign values to these instance variables either. Once instance variables have been assigned values by the constructor, those values can never be changed during the lifetime of the object. Classes whose internal state cannot be changed by the client, even through method calls, are said to be **immutable.** Immutable types have several extremely useful properties and will come up quite often in subsequent chapters.

6.6 Extending existing classes

If you look back at the definitions of the **Student** and **Rational** classes presented earlier in this chapter, you will discover that neither of the header lines includes an **extends** clause to specify a superclass. As a result, each of these classes becomes a direct subclass of Java's built-in **Object** class. This situation is a little unusual. In most cases, the new classes you define will extend an existing class, which enables the new class to inherit the superclass behavior. The new class typically extends that behavior by defining new methods and may also modify the behavior of the superclass by redefining existing methods. Because the process of extending an class is fundamental to Java's object-oriented structure, it is important to understand what happens when a new class extends an existing one.

Creating a class to represent filled rectangles

In Chapter 5, you learned how to use methods to simplify the creation of graphical objects that share a particular set of properties. The primary example presented in that chapter is the method **createFilledCircle**, which creates a circular **GOval** object that is automatically initialized to be filled with a color specified by the caller. You can achieve much the same goal by defining a new class that extends the behavior of one of the existing **GObject** subclasses.

Suppose that you are writing a graphical application and discover that almost all the rectangles you need to display are solidly filled rather than outlined. For that application, the behavior of the **GRect** class, which uses outline form by default, is not particularly helpful. You could, of course, implement a method **createFilledRect** along the lines of the **createFilledCircle** method from Chapter 5, but you might instead choose to solve the problem in a more object-oriented way. The **acm.graphics** package provides a class called **GRect** that initially appears as an outlined rectangle. For your purposes, it would have been better if the designers of that package had also defined a class called **FilledRect** that is essentially identical to **GRect** except that the rectangle is automatically filled instead of outlined.

Even though the designers of **acm.graphics** did not include a **FilledRect** class, there is nothing to prevent you from defining one. Intuitively, the new class is pretty much the same as the existing **GRect** class; the only difference is in the initialization. Instead of setting the filling indicator to be **false** in the way the **GRect** constructor does, the constructor for the **FilledRect** class would set it to be **true**. All the other methods in the **GRect** class would stay the same. In Java, the problem of keeping all the other methods the same is simple. All you have to do is make **FilledRect** be a subclass of **GRect**, and it will inherit the definition of every method in the **GRect** class. The header line for the class will therefore look like this:

```
public class FilledRect extends GRect
```

The only remaining question is how to change the constructor to add the necessary **setFilled** operation to the initialization code.

The first step in the process consists of deciding what you want the **FilledRect** constructor to look like in terms of its argument structure. The answer to that question comes immediately from the fact that a **FilledRect** is just a special kind of **GRect**. To create a **GRect** object, you need to supply the x and y coordinates of its upper left corner along with the width and height. The **FilledRect** constructor needs precisely the same information, so its header line must be

```
public FilledRect(double x, double y, double width,
                  double height)
```

At this point, the **FilledRect** constructor needs to invoke whatever operations the **GRect** constructor would perform to initialize its internal data structures. Those data structures represent the state of the object and are stored in instance variables. In keeping with good programming practice, those instance variables are private to the **GRect** class, which means that the **FilledRect** class can't manipulate them directly. The only thing that the **FilledRect** class can do is ask the **GRect** class to perform its standard initialization. Thus, the **FilledRect** constructor has to pass the **x, y, width**, and **height** information to the **GRect** constructor.

In Java, a class can invoke the constructor of its superclass by specifying the keyword **super** on the first line. In this context, **super** is written as if it were a method call and includes the arguments to the superclass constructor in parentheses. Since the **FilledRect** constructor wants to invoke the **GRect** constructor with exactly the arguments it received, the first line of the constructor looks like this:

```
super(x, y, width, height);
```

This line has the effect of initializing the **GRect** data structures. The **FilledRect** constructor can then continue with any further initialization required for its own operation. In this case, the only additional operation required is to set the filled state of the rectangle to **true**. The entire **FilledRect** constructor is therefore

```
public FilledRect(double x, double y, double width,
                  double height) {
   super(x, y, width, height);
   setFilled(true);
}
```

Given that all the **GRect** methods are inherited by the **FilledRect** class, you could stop at this point and include nothing in the body of the class definition beyond the new constructor. But you might also want to add some new functionality. If you tried to solve the exercises in Chapter 5 that used the **createFilledCircle** method, you probably discovered that it was quite convenient to be able to set the color of an object at the same time that you created it. To obtain the same convenience with the **FilledRect** class, you might want to add an additional constructor that took an extra argument specifying the color. As you saw in the **Rational** class presented in Figure 6-7, you can define more than one constructor as long as the Java compiler can tell which constructor you mean by looking at the arguments. If you add a new constructor that takes a fifth parameter indicating the color, Java will invoke that constructor whenever the caller supplies that argument.

One way to define the new constructor is simply to duplicate the code from the original constructor and add a **setColor** line, as follows:

```
public FilledRect(double x, double y, double width,
                              double height, Color color) {
    super(x, y, width, height);
    setFilled(true);
    setColor(color);
}
```

Although this code has the desired effect, it is not the optimal design. The problem is that the two constructors contain some duplicated code. Although the amount of duplication is admittedly small in this case, defining these two constructors independently can easily lead to maintenance problems. At some point in the future, someone might decide to add additional features to the **FilledRect** class. It is certainly possible that some of those extensions would require adding to the initialization code that occurs in the constructor. As things stand, anyone wanting to make those extensions would have to remember to incorporate those changes into both constructors. Such situations in which duplicated code forces maintainers to update the code in multiple places is a common source of trouble over the life cycle of a program.

If you take a closer look at the new constructor that includes the color argument, you will see that it divides into two conceptual pieces, as illustrated by the following definition, which is expressed in a combination of Java and English commonly known as **pseudocode:**

```
public FilledRect(double x, double y, double width,
                              double height, Color color) {
    Create a filled rectangle object using the first four arguments.
    Set the color of this object as indicated by the last argument.
}
```

You can rewrite the constructor so that it more closely follows this pseudocode outline. The first thing you want to do is call the original constructor for the **FilledRect** class and then set the color of this object as specified by the **color** argument. This approach leads to the following code:

```
        public FilledRect(double x, double y, double width,
                          double height, Color color) {
           this(x, y, width, height);
           setColor(color);
        }
```

The complete code for the **FilledRect** class appears in Figure 6-8. Using this class makes it possible to write some graphical programs much more compactly, as illustrated by the following **run** method:

```
        public void run() {
           double width = getWidth();
           double height = getHeight();
           double stripe = width / 3;
           add(new FilledRect(0, 0, stripe, height, Color.BLUE));
           add(new FilledRect(stripe, 0, stripe, height, Color.WHITE));
           add(new FilledRect(2 * stripe, 0, stripe, height, Color.RED));
        }
```

FIGURE 6-8   Definition of the **FilledRect** class

```
/*
 * File: FilledRect.java
 * ------------------------
 * This file defines a graphical object that appears as
 * a filled rectangle.
 */

import acm.graphics.*;
import java.awt.*;

/**
 * This class is a GObject subclass that is almost identical
 * to GRect except that it starts out filled instead of
 * outlined.
 */
public class FilledRect extends GRect {

/** Creates a new FilledRect with the specified bounds. */
   public FilledRect(double x, double y, double width, double height) {
      super(x, y, width, height);
      setFilled(true);
   }

/** Creates a new FilledRect with the specified bounds and color. */
   public FilledRect(double x, double y, double width, double height, Color color) {
      this(x, y, width, height);
      setColor(color);
   }

}
```

This method creates three vertical stripes, each one-third the width of the window, extending across the entire vertical space. The stripes are colored blue, white, and red, to create a picture of the French national flag:

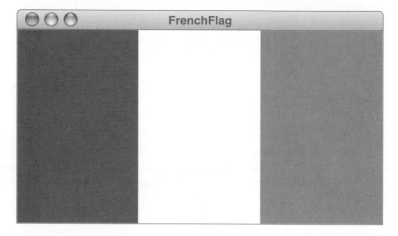

Rules for inherited constructors

Although they have much in common with methods, constructors in Java are somewhat more subtle. The reason for this subtlety comes from the fact that classes form hierarchies. Instances of the **FilledRect** class defined in the preceding section are also instances of **GRect**, **GObject**, and **Object** because each of these classes is a subclass of the next one in the list. To ensure that a new **FilledRect** object is correctly initialized, Java must make sure that the constructors for each of these classes is invoked during the construction process. The first step consists of initializing the data associated with every **Object** by calling the **Object** constructor. From there, Java must call the constructor of each subclass level, moving downward through the inheritance chain to **GObject**, **GRect**, and **FilledRect**. The **FilledRect** constructor invokes its superclass constructor explicitly, but most of the programming examples in this book have not done so. Even if that call is missing, it is essential for Java to invoke the superclass constructor to ensure that all invariants of the superclass are maintained.

To make sure that the superclass constructor is invoked, constructors in Java that don't explicitly include a call to **super** or **this** as their first line automatically act as if the constructor begins with the statement

```
super();
```

which invokes the superclass constructor with no arguments. The constructor with no arguments is called the **default constructor.** Thus, every constructor in a Java class will invoke the superclass constructor in one of three ways:

- Classes that begin with an explicit call to **this** invoke one of the other constructors for this class, delegating responsibility to that constructor for making sure that the superclass constructor gets called.

- Classes that begin with an explicit call to **super** invoke the constructor in the superclass that matches the argument list provided.

- Classes that begin with no call to either **super** or **this** invoke the default superclass constructor with no arguments.

The only remaining wrinkle lies in understanding how the superclass constructor gets defined. Just as class definitions in earlier chapters have not included explicit calls to the superclass constructor, those definitions have also not included a definition for a constructor that takes no arguments. How can Java invoke a superclass constructor if there isn't an appropriate constructor definition to call? The answer to this question is that Java automatically defines a default constructor if the class fails to define any constructors of its own. The automatically generated default constructor has an empty body, so it doesn't actually perform any initialization. Defining that constructor does, however, ensure that each class in the inheritance hierarchy has a constructor to call. Note, however, that the default constructor is not created if the class definition includes any other constructors. In such cases, the constructors for any subclasses must make explicit calls to one of the constructors in their superclass.

Rules for inherited methods

When you first encounter the concepts of inheritance and overriding, it is easy to get confused as to which version of a method should be called for a particular object. In Java, the rule is that the method that gets executed is the one that is closest in the inheritance hierarchy to the actual class of the object. Thus, given a method call to an object of class **FilledRect**, for example, the Java compiler will first look for a method with the appropriate name and argument structure in the **FilledRect** class itself. If the method is defined there, the compiler will use that version. If not, it will look for the method in the **GRect** class, which is the next class in the chain. The compiler continues in this way until it finds an appropriate definition or discovers that no such method exists.

The point that can be confusing is that Java always makes this decision on the basis of what the object actually *is* rather than on what you have declared it to be at that particular point in the program. Think back for a minute to the discussion of the **Student** class earlier in this chapter. In the section entitled "The **toString** method," you learned that calling

```
println("Top student = " + topStudent);
```

would automatically invoke the **toString** method in the **Student** class to produce the following easily readable output:

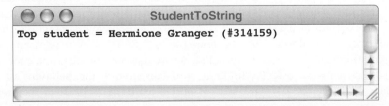

But what would happen if you instead executed the following lines?

```
Object obj = topStudent;
println("Top student = " + obj);
```

It is certainly legal to assign the **topStudent** variable to the variable **obj** because every Java class is a subclass of **Object**. The question now is which version of the **toString** method will be called when Java evaluates the argument to **println**. You know from the earlier example that **Object** has its own definition of **toString**. Given that the code is now declaring this value to be an **Object** rather than a **Student**, will Java go back to using the **Object** version of **toString** that produces such unreadable results? The answer is no. The value stored in the variable **obj** is still a **Student**, and the Java runtime system will correctly invoke the **Student** version of the method.

Although the ability to override methods provides considerable flexibility and power, it also carries with it a certain amount of risk. Suppose, for example, that you are designing a class in which one of your public methods calls another public method in the class. At the time that you write the code, you assume that the method you're calling has the particular effect that you designed. Unfortunately, if someone else declares a subclass of your class, they can invalidate that assumption by overriding the method on which your code depends. This situation can quickly become a maintenance nightmare. Worse still, if the problem occurs in privileged classes that perform operations unavailable to clients, the ability of other programmers to substitute one piece of code for another can easily become a security loophole.

As the caution box on the left suggests, it is best to use overriding sparingly and to limit your use of it to cases in which the designer of the original class has clearly allowed for that possibility. Class designers issue such invitations all the time. The comments for the **toString** method in the **Object** class, for example, begin as follows:

```
/**
 * Returns a string representation of the object. In
 * general, the toString method returns a string that
 * "textually represents" this object. The result should
 * be a concise but informative representation that is
 * easy for a person to read. It is recommended that all
 * subclasses override this method.
 */
```

The designers of the **Object** class don't merely invite you to override the **toString** method but actively recommend that you do so.

On some occasions, it is useful to be able to invoke the original definition of a method from inside the code that overrides it. This situation arises, for example, when a class defines an **init** method that performs initialization operations that are separate from those defined by the constructor. Subclasses may want to add additional initialization code, but must also ensure that any initialization code in the superclass remains in effect. In Java, you can invoke the behavior of your superclass by using the keyword **super** as if it were the receiver of the method.

COMMON PITFALLS

Be careful whenever you override a method in an existing class because your new definition can violate assumptions made by the original class. As a general rule, it makes sense to override methods only when the documentation for those methods specifically invites you to do so.

Thus, if you needed to write an extension of the **init** method provided by your superclass, you could do so by writing

```
public void init() {
    super.init();
    Code to perform any further initialization goes here.
}
```

The first line makes sure that all the initializations required for the superclass are complete, after which the method can perform any additional initialization operations required at this level.

Summary

The purpose of this chapter is to introduce the ideas of classes and objects at a holistic, conceptual level. In Java, a *class* represents a template for a set of values that have a common structure and behavior; an *object* is a particular example of that class. Thus, given a single class definition, there can be arbitrarily many *instances* of that class.

In addition to offering a more complete definition of objects and classes, this chapter includes the following important points:

- For the most part, computers operate *deterministically* in the sense that the output produced by a program is determined by its inputs, with the same inputs always generating the same results. For applications such as computer games and simulations, however, it is important to make programs operate *nondeterministically* by introducing randomness into their behavior. Because computing hardware typically does not support true randomness, most programming environments simulate random behavior by providing some method to produce *pseudorandom numbers*.
- The **acm.util** package includes a **RandomGenerator** class that offers several methods for simulating random events. The methods exported by the **RandomGenerator** class are listed in Figure 6-1.
- The **RandomGenerator** class defined in **acm.util** is actually a subclass of the **Random** class in **java.util** and therefore provides the full set of capabilities offered by the standard library class along with a few extensions. Because the new extensions of **RandomGenerator** are superimposed on top of the underlying capabilities of **Random**, these classes represent what is called a *layered abstraction*.
- Defining new classes in Java makes it possible for one programmer to provide useful services to other programmers who need to make use of those capabilities. The programmer who writes the code for the class is called the *implementor*. Programmers who use that class as a resource in programs of their own are called *clients*.
- Clients and implementors have different perspectives about a class. The client needs to know how to use the capabilities provided by a class but is generally unconcerned about the details of how those features actually work.

The implementor, by contrast, must understand those details. Moreover, to ensure that the client can work at an appropriately high level of abstraction, the implementor of a class should try to hide as much of the underlying detail as possible.

- The usual strategy for giving clients the information they need about a Java class is to use the **javadoc** documentation system. The **javadoc** application reads through the code for a class and automatically generates web pages that document the methods in that class.

- You can define your own classes by enclosing the definitions for that class in a block identified by the keyword **class**. Most class definitions specify the name of a specific superclass that the new class extends; in the absence of a specific superclass, the new class extends the **Object** class in **java.lang**, which is the root of the Java hierarchy.

- Class definitions typically contain *constructors, methods, named constants, and instance variables*. Constructors specify how to create new objects of the class, methods define the behavior of that class, named constants provide a mechanism (already discussed in Chapter 3) to assign more readable names to constant values, and instance variables allow each object to maintain its internal state. Collectively, these definitions are called *entries*.

- Each entry in a class can be marked using the keyword **public** or the keyword **private** to indicate who has access to that entry. Constructors, methods, and constants should be public only if a client would need to use them. In this book, all instance variables are private to ensure that the details of the internal state remain hidden from clients.

- A class can contain several constructors and methods with the same name as long as they have different argument structures that allow the compiler to determine which version is required. If more than one method definition exists for a particular name, that method name is said to be *overloaded*.

- A class can supply a new version of a method already defined in its superclass. This process is called *overriding*. Java always selects the version of the method that is appropriate to what the object actually is rather than what it is declared to be in that context.

- Java programmers are encouraged to override the definition of the **toString** method in every class so that the new definition produces a human-readable description of the object.

- Java defines the keyword **this** to mean the current object. You can use this keyword in expressions to refer to instance variables within the current object if there might otherwise be ambiguity. You can also use the keyword **this** in a constructor to invoke one of the other constructors for the class.

- Java defines the keyword **super** as referring to the superclass of the current object. This keyword is used to invoke constructors and methods in the superclass.

- Classes that do not allow clients to change any properties of an object once it has been created are called *immutable*. The **Rational** class in section 6-3 is an example of an immutable class, as are several of the classes introduced in later chapters.

Review questions

1. Why might it be useful for a program to behave nondeterministically?

2. What is meant by the term *pseudorandom number?*

3. This chapter encourages you to define an instance variable called **rgen** to hold the **RandomGenerator** object that generates each random value. What is the exact syntax of this line?

4. How would you use the methods in the **RandomGenerator** class to generate each of the following values?

    a) A random digit between 0 and 9
    b) A **double** between -1.0 and +1.0
    c) A **boolean** value that is **true** one-third of the time
    d) A random color value suitable for setting the color of a graphical object

5. Assuming that **d1** and **d2** have been declared as variables of type **int**, can you use the multiple assignment statement

            d1 = d2 = rgen.nextInt(1, 6);

    to simulate the process of rolling two dice?

6. In what circumstances is it useful to call the **setSeed** method?

7. Describe the differences in perspective between clients and implementors.

8. On what aspects of the design of a class do clients and implementors need to agree?

9. What is the role of the **javadoc** documentation system?

10. What is a *layered abstraction?*

11. Most class definitions include the keyword **extends** to specify the superclass. What happens if you omit this keyword?

12. What are the most common types of entries in a class definition?

13. True or false: All instance variables in this book and in the ACM library packages are defined using the keyword **private**.

14. What is the difference between *overloading* and *overriding?*

15. In Java, what do the keywords **this** and **super** signify? In what contexts are these keywords used in this chapter?

16. What property makes a class *immutable?*

17. Why is it useful to include a definition of the **toString** method in the definition of each new Java class?

Programming exercises

1. Write a program that displays the name of a card randomly chosen from a complete deck of 52 playing cards. Each card consists of a **rank** (Ace, 2, 3, 4, 5, 6, 7, 8, 9, 10, Jack, Queen, King) and a **suit** (Clubs, Diamonds, Hearts, Spades). Your program should display the complete name of the card, as shown in the following sample run:

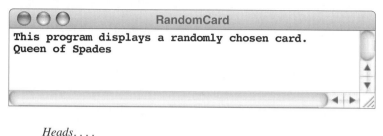

2.

> *Heads....*
> *Heads....*
> *Heads....*
> *A weaker man might be moved to re-examine his faith,*
> *if in nothing else at least in the law of probability.*
>
> —Tom Stoppard, *Rosencrantz and Guildenstern are Dead,* 1967

Write a program that simulates flipping a coin repeatedly and continues until three *consecutive* heads are tossed. At that point, your program should display the total number of times the coin was flipped. The following is one possible sample run of the program:

```
Tails
Heads
Heads
Tails
Tails
Heads
Tails
Heads
Heads
Heads
It took 10 flips to get 3 consecutive heads.
```

3. Although it is often easiest to think of random numbers in the context of games of chance, they have other, more practical uses in computer science and mathematics. For example, you can use random numbers to generate a rough approximation of the constant π by writing a simple program that simulates a dart board. Imagine that you have a dart board hanging on your wall. It consists of a circle painted on a square backdrop, as in the following diagram:

If you throw darts at this board in a random fashion, some will fall inside the circle. If the tosses are truly random, the ratio of the number of darts that land inside the circle to the total number of darts falling anywhere inside the square should be roughly equal to the ratio between the two areas. The ratio of the areas is independent of the actual size of the dart board, as illustrated by the following formula:

$$\frac{\text{darts falling inside the circle}}{\text{darts falling inside the square}} \cong \frac{\text{area of the circle}}{\text{area of the square}} = \frac{\pi r^2}{4r^2} = \frac{\pi}{4}$$

To simulate this process in a program, imagine that the dart board is drawn in the standard Cartesian coordinate plane you learned about in high school. You can model the process of throwing a dart randomly at the square by generating two random numbers, x and y, each of which lies between −1 and 1. This (x, y) point always lies somewhere inside the square. The point (x, y) lies inside the circle if

$$\sqrt{x^2 + y^2} < 1$$

You can, however, simplify this condition considerably by squaring each side of the inequality, which gives rise to the following more efficient test:

$$x^2 + y^2 < 1$$

If you perform this simulation many times and compute the fraction of darts that fall within the circle, the result will be somewhere in the neighborhood of $\pi/4$.

Write a program that simulates throwing 10,000 darts and then uses the simulation technique described in this exercise to generate and display an approximate value of π. Don't worry if your answer is correct only in the first few digits. The strategy used in this problem is not particularly accurate, even though it occasionally proves useful as a technique for making rough approximations. In mathematics, this technique is called *Monte Carlo integration*, after the gambling center that is the capital of Monaco.

4.
> *I shall never believe that God plays dice with the world.*
>
> —Albert Einstein, 1947

Despite Einstein's metaphysical objections, the current models of physics, and particularly of quantum theory, are based on the idea that nature does indeed involve random processes. A radioactive atom, for example, does not decay for any specific reason that we mortals understand. Instead, that atom has a random probability of decaying within a period of time. Sometimes it does, sometimes it doesn't, and there is no way to know for sure.

Because physicists consider radioactive decay a random process, it is not surprising that random numbers can be used to simulate the process. Suppose you start with a collection of atoms, each of which has a certain probability of decaying in any unit of time. You can then approximate the decay process by taking each atom in turn and deciding randomly whether it decays, considering the probability.

Write a program that simulates the decay of a sample that contains 10,000 atoms of radioactive material, where each atom has a 50 percent chance of decaying in a year. The output of your program should show the number of atoms remaining at the end of each year, which might look something like this:

```
● ● ●                    RadioactiveDecay
There are 10000 atoms initially
There are 4969 atoms at the end of year 1
There are 2464 atoms at the end of year 2
There are 1207 atoms at the end of year 3
There are 627 atoms at the end of year 4
There are 311 atoms at the end of year 5
There are 166 atoms at the end of year 6
There are 89 atoms at the end of year 7
There are 40 atoms at the end of year 8
There are 21 atoms at the end of year 9
There are 9 atoms at the end of year 10
There are 5 atoms at the end of year 11
There are 2 atoms at the end of year 12
There are 0 atoms at the end of year 13
```

As the numbers indicate, roughly half the atoms in the sample decay each year. In physics, the conventional way to express this observation is to say that the sample has a **half-life** of one year.

5. In casinos from Monte Carlo to Las Vegas, one of the most common gambling devices is the slot machine—the "one-armed bandit." A typical slot machine has three wheels that spin around behind a narrow window. Each wheel is marked with the following symbols: **CHERRY**, **LEMON**, **ORANGE**, **PLUM**, **BELL**, and **BAR**. The window, however, allows you to see only one symbol on each wheel at a time. For example, the window might show the following configuration:

If you put a silver dollar into a slot machine and pull the handle on its side, the wheels spin around and eventually come to rest in some new configuration. If the configuration matches one of a set of winning patterns printed on the front of the slot machine, you get back some money. If not, you're out a dollar. The following table shows a typical set of winning patterns, along with their associated payoffs:

BAR	BAR	BAR	pays	$250
BELL	BELL	BELL/BAR	pays	$20
PLUM	PLUM	PLUM/BAR	pays	$14
ORANGE	ORANGE	ORANGE/BAR	pays	$10
CHERRY	CHERRY	CHERRY	pays	$7
CHERRY	CHERRY	—	pays	$5
CHERRY	—	—	pays	$2

The notation **BELL/BAR** means that either a **BELL** or a **BAR** can appear in that position, and the dash means that any symbol at all can appear. Thus, getting a **CHERRY** in the first position is automatically good for two dollars, no matter what appears on the other wheels. The **LEMON** symbol never pays off, even if you happen to line up three of them.

Write a program that simulates playing a slot machine. Your program should provide the user with an initial stake of $50 and then let the user play until either the money runs out or the user decides to quit. During each round, your program should take away a dollar, simulate the spinning of the wheels, evaluate the result, and pay the user any appropriate winnings. For example, a user might be lucky enough to see the following sample run:

```
┌─────────────────────────────────────────────────────┐
│  ◯ ◯ ◯              SlotMachine                      │
├─────────────────────────────────────────────────────┤
│ Would you like instructions? no                      │
│ You have $50.  Would you like to play? yes           │
│ PLUM    LEMON  LEMON   -- You lose                   │
│ You have $49.  Would you like to play? yes           │
│ PLUM    BAR    LEMON   -- You lose                   │
│ You have $48.  Would you like to play? yes           │
│ BELL    LEMON  ORANGE  -- You lose                   │
│ You have $47.  Would you like to play? yes           │
│ CHERRY CHERRY ORANGE   -- You win $5                 │
│ You have $51.  Would you like to play? yes           │
│ LEMON   ORANGE BAR     -- You lose                   │
│ You have $50.  Would you like to play? yes           │
│ PLUM    BELL   PLUM    -- You lose                   │
│ You have $49.  Would you like to play? yes           │
│ BELL    BELL   BELL    -- You win $20                │
│ You have $68.  Would you like to play? no            │
└─────────────────────────────────────────────────────┘
```

Even though doing so is not realistic (and would make the slot machine unprofitable for the casino), you should assume that each of the six symbols is equally likely on each wheel.

6. As computers become more common in schools, it is important to find ways to use the machines to aid in the teaching process. This need has led to the development of an educational software industry which has produced many programs that help teach concepts to children.

   As an example of an educational application, write a program that poses a series of simple arithmetic problems for a student to answer, as illustrated by the following sample run:

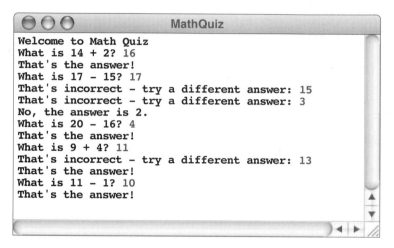

```
Welcome to Math Quiz
What is 14 + 2? 16
That's the answer!
What is 17 - 15? 17
That's incorrect - try a different answer: 15
That's incorrect - try a different answer: 3
No, the answer is 2.
What is 20 - 16? 4
That's the answer!
What is 9 + 4? 11
That's incorrect - try a different answer: 13
That's the answer!
What is 11 - 1? 10
That's the answer!
```

Your program should meet these requirements:

- It should ask a series of five questions. As with any such limit, the number of questions should be coded as a named constant so that it can easily be changed.
- Each question should consist of a single addition or subtraction problem involving just two numbers, such as "What is 2 + 3?" or "What is 11 − 7?". The type of problem—addition or subtraction—should be chosen randomly for each question.
- To make sure the problems are appropriate for students in the first or second grade, none of the numbers involved, including the answer, should be less than 0 or greater than 20. This restriction means that your program should never ask questions like "What is 11 + 13?" or "What is 4 − 7?" because the answers are outside the legal range. Within these constraints, your program should choose the numbers randomly.
- The program should give the student three chances to answer each question. If the student gives the correct answer, your program should indicate that fact in some properly congratulatory way and go on to the next question. If the student does not get the answer in three tries, the program should give the answer and go on to another problem.

7. Even though the program in exercise 6 was designed to offer encouragement when the student responds correctly, the monotonous repetition of a sentence like "That's the answer!" has the opposite effect after a while. To add variety to the interaction, modify your solution to exercise 6 so that it randomly chooses among four or five different messages when the student gets the right answer, as illustrated in this sample run:

```
○ ○ ○                MathQuiz
Welcome to Math Quiz
What is 14 + 2? 16
Correct!
What is 17 - 15? 2
You got it!
What is 20 - 16? 4
You got it!
What is 9 + 4? 13
Correct!
What is 11 - 1? 10
That's the answer!
```

8. Implement a new class called **Card** that includes the following entries:

- Named constants for the four suits (**CLUBS**, **DIAMONDS**, **HEARTS**, **SPADES**) and the four ranks that are traditionally represented in words (**ACE**, **JACK**, **QUEEN**, **KING**). The values of the rank constants should be 1, 11, 12, and 13, respectively.
- A constructor that takes a rank and a suit and returns a **Card** with those values.
- Getter methods named **getRank** and **getSuit** that retrieve the rank and suit components of a card.
- An implementation of the **toString** method that returns the complete name of the card, as in exercise 1. Remember that you can use the **+** operator to connect the different parts of the string together, as shown in the **toString** implementation for the **Rational** class in Figure 6-9.

9. Using the **Student** class from Figure 6-5 as a model, implement a new class called **LibraryRecord** that keeps track of the following information for a library book:

- The title
- The author
- The Library of Congress catalog number
- The publisher
- The year of publication
- Whether the book is circulating or noncirculating

Your class should export the following entries:

- A constructor that takes all six of these values and creates a new **LibraryRecord** object with them
- A second version of the constructor that takes only the first five values and initializes the book to be circulating
- Suitably named getter methods for each of the six fields
- A setter method for the circulating/noncirculating flag
- An appropriate implementation of the **toString** method

10. The implementation of the **Rational** class given in this chapter is not particularly useful in practice because it doesn't allow the numerator and denominator to exceed the size of an integer, even though larger values tend to occur quite often in rational arithmetic. One way to avoid the problem is to use the **BigInteger** class in the **java.math** package, which defines an extended type of integer that can take on arbitrarily large values. Rewrite the implementation of **Rational** so that the private instance variables **num** and **den** are declared as **BigInteger**s instead of **int**s, but without changing the argument and result types of any of the public methods. To learn how **BigInteger** works, you can consult the **javadoc** page.

CHAPTER 7
Objects and Memory

Yea, from the table of my memory
I'll wipe away all trivial fond records.
— William Shakespeare, *Hamlet*, c. 1600

Jay Forrester

After growing up on a Midwestern cattle ranch without electricity, Jay Forrester studied electrical engineering at the University of Nebraska and MIT, where he became director of the Navy's Project Whirlwind in 1944. Along with the ENIAC system at the Moore School in Philadelphia and the MARK I system at Harvard, Whirlwind played a central role in the early history of computers as they evolved from earlier analog designs to the digital systems that are standard in the industry today. Forrester's most significant contribution to computer hardware design was the development of core memory, in which small ferrite disks could be magnetized in one direction or the other to represent a binary 0 or 1. Magnetic core memory revolutionized hardware designs and was used in essentially all computers until it was replaced by integrated-circuit memory in the late 1970s. In 1956, Forrester joined the faculty of the Sloan School of Management, where he founded the new discipline of system dynamics, which attempts to focus holistically on large-scale systems and their interactions rather than looking only at their individual parts.

221

One of the enormous advantages of high-level languages like Java is that they free you from having to worry about the details of low-level representation inside the hardware of the machine. Managing the details of the internal representation is typically time-consuming, tedious, and susceptible to error; having the language keep track of these details can therefore increase programmer productivity. On the other hand, it is much more difficult to understand the programming process without having some idea of how that internal representation works. The structures that programmers have historically used—and that continue to form the foundation of languages like Java—reflect the capabilities of the hardware on which programs run. Knowing something about those low-level machine capabilities provides a conceptual framework for understanding programming at a higher, more abstract level.

Developing an intuitive feel for how data representation works inside the machine is particularly important when you begin to work with objects instead of primitive data. In Java, passing an object as an argument to a method seems very different from the corresponding process of using primitive types as arguments. If you understand how objects are represented inside the computer, however, the reasons for that apparent difference become much clearer and in fact turn out to be far more consistent that they might initially appear.

7.1 The structure of memory

In Chapter 1, you had the opportunity to learn a little bit about the internal structure of a computer, but only at a very abstract level. Figure 1-1 identified the major hardware components of a typical computer system, including the CPU, memory, secondary storage, and I/O devices. To develop a mental model of how objects are stored inside a computer, it is important to look at the structure of the memory system in more detail.

Bits, bytes, and words

At the most primitive level, all data values inside the computer are stored in the form of fundamental units of information called *bits*. A **bit** records the simplest possible value, which can be in one of two possible states. If you think of the circuitry inside the machine as if it were a tiny light switch, you might label those states as *off* and *on*. If you think of each bit as a Boolean value, you might instead use the labels *false* and *true*. However, because the word *bit* comes originally from a contraction of *binary digit*, it is more common to label those states using the values 0 and 1, which are the two digits used in the binary number system on which computer arithmetic is based.

Since a single bit holds so little information, the individual bits do not provide a convenient mechanism for storing data. To make it easier to store such traditional types of information as numbers or characters, bits are collected together into larger units that are then treated as integral units of storage. The smallest combined unit, called a **byte,** is composed of eight individual bits. On most machines, bytes are assembled into larger structures called **words**—defined to be four bytes in Java— that are large enough to hold an integer value.

The amount of memory available to a particular computer varies over a wide range. Early machines supported memories whose size was measured in kilobytes (KB); today's machines have memory sizes measured in megabytes (MB) or even gigabytes (GB). In most sciences, the prefixes *kilo, mega,* and *giga* stand for one thousand, one million, and one billion, respectively. In the world of computers, however, those base-10 values do not fit well into the internal structure of the machine. By tradition, therefore, these prefixes are taken to represent the power of two closest to their traditional interpretations. Thus, in programming, the prefixes *kilo, mega,* and *giga* have the following meanings:

$$\text{kilo (K)} = 2^{10} = 1{,}024$$
$$\text{mega (M)} = 2^{20} = 1{,}048{,}576$$
$$\text{giga (G)} = 2^{30} = 1{,}037{,}741{,}824$$

A 64KB computer from the early 1970s would have had 64 × 1024 or 65,536 bytes of memory. Similarly, a 512MB machine would have 512 × 1,048,576 or 536,870,912 bytes of memory.

Binary and hexadecimal representations

Each of the bytes inside a machine holds data whose meaning depends on how the system interprets the individual bits. Depending on the hardware instructions that are used to manipulate it, a particular sequence of bits can represent an integer, a character, or a floating-point value, each of which requires some kind of encoding scheme. The easiest encoding scheme to describe is that for integers, in which the bits are used to represent an integer represented in **binary notation,** in which the only legal values are 0 and 1, just as is true for the underlying bits. Binary notation is similar in structure to our more familiar decimal notation, but uses 2 rather than 10 as its base. The contribution that a binary digit makes to the entire number depends on its position within the number as a whole. The rightmost digit represents the units field, and each of the other positions counts for twice as much as the digit to its right.

Consider, for example, the eight-bit byte containing the following binary digits:

0	0	1	0	1	0	1	0

That sequence of bits represents the number forty-two, which you can verify by calculating the contribution for each of the individual bits, as follows:

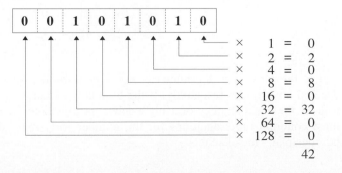

42

This diagram illustrates how to map an integer into bits using binary notation, but is not a particularly convenient representation. Binary numbers are cumbersome, mostly because they tend to be so long. Decimal representations are intuitive and familiar, but they make it difficult to understand how the number translates into bits. For applications in which it is useful to understand how a number translates into its binary representation without having to work with binary numbers that stretch all the way across the page, computer scientists tend to use **hexadecimal** (base 16) representation instead.

In hexadecimal notation, there are sixteen digits, representing values from 0 to 15. The decimal digits 0 through 9 are perfectly adequate for the first ten digits, but classical arithmetic does not define the extra symbols you need to represent the remaining six digits. Computer science traditionally uses the letters **A** through **F** for this purpose, as follows:

Hex digit	Value
A	10
B	11
C	12
D	13
E	14
F	15

What makes hexadecimal notation so attractive is that you can quickly move back and forth between hexadecimal values and the underlying binary representation. All you need to do is combine the bits into groups of four. For example, the number forty-two can be converted from binary to hexadecimal like this:

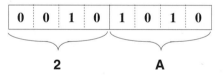

The first four bits represent the number 2, and the next four represent the number 10. Converting each of these to the corresponding hexadecimal digit gives **2A** as the base-16 form. You can then verify that this number still has the value 42 by adding up the independent digit values, as follows:

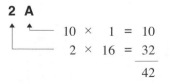

For the most part, the numeric representations that appear in this book use decimal notation for readability. If the base is not clear from the context, the text follows the usual strategy of using a subscript to denote the base. Thus, the three most common representations for the number forty-two—decimal, binary, and hexadecimal—look like this:

$$42_{10} = 101010_2 = 2A_{16}$$

Memory

The key point is that the number itself is always the same; the numeric base affects only the representation. Forty-two has a real-world interpretation that is independent of the base. That real-world interpretation is perhaps easiest to see in the representation an elementary school student might use, which is after all just another way of writing the number down:

The number of line segments in this representation is forty-two. The fact that a number is written in binary, decimal, or any other base is a property of the representation and not of the number itself.

Memory addresses

Within the memory system of a typical computer, every byte is identified by a numeric **address.** The first byte in the computer is numbered 0, the second is numbered 1, and so on, up to the number of bytes in the machine. For example, you can diagram the memory bytes of a tiny 64KB computer as shown along the right margin of this page. The numbering scheme, however, may seem unfamiliar at first, but only because the addresses are written using hexadecimal rather than decimal values. Hexadecimal notation was introduced in the preceding section, along with techniques for converting a hexadecimal value to its binary or decimal equivalent. The important thing to remember is that the addresses are simply numbers and that the base is relevant only to how those numbers are written down. The final address in the diagram is the address **FFFF**, which corresponds to the decimal value 65535. It would have been easy to write the addresses in decimal notation, which would have made them a little easier to read as numbers. This text, however, uses hexadecimal for the following reasons:

1. Address numbers are conventionally written in hexadecimal, and Java debuggers and runtime environments tend to display addresses in this form.
2. Writing address numbers in their hexadecimal form and using a sans-serif font makes it easier to recognize that a particular number represents an address rather than some unidentified integer.
3. Using hexadecimal values makes it easier to see why particular limits are chosen. When you write it as a decimal value, the number 65535 seems like a rather random value. If you express that same number in hexadecimal as **FFFF**, it becomes easier to recognize that this value is the largest value that can be represented in 16 bits.
4. Making the numbers seem less familiar may discourage you from thinking about them arithmetically. Java does a wonderful job of hiding the underlying address calculations from the programmer. What is important to understand is that addresses are represented as numbers. It is completely unimportant—and indeed usually impossible to determine—what those numbers are.

Memory	Address
	0000
	0001
	0002
	0003
	0004
	0005
	0006
	0007
	0008
	0009
	000A
	000B
	000C
	000D
	000E
	000F
	⋮
	1000
	1001
	1002
	1003
	1004
	1005
	1006
	1007
	1008
	1009
	100A
	100B
	100C
	100D
	100E
	100F
	⋮
	FFF0
	FFF1
	FFF2
	FFF3
	FFF4
	FFF5
	FFF6
	FFF7
	FFF8
	FFF9
	FFFA
	FFFB
	FFFC
	FFFD
	FFFE
	FFFF

In earlier days, byte values were useful in and of themselves because characters could be represented using a single byte. Today, bytes are too small to represent the large character sets found in a modern computer. The Unicode representation discussed in Chapter 8, for example, requires two bytes for each character. A value of type **char** therefore takes up two of these byte-sized units in memory, as illustrated by the shaded bytes in the following diagram:

FFF0
FFF1

Data values requiring multiple bytes are identified by the address of the first byte, so that the character represented by the shaded area is considered to be at address **FFF0**. As a second example, values of type **double** require eight bytes of memory, so a variable of type **double** stored at address **1000** would take up all the bytes between addresses **1000** and **1007**, inclusive:

1000
1001
1002
1003
1004
1005
1006
1007

Although addresses in memory are usually specified in terms of bytes, the fact that bytes are too small to be of much use has led hardware designers to group consecutive bytes into larger units. Typical architectures today include instructions for manipulating memory units in the following sizes: one byte (8 bits), two bytes (16 bits), four bytes (32 bits), and eight bytes (64 bits). These units correspond to the built-in Java types **byte**, **short**, **int**, and **long**. To save space, it is common to draw memory diagrams using these larger units instead of individual bytes. The **double** stored in the bytes numbered between **1000** and **1007** could therefore be diagrammed more compactly in the following form, in which the memory is divided into four-byte words:

1000
1004

Memory regions

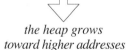

memory for
program code
and static data

pool of memory
available for objects
(the "heap")

*the heap grows
toward higher addresses*

*the stack grows
toward lower addresses*

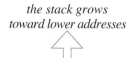

memory for
local variables
(the "stack")

7.2 The allocation of memory to variables

Whenever you declare a variable in a program, the compiler must reserve memory space to hold its value. The process of reserving memory space is called **allocation.** In Java, memory is allocated from one of three different sources depending on how it is declared, each of which is illustrated in the diagram to the left. The three allocation strategies are as follows:

1. *Static variables and constants.* Any variable whose declaration includes the **static** keyword applies to the class as a whole and not to an individual

object. These variables are typically allocated at the beginning of the memory space alongside the memory cells used to store the instructions for the program. In the examples included in this book, the only static declarations are those for named constants.

2. *Dynamically allocated objects.* All objects created using the **new** keyword are assigned storage from a region of memory called the **heap.** Although there is no explicit rule that enforces this convention, most implementations of the Java Virtual Machine assign heap memory beginning immediately after the fixed region assigned to the static declarations in a class, as illustrated in the diagram.

3. *Local variables.* All variables that are declared as local variables inside a method are allocated from a region of memory called the **stack,** which is typically implemented at least partially in hardware. In modern architectures, the stack begins at the highest legal address in memory and grows toward lower addresses as new methods are called. Calling a method increases the size of the stack by the amount needed to hold the local variables that method declares. As noted in Chapter 5, the memory assigned to the local variables for a method is called a **stack frame.** When a method returns, its stack frame is discarded, restoring the frame of its caller.

It is important to recognize that declaring an object variable is likely to reserve memory in both the stack and the heap. The local variable used to store the object appears on the stack just as if it were a local variable holding a primitive type. That particular variable, however, holds only the memory address of the object, which is stored in the heap. As noted in Chapter 6, that address is called a **reference.**

Memory diagrams for the `Rational` class

At this point, it is useful to consider a simple example to illustrate the relationship between heap storage and stack storage. Suppose that you have decided to use the **Rational** class introduced in section 6.3, which allows for a precise representation of fractional numbers. Internally, each **Rational** object declares two instance variables, **num** and **den**, to store the numerator and denominator of the fraction, respectively. The important question is then what happens inside the computer when you execute a declaration such as the following:

```
Rational half = new Rational(1, 2);
```

The variable **half** is a local variable and therefore appears in the stack frame for its caller. That variable, however, contains only enough storage to hold a memory address, which is typically four bytes on a machine with 32-bit addressing, although the growing number of 64-bit architectures means that the memory required will presumably grow to eight bytes over time. In any event, the amount of memory that appears on the stack is small. No matter how large the object itself turns out to be, a *reference* to that object can be stored in a single word.

The complete picture of what happens during the execution of this Java statement requires looking at what happens in both the heap and the stack. The evaluation of the initial-value expression on the right-hand side of the equal sign creates a new object in the heap. The heap storage for that object contains space for the integer values **num** and **den** along with some additional information common to all objects, which is used by the Java runtime system to manage objects in memory. From your perspective as a programmer, the details of that additional information are of no consequence, but it sometimes helps to know that objects take up more memory than you might expect from looking at the memory requirements of their instance variables. In this book, this extra management information is called the **object overhead** and is represented as a shaded area in memory diagrams. For example, the object created by the call to **new Rational(1, 2)** might look like this:

Once the new **Rational** object has been allocated in the heap, the next step in the declaration process is to store the address of that object in the variable **half**. That variable is allocated on the stack and therefore appears in a stack frame somewhere toward the high end of memory on most machines. Although there is no way to know what other values might exist in the stack frame without seeing the code for the entire method, the word assigned to **half** might look like this:

Once the new **Rational** object has been allocated in the heap, the next step in the declaration process is to store the address of that object in the variable **half**.

```
half    1000    FFC0
```

The value 1000 shown in the variable **half** is not intended as an integer but rather as the address at which the actual object is located. The choice of 1000—along with the addresses of every other heap and stack variable used in this book—is entirely arbitrary. In general, there is no way for you as a Java programmer to know the address of an object, nor is there any reason for you to do so. It is, however, important for you to remember that every object has some address and that Java programs can gain access to the data in the object by keeping track of the address where that object lives.

Even after you become more familiar with objects, you will discover that it often helps to create diagrams that make it easier to follow what's happening inside the memory. To illustrate this process, it is useful to try a somewhat more elaborate example. Consider the following **run** method, which first appeared in Chapter 6:

```java
public void run() {
    Rational a = new Rational(1, 2);
    Rational b = new Rational(1, 3);
    Rational c = new Rational(1, 6);
    Rational sum = a.add(b).add(c);
    println(a + " + " + b + " + " + c + " = " + sum);
}
```

The idea of this program, of course, is to add three **Rational** variables and display their sum. Our concern here, however, is simply to understand how these values are represented inside the machine.

The first three declarations are easy enough. As in the simple example of the variable **half**, each of these declarations constructs a new **Rational** object and assigns its address to a variable in the stack frame for the **run** method, giving rise to a memory diagram that looks like this:

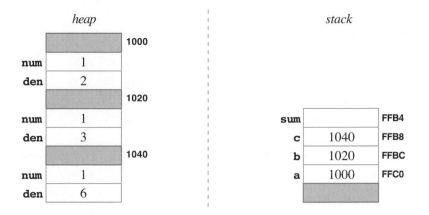

As in most languages, Java creates the complete stack frame for a method at the time the method is called, so all four local variables—**a**, **b**, **c**, and **sum**—have already been allocated on the stack, but only the first three have been initialized at this point in the execution. The value used to initialize **sum** is the result of the expression

```
a.add(b).add(c)
```

It is worth tracing this operation step by step.

The first step in the process is to invoke the **add** method on the **Rational** object **a**, passing it the value of **b** as a parameter. Because this operation is a method call, a new stack frame must be created for it, binding the formal parameters of the method to the values of the actual arguments included in the call. As you can see from Figure 6-9, the code for the **add** method appears as follows:

```
public Rational add(Rational r) {
    return new Rational(this.num * r.den + r.num * this.den,
                        this.den * r.den);
}
```

The formal parameter is named **r** inside the **add** method, which means that **r** must be assigned the value of the actual argument, which is named **b** in the calling frame. The value currently occupying the variable **b** is the number 1020, which is the address of the corresponding object in the heap. Java initializes the variable **r** in the new frame simply by copying the address, which means that the variable **r** in the new frame will also contain 1020.

For this example, it is important to note that the stack frame for any method invoked on a receiving object also contains a reference to that object, which Java identifies using the keyword **this**. Intuitively, it is best to think of **this** as simply a local variable that refers to the receiving object, which in this case is the value stored in the variable **a**. As with the argument value, the identity of the receiver is also copied into the new frame as a simple address. Thus, the state of the memory once the new frame has been created looks like this:

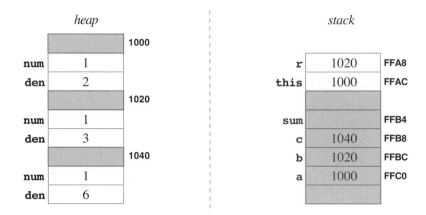

In this diagram, the stack region below the current frame is shown in gray to emphasize that the shaded region is inaccessible to the **add** method. The only variables accessible to **add** are the references stored in the variables **r** and **this** in the current frame. These reference variables are exactly what the **add** method needs to perform its computation. The **add** method returns a new **Rational** value whose numerator is given by the expression

```
this.num * r.den + r.num * this.den
```

and whose denominator has the value

```
this.den * r.den
```

Each term in these expressions denotes a selection operation that extracts one of the two fields, **num** or **den**, from the appropriate **Rational** value. For example, the term **r.den** specifies the selection of the **den** field of the value whose reference is stored in **r**. Since **r** contains the address 1020, the term **r.den** indicates the denominator component of the object stored at address 1020, which is the integer 3. Expanding the value for each term in a similar fashion reveals that the result of the **add** method is given by the expression

```
new Rational(1 * 3 + 1 * 2, 2 * 3)
```

which can be further simplified to

```
new Rational(5, 6)
```

This expression constructs a new **Rational** object with the indicated components in the heap and returns the address of that object as the value of the call **a.add(b)**, clearing away the stack frame for **add** as it returns.

Unlike the result of most of the computations you have seen so far, the new value computed by this method does not get stored in a variable. The calculation **a.add(b)** is only a subexpression of the longer expression

        a.add(b).add(c)

The value of **a.add(b)** therefore becomes the receiver of a new **add** call with the argument **c**. Setting up the frame for this new method call leaves the memory in the following state, with the new **Rational** object shown at address 1060 in the heap:

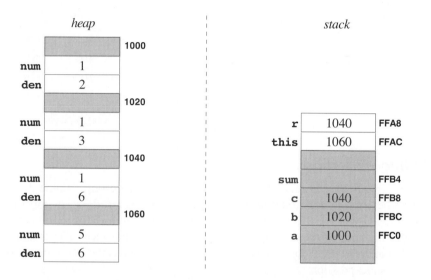

Once again, the evaluation of the **add** method requires determining the values of the fields in the two **Rational** values accessible from the current frame. This time, the straightforward expansion of the result expression indicates that the final value is equivalent to the constructor call

        new Rational(5 * 6 + 1 * 6, 6 * 6)

which works out to

        new Rational(36, 36)

Fortunately, the constructor for **Rational** provides additional simplification of the result by using Euclid's algorithm to reduce the fraction to lowest terms. Eliminating the common factor of 36 from both the numerator and the denominator gives rise to a new **Rational** object with 1 as the value of both its **num** and **den** fields. When that value is assigned to the variable **sum**, the heap and stack look like this:

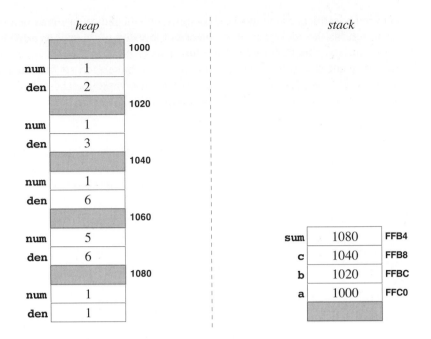

Garbage collection

The example from the preceding section illustrates an interesting wrinkle that often arises when objects are stored in memory. If you look carefully at the most recent diagram, you will see that the heap contains five different **Rational** objects even though only four of those objects have references on the stack. The fraction 5/6 stored at address 1060 was created during the calculation as the intermediate result from the subexpression

```
a.add(b)
```

While that value is necessary to complete the calculation, it becomes irrelevant once the final addition is performed. In the traditional parlance of computer science, that value is now **garbage.** Calculations in object-oriented languages often generate quite a bit of garbage along the way as intermediate results are computed as part of complex computations. Unfortunately, those values occupy space in the heap. If that garbage is allowed to remain, the heap will eventually fill up, even if there is plenty of room for the active data.

To get around the problem of having the heap fill up with objects that are no longer useful, the Java runtime system adopts a strategy called **garbage collection,** which does pretty much exactly what it sounds as if it does. Whenever the memory available in the heap seems to be running short, Java defers what it's doing, in order to collect any garbage in the heap and return that memory to the pool of assignable storage. To do so, Java uses a two-phase strategy that operates in more or less the following way, although the process presented here has been simplified to ensure that the basic idea remains clear:

1. Go through every variable reference on the stack and every variable reference in static storage and mark the corresponding object as being "in use" by setting a flag that lives in the object's overhead space. In addition, whenever you set the "in use" flag for an object, determine whether that object contains references to other objects and mark those objects as being "in use" as well.

2. Go through every object in the heap and delete any objects for which the "in use" flag has not been set, returning the storage used for that object to the heap for subsequent reallocation. It must be safe to delete these objects, because there is no way for the program to gain access to them, given that no references to those objects still exist in the program variables.

Because the garbage-collection algorithm operates in two phases—one to mark the objects that are in use and one to sweep through memory collecting inaccessible objects—this strategy is traditionally called a **mark-and-sweep collector.**

7.3 Primitive types versus objects

From a high-level conceptual perspective, you can often think about Java objects in much the same way that you think about the primitive types like **int** and **double**. If you declare an integer variable by writing

```
int three = 3;
```

you can diagram that variable by drawing a box named **three** and writing a 3 in the box, as follows:

To a certain extent, you can treat objects in the same way. For example, if you create a new **Rational** variable using the declaration

```
Rational third = new Rational(1, 3);
```

you can think about this variable conceptually as if it held the actual value, as shown in the following diagram:

It is, however, important to understand at what point this analogy breaks down. As you know from the discussion of internal representation earlier in this chapter, the variable **third** does not in fact contain the actual object but instead contains the address of that object. This mode of representing objects has several implications that it is important for you, as a budding programmer, to understand.

Parameter passing

One of the most important consequences of the representation scheme that Java uses for objects arises when you pass an object as a parameter to a method. At first glance, the rules for passing objects as parameters seem different from the corresponding rules for passing primitive values. Suppose, for example, that you have written the following pair of methods:

```java
public void run() {
    int x = 17;
    increment(x);
    println("x = " + x);
}

private void increment(int n) {
    n++;
    println("n = " + n);
}
```

Running this program produces the following output:

```
SimpleParameterTest
n = 18
x = 17
```

As you can see from the output, the **++** operator in the **increment** method affects only the value of the local variable **n** and not the value of **x** in the calling frame. The behavior simply reflects the way these values are stored on the stack. When **increment** is called, the value from the stack entry for the local variable **x** is copied into a new stack entry for the variable **n**, so that the stack looks something like this:

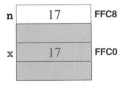

Changing the value of **n** inside the new frame has no effect on the original value.

But what would happen if these values were objects instead of simple integers? One way to answer that question is to design a simple class that contains an embedded integer value, as shown in Figure 7-1. The definition of the **EmbeddedInteger** class includes a constructor, a **setValue** method for setting the internal value, a **getValue** method for getting that value back, and a **toString** method to make it easier to display the object using **println**. Given these methods, you can write a similar test program that looks like this:

```
      public void run() {
         EmbeddedInteger x = new EmbeddedInteger(17);
         increment(x);
         println("x = " + x);
      }

      private void increment(EmbeddedInteger n) {
         n.setValue(n.getValue() + 1);
         println("n = " + n);
      }
```

FIGURE 7-1   Implementation of the EmbeddedInteger class

```
/**
 * This class allows its clients to treat an integer as an object.
 * The underlying integer value is set using setValue and returned
 * using getValue.
 */
public class EmbeddedInteger {

/**
 * Creates an embedded integer with the value n.
 */
   public EmbeddedInteger(int n) {
      value = n;
   }

/**
 * Sets the internal value of this EmbeddedInteger to n.
 */
   public void setValue(int n) {
      value = n;
   }

/**
 * Returns the internal value of this EmbeddedInteger.
 */
   public int getValue() {
      return value;
   }

/**
 * Overrides the toString method to make it return the string
 * corresponding to the internal value.
 */
   public String toString() {
      return "" + value;
   }

/* Private instance variable */
   private int value;        /* The internal value */

}
```

If you run this version of the program, the output is different than before:

```
ObjectParameterTest
n = 18
x = 18
```

In the object-based implementation, a change in the value of a field in the underlying object continues to be reflected after the method returns. This difference in behavior follows directly from the way objects are represented in memory. At the beginning of the call to **increment** in the new implementation, the heap and stack are in the following state:

In this case, changing the **value** field inside the object affects the conceptual value of both **n** and **x** because those two variables contain the same reference.

The intuitive effect of this difference in representation is that objects—in contrast to primitive values—are shared between the calling method and the method being called. The underlying mechanism, however, is exactly the same. Whenever a new local variable is initialized, the old value is copied into the stack location for the new variable. If that value is an object, what gets copied is the reference and not the underlying value.

Wrapper classes

The **EmbeddedInteger** class shown in Figure 7-1 is actually somewhat more than a simple illustration of parameter-passing in the object world. As you will discover in subsequent chapters, the Java library packages contain quite a few classes that are designed to work with any type of object. For example, the **ArrayList** class that you will learn about in Chapter 10 makes it possible to maintain an ordered list of objects. Given an **ArrayList**, you can add new values, remove existing ones, and perform a number of other useful operations that make sense in the abstract context of a list. The nature of the operations that manipulate the list turn out to be independent of the type of value the list contains. Thus, to make it possible to store any kind of object at all, the **ArrayList** class uses the universal class **Object** from which all other classes in the Java class hierarchy descend.

Unfortunately, being able to store any kind of object in an **ArrayList** does not provide quite as much flexibility as you might like. The Java primitive types are not objects and therefore cannot be used in conjunction with this marvelously convenient class. To get around this problem, Java defines a class, usually called a **wrapper class,** to go along with each of the eight primitive types, as follows:

Primitive type	Wrapper class
byte	Byte
short	Short
int	Integer
long	Long
float	Float
double	Double
boolean	Boolean
char	Character

Each of the wrapper classes has a constructor that creates a new object from the corresponding primitive type. For example, if the variable **n** is an **int**, the declaration

```
Integer nAsInteger = new Integer(n);
```

creates a new **Integer** object whose internal value is **n** and assigns it to **nAsInteger**. Each of the wrapper classes also defines a method to retrieve the underlying value. The name of that method is always the name of the primitive type followed by the suffix **Value**. Thus, once you have initialized the variable **nAsInteger**, you can get back the value stored inside it by writing

```
nAsInteger.intValue()
```

Because **nAsInteger** is a legitimate object, you can store that value in an **ArrayList** or any other compound structure.

Unlike the **EmbeddedInteger** class from the preceding section, however, the wrapper classes provide no method to set the value of the underlying variable in an existing object. The wrapper classes are in fact immutable, as defined in Chapter 6. Immutable classes have the wonderful property that it is always possible to think about them as if they represent pure values in the way that Java's primitive types do. With an immutable class, you don't have to worry whether a value is shared or copied when you pass it from one method to another. Because neither side can change that value, it turns out not to matter.

The wrapper classes also include several static methods that you are likely to find useful, particularly those in the **Integer** class that support numeric conversion in arbitrary bases. Figure 7-2 lists a few of the most important static methods for the classes **Integer** and **Double**; the even more useful static methods in the **Character** class are described in Chapter 8. Because these methods are static, you need to include the name of the class. Thus, to convert the integer 50 into a hexadecimal string, you would need to write

```
Integer.toString(50, 16)
```

FIGURE 7-2 **Numeric conversion methods in the Integer and Double classes**

Static methods in the **Integer** class

`static int parseInt(String str)`   *or*   `parseInt(String str, int radix)`
Converts a string of digits into an **int** using the specified radix, which defaults to 10.
`static String toString(int i)`   *or*   `toString(int i, int radix)`
Converts an **int** to its string representation for the specified radix, which defaults to 10.

Static methods in the **Double** class

`static double parseDouble(String str)`
Converts the string representation of a number into the corresponding **double**.
`static String toString(double d)`
Converts a **double** to its string representation.

Boxing and unboxing

If you are using the most recent versions of Java, you can often ignore the distinction between primitive types and wrapper classes. Beginning with Java 5.0, the compiler automatically converts back and forth between a primitive type and its associated wrapper class whenever the semantics of the language would require it. Thus, instead of forcing you to write a declaration like

```
Integer nAsInteger = new Integer(n);
```

Java 5.0 allows you to simplify the declaration to

```
Integer nAsInteger = n;
```

When the Java 5.0 compiler discovers that you are trying to assign a value of type **int** to a variable declared as type **Integer**, it automatically creates an **Integer** object with the appropriate value before performing the assignment. Conversely, if you use the variable **nAsInteger** in a context in which Java expects a value of type **int**, the Java 5.0 compiler automatically performs the necessary conversion in that direction as well. This process of adding or removing the wrapper classes as needed is called **boxing** and **unboxing.**

The advantage of implementing automatic boxing and unboxing is that doing so tends to create much more readable code. The constructors that create the wrapper classes and the methods that select the primitive contents from a wrapper object disappear completely. Such conversions are particularly valuable when you want to store primitive data as part of a collection, as discussed in Chapter 13.

The strategy of boxing and unboxing, however, also has a couple of significant disadvantages. One disadvantage is that hiding the fact that a primitive data value has been converted to an object makes it more difficult to understand how that value is represented in memory. As the examples involving the **EmbeddedInteger** class make clear, it is sometimes important to know whether a value passed as a parameter is an object or a primitive data value because the behavior in the two cases often appears to be quite different. By making it less clear whether a value is in fact an object, the technique of automatic boxing and unboxing can make a program's behavior more difficult to comprehend.

COMMON PITFALLS

Even if you have Java 5.0 available, you should exercise caution when using automatic boxing and unboxing. In particular, it is important to keep in mind that objects and primitive values sometimes behave differently, such as when they are passed as parameters or when they are tested for equality.

A second disadvantage is that Java applies automatic boxing and unboxing only if the values involved in an operation cannot be interpreted as they exist. As a result, some Java operations invoke automatic conversions, while others that initially seem similar do not. This situation is illustrated by the following **run** method compiled using Java 5.0:

```
public void run() {
    Integer x = 5;
    Integer y = new Integer(x);
    println("x == y -> " + (x == y));
    println("x < y  -> " + (x < y));
    println("x > y  -> " + (x > y));
}
```

The statements in this method create two values of type **Integer**, both of which have the value 5. The value assigned to **x** is created by automatic boxing; the value assigned to **y** is a newly constructed **Integer** whose initial value comes from unboxing the contents of **x**. The next three lines display the values of the relational expressions **x == y**, **x < y**, and **x > y**, respectively.

If you compile and run this program using Java 5.0, the output at first seems rather surprising:

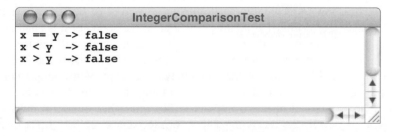

According to the rules of mathematics, exactly one of the expressions should be true, no matter what values have been assigned to **x** and **y**. The reason that all three of these comparisons are **false** is that the unboxing of the objects occurs only with the **<** and **>** operators; the equality operator **==** has a well-defined meaning when applied to objects of type **Integer**, which means that Java does not try to convert them into primitive values. When applied to objects, the equality operator returns **true** only if the values on each side of the **==** are the same object. In this case, **x** and **y** are *different* objects that happen to have the *same* internal value, as shown in the following heap-stack diagram:

▰▰ 7.4 Linking objects together

The fact that objects are represented internally as references has one more implication that seems important to consider in the context of this chapter, even though a full discussion of the topic must wait until much later in the book. Because references are small, an object can easily contain references to other objects. If objects were stored only in the complete form in which they appear in the heap, it would obviously be impossible for a small object to contain a larger one. Moreover, since every object requires some amount of overhead, it would even be impossible for one heap object to contain another object of the same size, because there would no longer be any room in which to store the bookkeeping information that Java needs. These restrictions, however, disappear completely if objects are stored as references. Although it is true that a small object cannot physically contain a larger object, there is nothing to prevent one object from containing a reference to another object no matter how much heap storage that object might consume. A reference, after all, is simply the address of an object in memory and can therefore be represented using just a few bytes. Thus, there is no problem in having one object contain a reference to another object of a different class, or even an object of the same class.

Creating an object that contains references to other objects is an extremely powerful programming technique. Such objects are said to be **linked.** Although an in-depth discussion of linked structures lies beyond the scope of this chapter, it is useful to present a simple example, both because that example will reinforce your understanding of how linked structures are represented in memory and because it offers a powerful illustration of the fundamental concept of **message-passing,** which is the metaphor Java uses to describe communication among the objects in a system. When an object needs to interact with some other object, it does so by invoking a method in the receiving object. In the context of the object-oriented paradigm, however, the act of calling that method is usually described as one of "sending a message" to the receiver. That message may in turn trigger a response in the receiver, such as a change in its state or the generation of additional messages that propagate that message to other objects. Even though the implementation of message-passing depends on method calls, it is important to keep the underlying metaphor in mind.

Message passing in linked structures: The beacons of Gondor

> *For answer Gandalf cried aloud to his horse. "On, Shadowfax! We must hasten. Time is short. See! The beacons of Gondor are alight, calling for aid. War is kindled. See, there is the fire on Amon Dîn, and flame on Eilenach; and there they go speeding west: Nardol, Erelas, Min-Rimmon, Calenhad, and the Halifirien on the borders of Rohan."*
> —J. R. R. Tolkien, *The Return of the King*, 1955

In adapting this scene for the concluding episode in his trilogy, Peter Jackson created what may be the most evocative and dramatic example of message-passing ever recorded on film. After the first beacon is lit in the towers of Minas Tirith, we see the signal pass from mountaintop to mountaintop as the keepers of each signal tower, ever vigilant, light their own fires when they see the triggering fire at the preceding station. The message of Gondor's danger thus passes quickly over the miles that separate it from Rohan, as illustrated by the following schematic diagram:

How would you go about simulating the lighting of the beacons of Gondor using the method-passing paradigm? Each signal tower is presumably a separate object that contains such information as the name of the tower. Each tower, however, must also be able to identify the next tower in the chain so that it knows where to send its message. The most straightforward strategy is to have each tower contain a reference to its successor. Thus, the object that represents Minas Tirith contains a reference to the object used to model Amon Dîn, which in turn contains a reference to the object that represents Eilenach, and so on. If you adopt this approach, the private data for each object must include—possibly along with other information required by the application as a whole—the following instance variables:

```
private String towerName;
private SignalTower nextTower;
```

The first variable contains the name of the tower, and the second is a reference to the next tower in sequence.

While this model makes sense for Minas Tirith and the intermediate towers in the chain, using this strategy to represent Rohan raises a minor issue by virtue of the fact that Rohan appears at the end of the chain. Like the other towers, Rohan has a **nextTower** field that is supposed to contain a reference to the next tower. Rohan doesn't have one, and the question is simply how to represent this fact. Fortunately, Java defines a special value called **null** for precisely this situation. The constant **null** represents a reference to a nonexistent value and can be assigned to any variable that holds an object reference. Thus, you can record the fact that Rohan is the last tower in the chain simply by making sure that its **nextTower** field is **null**.

Figure 7-3 contains a simple definition of a **SignalTower** class that implements the idea of passing a message along a chain of towers. The constructor takes the name of the tower and a reference to the next tower in sequence. The only other public method is **signal**, which is the action associated with the "Light your signal fire" message that propogates through the towers. When a tower receives the **signal** message, it lights its own signal fire and then passes the message along by sending the **signal** message to its successor, if any.

In the design of the **SignalTower** class shown in Figure 7-3, the process of lighting the current signal tower is the responsibility of the **lightCurrentTower** method. In this implementation, **lightCurrentTower** consists of the code

```
public void lightCurrentTower() {
   System.out.println("Lighting " + towerName);
}
```

FIGURE 7-3   Implementation of the SignalTower class

```java
/**
 * This class defines a signal tower object that passes a message
 * to the next tower in a line.
 */

public class SignalTower {

/**
 * Constructs a new signal tower with the following parameters:
 * @param name The name of the tower
 * @param link A link to the next tower, or null if none exists
 */
   public SignalTower(String name, SignalTower link) {
      towerName = name;
      nextTower = link;
   }

/**
 * This method represents sending a signal to this tower. The effect
 * is to light the signal fire here and to send an additional signal
 * message to the next tower in the chain, if any.
 */
   public void signal() {
      lightCurrentTower();
      if (nextTower != null) nextTower.signal();
   }

/**
 * This method lights the signal fire for this tower. This version
 * that simply prints the name of the tower to the standard output
 * channel. If you wanted to extend this class to be part of a
 * graphical application, for example, you could override this
 * method to draw an indication of the signal fire on the display.
 */
   public void lightCurrentTower() {
      System.out.println("Lighting " + towerName);
   }

/* Private instance variables */
   private String towerName;        /* The name of this tower    */
   private SignalTower nextTower;   /* A link to the next tower  */

}
```

---

which prints a message including the name of the tower on **System.out**, which is a standard output stream that is always available to Java programs. At some point in the future, you might want to rewrite the program so that the signal fires appear on the screen one after the other. In that case, you could rewrite the implementation of **lightCurrentTower** so that it performed the appropriate graphical operations instead. Better still, you could create a new subclass that overrides the definition of **lightCurrentTower**. The extended class can substitute its own version of this method but still rely on all the other features provided by the base class for linking the towers together. You will have a chance to animate this example in Chapter 9.

The constructor for the **SignalTower** class is simple and does nothing more than copy its arguments into the corresponding instance variables, as follows:

```
public SignalTower(String name, SignalTower link) {
    towerName = name;
    nextTower = link;
}
```

Because each invocation of the constructor for **SignalTower** requires you to specify the link to the next tower in the chain, it is easiest to create the data structure representing the chain of beacons in Gondor if you start at the end of the chain with Rohan and work backwards toward the front of the chain at Minas Tirith. If each of the towers is declared as an instance variable, the following method initializes each of those variables to reflect the structure of the signal tower chain:

```
private void createSignalTowers() {
    rohan = new SignalTower("Rohan", null);
    halifirien = new SignalTower("Halifirien", rohan);
    calenhad = new SignalTower("Calenhad", halifirien);
    minRimmon = new SignalTower("Min-Rimmon", calenhad);
    erelas = new SignalTower("Erelas", minRimmon);
    nardol = new SignalTower("Nardol", erelas);
    eilenach = new SignalTower("Eilenach", nardol);
    amonDin = new SignalTower("Amon Din", eilenach);
    minasTirith = new SignalTower("Minas Tirith", amonDin);
}
```

The internal representation of linked structures

After you call **createSignalTowers** to initialize the towers, the internal representation for the objects in the heap looks something like the diagram in Figure 7-4. Note that the order in which the signal towers appear is indicated only by the chain of references in the final memory cells within each structure and not by the order in which the cells appear in memory. To emphasize the internal connections within the chain, the diagram in Figure 7-4 includes arrows that link each cell to its successor. The only value stored in memory is the numeric address, which is sufficient to identify the next object in the chain.

Once you have established the data structure shown in Figure 7-4, all you need to do to get the process started is send a **signal** message to the first tower by invoking

```
minasTirith.signal();
```

The implementation of the **signal** method takes whatever action is necessary to simulate lighting the beacon in Minas Tirith and then passes the **signal** message to the object representing Amon Dîn. That object in turn passes the **signal** message to its successor, and the process continues until it reaches the Rohan tower, at which point the **null** in the **nextTower** field indicates that the signal has reached the end of the line.

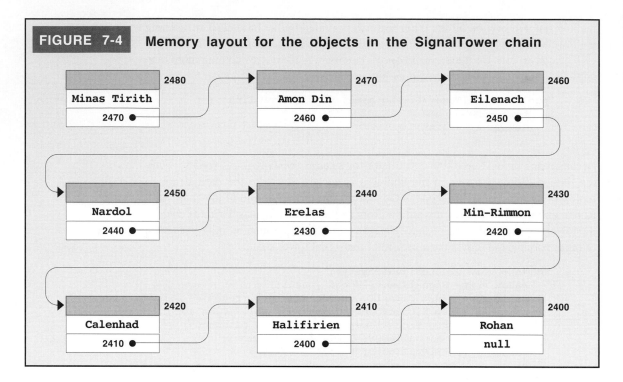

FIGURE 7-4 Memory layout for the objects in the SignalTower chain

Summary

Even though the object model is designed to promote a more abstract view of data, using objects effectively requires that you have a mental model of how objects are represented in memory. In this chapter, you have had a chance to see how those objects are stored and to get a sense of what goes on "under the hood" as you create and use objects in your programs.

The important points introduced in this chapter include:

- The fundamental unit of information in a modern computer is a *bit,* which can be in one of two possible states. The state of a bit is usually represented in memory diagrams using the binary digits 0 and 1, but it is equally appropriate to think of these values as *off* and *on* or *false* and *true,* depending on the application.

- Sequences of bits are combined inside the hardware to form larger structures, including *bytes,* which are eight bits long, and *words,* which contain four bytes or 32 bits.

- The internal memory of a computer is arranged into a sequence of bytes in which each byte is identified by its index position in that sequence, which is called its *address*.

- Computer scientists tend to write address values and the contents of memory locations in *hexadecimal* notation (base 16) because doing so makes it easy to identify the individual bits.

- The primitive types in Java require different amounts of memory. A value of type **char** requires two bytes, a value of type **int** requires four, and a value of type **double** requires eight. The address of a multibyte value is the address of the first byte it contains.

- Data values that you create in a Java program are allocated in three different regions of memory. Static variables and constants that apply to an entire class are allocated in a region of memory devoted to the program code and static data. Local variables are allocated in a region called the *stack,* which is apportioned into structures called *frames* that contain all of the local variables for a method. All objects are allocated in a region called the *heap,* which is simply a pool of available memory.

- When you declare a local variable of some object class and assign it an initial value by calling its constructor, memory is allocated in both the heap and the stack. The heap contains the storage for the actual data in the object. The stack entry for the variable contains only enough memory to hold the address of the object, which is called a *reference*.

- The stack frame for a method call includes an entry identified by the keyword **this** that identifies the object to which that method is applied.

- As a computation proceeds, objects on the heap are often used as temporary values that are no longer needed for the rest of the computation. Such values, however, continue to occupy memory in the heap and are referred to as *garbage*. The Java runtime system periodically undertakes a process called *garbage collection* to search through the heap and reclaim the space used by those objects.

- When an object is passed from one method to another, only the reference to that object is copied into the stack frame for the new method. Because this reference identifies exactly the same object as the identical reference in the caller, object values are shared between the calling and called methods.

- The primitive types in Java are not in fact objects and therefore cannot be used in contexts in which an object is required. To get around this problem, Java defines a set of *wrapper classes* that encapsulate each of the primitive types in a full-fledged object.

- Objects in Java can contain references to other objects. Such objects are said to be *linked*. Linked structures are used quite often in programming and will be covered in more detail in later chapters in this book.

Review questions

1. Define the following terms: *bit, byte,* and *word*.

2. What is the etymology of the word *bit?*

3. How many bytes of memory are there in a 384MB machine?

4. Convert each of the following decimal numbers to its hexadecimal equivalent:

   a) 17

   b) 256

   c) 1729

   d) 2766

5. Convert each of the following hexadecimal numbers to decimal:

    a) **17**   c) **CC**
    b) **64**   d) **FAD**

6. What is an *address?*

7. How many bytes does Java assign to a value of type **int**? How many bytes are required for a **double**?

8. What are the three memory regions in which values can be stored in a Java program?

9. Using the example in section 7.2 as a model, trace the heap and stack operations that occur in the execution of the following method:

    ```
    public void run() {
        Rational x = new Rational(4, 5);
        Rational y = new Rational(5, 2);
        Rational z = x.multiply(y).subtract(z);
        println(x + " x " + y + " - " + y + " = " + z);
    }
    ```

    Which objects on the heap are garbage when the **println** statement is reached?

10. True or false: When you pass a primitive data value from one method to another, Java always copies that value into the frame of the method being called.

11. True or false: When you pass an object from one method to another, Java copies the data in that object into the new frame.

12. Describe the two phases used by a simple mark-and-sweep garbage collector.

13. What is meant by the term *wrapper class?* What purpose do wrapper classes serve?

14. What methods can you use to convert between integers and the string representations of those integers in a particular base?

15. What property identifies a *linked structure?*

16. Given that objects of a particular class require a certain amount of space in memory, it is clear that an object in the heap could never physically contain another object of that same class and still have room for additional data. What can a Java programmer do to achieve the same effect?

17. Why is important for Java to include the special value **null?** What does this value represent?

Programming exercises

1. Use the static methods **Integer.parseInt** and **Integer.toString** to write a program that converts hexadecimal values into their decimal equivalents. Your program should continue to read hexadecimal values until the user enters a 0. A sample run of the program might look like this:

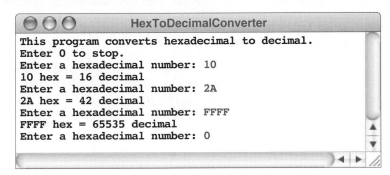

```
This program converts hexadecimal to decimal.
Enter 0 to stop.
Enter a hexadecimal number: 10
10 hex = 16 decimal
Enter a hexadecimal number: 2A
2A hex = 42 decimal
Enter a hexadecimal number: FFFF
FFFF hex = 65535 decimal
Enter a hexadecimal number: 0
```

2. The fact that the **Integer.parseInt** method allows a program to read user input as a string and then convert it to an integer makes it possible to write programs that use something other than an integer—such as a blank line—as a sentinel to signal the end of the input. Rewrite the **AverageList** program from exercise 4-6 so that it uses a blank line to mark the end of the input.

3. *But don't panic. Base 8 is just like base 10 really—if you're missing two fingers.*
   —Tom Lehrer, "The New Math," 1965

   Rewrite the Math Quiz program from exercise 6-5 so that it poses its questions in base 8 instead of base 10, as shown in the following sample run:

```
Welcome to the octal Math Quiz
What is 3 + 5 in base 8? 10
That's the answer!
What is 17 - 15 in base 8? 2
That's the answer!
What is 20 - 16 in base 8? 4
That's incorrect - try a different answer: 2
That's the answer!
What is 6 + 7 in base 8? 13
That's incorrect - try a different answer: 15
That's the answer!
What is 21 - 6 in base 8? 13
That's the answer!
```

4. The **Runtime** class in the **java.lang** package includes a few simple methods that may help you get a better sense of what Java's garbage collector does. A **Runtime** object maintains information about the state of the Java Virtual

Machine. If you want to look at that information, you can get the current runtime environment by calling the static method **getRuntime()** and storing the result in a variable, like this:

> **Runtime myRuntime = Runtime.getRuntime();**

Once you have this variable, you can find out how much free memory is available by calling

> **myRuntime.freeMemory();**

Because memory sizes can be large, the value returned by **freeMemory** is a **long** rather than an **int** and indicates the number of bytes available. You can also explicitly trigger the garbage collector by calling

> **myRuntime.gc();**

Write a program that allocates 10000 **Rational** objects without saving any of them in variables so they all become garbage. Once you've done so, measure the amount of free memory before and after garbage collection and use the difference to report how many bytes were freed, as shown in the following sample run:

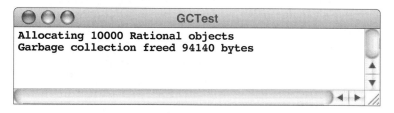

CHAPTER 8
Strings and Characters

Surely you don't think numbers are as important as words.

—King Azaz to the Mathemagician
Norton Juster, *The Phantom Tollbooth*, 1961

Herman Hollerith (1860-1929)

The idea of encoding text in machine-readable form dates back to the nineteenth century and the work of the American inventor Herman Hollerith. After studying engineering at City College of New York and the Columbia School of Mines, Hollerith spent a couple of years working as a statistician for the U.S. Census Bureau before accepting a teaching position at MIT. While at the Census Bureau, Hollerith had become convinced that the data produced by the census could be counted more quickly and accurately by machine. In the late 1880s, he designed and built a tabulating machine that was used to conduct the 1890 census in record time. The company he founded to commercialize his invention, originally called the Tabulating Machine Company, changed its name in 1924 to International Business Machines (IBM). Hollerith's card-based tabulating system pioneered the technique of textual encoding described in this chapter—a contribution that was reflected in the fact that early versions of the FORTRAN language used the letter **H** (for Hollerith) to indicate text data.

Throughout most of this book, the only data with which you have actually worked—in the traditional sense of using data as the basis of calculation—has been numeric data, as represented by the types `int` and `double`. As Juster's Mathemagician would insist, numbers are certainly important, but there are many other kinds of data in the world. Particularly since the development of the personal computer in the early 1980s, computers have worked less with numeric data than they have with **text data** composed of individual characters of the sort that appear on the keyboard and the screen. The ability of computers to process text data has led to the development of word processing systems, electronic mail, the World Wide Web, search engines, and a wide variety of other useful applications.

The concept of text data was introduced informally in Chapter 2, beginning with the first line of code in this book, which includes the string

```
"hello, world"
```

Since then, you have used string values from time to time but, in each case, you've looked at those strings only as an integrated whole. This perspective is an essential one, and will indeed be appropriate most of the time that you use string data. To unlock the full power of strings, you need to know how to manipulate strings in more sophisticated ways.

Because a string is composed of individual characters, it is important for you to understand how characters work and how they are represented inside the computer. Thus, this chapter focuses on the data type `char` as well as the built-in Java class `String`. Before examining the details of either type, however, it is helpful to begin by taking a more general look at how nonnumeric data can be represented inside the computer.

▆ 8.1 The principle of enumeration

As the use of computing technology grows, more and more information is stored electronically. To store information within a computer, it is necessary to represent the data in a form the machine can use. The representation of a particular item depends on its data type. Integers have one representation inside the computer, which you know from Chapter 7 consists of a sequence of bits that holds the number in binary representation. Floating-point numbers have a different representation that is beyond the scope of this text. There are, however, many types of useful data other than numbers, so computers must be able to represent nonnumeric data as well.

To gain insight into the nature of nonnumeric data, think for a moment about the information that you yourself provide to institutions and agencies over the course of a year. For example, if you live in the United States, you supply data to the Internal Revenue Service with your annual tax return. Much of that information is numeric—your salary, deductions, taxes, withholdings, and the like. Some consists of text data, such as your name, address, and occupation. But other items on your tax return cannot easily be classified into either of these forms. For example, one of the questions is

Filing status (check one):

☐ single

☐ married filing joint return

☐ married filing separate return

☐ head of household

☐ qualifying widow(er)

As with every other entry on the form, your answer represents data. Your response, however, is neither numeric data nor text data. The best way to describe the data type would be simply to call it *filing status data*—an entirely new data type whose domain consists of five values: *single, married filing joint return, married filing separate return, head of household,* and *qualifying widow(er)*.

You can easily imagine many other data types that have a similar structure. For example, other forms might ask you for your sex, ethnicity, or status as a student. In each case, you would choose a response from a list of possibilities that constitutes the domain of a distinct conceptual type. The process of listing all the elements in the domain of a type is called **enumeration.** A type defined by listing all of its elements is called an **enumerated type.**

Because the title of this chapter is "Strings and Characters," discussing enumerated types might seem like a digression. As it happens, though, characters are similar in structure to enumerated types. Understanding how enumerated types work will help you appreciate how characters work.

At this point, however, enumerated types are an abstract concept. To understand how the concept applies to programming, you need to learn how the computer represents such values internally. You must also learn how to use enumerated types in the context of a Java program. The next two sections address these issues.

Representing enumerated types inside the machine

When the Internal Revenue Service reviews your tax return, the first step in the process is to enter the data from your return into a computer system. To store that information, the computer must have a way of representing each of the different data items, including your filing status. If you were developing a strategy for recording a taxpayer's filing status, what would you do?

The insight you need to solve this problem comes from building on the capabilities you know computers have. Computers are good at working with integers. That's how they're built. As part of their basic hardware operation, they can store, add, subtract, compare, and do all sorts of other things with integers. The fact that computers are good at manipulating integers suggests a solution to the problem of representing an enumerated type. To represent a finite set of values of any type, all you have to do is give each value a number. For example, given the list of allowable filing status values, you could simply count them off, letting *single* be 1, *married filing joint return* be 2, *married filing separate return* be 3, and so on. (In fact, these numeric codes are listed directly on the tax form.) Assigning an integer to each of the different possibilities means that you can use that integer to represent the corresponding filing status.

Thus all you have to do to define a representation for any enumerated type is to number its elements. The process of assigning an integer to each element of an enumerated type is called **integer encoding**—the integer acts as a coded representation of the original value.

Representing enumerated types as integers

For most of Java's history, programmers have adopted the strategy of integer encoding in the most explicit way possible. Because the language lacked any higher-level support for enumerated types, the only mechanism that was available was to define named constants for each value you wanted to represent. Thus, in a program that needed to record the various filing categories offered by the Internal Revenue Service, you might expect to see the following definitions in a Java program:

```
public static final int SINGLE = 1;
public static final int MARRIED_FILING_JOINT_RETURN = 2;
public static final int MARRIED_FILING_SEPARATELY = 3;
public static final int HEAD_OF_HOUSEHOLD = 4;
public static final int QUALIFYING_WIDOW_OR_WIDOWER = 5;
```

These definitions make it possible to use these names in your program. For example, if you wanted to perform some code only if the filing status were *single,* you would use the following **if** statement:

```
if (filingStatus == SINGLE)
```

In using integer constants to represent enumerated types, there are a few cautions that you should keep in mind:

- The variables that hold the enumerated values must be declared as being of type **int**. In many ways, this fact is unfortunate because the conceptual domain of the value is by no means everything encompassed by the type **int**. It is not at all clear what a filing status of –1 or 999 might be, although those are legal integers.

- The definition of constants in the program does not permit you to use the constant names in input operations. In particular, if your program were to request the filing status by issuing the command

```
int filingStatus = readInt("Enter filing status: ");
```

  you could not enter **MARRIED_FILING_SEPARATELY** in response.

- There is no automatic mechanism for displaying the value of an enumerated type so that its name appears in the output. If the value of **filingStatus** were **SINGLE**, calling

```
println("filing status = " + filingStatus);
```

  would simply display a line indicating that the filing status was 1.

Despite these shortcomings, enumerated types are still valuable because they increase the readability of the code.

Defining new enumerated types

While the approach described in the preceding section is common in Java programs, it does not take full advantage of the facilities the language now offers. As of Java 5.0, it is possible to define an actual type name to represent an enumerated type. In its simplest form, the syntax for declaring an enumerated type takes the form shown in the box to the right. As an example, you could define a new type corresponding to the days of the week by writing

```
public enum Weekday {
    SUNDAY, MONDAY, TUESDAY, WEDNESDAY,
    THURSDAY, FRIDAY, SATURDAY
}
```

or a new type representing the primary compass directions by writing the definition

```
public enum Direction {
    NORTH, EAST, SOUTH, WEST
}
```

> **Syntax for defining an enumerated type**
>
> *access* **enum** *name* {
>   *elements*
> }
>
> where:
>   *access* is either **public** or empty.
>   *name* is the name of the new type.
>   *elements* is a list of names used to refer to the individual values that comprise the enumerated type. The elements in the list are separated by commas.

Inside the machine, defining an enumerated type has much the same effect as defining a named integer constant: each element of the enumerated type is represented by an integer code. From the programmer's point of view, however, defining enumerated types using the Java 5.0 strategy has the following advantages:

- The compiler is able to choose the integer codes, thereby freeing the programmer from this responsibility.

- The fact that there is a separate type name often makes the program easier to read because declarations can use a meaningful type name instead of the general-purpose designation **int**.

- The compiler can check whether the value of an enumerated type matches the declaration of the variable to which that value is assigned.

- Enumerated values are displayed using their names.

When you use an enumerated type constant in your program, you typically need to include the enumerated type name as a qualifier. Thus, if you wanted to declare a variable **dir** of type **Direction** and initialize it to the value **NORTH**, you would need to write

```
Direction dir = Direction.NORTH;
```

There is, however, one context in which Java does not use the name of the enumerated type as a qualifier. If you use an enumerated value as the expression in a **switch** statement, Java requires you to use the *unqualified* element names in the **case** clauses. For example, the following method returns **true** if the argument is a weekend day:

```
private boolean isWeekendDay(Weekday day) {
   switch (day) {
      case SATURDAY: case SUNDAY: return true;
      default: return false;
   }
}
```

If you were to write the same method using Boolean logic, you would need to include the enumerated type name, as follows:

```
private boolean isWeekendDay(Weekday day) {
   return day == Weekday.SATURDAY || day == Weekday.SUNDAY;
}
```

8.2 Characters

Characters form the basis of all text data processing. Although strings occur more often in programs than single characters, characters are the fundamental type—the "atoms" used to construct all other forms of text data. Understanding how characters work is therefore critical to understanding all other aspects of text processing. In a sense, characters constitute a built-in enumerated type, although the complete list of possible characters is too large to list in its entirety. It is more appropriate to describe the domain of all characters as a **scalar type,** which is any type that can be interpreted as an integer. Scalar types are extremely useful in Java because you can use them in any context in which an integer might appear. For example, a variable of a scalar type can be used as the control expression in a `switch` statement.

The data type `char`

In Java, single characters are represented using the data type `char`, which is one of the predefined data types. Like all the primitive types introduced in Chapter 3, the type `char` consists of a domain of legal values and a set of operations for manipulating those values. Conceptually, the domain of the data type `char` is the set of symbols that can be displayed on a screen or typed on a keyboard. These symbols—the letters, digits, punctuation marks, spacebar, Return key, and so forth—are the building blocks for all text data.

Because `char` is a scalar type, the set of operations available for characters is the same as that for integers. Understanding what those operations mean in the character domain, however, requires looking more closely at how characters are represented inside the machine.

The ASCII and Unicode coding systems

Single characters are represented inside the machine just like any other scalar type. The fundamental idea is that you can assign every character a number by writing them all down in a list and then counting them off one at a time. The code used to represent a particular character is called its **character code.** For example, you could let the integer 1 represent the letter *A*, the integer 2 represent the letter *B*, and so on. After you got to the point of letting 26 represent the letter *Z*, you could then keep going and number each of the lowercase letters, digits, punctuation marks, and other characters with the integers 27, 28, 29, and so on.

Even though it is technically possible to design a computer in which the number 1 represents the letter *A*, it would certainly be a mistake to do so. In today's world, information is often shared between different computers: you might copy a program from one machine to another on a memory stick or arrange to have your computer communicate directly with others over a national or international network. To make that kind of communication possible, computers must be able to communicate with one another in a common language. An essential feature of that common language is that the computers use the same codes to represent characters, so that the letter *A* on one machine does not come out as a *Z* on another.

In the early days of computing, different computers actually used different character codes. The letter *A* might have a particular integer representation on one machine but an entirely different representation on a computer made by some other manufacturer. Even the set of available characters was subject to change. One computer, for example, might have the character ¢ on its keyboard, while another computer would not be able to represent that character at all. Computer communication was plagued by all the difficulties that people speaking different languages encounter.

Over time, however, the enormous advantage that comes from enabling computers to communicate effectively led to the adoption of a coding system for characters called **ASCII,** which stands for the *American Standard Code for Information Interchange*. The ASCII coding system became quite widespread in the 1980s and represented something of a standard. It was, however, more closely tied to the characters used in English than to those used for other languages in the world. Particularly with the rise of the World Wide Web in the 1990s, it became necessary to expand the domain of the character type to encompass a much broader collection of languages. The result of that expansion was a new coding system called **Unicode,** which is intended to be broader in its application. Java was one of the first languages to adopt Unicode as its representation for characters, which makes it more appropriate for the international framework in which computers operate today.

The Unicode system does make it a little harder to illustrate the principle of enumeration, because there is no way to list all the characters. The ASCII code supported only 256 possible characters, of which only the first 128 were fully standardized. A character set of that size was by no means sufficient to represent all available languages, but it was nonetheless easy to make a table of ASCII values. Unicode has space for 65,536 characters, although not all of those characters have yet been defined. This limit may still prove too small, but it is certainly an improvement in flexibility over the far more limited range of ASCII.

Fortunately, the designers of Unicode decided to incorporate the standard ASCII characters as the first 128 elements in the Unicode set. These characters and their codes appear in Figure 8-1, which shows the ASCII portion of the Unicode table. Most of the entries in the table are familiar characters that appear on the keyboard,

FIGURE 8-1	The ASCII portion of the Unicode table

	0	1	2	3	4	5	6	7
00x	\000	\001	\002	\003	\004	\005	\006	\007
010	\b	\t	\n	\013	\f	\r	\016	\017
020	\020	\021	\022	\023	\024	\025	\026	\027
030	\030	\031	\032	\033	\034	\035	\036	\037
040	space	!	"	#	$	%	&	'
050	(	)	*	+	,	-	.	/
060	0	1	2	3	4	5	6	7
070	8	9	:	;	<	=	>	?
100	@	A	B	C	D	E	F	G
110	H	I	J	K	L	M	N	O
120	P	Q	R	S	T	U	V	W
130	X	Y	Z	[	\	]	^	_
140	`	a	b	c	d	e	f	g
150	h	i	j	k	l	m	n	o
160	p	q	r	s	t	u	v	w
170	x	y	z	{	|	}	~	\177

but there are several less familiar entries represented by a backward slash (\), usually called a **backslash,** followed by a single letter or a sequence of digits. These entries are called **special characters** and are discussed in a separate section later in this chapter.

There is, however, another aspect of the table that is likely to be even more confusing than the special characters. The column headings run from 0 to 7 instead of the 0 to 9 one might expect in a table whose entries specify numeric codes. Similarly, the row headings at first appear to be increasing at a predictable rate but then jump from 070 to 100. The reason for this behavior is that ASCII and Unicode values are not typically presented in decimal (base 10), but rather in a base that is easier to convert to the internal representation of numbers as a sequence of bits. The bases that permit this kind of easy translation are those that derive from a power of two, of which the most common—and the only ones supported directly by Java—are **octal** (base 8) and **hexadecimal** (base 16). Figure 8-1 uses octal notation, in which the only digits fall in the range from 0 to 7. Numeric bases were discussed briefly in section 7.1; for now, the only thing you need to remember about base-8 notation is that every digit position is worth 8 times as much as the digit to its right. For example, the octal number 177 corresponds to the integer

$$1 \times 64 + 7 \times 8 + 7$$

which works out to be 127 in traditional decimal notation. In this text, numbers that are written in a base other than decimal will be marked with a subscript indicating the base. Thus, the notation 177_8 specifies an octal value.

In Java, you can write integer constants in decimal, octal, or hexadecimal. Octal constants begin with a leading **0**; hexadecimal constants begin with the characters **0x**. For example, the number forty-two can be written as **42**, **052**, or **0x2A**.

The internal code for each character in Figure 8-1 is the sum of the octal row and column number associated with that entry. For example, the letter A halfway down the chart is in the row labeled 100 and the column labeled 1. The Unicode value for the letter A is therefore $100_8 + 1_8$, which works out to be 101_8 or 65_{10}. You can use the table to find the code for any character in this same way. In most cases, however, you will not need to do so. Although it is important to know that characters are represented internally using a numeric code, it is not generally useful to know what numeric value corresponds to a particular character. When you type the letter A, the hardware logic built into the keyboard automatically translates that character into the Unicode value 65 which is then sent to the computer. Similarly, when the computer sends the Unicode value 65 to the screen, the letter A appears.

Character constants

When you want to refer to a specific character in a Java program, the standard approach is to specify a **character constant,** which is written by enclosing the desired character in single quotation marks. For example, to indicate the Unicode representation for the letter A, all you have to write is **'A'**. The Java compiler knows that this notation means to use the Unicode value for the letter A, which happens to be 65. Similarly, you can indicate the space character by writing **' '** or the digit 9 by writing **'9'**. Note that the constant **'9'** refers to a *character* and should not be confused with the *integer* value 9. As an integer, the value **'9'** is the value for that character given in the Unicode table, which is 71_8 or 57.

Since Java represents characters internally as their integer codes in the Unicode table, you could in most cases replace the character constant **'A'** with the integer 65. The program would work in exactly the same way but would be much harder to read. You need to keep in mind that some other programmer will eventually come along and have to make sense out of what you've written. Unless that programmer has memorized the Unicode table, seeing the integer 65 written as part of the program won't immediately conjure up an image of the letter A. On the other hand, the character constant **'A'** conveys that meaning directly.

This text includes Figure 8-1 to give you a more concrete understanding of how characters are represented inside the machine. As soon as you have that idea in mind, you should forget about the specific character codes and concentrate instead on the characters themselves.

Important properties of the Unicode representation

Even though it is important not to think about specific character codes, the following two structural properties of the Unicode table are worth remembering:

> **COMMON PITFALLS**
>
> Avoid using integer constants to refer to Unicode characters in a program. All character constants should be indicated by enclosing the character in single quotation marks, as in **'A'** or **'*'**.

1. The codes for the characters representing the digits 0 through 9 are consecutive. Even though you do not need to know exactly what code corresponds to the digit character `'0'`, you know that the code for the digit `'1'` is the next larger integer. Similarly, if you add 9 to the code for `'0'`, you get the code for the character `'9'`.

2. The letters in the alphabet are divided into two separate ranges: one for the uppercase letters *(A–Z)*, and one for the lowercase letters *(a–z)*. Within each range, however, the Unicode values are consecutive, so you can count through the letters one at a time in order.

Each of these properties will prove useful in programs later in this text.

Special characters

Most of the characters in Figure 8-1 are the familiar ones that can be displayed on the screen. These characters are called **printing characters.** The Unicode table, however, also includes **special characters,** which are typically used to control formatting. In Java, special characters are written using an **escape sequence,** which consists of a backslash followed by a character or a sequence of digits. Figure 8-2 lists the predefined escape sequences.

You can include special characters in character constants by writing the escape sequence as part of the constant. Although an escape sequence consists of several characters, each sequence is translated into a single Unicode value inside the machine. The internal codes for the special characters are included in Figure 8-1.

When the compiler sees the backslash character, it expects it to be the first character in an escape sequence. If you want to represent the backslash character itself, you therefore have to use two consecutive backslashes inside single quotation marks like this: `'\\'`. Similarly, the single quotation mark, when used as a character constant, must also be preceded by a backslash: `'\''`.

FIGURE 8-2	Escape sequences used in character and string constants
Sequence	**Interpretation**
`\b`	Backspace
`\f`	Formfeed (starts a new page)
`\n`	Newline (moves to the beginning of the next line)
`\r`	Return (returns to the beginning of the line without advancing)
`\t`	Tab (moves horizontally to the next tab stop)
`\0`	Null character (the character whose Unicode value is 0)
`\\`	The character \ itself
`\'`	The character ' (requires the backslash only in character constants)
`\"`	The character " (requires the backslash only in string constants)
`\ddd`	The character whose Unicode value is the octal number *ddd*
`\uxxxx`	The character whose Unicode value is the hexadecimal number *xxxx*

Special characters can also be used in string constants. The fact that a double quotation mark is used to indicate the *end* of a string means that the double quotation mark must be marked as a special character if it is *part* of a string. For example, if you write a program containing the line

```
println("\"Bother,\" said Pooh.");
```

the output is

```
"Bother," said Pooh.
```

Many of the special characters in Unicode do not have explicit names and are instead represented in programs using their internal numeric codes. You can specify those characters in octal using the format *ddd* or in hexadecimal as \\u*xxxx*.

Character arithmetic

In Java, you can use the arithmetic operators with character values just as you do with integers. You don't need a type cast to convert a character to its integer equivalent, although specifying such casts can sometimes make your programs easier to read. When you use a character value in an expression, the result is defined according to the internal Unicode values. For example, Java treats the character `'A'`, which is represented internally using the Unicode value 65, as the integer 65 whenever that character appears in an arithmetic context. Conversions from integers to characters use the same strategy of relying on the internal Unicode values. In Java, you do need a type cast to convert an integer into a character because the range of type **char** is smaller than the range of type **int**. Java's designers were careful to require explicit type casts in cases where information might be lost in the conversion.

You can use the convertibility of integers and characters to write a **randomLetter** method that returns a randomly chosen uppercase letter. The simplest implementation is

```
private char randomLetter() {
    return (char) rgen.nextInt('A', 'Z');
}
```

where **rgen** is an instance variable containing a **RandomGenerator**, as described in section 6.1. This implementation, however, may end up confusing readers who expect the call to **rgen.nextInt** to take integers as parameters rather than characters. For the benefit of those readers, it is probably better to make the conversions explicit by introducing type casts, as follows:

```
private char randomLetter() {
   return (char) rgen.nextInt((int) 'A', (int) 'Z');
}
```

Even though it is legal to apply any arithmetic operation to values of type **char**, not all operations are meaningful in that domain. For example, it is legal to multiply **'A'** by **'B'** as part of a program. To determine the result, the computer takes the internal codes, 65 and 66, and multiplies them to get 4290. The problem is that this integer means nothing in the character world. Only a few of the arithmetic operations are likely to be useful when applied to characters. The operations that generally make sense are:

- *Adding an integer to a character.* If **c** is a character and **n** is an integer, the expression **c + n** represents the character code that comes **n** characters after **c** in the coding sequence. For example, the expression **'0' + n** computes the character code of the nth digit, if **n** is between 0 and 9. Thus **'0' + 5** computes the character code for **'5'**. Similarly, the expression **'A' + n − 1** computes the character code of the nth letter in the alphabet, assuming that **n** is between 1 and 26. The result of this operation is logically a **char**.

- *Subtracting an integer from a character.* The expression **c − n** represents the code of the character that comes **n** characters before **c** in the coding sequence. For example, the expression **'Z' − 2** computes the character code for **'X'**. The result of this operation is logically a **char**.

- *Subtracting one character from another.* If **c1** and **c2** are both characters, the expression **c1 − c2** represents the distance between those characters in coding sequence. For example, if you look back to Figure 8-1 and compute the Unicode values of each character, you can determine that **'a' − 'A'** is 32. More importantly, the distance between a lowercase character and its uppercase counterpart is constant, so that **'z' − 'Z'** is also 32. The result of this operation is logically an **int**.

- *Comparing two characters against each other.* Comparing two character values using any of the relational operators is a common operation, often used to determine alphabetical ordering. For example, the expression **c1 < c2** is **true** if **c1** comes before **c2** in the Unicode table.

To see how these operations apply to practical problems, consider how the computer executes a method like **readInt**. When a user types a number, such as 102, the computer receives the individual keystrokes as characters and must therefore work with the input values **'1'**, **'0'**, and **'2'**. Because the **readInt** method must return an integer, it needs to translate the character into the integers they represent. To do so, **readInt** takes advantage of the fact that the digits are consecutive in the Unicode sequence.

As an illustration, suppose that **readInt** has just read a character from the keyboard and stored it in the variable **ch**. It can convert the character to its numeric form by evaluating the expression

```
ch − '0'
```

Assuming that **ch** contains a digit character, the difference between its Unicode value and the Unicode value for the digit **'0'** must correspond to the decimal value of that digit. Suppose, for example, that the variable **ch** contains the character **'9'**. If you consult the Unicode table, you can determine that the character **'9'** has the internal code 57. The digit **'0'** has the Unicode value 48, and 57 – 48 is 9. The key point is that the method makes no assumption that **'0'** has the Unicode value 48, which means that the same method would work even if Java someday decided to use a different character set. The only assumption is that the codes for the digits form a consecutive sequence.

But how can **readInt** determine whether the character **ch** is in fact a digit? Once again, it can take advantage of the fact that the digits are consecutive in the Unicode table. The statement

```
if (ch >= '0' && ch <= '9') . . .
```

distinguishes the digit characters from the rest of the Unicode set. Similarly, the statement

```
if (ch >= 'A' && ch <= 'Z') . . .
```

identifies the uppercase letters, and

```
if (ch >= 'a' && ch <= 'z') . . .
```

identifies the lowercase letters.

Useful methods in the **Character** class

As it happens, you won't usually encounter the **if** statements used at the end of the preceding section in a typical Java program. The operations for checking whether a character is a digit or a letter are so common that the designers of Java made them methods in the **Character** class, which is defined in the package **java.lang** and is therefore available in any Java program without an **import** statement.

The **Character** class declares several useful methods for manipulating character values, the most important of which appear in Figure 8-3. Like the methods in the **Math** class, these methods are declared to be static, which means that they don't operate on an object but instead act more like traditional functions in mathematics. For example, you can convert a lowercase character **ch** into its uppercase equivalent by writing

```
ch = Character.toUpperCase(ch);
```

Although **toLowerCase** and **toUpperCase** are already available in the **Character** class, you will be able to appreciate their operation more if you try to implement them from scratch. Once again, you can ignore the actual Unicode values involved and rely only on the fact that letters are contiguous. If **ch** contains a character code for an uppercase letter, you can convert it to its lowercase form by adding the constant difference in value that separates the uppercase and lowercase

FIGURE 8-3	Useful static methods in the `Character` class

`static boolean isDigit(char ch)`   Determines if the specified character is a digit.
`static boolean isJavaIdentifierPart(char ch)`   Determines if the specified character may be part of a Java identifier.
`static boolean isJavaIdentifierStart(char ch)`   Determines if the specified character is permissible as the first character in a Java identifier.
`static boolean isLetter(char ch)`   Determines if the specified character is a letter.
`static boolean isLetterOrDigit(char ch)`   Determines if the specified character is a letter or digit.
`static boolean isLowerCase(char ch)`   Determines if the specified character is a lowercase character.
`static boolean isUpperCase(char ch)`   Determines if the specified character is an uppercase character.
`static boolean isWhitespace(char ch)`   Determines if the specified character is **whitespace** (that is, invisible in print, like spaces or tabs).
`static char toLowerCase(char ch)`   Converts **ch** to its lowercase equivalent, if one exists. If not, **ch** is returned unchanged.
`static char toUpperCase(char ch)`   Converts **ch** to its uppercase equivalent, if one exists. If not, **ch** is returned unchanged.

characters. Rather than write that difference as an explicit constant, however, the program is easier to read if you express it using character arithmetic as `'a' - 'A'`. Thus, you could implement the **toLowerCase** method as follows:

```
public static char toLowerCase(char ch) {
   if (ch >= 'A' && ch <= 'Z') {
      return ch + 'a' - 'A';
   } else {
      return ch;
   }
}
```

The method **toUpperCase** has a similar implementation. Given that the point of this example is to match the implementation in the **Character** class, this method is declared to be **public** rather than the traditional **private**; the corresponding method in the **Character** class must certainly be public, or you would not be able to call it. Similarly, the method is declared to be **static**, as in the **Character** class.

Even though the methods defined in the **Character** class are easy to implement, it is good programming practice to use the library methods instead of writing your own. There are four principal reasons for doing so.

1. Because the methods from the **Character** class are standard, programs you write will be easier for other programmers to read. Assuming those programmers are at all experienced in Java, they will recognize the methods in that class and know exactly what they mean.

2. It is easier to rely on library methods for correctness than on your own. Because the Java libraries are used by millions of client programmers, there is considerable pressure on the implementors to get the methods right. If you rewrite library methods yourself, the chance of introducing a bug into your program is much larger.

3. The code you write yourself will not take advantage of the international applicability of Unicode. The do-it-yourself implementation of **toLowerCase** shown earlier assumes that the characters are in the Roman alphabet, which is no longer a reasonable assumption. Other alphabets also have uppercase and lowercase characters, and the implementation in the **Character** class knows how to convert characters in those alphabets as well.

4. The implementations of methods in the library packages are typically more efficient than those you would write yourself. How these more efficient implementations work is beyond the scope of this chapter, but the important point is that you can take advantage of that added efficiency by using the library forms.

Control statements involving characters

Because **char** is a scalar type, you can use it in all the statement forms in which integers appear. For example, if **ch** is declared to be of type **char**, you can use the following **for** header line to execute a loop 26 times, once for each uppercase letter in the alphabet:

```
for (char ch = 'A'; ch <= 'Z'; ch++)
```

Similarly, you can use a character as the control expression in a **switch** statement. For example, the following predicate method returns **true** if its argument is a vowel in the English language:

```
private boolean isEnglishVowel(char ch) {
   switch (Character.toLowerCase(ch)) {
      case 'a': case 'e': case 'i': case 'o': case 'u':
         return true;
      default:
         return false;
   }
}
```

Note that the implementation uses the **toLowerCase** method to recognize vowels in both their uppercase and lowercase forms.

▉ 8.3 Strings as an abstract idea

The real power of using characters comes from the fact that you can string them together to form a sequence of characters called a **string,** which is represented in Java by a class in the always-imported **java.lang** package called **String**. Because English explanations of the **String** class get much harder to read if every occurrence of the noun that means a sequence of characters is written in its Java form, I will usually talk about strings in an abstract sense and just call them strings with no uppercase **s** and no special code font. I leave it to you to remember that strings—as an abstract idea—are represented in Java by a class named **String**. As noted in the introduction to this chapter, you have been using strings since the very first program in the book to display messages. As you will discover, however, there is a lot more you need to learn about strings in order to unlock the enormous power they bring to programming. To understand strings in their entirety, you must consider them from more than one perspective at different levels of detail.

Holistic and reductionist views of strings

As you have found many times in this text, you can approach programming from both a reductionistic and a holistic perspective. When you concern yourself with the internal details of data representation, you are taking the reductionistic view. From this perspective, your job is to understand how characters are stored in the computer's memory, how a sequence of those characters can be stored to form a string, and how, for example, a 200-character string can fit inside the same variable that holds a 2-character string. These are all interesting questions, and you will discover the answers in due course. When you consider strings from the holistic perspective, however, your job is to understand how to manipulate a string as a single logical unit. By focusing on the abstract behavior of strings, you can learn how to use them effectively without getting bogged down in details.

To a certain extent, Java forces a holistic view of strings because the **String** class provides you with very little access to the underlying representation. Even so, it is possible to contrast the reductionistic view in which you think about the individual characters with the more holistic view in which you don't. So far in this text, you have been working entirely at the holistic level. The remainder of this chapter describes methods in the **String** class that operate at both the character and the whole-string levels.

The notion of an abstract type

The principal advantage of the **String** class—and of object-oriented class definitions in general—is that the definition makes it possible to work with strings as an **abstract type** in which the fundamental operations are defined only by their *behavior* and not in terms of the underlying *representation*. In Java, abstract types correspond to class definitions that specify the operations which can be performed on objects of that type. The legal operations for a particular abstract type are called its **primitive operations** and are defined as public methods. Details of how those operations work and how the information is represented internally are hidden away in the implementation of the class. Whenever a client wants to manipulate values of an abstract type, the client must use the methods provided by the class.

In the context of strings, what are the primitive operations that you might want to perform? To begin with, you already know how to specify a string constant in a program, to combine strings using concatenation, and to perform string input and output using the **println** and **readLine** methods.

What else might you want to do? When working with strings, you might, for example, want to perform any of the following operations:

- Find out how long a string is
- Select the ith character from a string
- Extract a piece of a string to form a shorter one
- Determine whether two strings contain the same characters
- Compare two strings to see which comes first in alphabetical order
- Determine whether a string contains a particular character or set of characters

There are other operations you might consider, but this list offers an interesting and useful start. Each of these operations is implemented by a method in the **String** class, which gives you the tools you need to use strings without requiring you to comprehend the details of the underlying representation. The fact that you do not need to understand those details is the essence of data abstraction.

8.4 Using the methods in the String class

As noted in Chapter 6, the best way to learn about a class and its methods is to consult the **javadoc** documentation. If you do so, you will find that the **String** class implements lots of methods, many of which you will probably never have occasion to use. The ones that you are most likely to encounter are shown in Figure 8-4 and described in the sections that follow.

As you read through the descriptions of these methods, it is important to keep in mind that the **String** class is **immutable,** which simply means that none of its methods ever change the internal state. For many students, this behavior—which is actually quite useful—seems counterintuitive. After discovering that the list in Figure 8-4 includes a **toLowerCase** method, many students expect that the line

```
str.toLowerCase()
```

will convert the characters in the string **str** to lower case. As the bug symbol suggests, however, this expectation is incorrect. What the **toLowerCase** method in fact does is *return* a new string in which those conversions have been performed. Thus, to change the value stored in the string variable **str** so that all letters within it appear in lowercase, you need to use an assignment statement, such as

```
str = str.toLowerCase();
```

Determining the length of a string

When writing programs to manipulate strings, you often need to know how many characters a particular string contains. The total number of characters in a string—counting all letters, digits, spaces, punctuation marks, and special characters—is called the **length** of the string.

Using the **String** class, you can obtain the length of a string **s** by calling the method **length**. For example, the first string you encountered in this book was

FIGURE 8-4	Useful methods available in the `String` class

`int length()`
Returns the length of the string.
`char charAt(int index)`
Returns the character at the specified index.
`String concat(String s2)`
Concatenates **s2** to the end of the receiver, returning a new string with the receiver unchanged.
`String substring(int p1, int p2)`
Returns the substring beginning at **p1** and extending up to but not including **p2**.
`String substring(int p1)`
Returns the substring beginning at **p1** and extending through the end of the string.
`String trim()`
Returns the substring formed by deleting any white space at the beginning or end of the string.
`boolean equals(String s2)`
Returns **true** if the string **s2** is equal to the receiver.
`boolean equalsIgnoreCase(String s2)`
Returns **true** if the string **s2** is equal to the receiver, ignoring distinctions in case.
`int compareTo(String s2)`
Returns a number whose sign indicates how the strings compare in lexicographic order.
`int indexOf(char c)` *or* `indexOf(String s)`
Returns the index of the first occurrence of the character or string, or -1 if it does not appear.
`int indexOf(char c, int start)` *or* `indexOf(String s, int start)`
Like **indexOf** with one argument, but starts at the specified index position.
`boolean startsWith(String prefix)`
Returns **true** if the string starts with the specified prefix.
`boolean endsWith(String suffix)`
Returns **true** if the string ends with the specified suffix.
`string toUpperCase()`
Converts the string to uppercase.
`string toLowerCase()`
Converts the string to lowercase.

      `"hello, world"`

This string has length 12—five characters in the word **hello**, five more in **world**, one comma, and one space. Thus, if you assigned that string to the variable **message** by writing

      `String message = "hello, world";`

you could then compute its length by writing

      `message.length()`

As this example makes clear, the **String** class uses the object-oriented receiver notation. If you want to determine the length of a **String** variable, you send that string a message asking it to respond by reporting its length. That response is then returned as the value of the method.

Selecting characters from a string

In Java, positions within a string are numbered starting from 0. For example, the individual characters in the string **"hello, world"** are numbered as in the following diagram:

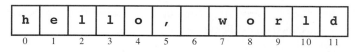

The position number written underneath each character in the string is called its **index.**

To enable you to select a particular character in a string given its index, the **String** class provides a method called **charAt** that takes an integer representing the index and returns a character. For example, if the variable **str** contains the string **"hello, world"**, calling

        str.charAt(0)

returns the character **'h'**. Similarly, calling **str.charAt(5)** returns **','**. Be sure to remember that Java numbers characters starting with 0, not 1. It is easy to forget this rule and assume that **str.charAt(5)** will return the fifth character in the string; what happens instead is that **str.charAt(5)** returns the character at index position 5, which is the *sixth* character as we number character positions in English.

Concatenation

One of the most useful operations available for strings is **concatenation,** which consists of combining two strings end to end with no intervening characters. As you can see from Figure 8-4, the **String** class implements a **concat** method that performs this operation. For example, if **str** contains **"hello, world"**, you could generate a new string that included an exclamation point on the end by writing

        str.concat("!")

It is critical to note, however, that this method call simply returns a new string value and does not change the value of the variable **str**. To do so using the **concat** method, you would have to write

        str = str.concat("!");

In Java, no one actually uses the **concat** method because its function is built into Java in the form of the + operator. Thus, what you would be more likely to see is

        str = str + "!";

or, even more compactly,

        str += "!";

In either form, concatenation always combines the two strings with no intervening space. If you want to put a space between two words represented as string values, you have to perform an additional concatenation step. For example, if the variable **word1** contains **"hello"** and the variable **word2** contains **"world"**, you need to write

```
word1 + " " + word2
```

to get the string **"hello world"**. You could also write this expression so that it invoked the **concat** method explicitly, like this:

```
word1.concat(" ").concat(word2)
```

The ungainly appearance of this expression should quickly convince you of the value of the + operator.

The + operator also has the wonderful property that it converts any operands that are not strings to their string representation, which is why you can write statements like

```
println("The answer is " + answer);
```

This statement works no matter what type the variable **answer** is. Before Java concatenates the two values, it converts **answer** to its string representation.

When you write expressions involving the + operator, you need to keep Java's precedence rules in mind. In the statement

```
println("The answer is " + 6 * 7);
```

the * operator is evaluated before the + operator, so the output will look like this:

At first glance, it would seem that the statement

```
println("The answer is " + 15 + 25);
```

would behave similarly and produce the same output. In this case, however, the two instances of the + operator are evaluated from left to right in accordance with Java's rules of precedence. The effect is that the string version of 15 gets concatenated to the string first, and then the string version of 25 is concatenated to that, producing the following output:

COMMON PITFALLS

Remember to consider Java's rules of precedence when you use the + operator to signify concatenation. Failure to think about precedence can lead to some surprising results.

As a simple example of the use of concatenation, the following method returns a string consisting of a specified number of copies of the string passed as the second argument:

```
private String concatNCopies(int n, String str) {
    String result = "";
    for (int i = 0; i < n; i++) {
        result += str;
    }
    return result;
}
```

This method is particularly handy if you want to generate separators in console output. For example, the statement

```
println(concatNCopies(72, "-"));
```

prints a line of 72 hyphens.

In a way, the implementation strategy used in **concatNCopies** is similar to that used in the **factorial** method presented in Chapter 5. In both cases, the method uses a local variable to keep track of the partially computed result during each cycle of a **for** loop. In the **concatNCopies** method, each cycle in the **for** loop concatenates the value of **str** onto the end of the previous value of **result**. Because each cycle adds one copy of **str** to the end of **result**, the final value of **result** after **n** cycles must consist of **n** copies of that string.

In each of the two methods—**factorial** and **concatNCopies**—the initialization of the variable used to hold the result is worthy of some note. In the **factorial** method, the **result** variable is initialized to 1, so multiplying it by each successive value of **i** properly keeps track of the result as the computation proceeds. In the case of **concatNCopies**, the corresponding statement initializes the string variable **result** so that it grows through concatenation. After the first cycle of the loop, the variable **result** must consist of one copy of the string **str**. Prior to the first cycle, therefore, **result** must contain zero copies of the string, which means it has no characters at all. The string with no characters at all is called the **empty string** and is written in Java using adjacent double quotes: `""`. Whenever you need to construct a new string by concatenating successive parts onto an existing string variable, you should initialize that variable to the empty string.

Extracting parts of a string

Concatenation makes longer strings from shorter pieces. You often need to do the reverse: separate a string into the shorter pieces it contains. A string that is part of a longer string is called a **substring.** The **String** class provides a method **substring** that takes two arguments representing index positions in the string. The effect of invoking **s.substring(p1, p2)** is to extract the characters in **s** lying between positions **p1** up to but not including **p2**. Thus if **str** contains the string `"hello world"`, the method call

```
str.substring(1, 4)
```

returns the string `"ell"`. As you know, numbering in Java begins at 0, so the character at index position 1 is the character `'e'`.

The second argument in the **substring** method is optional. If it is missing, substring returns the characters starting at the index position specified by the first argument and continuing through the end of the string.

As an example of the use of **substring**, the method **secondHalf(s)** returns the substring consisting of the last half of the characters in **s**, including the middle character if the length of the string is odd:

```
private String secondHalf(String str) {
   return str.substring(str.length() / 2);
}
```

Comparing one string with another

At many times in your programming, you will need to check to see whether two strings have the same value. When you do, you are almost certain to code this test at least once in the following incorrect form:

```
if (s1 == s2) . . .
```

The problem here is that strings are objects in Java and the relational operators like == are defined in the conventional mathematical way only for the primitive Java types like **int** and **char**. What makes this problem all the more insidious is that the == operator does something when applied to strings, but not what you'd initially expect. For objects, the == operator tests whether the two sides are the same object. What you want in this case, however, is to test whether two different **String** objects have the same value.

To accomplish what you need, the **String** class defines a method called **equals**, which you can use to test two strings for equality. Like the other methods in the **String** class, **equals** is applied to a receiver object, which means that the syntax for an equality test looks like this:

```
if (s1.equals(s2)) . . .
```

There is also a method **equalsIgnoreCase** that checks whether two strings are equal independent of uppercase/lowercase distinctions.

You will sometimes also find it useful to determine how two strings relate to each other in alphabetical order. The **String** class provides the method **compareTo** for this purpose. You call the **compareTo** method in typical receiver-based fashion:

```
s1.compareTo(s2)
```

The result of the call is an integer whose sign indicates the relationship between the two strings, as follows:

> **COMMON PITFALLS**
>
> When comparing string values in Java, remember to use the **equals** and **compareTo** methods, and not the relational operators. The compiler will not detect this error, but the test will have unpredictable results.

- If **s1** precedes **s2** in alphabetical order, **compareTo** returns a negative integer.
- If **s1** follows **s2** in alphabetical order, **compareTo** returns a positive integer.
- If the two strings are exactly the same, **compareTo** returns 0.

Thus, if you want to determine whether **s1** comes before **s2** in alphabetical order, you need to write

```
if (s1.compareTo(s2) < 0) . . .
```

The "alphabetical order" computers use is different from the order that dictionaries use in certain respects. When **compareTo** compares two strings, it compares them using the numeric ordering imposed by the underlying character codes. This order is called **lexicographic order** and differs from traditional alphabetical order in several respects. For example, in an alphabetical index, you will find the entry for *aardvark* before the entry for *Achilles,* because traditional alphabetical ordering does not consider uppercase and lowercase letters separately. If you apply **compareTo** to the strings **"aardvark"** and **"Achilles"**, the method simply compares the Unicode values. In Unicode, the lowercase character **'a'** comes after an uppercase **'A'**. In lexicographic order, the string **"Achilles"** comes first. Thus the method call

```
"aardvark".compareTo("Achilles")
```

returns a positive integer.

When you call **compareTo**, it compares the strings starting with the first character in each. If those characters are different, **compareTo** considers how the two character values relate to each other in the Unicode sequence and returns an integer that indicates that result. If the first characters match, **compareTo** goes on to look at the second characters, continuing this process until it detects a difference. If **compareTo** runs out of characters in one of the two strings, that string is automatically considered to precede the longer one, just as in traditional alphabetical ordering. For example,

```
"abc".compareTo("abcdefg")
```

returns a negative integer. Only if the two strings match all the way down the line and end at the same place does **compareTo** return the value 0.

Searching within a string

From time to time, you will find it useful to search a string to see whether it contains a particular character or substring. To enable you to do so, the **String** class provides a method called **indexOf**, which comes in several forms. The simplest form of the call is illustrated by the statement

```
int pos = str.indexOf(search);
```

where *search* is what you are looking for, which can be either a string or a character. When **indexOf** is called, the method searches through the string **str** looking for the first occurrence of the search value. If the search value is found, **indexOf** returns the index position at which the match begins. If the character does not appear before the end of the string, **indexOf** returns the value −1.

The **indexOf** method also takes an optional second argument that indicates the index position at which to start the search. The effect of both styles of the **indexOf** method is illustrated by the following examples, which assume that the variable **str** contains the string "**hello, world**":

`str.indexOf('o')`	*returns*	4
`str.indexOf('o', 5)`	*returns*	8
`str.indexOf('x')`	*returns*	−1

As with string comparison, the methods for searching a string consider uppercase and lowercase characters to be different.

You can use **indexOf** to implement a method that generates an **acronym,** which is a new word formed by combining, in order, the initial letters of a series of words. For example, the word *scuba* is an acronym formed from the first letters in *self contained underwater breathing apparatus*. The method **acronym** takes a string composed of separate words and return its acronym. Thus, calling the method

```
acronym("self contained underwater breathing apparatus")
```

returns "**scuba**".

Provided that the words are separated by a single space and that no extraneous characters appear, the implementation of **acronym** can simply take the very first letter and then go into a loop searching for each space. Whenever it finds one, it can concatenate the next character onto the end of the string variable used to hold the result. When no more spaces appear in the string, the acronym is complete. This strategy can be translated into a Java implementation as follows:

```java
private String acronym(String str) {
   String result = str.substring(0, 1);
   int pos = str.indexOf(' ');
   while (pos != -1) {
      result += str.substring(pos + 1, pos + 2);
      pos = str.indexOf(' ', pos + 1);
   }
   return result;
}
```

The Java **String** class also contains two useful methods for checking to see whether a string begins or ends with a particular substring. The **startsWith** method returns **true** if the string on which it is invoked begins with the string passed as an argument. Thus, the statements

```java
String answer = readLine("Would you like to play a game? ");
if (answer.startsWith("y") || answer.startsWith("Y")) {
   . . . code to play the game . . .
}
```

executes the body of the **if** statement only if the user enters an answer to the question that begins with an upper- or lowercase **Y**. The **String** class also contains a symmetric **endsWith** method that returns **true** if the string ends with the specified substring.

Case conversion

The **String** class includes two methods, **toUpperCase** and **toLowerCase**, that convert the case of any alphabetic characters to the indicated case. For example, if **str** contains the string **"hello, world"**, calling the method

```
str.toUpperCase()
```

returns the string **"HELLO, WORLD"**. Any nonalphabetic characters appearing in the string—such as the comma, space, and period in this example—remain unaffected.

8.5 A case study in string processing

To give you more of a sense of how to implement string-processing problems in Java, this section walks you through the development of a **ConsoleProgam** that reads lines of text from the user and then translates each word in the line from English into Pig Latin. Pig Latin is an invented language formed by transforming each English word according to the following simple rules:

1. If the word begins with a consonant, you form its Pig Latin equivalent by moving the initial consonant string (that is, all the letters up to the first vowel) from the beginning of the word to the end and then adding the suffix *ay*.
2. If the word begins with a vowel, you simply add the suffix *way*.

For example, suppose the word is *scram*. Because the word begins with a consonant, you divide it into two parts: one consisting of the letters before the first vowel and one consisting of that vowel and the remaining letters:

$$\boxed{s\ c\ r}\quad \boxed{a\ m}$$

You then interchange these two parts and add *ay* at the end, as follows:

$$\boxed{a\ m}\quad \boxed{s\ c\ r}\quad \boxed{a\ y}$$

creating the Pig Latin word *amscray*. For a word that begins with a vowel, such as *apple,* you simply add *way* to the end, which leaves you with *appleway*.

Applying top-down design

Since the problem is to translate an entire line of English text into Pig Latin, the program should be able to produce sample runs like this one:

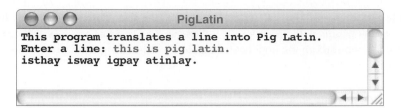

As with most programming problems, the best approach is to begin by applying top-down design, as described in the section on "Stepwise refinement" in Chapter 5. With top-down design, you start at the level of the **run** method and work your way down through a series of subsidiary methods, each of which solves a successively simpler part of the entire problem. At the initial stage, you define the **run** method as a sequence of high-level steps that have yet to be implemented. Although it is often possible to code the steps directly as method calls, it is usually easier to write them in English first. For example, as long as you are designing your program on paper, you can write a rough draft of the Pig Latin program using pseudocode:

```
public void run() {
    Tell the user what the program does.
    Ask the user for a line of text.
    Translate the line into Pig Latin and print it on the console.
}
```

Even though it makes no sense to the compiler, pseudocode is useful for you as a programmer because it enables you to keep track of the stepwise refinement process. After you write out the complete program as a sequence of English steps, you can go back through the pseudocode statements and substitute the actual Java code necessary to implement them. In this case, for example, it is easy to translate the first two pseudocode statements into Java because they match programming idioms you have been using since Chapter 2. After you fill in the details of those two statements, the pseudocode version of the program looks like this:

```
public void run() {
    println("This program translates a line into Pig Latin.");
    String line = readLine("Enter a line: ");
    Translate the line into Pig Latin and print it on the console.
}
```

The result is still pseudocode, but you have made progress. The remaining English statement is harder to code, so the best strategy is to apply stepwise refinement, replacing the line of pseudocode with a new method that has the effect of the English sentence. In this case, you want a method that will "translate the line into Pig Latin," which you might choose to name **translateLine**. Using that name, you can complete the implementation of the **run** method as follows:

```
public void run() {
    println("This program translates a line into Pig Latin.");
    String line = readLine("Enter a line: ");
    println(translateLine(line));
}
```

At this level of detail, the program is satisfyingly simple: you give the user an idea of what the program does, read in a line of text as a Java string, call **translateLine** to convert the string into its Pig Latin equivalent, and finally print the translated line to the console.

Although you haven't yet written **translateLine**, you can say something about its behavior from the caller's point of view. Because you know it takes a string from the caller and returns a new string containing the translated line, the header line for **translateLine** must look like this:

```
private String translateLine(String line)
```

Implementing **translateLine**

After reaching this point, you are ready to begin implementing **translateLine**, which is still complex enough that it makes sense to decompose it further. As is often true in programming, there are many strategies for doing so, some of which work better than others. In most cases, however, no particular strategy for decomposition is clearly the "correct" one. You will usually need to consider several ways of subdividing the problem and try to balance the various tradeoffs. Your first decomposition strategy will often lead down a blind alley, forcing you to back up and start again. Such detours are all part of the programming process.

In implementing **translateLine**, you need to solve the problem of how to divide a string into words, translate each word into Pig Latin, and then recombine the words to form the translated string. This statement of the problem suggests the following conceptual decomposition:

```
private String translateLine(String line) {
    Divide the line into words.
    Translate each word into Pig Latin.
    Concatenate each of the translated words together.
    Return the concatenated string as a result.
}
```

This decomposition is reasonable in theory but raises certain practical questions. As written, the first step requires you to store the entire list of words, which you won't know how to do until Chapter 12. If you think carefully about the problem, however, you will discover that you don't need to keep track of all the words at once. As soon as you find one word, you can translate that word and then immediately concatenate it onto the string that holds the translated line. This observation suggests a second strategy:

```
private String translateLine(String line) {
    Initialize a variable to hold the result and set it to the empty string.
    while (there are any words left on the line) {
        Get the next word.
        Translate that word into Pig Latin.
        Append the translated word to the result variable.
    }
    Return the value of the result variable to the caller.
}
```

There are several details missing from the pseudocode version of the strategy, but the overall idea seems to make sense and avoids the problem of having to keep track of an entire list of words.

Taking spaces and punctuation into account

The strategy used in the pseudocode version of **translateLine** has a small problem. Suppose, for example, that the user enters the following input line when the program is run:

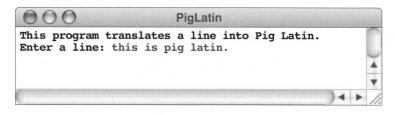

If you conceive of the input as being the four words **"this"**, **"is"**, **"pig"**, and **"latin"**, the output of the program, assuming that all the English steps work exactly as they are supposed to, would be

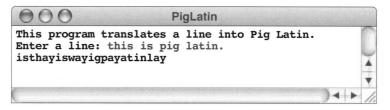

This output is not really what you want. All the words run together because the spaces and punctuation marks have disappeared. The pseudocode version of **translateLine** doesn't take spacing and punctuation into account. On the other hand, neither did the original English statement of the problem. The problem was incompletely specified.

One of the realities of programming is that English descriptions of problems are usually incompletely specified. As a programmer, you will often trip over some detail that the framers of the problem either overlooked or considered too obvious to mention. In some cases, the omission is serious enough that you have to discuss it with the person who assigned you the programming task. In many cases, however, you will have to choose for yourself a policy that seems reasonable.

Deciding what seems reasonable, however, can sometimes be tricky. In this case, you might decide to print a space between each word in the output, ignoring any other punctuation. This strategy is simple and might be reasonable in this context. On the other hand, it is probably not the best strategy. Punctuation helps make output readable. Because the punctuation marks and spaces convey meaning, it would be better to display them in precisely the same places where they appear in the input. Thus you probably want the output to look like this:

```
 ○ ○ ○                    PigLatin
This program translates a line into Pig Latin.
Enter a line: this is pig latin.
isthay isway igpay atinlay.
```

There are many ways to redesign the program so that punctuation marks appear correctly in the output. One approach, for example, is to change the loop in the **run** method so that it goes through the string character by character instead of word by word. If you use this strategy, the pseudocode for the implementation has the following structure:

```
private String translateLine(String line) {
    Initialize a variable to hold the result and set it to the empty string.
    for (int i = 0; i < line.length(); i++) {
        if (the iᵗʰ character in the line is some kind of separator) {
            Append that character to the result variable.
        } else if (the iᵗʰ character is the end of a word) {
            Extract the word as a substring.
            Translate the word to Pig Latin.
            Append the translated word to the result variable.
        }
    }
    Return the value of the result variable to the caller.
}
```

With some amount of effort, you can get this strategy to work (and will indeed have the opportunity to do so in exercise 17). Such a strategy, however, has several drawbacks. One is that the program structure has become more complicated. The original pseudocode design was shorter, in part because it allowed you to work with the string in larger units.

A more serious problem, however, shows up in the decomposition. The version of the pseudocode presented in the preceding section contains the English statement

Get the next word.

That statement has disappeared in the most recent version. If you think like a programmer, you will recognize that the operation "get the next word" is a useful general tool, one that has application far beyond a simple Pig Latin program. Many problems require you to break up text into words. If you can develop a general method that performs this operation, you will have a tremendous head start toward solving those problems. On the other hand, simply being able to get the next word does not solve the punctuation problem. To be useful in the current application, the method that returns the next word must be able to return the spaces and punctuation marks as well.

The easiest way to fix the psuedocode version of **translateLine** begins by redefining the notion of what constitutes a word. If you look at the input line

this is pig latin.

you might simply see it as the four words, *this, is, pig,* and *latin*. Alternatively, you can also choose to think about the line as being composed of eight separate pieces, as follows:

In this view of the line, the spaces and punctuation marks are interpreted as distinct entities, just like the words. In computer science, a sequence of characters that acts as a coherent unit is called a **token.** Thus, each of the boxed units in the preceding diagram constitutes a token.

Considering spaces and punctuation characters as separate tokens makes it easy to modify the **translateLine** strategy so these characters are included in the returned string. The revised pseudocode strategy is

```
private String translateLine(String line) {
    Initialize a variable to hold the result and set it to the empty string.
    while (there are any tokens left on the line) {
        Get the next token.
        if (the token is a word) {
            Translate the token to Pig Latin.
        }
        Append the token to the result variable.
    }
    Return the value of the result variable to the caller.
}
```

The strategy is still quite simple. Moreover, the individual operations of getting a token and testing to see whether tokens remain on the line are likely to be useful in a variety of applications.

The **StringTokenizer** class

In fact, the ability to divide a string into tokens is so useful that the Java libraries include several different classes to accomplish this task. Of these, the simplest is the **StringTokenizer** class that is part of the **java.util** package. This class makes it possible to read tokens from a string that you provide to the **StringTokenizer** constructor. Once you create the tokenizer, you can use it to read successive tokens from the original string, one at a time. The sequence of tokens that you read from the tokenizer is called a **token stream.**

The most important methods in the **StringTokenizer** class are listed in Figure 8-5. As you can see, the constructor for **StringTokenizer** appears in three forms. The simplest form is illustrated by the following declaration, which reads its tokens from a string-valued variable named **line**:

```
StringTokenizer tokenizer = new StringTokenizer(line);
```

When you use this form of the constructor, the tokenizer divides the string into tokens using spaces and tabs—or in fact any character for which the **Character.isWhitespace** method returns **true**—to mark the boundaries of each token. The spaces that separate the tokens are not considered tokens in their own right and are never returned as part of the token stream.

FIGURE 8-5   Useful methods exported by the `StringTokenizer` class

Constructor

> `new StringTokenizer(String str)`
> Creates a new `StringTokenizer` object that reads whitespace-separated tokens from `str`.

> `new StringTokenizer(String str, String delims)`
> Creates a `StringTokenizer` that uses the characters in `delims` as token separators.

> `new StringTokenizer(String str, String delims, boolean returnDelims)`
> Creates a `StringTokenizer` that returns delimiters as tokens if the third argument is `true`.

Methods to read tokens from the token stream

> `boolean hasMoreTokens()`
> Returns `true` if there are more tokens to read from this `StringTokenizer`.

> `String nextToken()`
> Returns the next token from the token stream, signaling an error if no tokens remain.

The second form of the constructor allows you to specify the set of characters that separate individual tokens; these characters are called **delimiters.** For example, if you want to create a tokenizer that uses either spaces or commas to separate individual tokens, you can do so by rewriting the declaration like this:

```
StringTokenizer tokenizer = new StringTokenizer(line, " ,");
```

As in the single-argument version of the `StringTokenizer` constructor, the tokenizer created by this declaration uses the space and comma characters to separate tokens, but does not include them as part of the token stream. As it currently stands, the pseudocode for the Pig Latin example requires a scanner that can return the delimiter characters as well. That capability is provided by the third form of the constructor, which includes a third argument that determines whether the delimiters should be returned as tokens. If this argument is `false`, the tokenizer operates exactly as it does in the two-argument form. If the argument is `true`, the token stream includes each of the delimiter characters as a single-character token.

In the `PigLatin` program, what you need is a tokenizer that interprets any punctuation marks as delimiters and returns those delimiters as tokens. The easiest way to create such a tokenizer is to define a named constant called `DELIMITERS` that contains all the legal punctuation symbols and then declare the tokenizer using the following code:

```
StringTokenizer tokenizer =
    new StringTokenizer(line, DELIMITERS, true);
```

Once you have declared the tokenizer, your code can then read the tokens from the token stream by calling the `nextToken` method to obtain each token in turn. To determine when you have reached the end of the token stream, you need to use the `hasMoreTokens` method, which returns `true` as long as there are additional tokens to read. These methods make it possible to replace most of the pseudocode in `translateLine` with the actual Java code necessary to implement the method. If you then replace the last remaining bits of pseudocode with calls to the as-yet-unimplemented methods `isWord` and `translateWord`, the code for `translateLine` looks like this:

```
private String translateLine(String line) {
    String result = "";
    StringTokenizer tokenizer =
      new StringTokenizer(line, DELIMITERS, true);
    while (tokenizer.hasMoreTokens()) {
        String token = tokenizer.nextToken();
        if (isWord(token)) {
            token = translateWord(token);
        }
        result += token;
    }
    return result;
}
```

Completing the implementation

At this point, only two methods remain unimplemented: `isWord` and `translateWord`. The simplest of the two is the predicate method `isWord`, which determines whether the token returned by `nextToken` is a word that should be translated into Pig Latin or whether it is simply part of the punctuation. The rules of Pig Latin make sense only if a word consists entirely of letters. It therefore seems reasonable to have `isWord(token)` return `true` if every character in `token` is a letter. By now, you should be familiar enough with strings and characters to implement this method immediately, as follows:

```
private boolean isWord(String token) {
    for (int i = 0; i < token.length(); i++) {
        char ch = token.charAt(i);
        if (!Character.isLetter(ch)) return false;
    }
    return true;
}
```

The process of translating a single word is only slightly harder. In pseudocode, the structure of `translateWord` mirrors the rules for Pig Latin:

```
private String translateWord(String word) {
    Find the position of the first vowel.
    if (the vowel appears at the beginning of the word) {
        Return the word concatenated with "way".
    } else {
        Extract the initial substring up to the vowel and call it the "head."
        Extract the substring from that position onward and call it the "tail."
        Return the tail, concatenated with the head, concatenated with "ay".
    }
}
```

The first English statement in the pseudocode requires the most code to implement and is the only one for which it makes sense to define a new method. That method,

findFirstVowel(word), returns the index position of the first vowel in **word**. Thus the first statement in the **translateWord** implementation can be written as follows:

```
int vp = findFirstVowel(word);
```

If you're being careful in your design, you may notice that the method **findFirstVowel(word)** is incompletely specified. The informal description does not cover all the possible cases. What happens if there aren't any vowels in **word**? In that case, **findFirstVowel** must still return something. Given that the various search methods in the **String** class use −1 as a sentinel to indicate that the value for which the method is searching does not exist in the string, it makes sense to employ the same strategy here.

When **findFirstVowel** returns −1, **translateWord** must respond reasonably. Since the result of translating a word containing no vowels was never defined explicitly, you need to decide what action **translateWord** should take. The easiest approach is for **translateWord** to return the original word unchanged. Incorporating this design decision into the pseudocode version of **translateWord** results in the following, more complete implementation:

```
private String translateWord(String word) {
    int vp = findFirstVowel(word);
    if (vp == -1) {
        return (word);
    } else if (vp == 0) {
        Return the word concatenated with "way".
    } else {
        Extract the initial substring up to the vowel and call it the "head."
        Extract the substring from that position onward and call it the "tail."
        Return the tail, concatenated with the head, concatenated with "ay".
    }
}
```

The remaining steps in **translateWord** are simply calls to the appropriate methods from the **String** class, which makes it easy to complete the coding process, like this:

```
private String translateWord(String word) {
    int vp = findFirstVowel(word);
    if (vp == -1) {
        return word;
    } else if (vp == 0) {
        return word + "way";
    } else {
        String head = word.substring(0, vp);
        String tail = word.substring(vp);
        return tail + head + "ay";
    }
}
```

Coding **findFirstVowel** is also easy, particularly when you remember that you already have a method **isEnglishVowel**, defined in the section on "Control statements involving characters" earlier in this chapter, to determine whether a character is a vowel. The implementation of **findFirstVowel** is then

```
private int findFirstVowel(String word) {
   for (int i = 0; i < word.length(); i++) {
      if (isEnglishVowel(word.charAt(i))) return i;
   }
   return -1;
}
```

The complete code for the **PigLatin** program appears in Figure 8-6.

FIGURE 8-6   **Complete implementation of the Pig Latin translator**

```
/*
 * File: PigLatin.java
 * ---------------------
 * This file takes a line of text and converts each word into Pig Latin.
 * The rules for forming Pig Latin words are as follows:
 * - If the word begins with a vowel, add "way" to the end of the word.
 * - If the word begins with a consonant, extract the set of consonants up
 *   to the first vowel, move that set of consonants to the end of the word,
 *   and add "ay".
 */

import acm.program.*;
import java.util.*;

public class PigLatin extends ConsoleProgram {

   public void run() {
      println("This program translates a line into Pig Latin.");
      String line = readLine("Enter a line: ");
      println(translateLine(line));
   }

/* Translates a line to Pig Latin, word by word */
   private String translateLine(String line) {
      String result = "";
      StringTokenizer tokenizer =
        new StringTokenizer(line, DELIMITERS, true);
      while (tokenizer.hasMoreTokens()) {
         String token = tokenizer.nextToken();
         if (isWord(token)) {
            token = translateWord(token);
         }
         result += token;
      }
      return result;
   }
```

☞

| FIGURE 8-6 | Complete implementation of the Pig Latin translator (continued) |

```
/* Translates a word to Pig Latin and returns the translated word */
    private String translateWord(String word) {
        int vp = findFirstVowel(word);
        if (vp == -1) {
            return word;
        } else if (vp == 0) {
            return word + "way";
        } else {
            String head = word.substring(0, vp);
            String tail = word.substring(vp);
            return tail + head + "ay";
        }
    }

/* Returns the index of the first vowel in the word (-1 if none) */
    private int findFirstVowel(String word) {
        for (int i = 0; i < word.length(); i++) {
            if (isEnglishVowel(word.charAt(i))) return i;
        }
        return -1;
    }

/* Returns true if the character is a vowel */
    private boolean isEnglishVowel(char ch) {
        switch (Character.toLowerCase(ch)) {
            case 'a': case 'e': case 'i': case 'o': case 'u':
                return true;
            default:
                return false;
        }
    }

/* Returns true if token is a "word" (all character are letters) */
    private boolean isWord(String token) {
        for (int i = 0; i < token.length(); i++) {
            char ch = token.charAt(i);
            if (!Character.isLetter(ch)) return false;
        }
        return true;
    }

/* Defines the characters that delimit a token */
    private static final String
        DELIMITERS = "!@#$%^&*()_-+={[}]:;\"'<,>.?/~`|\\ ";

}
```

Summary

With this chapter, you have begun the process of understanding how to work with *text data*. In Java, the most common form of text data is a *string,* which is an ordered collection of individual characters. Individual characters are represented using the data type **char**, which is one of the primitive types defined in Java. Characters are represented inside the hardware as numeric values using an encoding system called Unicode. Strings themselves are represented using the class **String**, which is defined formally as part of the **java.lang** package, but is in fact integrated directly into the language in many ways.

In this chapter, you learned how to manipulate strings using the methods provided by the **String** class, which allows you to focus on the abstract behavior of a string without having to be concerned about its concrete representation.

Important points raised in this chapter include:

- Types whose conceptual values are not numbers can usually be represented inside the computer by numbering the elements in the domain of the type and then using those numbers as codes for the original values. Types defined by counting off their elements are called *enumerated types.*

- Java makes it possible to define new enumerated types in two ways. The older strategy is simply to use **int** for such types and to define named constants for the specific values. The more modern strategy is to use the **enum** keyword introduced in Java 5.0.

- Characters are represented internally as integers according to a predefined coding scheme called *Unicode,* which makes it possible to represent characters from a wide range of languages. Those values are represented in Java by the primitive type **char**.

- Character values can be manipulated using the standard operations of arithmetic. No type cast is required to convert a **char** to an **int**, but Java requires casts to convert in the opposite direction.

- The **Character** class contains several methods for classifying and changing the case of individual characters.

- The **String** class makes it possible to work with strings as an *abstract type.*

- The **String** class defines several methods for manipulating strings. These methods are summarized in Figure 8-4.

- The **java.util** package includes a **StringTokenizer** class that makes it easy to divide a string into substrings that make sense as a unit. These methods are summarized in Figure 8-5.

Review questions

1. In your own words, state the principle of enumeration.

2. What are the two options mentioned in this chapter for representing enumerated types in Java? Why does this text currently rely on the older strategy?

3. What is a *scalar type?*

4. How do you include a double quotation mark inside a string constant?

5. What does *ASCII* stand for?

6. What is the relationship between ASCII and Unicode?

7. By consulting Figure 8-1, determine the octal Unicode values of the characters `'$'`, `'@'`, `'\t'`, and `'x'`. Convert these values to their decimal equivalents.

8. Why is it useful to know that the digit characters are consecutive in the Unicode table?

9. What four arithmetic operations does this chapter argue make the most sense for characters?

10. What is the result of calling `Character.isDigit(5)`? What if the call were `Character.isDigit('5')`? Is it legal to call `Character.isDigit("5")`?

11. What is the result of calling `Character.toUpperCase('5')`?

12. What four reasons are given in the chapter for using the methods in the `Character` class in preference to writing those methods on your own?

13. True or false: It is legal to use character constants as `case` expressions within a `switch` statement.

14. What effect does the following statement have on the value of `str`?

        str.trim()

15. What is the correct way to achieve the effect clearly intended by the expression in the preceding question?

16. What is meant by the term *immutable?*

17. What is the result of each of the following expressions?

    a) `"ABCDE".length()`
    b) `"".length()`
    c) `"\t".length()`
    d) `"ABC".charAt(2)`
    e) `"ABCDE".substring(0, 3)`
    f) `"ABCDE".substring(2)`
    g) `"ABCDE".indexOf("C")`
    h) `"ABCDE".indexOf('Z')`
    i) `"XYZZY".indexOf('Z', 3)`
    j) `"ABCDE".toLowerCase()`

18. What is the most important caution to keep in mind when comparing strings?

19. What is the result of each of the following expressions? (For calls to `compareTo`, simply indicate the sign of the result.)

    a) `"ABCDE".equals("abcde")`
    b) `"ABCDE".equalsIgnoreCase("abcde")`
    c) `"ABCDE".compareTo("ABCDE")`
    d) `"ABCDE".compareTo("ABC")`
    e) `"ABCDE".compareTo("abcde")`
    f) `"ABCDE".startsWith("a")`

20. What is the purpose of the third argument in the **StringTokenizer** constructor?

21. Describe the operation of the **nextToken** and **hasMoreTokens** methods of the **StringTokenizer** class.

Programming exercises

1. Implement the method **isEnglishConsonant(ch)**, which returns **true** if **ch** is a consonant in English, that is, any letter except one of the five vowels: **'a'**, **'e'**, **'i'**, **'o'**, and **'u'**. Like **isEnglishVowel**, your method should recognize consonants of both cases. Write a **ConsoleProgram** that displays all the uppercase consonants.

2. Write a method **randomWord** that returns a randomly constructed "word" consisting of randomly chosen letters. The number of letters in the word should also be chosen randomly by picking a number between the values of the named constants **MIN_LETTERS** and **MAX_LETTERS**. Write a **ConsoleProgram** that tests your method by displaying five random words.

3. Implement a method **capitalize(str)** that returns a string in which the initial character is capitalized (if it is a letter) and all other letters are converted so that they appear in lowercase form. Characters other than letters should not be affected; thus, **capitalize("BOOLEAN")** and **capitalize("boolean")** should each return the string **"Boolean"**.

4. Write a method **createDateString(day, month, year)** that returns a string consisting of the day of the month, a hyphen, the first three letters in the name of the month, another hyphen, and the last two digits of the year. For example, calling the method

   ```
   createDateString(22, 11, 1963)
   ```

   should return the string **"22-Nov-63"**.

5. In most word games, each letter in a word is scored according to its point value, which is inversely proportional to its frequency in English words. In Scrabble™, the points are allocated as follows:

Points	Letters
1	A, E, I, L, N, O, R, S, T, U
2	D, G
3	B, C, M, P
4	F, H, V, W, Y
5	K
8	J, X
10	Q, Z

   For example, the Scrabble word **"FARM"** is worth 9 points: 4 for the *F*, 1 each for the *A* and the *R*, and 3 for the *M*. Write a **ConsoleProgram** that reads in words and prints out their score in Scrabble, not counting any of the other bonuses that occur in the game. You should ignore any characters other than uppercase letters in computing the score. In particular, lowercase letters are assumed to represent blank tiles, which can stand for any letter but which have a score of 0.

6. A **palindrome** is a word that reads identically backward and forward, such as *level* or *noon*. Write a predicate method `isPalindrome(str)` that returns `true` if the string `str` is a palindrome. In addition, design and write a test program that calls `isPalindrome` to demonstrate that it works. In writing the program, concentrate on how to solve the problem simply rather than how to make your solution more efficient.

7. The concept of a palindrome introduced in exercise 6 is often extended to full sentences by ignoring punctuation and differences in the case of letters. For example, the sentence

   Madam, I'm Adam.

   is a sentence palindrome, because if you only look at the letters and ignore any distinction between uppercase and lowercase letters, it reads identically backward and forward. Write a predicate method `isSentencePalindrome(str)` that returns `true` if the string `str` fits this definition of a sentence palindrome. For example, you should be able to use your method to write a main program capable of producing the following sample run:

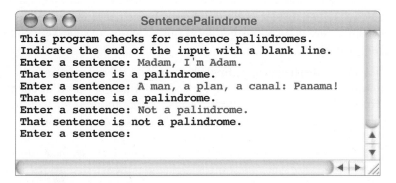

```
                    SentencePalindrome
This program checks for sentence palindromes.
Indicate the end of the input with a blank line.
Enter a sentence: Madam, I'm Adam.
That sentence is a palindrome.
Enter a sentence: A man, a plan, a canal: Panama!
That sentence is a palindrome.
Enter a sentence: Not a palindrome.
That sentence is not a palindrome.
Enter a sentence:
```

8. Write a method `createRegularPlural(word)` that returns the plural of `word` formed by following these standard English rules:

   a) If the word ends in *s, x, z, ch,* or *sh,* add *es* to the word.
   b) If the word ends in *y* and the *y* is preceded by a consonant, change the *y* to *ies.*
   c) In all other cases, add just an *s.*

   Write a test program and design a set of test cases to verify that your program works.

9. In English, the notion of a present action that is continuing into the future is expressed using the present progressive tense, which involves the addition of an *ing* suffix to the verb. For example, the sentence *I think* conveys a sense that one is capable of thinking; by contrast, the sentence *I am thinking* conveys the impression that one is actually in the process of thinking. The *ing* form of the verb is called the **present participle.**

    Unfortunately, creating the present participle is not always as simple as adding the *ing* ending. One common exception is words that end in a silent *e*, such as *cogitate*. In such cases, the *e* is usually dropped, so that the participle form becomes *cogitating*. Another common exception involves words that end with a single consonant, which typically gets doubled in the participle form. For example, the verb *program* becomes *programming*.

    Although there are many exceptions, you can construct a large fraction of the legal participle forms in English by applying the following rules:

    a) If the word ends in an *e* preceded by a consonant, take the *e* away before adding the *ing* suffix. Thus, *move* should become *moving*. If the *e* is not preceded by a consonant, it should remain in place, so that *see* becomes *seeing*.

    b) If the word ends in a consonant preceded by a vowel, insert an extra copy of that consonant before adding the *ing* suffix. Thus, *jam* should become *jamming*. If, however, there is more than one consonant at the end of the word, no such doubling takes place, so that *walk* becomes *walking*.

    c) In all other circumstances, simply add the *ing* suffix.

    Write a method `createPresentParticiple` that takes an English verb, which you may assume is entirely lowercase and at least two characters long, and forms the participle using these rules. Write a `ConsoleProgram` to test your method.

10. Like most other languages, English include two types of numbers: **cardinal numbers** (such as *one, two, three,* and *four*) that are used in counting, and **ordinal numbers** (such as *first, second, third,* and *fourth*) that are used to indicate a position in a sequence. In numeric form, ordinals are usually indicated by writing the digits in the number, followed by the last two letters of the English word that names the corresponding ordinal. Thus, the ordinal numbers *first, second, third,* and *fourth* often appear in print as *1st, 2nd, 3rd,* and *4th*.

    The general rule for determining the suffix of an ordinal can be defined as follows:

    > Numbers ending in the digit 1, 2, and 3, take the suffixes `"st"`, `"nd"`, and `"rd"`, respectively, *unless* the number ends with the two-digit combination 11, 12, or 13. Those numbers, and any numbers not ending with a 1, 2, or 3, take the suffix `"th"`.

    Your task in this problem is to write a method `createOrdinalForm(n)` that takes an integer **n** and returns a string indicating the corresponding ordinal number. For example, your method should return the following values:

`createOrdinalForm(1)`	*returns the string*	`"1st"`
`createOrdinalForm(2)`	*returns the string*	`"2nd"`
`createOrdinalForm(3)`	*returns the string*	`"3rd"`
`createOrdinalForm(10)`	*returns the string*	`"10th"`
`createOrdinalForm(11)`	*returns the string*	`"11th"`
`createOrdinalForm(12)`	*returns the string*	`"12th"`
`createOrdinalForm(21)`	*returns the string*	`"21st"`
`createOrdinalForm(42)`	*returns the string*	`"42nd"`
`createOrdinalForm(101)`	*returns the string*	`"101st"`
`createOrdinalForm(111)`	*returns the string*	`"111th"`

11. One of the simplest types of codes used to make it harder for someone to read a message is a **letter-substitution cipher,** in which each letter in the original message is replaced by some different letter in the coded version of that message. A particularly simple type of letter-substitution cipher is a **Caesar cipher**—so named because the Roman historian Suetonius records that Julius Caesar used such a cipher—in which each letter is replaced by another letter that is a fixed distance ahead in the alphabet. A Caesar cipher is *cyclic* in the sense that any operations that shift a letter beyond *Z* simply circle back to the beginning and start over again with *A*.

    As an example, suppose you wanted to encode a message by shifting every letter ahead four places. In that Caesar cipher, each *A* becomes an *E*, *B* becomes *F*, *Z* becomes *D* (because it cycles back to the beginning), and so on.

    To solve this problem, you should first define a method

    ```
    private String encodeCaesarCipher(String str, int shift)
    ```

    that returns a new string formed by shifting every letter in `str` forward the number of letters indicated by `shift`, cycling back to the beginning of the alphabet if necessary. After you have implemented `encodeString`, write a `ConsoleProgram` that duplicates the examples shown in the following sample run:

    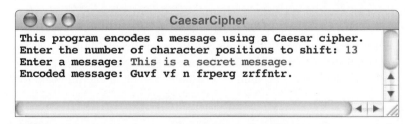

    Note that the coding operation applies only to letters; any other character is included unchanged in the output. Moreover, the case of letters is unaffected: lowercase letters come out as lowercase, and uppercase letters come out as uppercase.

    Write your program so that a negative value of `shift` means that letters are shifted toward the beginning of the alphabet instead of toward the end, as illustrated by the following sample run:

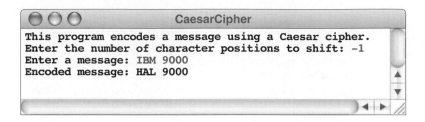

12. Suppose that the **ConsoleProgram** class did not include the **readInt** method to read an integer from the console and supported only the **readString** method. Write a method

    private int myReadInt(String prompt)

    that simulates the operation of **readInt** by reading in a line and then translating the characters from that line into an integer. Your implementation of **myReadInt** should allow the input to begin with a **–** character to signal a negative value. Except for that special case, however, your implementation should indicate an error if it finds any characters other than the standard decimal digits. As with the **readInt** method in **acm.io**, your implementation should note that error by printing a message and asking the user to enter a new value, as shown in the following sample run of the **Add2Integers** program from Chapter 2:

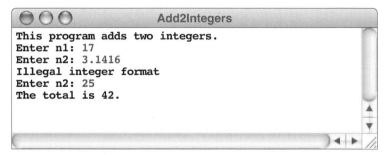

13. When large numbers are written out on paper, it is traditional—at least in the United States—to use commas to separate the digits into groups of three. For example, the number one million is usually written in the following form:

    1,000,000

    To make it easier for programmers to display numbers in this fashion, implement a method

    private String addCommas(String digits)

    that takes a string of decimal digits representing a number and returns the string formed by inserting commas at every third position, starting on the right. For example, if you were to execute the main program

```
public void run() {
   while (true) {
      String digits = readLine("Enter a number: ");
      if (digits.length() == 0) break;
      println(addCommas(digits));
   }
}
```

your implementation of the **addCommas** method should be able to produce the
following sample run:

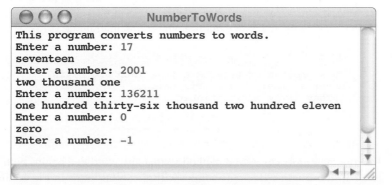

```
                       AddCommas
Enter a number: 17
17
Enter a number: 1001
1,001
Enter a number: 12345678
12,345,678
Enter a number: 999999999
999,999,999
Enter a number:
```

14. When you write a check, it is conventional to record the amount of the check
    both in figures and in words. Thus, if you were writing a check for $1,729
    dollars, you would write the amount out in words like this:

    one thousand seven hundred and twenty-nine

    Implement a method

    private String numberToWords(int n)

    that takes an integer—which you may assume is between 0 and 999,999—and
    returns a string that represents that number in words. Test your method by
    writing a **run** method that repeatedly reads in an integer and converts that
    number into words, stopping when a negative number is entered, as illustrated
    in the following sample run:

```
                      NumberToWords
This program converts numbers to words.
Enter a number: 17
seventeen
Enter a number: 2001
two thousand one
Enter a number: 136211
one hundred thirty-six thousand two hundred eleven
Enter a number: 0
zero
Enter a number: -1
```

Note that there is no magical way to convert a digit like 1 into the English word *one*. To implement that correspondence, you will need to include explicit code—probably in the form of a **switch** statement—that converts each digit to its English equivalent. The important thing to think about in this assignment is how to decompose the problem so that you can reuse the same methods to translate different parts of the number.

15. Implement a method

    ```
    private String longestWord(String line)
    ```

    that returns the longest word in **line**, where a word is defined as a consecutive string of letters, as in the **PigLatin** program. Test your implementation by writing a **ConsoleProgram** that can duplicate this sample run:

    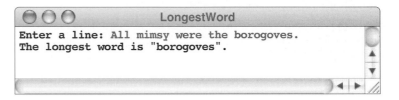

    ```
    LongestWord
    Enter a line: All mimsy were the borogoves.
    The longest word is "borogoves".
    ```

16. Rewrite the **acronym** method described in the section on "Searching within a string" so that it uses the **StringTokenizer** class to separate the words in the argument. This change will allow the acronym method to return the correct result even if the words are not separated by spaces. As an example, your implementation should be able to form the acronym *scuba* from the string *self-contained underwater breathing apparatus,* even though the first two words are separated by a hyphen rather than a space.

17. Rewrite the **PigLatin** program in this chapter so that it uses the algorithmic strategy of going through the line character by character rather than word by word. The pseudocode version of this strategy appears in the section on "Taking spaces and punctuation into account."

18. As written, the **PigLatin** program in Figure 8-6 behaves somewhat oddly if you enter a string that includes words that begin with an uppercase letter. For example, if you were to capitalize the first word in the sentence and the name of the Pig Latin language, you would see the following output:

    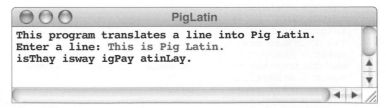

    ```
    PigLatin
    This program translates a line into Pig Latin.
    Enter a line: This is Pig Latin.
    isThay isway igPay atinLay.
    ```

    Rewrite the **translateWord** method so that any word that begins with a capital letter in the English line still begins with a capital letter in Pig Latin. Thus, after making your changes in the program, the output should look like this:

```
 ◯ ◯ ◯                    PigLatin
This program translates a line into Pig Latin.
Enter a line: This is Pig Latin.
Isthay isway Igpay Atinlay.
```

19. Most people—at least those in English-speaking countries—have played the Pig Latin game at some point in their lives. There are, however, other invented "languages" in which words are created using some simple transformation of English. One such language is Obenglobish, in which words are created by adding the letters *ob* before the vowels in an English word. For example, given this rule, the word *english* is transformed by adding *ob* before the two vowels to form *obenglobish,* which is how the language gets its name.

In official Obenglobish, the letters *ob* are added only before vowels that are pronounced, which means that a word like *game* would become *gobame* rather than *gobamobe* because the final *e* is silent. While it is impossible to implement this rule perfectly, you can do a pretty good job by adopting the rule that the *ob* should be added before every vowel in the English word *except*

- Vowels that follow other vowels
- An *e* that occurs at the end of the word

Write a method **obenglobish** that takes an English word and returns its Obenglobish equivalent, using the translation rule given above. For example, if you used your function with the **run** method

```java
public void run() {
   while (true) {
      String word = readLine("Enter a word: ");
      if (word.equals("")) break;
      println(word + " -> " + obenglobish(word));
   }
}
```

you should be able to generate the following sample run:

```
 ◯ ◯ ◯                 Obenglobish
Enter a word: english
english -> obenglobish
Enter a word: hobnob
hobnob -> hobobnobob
Enter a word: gooiest
gooiest -> gobooiest
Enter a word: amaze
amaze -> obamobaze
Enter a word: rot
rot -> robot
Enter a word:
```

20. The genetic code for all living organisms is carried in its DNA—a molecule with the remarkable capacity to replicate its own structure. The DNA molecule itself consists of a long strand of chemical bases wound together with a similar molecule to form a double helix pattern. DNA's ability to replicate comes from the fact that the four bases in its structure—adenosine, cytosine, guanine, and thymine—combine with each other only in the following ways:

    • Adenosine links only with thymine, and vice versa.

    • Cytosine links only with guanine, and vice versa.

    Typically, biologists abbreviate the names of the bases so that each is represented by its initial letter: **A**, **C**, **G**, or **T**.

    Inside the cell, a DNA strand acts as a template to which other DNA strands can attach themselves. As an example, suppose that you have the following DNA strand, in which the position of each base has been numbered as it would be in a Java string:

    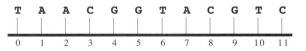

    One of problems that biologists need to solve is finding where a short DNA strand can attach itself to a longer one. If, for example, you are trying to find a match for the strand

    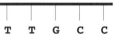

    the rules for DNA replication dictate that this strand can bind to the longer one at position 1:

    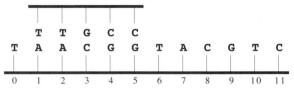

    Write a method **findFirstMatchingPosition(shortDNA, longDNA)** that takes two strings of letters representing the bases in DNA strands. The method should return the first index position at which the first DNA strand would bind onto the second, or −1 if no matching position exists.

21. Even though the **StringTokenizer** class is already part of the **java.util** package, you can learn a great deal about both string manipulation and class design by reimplementing **StringTokenizer** on your own. Write a new implementation of this class that implements the constructors and methods shown in Figure 8-5. The only aspect of the design that you don't yet know how to implement is the feature in which calling **nextToken** when no tokens are available generates an error. To get around that problem, write your version of **nextToken** so that it returns **null** if no additional tokens exist.

CHAPTER 9
Object-oriented Graphics

In pictures, if you do it right, the thing happens, right there on the screen.
—Director John Huston, as quoted in
—James Agee, *Agee on Film*, 1964

Ivan Sutherland

Ivan Sutherland was born in Nebraska and developed a passion for computers while still in high school, when a family friend gave him the opportunity to program a tiny relay-based machine called SIMON. Since computer science was not yet an academic discipline, Sutherland majored in electrical engineering at Pittsburgh's Carnegie Institute of Technology (now Carnegie Mellon University) and then went on to get a Master's degree at Caltech and a Ph.D. from MIT. His doctoral thesis, "Sketchpad: A man-machine graphical communications system," became one of the cornerstones of computer graphics and introduced the idea of the graphical user interface, which has become an essential feature of modern software. After completing his degree, Sutherland held faculty positions at Harvard, the University of Utah, and Caltech before leaving academia to found a computer-graphics company. Sutherland received the ACM Turing Award in 1988.

Although you have already seen several of the classes and methods in the `acm.graphics` package, you have not yet had the chance to consider that collection of classes as a whole. Rather than continuing to present the package in bits and pieces, this chapter examines `acm.graphics` as an integrated set of tools. Doing so has two main purposes. First, you will learn a lot more about the graphical capabilities that the package provides. That understanding will help you write more interesting graphics programs, which ought to be an exciting prospect. But there is a subtler purpose as well. The object-oriented approach to programming has less to do with styles of coding than it does with strategies of design. By focusing on `acm.graphics` as a coherent package, you will gain a more detailed sense of how to approach the design of classes and packages, which will make it easier to write them on your own.

9.1 The `acm.graphics` model

Before you can appreciate the classes and methods available in `acm.graphics`, you need to understand the assumptions, conventions, and metaphors on which the package is based. Collectively, these ideas that define the appropriate mental picture for a package are called a **model.** The model for a package allows you to answer various questions about how you should think about working in that domain. Before using a graphics package, for example, you need to be able to answer the following sorts of questions:

- What units do you use to specify lengths and positions on the screen?
- What real-world analogies and metaphors underlie the package design?

You already know the answer to the first question from the section on "The Java coordinate system" in Chapter 2. In the `acm.graphics` model, all coordinate positions and lengths are expressed in terms of **pixels,** which are the individual dots that appear on the screen. Points on the screen are identified by specifying their coordinates in both the *x* and *y* directions, with *x* values increasing as you move rightward across the canvas and *y* values increasing as you move downward from the top. The interpretation of the *x* coordinate is therefore the same as in traditional Cartesian geometry, but the *y* coordinate is inverted. Because *y* values increase as you move downward, the designers of the Java graphics model put the point $(0, 0)$ in the upper left corner of the window. That point is called the **origin.**

The `acm.graphics` package adopts this coordinate model—as opposed to a Cartesian coordinate system—to match the coordinate system used in other Java packages. Maintaining a consistent model across packages makes it easier to move from one package to another.

In the case of `acm.graphics`, the second question—what analogies and metaphors are appropriate for the package—is in many ways more important. Many real-world analogies are possible for computer graphics, in part because there are many different ways to create visual art. One possible metaphor is that of painting, in which the artist selects a paintbrush and a color and then draws images by moving the brush across a screen that represents a virtual canvas. If you instead imagine yourself drawing with a pencil, you might develop a different style of graphics in which line drawings predominate and in which it is possible to erase things you have previously drawn. You might conceivably design a graphics package based on an engraving metaphor in which the artist uses a stylus to etch out a drawing; erasing would presumably not make sense according to that metaphor. There are many other possible metaphors, just as there are many artistic techniques.

To support the concept of object-oriented design, the `acm.graphics` package uses the metaphor of a **collage.** A collage artist works by taking various objects and assembling them on a background canvas. In the real world, those objects might be geometrical shapes, words clipped from newspapers, lines formed from bits of string, or images taken from magazines. The `acm.graphics` package offers counterparts for all of these objects.

The notion that the image is a collage has important implications for the way you describe the process of creating a design. If you are painting, you might talk about making a brush stroke in a particular position or filling an area with paint. In the collage model, the key operations are adding and removing objects, along with repositioning them on the background canvas.

Collages also have the property that some objects can be positioned on top of other objects, obscuring whatever is behind them. Removing those objects reveals whatever used to be underneath. The back-to-front ordering of objects in the collage is called the **stacking order** in this book, although you will sometimes see it referred to as *z-ordering* in more formal writing. The name *z-ordering* comes from the fact that the stacking order occurs along the axis that comes out of the two-dimensional plane formed by the x and y axes. In mathematics, that perpendicular axis coming out of the plane is called the **z-axis.**

9.2 Structure of the `acm.graphics` package

Although you have been using several of the classes from the `acm.graphics` package since Chapter 2, there is still much to learn about the package as a whole. The goal of this chapter is to give you a more complete understanding of what the `acm.graphics` package offers in the way of graphical tools. Figure 9-1 begins that process by presenting a diagram of the class structure within `acm.graphics`. The subsections that follow describe the individual classes and how to use them.

The `GCanvas` class

The first new class shown in Figure 9-1 is the `GCanvas` class. Even though the `GCanvas` class has not yet been mentioned in this book, you have used a `GCanvas` object in every `GraphicsProgram` you have written. The `GCanvas` class represents the background to which you add the individual `GObject`s. In the world of a collage artist, that background is a physical canvas. In the world of the `acm.graphics` package, that background is a window displayed on the screen.

Although you can construct new instances of the `GCanvas` class by calling its constructor, you ordinarily won't have to do so explicitly. The `GraphicsProgram` class automatically creates a `GCanvas` and positions it so that it completely fills the program window. Whenever you call the `add` method in one of your progams, the

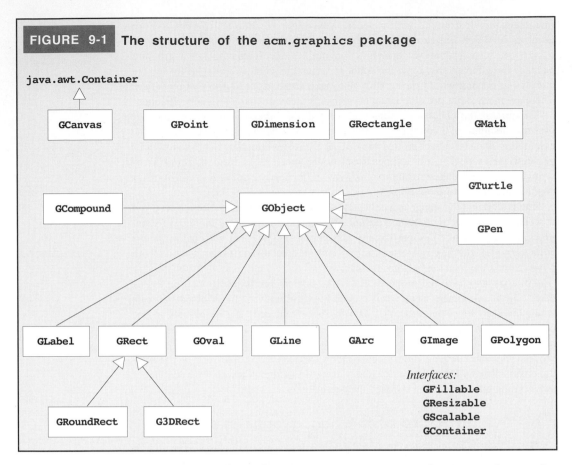

FIGURE 9-1 The structure of the `acm.graphics` package

`java.awt.Container`

GCanvas · GPoint · GDimension · GRectangle · GMath

GCompound · GObject · GTurtle · GPen

GLabel · GRect · GOval · GLine · GArc · GImage · GPolygon

GRoundRect · G3DRect

Interfaces:
GFillable
GResizable
GScalable
GContainer

implementation of **add** in **GraphicsProgram** passes that request along to the underlying **GCanvas**. Thus, when the **HelloProgram** in Chapter 2 executes the line

```
add(new GLabel("hello, world", 100, 75));
```

it sends the same message to the **GCanvas**, asking it to add the newly generated label. The **GraphicsProgram** class treats other method calls pertaining to the underlying canvas in exactly the same way: it simply passes the request along to the **GCanvas**, which implements the actual operation. That process is called **forwarding.**

The most important methods available to the **GCanvas** class—which you can invoke either by calling them explicitly on a **GCanvas** object or by having your **GraphicsProgram** forward them—are shown in Figure 9-2. The first set of methods is concerned with adding and removing graphical objects. These methods are easy to understand, particularly if you keep the collage metaphor in mind. Adding graphical objects to a **GCanvas** corresponds to adding physical objects to a collage. In the process, those objects may obscure other objects that are behind the

---

FIGURE 9-2   **Useful methods in the `GCanvas` and `GraphicsProgram` classes**

Methods to add and remove graphical objects

`void add(GObject gobj)`
  Adds a graphical object to the canvas at its internally stored location.

`void add(GObject gobj, double x, double y)`
  Adds a graphical object to the canvas at the specified location.

`void remove(GObject gobj)`
  Removes the specified graphical object from the canvas.

`void removeAll()`
  Removes all graphical objects from the canvas.

Method to find the graphical object at a particular location

`GObject getElementAt(double x, double y)`
  Returns the topmost object containing the specified point, or `null` if no such object exists.

Method to support graphical animation (available in `GraphicsProgram` only)

`void pause(double milliseconds)`
  Suspends program execution for the specified time interval, which is measured in milliseconds.

`void waitForClick()`
  Suspends program execution until the user clicks the mouse anywhere in the canvas.

Useful methods inherited from superclasses

`int getWidth()`
  Returns the width of the canvas, in pixels.

`int getHeight()`
  Returns the height of the canvas, in pixels.

`void setBackground(Color bg)`
  Changes the background color of the canvas.

---

new ones in the stacking order. Removing an object takes it off the canvas, revealing any objects that were behind it.

The **add** method comes in two forms. The first is useful when the constructor for the **GObject** has already established the location of the object, as it has in the examples you have seen. The second form is used when you want to place the object on the screen in a way that depends on its size or other properties. In that case, you typically need to create a **GObject** without specifying a location, figure out where it should go, and then add it to the canvas at that explicit *x* and *y* location. The most common example of this style of positioning occurs when you want to center a **GLabel** at some location; the section on "The **GLabel** class" later in this chapter describes how it works.

The **getElement** method in the **GCanvas** class returns the graphical object on the canvas that includes a specified point. This method is particularly useful when you want to select an object using the mouse. Because the description fits better in that context, the details of **getElement** are described in Chapter 10.

You have already seen the **pause** method, which delays the execution of the program for the number of milliseconds specified by the argument. As you learned in Chapter 4, you can animate a program by making small changes to the graphical objects on the canvas and then calling **pause** to ensure that the program doesn't run through the entire animation faster than the human eye can follow. Programs that use animation typically have the following form:

```
public void run() {
    Initialize the graphical objects in the display.
    while (as long as you want to run the animation) {
        Update the properties of the objects that you wish to animate.
        pause(delay time);
    }
}
```

The **waitForClick** method is useful when you want to suspend a graphical program until the user clicks the mouse anywhere in the canvas. This strategy allows the user to determine when execution continues.

As is often the case in object-oriented class hierarchies, several of the most useful methods in the **GCanvas** class are not defined in **GCanvas** itself but are instead inherited from its superclasses. The **GCanvas** class extends a class called **Container** in the **java.awt** package. Because any **GCanvas** is a **Container**—and a **Component** if you climb still higher on the inheritance chain—a **GCanvas** can be displayed in a window, which is what makes it visible on the screen. Like any other **Component**, a **GCanvas** responds to the methods **getWidth** and **getHeight**, which tell you the dimensions of the canvas on the screen. You can also change the background color of a **GCanvas** by calling **setBackground(bg)**, where **bg** is the new background color. You specify the new color using an object of the **Color** class, just as you do when you set the color of a **GObject**.

Further details about the `Color` class

As long as we're on the subject of colors, it is useful to cover a few additional details about the **Color** class. So far, the only colors that have appeared in this text are the 13 colors defined as named constants in the **Color** class, which were introduced in Chapter 2. As is the case with any modern graphics package, the **Color** class in the **java.awt** package offers a much richer set of colors than those you can easily name. To give you the option of choosing colors more finely, this section describes how to use the constructor in the **Color** class to create millions of different colors.

Although Java offers several models for defining colors, the most common is the **RGB model,** in which a color is defined by the proportions it contains of red, green, and blue—the three primary colors of light. The values of the red, green, and blue components of a color are each represented as an integer between 0 and 255, where 0 means that none of that color appears and 255 means that the color is present at its full intensity. For example, a color in which the red component is 255 and the other components are 0 defines the color **RED**. Similarly, a color in which each of the red, green, and blue components is 128 means that each color is present at half its maximum intensity, which defines the color **GRAY**. Given a color, you can determine its components by calling the methods **getRed**, **getGreen**, and **getBlue.**

The simplest version of the **Color** constructor takes three integer arguments that specify the red, green, and blue intensities, respectively. In existing Java code, however, you will often see the color components expressed using a six-digit hexadecimal number in which the first two digits specify the red component, the next two specify the green component, and the last two specify the blue component. The constructor calls that define the standard color constants appear in Figure 9-3, which also shows the hexadecimal specification in the comments.

If you want to create other colors, you can experiment with different values for these three intensities. As a general rule, you can create darker colors by reducing the intensity values of its dominant components and brighter ones by increasing the proportion of the other components. For example, you can create a darker red by reducing the value of the red component and a brighter red by increasing the values of the green and blue components.

The `GPoint`, `GDimension`, and `GRectangle` classes

As noted in the section on "Encapsulation" in Chapter 6, it is often convenient to combine inidividual *x* and *y* coordinate values into a single encapsulated unit that represents a point on the canvas. In much the same way, it is useful to combine a *width* and a *height* value to represent the dimensions of an object, or to combine all four of these values to represent both the location and size of a rectangle. The **acm.graphics** package defines the classes **GPoint**, **GDimension**, and **GRectangle** for precisely this purpose. The primary advantage of encapsulating the individual values into a composite object is that the object can then be passed from one method to another as a single entity.

As an example, the declaration

```
GPoint center = new GPoint(getWidth() / 2, getHeight() / 2);
```

introduces the variable **center** and initializes it to a **GPoint** object whose coordinates are at the center of the canvas. You could similarly define a **GRectangle** variable **bounds** to indicate the boundaries of the canvas like this:

```
GRectangle bounds =
    new GRectangle(0, 0, getWidth(), getHeight());
```

FIGURE 9-3   **Definitions of the Color constants**

```
/* Public constants in the Color class from java.awt */
    public final static Color WHITE = new Color(255, 255, 255);      /* 0xFFFFFF */
    public final static Color LIGHT_GRAY = new Color(192, 192, 192);  /* 0xC0C0C0 */
    public final static Color GRAY = new Color(128, 128, 128);        /* 0x808080 */
    public final static Color DARK_GRAY = new Color(64, 64, 64);      /* 0x404040 */
    public final static Color BLACK = new Color(0, 0, 0);             /* 0x000000 */
    public final static Color RED = new Color(255, 0, 0);             /* 0xFF0000 */
    public final static Color YELLOW = new Color(255, 255, 0);        /* 0xFFFF00 */
    public final static Color GREEN = new Color(0, 255, 0);           /* 0x00FF00 */
    public final static Color CYAN = new Color(0, 255, 255);          /* 0x00FFFF */
    public final static Color BLUE = new Color(0, 0, 255);            /* 0x0000FF */
    public final static Color MAGENTA = new Color(255, 0, 255);       /* 0xFF00FF */
    public final static Color PINK = new Color(255, 175, 175);        /* 0xFFAFAF */
    public final static Color ORANGE = new Color(255, 200, 0);        /* 0xFFC800 */
```

Although the **GPoint**, **GDimension**, and **GRectangle** classes export a number of useful methods to simplify common geometric operations, listing them all in this book would provide much more detail than you need. The most important operations are the constructors that create the composite objects and the methods that retrieve the individual coordinate values. These methods are listed in Figure 9-4. To find out about the other methods available in these classes, you can explore the **javadoc** pages.

The GMath class

Computing the positions and sizes of objects in a graphical figure can sometimes require the use of simple mathematical functions. Although Java's **Math** class defines methods to compute trigonometric functions such as **sin** and **cos**, these methods are often confusing because they adopt a coordinate model that is in some ways incompatible with the one Java uses for its graphics packages. In Java's graphics libraries, angles are measured in degrees; in the **Math** class, angles must be specified in radians.

To minimize the confusion associated with this inconsistency of representation, the **acm.graphics** package includes a class called **GMath**, which exports the methods in Figure 9-5. As with the methods in Java's math class, the methods

---

FIGURE 9-4 **Essential methods in the GPoint, GDimension, and GRectangle classes**

GPoint constructors and methods

new GPoint(double x, double y)
Creates a new **GPoint** object containing the coordinate values **x** and **y**.

double getX()
Returns the **x** component of a **GPoint**.

double getY()
Returns the **y** component of a **GPoint**.

GDimension constructors and methods

new GDimension(double width, double height)
Creates a new **GDimension** object containing the values **width** and **height**.

double getWidth()
Returns the **width** component of a **GDimension**.

double getHeight()
Returns the **height** component of a **GDimension**.

GRectangle constructors and methods

new GRectangle(double x, double y, double width, double height)
Creates a new **GRectangle** object containing the four specified values.

double getX()
Returns the **x** component of a **GRectangle**.

double getY()
Returns the **y** component of a **GRectangle**.

double getWidth()
Returns the **width** component of a **GRectangle**.

double getHeight()
Returns the **height** component of a **GRectangle**.

FIGURE 9-5 Static methods in the `GMath` class

Trigonometric methods in degrees

`double sinDegrees(double angle)`
  Returns the trigonometric sine of an angle measured in degrees.

`double cosDegrees(double angle)`
  Returns the trigonometric cosine of an angle measured in degrees.

`double tanDegrees(double angle)`
  Returns the trigonometric tangent of an angle measured in degrees.

`double toDegrees(double radians)`
  Converts an angle from radians to degrees.

`double toRadians(double degrees)`
  Converts an angle from degrees to radians.

Methods to simplify the conversion to polar coordinates

`double distance(double x, double y)`
  Returns the distance from the origin to the point (x, y).

`double distance(double x0, double y0, double x1, double y1)`
  Returns the distance between the points $(x0, y0)$ and $(x1, y1)$.

`double angle(double x, double y)`
  Returns the angle between the origin and the point (x, y), measured in degrees.

Method to round a `double` to an `int`

`int round(double x)`
  Rounds a **double** to the nearest **int** (rather than to a **long** as in the **Math** class).

---

exported by **GMath** are static. Calls to these methods therefore need to include the name of the class, as in

```
double cos45 = GMath.cosDegrees(45);
```

which sets the variable **cos45** to the cosine of 45 degrees.

The first few methods in Figure 9-5 compute trigonometric functions of angles in degrees. The **distance** and **angle** methods make it easy to convert traditional *x-y* coordinates into **polar coordinates,** in which points are defined in terms of their distance and direction from the origin. The distance is usually denoted by the letter *r,* which comes from the observation that a particular value of *r* corresponds to the points lying on a circle with that radius. The angle—typically written using the Greek letter θ in mathematics and represented using the variable name **theta**—is measured in degrees counterclockwise from the +*x* axis, just as it is in classical geometry.

The last method listed in Figure 9-5 is **round**, which rounds a **double** to the nearest **int**. Although Java's **Math** class also exports a method called **round**, that version returns a **long**, which makes it less convenient to use.

The `GObject` class and its subclasses

If you look back at the arrows in Figure 9-1, it is immediately clear that the **GObject** class plays a central role in the **acm.graphics** package. Just as all roads led to

Rome in the days of its empire, all the paths from subclasses to their superclasses lead to **GObject**, which represents the universe of all graphical objects. In the framework of the collage model, the **GObject** class represents the generic designation for the set of objects that you can add to the collage. Some of those objects might be cutout shapes like rectangles or ovals; others might be images or words clipped from a magazine. What those objects share is the property that you can add them to the canvas. In the **acm.graphics** world, a **GObject** is simply an object that you can add to a **GCanvas**.

In Figure 9-1, the name of the **GObject** class appears in italic type. In class diagrams, italics are used to identify **abstract classes,** which are classes that cannot be constructed on their own but instead serve as a template for a collection of subclasses. Thus, there are no graphical objects that have **GObject** as their primary class. Instead, every object you put on the screen is a **GLabel**, **GRect**, **GOval**, or one of the other subclasses that extends **GObject**. The structure of Java's class hierarchy, however, dictates that any of those objects is also a **GObject**, even though you will never see a declaration of the form

```
GObject gobj = new GObject();
```

Such a declaration is illegal because you cannot construct an instance of any abstract class on its own. It is, however, perfectly legal to construct an instance of a specific **GObject** subclass and then assign it to a **GObject** variable, as in

```
GObject gobj = new GLabel("hello, world");
```

The **GObject** class itself defines the set of methods shown in Figure 9-6. As it happens, you've already seen many of them. Here are brief descriptions of a few of the new ones:

- The **setLocation**, **move**, and **movePolar** methods allow you to change the location of an object on the canvas. You use the **setLocation** method if you know the precise coordinates of the new location. If, however, you want to move the object a specific distance from where it is now, you can use the **move** or **movePolar** method. For example, if you wanted to move the object stored in the variable **gobj** ten pixels to the right, you can do so by calling

  ```
  gobj.move(10, 0);
  ```

  If you instead want to move the object 100 pixels northeast, you can call

  ```
  gobj.movePolar(100, 45);
  ```

  The second parameter to **movePolar** is the direction in which you want to move expressed as an angle in polar coordinates. For example, the argument 45 in this example represents the direction 45 degrees counterclockwise from the +x axis.

- The predicate method **contains** allows you to determine whether an object contains a particular point.

| FIGURE 9-6 | Methods supported by all `GObject` subclasses |

`void setLocation(double x, double y)`   Sets the location of this object to the specified point.
`void move(double dx, double dy)`   Moves the object using the displacements **`dx`** and **`dy`**.
`void movePolar(double r, double theta)`   Moves the object **`r`** units in direction **`theta`**, measured in degrees.
`double getX()`   Returns the x-coordinate of the object.
`double getY()`   Returns the y-coordinate of the object.
`double getWidth()`   Returns the width of the object.
`double getHeight()`   Returns the height of the object.
`boolean contains(double x, double y)`   Checks to see whether a point is inside the object.
`void setColor(Color c)`   Sets the color of the object.
`Color getColor()`   Returns the object color.
`void setVisible(boolean visible)`   Sets whether this object is visible.
`boolean isVisible()`   Returns **`true`** if this object is visible.
`void sendToFront()`   Sends this object to the front of the canvas, where it may obscure objects further back.
`void sendToBack()`   Sends this object to the back of the canvas, where it may be obscured by objects in front.
`void sendForward()`   Sends this object forward one position in the stacking order.
`void sendBackward()`   Sends this object backward one position in the stacking order.

- The **`setVisible`** method makes it possible to hide an object on the screen. If you call **`setVisible(false)`**, the object disappears from the display until you call **`setVisible(true)`**. The predicate method **`isVisible`** allows you to determine whether an object is visible.

- The various **`send`** methods allow you to change the stacking order. When you add a new object to the canvas, it goes on top of the other objects and can therefore obscure the objects behind it. If you call **`sendToBack`**, the object goes to the back of the stack. Conversely, **`sendToFront`** brings it to the front. You can also change the order by calling **`sendForward`** and **`sendBackward`**, which move an object one step forward or backward, respectively, in the stack.

Although it is useful to know about these new methods, it may be momentarily disconcerting to discover that some of the methods you've been using don't appear at all in Figure 9-6. There is no **setFilled** method, even though you've been filling **GOval**s and **GRect**s all along. Similarly, the list does not include **setFont**, although you've been using that method in the context of **GLabel**s. The absence of these methods from Figure 9-6, however, should not be a cause for concern. As the caption on the figure makes clear, the methods defined at the **GObject** level are the ones that apply to *all* subclasses of **GObject**. This is not the case, for example, with **setFont**, which applies to the **GLabel** class and is therefore defined at that level.

The case of the **setFilled** method is more interesting. Because it makes sense to fill an oval, a rectangle, a polygon, and an arc, there are four classes (plus the extended **GRoundRect** and **G3DRect** subclasses) for which **setFilled** would be appropriate. It is not at all clear, however, what one might mean by filling a line, an image, or a label. Since there are some classes for which no meaningful interpretation of **setFilled** exists, it would not be appropriate to define it at the **GObject** level, which is reserved for methods that are common to all subclasses. At the same time, it seems redundant to define **setFilled** independently in each of the subclasses for which it is meaningful. It would certainly be convenient for **setFilled** to work the same way for each of the fillable classes.

In Java, the best way to define a suite of methods that are shared by a subset of classes in a hierarchy is to define what Java calls an **interface,** which is a listing of the methods that a set of classes share. In Java, a class that exports all the methods in an interface is said to **implement** that interface. You will learn more about the structure of an interface in Chapter 13. For now, it is enough to understand that you can call the methods defined by an interface in any class that implements it.

In the **acm.graphics** package, the classes **GOval**, **GRect**, **GPolygon**, and **GArc** implement an interface called **GFillable**, which specifies the behavior of any fillable object. In addition to **GFillable**, the **acm.graphics** package includes an interface called **GResizable** that allows you to reset the bounds of an object and an interface called **GScalable** that allows you to scale an object by a scaling factor. The methods specified by these three interfaces appear in Figure 9-7.

The remaining classes in Figure 9-7 fall into a few recognizable groups:

- The **GCompound** class is used to combine various **GObject**s into a single object that you can then manipulate as a unit. In a way, the **GCompound** class is a combination of the **GCanvas** and **GObject** models. As with a **GCanvas**, you can add graphical objects to a **GCompound**. As with any other **GObject**, you can add a **GCompound** to a **GCanvas** so that it appears on the screen. The **GCompound** class is useful in many contexts and is described in detail in section 9.4.

- The **GPen** and **GTurtle** classes are not covered in this book, even though they are part of the **acm.graphics** package. The **GPen** class makes it easy to draw certain kinds of figures for which a pen-on-paper analogy is more appropriate than the collage model used in the rest of the package. The **GTurtle** class is similar in many ways to **GPen** but is specifically designed to teach children about graphical programming. The inspiration for the **GTurtle** class comes from Project LOGO at MIT, which is described in detail in Seymour Papert's book *Mindstorms*.

FIGURE 9-7 Methods specified by the graphical interfaces

GFillable (implemented by **GArc**, **GOval**, **GPolygon**, and **GRect**)

> **void setFilled(boolean fill)**
> Sets whether this object is filled (**true** means filled; **false** means outlined).

> **boolean isFilled()**
> Returns **true** if the object is filled.

> **void setFillColor(Color c)**
> Sets the color used to fill this object. If the color is **null**, filling uses the color of the object.

> **Color getFillColor()**
> Returns the color used to fill this object.

GResizable (implemented by **GImage**, **GOval**, and **GRect**)

> **void setSize(double width, double height)**
> Changes the size of this object to the specified width and height.

> **void setBounds(double x, double y, double width, double height)**
> Changes the bounds of this object as specified by the individual parameters.

GScalable (implemented by **GArc**, **GCompound**, **GImage**, **GLine**, **GOval**, **GPolygon**, and **GRect**)

> **void scale(double sf)**
> Resizes the object by applying the scale factor in each dimension, leaving the location fixed.

> **void scale(double sx, double sy)**
> Scales the object independently in the *x* and *y* dimensions by the specified scale factors.

- The classes at the bottom of the diagram—**GLabel**, **GRect**, **GOval**, **GLine**, **GArc**, **GImage**, and **GPolygon**, along with the **GRoundRect** and **G3DRect** subclasses of **GRect**—are collectively known as the **shape classes.** These classes are the concrete realizations of the abstract **GObject** class, each of which defines one of the shapes that you can add to the collage. The shape classes are the ones that show up most often in graphical programming and are important enough to warrant a major section of their own.

9.3 Using the shape classes

As defined at the end of the preceding section, the shape classes are the concrete subclasses of **GObject** used to represent the actual objects on the screen. There are several different shape classes corresponding to the variety of graphical objects—labels, rectangles, ovals, lines, arcs, images, and polygons—that you might display on a canvas. Each of the shape classes inherits the methods from **GObject**, but usually defines additional methods that are specifically appropriate to that subclass. The sections that follow describe each of the shape classes in more detail.

The **GLabel** class

The **GLabel** class is the first class you encountered in this text, even though it is in some respects the most idiosyncratic of the shape classes. For one thing, **GLabel** does not implement any of the graphical interfaces from Figure 9-7. For another, it uses a different geometric model than the other graphical objects in that the location of a **GLabel** is not defined by its upper left corner. The **GLabel** class instead uses the geometric model illustrated in Figure 9-8.

The geometric model for the **GLabel** class is similar to the one that typesetters have used over the centuries since Gutenberg's invention of the printing press. The notion of a font, of course, originally comes from printing. Printers would load different sizes and styles of type into their presses to control the way in which characters appeared on a page. The terminology that Java uses to describe both fonts and labels also derives from the typesetting world. You will find it easier to understand the behavior of the **GLabel** class if you learn the following terms:

- The **baseline** is the imaginary line on which characters sit.
- The **origin** is the point at which the text of a label begins. In languages that read left to right, the origin is the point on the baseline at the left edge of the first character, as shown in Figure 9-8. In languages that read right to left, the origin is the point at the right edge of the first character, at the right end of the line.
- The **height** of a font is the distance between successive baselines in multiline text.
- The **ascent** of a font is the maximum distance characters extend above the baseline.
- The **descent** of a font is the maximum distance characters extend below the baseline.

The methods exported by the **GLabel** class appear in Figure 9-9. The first entries in this list are for the constructor, which comes in two forms. The first version of the constructor is the one you have already seen, which takes the string for the label along with the *x* and *y* coordinates of the origin. The second version leaves out the origin point, which has the effect of setting the origin to the default value of $(0, 0)$.

At first glance, this second version of the constructor seems to have little use. After all, if you actually displayed a **GLabel** at the point $(0, 0)$, everything above the

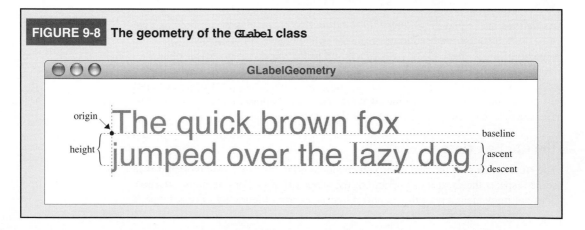

FIGURE 9-8   **The geometry of the GLabel class**

FIGURE 9-9	**Useful methods exported by the GLabel class**

Constructor

new GLabel(String str, double x, double y)
Creates a new **GLabel** object containing the string **str** whose origin is the point (**x**, **y**).

new GLabel(String str)
Creates a new **GLabel** object containing **str** at the point (0, 0); the actual location is set later.

Methods to get and set the text displayed by the label

void setLabel(String str)
Changes the string displayed by the label to **str**.

String getLabel()
Returns the text string currently being dispayed.

Methods to get and set the font

void setFont(Font f)   *or*   **setFont(String description)**
Sets the font to a Java **Font** object or a string in the form **"Family-style-size"**

Font getFont()
Returns the current font.

Methods to retrieve geometric properties of the label and its font

double getWidth()
Returns the horizontal extent of the label when displayed in its current font.

double getHeight()
Returns the height of the **GLabel** object, which is defined to be the height of its font.

double getAscent()
Returns the distance the characters in the current font extend above the baseline.

double getDescent()
Returns the distance the characters in the current font extend below the baseline.

---

baseline would disappear off the top of the canvas. In fact, the second version is often considerably more convenient, particularly if you don't yet know exactly where the label should be placed at the time you create it.

Many of the shape classes, including **GLabel**, export one version of the constructor that includes the initial coordinates and another that does not. You use the constructor that includes the coordinates when you know the location at the time you create the object. If you instead need to perform some calculation to determine the location, the easiest approach is to create it without specifying a location, perform the necessary calculations to figure out where it should go, and then add it to the canvas using the version of the **add** method that includes the x and y coordinates of the object. You will see several examples of this approach later in the chapter.

The **getLabel** and **setLabel** methods allow you to retrieve or change the contents of a **GLabel** after it has been created. Suppose, for example, that you want to include a **GLabel** on the screen to keep track of the user's score in an interactive game. You might start things off by defining a **GLabel** called **scoreLabel** like this:

```
GLabel scoreLabel = new GLabel("Score: 0");
```

If you add this **GLabel** to the canvas at an appropriate location, it displays the score in the format indicated by the argument string. As the game proceeds, however, the user's score will presumably change. If the program keeps track of the score in an instance variable named **score**, you can update the label by making the following call:

```
scoreLabel.setLabel("Score: " + score);
```

The **setFont** and **getFont** methods allow you to control the font used to display the label. As you know from Chapter 2, you can specify the font as a string consisting of three parts—the font family, the style, and the point size—separated by hyphens. For example, you can set the font for **scoreLabel** to be a 24-point bold sans-serif font by calling

```
scoreLabel.setFont("SansSerif-bold-24");
```

You could also supply a Java **Font** object as the argument to **setFont**, but the string version is usually easier to read.

You can obtain information about the geometric parameters of a **GLabel** by calling the methods **getWidth**, **getHeight**, **getAscent**, and **getDescent**. The **getWidth** method returns the number of pixels the label occupies in the horizontal dimension. Note that this result depends on both the properties of the font and the value of the string stored in the **GLabel**; the values of the other three methods are independent of the value of the string and are determined by the font alone.

These properties are useful for centering a **GLabel** at a particular location. Suppose, for example, that you want to rewrite the **HelloProgram** example from Chapter 2 so that it centered its message on the canvas. You can do so by rewriting the **run** method as follows:

```
public void run() {
    GLabel label = new GLabel("hello, world");
    double x = (getWidth() - label.getWidth()) / 2;
    double y = (getHeight() + label.getAscent()) / 2;
    add(label, x, y);
}
```

In order to center the **GLabel** horizontally, you must shift the origin left by half the width of the label. That calculation is accomplished by the declaration of **x** in the second line of the **run** method. Centering the label in the vertical dimension is a bit trickier. If you want the center line on the canvas to run through the middle of the typical uppercase character, you need to set the baseline so that it is half the font ascent below the center line. That calculation is expressed in the declaration of **y**. This line *adds* the adjustment for the font ascent because *y* values increase as you move downward.

If you're a stickler for aesthetic detail, you may find that using **getAscent** to center a **GLabel** vertically doesn't always produce the optimal result. Most labels that you display on the canvas will appear to be a few pixels too low. The reason is that **getAscent** returns the *maximum* ascent of the font and not the distance the text of this particular **GLabel** happens to rise above the baseline. For most fonts, certain characters—most notably the parentheses and accent marks—extend above the tops of the uppercase letters and therefore increase the font ascent beyond what it appears to be for a typical string. If you want things to look perfect, you may have to adjust the vertical centering by a pixel or two.

The GRect class and its subclasses (GRoundRect and G3DRect)

If **GLabel** is the most idiosyncratic class in the **acm.graphics** package, **GRect** is the most conventional. It implements all three of the special interfaces—**GFillable**, **GResizable**, and **GScalable**—but otherwise defines no methods except those that are common to the entire **GObject** hierarchy.

Like the **GLabel** class described in the preceding section, the **GRect** class exports two versions of the constructor. The one you have been using up to now has the form

```
new GRect(x, y, width, height)
```

and includes the coordinates of the upper left corner along with the dimensions of the rectangle. The second form is

```
new GRect(width, height)
```

which creates a new rectangle of the specified size but leaves it positioned at the origin. If you use this form, you will ordinarily specify the location of the **GRect** when you add it to the canvas. To understand the relationship between the two forms of the constructor, it is useful to keep in mind that the code

```
GRect rect = new GRect(x, y, width, height);
add(rect);
```

is identical in effect to

```
GRect rect = new GRect(width, height);
add(rect, x, y);
```

Depending on the circumstances, one of these approaches may be more convenient than the other. Having them both available makes it possible to use whichever one best fits the problem at hand.

If you look back to the class diagram for the **acm.graphics** library in Figure 9-1, you will see that **GRect** has two subclasses—**GRoundRect** and **G3DRect**—which represent two slightly different types of rectangles that differ from **GRect** only in their appearance on the display. The **GRoundRect** class has rounded corners, and the **G3DRect** class includes a shaded border that gives it a three-dimensional appearance. Neither of these classes is used in this book, but you can experiment with them if you'd like to find out more about how they work.

The GOval class

The **GOval** class is almost as straightforward as **GRect** and operates in much the same way. Particularly since you've been using the **GOval** class since Chapter 2, there is not a great deal of new information to cover.

The only aspect of the **GOval** that tends to cause confusion is the fact that using the upper left corner as the location makes less sense for ovals than it does for rectangles, given that this point is not inside the figure. Somehow, the confusion seems most acute when the oval happens to be a circle. In mathematics, a circle is conventionally defined in terms of its center and radius and not by the dimensions of the square that encloses it. As you saw with the **createFilledCircle** method that appeared in Figure 5-3, you can define methods that restore the conventional mathematical interpretation.

Despite the confusion that sometimes arises from defining ovals in terms of their bounding rectangle, there is a compelling reason for adopting that design decision in the **acm.graphics** package. The classes in the standard **java.awt** package use the bounding-rectangle approach. Maintaining consistency with the standard Java model makes it easier to move back and forth between the two. Although Emerson may have been correct in his observation that "a foolish consistency is the hobgoblin of little minds," there is enough justification behind this particular consistency to move it beyond the foolish category.

The GLine class

The **GLine** class is used to construct line drawings in the **acm.graphics** package. The **GLine** class implements **GScalable** (which is implemented so that the starting point of the line remains fixed and the line expands outward from there), but not **GFillable** or **GResizable**. The **GLine** class also defines several additional methods, as shown in Figure 9-10. The **setStartPoint** method allows clients to change the first endpoint of the line without changing the second; conversely, **setEndPoint** gives clients access to the second endpoint without affecting the first. These methods are therefore different in their operation from **setLocation**, which moves the entire line without changing its length or orientation. The corresponding **getStartPoint** and **getEndPoint** methods return the coordinates as a **GPoint**, which combines the individual *x* and *y* values into a single object.

FIGURE 9-10 **Useful methods exported by the GLine class**

Constructor

```
new GLine(double x0, double y0, double x1, double y1)
```
Creates a new **GLine** object connecting the points (**x0**, **y0**) and (**x1**, **y1**).

Methods to get and set the endpoints independently

```
void setStartPoint(double x, double y)
```
Resets the coordinates of the initial point of the line to (**x**, **y**) without changing the end point.

```
GPoint getStartPoint()
```
Returns the coordinates of the initial point in the line.

```
void setEndPoint(double x, double y)
```
Resets the coordinates of the end point of the line to (**x**, **y**) without changing the starting point.

```
GPoint getEndPoint()
```
Returns the coordinates of the end point in the line.

One other property of the **GLine** class that is worth highlighting is the way it interprets the **contains** method, which is defined for all **GObject** subclasses. For the **GRect** and **GOval** class, containment has an obvious meaning since the shapes have a bounded interior. Mathematically, however, a line is infinitely thin and therefore has no interior. In practice, however, it makes sense to define a point as being contained within a line if it is "close enough" to be considered as part of that line. In the **acm.graphics** package, that distance is specified by the constant **LINE_TOLERANCE** in the **GLine** class, which is defined to be a pixel and a half.

The GArc class

The **GArc** class is used to display an arc formed by selecting part of the perimeter of an oval. In Java, you define the location and size of an arc by specifying the location and dimensions of the rectangle that bounds the oval from which the arc is taken. In addition, you also have to indicate the part of the oval you're interested in by specifying the angle at which the arc begins and the angle through which the arc extends as it moves around the perimeter. These two values are called the **start angle** and the **sweep angle,** respectively. Like all angles in the **acm.graphics** package, start and sweep angles are measured in degrees counterclockwise from the +*x* axis. The complete geometry of an arc is therefore indicated by six parameters: *x, y, width, height, start,* and *sweep.* The relationship of these parameters is illustrated in Figure 9-11.

The effect of these parameters, however, is more easily illustrated by example. The four sample runs in Figure 9-12 show the effect of the code that appears below

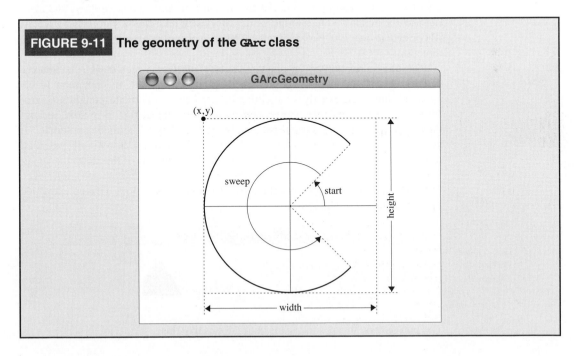

FIGURE 9-11 **The geometry of the GArc class**

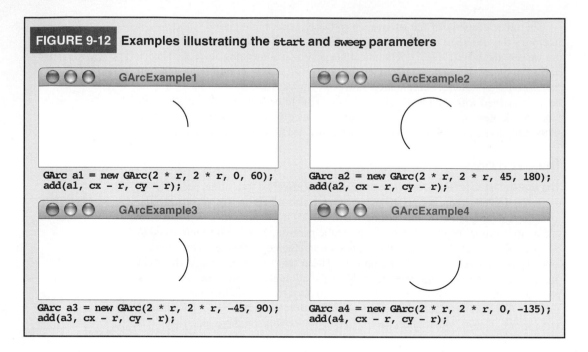

FIGURE 9-12 Examples illustrating the start and sweep parameters

GArcExample1

```
GArc a1 = new GArc(2 * r, 2 * r, 0, 60);
add(a1, cx - r, cy - r);
```

GArcExample2

```
GArc a2 = new GArc(2 * r, 2 * r, 45, 180);
add(a2, cx - r, cy - r);
```

GArcExample3

```
GArc a3 = new GArc(2 * r, 2 * r, -45, 90);
add(a3, cx - r, cy - r);
```

GArcExample4

```
GArc a4 = new GArc(2 * r, 2 * r, 0, -135);
add(a4, cx - r, cy - r);
```

each diagram. Those code fragments create and display arcs using different values for **start** and **sweep**. Each of the arcs is centered at the point (**cx**, **cy**) and has a radius of **r** pixels. Note that the values of **start** and **sweep** can be negative, as illustrated in the last two examples. Negative angles extend in the clockwise direction.

The **GArc** class implements the **GFillable** interface, which means that you can call the **setFilled** method to control whether the arc is filled. It is not immediately apparent, however, exactly what filling an arc means. The interpretation of arc-filling that Java's designers chose seems a bit confusing at first, primarily because the unfilled version of a **GArc** is not simply the boundary of its filled counterpart. If you display an unfilled **GArc**, only the arc itself is shown. If you call **setFilled(true)** on that arc, Java connects the endpoints of the arc to the center from which the arc was drawn and then fills the interior of that region. The following sample run illustrates the difference by showing both unfilled and filled version of the same 60-degree arc:

UnfilledAndFilledArcs

The **run** method that produces this output looks like this:

```
public void run() {
    double r = 50;
    GArc openArc = new GArc(2 * r, 2 * r, 0, 60);
    add(openArc, 0.3 * getWidth() - r, (getHeight() - r) / 2);
    GArc filledArc = new GArc(2 * r, 2 * r, 0, 60);
    filledArc.setFilled(true);
    add(filledArc, 0.7 * getWidth() - r, (getHeight() - r) / 2);
}
```

The important lesson to take from this example is that the geometric boundary of a
GArc changes if you set it to be filled. A filled arc is a wedge-shaped region that has
a well-defined interior. An unfilled arc is simply a section taken from the perimeter
of an ellipse.

As in the case of a line segment, an unfilled arc doesn't enclose any points. As a
result, the interpretation of the **contains** method for the **GArc** class also depends on
whether the arc is filled. For an unfilled arc, containment implies that the arc point
is actually on the arc, subject to the same interpretation of "closeness" as described
for a point on a line in the preceding section. For a filled arc, containment implies
inclusion in the wedge.

If you want to display the outline of a wedge using the **GArc** class, the simplest
approach is to create the arc, set it to be filled, and then set its fill color to match the
background. Thus, you can create an outlined version of the same 60-degree arc
using a **run** method that looks like this:

```
public void run() {
    double r = 50;
    GArc outlinedArc = new GArc(2 * r, 2 * r, 0, 60);
    outlinedArc.setFilled(true);
    outlinedArc.setFillColor(Color.WHITE);
    add(outlinedArc, getWidth() / 2 - r, getHeight() / 2 - r);
}
```

This code produces the following output on the screen:

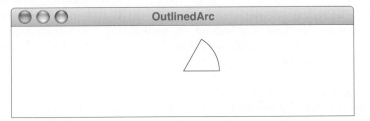

Although the examples of **GArc** you have seen so far in this chapter have all used
circular arcs, it is possible to produce elliptical arcs as well. One way to create this
effect is to use different width and height values in the constructor. Another is to
exploit the fact that **GArc** implements the **GScalable** interface. The fact that arcs
are scalable allows you to create a circular arc and then stretch it so that it becomes
an ellipse. You could, for example, make the arc in the preceding example four
times as long as it is high by calling

```
outlinedArc.scale(4, 1);
```

If you then added this rescaled arc to the canvas (after adjusting the location so that the center of the ellipse still fell at the center of the window), you would see the following display:

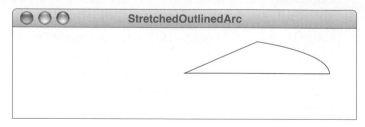

This figure illustrates the interesting property that the start and sweep angles for an elliptical arc do not always correspond to the geometry of the figure that appears on the screen. As you can tell from the parameters to the **GArc** constructor, this arc has a sweep of 60 degrees. As long as the arc is circular, the angle formed by the two radial segments of the wedge is also 60 degrees. When the arc is elliptical, however, that angle changes. In the preceding sample run, the angle at the center of the canvas is clearly much smaller than 60 degrees. What remains true is that the arc has continued through one sixth (60 / 360) of the perimeter of the ellipse, even though the scaling reduces the size of the actual angle. In practice, the easiest way to think about arc scaling is to determine how particular values for the start and sweep angles would appear on a circle and then scale each coordinate to find the corresponding endpoints on an ellipse.

The **GArc** class includes several methods beyond those defined in the **GFillable** and **GScalable** interfaces. Those methods appear in Figure 9-13.

The **GImage** class

The **GImage** class is used to display an image stored in a data file that contains data encoded using one of the standard image formats. The two most common are the Graphics Interchange Format (GIF) and the Joint Photographic Experts Group (JPEG) format. Although most Java environments are capable of displaying images encoded in other formats as well, you can maximize the portability of your program by sticking with the most common formats.

The first step in displaying an image is to create an image file in one of the standard formats. The name of the image file should end with an extension that identifies the encoding format, which is typically either **.gif** or **.jpg**. You then need to store that file on your computer in the same directory as the Java program in which you want to use it or in a subdirectory of that directory called **images**. In your program, you then create a **GImage** object and add it to the canvas, just as you would with any of the other **GObject** subclasses. For example, if you have an image file called **MyImage.gif**, you can display that image in the upper left corner of the canvas using the following **run** method:

```
public void run() {
   add(new GImage("MyImage.gif"));
}
```

| FIGURE 9-13 | Methods exported by the `GArc` class |

Constructor

```
new GArc(double x, double y, double width, double height,
         double start, double sweep)
```
Creates a new **GArc** object as specified by the six parameters.

```
new GArc(double width, double height, double start, double sweep)
```
Creates a new **GArc** object with a default location of (0, 0).

Methods to get and set the start and sweep angles

```
void setStartAngle(double theta)
```
Resets the start angle used to define the arc.

```
double getStartAngle()
```
Returns the current value of the start angle.

```
void setSweepAngle(double theta)
```
Resets the sweep angle used to define the arc.

```
double getSweepAngle()
```
Returns the current value of the sweep angle.

Methods to retrieve the endpoints of the arc

```
GPoint getStartPoint()
```
Returns the coordinates of the initial point in the arc.

```
GPoint getEndPoint()
```
Returns the coordinates of the end point in the arc.

Methods to retrieve or reset the framing rectangle that encloses the arc

```
GRectangle getFrameRectangle()
```
Returns the rectangle that bounds the ellipse from which the arc is taken.

```
void setFrameRectangle(GRectangle bounds)
```
Resets the rectangle that bounds the arc.

If you wanted to center the image in the canvas instead, you could rewrite the **run** method as follows:

```
public void run() {
   GImage image = new GImage("MyImage.gif");
   double x = (getWidth() - image.getWidth()) / 2;
   double y = (getHeight() - image.getHeight()) / 2;
   add(image, x, y);
}
```

As these examples make clear, the mechanical details of using images are not particularly complicated, because Java takes care of the work necessary to display the actual image on the screen. All you have to do is put the image data into a file and then tell Java the name of that file.

A more interesting question is where these images come from in the first place. One possibility is to create images of your own. To do so, you need to use a digital camera or some kind of image-creation software. The second possibility is to download existing images from the web. Most web browsers make it possible for you to download the corresponding image file whenever an image appears on the screen.

If you do use existing images, however, you need to be aware of possible restrictions on the use of intellectual property. Most of the images you find on the web are protected by copyright. Under copyright law, you must obtain the permission of the copyright holder in order to use the image, unless your use of the image satisfies the guidelines for "fair use"—a doctrine that has unfortunately become much more murky in the digital age. Under "fair use" guidelines, you could almost certainly use a copyrighted image in a paper that you write for a class. On the other hand, you could not put that same image into a commercially published work without first securing—and probably paying for—the right to do so.

Even in cases in which your use of an image falls within the "fair use" guidelines, it is important to give proper credit to the source. As a general rule, whenever you find an image on the web that you would like to use, you should first check to see whether that web site explains its usage policy. Many of the best sources for images on the web have explicit guidelines for using their images. Some images are absolutely free, some are free for use with citation, some can be used in certain contexts but not others, and some are completely restricted. For example, the web site for the National Aeronautics and Space Administration (**http://www.nasa.gov**) has an extensive library of images about the exploration of space. As the web site explains, you can use these images freely as long as you include the citation "Courtesy NASA/JPL-Caltech" along with the image.

The code for the **EarthImage** program in Figure 9-14 illustrates the use of the **GImage** class as well as the strategy of using a **GLabel** to include the requested citation. The image, which shows the Earth as seen by the Apollo 17 astronauts on their way to the moon in December 1972, is stored in an image file named **EarthFromApollo17.jpg**. The **EarthImage** program reads that image file into a **GImage** object and then adds that object to the canvas, along with the citation. The effect is to produce the following display:

| FIGURE 9-14 | Program to display an image of the earth |

```
/*
 * File: EarthImage.java
 * -----------------------
 * This program displays an image of the earth from space.
 * The image appears through the courtesy of NASA/JPL-Caltech.
 */

import acm.graphics.*;
import acm.program.*;

public class EarthImage extends GraphicsProgram {

    public void run() {
        add(new GImage("EarthFromApollo17.jpg"));
        addCitation("Courtesy NASA/JPL-Caltech");
    }

/* Adds a citation label at the lower right of the canvas */
    private void addCitation(String text) {
        GLabel label = new GLabel(text);
        label.setFont(CITATION_FONT);
        double x = getWidth() - label.getWidth();
        double y = getHeight() - CITATION_MARGIN + label.getAscent();
        add(label, x, y);
    }

/* Private constants */
    private static final String CITATION_FONT = "SansSerif-10";
    private static final int CITATION_MARGIN = 13;

/* Set the dimensions of the window */
    public static final int APPLICATION_WIDTH = 640;
    public static final int APPLICATION_HEIGHT = 640 + CITATION_MARGIN;

}
```

The **EarthImage** program also illustrates another useful technique that allows you to set the window size for any program that extends one of the **Program** classes in the **acm.program** package. The initialization of the **Program** class checks to see whether this particular subclass defines the constants **APPLICATION_WIDTH** and **APPLICATION_HEIGHT**. If so, the **Program** class uses the values of those constants to determine the size of the program window. If the values are undefined, the **Program** class creates a window with a standard default size. In this example, the size of the program window is set so that the image of the earth, which happens to be 640 × 640 pixels, fills the entire window after leaving **CITATION_MARGIN** pixels at the bottom free for the citation.

But what if you don't know the size of the image in advance and instead simply want it to fill the available area on the screen? As it happens, adjusting the size of an image is very easy in Java. The **GImage** class implements both the **GScalable** and **GResizable** interfaces, which means that you can change the size of an image either by applying a scaling factor or by calling **setSize** with a new height and width. Thus, you could make sure that the image of the earth and its citation always filled the screen by rewriting the **run** method as follows:

```
public void run() {
    GImage image = new GImage("EarthFromApollo17.jpg");
    image.setSize(getWidth(), getHeight() - CITATION_MARGIN);
    add(image);
}
```

Although this code achieves the goal of filling the screen with the image, it might not always have the desired aesthetic effect. For most images, scaling works well only if you scale the image by the same factor in each dimension. Scaling an image by the same factor in both the *x* and *y* directions preserves its **aspect ratio,** which is simply the width of the image divided by its height. If you allow the aspect ratio to vary too much, the image will appear stretched in one dimension or the other. For example, if you were to display the **EarthFromApollo17.jpg** image in a window in which the width was substantially larger than the height, you would see a display that looked something like this:

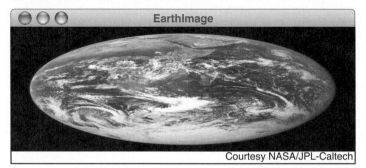

The picture is now barely recognizable as the Earth and no longer conveys the same impression of a celestial sphere floating in the heavens.

There are, however, some images in which differential scaling—at least within modest limits—doesn't adversely affect their appearance. One example is a line graph in which rescaling the image is simply a matter of changing the size of a unit along each axis. Suppose, for example, that you have an image file called **GlobalTemperatures.gif** that contains the following graph of the average annual temperature from 1880 to 2005:

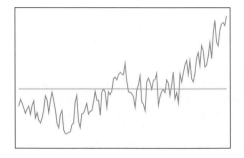

With images of this sort, changing the aspect ratio doesn't make much difference. The following sample run shows the result of displaying this graph so that it fills a larger window, leaving room for a citation indicating the source of the data:

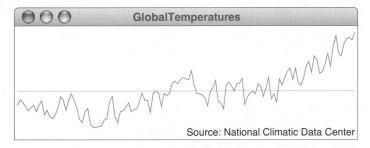

The **GImage** class exports a few useful methods beyond the ones described in this chapter. For the most part, those methods are designed to support image-processing strategies that make it possible to manipulate the individual pixels in the image. Those strategies, along with the methods that **GImage** exports to enable them, are introduced in Chapter 11.

The **GPolygon** class

The **GPolygon** class makes it possible to display a **polygon,** which is simply the mathematical name for a closed shape whose boundary consists of straight lines**.** The line segments that form the outline of a polygon are called **edges.** The point at which a pair of edges meets is called a **vertex.** Many polygonal shapes are familiar from the real world. Each cell in a honeycomb is a hexagon, which is the common name for a polygon with six sides. A stop sign is an octagon with eight identical sides. Polygons, however, are not required to be so regular. The figures in the right margin, for example, illustrate four polygons that fit the general definition.

The **GPolygon** class is relatively easy to use as long as you keep a couple of points in mind:

- Unlike the constructors for the other shape classes, the constructor for the **GPolygon** class does not create the entire figure. What happens instead is that the constructor creates an empty **GPolygon** that contains no vertices. Once you have created the empty polygon, you then add vertices to it by calling various other methods described later in this section.
- The location of a **GPolygon** is not defined to be its upper left corner. Many polygons, after all, don't have an upper left corner. What happens instead is that you—as the programmer who is creating the specific polygon—choose a **reference point** that defines the location of the polygon as a whole. You then specify the coordinates for each vertex in terms of where they lie relative to the reference point. The advantage of this design is that you don't have to recompute the coordinates of each vertex if you move the **GPolygon** on the canvas. All you have to do is move the reference point. Because the vertices are defined relative to the reference point, the code that redraws the polygon will shift all the vertices to their correct locations.

diamond

trapezoid

T-shape

five-pointed star

The creation of a **GPolygon** is easiest to illustrate by example. Suppose that you want to create a **GPolygon** representing the diamond-shaped figure shown in the earlier example. Your first design decision consists of choosing where to put the reference point. For most polygons, the most convenient point is the geometric center of the figure. If you adopt that model, you then need to create an empty **GPolygon** and add four vertices to it, specifying the coordinates of each vertex relative to the coordinates of the center. Assuming that the width and height of the diamond are stored in the constants **DIAMOND_WIDTH** and **DIAMOND_HEIGHT**, you can create the diamond-shaped **GPolygon** using the following code:

```
GPolygon diamond = new GPolygon();
diamond.addVertex(-DIAMOND_WIDTH / 2, 0);
diamond.addVertex(0, DIAMOND_HEIGHT / 2);
diamond.addVertex(DIAMOND_WIDTH / 2, 0);
diamond.addVertex(0, -DIAMOND_HEIGHT / 2);
```

You can then add the diamond at the center of the canvas by executing the following statement:

```
add(diamond, getWidth() / 2, getHeight() / 2);
```

The graphics window would then look like this:

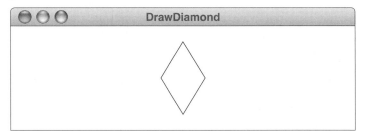

When you use the **addVertex** method to construct a polygon, the coordinates of each vertex are expressed relative to the reference point. In some cases, it is easier to specify the coordinates of each vertex in terms of the preceding one. To enable this approach, the **GPolygon** class offers an **addEdge** method, which is similar to **addVertex** except that the parameters specify the displacement from the previous vertex to the current one. You can therefore draw the same diamond by making the following sequence of calls:

```
GPolygon diamond = new GPolygon();
diamond.addVertex(-DIAMOND_WIDTH / 2, 0);
diamond.addEdge(DIAMOND_WIDTH / 2, DIAMOND_HEIGHT / 2);
diamond.addEdge(DIAMOND_WIDTH / 2, -DIAMOND_HEIGHT / 2);
diamond.addEdge(-DIAMOND_WIDTH / 2, -DIAMOND_HEIGHT / 2);
diamond.addEdge(-DIAMOND_WIDTH / 2, DIAMOND_HEIGHT / 2);
```

Note that the first vertex must still be added using **addVertex**, but that subsequent ones can be defined by specifying the edge displacements.

As you work with the **GPolygon** class, you will discover that some polygons are easier to define with successive calls to **addVertex**, while others are easier to define using **addEdge**. For many polygonal figures, however, it is even more convenient to define the edges using polar coordinates. The **GPolygon** class supports this style through the method **addPolarEdge**. This method is identical to **addEdge** except that its arguments are the length of the edge and its direction is expressed in degrees counterclockwise from the +*x* axis.

The **addPolarEdge** method makes it easy to create figures in which you know the angles of the edges but would need trigonometry to calculate the vertices. The following method, for example, uses **addPolarEdge** to create a regular hexagon in which the length of each edge is determined by the parameter **size**:

```
private GPolygon createHexagon(double side) {
   GPolygon hex = new GPolygon();
   hex.addVertex(-side, 0);
   int angle = 60;
   for (int i = 0; i < 6; i++) {
      hex.addPolarEdge(side, angle);
      angle -= 60;
   }
   return hex;
}
```

As always, the first vertex is added using **addVertex**. Here, the initial vertex is the one at the left edge of the hexagon. The first edge then extends from that point at an angle of 60 degrees. Each subsequent edge has the same length, but sets off at an angle 60 degrees to the right of the preceding one. When all six edges have been added, the final edge will end up at the original vertex, thereby closing the polygon.

Once you have defined this method, you can use it to create a **GPolygon** that represents a regular hexagon of any size. For example, if you were to combine the definition of **createHexagon** with the **run** method

```
public void run() {
   add(createHexagon(50), getWidth() / 2, getHeight() / 2);
}
```

you would see the following display:

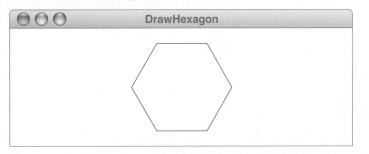

The **GPolygon** class implements the **GFillable** and **GScalable** interfaces, but not **GResizable**. Moreover, as with any **GObject**, you can set the color of a **GPolygon** using the **setColor** method. These capabilities make it easy, for example, to draw a traditional stop sign that looks like this:

The code for this program appears in Figure 9-15.

FIGURE 9-15   **Program to display a stop sign**

```java
import acm.graphics.*;
import acm.program.*;
import java.awt.*;

public class StopSign extends GraphicsProgram {

   public void run() {
      double cx = getWidth() / 2;
      double cy = getHeight() / 2;
      GPolygon sign = createOctagon(EDGE_LENGTH);
      sign.setFilled(true);
      sign.setColor(Color.RED);
      add(sign, cx, cy);
      GLabel stop = new GLabel("STOP");
      stop.setFont("SansSerif-bold-36");
      stop.setColor(Color.WHITE);
      add(stop, cx - stop.getWidth() / 2, cy + stop.getAscent() / 2);
   }

/* Creates a regular octagon with the specified side length */
   private GPolygon createOctagon(double side) {
      GPolygon octagon = new GPolygon();
      octagon.addVertex(-side / 2, side / 2 + side / Math.sqrt(2));
      int angle = 0;
      for (int i = 0; i < 8; i++) {
         octagon.addPolarEdge(side, angle);
         angle += 45;
      }
      return octagon;
   }

/* Private constants */
   private static final double EDGE_LENGTH = 50;

}
```

In much the same fashion as the **createHexagon** example earlier in this section, the **StopSign** program in Figure 9-15 uses a **createOctagon** method to initialize a polygon of the desired shape. Separating the code that creates the polygon from the rest of the program is a good illustration of procedural decomposition in which the details of the **GPolygon** class are encapsulated within a single method. Other methods within the program can then create an octagonal shape without forcing you to worry about those details.

There is, however, another approach to encapsulating this complexity that fits more closely into the object-oriented paradigm. Instead of defining a method that creates a particular polygon, you can define a subclass of **GPolygon** that does the same work in its constructor. This strategy is illustrated in Figure 9-16, which defines a **GStar** class that represents a five-pointed star with its reference point at the center. The code for the constructor automatically starts off with an empty **GPolygon** created by an implicit call to the constructor for the **GPolygon** superclass. All the **GStar** constructor does is add the necessary vertices to create a five-pointed star.

Unfortunately, the five-pointed star is much more complicated mathematically than the diamond, hexagon, and octagon examples you have seen so far. The first two lines of the constructor declare the variables **dx** and **dy** and initialize them to the distance along each axis from the center of the star to the starting point, which is the

---

FIGURE 9-16   **GPolygon subclass that displays a five-pointed star**

```
import acm.graphics.*;

/**
 * Defines a new GObject class that appears as a five-pointed star.
 */
public class GStar extends GPolygon {

/**
 * Creates a new GStar centered at the origin with the specified
 * horizontal width.
 * @param width The width of the star
 */
   public GStar(double width) {
      double dx = width / 2;
      double dy = dx * GMath.tanDegrees(18);
      double edge = width / 2 - dy * GMath.tanDegrees(36);
      addVertex(-dx, -dy);
      int angle = 0;
      for (int i = 0; i < 5; i++) {
         addPolarEdge(edge, angle);
         addPolarEdge(edge, angle + 72);
         angle -= 72;
      }
   }
}
```

leftmost vertex. Calculating the distance in the *x* direction is the easy part, since the starting point is simply half the width of the star to the left of its center. Calculating the distance in the *y* direction requires a bit of trigonometry, which can be illustrated as follows:

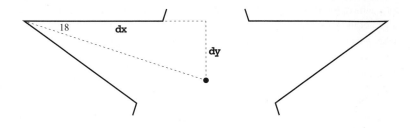

Each of the points around the periphery of a five-pointed star forms an angle that is a tenth of a complete circle, which is 36 degrees. If you draw a line that bisects that angle—leaving 18 degrees on either side—that line will hit the geometric center of the star, forming the right triangle shown in the diagram. The value of **dy** is therefore equal to **dx** multiplied by the tangent of 18 degrees.

The third line in the constructor declares the variable **edge** and assigns it the length of the line segments that form the outline of the star. The calculation necessary to compute this value is illustrated in the following diagram:

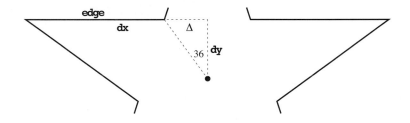

To determine the value of **edge**, you need to subtract the dotted portion of the horizontal line from its entire length, which is given by **dx**. The length of the dotted portion, shown here using the Greek letter Δ, can also be computed using trigonometry. In this case, the value of Δ is equal to **dy** multiplied by the tangent of 36 degrees.

Once you have computed these initial values, the rest of the **GStar** constructor is relatively straightforward. Each cycle of the **for** loop uses **addPolarEdge** to add two line segments to the polygon. At the end of each cycle, the **for** loop adds 72 to the value of **angle** so that the next two edges are rotated by a fifth of a complete circle ($72° = 360° / 5$).

In addition to the **addVertex**, **addEdge**, and **addPolarEdge** methods, the **GPolygon** class exports one other method for adding edges to a polygon. That method is **addArc**, which at first seems contrary to the mathematical conception of a polygon, given that a polygon is defined to be bounded by straight lines. What **addArc** does, however, is to add a series of short edges to a **GPolygon** that *simulate* the desired arc. As a result, **addArc** makes it possible to create fillable shapes that appear to have curved edges. The arguments to **addArc** are the same as those for the **GArc** constructor, specifying the width and height of the ellipse from which the arc is taken, along with the start and sweep angle of the arc. The coordinates of the arc, however, are not explicitly specified. When you call **addArc**, the segments that approximate the arc boundary are positioned so that they connect to the most recent vertex in the **GPolygon**.

The use of **addArc** is most easily illustrated by example. Suppose that you want to draw a doorway in which the upper portion of the door is a semicircular arc, as shown in the following sample run:

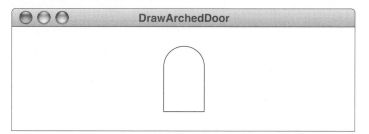

This door can be represented as a **GPolygon** with three straight edges and a series of tiny edges that curve across the top of the archway. You can implement this shape as a **GPolygon** subclass by writing the following class definition:

```
public class GArchedDoor extends GPolygon {
    public GArchedDoor(double width, double height) {
        double lengthOfVerticalEdge = height - width / 2;
        addVertex(-width / 2, 0);
        addEdge(width, 0);
        addEdge(0, -lengthOfVerticalEdge);
        addArc(width, width, 0, 180);
        addEdge(0, lengthOfVerticalEdge);
    }
}
```

The constructor for the **GArchedDoor** class takes the width and height of the door, where the height is measured from the base to the top of the arch. The reference point for the polygon is the point at the center of the door's base. The construction of the **GPolygon** begins by calling **addVertex** with the coordinates of the lower left corner and then uses **addEdge** to create the bottom and right edges of the door. The **addArc** call then adds the semicircular arc across the top, which has a diameter equal to the width of the door, a start angle of 0°, and a sweep angle of 180°. After adding the arc, the constructor calls **addEdge** to add the left edge of the door, thereby completing the polygonal outline.

Although the methods outlined in this section are sufficient for the examples used in this book, the **GPolygon** class exports several additional methods as well. These methods are included in the table shown in Figure 9-17. For more

---

FIGURE 9-17   **Methods exported by the `GPolygon` class**

Constructor

`new GPolygon()`
Creates an empty **GPolygon** object with its reference point at $(0, 0)$.

`new GPolygon(double x, double y)`
Creates an empty **GPolygon** object with its reference point at (x, y).

Methods to add edges to the polygon

`void addVertex(double x, double y)`
Adds a vertex at (x, y) relative to the reference point of the polygon.

`void addEdge(double dx, double dy)`
Adds a new vertex whose coordinates are shifted by **dx** and **dy** from the previous vertex.

`void addPolarEdge(double r, double theta)`
Adds a new vertex whose location is expressed in polar coordinates relative to the previous one.

`void addArc(double arcWidth, double arcHeight, double start, double sweep)`
Adds a series of edges that simulates an arc specified in the style of the **GArc** constructor.

Other useful methods

`void rotate(double theta)`
Rotates the polygon around its reference point by the angle **theta**, measured in degrees.

`void recenter()`
Adjusts the vertices of the polygon so that the reference point is at the geometric center.

`GPoint getCurrentPoint()`
Returns the coordinates of the last vertex added to the polygon, or **null** if the polygon is empty.

---

information on the methods that are not described in this book, the best approach is to consult the **javadoc** pages.

9.4 Creating compound objects

The class from the **acm.graphics** hierarchy that has not yet been discussed is the **GCompound** class, which turns out to be so useful that it is worth a section of its own. The **GCompound** class makes it possible to collect several **GObject**s together into a single unit, which is itself a **GObject**. This feature extends the notion of abstraction into the domain of graphical objects. In much the same way that methods allow you to assemble many statements into a single unit, the **GCompound** class allows you to put together graphical objects into a single unit that has its own integrity as a graphical object.

The methods available in the **GCompound** class are listed in Figure 9-18. The sections that follow introduce a series of examples that illustrate the use of these methods.

A simple GCompound example

To understand how the **GCompound** class works, it is easiest to start with a simple example. Imagine that you want to assemble an abstract face on the canvas that looks something like this:

FIGURE 9-18	Methods exported by the `GCompound` class

Constructor

`new GCompound()`
Creates a new **GCompound** that contains no objects.

Methods to add and remove graphical objects from a compound

`void add(GObject gobj)`
Adds a graphical object to the compound.

`void add(GObject gobj, double x, double y)`
Adds a graphical object to the compound at the specified location.

`void remove(GObject gobj)`
Removes the specified graphical object from the compound.

`void removeAll()`
Removes all graphical objects and components from the compound.

Miscellaneous methods

`GObject getElementAt(double x, double y)`
Returns the frontmost object containing the specified point, or **null** if no such object exists.

`GPoint getLocalPoint(double x, double y)`   *or*   `getLocalPoint(GPoint pt)`
Returns the point in the local coordinate space corresponding to **pt** in the canvas.

`GPoint getCanvasPoint(double x, double y)`   *or*   `getCanvasPoint(GPoint pt)`
Returns the point on the canvas corresponding to **pt** in the local coordinate space.

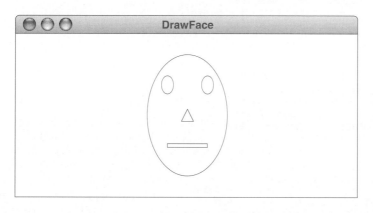

The face consists of several independent features—a **GOval** for the head, two **GOval**s for the eyes, a **GRect** for the mouth, and a **GPolygon** for the nose—which you then need to add in the appropriate places. You can, of course, add each of these objects to the canvas just as you have all along. If you do so, however, you will find it hard to manipulate the face as a unit. Suppose, for example, that you want to move the face to a different position on the canvas. If you added each of the features independently, moving the face would require then moving every feature. It would be much better if you could simply tell the entire face to move.

The code in Figure 9-19 uses the **GCompound** class to do just that. The **GFace** class extends **GCompound** to create a face object containing the necessary features.

FIGURE 9-19 **A "graphical face" class defined using GCompound**

```java
/*
 * File: GFace.java
 * -------------------
 * This file defines a compound GFace class.
 */

import acm.graphics.*;

public class GFace extends GCompound {

/** Creates a new GFace object with the specified dimensions */
   public GFace(double width, double height) {
      head = new GOval(width, height);
      leftEye = new GOval(EYE_WIDTH * width, EYE_HEIGHT * height);
      rightEye = new GOval(EYE_WIDTH * width, EYE_HEIGHT * height);
      nose = createNose(NOSE_WIDTH * width, NOSE_HEIGHT * height);
      mouth = new GRect(MOUTH_WIDTH * width, MOUTH_HEIGHT * height);
      add(head, 0, 0);
      add(leftEye, 0.25 * width - EYE_WIDTH * width / 2,
                   0.25 * height - EYE_HEIGHT * height / 2);
      add(rightEye, 0.75 * width - EYE_WIDTH * width / 2,
                    0.25 * height - EYE_HEIGHT * height / 2);
      add(nose, 0.50 * width, 0.50 * height);
      add(mouth, 0.50 * width - MOUTH_WIDTH * width / 2,
                 0.75 * height - MOUTH_HEIGHT * height / 2);
   }

/* Creates a triangle for the nose */
   private GPolygon createNose(double width, double height) {
      GPolygon poly = new GPolygon();
      poly.addVertex(0, -height / 2);
      poly.addVertex(width / 2, height / 2);
      poly.addVertex(-width / 2, height / 2);
      return poly;
   }

/* Constants specifying feature size as a fraction of the head size */
   private static final double EYE_WIDTH    = 0.15;
   private static final double EYE_HEIGHT   = 0.15;
   private static final double NOSE_WIDTH   = 0.15;
   private static final double NOSE_HEIGHT  = 0.10;
   private static final double MOUTH_WIDTH  = 0.50;
   private static final double MOUTH_HEIGHT = 0.03;

/* Private instance variables */
   private GOval head;
   private GOval leftEye, rightEye;
   private GPolygon nose;
   private GRect mouth;
}
```

These features are created and then added in the appropriate places by the **GFace** constructor. The constructor is coded in such a way that the size of each feature is expressed in terms of the width and height of the face as a whole, so that small faces have, for example, eyes of the appropriately small size.

Once the constructor has created each of the features, it then adds each of them in turn, using calls like

```
add(nose, 0.50 * width, 0.50 * height);
```

This statement adds the nose so that its appears at the center of the face. The important thing to recognize, however, is that this **add** call does not add the nose to the canvas, but rather to the **GCompound**. The **add** method you've been using up to now is the one defined in **GraphicsProgram**. Because the **GFace** class extends **GCompound**, it uses the **add** method defined in its superclass. Adding objects to a **GCompound** is intuitively analogous to the same operation at the canvas level except that the objects stay together as a unit. You can move everything in the **GCompound** simply by moving the **GCompound** itself.

The **GCompound** coordinate system

Like the **GPolygon** class, the **GCompound** class defines its own coordinate system in which all coordinate values are expressed relative to a reference point. This design makes it possible for you to define a **GCompound** without having to know exactly where it is going to appear on the canvas. When the components of a **GCompound** actually get drawn, they are shifted to the appropriate position. If you need to convert coordinates back and forth between the local coordinate system of the **GCompound** and the coordinate system of the canvas as a whole, you can use the methods **getCanvasPoint** and **getLocalPoint**, which appear in the table of **GCompound** methods in Figure 9-18.

The fact that the **GCompound** class maintains its own coordinate system turns out to be extremely useful, because it allows you to change the reference point for a graphical object in a way that simplifies common mathematical and physical calculations. As an example, consider how you might represent a bouncing ball on the canvas. The obvious solution is to use a **GOval** with equal width and height so that it appears as a circle. The problem with that strategy, however, is that the reference point of a **GOval** is in the upper left corner. If you want to perform any physical calculations involving the ball, it would be far better if you could define the location of the ball to be its center.

The simplest way to change the reference point for the ball from the corner to the center is to use the **GCompound** class. The code in Figure 9-20, for example, defines a new **GBall** class whose location is always at the center of the ball.

Object decomposition using **GCompound**

In the discussion of decomposition in Chapter 5, the primary example consists of drawing a three-car train that looks like this:

FIGURE 9-20   **Using GCompound to create a ball defined by its center**

```
/*
 * File: GBall.java
 * -------------------
 * This file defines a GObject class that represents a ball.
 */

import acm.graphics.*;

/**
 * This class defines a GObject subclass that represents a ball
 * whose reference point is the center rather than the upper
 * left corner.
 */
public class GBall extends GCompound {

/** Creates a new ball with radius r centered at the origin */
   public GBall(double r) {
      GOval ball = new GOval(2 * r, 2 * r);
      ball.setFilled(true);
      add(ball, -r, -r);
      markAsComplete();
   }

/** Creates a new ball with radius r centered at (x, y) */
   public GBall(double r, double x, double y) {
      this(r);
      setLocation(x, y);
   }
}
```

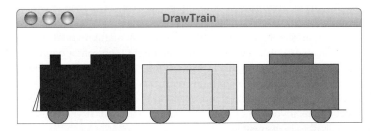

As you learned in that discussion, the **DrawTrain** program provides many opportunities to decompose the problem into a set of simpler methods, not only as a strategy for reducing the complexity of the problem but also as a way to take advantage of common elements within the structure.

Although stepwise refinement of individual methods remains important in the object-oriented world, it is not the only decomposition strategy available. In many cases—including the **DrawTrain** example—it is far more useful to decompose the problem by creating a hierarchy of classes whose structure reflects the relationship among the objects.

If you think about the elements of the train diagram as objects, the cars come in three different classes: engines, boxcars, and cabooses. What unifies each of these classes is that they are all train cars and share certain properties of that more general class. Looking at the problem in this way suggests the following class hierarchy:

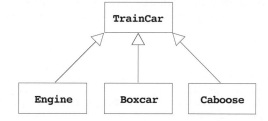

Each of the concrete classes—**Engine**, **Boxcar**, and **Caboose**—is a subclass of the abstract class **TrainCar**, which defines the properties that all train cars share.

This class diagram, however, does not yet show a superclass for **TrainCar** itself. To get a sense of what that superclass must be, it is important for you to think about what operations you want to do with objects that are instances of the **TrainCar** class. Although there may be other operations that make sense for train cars, one of the things you need to do with a train car is to display it on a **GCanvas** so that it appears on the screen. Thus, a **TrainCar** must be a **GObject** of some kind. Moreover, because each train car is composed of graphical objects that make up the picture, the most natural choice of a superclass for **TrainCar** is **GCompound**, since that is the subclass of **GObject** that can contain other **GObject**s. Thus, a more complete picture of the class hierarchy looks like this:

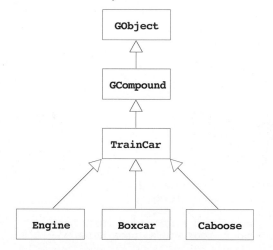

In implementing the classes at the bottom of this hierarchy, you can take advantage of the same commonalities among the different train car types that made it useful to define the **drawCarFrame** method in Chapter 5. The constructor for the **TrainCar** class can add the graphical objects that are common to all train cars, and the constructors in the **Engine**, **Boxcar**, and **Caboose** classes can the add whatever additional objects are necessary to complete the diagram. To give you a sense of how this works, the definitions of the **Boxcar** and **TrainCar** classes appear in Figures 9-21 and 9-22. The corresponding definitions of **Engine** and **Caboose** are left for you to implement in exercise 13.

Once you have defined these classes, you can then create a three-car train centered along the bottom edge of the window using the following **run** method:

```
public void run() {
    double trainWidth = 3 * TrainCar.CAR_WIDTH
                        + 4 * TrainCar.CONNECTOR;
    double x = (getWidth() - trainWidth) / 2;
    double y = getHeight();
    double dx = TrainCar.CAR_WIDTH + TrainCar.CONNECTOR;
    add(new Engine(), x, y);
    add(new Boxcar(Color.GREEN), x + dx, y);
    add(new Caboose(), x + 2 * dx, y);
}
```

FIGURE 9-21   **Code for the Boxcar class**

```
/*
 * File: Boxcar.java
 * ------------------
 * This file defines the boxcar class as a subclass of the more
 * general TrainCar class.
 */

import acm.graphics.*;
import java.awt.*;

/**
 * This class represents a boxcar.  Like all TrainCar subclasses,
 * a Boxcar is a graphical object that you can add to a GCanvas.
 */
public class Boxcar extends TrainCar {

/**
 * Creates a new boxcar with the specified color.
 * @param color The color of the new boxcar
 */
    public Boxcar(Color color) {
        super(color);
        double xRightDoor = CONNECTOR + CAR_WIDTH / 2;
        double xLeftDoor = xRightDoor - DOOR_WIDTH;
        double yDoor = -CAR_BASELINE - DOOR_HEIGHT;
        add(new GRect(xLeftDoor, yDoor, DOOR_WIDTH, DOOR_HEIGHT));
        add(new GRect(xRightDoor, yDoor, DOOR_WIDTH, DOOR_HEIGHT));
    }

/* Dimensions of the door panels on the boxcar */
    private static final double DOOR_WIDTH = 18;
    private static final double DOOR_HEIGHT = 32;

}
```

FIGURE 9-22 Code for the `TrainCar` class

```java
/*
 * File: TrainCar.java
 * ---------------------
 * This file defines the abstract superclass for all train cars.
 */

import acm.graphics.*;
import java.awt.*;

/** This abstract class defines what is common to all train cars */
public abstract class TrainCar extends GCompound {

/**
 * Creates the frame of the car using the specified color.
 * @param color The color of the new boxcar
 */
    public TrainCar(Color color) {
        double xLeft = CONNECTOR;
        double yBase = -CAR_BASELINE;
        add(new GLine(0, yBase, CAR_WIDTH + 2 * CONNECTOR, yBase));
        addWheel(xLeft + WHEEL_INSET, -WHEEL_RADIUS);
        addWheel(xLeft + CAR_WIDTH - WHEEL_INSET, -WHEEL_RADIUS);
        double yTop = yBase - CAR_HEIGHT;
        GRect r = new GRect(xLeft, yTop, CAR_WIDTH, CAR_HEIGHT);
        r.setFilled(true);
        r.setFillColor(color);
        add(r);
    }

/* Adds a wheel centered at (x, y) */
    private void addWheel(double x, double y) {
        GOval wheel = new GOval(x - WHEEL_RADIUS, y - WHEEL_RADIUS,
                                2 * WHEEL_RADIUS, 2 * WHEEL_RADIUS);
        wheel.setFilled(true);
        wheel.setFillColor(Color.GRAY);
        add(wheel);
    }

/* Dimensions of the frame of a train car */
    protected static final double CAR_WIDTH = 75;
    protected static final double CAR_HEIGHT = 36;

/* Distance that the bottom of a train car rides about the track */
    protected static final double CAR_BASELINE = 10;

/* Width of the connector, which overlaps between successive cars */
    protected static final double CONNECTOR = 6;

/* Radius of the wheels on each car */
    protected static final double WHEEL_RADIUS = 8;

/* Distance from the edge of the frame to the center of the wheel */
    protected static final double WHEEL_INSET = 16;

}
```

This method is the same as the one from Chapter 5 except for two things:

1. The named constants **CAR_WIDTH** and **CONNECTOR** are now defined in the **TrainCar** class and must therefore be marked with the name of that class, as in **TrainCar.CAR_WIDTH**.

2. Instead of calling methods to draw the individual cars, the last three statements in the program call the appropriate constructors to create the individual cars and then add each car to the canvas.

This implementation of the **run** method, however, has some very real drawbacks. For one thing, the code has to calculate the coordinates for each of the train cars. The expressions that perform that calculation actually take up more than half the code and make it harder to read. More significantly, those expressions would have to change if you decided to add a new car to the train. It would be far better if those calculations could be integrated into the code for creating the graphical objects. The most effective strategy for doing so is to define a new **Train** class that can contain the individual **TrainCar** objects, as described in the following section.

Nesting **GCompound** objects

One of the most useful features of the **GCompound** class is that it can contain other **GCompound** objects. This fact makes it possible to assemble hierarchical graphical structures. The problem of drawing a train offers a particularly compelling example of how such hierarchies can be useful. In all likelihood, the client of the various train classes is more interested in drawing a complete train than in drawing individual cars. Defining a **Train** class as a **GCompound** that can contain the individual **TrainCar** objects makes it much easier to work with trains as a whole and substantially simplifies the programming process.

The basic idea behind this design is to define a **Train** class whose constructor creates an empty train. Once you have created a **Train** object, you can then adds cars to the end of the train by calling the **append** method. Thus, to create the three-car train consisting of an engine, a green boxcar, and a caboose, you can use the following code:

```
Train train = new Train();
train.append(new Engine());
train.append(new Boxcar(Color.GREEN));
train.append(new Caboose());
```

To center the train at the base of the window, you can take advantage of the fact that the **getWidth** method in the **GObject** class works for **GCompound** objects, just as it does for other graphical objects. You can therefore simply ask the train how long it is and then subtract half its width from the coordinates of the center of the canvas. Thus, the code to center the train on the baseline looks like this:

```
double xc = getWidth() / 2;
add(train, xc - train.getWidth() / 2, getHeight());
```

You can also take advantage of the **getWidth** method in the implementation of the **Train** class itself. When you add the first car to the train, its reference point should be at $(0, 0)$ in the coordinate system of the compound. When you add each subsequent car, you need to make sure that the new car is added at the end of the train. To do so, you can simply take the width of the existing train and subtract the width of the connector, because the connectors overlap on adjacent cars. This insight is all you need to implement the **Train** class, which is shown in Figure 9-23.

The biggest advantage of using the **Train** class is not that it saves calculating the coordinates of the individual cars, but rather that it lets you manipulate the entire train as a unit. This fact makes it easy, for example, to animate the train so that it moves across the screen. As an example, the following **run** method creates a three-car train, centers it in the window, waits for the user to click the mouse, and then moves the train leftward across the canvas until it disappears from the window:

FIGURE 9-23   **Code for the Train class**

```
/*
 * File: Train.java
 * ------------------
 * This file defines the Train class, which can contain any
 * number of train cars linked end to end.
 */

import acm.graphics.*;

/**
 * This class defines a GCompound that represents a train.
 * The primary operation is append, which adds a TrainCar
 * at the end of the train.
 */
public class Train extends GCompound {

/**
 * Creates a new train that contains no cars.  Clients can add
 * cars at the end by calling append.
 */
   public Train() {
       /* No operations necessary */
   }

/**
 * Adds a new car to the end of the train.
 * @param car The new train car
 */
   public void append(TrainCar car) {
       double width = getWidth();
       double x = (width == 0) ? 0 : width - TrainCar.CONNECTOR;
       add(car, x, 0);
   }
}
```

```
public void run() {
    double xc = getWidth() / 2;
    Train train = new Train();
    train.append(new Engine());
    train.append(new Boxcar(Color.GREEN));
    train.append(new Caboose());
    add(train, xc - train.getWidth() / 2, getHeight());
    waitForClick();
    while (train.getX() + train.getWidth() >= 0) {
        train.move(-DELTA_X, 0);
        pause(PAUSE_TIME);
    }
}
```

The constants **PAUSE_TIME** and **DELTA_X** control the speed of the animation, just as they have in earlier examples. If, for example, you wanted the train to move two pixels per time step and to have the **while** loop sleep for 20 milliseconds between cycles, you would use the following definitions for these constants:

```
private static final double PAUSE_TIME = 20;
private static final double DELTA_X = 2;
```

If you go back to the earlier implementations of the **DrawTrain** program, you will quickly discover that it is extremely difficult to animate the train using these earlier designs. By making use of the power provided by the **GCompound** class, however, you can easily manipulate the entire train in a single method call.

Summary

In this chapter, you have had the chance to explore the **acm.graphics** package in more detail and to develop an appreciation of the entire package as an integrated collection of tools. Along the way, you have also had the opportunity to think holistically about the design of the graphics package and the assumptions, conventions, and metaphors on which the package is based.

Important points introduced in this chapter include:

- The set of assumptions, conventions, and metaphors that underlie the design of a package represent its conceptual *model*. Before you can use a package effectively, you must take the time to understand its underlying model.
- An essential part of the model for the **acm.graphics** package is the coordinate system. The **acm.graphics** package follows the conventions of the standard graphics packages in Java by specifying coordinates in *pixels* and placing the *origin* in the upper left corner of a canvas. This coordinate system is different from the Cartesian plane used in high-school geometry classes, which has its origin in the lower left.
- The foundation of the **acm.graphics** package is the **GObject** class, which is the common superclass of all objects that can be displayed on a canvas. The **GObject** class itself is an *abstract class*, which means that there are no objects whose primary class is **GObject**. When you create a graphical image

on a canvas, the classes that you actually use are the subclasses of **GObject** called *shape classes:* **GArc**, **GImage**, **GLabel**, **GLine**, **GOval**, **GPolygon**, **GRect**, **GRoundRect**, and **G3DRect**.

- Each of the shape classes inherits a set of methods from **GObject** that all graphical objects share. In addition, each shape class includes additional methods that define its particular behavior. Several of the shape classes also share common behavior by virtue of implementing one or more of the interfaces **GFillable**, **GResizable**, and **GScalable**.

- To display a graphical object, you need to add it to a **GCanvas**, which serves as the background for a "collage" of **GObject**s. In most cases, that **GCanvas** will be provided automatically as part of a **GraphicsProgram**, although you can also create your own **GCanvas** objects and use them independently of the **acm.program** package.

- You can use the **GCompound** type to assemble individual objects into larger structures that you can then manipulate as a unit.

Review questions

1. Why does the text describe the graphical framework used in the **acm.graphics** package as a "collage" model?

2. What unit of measurement is used to specify coordinates in **acm.graphics**?

3. Where is the origin located in the **acm.graphics** coordinate system?

4. The text of the chapter emphasizes that **GObject** is an *abstract class*. What is the significance of that designation?

5. Without looking back at the figure in this chapter, draw a diagram that shows the class hierarchy formed by the **GObject** class and the shape classes **GArc**, **GImage**, **GLabel**, **GLine**, **GOval**, **GPolygon**, **GRect**, **GRoundRect**, and **G3DRect**.

6. What methods are defined by the **GFillable** interface? Which of the shape classes implement **GFillable**?

7. What is the difference between the **GResizable** and **GScalable** interfaces? Which of the shape classes are scalable but not resizable?

8. In terms of the geometric characteristics of **GLabel**s displayed on a canvas, explain the significance of the values returned by each of the following methods: **getWidth**, **getHeight**, **getAscent**, and **getDescent**.

9. Describe the significance of the **start** and **sweep** parameters in the constructor for the **GArc** class.

10. How does the **acm.graphics** package interpret filling in the case of the **GArc** class?

11. Describe the arcs produced by each of the following calls to the **GArc** constructor:

a) `new GArc(2.0, 2.0, 0, 270);`
b) `new GArc(2.0, 2.0, 135, -90);`
c) `new GArc(2.0, 2.0, 180, -45);`
d) `new GArc(3.0, 1.0, -90, 180);`

12. What does it mean if the **sweep** argument to the **GArc** constructor is negative?

13. For the **GLine** class, how do the methods **setLocation** and **setStartPoint** differ?

14. Write the Java statements necessary to create each of the following polygonal shapes as a single **GPolygon**:

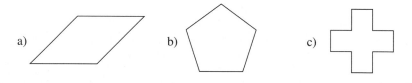

15. How can you obtain the coordinates of the center of the drawing canvas used by a **GraphicsProgram**?

16. In your own words, describe the purpose of the **GCompound** class.

Programming exercises

1. Download or scan one of your favorite pictures or cartoons into an image file and then write a **GraphicsProgram** that displays it on the screen, along with a citation indicating the source.

2. Write a **GraphicsProgram** that draws a filled black square in the center of the canvas. Once you have that part of the program working, animate your program so that the color of the square changes once a second to a new color chosen randomly by calling the **nextColor** method in the **RandomGenerator** class.

3. Write a **GraphicsProgram** that creates **GLabel**s for each of the color names **RED**, **ORANGE**, **YELLOW**, **GREEN**, **CYAN**, **BLUE**, and **MAGENTA**, and then puts those labels up on the screen in a random position. The color of each label, however, should be randomly chosen from the other colors in this list, so that the **GLabel** for **GREEN** is allowed to be any color *except* green. Some people find it hard to identify the color of a label when the text says one thing, but the color says another.

4. Using the **GStar** class from 9-16 as a model, define new classes **GDiamond**, **GTrapezoid**, and **GTShape** that extend **GPolygon** to produce the other polygon examples shown in the margin of page 277. Part of the problem is figuring out what parameters are appropriate for each of the constructors.

5. Write a **GraphicsProgram** that draws a picture of the Halloween pumpkin shown in the following sample run:

The head is an orange circle, and the eyes, nose, and mouth are filled polygons. The stem is a **GRect**. Use named constants in your program to define the sizes of the various features.

6. Besides jack-o'-lanterns, one of the things you can make with pumpkins is pumpkin pie. Write a **GraphicsProgram** program that draws a picture of a pumpkin pie divided into equal wedge-shaped pieces where the number of pieces is indicated by the constant **N_PIECES**. Each wedge should be a separate **GArc**, filled in orange and outlined in black. The following sample run, for example, shows the diagram when **N_PIECES** is 6.

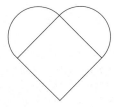

7. One way to draw a heart-shaped figure is by drawing two semicircles on top of a square that is positioned so that its sides run diagonally, as illustrated by the following diagram:

Write a **GraphicsProgram** that uses this construction to draw a heart on the screen using the classes **GArc** and **GLine**. Your program should display the heart without drawing the interior lines that form the top of the square, so that the output looks like this:

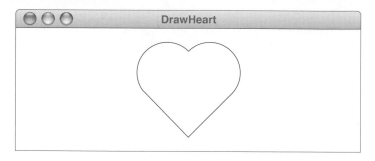

8. Rewrite the **DrawHeart** program from the preceding exercise so that it draws the entire heart as a **GPolygon** that includes both traditional straight-line edges and arc approximations generated by the **addArc** method. The advantage of this style is that the heart is now fillable, which means that you can produce a filled red heart like this:

9. Write a **GraphicsProgram** that draws a simple calendar similar to the one shown in the following diagram:

SUN	MON	TUE	WED	THU	FRI	SAT
					1	2
3	4	5	6	7	8	9
10	11	12	13	14	15	16
17	18	19	20	21	22	23
24	25	26	27	28	29	30
31						

Your program should use the following named constants to control the format of the calendar:

```
/* The number of days in the month */
    private static final int DAYS_IN_MONTH = 31;

/* The day of the week on which the month starts */
/* (Sunday = 0, Monday = 1, Tuesday = 2, and so on) */
    private static final int DAY_MONTH_STARTS = 5;
```

Your program should generate exactly the number of rows necessary to display the days of the month. Here, in a 31-day month that begins on a Friday, the calendar needs six rows; if you were generating a calendar for a non-leap-year February that began on a Sunday, the calendar would require only four rows. The boxes for the days on the calendar display should fill the available space in both dimensions.

10. Chapter 5 introduced the function **combinations(n, k)**, which returns the number of ways in which one can choose **k** items out of a set of **n** distinct objects. One of the classic ways to visualize the **combinations** function is called Pascal's Triangle after the seventeenth-century French mathematician Blaise Pascal, even though it was known by Chinese mathematicians over 2000 years ago. The top row of the triangle contains the entry **combinations(0, 0)**. The next row contains **combinations(1, 0)** and **combinations(1, 1)**. The pattern continues from there, with **n** increasing as you move downward and **k** increasing as you move across the triangle from left to right, as shown in the following diagram:

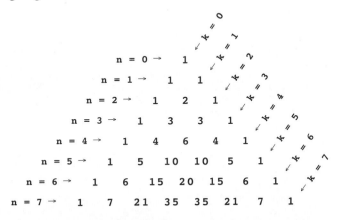

In the triangle, each value along the left or right edge is simply 1, and each value in the interior of the triangle is the sum of the two values diagonally above it to the left and right.

Write a **GraphicsProgram** that displays the first several rows of Pascal's Triangle as shown in the following sample run:

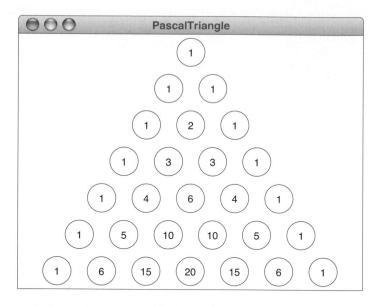

The top circle should be centered horizontally a few pixels below the top of the window. Your program should then generate additional rows of the triangle as long as all the circles in the new row will fit on the canvas. As soon as the circles in a row would extend past the sides or the bottom of the window, your program should stop.

11. Write a **GraphicsProgram** that draws a sampler quilt that looks like this:

This quilt consists of three different block types, as follows:

- *Log cabin block*. The first block in the quilt uses a pattern that is popular in traditional quilting. The log cabin block is composed of a series of frames, each of which is nested inside the next larger one. Each frame is in turn composed of four rectangles—colored green in this example—laid out to form a square.

- *Nested square block*. The second block also follows a traditional pattern in which squares in alternating colors are stacked so that each new square is rotated 45° from the preceding one and then resized so that it fits entirely inside its predecessor. In this diagram, the squares are filled in cyan and magenta.

- *I Love Java block*. While this block is anything but traditional, it gives you a chance to work with more **GObject** classes. Each quilt square in this pattern contains a red heart superimposed on a pink background. Centered on each heart is the message "I Love Java" with one word per line.

One particularly effective way to organize the implementation is to define an abstract class named **QuiltBlock** that extends **GCompound**. Each of the quilt blocks can then be defined as subclasses of **QuiltBlock**, in much the same way that the individual train cars are subclasses of a more general abstract class.

12. The title character in the PacMan series of games is easy to draw in Java using a filled **GArc**. As a first step, write a **GraphicsProgram** that adds a PacMan figure at the extreme left edge of the canvas, as follows:

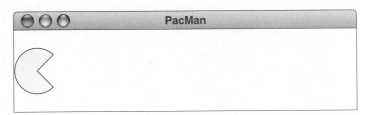

Once you have this part working, add the code to make the PacMan figure move rightward until it disappears off the edge of the canvas. As it moves, change the start and sweep angles so that the mouth appears to open and close as illustrated in the following sequence of images:

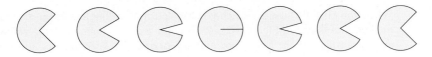

13. Complete the implementation of the object-oriented **DrawTrain** program by writing the definitions of the **Engine** and **Caboose** classes.

14. The slot machine program introduced as exercise 5 in Chapter 6 becomes much more exciting if you change it from a **ConsoleProgram** to a **GraphicsProgram**. Suppose that you have the following image files:

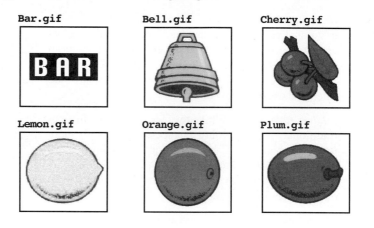

In addition to these six images, it is also useful to have a image file called **Empty.gif** that is simply an empty box of the same size.

   Rewrite the slot machine program so that it uses these images along with a few **GLabel** objects to display the outcome of each spin of the machine. Your program should begin by putting up three boxes containing the **Empty.gif** image to create a display that looks like this:

When you click the mouse (which you can detect by calling the **waitForClick** method introduced in Figure 9-2), you should generate three random symbols and install them in the boxes, updating the **GLabel**s to keep the user informed of the progress of the game. For example, after clicking the mouse, you might see the following configuration:

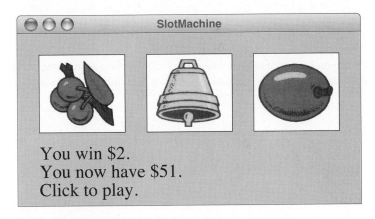

You can add suspense to the game by resetting the boxes to the empty symbol before each spin and then calling **pause** after displaying each new symbol.

15. Define a new **GLens** class to represent a convex lens that looks something like this:

Geometrically, the lens is formed by the interersection of two somewhat larger circles as you can see from this diagram:

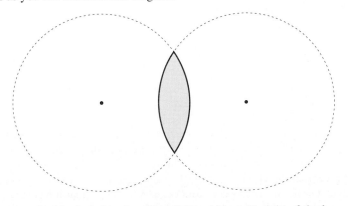

The radius of each circle is a function of the width and height of the lens. You can easily work out the relationship by using the Pythagorean Theorem along with a little algebra; to save you the trouble, the formula for the radius r is

$$r \quad = \quad \frac{h^2 + w^2}{4w}$$

Once you know the radius, you can calculate the location of the center of each circle by using the geometrical relationship shown in the following diagram:

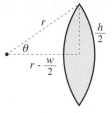

In terms of the implementation, the **GLens** class should extend **GPolygon** and use the **addArc** method to construct the outline. The constructor should take the width and height of the lens as parameters. To compute the angle θ, you can either use trigonometry or call the **GMath.angle** method shown in Figure 9-5. Write a test program that draws several lenses on the display, using different values for the width and height of each lens.

16. You can use the **GLens** class from the preceding exercise to illustrate how lenses form images. Light rays that enter a lens parallel to its horizontal axis are bent so that they pass through a single point called the **focal point** of the lens; the distance from the center of the lens to the focal point is called the **focal length.** Those light rays continue on and form an upside-down image to an observer on the far side of the focal point, as shown in the following sample run:

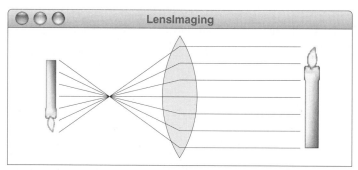

Write a **GraphicsProgram** that produces this illustration. Assume you have two image files—**Candle.gif** and **InvertedCandle.gif**—that contain the candle image on the right side of this diagram and that same image flipped in the vertical direction, but with the same size as the original. Your program should scale the **InvertedCandle.gif** image so that it has the correct size, given the position of the observer. In Chapter 11, you will learn how to invert an image, which will make it possible to use only a single image file for this problem.

CHAPTER 10
Event-driven Programs

I claim not to have controlled events, but confess
plainly that events have controlled me.
— Abraham Lincoln, letter to Albert Hodges, 1864

Alan Kay

Alan Kay was introduced to computer programming while serving in the United States Air Force, where his high score on a programming-aptitude test got him a post programming an early IBM 1401 computer. After finishing his military service, Kay completed his undergraduate degree and then went on to earn a Ph.D. at the University of Utah. His doctoral thesis, "The Reactive Engine," extended Ivan Sutherland's early vision of computer graphics by showing how programming languages—and in particular the object-oriented ideas pioneered in SIMULA—could be used to create flexible graphical systems. In 1971, Kay accepted a research position at the Xerox 's legendary Palo Alto Research Center, which pioneered many of the fundamental ideas that have shaped modern computing. With his colleagues Adele Goldberg and Dan Ingalls, Kay developed Smalltalk, which was the first object-oriented programming language to support interactive graphics. Kay received the ACM Turing Award in 2003.

In Chapter 4, you learned a simple strategy by which you can animate a graphical program so that the display changes with time. If you want to write programs that operate more like the computing applications you use every day, you will also need to learn how to make those programs interactive by having them respond to actions taken by the user.

In some ways, the `ConsoleProgram` examples in the earlier chapters could be classified as interactive, in the sense that most of them require input from the user. That style of interactivity, however, differs from that used in modern applications in at least one important respect. In a `ConsoleProgram`, the user has the opportunity to provide input to the program only at certain well-defined points in its execution history, most commonly when the program calls a method like `readInt` and then waits for a response. This style of interaction is called **synchronous,** because user input is synchronized with the program operation. Modern user interfaces, by contrast, are **asynchronous,** in that they allow the user to intercede at any point, typically by using the mouse or the keyboard to trigger a particular action. Actions that occur asynchronously with respect to the program operation, such as clicking the mouse or typing on the keyboard, are generically referred to as **events.** Interactive programs that operate by responding to these events are said to be **event-driven.** The primary goal of this chapter is to teach you how to write simple event-driven programs.

In addition to being event-driven, most modern applications offer a **graphical user interface**—usually shortened to the acronym **GUI,** which is pronounced like *gooey*—that allows the user to control a program by manipulating interactive components on the screen. Typical interactive components include buttons you can click, fields into which you can enter data, sliders that allow you to adjust some setting, and popup menus that let you choose from a list of options. Collectively, such interactive components are called **interactors,** because they make it possible for the user to interact with a running program in a convenient way. The Java libraries include a variety of interactor classes that support the development of GUI-based applications, and this chapter introduces you to the most important of them.

10.1 The Java event model

As was true for the `acm.graphics` package described in Chapter 9, the first step in learning how event-driven programs work is understanding the underlying conceptual model. In Java, every event is represented by an object that is a subclass of the `EventObject` class in the `java.util` package. The individual subclasses of `EventObject` represent particular types of events. In this chapter, for example, you will learn about the following event classes:

- `MouseEvent`, which is used to represent an action taken with the mouse, such as moving or dragging it from one position to another or clicking the mouse button.
- `KeyEvent`, which is used to represent pressing a key on the keyboard.
- `ActionEvent`, which is used to represent a user-interface action taken by the user, such as clicking a button on the screen.

Because these event objects contain different information, most of the methods that apply to the individual subclasses are particular to that class. If you have a **MouseEvent**, for example, you need to know the coordinates of the mouse on the screen and some indication as to the type of mouse action (clicking, moving, dragging, and so forth). If you have a **KeyEvent**, you need to know what key was pressed. For an **ActionEvent**, you need to be able to determine which interactor generated the event so that you can figure out how to respond. The methods that provide this information are described in later sections that cover the individual classes in detail.

In the Java event model, event objects do not themselves perform any actions. What happens instead is that events are delivered to some other object that is charged with responding to that particular type of event. Such an object is called a **listener.** As you might expect, there are different kinds of listeners that correspond to the different types of events. Thus, you will need a mouse listener to respond to mouse events, a key listener to respond to keyboard events, and an action listener to respond to user-interface actions such as pressing a button.

Unlike events, the various listener types are not implemented as classes in Java. Instead, each listener type is defined as an interface. As you know from the discussion of the **GFillable**, **GResizable**, and **GScalable** interfaces in Chapter 9, an interface is a collection of methods that define a particular behavior. Any class that supplies definitions for those methods can declare that it implements that interface by including the name of the interface in an **implements** clause as part of the class header. For example, if you wanted to write a **GraphicsProgram** that could respond to mouse events, you could use the header line

```
public class MyProgram extends GraphicsProgram
    implements MouseListener
```

and then implement each of the methods required by the **MouseListener** interface.

As it happens, that definition is unnecessary when you use the **acm.program** package. The **Program** class declares itself to be a listener for mouse, key, and action events and provides default definitions for each of the required methods in the corresponding interface. The default version of each method does nothing, but you can override the default implementation in your program so that the method performs some meaningful action. This design decision simplifies considerably the task of responding to events because you never have to implement any listener methods beyond the ones you actually need. You will, however, need to import the definitions of the event classes, which are defined in the **java.awt.event** package. Thus, most interactive programs will include the import line

```
import java.awt.event.*;
```

10.2 A simple event-driven program

Before getting into the details of the various event classes and listener interfaces, it is useful to introduce a simple event-driven example that will illustrate the underlying event model. The **DrawStarMap** program in Figure 10-1 uses mouse

> FIGURE 10-1   **Program to illustrate simple mouse events**
>
> ```
> import acm.graphics.*;
> import acm.program.*;
> import java.awt.*;
> import java.awt.event.*;
>
> /**
>  * This program creates a five-pointed star every time the
>  * user clicks the mouse on the canvas.
>  */
> public class DrawStarMap extends GraphicsProgram {
>
> /* Initializes the mouse listeners */
>     public void init() {
>         addMouseListeners();
>     }
>
> /* Called whenever the user clicks the mouse */
>     public void mouseClicked(MouseEvent e) {
>         GStar star = new GStar(STAR_SIZE);
>         star.setFilled(true);
>         add(star, e.getX(), e.getY());
>     }
>
> /* Private constants */
>     private static final double STAR_SIZE = 20;
>
> }
> ```

events to draw a five-pointed star at the current mouse position whenever the user clicks the mouse on the canvas. For example, if you were to click the mouse near the upper left corner of the canvas, the program will draw a star in that position centered at the current mouse position, as shown in the following diagram:

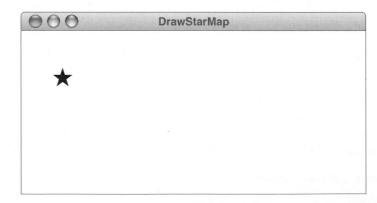

If you then go on to click the mouse in other positions, stars will appear there as well. You could, for example, draw a picture of the constellation Ursa Major or the

Great Bear, which is more commonly known as the Big Dipper. All you have to do is click the mouse once for each of the seven stars, as follows:

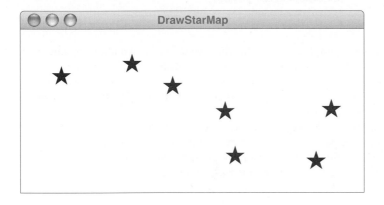

The code in Figure 10-1 is quite short, with just two methods and a couple of constant definitions. Even so, the program is different enough from the ones that you've seen so far that it makes sense to go through it in detail.

The most obvious difference between the **DrawStarMap** program and the other programs you've seen is that **DrawStarMap** has no **run** method. In its place, there is a method called **init**. The **init** method is used to specify initialization code that needs to be executed before the program starts. The **run** method, if it exists, specifies what the program does when it runs. An event-driven program often doesn't do anything particularly active when you start it up. The typical pattern for an event-driven program is to set up some initial configuration of the canvas and then wait for events to occur. That type of operation is precisely the one for which the **init** method was designed.

The **init** method in the **DrawStarMap** program looks like this:

```
public void init() {
    addMouseListeners();
}
```

The call to **addMouseListeners** registers the program as a listener for all mouse events that occur within the canvas. Given that the **Program** class already defines the necessary methods and declares itself to be a **MouseListener**, any subclass of **Program** is entitled to act as a mouse listener. All it needs to do is redefine any methods that are important for this particular application. In this case, the program is supposed to add a star to the canvas whenever the user clicks the mouse. To do so, all the **DrawStarMap** program has to do is write a definition for the **mouseClicked** method, which is called whenever a mouse click occurs anywhere inside the program window.

For the **DrawStarMap** program, the **mouseClicked** method—which must be public because listener methods are invoked from the Java runtime system—has the following implementation:

```
public void mouseClicked(MouseEvent e) {
   GStar star = new GStar(STAR_SIZE);
   star.setFilled(true);
   add(star, e.getX(), e.getY());
}
```

For the most part, the code is straightforward and uses nothing beyond the graphics methods you have already seen. The first statement creates a **GStar** object, relying on the definition of the **GStar** class presented in Figure 9-16. The next statement makes sure that the star is filled rather than outlined. The final statement then adds the star to the canvas.

The only new feature in this implementation of **mouseClicked** is the **MouseEvent** parameter, which provides information about where the click occurred. That information is stored inside the **MouseEvent** object **e**, and you can retrieve it by calling **e.getX()** and **e.getY()**. In this example, the goal is to have the star appear precisely where the mouse is pointing, so these values are precisely what you need to set the location of the star.

10.3 Responding to mouse events

The **mouseClicked** method in the **DrawStarMap** program is only one of several listener methods you can use to respond to mouse events. The complete set of listener methods called in response to mouse events appears in Figure 10-2. Each method allows you to respond to a specific type of action with the mouse, most of which will probably seem familiar from using your computer. Dragging the mouse, for example, consists of moving the mouse while holding the button down. Applications tend to use dragging when they want to move an object from one place

---

FIGURE 10-2   **Standard listener methods for responding to mouse events**

MouseListener interface

> **void mousePressed(MouseEvent e)**
> Called whenever the mouse button is pressed.

> **void mouseReleased(MouseEvent e)**
> Called whenever the mouse button is released.

> **void mouseClicked(MouseEvent e)**
> Called when the mouse button is "clicked" (pressed and released within a short span of time).

> **void mouseEntered(MouseEvent e)**
> Called whenever the mouse enters the canvas.

> **void mouseExited(MouseEvent e)**
> Called whenever the mouse exits the canvas.

MouseMotionListener interface

> **void mouseMoved(MouseEvent e)**
> Called whenever the mouse is moved with the button up.

> **void mouseDragged(MouseEvent e)**
> Called whenever the mouse is moved with the button down.

to another. Typically, you press the mouse button over the object you want to move and then drag it to its new position.

The **MouseListener** and **MouseMotionListener** interfaces

As you may have observed from the captions in Figure 10-2, Java defines two different listener interfaces for responding to mouse events. The first is **MouseListener**, which makes it possible to listen for a set of user actions that for the most part involve the mouse button; the second is **MouseMotionListener**, which is used to track the mouse as it moves. The reason for separating these two types of listeners is that mouse motions generate many more events than button-oriented actions do. If your application is driven only by mouse clicks and never has to track the mouse itself, that application will run more efficiently if it does not have to respond to frequent motion events in which it has no interest. Calling **addMouseListeners** in a program enables both types of listeners, and you don't need to pay any attention to the fact that the listener methods come from two distinct interfaces. In the context of the **Program** class, everything looks the same.

Overriding listener methods

As noted in the preceding section, the **Program** class declares itself to be both a **MouseListener** and a **MouseMotionListener** by defining implementations for each of the listener methods in Figure 10-2. The implementations provided by the **Program** class, however, do nothing at all. For example, the standard definition of **mouseClicked** is simply

```
public void mouseClicked(MouseEvent e) {
    /* Empty */
}
```

Thus, unless you take some action to the contrary, a program will simply ignore mouse clicks, along with all the other mouse events. If, however, you want to change the behavior for a particular event, all you need to do is add a new definition for that method. This new definition supersedes the original definition and will be called instead of the empty one. Any methods that you don't override continue to do what they did by default, which was nothing. Thus, you need to override only those methods that your program actually uses.

Each of the methods listed in Figure 10-2 takes as its argument an object of type **MouseEvent**, which is a class defined as part of Java's standard window system toolkit. Like the listener interfaces themselves, the **MouseEvent** class lives in the package **java.awt.event**.

Although Java's **MouseEvent** class includes several methods that help in designing sophisticated user interfaces, this text uses only two of those methods. Given a **MouseEvent** stored in a variable named **e**, you can determine the location of the mouse—the point at the tip of the mouse cursor—by calling **e.getX()** and **e.getY()**. Being able to detect the location at which a mouse event occurred is all you need to write many mouse-driven applications, as illustrated by the examples in the two subsections that follow.

A line-drawing program

The first example of mouse interaction is a simple line-drawing program that operates—at least for straight lines—in the way commercial figure-drawing applications do. To create a line on the canvas, you press the mouse at its starting point. From there, you hold the mouse button down and drag the mouse to the other endpoint. As you do so, the line keeps itself updated on the canvas so that it connects the starting point with the current position of the mouse.

As an example, suppose that you press the mouse button somewhere on the screen and then drag the mouse rightward an inch, holding the button down. What you'd like to see is the following picture:

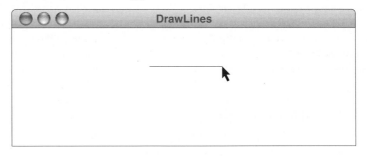

If you then move the mouse downward without releasing the button, the displayed line will track the mouse, so that you might see the following picture:

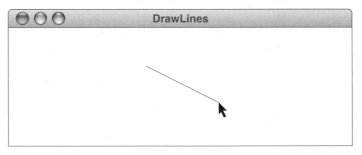

When you release the mouse, the line stays where it is. If you then press the mouse button again on that same point, you can go ahead and draw an additional line segment by dragging the mouse to the endpoint of the new line, as follows:

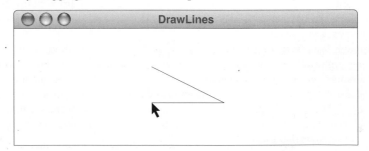

Alternatively, you could move the mouse to an entirely new location and draw a disconnected line in some other part of the canvas.

While you are dragging the line with the mouse, the line that joins the initial point and the current mouse position will stretch, contract, and change direction as the mouse moves. Because the effect is what you would expect if you joined the initial point and the mouse cursor with a stretchy elastic line, this technique is called **rubber-banding.**

The code for a line-drawing program that uses rubber-banding appears in Figure 10-3. Despite the fact that the program seems to perform a reasonably interesting task, the code is surprisingly short—the bodies of the three methods in the program contain a grand total of four lines, but it is nonetheless worth going through each of the methods in turn.

As in the case of the **DrawStarMap** program from Figure 10-1, the **DrawLines** program includes an **init** method instead of a **run** method. Once again, the only initialization necessary is to enable the program as a listener for mouse events, which is accomplished through the call to **addMouseListeners**.

The **mousePressed** method is called whenever the user presses the mouse button. In the line-drawing program, the body of the **mousePressed** method creates a new **GLine** object that starts and ends at the current mouse position. This **GLine** appears on the canvas as a dot. The **GLine** is stored in the private instance variable

---

FIGURE 10-3   **Program to create lines using the mouse**

```java
import acm.graphics.*;
import acm.program.*;
import java.awt.event.*;

/* This class allows users to draw lines on the canvas */
public class DrawLines extends GraphicsProgram {

/* Initializes the program by enabling the mouse listeners */
    public void init() {
        addMouseListeners();
    }

/* Called on mouse press to create a new line */
    public void mousePressed(MouseEvent e) {
        line = new GLine(e.getX(), e.getY(), e.getX(), e.getY());
        add(line);
    }

/* Called on mouse drag to reset the endpoint */
    public void mouseDragged(MouseEvent e) {
        line.setEndPoint(e.getX(), e.getY());
    }

/* Private instance variables */
    private GLine line;
}
```

line, which means that other methods in the class have access to it. In particular, dragging the mouse with the button down calls the **mouseDragged** method, which resets the endpoint of the line to the current mouse position.

Dragging objects on the canvas

The **DragObjects** program in Figure 10-4 offers a slightly more sophisticated example of an event-driven program that uses the mouse to reposition objects on the display. This example begins by creating two graphical objects—a red rectangle and a green oval similar to those in the examples from Chapter 2—and then adds those objects to the canvas. It then calls **addMouseListeners** to register the program as a listener for mouse events.

The first listener method defined in Figure 10-4 is **mousePressed**, which is called when the mouse button goes down, as you know from the preceding example. In this application, the **mousePressed** method looks like this:

```
public void mousePressed(MouseEvent e) {
    lastX = e.getX();
    lastY = e.getY();
    gobj = getElementAt(lastX, lastY);
}
```

The first two statements simply record the *x* and *y* coordinates of the mouse in the variables **lastX** and **lastY**. As you can see from the program, these variables are declared as instance variables for the object and not as local variables of the sort that you have seen in most methods. It turns out that you will need these values later when you try to drag the object. Because local variables disappear when a method returns, you have to store these values in instance variables associated with the object as a whole.

The last statement in **mousePressed** checks to see what object on the canvas contains the current mouse position. Here, it is important to recognize that there are two possibilities. First, you could be pressing the mouse button on top of an object, which means that you want to start dragging it. Second, you could be pressing the mouse button somewhere else on the canvas at which there is no object to drag. The **getElementAt** method looks at the specified position and returns the object it finds there. If there is more than one object covering that space, it chooses the one that is in front of the others in the stacking order. If there are no objects at that location, **getElementAt** returns the special value **null**, which signifies an object that does not exist. The other methods will check for this value to determine whether there is an object to drag.

The **mouseDragged** method consists of the following code:

```
public void mouseDragged(MouseEvent e) {
    if (gobj != null) {
        gobj.move(e.getX() - lastX, e.getY() - lastY);
        lastX = e.getX();
        lastY = e.getY();
    }
}
```

| FIGURE 10-4 | Program to drag objects on the canvas |

```java
import acm.graphics.*;
import acm.program.*;
import java.awt.*;
import java.awt.event.*;

/** This class displays a mouse-draggable rectangle and oval */
public class DragObjects extends GraphicsProgram {

/* Initializes the program */
   public void init() {
      GRect rect = new GRect(100, 100, 150, 100);
      rect.setFilled(true);
      rect.setColor(Color.RED);
      add(rect);
      GOval oval = new GOval(300, 115, 100, 70);
      oval.setFilled(true);
      oval.setColor(Color.GREEN);
      add(oval);
      addMouseListeners();
   }

/* Called on mouse press to record the coordinates of the click */
   public void mousePressed(MouseEvent e) {
      last = new GPoint(e.getPoint());
      gobj = getElementAt(last);
   }

/* Called on mouse drag to reposition the object */
   public void mouseDragged(MouseEvent e) {
      if (gobj != null) {
         gobj.move(e.getX() - last.getX(), e.getY() - last.getY());
         last = new GPoint(e.getPoint());
      }
   }

/* Called on mouse click to move this object to the front */
   public void mouseClicked(MouseEvent e) {
      if (gobj != null) gobj.sendToFront();
   }

/* Private instance variables */
   private GObject gobj;          /* The object being dragged */
   private GPoint last;           /* The last mouse position  */

}
```

The **if** statement simply checks to see whether there is an object to drag. If the value of **gobj** is **null**, there is nothing to drag, and the rest of the method is simply skipped. If there is an object, you need to move it by some distance in each direction. That distance does not depend on where the mouse is in an absolute sense but rather on how far it has moved from where you last took stock of its position. Thus, the arguments to the **move** method are—for both the *x* and *y* components—the location where the mouse is now minus where it used to be. Once you have moved it, you then have to record the mouse coordinates again so that you can update the location correctly on the next call to **mouseDragged**.

The final listener method specified in Figure 10-4 is **mouseClicked**, which looks like this:

```
public void mouseClicked(MouseEvent e) {
    if (gobj != null) gobj.sendToFront();
}
```

The intent of this method is to allow the user to move an object to the front by clicking on it, thereby bringing it out from under the other objects on the canvas. The body of the method is almost readable as the English sentence

If there is a current object, send it to the front of the canvas display.

The only question you might have is how the instance variable **gobj**, which holds the current object, gets initialized in this case. If the **mouseClicked** event were generated by itself, clicking on a graphical object would never set this variable. The answer depends on the fact that the Java runtime system generates a **mousePressed** and a **mouseReleased** event in conjunction with every **mouseClicked** event. The **gobj** variable is therefore set by **mousePressed**, just as if you were going to drag it. Both the **mousePressed** and **mouseReleased** events precede the **mouseClicked** event, because the system doesn't know that a click has occurred until the mouse button comes up.

10.4 Responding to keyboard events

The interactive examples so far have all used the mouse as the source for events. Pressing a key on the keyboard also generates an event, which can be used in a similar way. Pressing the key generates a **KeyEvent**, which is then delivered to any object that has registered itself as a **KeyListener**. The easiest way to field key events in a program is to register the program itself as a key listener by calling **addKeyListeners**, which works in much the same way as the **addMouseListeners** call in the earlier examples. Once you have called **addKeyListeners**, any events generated by typing on the keyboard are sent to the program, where they trigger calls to the methods shown in Figure 10-5.

The methods shown in Figure 10-5 support two different disciplines for working with the keyboard. The **keyPressed** and **keyReleased** methods provide a lower level of control and invoke the listener both when a key goes down and when it comes back up. These methods are therefore appropriate for applications in which

| FIGURE 10-5 | Standard listener methods for responding to keyboard events |

`void keyPressed(KeyEvent e)`   Called whenever a key is pressed.
`void keyReleased(KeyEvent e)`   Called whenever a key is released.
`void keyTyped(KeyEvent e)`   Called when a key is "typed" (pressed and released).

it matters how long you hold a key down. The `keyTyped` method provides a slightly higher level of control and makes sense for applications in which you use the keyboard to enter text.

The methods that you call to extract information from a `KeyEvent` depend on which of these styles you are using. In the `keyPressed` and `keyReleased` methods, you can find out which key was pressed by calling the `getKeyCode` method on the `KeyEvent`. The return value, however, is not a character but an integer code representing what the designers of Java's event model called a **virtual key.** The constant names defined by `KeyEvent` for the most common virtual key codes appear in Figure 10-6.

When you use the `keyTyped` method, you can determine the actual character entered on the keyboard by calling the `getKeyChar` method on the `KeyEvent`. In this case, the `getKeyChar` method automatically takes account of modifier keys like SHIFT, so that holding down the SHIFT key and typing the A key delivers the expected uppercase character `'A'`. The `getKeyChar` method is not available if you are using the `keyPressed` and `keyReleased` methods. If you need to take account of modifier keys, you need to call other methods in the `KeyEvent` class that are beyond the scope of this text.

So that you have a chance to see at least one illustration of key listeners, it is useful to extend the `DragObjects` program from Figure 10-4 so that you can move the currently selected object either by dragging it with the mouse or by using the

| FIGURE 10-6 | Virtual key constants defined in the `KeyEvent` class |

`VK_A` *through* `VK_Z`	`VK_F1` *through* `VK_F12`	`VK_UP`
`VK_0` *through* `VK_9`	`VK_NUMPAD0` *through* `VK_NUMPAD9`	`VK_DOWN`
`VK_COMMA`	`VK_BACK_SPACE`	`VK_LEFT`
`VK_PERIOD`	`VK_DELETE`	`VK_RIGHT`
`VK_SLASH`	`VK_ENTER`	`VK_PAGE_UP`
`VK_SEMICOLON`	`VK_TAB`	`VK_PAGE_DOWN`
`VK_EQUALS`	`VK_SHIFT`	`VK_HOME`
`VK_OPEN_BRACKET`	`VK_CONTROL`	`VK_END`
`VK_BACK_SLASH`	`VK_ALT`	`VK_ESCAPE`
`VK_CLOSE_BRACKET`	`VK_META`	`VK_PRINTSCREEN`
`VK_BACK_QUOTE`	`VK_NUM_LOCK`	`VK_INSERT`
`VK_QUOTE`	`VK_SCROLL_LOCK`	`VK_HELP`
`VK_SPACE`	`VK_CAPS_LOCK`	`VK_CLEAR`

arrow keys, which are often more appropriate for fine adjustments. The only changes you need to make in the program are to add the line

```
addKeyListeners();
```

to the end of the **init** method and then to include the following definition of the **keyPressed** method:

```
public void keyPressed(KeyEvent e) {
    if (gobj != null) {
        switch (e.getKeyCode()) {
            case KeyEvent.VK_UP:    gobj.move(0, -1); break;
            case KeyEvent.VK_DOWN:  gobj.move(0, +1); break;
            case KeyEvent.VK_LEFT:  gobj.move(-1, 0); break;
            case KeyEvent.VK_RIGHT: gobj.move(+1, 0); break;
        }
    }
}
```

This method reads the key code from the event and then uses a **switch** statement to choose the appropriate action. If the code matches the virtual key value for one of the arrow keys, the method calls **move** to shift the current object one pixel in the corresponding direction. All other key codes are ignored.

10.5 Creating a simple GUI

Arthur listened for a short while, but being unable to understand the vast majority of what Ford was saying he began to let his mind wander, trailing his fingers along the edge of an incomprehensible computer bank, he reached out and pressed an invitingly large red button on a nearby panel. The panel lit up with the words "Please do not press this button again."

—Douglas Adams, *Hitchhiker's Guide to the Galaxy,* 1979

Now that you know how to use events and listeners to respond to mouse and keyboard events, it is time to turn to the question of how to design a graphical user interface using the standard GUI interactors that Java provides. Before doing so, however, it makes sense to consider a simple example that illustrates the basic idea.

Let's imagine that you want to write a program to simulate the vignette from *Hitchhiker's Guide to the Galaxy* at the beginning of this section. You need to put a button on the screen, which for the purposes of the illustration can be labeled with its color, like this:

Before you can use such a button, however, you need to answer several questions:

1. How can you construct the object that represents the button?
2. How can you place the button on the screen?
3. How can you set things up so that the program responds appropriately when the button is clicked?

The first question is the easiest. The standard Java class that represents buttons on the screen is called **JButton**. This class—along with most of the other interactors defined in this chapter—is part of a general interactor library called Swing that is discussed in detail in the next section. In its most common form, the constructor for the **JButton** class takes the label on the button as a string. Thus, you can create the button and assign it to a local variable like this:

```
JButton redButton = new JButton("Red");
```

The question about how to place the button on the screen is more complicated. Later in this chapter, you will learn how to use layout managers to arrange interactors in a way that makes sense in terms of your GUI design. For the moment, the best approach is to use the facilities provided by the **Program** class, which makes it easy to add interactors to the borders of a program window.

Suppose, for example, that you want to add this button at the bottom of the window, which Java describes as the **SOUTH** border. All you need to do is add the button to that border by executing the following statement:

```
add(redButton, SOUTH);
```

The names of the four compass directions (**NORTH**, **SOUTH**, **EAST**, and **WEST**) are defined as constants in the **Program** class.

If you never add anything to a border region, that border won't appear on the screen at all. If, however, you add an interactor to a border region, the **Program** class will display that interactor in the center of the appropriate border. Thus, if you create a **ConsoleProgram** and add **redButton** to the **SOUTH** border, the window will look like this:

If you add more than one interactor to the same border, the **Program** class arranges those interactors so that they form a line along the appropriate axis, which is horizontal for the **NORTH** and **SOUTH** borders and vertical for the **EAST** and **WEST** borders. These interactors are then centered in the appropriate region.

In this chapter, most of the programs install their interactors along the **SOUTH** border, just as in the **HitchhikerButton** example. The collection of interactors along the bottom serves as the graphical user interface for this style of program. In these examples, the border region at the bottom that contains these interactors is called the **control bar.**

The last question you need to consider is how to respond when the user clicks the button. As with other events in the Java framework, the appropriate strategy is to declare a listener that listens to the button. In this case, you need to implement the **actionPerformed** method, which has the following header line:

```
public void actionPerformed(ActionEvent e)
```

Writing the code that responds to the action event consists of two parts. First, you have to register the program as a listener for action events. You can do so by including the following call in the **init** method, which adds the program as an action listener to every button currently installed in the program window:

```
addActionListeners();
```

You must then implement **actionPerformed** so that it performs the desired action. Although there is only one button in this example, there will typically be more than one on the screen. The code for **actionPerformed** must therefore figure out which button triggered the event. The easiest strategy is to call **getActionCommand** on the event, which returns the name of the button. You can then use the **equals** method to check for each button name.

Figure 10-7 shows a complete implementation of the program. If you run the program and click the button, you will see the following message on the screen:

FIGURE 10-7   The **HitchhikerButton** example

```
import acm.program.*;
import java.awt.event.*;
import javax.swing.*;

/*
 * This program puts up a button on the screen, which triggers a
 * message inspired by Douglas Adams's novel.
 */
public class HitchhikerButton extends ConsoleProgram {

/* Initializes the user-interface buttons */
   public void init() {
      add(new JButton("Red"), SOUTH);
      addActionListeners();
   }

/* Responds to a button action */
   public void actionPerformed(ActionEvent e) {
      if (e.getActionCommand().equals("Red")) {
         println("Please do not press this button again.");
      }
   }
}
```

Were you to ignore the injunction and press the button again, the `actionPerformed` method would be executed a second time, thereby repeating the message on the screen, as follows:

10.6 The Swing interactor hierarchy

Most of the interactors that Java programmers use to build graphical user interfaces are part of a library called **Swing** that was added to Java in 1997. The principal classes in the Swing package are all part of a large package called `javax.swing`, which means that programs that use these classes need to include the line

```
import javax.swing.*;
```

In an introductory text, it doesn't make sense to try to cover all of Swing. This book focuses instead on the interactor classes shown in Figure 10-8, which also shows the hierarchical relationships among the different classes. The individual interactor classes are described in the sections that follow. If you want more information about Swing classes that are not included here, you can refer to their **javadoc** pages.

The `JButton` class

The `JButton` class is used to create buttons that trigger some action when you click them with the mouse. You have already seen an example of a `JButton` in the `HitchhikerButton` program, which used a `JButton` to print a warning message on the screen whenever the button was clicked. That example illustrated the standard pattern for using buttons, which consists of the following steps:

1. Create each new button by calling the `JButton` constructor with the string you want to appear in the button.
2. Add each `JButton` to the user interface, which for now means adding each button to a control bar along the border.
3. Assign the program as an `ActionListener` for each `JButton`. You can make this assignment for each button by calling its `addActionListener` method, but it is usually simpler to perform this step for all the buttons in the program by calling `addActionListeners` at the end of the `init` method.
4. Implement an `actionPerformed` method that checks for the name of each button by comparing each button name with the string returned by calling `getActionCommand` on the `ActionEvent`.

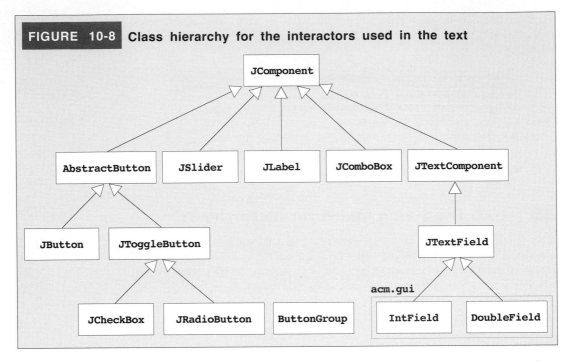

FIGURE 10-8 Class hierarchy for the interactors used in the text

So that you have a chance to see a second example of this pattern, the next few paragraphs show how you can add a button to the **DrawStarMap** program from Figure 10-1 that clears the screen by deleting all the stars from the display. The first three steps in the programming pattern for working with buttons can be accomplished by adding the following lines to the **init** method:

```
add(new JButton("Clear"), SOUTH);
addActionListeners();
```

The first line creates a button labeled **Clear** and adds it to the control bar at the bottom of the program window, creating a user interface that looks like this:

The second line then makes sure that the program becomes an action listener for every button in the window, even though there is only one in this example.

The final step is to specify the response to the button by implementing the **addActionListeners** method. Here, once you discover that the name of the button is **"Clear"**, all you need to do is call the **removeAll** method, which removes all graphical objects from the canvas. The implementation of **addActionListeners** therefore looks like this:

```
public void actionPerformed(ActionEvent e) {
    if (e.getActionCommand().equals("Clear")) removeAll();
}
```

In some applications, it is useful to change the label on a **JButton** as the program runs. To do so, you can call the **setText** method with the new button name. Conversely, calling **getText** on a **JButton** returns its current label.

Although the **JButton** examples in this text are usually labeled with a string, the Swing implementation of **JButton**—and in fact all of the classes in the hierarchy that extend **AbstractButton**—also supports the use of buttons containing a visual icon. To create such a button, you need to replace the button name in the **JButton** constructor with an **ImageIcon** object. For example, if you have an image file called **RedSquare.gif** that contains a small red square, you can modify the **HitchhikerButton** program by replacing the first line with the following code:

```
ImageIcon icon = new ImageIcon("RedSquare.gif");
JButton button = new JButton(icon);
button.setActionCommand("Red");
add(button, SOUTH);
```

If you run this version of the program and click the button, you will see a program window that looks like this:

Note that the iconic version of the button doesn't have a label, so you need to call **setActionCommand** to set the action command explicitly.

The **JToggleButton** class

The **JButton** class creates buttons that are executed for their effect. Each time you click a **JButton**, it generates an action event and delivers it to any listeners that are waiting for that event. Although the appearance of the **JButton** changes while the mouse button is down, it returns to its previous state as soon as you release the mouse button. By contrast, clicking a **JToggleButton** changes its state. The first click selects the button and highlights it on the screen; clicking it again turns off the selection. The button therefore toggles back and forth between the selected and unselected state each time it is clicked. You can then call **isSelected** to determine whether a **JToggleButton** is selected. The **isSelected** method returns a Boolean value that you can use to control the operation of your program.

In all likelihood, however, you will not have much use for the **JToggleButton** class on its own. Most applications that need the sort of on/off switch that toggle buttons provide will instead use one of its principal subclasses—**JCheckBox** and **JRadioButton**—which are described in the two sections that follow.

The **JCheckBox** class

The most common form of toggle button is the **JCheckBox** class. Because it extends **JToggleButton**, the **JCheckBox** class inherits the behavior of its superclass. Thus, clicking a **JCheckBox** once turns it on, and clicking it again turns it off. The only difference between **JCheckBox** and its superclass is the way these objects are displayed. A **JToggleButton** looks just like a **JButton** except for the fact that the button is highlighted whenever it is selected. A **JCheckBox** appears as a small squarish box that contains a check mark whenever it is selected. The label for a **JCheckBox** appears to the right of the box.

You can use the **JCheckBox** class to add another feature to the **DrawStarMap** program. As the program now stands, all stars are filled when they appear on the screen. If you wanted to call attention to particular stars, you might want some of them to be filled while others are left as outlines. Because the decision of whether to fill a star has only two possible answers—yes and no—a **JCheckBox** is an appropriate way to represent this option in the user interface.

To implement this extension, you need to declare a **JCheckBox** variable and use it to hold the state of whether stars should be filled. In the program, you need to initialize the **JCheckBox** variable in the **init** method, but you need to refer to that variable in the **mouseClicked** method when you create a new star. Given that the variable is initialized in one method and used in another, you must declare it as an instance variable rather than as a local variable. The declaration therefore appears outside of any method and looks like this:

```
private JCheckBox fillCheckBox;
```

The **init** method must then create the actual check box, assign it to the instance variable, and add it to the collection of interactors in the control bar. If you also want to ensure that the check box starts out in the "on" position, you can add the following lines to the **init** method:

```
fillCheckBox = new JCheckBox("Filled");
fillCheckBox.setSelected(true);
add(fillCheckBox, SOUTH);
```

These statements create a control bar that looks like this:

The one remaining change that you need to make is to modify the definition of the **mouseClicked** method so that it sets the star to be filled only if **fillCheckBox** is selected. You can accomplish that goal by rewriting the call to **setFilled** as follows:

```
star.setFilled(fillCheckBox.isSelected());
```

Making this change allows you to create a display in which some stars are outlined and others are filled. For example, if you wanted to draw a diagram of the constellation Lyra (the lyre) that emphasized Vega—Lyra's most prominent star and one of the brightest stars in the night sky—you could click on the map to create Vega and then turn off the check box before creating the other stars, producing an image that looks like this:

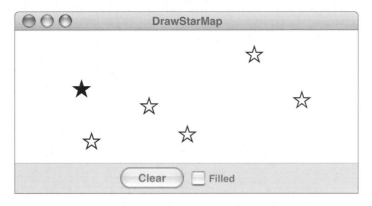

The **JRadioButton** and **ButtonGroup** classes

Unfortunately, having filled and unfilled stars does not give you the flexibility you need to create a useful star chart. What you really want is to be able to display stars of different sizes. One possibility is to make the brightest stars big and the faintest stars small, leaving a medium-sized option for stars that fall in the intermediate range. Given that there are now three possible sizes, a check box no longer works. You need instead to be able to select from a set of three options.

One strategy for choosing among a small set of options is to use an interactor called a **radio button,** which is named for the controls on car radios that allow you to select a preset station by pressing one of five buttons. The defining feature of a radio button is that the choices are *exclusive,* in the sense that only one button can be selected at a time. Pressing one button automatically clears any previous selection.

Radio buttons are implemented in Swing using two classes: **JRadioButton** and **ButtonGroup**. The interactor itself is a **JRadioButton**, which looks almost the same as a **JCheckBox**. The only differences are that a **JRadioButton** is drawn with a circle instead of a box and is marked as selected using a dot instead of a check mark. The **ButtonGroup** class is used to designate a set of radio buttons in which only one button may be selected at a time.

You can use the following steps to create a set of radio buttons:

1. Create a **JRadioButton** for each option and store it in an instance variable.
2. Create a new **ButtonGroup**, which is initially empty.
3. Add the buttons to the group using the **add** method in the **ButtonGroup** class.
4. Call **setSelected** on the button you want to be enabled initially.
5. Add each of the radio buttons to the user interface.

Applying this strategy to the **DrawStarMap** program gives rise to the following code:

```
smallButton = new JRadioButton("Small");
mediumButton = new JRadioButton("Medium");
largeButton = new JRadioButton("Large");
ButtonGroup sizeGroup = new ButtonGroup();
sizeGroup.add(smallButton);
sizeGroup.add(mediumButton);
sizeGroup.add(largeButton);
mediumButton.setSelected(true);
add(smallButton, SOUTH);
add(mediumButton, SOUTH);
add(largeButton, SOUTH);
```

If you add these statements to the **init** method in place of the **fillCheckBox** code, you create a control bar that looks like this:

The only other change you need to make in the program is to change the first line of the **mouseClicked** method so that it uses the currently selected size in place of the constant **STAR_SIZE**. If you take the opportunity to decompose the program by writing a private helper method, you can replace the first line with

```
GStar star = new GStar(getCurrentSize());
```

and then implement **getCurrentSize** as follows, assuming that the names **SMALL_SIZE**, **MEDIUM_SIZE**, and **LARGE_SIZE** have been defined with suitable values:

```
private double getCurrentSize() {
    if (smallButton.isSelected()) return SMALL_SIZE;
    if (largeButton.isSelected()) return LARGE_SIZE;
    return MEDIUM_SIZE;
}
```

Making this change would enable you to draw the following picture of the constellation Gemini (the twins):

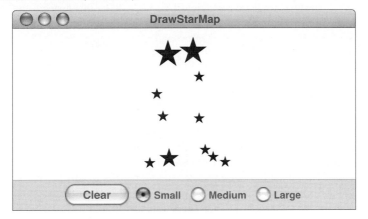

The two large stars are Castor on the right and Pollux on the left, which are named for the famous twins from classical mythology. The medium-sized star near the bottom is Almeisan, which is Arabic for "the shining one."

The `JSlider` and `JLabel` classes

At some point, you may decide that having only three choices for the size of a star does not provide enough precision to draw star maps with as much detail as you'd like. It would be better if you could add an interactor to the control bar that allowed you to draw stars as small as one pixel or as large as fifty pixels. For that, you would need a different type of interactor, one that allows for continuous variation. In the Swing library, the most common choice for such an interactor is the `JSlider` class, which implements a linear bar with a control knob that you can drag from one setting to another.

Although the `JSlider` constructor comes in many different forms, the easiest one to use takes three integer arguments: the minimum value, the maximum value, and the initial value. Thus, to create a `JSlider` that could vary between 1 and 50 with an initial value of 16, you could call **new JSlider(1, 50, 16)** and store the result in an instance variable declared as a `JSlider`. In practice, of course, it would be better to declare the values 1, 50, and 16 as named constants so that they would be easy to change as the program evolved. If you add `sizeSlider` to the control bar, the user interface will appear as follows:

Although the slider is reasonably attractive, it doesn't offer the user much guidance in the way of telling what it's for. What would help is to add some explanatory labels to the control bar so that the user interface looked like this instead:

To accomplish this goal, you need the **JLabel** class.

Although it is included in the interactor hierarchy, the **JLabel** class is a funny kind of interactor because it is completely inert and doesn't react to anything. Its purpose is simply to add labels to other interactors that need them, such as sliders.

The code to create the interactors in the control bar looks like this:

```
add(new JButton("Clear"), SOUTH);
sizeSlider = new JSlider(MIN_SIZE, MAX_SIZE, INITIAL_SIZE);
add(new JLabel("  Small"), SOUTH);
add(sizeSlider, SOUTH);
add(new JLabel("Large"), SOUTH);
```

The spaces at the beginning of the first label increase the distance between the button and the label because doing so makes it easier for the user to see that the label goes with the slider rather than the button.

As in the previous examples, the final step in implementing this extension is to change the code that creates the stars to take account of the current size. With the slider, this change is easy because the value stored in the slider is exactly the value you want to use for the size. Thus, the only thing you need to do is change the code for the helper method **getCurrentSize** as follows:

```
public double getCurrentSize() {
   return sizeSlider.getValue();
}
```

The JComboBox class

The only other interactor that makes sense to include in the **DrawStarMap** program is the **JComboBox** class, which is useful in contexts that offer too many options to use radio buttons but for which the range of values is not continuous as it is with a slider. A **JComboBox** is a small interactor that contains a menu of the available choices. Pressing the mouse button on the **JComboBox** pops up the menu and allows the user to select one of the available options. Because they allow you to choose among a set of options, **JComboBox** interactors are often informally called **choosers.**

The simplest programming pattern for using a **JComboBox** consists of the following steps:

1. Create an empty **JComboBox** and store it in an instance variable.
2. Add the names of each option to the **JComboBox** by calling its **add** method.
3. Call **setSelectedItem** on the **JComboBox** to set its initial selection.
4. Add the **JComboBox** to the user interface.

One application for the **JComboBox** class in the **DrawStarMap** program is to use it to select the color of the star. The following method initializes the instance variable **colorChooser** to be an empty **JComboBox** and then adds seven colors to it:

```
private void initColorChooser() {
    colorChooser = new JComboBox();
    colorChooser.addItem("White");
    colorChooser.addItem("Red");
    colorChooser.addItem("Yellow");
    colorChooser.addItem("Orange");
    colorChooser.addItem("Green");
    colorChooser.addItem("Blue");
    colorChooser.addItem("Black");
    colorChooser.setEditable(false);
    colorChooser.setSelectedItem("White");
}
```

The call to **setEditable** in the second-to-last line makes it illegal for the user to type a new value into the color field. This statement is important because the program is not prepared to use any values other than the ones explicitly included as items in the list. The final line sets the currently selected item in the **JComboBox** to be the string **"White"**.

Although white seems like a natural color for a star, it would be invisible against the white background used in the previous versions of the program. To make it possible to draw white stars, it makes sense to change the background color of the **GCanvas** by calling

```
setBackground(Color.GRAY);
```

to represent the night sky.

The only thing left to do is to find a way to set the color of the star from the current value stored in the **JComboBox**. Unfortunately, there is no automatic way to translate the string values in the **JComboBox** into the corresponding colors. The most straightforward approach is to read the name of the color from the **JComboBox** and then to compare it to the list of colors using a helper method like this:

```
private Color getCurrentColor() {
    String name = (String) colorChooser.getSelectedItem();
    if (name.equals("Red")) return Color.RED;
    if (name.equals("Yellow")) return Color.YELLOW;
    if (name.equals("Orange")) return Color.ORANGE;
    if (name.equals("Green")) return Color.GREEN;
    if (name.equals("Blue")) return Color.BLUE;
    if (name.equals("Black")) return Color.BLACK;
    return Color.WHITE;
}
```

The type cast in the first line is required because the values in the **JComboBox** class are not necessarily strings but can in fact be any object. (The ability of the **JComboBox** class to store objects of any class makes it possible to use a more object-oriented approach to this problem, as described in exercise 6.)

Although it is not necessary in this example, you can set up the program to detect when the value of a **JComboBox** changes. When you select a value in a **JComboBox**, it generates an action event to which listeners can respond.

Completing this extension makes it easy to draw the constellation Orion (the hunter), in which the red giant Betelgeuse appears in red in the upper left. The other large star in the lower right is Rigel.

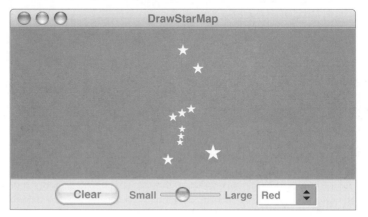

To help you keep track of the extensions described in this chapter, Figure 10-9 contains the code for the current version of the **DrawStarMap** program.

The **JTextField**, **IntField**, and **DoubleField** classes

The only classes from Figure 10-8 that remain to be covered are those that extend **JTextComponent**. Beyond what the figure shows, the **JTextComponent** hierarchy contains an extensive set of powerful classes, including, for example, editing windows that enable the user to display and modify formatted text. Those more sophisticated interactors, however, lie outside the scope of this text, which limits itself to the **JTextField** class and the closely related **IntField** and **DoubleField** subclasses defined in the **acm.gui** package. These classes allow you to accept input of a single line of text, an integer value, and a floating-point value, respectively. In a sense, these classes represent the interactor versions of the **readLine**, **readInt**, and **readDouble** methods you have been using since Chapter 2. If you want to write a GUI-based program that needs, for example, to read a string from the user, all you need to do is create a **JTextField** object and add it to the control bar. The user can then enter text into this field to give the program the information it needs.

Although it is possible to make use of a **JTextField** in the **DrawStarMap** program (as you will see in exercise 7), the time seems right for a new example. Because most modern computers come with a large collection of fonts, it is useful to have an application that lets you see what a particular font looks like on the screen.

FIGURE 10-9   Extended version of the `DrawStarMap` application

```java
import acm.graphics.*;
import acm.program.*;
import java.awt.*;
import java.awt.event.*;

/**
 * This program creates a five-pointed star every time the
 * user clicks the mouse on the canvas.  This version includes
 * a JButton to clear the screen, a JSlider to choose the size,
 * and a JComboBox to choose the color.
 */
public class DrawStarMap extends GraphicsProgram {

/* Initializes the graphical user interface */
   public void init() {
      setBackground(Color.GRAY);
      add(new JButton("Clear"), SOUTH);
      sizeSlider = new JSlider(MIN_SIZE, MAX_SIZE, INITIAL_SIZE);
      add(new JLabel("  Small"), SOUTH);
      add(sizeSlider, SOUTH);
      add(new JLabel("Large  "), SOUTH);
      initColorChooser();
      add(colorChooser, SOUTH);
      addMouseListeners();
      addActionListeners();
   }

/* Initializes the color chooser */
   private void initColorChooser() {
      colorChooser = new JComboBox();
      colorChooser.addItem("White");
      colorChooser.addItem("Red");
      colorChooser.addItem("Yellow");
      colorChooser.addItem("Orange");
      colorChooser.addItem("Green");
      colorChooser.addItem("Blue");
      colorChooser.addItem("Black");
      colorChooser.setEditable(false);
      colorChooser.setSelectedItem("White");
   }

/* Returns the current color */
   private Color getCurrentColor() {
      String name = (String) colorChooser.getSelectedItem();
      if (name.equals("Red")) return Color.RED;
      if (name.equals("Yellow")) return Color.YELLOW;
      if (name.equals("Orange")) return Color.ORANGE;
      if (name.equals("Green")) return Color.GREEN;
      if (name.equals("Blue")) return Color.BLUE;
      if (name.equals("Black")) return Color.BLACK;
      return Color.WHITE;
   }
```

FIGURE 10-9 **Extended version of the DrawStarMap application** (continued)

```
/* Returns the current size */
    private double getCurrentSize() {
        return sizeSlider.getValue();
    }

/* Called whenever the user clicks the mouse */
    public void mouseClicked(MouseEvent e) {
        GStar star = new GStar(getCurrentSize());
        star.setFilled(true);
        star.setColor(getCurrentColor());
        add(star, e.getX(), e.getY());
    }

/* Called whenever an action event occurs */
    public void actionPerformed(ActionEvent e) {
        if (e.getActionCommand().equals("Clear")) {
            removeAll();
        }
    }

/* Private constants */
    private static final int MIN_SIZE = 1;
    private static final int MAX_SIZE = 50;
    private static final int INITIAL_SIZE = 16;

/* Private instance variables */
    private JSlider sizeSlider;
    private JComboBox colorChooser;
}
```

The **FontSampler** program in Figure 10-9 does precisely that. It begins by creating a **JTextField** for the font and adding it to the control bar, along with a **JLabel** that tells the user what the field is for. It then displays a string that uses all the alphabetic characters in the default font that the Java runtime system uses for **GLabel** objects. The resulting screen display looks like this:

The **JTextField** is the long rectangular box in the control strip, which is created by the statement

```
fontField = new JTextField(MAX_FONT_NAME);
```

FIGURE 10-9   Program to display a standard string in a font chosen by the user

```
import acm.program.*;
import acm.graphics.*;
import java.awt.*;
import java.awt.event.*;

/**
 * This program allows the user to type in a font name and
 * then displays a line of text using that font.
 */
public class FontSampler extends GraphicsProgram {

    public void init() {
        fontField = new JTextField(MAX_FONT_NAME);
        fontField.addActionListener(this);
        add(new JLabel("Font"), SOUTH);
        add(fontField, SOUTH);
        lastY = 0;
        lastLabel = new GLabel(TEST_STRING);
        addGLabel(lastLabel);
    }

/* Called when any action event is generated */
    public void actionPerformed(ActionEvent e) {
        if (e.getSource() == fontField) {
            GLabel label = new GLabel(TEST_STRING);
            label.setFont(lastLabel.getFont());
            label.setFont(fontField.getText());
            addGLabel(label);
            lastLabel = label;
        }
    }

/* Adds a GLabel on the next line, adjusting for different sizes */
    private void addGLabel(GLabel label) {
        lastY += label.getHeight();
        lastY += lastLabel.getDescent() - label.getDescent();
        add(label, LEFT_MARGIN, lastY);
    }

/* Private constants */
    private static final int MAX_FONT_NAME = 30;
    private static final int LEFT_MARGIN = 3;
    private static final String TEST_STRING =
        "The quick brown fox jumped over the lazy dog.";

/* Private instance variables */
    private JTextField fontField;
    private GLabel lastLabel;
    private double lastY;
}
```

where **MAX_FONT_NAME** is a constant indicating the maximum number of characters that can be entered in the field. The value of this argument determines the width of the **JTextField** box, although it often appears wider than it needs to be when you enter data. The reason the box often seems too wide is that the implementation reserves enough space for the requested number of characters assuming that all of them might be as wide as the **m** character, which has the greatest horizontal extent of any alphabetic character. Because most characters are narrower than an **m**, there will usually be a fair amount of extra space at the end of the field.

When you run a program containing a **JTextField**, you can type characters into the field. When you type the ENTER key to signal the end of the input, the **JTextField** sends an action event to its associated listeners. Because the **addActionListeners** method adds the program as a listener only to *buttons,* you have to make an explicit call to assign the program as a listener to each **JTextField** you introduce, as illustrated by the following call:

> **fontField.addActionListener(this);**

In this example, the code for the **actionPerformed** method uses a different strategy for identifying the source of the event than the earlier button-based examples do. Rather than check for a particular action command string, this implementation looks at the source of the action event to see whether it is the text field. Although you could also use this approach for buttons, doing so usually increases the size of the program because you then have to store each button in an instance variable. In this case, checking the source is easier because the action event generated by a **JTextField** is not ordinarily associated with a useful action command the way buttons are.

When the action event occurs and has been determined to come from the **fontField** interactor, the program executes the statements

```
GLabel label = new GLabel(TEST_STRING);
label.setFont(lastLabel.getFont());
label.setFont(fontField.getText());
addGLabel(label);
lastLabel = label;
```

where the helper method **addGLabel** looks like this:

```
private void addGLabel(GLabel label) {
    lastY += label.getHeight();
    lastY += lastLabel.getDescent() - label.getDescent();
    add(label, LEFT_MARGIN, lastY);
}
```

The effect of this code is to add a new **GLabel** to the canvas one line below the most recent label, using a bit more computation than you might expect to ensure that the lines stay separated. The rationale behind the computation of the **lastY** variable that indicates the *y* coordinate of the label is explained later in this section. The label appears in the font specified in the **fontField** interactor. Thus, if you typed in **Serif-14** and then hit the ENTER key, the display would add a new line to the canvas set in a 14-point Serif font, as follows:

```
 _____
| ⊖ ⊖ ⊖           FontSampler               |
|-------------------------------------------|
| The quick brown fox jumped over the lazy dog. |
| The quick brown fox jumped over the lazy dog. |
|                                           |
|                                           |
|  Font | Serif-14                        | |
|_____|_____|_|
```

Although much of the code to display the label is a straightforward application of the tools provided by the **acm.graphics** library, a couple of subtleties are worth noting. First, the program needs to maintain the *y* coordinate for the baseline of the last label it displayed so that it knows how to position the next label. To do so, the program uses the instance variables **lastLabel** and **lastY** to hold the most recent **GLabel** added to the canvas and the position of its baseline.

At first, it might seem that you don't need to remember the last label to position the next one correctly. After all, in a program that uses only a single font, you can move from line to line simply by adding the height of the font. In this program, however, the fonts on the each line are different. As a result, the program needs to take account of the fact that the separation between successive lines depends not only on the font used in the *current* line, but also on how far characters descend below the baseline on the *preceding* line. The code in Figure 10-9 implements the baseline computation by adjusting the new baseline so that it includes the font descent from **lastLabel** rather than from the new label.

The second aspect of the program that merits additional explanation is the code to set the font of the new label, which consists of two successive calls to **setFont**. It seems as if the first call to **setFont** is extraneous, given that the second goes on to change the font again. The reason for this implementation strategy is that the second call to **setFont**—the one that uses a string argument—need not specify every aspect of the new font. If, for example, the point size or style is omitted from the string, the **GLabel** uses the value from its current font. Thus, if the user were to type in a new font family name and leave out the point-size information, the implementation of the **FontSampler** program in Figure 10-9 would change the font family without changing the point size. In the current example, you could set the font to Lucida Blackletter, without changing the point size, like this:

```
 _____
| ⊖ ⊖ ⊖           FontSampler               |
|-------------------------------------------|
| The quick brown fox jumped over the lazy dog. |
| The quick brown fox jumped over the lazy dog. |
| The quick brown fox jumped over the lazy dog. |
|                                           |
|  Font | Lucida Blackletter              | |
|_____|_____|_|
```

To simplify the process of reading numeric data from a text field, the **acm.gui** package includes two new classes—**IntField** and **DoubleField**—that allow the user to enter a numeric value of the appropriate type. These classes extend **JTextField** but provide additional methods that hide the complexity involved in numeric conversion and in checking the input for errors. The most useful methods available for **DoubleField** appear in Figure 10-10; the methods for **IntField** are the same except for the expected changes in the argument and result types. You will have the chance to see examples of these classes later in this chapter.

10.7 Managing component layout

Although the control-bar model used in the earlier interactive examples can be used to good effect in a variety of applications, most GUI-based applications do not banish their interactors to the borders of the window. What one would prefer is the ability to place interactors anywhere within the application window so as to create an integrated graphical user interface that is appropriate to a particular application.

The Java windowing hierarchy

Before you can create programs that allow interactors to appear anywhere inside the application window, you need to learn a bit more about how Java displays windows on the computer screen and arranges their internal contents. As is often the case when you are learning about the structure of a Java package, one of the first steps consists of understanding the relevant class hierarchy. In trying to make sense of Java's window system, the most important classes to understand are the ones that appear in Figure 10-11.

Although much of this structure is new, you have already seen several of the classes in Figure 10-11. The **Program** class at the bottom of the left column is the superclass for all programs, and has **JApplet** and **Applet** as its two immediate ancestors, as you learned in Chapter 2. The hierarchy, however, continues upward

---

FIGURE 10-10   **Methods defined in the DoubleField class**

Constructor

> `DoubleField()`
> Creates a **DoubleField** object with no initial value.

> `DoubleField(double value)`
> Creates a **DoubleField** object with the specified initial value.

Methods to set and get the value of the field

> `void setValue(double value)`
> Sets the value of the field and updates the display.

> `double getValue()`
> Returns the value in the field. If the value is out of range, errors or retries occur here.

Methods to control formatting

> `void setFormat(String format)`
> Sets the format string for the field in the style of **DecimalFormat** (see the **javadoc** for details).

> `String getFormat()`
> Returns the current format string.

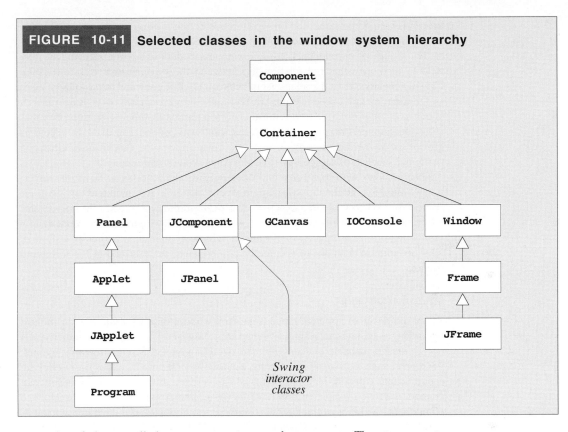

FIGURE 10-11 Selected classes in the window system hierarchy

to a series of classes called **Panel**, **Container**, and **Component**. The **JComponent** class in the next column forms the basis not only for all Swing interactors like **JButton**, but also for the **JPanel** class, which is useful in creating interactor hierarchies. Along with **Panel** and **JComponent**, the **GCanvas** and **IOConsole** classes extend **Container** and are therefore both **Container**s and **Component**s. And although these classes fall outside the scope of this text, the portion of the class hierarchy consisting of **Window**, **Frame**, and **JFrame** (which is used to create most standalone Java applications) are also part of the class hierarchy that begins with the **Component** and **Container** classes.

The **Component** and **Container** classes are critical to a detailed understanding of Java's window system, even though you will rarely have any opportunity to use them directly. The **Component** class represents the set of all Java classes that can appear in a window. As the hierarchy in Figure 10-11 shows, every **Applet** is a **Component**, as is everything else in the diagram. The **Container** class is a particular type of **Component** that can contain other **Component**s. For example, the fact that **Program** is a subclass of **Container** means that you can add components to a program. The standard subclasses of **Program** do just that. When you run a **GraphicsProgram**, it creates a **GCanvas** and adds it to the program window so that the **GCanvas** fills the available space. When you run a **ConsoleProgram**, the process is much the same; the only difference is that a **ConsoleProgram** fills the program window with an **IOConsole** instead of a **GCanvas**.

If the idea of components inside containers begins to seem confusing, it may help to recognize that the relationship between the **Component** and **Container** classes is analogous to the relationship between the **GObject** and **GCompound** classes in the **acm.graphics** package. Everything that can appear on a **GCanvas** is a subclass of **GObject**; the **GCompound** class is a particular subclass of **GObject** that can contain other **GObject**s. In much the same way, everything that can appear as part of the window system is ultimately a **Component**; the **Container** class is a particular subclass of **Component** that can contain other **Component**s.

The analogy with **GObject** and **GCompound** begins to break down, however, when you look at the question of how components are arranged inside their containers. When you add a **GObject** to a **GCompound**, you specify the coordinates of the **GObject** explicitly. By contrast, when you add a **Component** to a **Container**, you do not ordinarily specify the location. What you do instead is specify a strategy that the container can use to arrange its components, as described in the following section.

Layout managers

When the designers of Java created the first version of Java's windowing toolkit, they recognized that the graphical windows used as the foundation for modern GUI design must be capable of changing their size. In a typical windowing environment, you can change the size of an existing window by dragging its edges or by clicking a button that extends the window to fill the screen. If the size of a window can change, it doesn't make sense to have the programmer specify the locations of the components within a container, because the optimal position of each component—and often its size as well—depends on the size of the window in which it appears.

To make it easier for applications to respond to changes in their size, Java's designers adopted the strategy of using **layout managers,** which are classes that take responsibility for the arrangement of the components within a container. That arrangement depends on the following factors:

- *The strategy used by the layout manager.* Each layout manager adopts a particular strategy for laying out the components within its container. Different layout managers use different strategies; part of your job as a GUI designer is to choose a layout manager that arranges its components in a way that is appropriate to the application.
- *The amount of space available in the container.* The primary job of the layout manager is to make effective use of the space within the container. As the size of the container changes, the layout typically changes as well.
- *The preferred size for each component.* Every component has a **preferred size,** which is the ideal amount of space for that component if there were no constraints on its size. A **JButton**, for example, defines its preferred size so that it is wide enough to display the full text of its label, with a little extra space on each side. Typically, layout managers take these preferred sizes into account when deciding how to arrange the components.

- *Any constraints specified for the component when you add it to its container.* The **add** method that adds a component to its container takes an optional second argument used to convey information to the layout manager about the optimal placement for that component. You will see examples of constraints in the sections on the **BorderLayout** and **TableLayout** managers later in this chapter.

The sections that follow offer brief descriptions of the most common layout managers available in the **java.awt** package along with simple examples of their use. The example of the **BorderLayout** manager in the next section shows how to assign a layout manager to a **JPanel** that you create independently. The examples in the subsequent sections assign a new layout manager to the program itself.

The **BorderLayout** manager

Although the details have been hidden, you have already seen one of the standard layout managers in operation. The window assigned to any **Program** subclass uses a **BorderLayout** to create the control bars along the borders of the window. When a container uses a **BorderLayout**, the container is divided into five regions as shown in the following diagram:

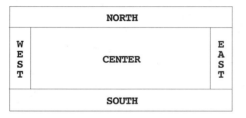

When you add a component to a container managed by a **BorderLayout**, you must specify the border to which you wish to add that component by supplying the name of that region as the second argument to the **add** method. The region names— **NORTH**, **SOUTH**, **EAST**, **WEST**, and **CENTER**—are defined as constants in the **BorderLayout** class. For convenience, these constants are also defined in the **Program** class, which makes it possible for you to use them in the context of a program without supplying **BorderLayout** as a qualifier.

When a **BorderLayout** manager lays out the components in its container, it goes through the following steps in order:

1. Change the size of the components along the **NORTH** and **SOUTH** border so that they extend horizontally for the full width of the container, giving each border the vertical space indicated by its preferred size.
2. Change the size of the components along the **EAST** and **WEST** border so that they extend vertically for what remains of the container height after taking account of the borders that have already been assigned. The preferred size of each component determines the width of these regions.
3. Change the size of the **CENTER** component so that it takes up all the space that remains after the border regions are assigned.

If any of the components are missing, those regions are assigned no space at all.

The following program illustrates the use of both the **BorderLayout** manager and the **JPanel** class, which is the container class traditionally used to assemble components under the control of a layout manager:

```
public class BorderLayoutExample extends Program {
    public void init() {
        JPanel panel = new JPanel();
        panel.setLayout(new BorderLayout());
        panel.add(new JButton("NORTH"), BorderLayout.NORTH);
        panel.add(new JButton("SOUTH"), BorderLayout.SOUTH);
        panel.add(new JButton("WEST"), BorderLayout.WEST);
        panel.add(new JButton("EAST"), BorderLayout.EAST);
        panel.add(new JButton("CENTER"), BorderLayout.CENTER);
        add(panel);
    }
}
```

The first thing to notice about this program is that it extends the **Program** class directly. Up to now, the examples you have seen in this book have extended one of the **Program** subclasses, such as **GraphicsProgram** or **ConsoleProgram**. As noted in the preceding section, these subclasses automatically install a component in the program window. If you are building your own GUI-based application, you want to assemble the contents of the program window on your own.

The first line of the **init** method creates a new **JPanel**. As was the case for the **GCompound** class in Chapter 9, the new **JPanel** is initially empty. To put together the contents you want, you use the **add** method to assemble the panel one component at a time. Before doing so, you need to assign a layout manager to the panel to control how those components are arranged. In this example, the second line of the **init** method sets the layout manager to be a **BorderLayout** object. The next several lines add five **JButton**s to the container, so that the label on each button corresponds to the border region to which it is assigned. Finally, the last statement in the **init** method adds the entire panel to the program window where, by default, it takes up the entire space.

When you run the **BorderLayoutExample** program, the layout manager for the **JPanel** will arrange its components according to the **BorderLayout** strategy, producing a program window that looks like this:

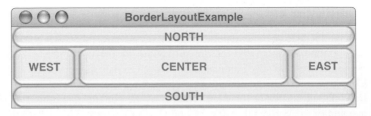

The **NORTH** and **SOUTH** buttons are stretched horizontally to fill the panel, and the **WEST** and **EAST** buttons are stretched vertically to occupy the space that remains. The **CENTER** button is stretched in both dimensions.

At this point, you may be wondering why the interactors that you added to control strips earlier in the chapter did not stretch to fill the space the way the buttons in this example do. The answer is that even though the **Program** class uses a **BorderLayout** manager to arrange the border regions, there is actually a little more going on. In a **Program**, each of the border regions is a **JPanel**, which means that it can hold multiple components. The **JPanel** is stretched to fill the space, but the arrangement of the individual interactors within the **JPanel** is controlled by its layout manager, and not by the layout manager of the program as a whole. The **Program** class overrides the **add** method so that adding a component to one of the border regions forwards that request to the appropriate **JPanel** object.

To use layout managers effectively, you also need to have some idea when the layout process occurs. In Java, the layout manager for a container is invoked by calling the **validate** method on the container. A call to **validate** occurs automatically after the **init** method in a program or whenever the program window changes size, so you don't have to invoke this method explicitly unless you change the contents of a container at some other point in the program.

The **FlowLayout** manager

Another common layout manager is **FlowLayout**, which is probably the easiest manager to use. When a **FlowLayout** manager arranges the components within its container, it starts at the top of the window and lays out components in horizontal rows, using exactly the space that each component designates as its preferred size. Whenever the next component will not fit on the current row, the **FlowLayout** manager moves on to the next row and continues to place additional components on that row until it again runs out of space. By default, the **FlowLayout** manager centers each row of components within the window.

To get a sense of how **FlowLayout** works, it helps to consider a simple example. The following program uses its **init** method to install a **FlowLayout** manager and then adds six **JButton** objects to the program window:

```
public class FlowLayoutExample extends Program {

   public void init() {
      setLayout(new FlowLayout());
      add(new JButton("Button 1"));
      add(new JButton("Button 2"));
      add(new JButton("Button 3"));
      add(new JButton("Button 4"));
      add(new JButton("Button 5"));
      add(new JButton("Button 6"));
   }

}
```

This program takes a different approach than the earlier **BorderLayout** example. Instead of creating a new **JPanel**, the **init** method in this example simply assigns a new layout manager to the program itself.

The results of running **FlowLayoutExample** depend on the window size. Here is one possible sample run:

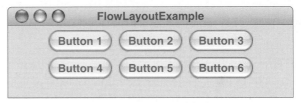

Given a window of this size, the **FlowLayout** manager lays out the first four buttons in the top row of the layout. At that point, there is no room to place the fifth button in that row, so the layout manager moves to the next row for the last two buttons. It then centers each of the rows to produce the layout shown in the sample run.

If you change the size of the window, the layout manager automatically repositions the buttons on the display. For example, if you make the window a little narrower, there will be room for only three buttons on each row, as follows:

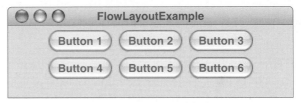

Conversely, if you make the window wider, you will eventually reach the point at which all the buttons fit on the top row.

The primary advantage of the **FlowLayout** manager is that it usually produces a layout that is readable while remaining easy to use. The disadvantage is that you have very little control over the layout. In particular, the **FlowLayout** manager does not allow you to specify where the row boundaries occur, which may be important in some applications.

As an example of how things can go wrong with a **FlowLayout** manager, suppose that you want to include a slider as one of the interactors in your user interface, as you did in the **DrawStarMap** program earlier in this chapter. As is usually the case, the slider in that program is associated with two **GLabel**s, one on each side, so that the user has some idea what the slider controls. In the **DrawStarMap** program, the labels and the slider together look like this:

If you use a **FlowLayout** manager to arrange these interactors, there will be some window sizes for which the boundary between rows in the layout comes *between* one of the labels and the slider, thereby destroying the visual effect.

The **GridLayout** manager

One way to gain control over which interactors are assigned to a particular row is to use the **GridLayout** manager, which arranges its components in a two-dimensional grid. You specify the number of rows and columns when you call the **GridLayout** constructor. For example, the constructor

```
new GridLayout(2, 3)
```

creates a grid with two rows and three columns. When the **GridLayout** manager lays out the components in its container, it fills each row before moving on to the next. Each of the components is stretched to fill its space in the grid, which is itself expanded to fill all the space available in the container. Thus, in a grid with two rows and three columns, each component will get a third of the available horizontal space and half of the vertical space.

As an example of how **GridLayout** works, the **init** method

```
public void init() {
    setLayout(new GridLayout(2, 3));
    add(new JButton("Button 1"));
    add(new JButton("Button 2"));
    add(new JButton("Button 3"));
    add(new JButton("Button 4"));
    add(new JButton("Button 5"));
    add(new JButton("Button 6"));
}
```

produces a layout that looks like this:

If you change the size of this window, the buttons will stretch in each dimension, but the overall structure of the grid will remain intact.

The inadequacy of the standard layout managers

Although the standard layout managers described in the preceding sections are useful in many contexts, they don't provide the flexibility you need to design anything beyond the simplest GUI layouts. To create sophisticated layouts of the sort you find in commercial applications, you need to use a more sophisticated layout manager. Unfortunately, the most general layout manager that Java provides—the **GridBagLayout** class in the **java.awt** package—is too complicated to teach to beginning programmers. It is, moreover, so poorly designed that experienced Java programmers tend to avoid it.

The fact that **GridBagLayout** is not appropriate at the introductory level creates a dilemma. The layout managers that are easy to learn are not powerful enough to create interesting layouts. Conversely, the layout managers that have the necessary power are extremely difficult to learn. To solve this problem, the ACM Java Task Force developed a new layout manager called **TableLayout**, which makes it easy to arrange components in a flexible two-dimensional grid. The **TableLayout** manager provides all the capabilities of **GridBagLayout** but eliminates most of the complexity. The capabilities of the **TableLayout** class, however, are substantial enough that it makes sense to give it a section of its own.

10.8 Using the **TableLayout** class

As noted at the end of the preceding section, the difficulties involved in using existing layout managers led the ACM Java Task Force to design a new layout manager called **TableLayout**, which makes it possible to design sophisticated layouts much more easily. In certain respects, the **TableLayout** class is similar to the **GridLayout** class, particularly in that it arranges its interactors into a two-dimensional grid. It differs from **GridLayout** in the following respects:

- The cells in a **TableLayout** can vary in size. By default, rows and columns are given enough space to hold the largest item in that row or column.
- The **TableLayout** manager calculates the size of the grid from the preferred sizes of the components and does not ordinarily try to expand the grid to fill the available space.
- The **TableLayout** manager makes it possible to associate constraints with individual components to guide the layout process. The use of constraints is described in the section entitled "Specifying constraints" later in this chapter.

The sections that follow explain how the **TableLayout** manager works and how you can use it effectively in your programs.

Comparing **GridLayout** and **TableLayout**

The easiest way to see how the **GridLayout** and **TableLayout** managers differ is to run the same program changing only the layout manager. The program example used to illustrate **GridLayout** set up a grid layout with two rows and three columns and then added six **JButton**s to the program window. Adapting the program to use **TableLayout** changes only the **setLayout** call from

```
setLayout(new GridLayout(2, 3));
```

to

```
setLayout(new TableLayout(2, 3));
```

Running this modified version of the program produces the following arrangement of the buttons:

As you can see if you compare this sample run to the earlier one produced by **GridLayoutExample** on page 386, the buttons have been restored to their preferred size and no longer expand to fill the program window.

Using **TableLayout** to create a temperature converter

To get a better sense of the flexibility offered by **TableLayout**, you will need to look at a more sophisticated example, such as the **TemperatureConverter** program in Figure 10-12. The user interface for the **TemperatureConverter** program looks like this:

The user can convert temperatures in either direction by entering a value in either of the numeric fields and then clicking the corresponding button. For example, to find out what 20 degrees Celsius corresponds to on the Fahrenheit scale, the user would simply enter the value 20 in the **Degrees Celsius** box and then click the button labeled **C -> F**, which would give rise to the following display:

As in the preceding examples, the **init** method is responsible for setting up the graphical user interface. In this case, the **init** method begins by calling

```
setLayout(new TableLayout(2, 3));
```

which creates a table with two rows running horizontally and three columns running vertically. Once the layout manager is in place, the rest of the **init** method creates the interactors and adds them to the table, filling each row from left to right and then each row from top to bottom. In the **TemperatureConverter** example, the calls to **add** create the Fahrenheit row of the table using the lines

```
add(new JLabel("Degrees Fahrenheit"));
add(fahrenheitField);
add(new JButton("F -> C"));
```

and the corresponding Celsius row using the lines

```
add(new JLabel("Degrees Celsius"));
add(celsiusField);
add(new JButton("C -> F"));
```

FIGURE 10-12 **GUI-based temperature conversion program**

```java
import acm.graphics.*;
import acm.gui.*;
import acm.program.*;
import java.awt.event.*;
import javax.swing.*;

/**
 * This program allows users to convert temperatures back and forth
 * from Fahrenheit to Celsius.
 */
public class TemperatureConverter extends Program {

/* Initializes the graphical user interface */
   public void init() {
      setLayout(new TableLayout(2, 3));
      fahrenheitField = new IntField(32);
      fahrenheitField.setActionCommand("F -> C");
      fahrenheitField.addActionListener(this);
      celsiusField = new IntField(0);
      celsiusField.setActionCommand("C -> F");
      celsiusField.addActionListener(this);
      add(new JLabel("Degrees Fahrenheit"));
      add(fahrenheitField);
      add(new JButton("F -> C"));
      add(new JLabel("Degrees Celsius"));
      add(celsiusField);
      add(new JButton("C -> F"));
      addActionListeners();
   }

/* Listens for a button action */
   public void actionPerformed(ActionEvent e) {
      String cmd = e.getActionCommand();
      if (cmd.equals("F -> C")) {
         int f = fahrenheitField.getValue();
         int c = GMath.round((5.0 / 9.0) * (f - 32));
         celsiusField.setValue(c);
      } else if (cmd.equals("C -> F")) {
         int c = celsiusField.getValue();
         int f = GMath.round((9.0 / 5.0) * c + 32);
         fahrenheitField.setValue(f);
      }
   }

/* Private instance variables */
   private IntField fahrenheitField;
   private IntField celsiusField;
}
```

If you look at the sample run this code produces, you will see that the sizes of the various interactors in the table have been adjusted according to the constraints imposed by the grid. The **JLabel** objects have different sizes, but the **TableLayout** manager makes sure that there is enough space in the first column to hold the longer of the two labels. By default, each component is expanded to fill its grid cell, even though the cell is not expanded to fill the container.

When you create a **TableLayout** object, you can also use 0 in place of *either* the number of rows or the number of columns to indicate an unspecified value, but not both. For example, the call

```
setLayout(new TableLayout(0, 7));
```

specifies a table with seven columns and as many rows as needed to display the components in the table. You could use such a layout to create a calendar in which there are always seven columns for the days but in which the number of rows varies depending on the month.

The code for **TemperatureConverter** calls the **addActionListeners** method to designate the program as an action listener for all buttons within it. The individual calls to **addActionListener** and **setActionCommand** make it possible for the user to trigger a conversion either by clicking the appropriate button or by typing the ENTER key in the interactor itself. Each of these actions generates an **ActionEvent** whose action command is either the string **"F -> C"** or **"C -> F"** depending on which button or interactor generated the event. The **actionPerformed** method responds to these action events by performing the necessary conversion and then updating the value of the corresponding field.

Specifying constraints

Although the default behavior of the **TableLayout** manager is useful in its own right, its most important feature is that you can specify additional constraints as you add new components. Such constraints can, for example, allow you to set the minimum width and height of the row and column containing that table cell, specify the way in which components change their size as the cell size changes, or indicate that a particular cell spans several rows or columns.

When you add a component to a **TableLayout** grid, you can specify these constraints in the form of a string passed as the second argument to the **add** method. The format of that string is a sequence of one or more specifications of the form

constraint=value

where *constraint* is the name of one of the available constraint options and *value* is the corresponding value for that option. For example, if you wanted to give the current table row a minimum height of 50 pixels, you could do so by specifying

```
"height=50"
```

Similarly, if you wanted the component to take up three columns in the grid, you could specify the constraint string

```
"gridwidth=3"
```

You can include more than one constraint in the same call to **add** by including multiple *constraint=value* entries in the same string, separated by at least one space.

Figure 10-13 describes the set of constraints you can specify when adding constraints to a container managed using the **TableLayout** strategy. This book uses only the first two options (**gridwidth**/**gridheight** and **width**/**height**), but the other constraint options are worth exploring on your own.

Using **TableLayout** to create a simple calculator

The **TableLayout** class is useful in a wide variety of GUI designs. To get a sense of how it works in the context of a larger example, let's suppose you want to create an application that simulates a traditional four-function calculator that works with integer values. Both the layout and operation of the calculator are illustrated in Figure 10-14, which shows the steps involved when you use the calculator to add the integers 25 and 17.

This program is sophisticated enough to raise several design issues. The issue most germane to this chapter is how to arrange the buttons and interactors. The buttons themselves form a 4 × 4 grid, in which each of the buttons is a square. To make it easy to change the dimensions of the calculator, it makes sense to define the square size as a constant, presumably called something like **BUTTON_SIZE**.

The numeric display at the top of the calculator is also part of the grid. Its vertical dimension is the same as that for the buttons, but it spans all four columns along the horizontal axis. The **init** method for this application will therefore look

---

FIGURE 10-13 | **Constraint options available for use with the TableLayout class**

gridwidth=*columns* *or* **gridheight**=*rows*
Indicates that this table cell should span the indicated number of columns or rows.

width=*pixels* *or* **height**=*pixels*
The **width** specification indicates that the width of this column should be the specified number of pixels. If different widths are specified for cells in the same column, the column width is defined to be the maximum. In the absence of any **width** specification, the column width is the largest of the preferred widths. The **height** specification is interpreted symmetrically for row heights.

weightx=*weight* *or* **weighty**=*weight*
If the total size of the table is less than the size of its enclosure, **TableLayout** will ordinarily center the table in the available space. If any of the cells, however, are given nonzero **weightx** or **weighty** values, the extra space is distributed along that axis in proportion to the weights specified. The weights are interpreted as floating-point values.

fill=*fill*
Indicates how the component in this cell should be resized if its preferred size is smaller than the cell size. The legal values are **NONE**, **HORIZONTAL**, **VERTICAL**, and **BOTH**, indicating the axes along which stretching should occur. The default is **BOTH**.

anchor=*anchor*
If a component is not being filled along a particular axis, the **anchor** specification indicates where the component should be placed in its cell. The default value is **CENTER**, but you may also use any of the standard compass directions (**NORTH**, **SOUTH**, **EAST**, **WEST**, **NORTHEAST**, **NORTHWEST**, **SOUTHEAST**, or **SOUTHWEST**).

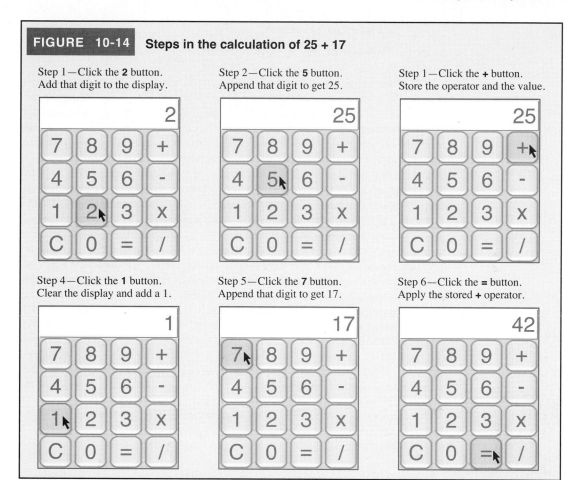

FIGURE 10-14 Steps in the calculation of 25 + 17

Step 1—Click the **2** button.
Add that digit to the display.

Step 2—Click the **5** button.
Append that digit to get 25.

Step 1—Click the **+** button.
Store the operator and the value.

Step 4—Click the **1** button.
Clear the display and add a 1.

Step 5—Click the **7** button.
Append that digit to get 17.

Step 6—Click the **=** button.
Apply the stored **+** operator.

something like this, where **CalculatorDisplay** is an as-yet-undefined class that implements the numeric display:

```
public void init() {
    setLayout(new TableLayout(5, 4));
    display = new CalculatorDisplay();
    add(display, "gridwidth=4 height=" + BUTTON_SIZE);
    Add the 16 buttons that occupy the next four rows.
    Enable the action listeners for those buttons.
}
```

The method call that adds the display to the program window uses the expression

```
"gridwidth=4 height=" + BUTTON_SIZE
```

to specify the **TableLayout** constraint. This expression uses the concatenation operator **+** to insert the value of the constant **BUTTON_SIZE** into the constraint string. If **BUTTON_SIZE** has the value 40, this constraint specification is equivalent to

```
"gridwidth=4 height=40"
```

which indicates that the calculator display should span four columns and have a height of 40 pixels, just as it does in the diagram.

The other important design decision is how to represent the buttons as Java objects. The brute force approach would be to make each of the 16 buttons an instance of the **JButton** class itself. If you did so, you could implement the **actionPerformed** listener method so that it checked for each possible action command and responded as necessary. That approach, however would not take into account the fact that the buttons fall into distinct logical groups: there are ten digit buttons (**0** through **9**), four operator buttons (**+**, **−**, **x**, and **/**), and a couple of buttons (**C** and **=**) that don't fall into either category. This structural relationship suggests that the buttons fit naturally into a class hierarchy of the sort shown in Figure 10-15.

Using a class hierarchy allows you to write a much simpler implementation of the **actionPerformed** method. If each button is an instance of a separate class, you no longer need to write **if** statements that check for the various action commands. You can instead adopt a more object-oriented approach. The first step is to use **getSource** to determine the source of the action event, which is presumably the button that caused it. If the source is an instance of one of the buttons in the **CalculatorButton** hierarchy, you can let that button specify its own response. All the **actionPerformed** method needs to do is call a particular method—which you might call **action**—on the button that caused the event. Each class in the hierarchy can then define its own version of **action** to execute whatever operations are required. The **DigitButton** class defines **action** so that it appends a digit to the value in the display, the **AddButton** class defines **action** so that it performs an addition, and so on.

A complete implementation of the **Calculator** program appears in Figure 10-16, which extends over the next four pages.

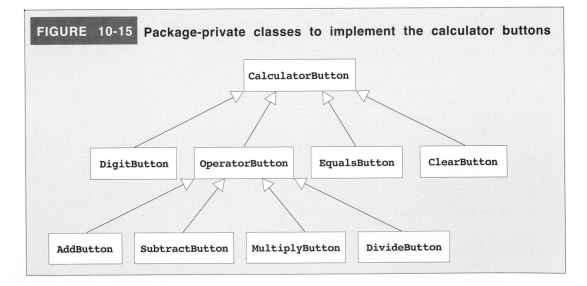

FIGURE 10-15 Package-private classes to implement the calculator buttons

FIGURE 10-16   Implementation of the calculator program

```
import acm.gui.*;
import acm.program.*;
import acm.util.*;
import java.awt.*;
import java.awt.event.*;
import javax.swing.*;

/** This program implements a simple four-function calculator */
public class Calculator extends Program {

/* Initializes the user interface */
   public void init() {
      setLayout(new TableLayout(5, 4));
      display = new CalculatorDisplay();
      add(display, "gridwidth=4 height=" + BUTTON_SIZE);
      addButtons();
      addActionListeners();
   }

/* Called on each action event; the response is determined by the button */
   public void actionPerformed(ActionEvent e) {
      Object source = e.getSource();
      if (source instanceof CalculatorButton) {
         ((CalculatorButton) source).action(display);
      }
   }

/* Adds the buttons to the calculator */
   private void addButtons() {
      String constraint = "width=" + BUTTON_SIZE + " height=" + BUTTON_SIZE;
      add(new DigitButton(7), constraint);
      add(new DigitButton(8), constraint);
      add(new DigitButton(9), constraint);
      add(new AddButton(), constraint);
      add(new DigitButton(4), constraint);
      add(new DigitButton(5), constraint);
      add(new DigitButton(6), constraint);
      add(new SubtractButton(), constraint);
      add(new DigitButton(1), constraint);
      add(new DigitButton(2), constraint);
      add(new DigitButton(3), constraint);
      add(new MultiplyButton(), constraint);
      add(new ClearButton(), constraint);
      add(new DigitButton(0), constraint);
      add(new EqualsButton(), constraint);
      add(new DivideButton(), constraint);
   }

/* Private constants and instance variables */
   private static final int BUTTON_SIZE = 40;
   private CalculatorDisplay display;

}
```

FIGURE 10-16 Implementation of the calculator program (continued)

```
/*
 * This class defines the display for the calculator.
 *
 * Implementation notes:
 *   This class does most of the work for the calculator application and keeps
 *   track not only of the number currently in the display but also the previous
 *   operator button (op) and the previous value from the display (memory), which
 *   will become the left operand of the operator.  When a new operator button is
 *   pressed, this class calculates the new value of the display by applying
 *   that operator to the value in memory and the current value in the display.
 *
 *   It is also important to note that the behavior of digit buttons depends on
 *   whether an operator button is clicked.  If the last click was an operator
 *   button, the digit buttons must clear the display to start a new value.  If
 *   not, the digit is added to the end of the existing value.  The code uses the
 *   boolean variable startNewValue to record this state.
 */
class CalculatorDisplay extends IntField {

/* Creates a new calculator display that is not directly editable by the user */
    public CalculatorDisplay() {
        setEditable(false);
        setFont(new Font("SansSerif", Font.PLAIN, 24));
        setValue(0);
        startNewValue = false;
        op = null;
    }

/* Adds a digit to the display, clearing the old value if startNewValue is set */
    public void addDigit(int digit) {
        int value = (startNewValue) ? 0 : getValue();
        setValue(10 * value + digit);
        startNewValue = false;
    }

/* Sets a new operator, applying the previous one if one exists */
    public void setOperator(OperatorButton button) {
        if (op == null) {
            memory = getValue();
        } else {
            memory = op.apply(memory, getValue());
            setValue(memory);
        }
        op = button;
        startNewValue = true;
    }

/* Private instance variables */
    private OperatorButton op;          /* The last operator button pressed */
    private int memory;                 /* The value to which the operator is applied */
    private boolean startNewValue;      /* Set after an operator to start a new value */
}
```
☞

FIGURE 10-16 **Implementation of the calculator program** (continued)

```
/*
 * This abstract class is the superclass for every calculator button. Every button
 * must define an action method, which is called whenever the button is clicked.
 */
abstract class CalculatorButton extends JButton {

/* Creates a new CalculatorButton with the specified name */
   public CalculatorButton(String name) {
      super(name);
      setFont(new Font("SansSerif", Font.PLAIN, 24));
   }

/* Called when the button is clicked (every subclass must implement this method) */
   public abstract void action(CalculatorDisplay display);

}

/*
 * This class is used for each of the digit buttons.  The action consists of
 * adding the digit used as a label on the button, which is returned by getText.
 */
class DigitButton extends CalculatorButton {

/* Creates a new DigitButton for the digit n */
   public DigitButton(int n) {
      super("" + n);
   }

/* Adds this digit to the display */
   public void action(CalculatorDisplay display) {
      display.addDigit(Integer.parseInt(getText()));
   }
}

/*
 * This abstract class is the superclass of the various operator buttons.
 * Each concrete subclass must override the apply method.
 */
abstract class OperatorButton extends CalculatorButton {

/* Creates a new OperatorButton with the specified name */
   public OperatorButton(String name) {
      super(name);
   }

/* Informs the display that this operator button has been clicked */
   public void action(CalculatorDisplay display) {
      display.setOperator(this);
   }

/* Applies this operator (every subclass must implement this method) */
   public abstract int apply(int lhs, int rhs);
}
```

> **FIGURE 10-16** **Implementation of the calculator program** (continued)
>
> ```
> /*
>  * The classes AddButton, SubtractButton, MultiplyButton, and DivideButton
>  * are the same except for their label and the implementation of apply.
>  */
> class AddButton extends OperatorButton {
>    public AddButton() { super("+"); }
>    public int apply(int lhs, int rhs) { return lhs + rhs; }
> }
>
> class SubtractButton extends OperatorButton {
>    public SubtractButton() { super("-"); }
>    public int apply(int lhs, int rhs) { return lhs - rhs; }
> }
>
> class MultiplyButton extends OperatorButton {
>    public MultiplyButton() { super("x"); }
>    public int apply(int lhs, int rhs) { return lhs * rhs; }
> }
>
> class DivideButton extends OperatorButton {
>    public DivideButton() { super("/"); }
>    public int apply(int lhs, int rhs) { return lhs / rhs; }
> }
>
> /*
>  * The EqualsButton class displays the current value.  As it happens, this
>  * operation can be implemented simply by setting the operator to null.
>  */
> class EqualsButton extends CalculatorButton {
>    public EqualsButton() {
>       super("=");
>    }
>
>    public void action(CalculatorDisplay display) {
>       display.setOperator(null);
>    }
> }
>
> /*
>  * The ClearButton class resets the calculator by setting the operator to
>  * null and the display value to 0.
>  */
> class ClearButton extends CalculatorButton {
>    public ClearButton() {
>       super("C");
>    }
>
>    public void action(CalculatorDisplay display) {
>       display.setOperator(null);
>       display.setValue(0);
>    }
> }
> ```

Although much of the code in Figure 10-16 simply follows the design described earlier in this section, it is also worth noting the following aspects of the program:

- *Package-private classes.* Up to this point in the text, classes have always been designated as **public**. When you use class-level decomposition to define the structure of a problem, it is often the case that many of those classes are of interest only within the implementation, just as private helper methods are of interest only within the class that defines them. Java supports this kind of "helper class" by allowing you to eliminate the **public** keyword in the class definition. Such classes are known as **package-private classes** and are accessible only from the package in which you define them. Java requires that all public classes be defined in a separate source file; by contrast, a single source file can include many package-private classes.

- *Checking whether an object is an instance of a class.* In case some future implementor decides to add new buttons to the calculator that fall outside the **CalculatorButton** hierarchy, the implementation of **actionPerformed** should check that the source of the event is really a **CalculatorButton** before calling its **action** method. Java allows you to implement such a check by invoking the built-in **instanceof** operator, which takes a value on its left and a class name on its right. The **instanceof** operator returns **true** if the value is a legal instance of the specified class and is not equal to **null**.

- *Abstract methods.* When you define an abstract class, you often want to specify that a particular method exists without writing the implementation. In this example, the abstract class **CalculatorButton** wants to specify that there is an **action** method, even though it leaves the precise implementation of that method to each of its subclasses. You can declare such a method by specifying the keyword **abstract** and replacing the body with a semicolon.

Summary

In this chapter, you have had the chance to learn several techniques for writing interactive programs, particularly those that involve *graphical user interfaces* or *GUIs*. The most important points in the chapter include the following:

- Modern applications are typically designed so that they respond to actions taken by the user that can happen at any time, and not simply when the program requests them. User actions that happen outside the normal sequential flow of a program are called *events*. Programs that operate in response to such events are called *event-driven*.

- In Java, programs respond to events by designating an object as a *listener* for a particular event type. Event listeners must implement one or more of the interfaces defined in the package **java.awt.event**. This chapter covers the listener interfaces **MouseListener**, **MouseMotionListener**, **KeyListener**, and **ActionListener**.

- The **Program** class implements each of these four interfaces by supplying empty definitions for each of the required methods. If you want to change the action for one of these methods, all you need to do is supply a new definition for that method in your program class. Your new definition will override the default implementation.

- Event-driven programs tend to include an **init** method rather than a **run** method. The **init** method specifies initialization code that must be executed before a program starts. The **run** method specifies the actions a program takes as it runs.

- You can respond to mouse events in a **GraphicsProgram** by implementing one or more of the listener methods defined in Figure 10-2 and then calling **addMouseListeners** as part of the **init** method. Similarly, you can respond to keyboard events by implementing the listener methods defined in Figure 10-5 and calling **addKeyListeners**.

- The **javax.swing** and **acm.gui** packages define a number of classes that respond to user actions. Collectively, instances of these classes are called *interactors*. This text uses the following interactor classes:

JButton	Triggers a particular action
JCheckBox	Specifies an option as either on or off
JRadioButton	Selects from a mutually exclusive set of options
JSlider	Adjusts a parameter within a continuous range
JLabel	Adds an inactive message to guide the user
JComboBox	Pops up a menu of choices
JTextField	Allows the user to enter text
IntField	Allows the user to enter an integer
DoubleField	Allows the user to enter a floating-point value

- When you click on an instance of the **JButton** class, it generates an action event. You respond to that event by defining an **actionPerformed** method, which implements the **ActionListener** interface. You can add the program as an action listener to all buttons within its window by calling **addActionListeners** in the **init** method.

- You can determine which button caused an action event in either of two ways. One approach is to call **getSource** on the event, which returns the object that caused the event. Alternatively, you can call **getActionCommand** on the event and then use the resulting string to determine your response. For a **JButton**, the action command is defined by default to be the button label.

- The easiest way to add interactors to a program is to add them to a *control bar* along one of the borders of a program window.

- Arranging interactors in the interior of a window typically requires the use of a *layout manager,* which is responsible for arranging components within a container. This chapter describes the standard **BorderLayout**, **FlowLayout**, and **GridLayout** managers in the **java.awt** package along with the more flexible **TableLayout** manager in **acm.gui**.

- The **TableLayout** manager makes it possible to specify constraints that control the layout of individual components. The options supported in constraint specifications are described in Figure 10-13.

- In many applications, the best way to define the behavior of an interactor is to create a hierarchy in which each subclass defines its own behavior by overriding the definition of a method common to all classes in the hierarchy.

- When you design an application using class-level decomposition, the subsidiary classes in the hierarchy are typically relevant only to the implementation and of no use to clients. In such situations, it usually makes sense to use *package-private classes,* which are defined without the keyword **public**. Package-private classes may be included in the same source file as the public class to which they apply.

Review questions

1. Define the terms *event* and *event-driven.*

2. What is an event listener?

3. In what package are **MouseEvent**, **KeyboardEvent**, and **ActionEvent** defined?

4. True or false: The **Program** class defines a set of listener methods that do nothing at all.

5. What is the difference in function between the **init** and **run** methods in a **Program**?

6. What two interfaces does the Java event model use for responding to mouse events? What is the reason for making this distinction?

7. True or false: A **MouseClicked** event is always preceded by a **MousePressed** event and followed by a **MouseReleased** event.

8. Describe the effect of the methods **addMouseListeners**, **addKeyListeners**, and **addActionListeners**.

9. In a sentence or two each, describe the circumstances under which you would use the following interactors: **JButton**, **JCheckBox**, **JRadioButton**, **JSlider**, **JLabel**, **JComboBox**, **JTextField**, **IntField**, and **DoubleField**.

10. What type of event is generated when you click a **JButton** object?

11. When you construct a new **JButton**, what value is used as its default action command?

12. What happens if you add more than one interactor to a control bar positioned along the **SOUTH** border of a program window?

13. What classes in the **acm.graphics** package are analogous to the **Component** and **Container** classes in Java's windowing hierarchy?

14. What is a layout manager?

15. Describe the layout policy used by each of the **BorderLayout**, **FlowLayout**, and **GridLayout** managers.

16. What are the names of the five regions defined in the **BorderLayout** class?

17. When a **BorderLayout** manager arranges its components, does it give the corner space to the left and right borders or the top and bottom borders?

18. Describe the difference between the **width** and **gridwidth** options in the **TableLayout** class.

19. For each of the following **init** methods, make a rough sketch of the program window after the initialization process is complete:

a)
```
public void init() {
    add(new JButton("Button 1"), SOUTH);
    add(new JButton("Button 2"), SOUTH);
    add(new JCheckBox("Finished"), SOUTH);
}
```

b)
```
public void init() {
    setLayout(new GridLayout(2, 1));
    add(new JButton("Button 1"));
    add(new JButton("Button 2"));
}
```

c)
```
public void init() {
    setLayout(new TableLayout(3, 2));
    add(new JButton("Button 1"), "gridwidth=2");
    add(new JButton("Button 2"), "gridheight=2");
    add(new JButton("Button 3"));
    add(new JButton("Button 4"));
}
```

20. What is a package-private class?

Programming exercises

1. Modify the **RandomColorLabel** program from exercise 3 in Chapter 9 so that pressing the mouse button on top of one of the **GLabel**s temporarily resets its color to the one that matches its name. Releasing the mouse button should choose a new random color for the label.

2. Write a **GraphicsProgram** that uses a **GLabel** to display the coordinates of the mouse as you move or drag it in the window. The **GLabel** should always appear slightly to the left of the current mouse position, as shown in the following diagram:

If you then move the mouse, the label should follow it, updating the values of the coordinates as it goes.

3. Rewrite the **DrawFace** program from section 9.4 so that the eyes have circular pupils that always appear to look at the position of the mouse. For example, if

the cursor is below eye-level to the right of the face, the eyes should appear to be looking down and to the right, like this:

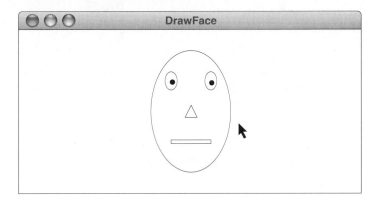

As you move the mouse, the eyes should follow the cursor position. Although it doesn't matter much as long as the cursor is outside the face, it is important to compute the position of the pupil independently for each eye. If you move the mouse between the eyes, for example, the pupils should point in opposite directions so that the face appears cross-eyed.

4. In addition to line drawings of the sort generated by the **DrawLines** program, interactive drawing programs allow you to draw other shapes on the canvas. In a typical drawing application, you would create a rectangle by pressing the mouse at one corner and then dragging it to the opposite corner. For example, if you pressed the mouse at the location in the left diagram and then dragged it to the position in which you see it in the right diagram, the program would create the rectangle shown:

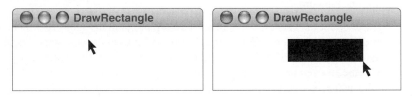

The rectangle grows as you drag the mouse. When you release the mouse button, the rectangle is complete and stays where it is. You can then go back and add more rectangles in the same way.

Although the code for this exercise is quite short, there is one important consideration that you will need to take into account. In the example above, the initial mouse click is in the upper left corner of the rectangle. Your program, however, has to work just as well if you drag the mouse in some other direction besides to the right and down. For example, you should also be able to draw a rectangle by dragging to the left, as shown in the following illustration:

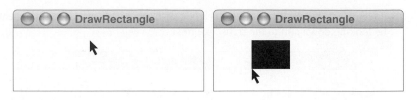

5. Using the **DrawLines** and **DrawRectangle** programs as a starting point, create a more elaborate drawing program that includes a palette of the five shapes—a filled rectangle, an outlined rectangle, a filled oval, an outlined oval, and a straight line—along the left side of the canvas as shown in the following diagram:

Clicking on one of the squares in the palette chooses that shape as a drawing tool. Thus, if you click on the filled oval in the middle of the palette, your program should draw filled ovals. Clicking and dragging in an empty area outside of the palette should draw the currently selected shape. Clicking and dragging inside an existing shape should move that shape on the canvas. Clicking on a shape without dragging should move that shape to the front of the stacking order.

6. The code for the version of the **DrawStarMap** program in Figure 10-9 includes a **JComboBox** that allows the user to select the color used for new stars. As things stand, the process of determining the actual color from the name used in the **JComboBox** requires a long series of **if** statements that look for the various color names and return the corresponding **Color** object. In addition to being tedious, that strategy has the weakness that adding a new color requires changing two parts of the program: the code in the **initColorChooser** method that creates the color chooser and the code for **getCurrentColor** that interprets the color name. If someone tried to add new colors but failed to make the change in both places, the program would not operate correctly.

The fact that the options in a **JComboBox** need not be strings offers some hope for a more efficient implementation, but the solution is not immediate. If you put the Java color values directly into the **JComboBox**, you could then set the current color simply by getting the current item and casting it to a **Color**, thereby eliminating the need for the **if** statements altogether. The problem is that the labels for the **JComboBox** options would no longer be particularly readable, because the **JComboBox** class uses each item's **toString** method to create its label. Instead of seeing **RED** in the list of choices, you would instead see the string

```
java.awt.Color[r=255,g=0,b=0]
```

Someone who knew enough Java to understand the color model would be able to figure out that this color would indeed appear red, but most users would be completely confused. You can, however, fix this problem by defining a **LabeledColor** class that extends the standard **Color** class but also takes a name to use as the result of the **toString** method. If you use this extended class you could add a color to the color chooser by writing

```
colorChooser.addItem(new LabeledColor(Color.RED, "Red"));
```

Implement the **LabeledColor** class and incorporate it into **DrawStarMap**.

7. Incorporate the following extensions into the **DrawStarMap** application:

   - Make it possible for the user to drag stars on the canvas. If the mouse pressed event occurs outside of an existing star, it should create a new one as in the original version of the program. If, however, the mouse pressed event occurs within an existing star, your program should set things up so that dragging the mouse moves that star along with it, as in the **DragObjects** program in Figure 10-4.
   - Add a key listener so that pressing the arrow keys moves the current star one pixel in the corresponding direction. In addition, pressing the DELETE key should remove the current star from the canvas altogether.
   - Add a **JTextField** to the control strip that allows the user to enter the name of a star. When the user types the ENTER key at the end of the name, the **DrawStarMap** program should add that name as a **GLabel** just to the right of the most recent star. The label should use the color specified by the color chooser, which will be the same as that for the star unless the user has made an explicit change. Make sure that it is possible to drag the **GLabel** on the canvas in much the same fashion as the stars.

8. Write the **init** method for **GraphicsProgram** that creates the control bar shown at the bottom of the following sample run:

9. Incorporate the speed control bar from the preceding exercise into the code for the **BouncingBall** program from exercise 15 in Chapter 4. The program should use the **run** method to implement an animation loop, but should not

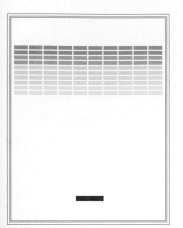

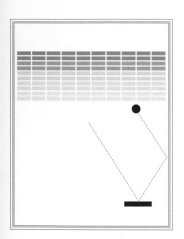

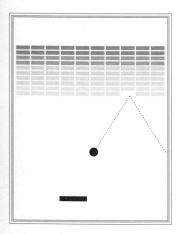

actually move the ball until the user clicks the start button. Although there are better strategies for controlling animation that you will learn in Chapter 14, the simplest way to implement this program is to declare a flag variable. If the flag is **true**, the program should move the ball on each animation cycle. If the flag is **false**, the program should leave the ball where it is. In either case, however, the program should call the **pause** method to ensure that your program doesn't keep the computer busy on every CPU cycle.

The purpose of the slider in the control bar is to allow the user to change the speed of the animation. For example, when the control is set all the way over at the slow end of the slider, your program should pause for a relatively long time so that the ball appears to move slowly. As you move the control toward the fast end of the slider, the pause time should get shorter. Moreover, if you want the ball to move at all quickly, you will also need to change how much the ball moves in each time step.

10. Write a program to play the classic arcade game of Breakout, which was developed in 1976 by Steve Wozniak, who would later become one of the founders of Apple. In Breakout, your goal is to clear a collection of bricks by hitting each of them with a bouncing ball.

The initial configuration of the Breakout game appears in the top diagram in the margin. The colored rectangles in the top part of the screen are bricks, two rows each of red, orange, yellow, green, and cyan. The slightly larger rectangle at the bottom is the paddle. The paddle is in a fixed position in the vertical dimension, but moves back and forth across the screen along with the mouse until it reaches the edge of its space.

A complete Breakout game consists of three turns. On each turn, a ball is launched from the center of the window toward the bottom of the screen at a random angle. That ball bounces off the paddle and the walls of the world. Thus, after two bounces—one off the paddle and one off the right wall—the ball might have the trajectory shown in the second diagram. (Note that the dotted line used to show the ball's path won't appear on the screen.)

As you can see from the second diagram, the ball is about to collide with one of the bricks on the bottom row. When that happens, the ball bounces just as it does on any other collision, but the brick disappears. The third diagram shows what the game looks like after that collision and after you have moved the paddle to line it up with the oncoming ball. The play continues in this way until one of the following conditions occurs:

- The ball hits the lower wall, which means that you must have missed it with the paddle. In this case, the turn ends and the next ball is served, assuming that you have not already exhausted your allotment of three turns. If you have, the game ends in a loss.
- The last brick is eliminated. In this case, the game ends immediately, and you can retire in victory.

After all the bricks in a particular column have been cleared, a path will open to the top wall. When this delightful situation occurs, the ball will often bounce back and forth several times between the top wall and the upper line of bricks without the user ever having to worry about hitting the ball with the paddle. This condition is a reward for "breaking out" and gives meaning to the name of the game. The diagram on the right shows the situation shortly after the first ball has broken through the wall. That ball will go on to clear several more bricks before it comes back down the open channel.

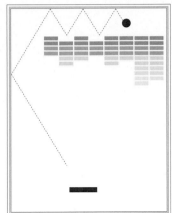

It is important to note that, even though breaking out is a very exciting part of the player's experience, you don't have to do anything special in your program to make it happen. The game is operating by the same rules as always: bouncing off walls, clearing bricks, and obeying the laws of physics.

The only part of the implementation that does require some explanation is the problem of checking to see whether the ball has collided with a brick or the paddle. The easiest strategy to adopt is to call `getElementAt(x, y)`, which returns the object that covers the point (**x**, **y**) on the canvas. particular *x* and *y* coordinate. If there are no graphical objects at that position, `getElementAt` returns the constant **null**. If there is more than one, `getElementAt` always chooses the one closest to the front in the stacking order.

Given that the ball is not a single point, it is not sufficient to check only the coordinates of the center. In this program, the simplest strategy is to check the four corner points on the square in which the ball is inscribed. The fact that a **GOval** is defined in terms of its bounding rectangle means that if the upper left corner of the ball is at the point (x, y), the other corners will be at the locations shown in this diagram:

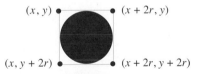

These points have the advantage of being outside the ball—which means that `getElementAt` can't return the ball itself—but nonetheless close enough to make it appear that collisions have occurred. Thus, for each of these four points, you need to call `getElementAt` on that location to see whether anything is there. If the value you get back is not **null**, you need look no further and can take that value as the **GObject** with which the collision occurred. If `getElementAt` returns **null** at all four corners, no collision exists.

11. Although Congress adopted a law in 1866 declaring it lawful "to employ the weights and measures of the metric system in all contracts, dealings or court proceedings," the traditional English system of units still prevails in the United States, except in scientific research. As a result, Americans still have to learn the conversion rules for English units, at least to the point of knowing the familiar rules on the left and possibly also the more esoteric rules on the right:

12 inches	= 1 foot	6 feet	= 1 fathom
3 feet	= 1 yard	16.5 feet	= 1 rod
5280 feet	= 1 mile	220 yards	= 1 furlong

To help users make sense of all these units, write a **LengthConverter** program that translates back and forth between the various units. The user interface for your program should look like this:

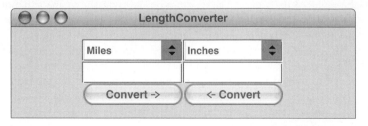

Each of the choosers on the top row should allow the user to select any of the seven possible units: inches, feet, yards, fathoms, rods, furlongs, and miles. To perform a conversion, the user should select the units, enter a number into either of the numeric fields, and then click the appropriate conversion button. For example, if you wanted to convert 18 inches to feet, you could change the left chooser to indicate feet, enter the value 18 into the numeric field on the right, and then click the button below that field. The program should use the **JComboBox** settings to determine the conversion factor and then compute a new result to store in the other numeric field, like this:

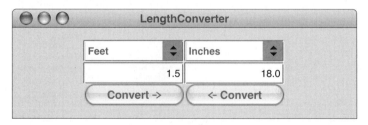

As with the **TemperatureConverter** program in Figure 10-12, your program should also allow the user to trigger the conversion by typing the ENTER key in either of the fields.

The easiest strategy for coping with the fact that this program allows the user to choose two different units is to convert the value from the input field into inches and then perform a second conversion to get the final value. To implement this strategy, you will need to include some mechanism in the code for determining the conversion factor for each of the units to the equivalent number of inches. One strategy is to code this information explicitly in a series of **if** statements. You could, however, also adopt the strategy from exercise 6 to store the conversion factor along with the chooser item.

12. Extend the **Calculator** program so that it uses floating-point numbers instead of integers. Solving this problem includes making design decisions (such as where to add the decimal point key) as well as implementation changes that require at least some changes in several parts of the existing structure.

CHAPTER 11
Arrays and ArrayLists

Little boxes on a hillside, little boxes made of ticky-tacky
Little boxes, little boxes, little boxes all the same
There's a green one and a pink one and a blue one and a yellow one
And they're all made out of ticky-tacky and they all look just the same
—Malvina Reynolds, "Little Boxes," 1962

Bob Frankston and Dan Bricklin

In modern computing, one of the most visible applications of the array structure described in this chapter is the electronic spreadsheet, which uses a two-dimensional array to store tabular data. The first electronic spreadsheet was VisiCalc, which was released in 1979 by Software Arts Incorporated, a small startup company founded by MIT graduates Dan Bricklin and Bob Frankston. VisiCalc proved to be a popular application, leading many larger firms to develop competing products, including Lotus 1 2 3 and, more recently, Microsoft Excel.

Up to now, most of the programs in this book have worked with individual data items. The real power of computing, however, comes from the ability to work with collections of data. This chapter introduces the idea of an **array,** which is an ordered collection of values of the same type. Arrays are important in programming largely because such collections occur quite often in the real world. Whenever you want to represent a set of values in which it makes sense to think about those values as forming a sequence, arrays are likely to play a role in the solution.

At the same time, arrays, in and of themselves, are becoming less important because Java's library packages include classes that do everything that arrays do and more. Because they represent collections of individual data values, the classes that fill the traditional role of arrays are called **collection classes.** Increasingly, Java programmers rely on these collection classes to represent the kinds of data that would once have been stored in an array. Understanding collection classes, however, is much easier if you understand the array model, which forms the conceptual foundation for many of the collection classes. This chapter therefore begins with a discussion of arrays as they have been used since the early days of programming. The point, however, is less to ensure that you understand the details of array processing than it is to provide you with the intuition you need to understand how Java's collection classes work.

To give you a preview of the collection classes, this chapter include a discussion of the **ArrayList** class, which is the collection class most closely analogous to arrays themselves. A more complete discussion of Java's collection classes appears in Chapter 13.

11.1 Introduction to arrays

An **array** is a collection of individual values with two distinguishing characteristics:

1. *An array is ordered.* You must be able to enumerate the individual values in order: here is the first, here is the second, and so on.
2. *An array is homogeneous.* Every value stored in an array must be of the same type. Thus, you can define an array of integers or an array of floating-point numbers but not an array in which the two types are mixed.

From a holistic perspective, it is best to think of an array as a sequence of boxes, with one box for each data value in the array. Each of the values in an array is called an **element.** The following diagram, for example, represents an array with five elements:

Every array has two fundamental properties that apply to the array as a whole:

- The **element type,** which indicates what values may be stored in the elements
- The **length,** which is the number of elements the array contains

In Java, it is possible to specify these properties at different times. You define the element type when you declare the array variable; you set the length when you create the initial value. In most cases, however, you specify both properties in the same declaration, as described in the following section.

Array declaration

Like any other variable in Java, an array must be declared before it is used. The most common form for an array declaration is shown in the syntax box to the right. For example, the declaration

```
int[] intArray = new int[10];
```

declares an array named **intArray** with 10 elements, each of which is of type **int**. You can represent this declaration graphically by drawing a row of 10 boxes and giving the entire collection the name **intArray**:

> **Typical syntax for array declarations**
>
> *type*[] *identifier* = **new** *type*[*length*];
>
> where:
> *type* is the type of each element
> *name* is the name of the variable being declared as an array
> *length* is the number of elements that are allocated as part of the array

intArray

0	0	0	0	0	0	0	0	0	0
0	1	2	3	4	5	6	7	8	9

When Java creates a new array, it initializes each of its elements to the default value for its type. For numbers, that default value is zero, which is why a 0 appears in each element of **intArray**. All other types have a default value as well. For example, the default value for **boolean** is **false**, and the default for objects is **null**.

Each element in the array is identified by a numeric value called its **index.** In Java, the index numbers for an array always begin with 0 and run up to one less than the length of the array. Thus, in an array with 10 elements, the index numbers are 0, 1, 2, 3, 4, 5, 6, 7, 8, and 9, as the preceding diagram shows.

Although it is possible to use integer values—such as the 10 in the preceding example—to specify the length of an array, it is much more common to use named constants for this purpose. Suppose, for example, that you have been asked to define an array capable of holding the scores for a sporting event, such as gymnastics or figure skating, in which scores are assigned by a panel of judges. Each judge rates the performance on a scale from 0 to 10, with 10 being the highest. Because a score may include a decimal fraction, as in 9.9, each element of the array must be of type **double**. Moreover, because the number of judges might change from application to application, it makes sense to declare the length of the array using a named constant. In this case, the declaration of an array called **scores** might look like this:

```
private static final int N_JUDGES = 5;

double[] scores = new double[N_JUDGES];
```

This declaration introduces a new array called **scores** with five elements, as shown in the following diagram:

scores

0.0	0.0	0.0	0.0	0.0
0	1	2	3	4

In Java, the value used to specify the length of an array need not be a constant. If you want to make your sports-scoring program more general, you can read the number of judges from the user, as follows:

```
int nJudges = readInt("Enter number of judges: ");
double[] scores = new double[nJudges];
```

Array selection

Although there are some cases in which you can use an array value as a single entity, you will usually need to manipulate the individual elements. The process of identifying a particular element within an array is called **selection.** To specify the selection of an individual element, you first supply the name of the array and then follow it with the index written in square brackets. The result is a **selection expression,** which has the following form:

array[*index*]

Within a program, a selection expression acts just like a simple variable. You can use it in an expression, and, in particular, you can assign a value to it. Thus, if the first judge (judge #0, since Java counts array elements beginning at zero) awarded the contestant a score of 9.2, you could assign that score to the initial element of the array by writing the assignment statement

```
scores[0] = 9.2;
```

The effect of this assignment can be diagrammed as follows:

scores

9.2	0.0	0.0	0.0	0.0
0	1	2	3	4

You could then go ahead and assign scores for each of the other four judges using, for example, the statements

```
scores[1] = 9.9;
scores[2] = 9.7;
scores[3] = 9.0;
scores[4] = 9.6;
```

Executing these statements results in the following picture:

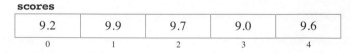

scores

9.2	9.9	9.7	9.0	9.6
0	1	2	3	4

In working with arrays, it is essential to understand the distinction between the *index* of an array element and the *value* of that element. For instance, the first box in the array has index 0, and its value is 9.2. It is also important to remember that you can change the values in an array but never the index numbers.

The power of array selection comes from the fact that the index value need not be constant, but may in fact be any expression that evaluates to an integer or any other scalar type. In many cases, the selection expression is the index variable of a **for** loop, which makes it easy to perform an operation on each element of the array in turn. For example, you can set each element in the **scores** array to 0.0 with the following statement:

```
for (int i = 0; i < nJudges; i++) {
   scores[i] = 0.0;
}
```

An example of a simple array

The program **GymnasticsJudge** given in Figure 11-1 provides a simple example of array manipulation. This program asks the user to enter the score for each judge and then displays the average score.

Running the **GymnasticsJudge** program with the data used in the examples in the preceding section produces the following sample run:

FIGURE 11-1   **Program to average an array of gymnastics scores**

```
/*
 * File: GymnasticsJudge.java
 * ---------------------------
 * This file reads in an array of scores and computes the
 * average.
 */

import acm.program.*;

public class GymnasticsJudge extends ConsoleProgram {

    public void run() {
        int nJudges = readInt("Enter number of judges: ");
        double[] scores = new double[nJudges];
        for (int i = 0; i < nJudges; i++) {
            scores[i] = readDouble("Score for judge " + i + ": ");
        }
        double total = 0;
        for (int i = 0; i < nJudges; i++) {
            total += scores[i];
        }
        double averageScore = total / nJudges;
        println("The average score is " + averageScore);
    }

}
```

```
 ● ● ●                    GymnasticsJudge
 Enter number of judges: 5
 Score for judge 0: 9.2
 Score for judge 1: 9.9
 Score for judge 2: 9.7
 Score for judge 3: 9.0
 Score for judge 4: 9.6
 The average score is 9.48
```

Changing the index range

In Java, the first element in every array is at index position 0. In many applications, however, this design may cause confusion for the user. To a nontechnical person using the **GymnasticsJudge** program, the fact that it asks about judge 0 is likely to be disconcerting. In the real world, we tend to number elements in a list beginning at 1. It would therefore be more natural for the program to ask the user to enter the scores for judges numbered from 1 to 5 instead.

There are two standard approaches for changing the index value the user sees:

1. Use the indices 0 to 4 internally, but add 1 to each index value when requesting data from the user or displaying output data. If you adopt this approach, the only part of the **GymnasticsJudge** program that needs to change is the **readDouble** statement that reads in each input value, which becomes

```
scores[i] = readDouble("Score for judge " + (i + 1) + ": ");
```

2. Declare the array with an extra element so that its indices run from 0 to 5, and then ignore element 0 entirely. Using this approach, the **run** method becomes

```
public void run() {
   int nJudges = readInt("Enter number of judges: ");
   double[] scores = new double[nJudges + 1];
   for (int i = 1; i <= nJudges; i++) {
      scores[i] = readDouble("Score for judge " + i + ": ");
   }
   double total = 0;
   for (int i = 1; i <= nJudges; i++) {
      total += scores[i];
   }
   double averageScore = total / nJudges;
   println("The average score is " + averageScore);
}
```

To allocate the extra element, this version of the **run** method declares the **scores** array using **nJudges + 1** to specify the array size.

The advantage of the first approach is that the internal array indices still begin with 0, which often makes it easier to use existing methods that depend on that assumption. The disadvantage is that the program requires two different sets of indices: an external set for the user and an internal set for the programmer. Even though the user sees a consistent and familiar index pattern, having to think about both sets of indices can complicate the programming process. The advantage of the second approach is that the programmer's indices match the user's.

Arrays of objects

The elements of an array are not restricted to the primitive types like **double** used in the **GymnasticsJudge** example but can equally well be objects of any Java class. For example, suppose that you want to declare an array to store the top five students in a class, where the individual elements are instances of the **Student** class defined in section 6.4. You could declare such an array as follows:

```
Student[] topStudents = new Student[5];
```

The effect of this declaration is to introduce an array in which each of the five elements is capable of holding a **Student** object. Those elements, however, are initialized to **null**, which is the default value for all objects. The array diagram after executing the declaration of **topStudents** therefore looks like this:

topStudents

null	null	null	null	null
0	1	2	3	4

You can assign new values to the elements of the **topStudents** array just as you would with an array of primitive values. For example, executing the statement

```
topStudents[0] = new Student("Hermione Granger", 314159);
```

replaces the **null** in the initial element with a new student object corresponding to Hermione Granger.

Using arrays in graphical programs

As you will see in several of the exercises at the end of this chapter, arrays are often useful in **GraphicsProgram**s. The implementation of the **acm.graphics** package itself uses arrays in several contexts. For example, the vertices of a **GPolygon** are stored internally as an array of **GPoint** objects. Creating an array of **GPoint** objects often makes sense at the application level as well.

As an example, the **YarnPattern** program in Figure 11-2 creates beautiful graphical patterns using only **GLine** objects. Each of the **GLine** objects connects two **GPoint**s stored in an array. The model for the pattern comes from a process that you can easily carry out in the real world as well. You begin by taking a rectangular board and arranging pegs or nails around the edges so that they are evenly spaced along all four edges. The code for the **YarnPattern** program defines the dimensions using the constants **N_ACROSS** and **N_DOWN**. The total number of pegs—given that **N_ACROSS** and **N_DOWN** are defined so that they don't count the corners twice—can then be defined as follows:

```
private static final int N_PEGS = 2 * N_ACROSS + 2 * N_DOWN;
```

FIGURE 11-2 **Program to create an intricate pattern of lines on the canvas**

```java
import acm.graphics.*;
import acm.program.*;
import java.awt.*;

/**
 * This program creates a pattern that simulates the process of winding a piece
 * of colored yarn around an array of pegs along the edges of the canvas.
 */
public class YarnPattern extends GraphicsProgram {

    public void run() {
        initPegArray();
        int thisPeg = 0;
        int nextPeg = -1;
        while (thisPeg != 0 || nextPeg == -1) {
            nextPeg = (thisPeg + DELTA) % N_PEGS;
            GPoint p0 = pegs[thisPeg];
            GPoint p1 = pegs[nextPeg];
            GLine line = new GLine(p0.getX(), p0.getY(), p1.getX(), p1.getY());
            line.setColor(Color.MAGENTA);
            add(line);
            thisPeg = nextPeg;
        }
    }

/* Initializes the array of pegs */
    private void initPegArray() {
        int pegIndex = 0;
        for (int i = 0; i < N_ACROSS; i++) {
            pegs[pegIndex++] = new GPoint(i * PEG_SEP, 0);
        }
        for (int i = 0; i < N_DOWN; i++) {
            pegs[pegIndex++] = new GPoint(N_ACROSS * PEG_SEP, i * PEG_SEP);
        }
        for (int i = N_ACROSS; i > 0; i--) {
            pegs[pegIndex++] = new GPoint(i * PEG_SEP, N_DOWN * PEG_SEP);
        }
        for (int i = N_DOWN; i > 0; i--) {
            pegs[pegIndex++] = new GPoint(0, i * PEG_SEP);
        }
    }

/* Private constants */
    private static final int DELTA = 67;        /* How many pegs to advance        */
    private static final int PEG_SEP = 10;      /* Pixels separating each peg      */
    private static final int N_ACROSS = 50;     /* Pegs across (minus one corner) */
    private static final int N_DOWN = 30;       /* Pegs down (minus one corner)   */
    private static final int N_PEGS = 2 * N_ACROSS + 2 * N_DOWN;

/* Private instance variables */
    private GPoint[] pegs = new GPoint[N_PEGS];

}
```

The process of generating the diagram consists of winding a piece of colored yarn around the pegs, starting with the peg in the upper left corner and then stretching it to a peg a fixed distance away around the perimeter. That distance is given by the parameter **DELTA**, which is typically larger than **N_ACROSS** or **N_DOWN**, but less than their sum. From this peg, the process continues by moving forward **DELTA** steps in the peg array each time until the yarn loops back to its starting point. The output of the **YarnPattern** program given the constant values shown in the code appears in Figure 11-3. By changing those constants, you can create other interesting patterns composed entirely of straight lines.

A digression on the ++ and –– operators

The **YarnPattern** program introduces a new feature of Java that you will undoubtedly encounter if you find yourself reading existing Java code. That feature appears in the statement

```
pegs[pegIndex++] = new GPoint( . . . );
```

which occurs four times in the **initPegArray** method with different arguments for the **GPoint** constructor.

Up to now, the programs in this text have executed the **++** and **––** operators only for the effect on their operands—they either add or subtract one from the variable to which they are applied. As it happens, these operators are much more versatile than

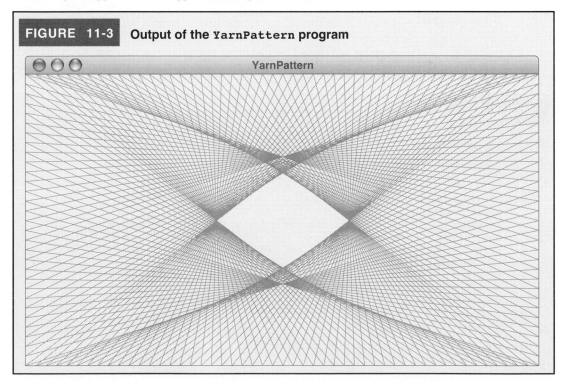

FIGURE 11-3 **Output of the YarnPattern program**

YarnPattern

the examples you have seen would suggest. First of all, each of these operators can be written in either of two ways. The operator can come after the operand to which it applies, as in the familiar

   x++

or before the operand, as in

   ++x

The first form, in which the operator follows the operand, is called the **postfix** form, and the second is called the **prefix** form.

   If all you do is execute the **++** operator in isolation—as you do if it acts as a separate statement or as the increment operator in a **for** loop—the prefix and postfix operators have precisely the same effect. The difference comes into play only if you use these operators as part of a larger expression. Like all operators, the **++** operator returns a value, but the value depends on where the operator is written relative to the operand. The two cases are as follows:

x++   Calculates the value of **x** first and then increments it. The value returned to the surrounding expression is the original value *before* the increment operation is performed.

++x   Increments the value of **x** first and then uses the new value as the value of the **++** operation as a whole.

The **--** operator behaves similarly, except that the value is decremented rather than incremented.

   The program in Figure 11-4 illustrates the difference between the prefix and postfix forms of the **++** operator, explaining its operation as it goes. The first four

---

FIGURE 11-4   **Program to illustrate the result of applying the ++ operator**

```
import acm.program.*;

/** This program illustrates the prefix and postfix forms of the ++ operator */
public class IncrementOperatorExample extends ConsoleProgram {

    public void run() {
        int x = INITIAL_VALUE;
        println("If x initially has the value " + x + ", evaluating ++x");
        int result = ++x;
        println("changes x to " + x + " and returns the value " + result + ".");
        x = INITIAL_VALUE;
        println("Conversely, if x has the value " + x + ", evaluating x++");
        result = x++;
        println("changes x to " + x + " but returns the value " + result + ".");
    }

/* Private constants */
    private static final int INITIAL_VALUE = 5;

}
```

statements trace the computation of the prefix form of the **++** operator, and the next four do the same for the postfix form. The output of the program looks like this:

```
●●●                    IncrementOperatorExample
If x initially has the value 5, evaluating ++x
changes x to 6 and returns the value 6.
Conversely, if x has the value 5, evaluating x++
changes x to 6 but returns the value 5.
```

The effect, therefore, of the statement

```
pegs[pegIndex++] = new GPoint( . . . );
```

is to assign the **GPoint** value to the element of the **pegs** array at the index specified by the *current* value of **pegIndex**, but then to increment **pegIndex** so that it indicates the next element position for the next cycle of the loop.

11.2 Internal representation of arrays

Although the various examples earlier in this chapter give you a sense of how to use arrays in your programs, the programs are too simple to illustrate certain important issues that arise when using arrays. In particular, none of the programs you have seen so far include methods that take arrays as arguments or return an array as a result. In order to write more sophisticated programs that use arrays, you will need to learn how to pass array information back and forth from one method to another.

Before you can appreciate the details of how array data can be communicated between two methods, it is important to understand how arrays are represented in memory. In Java, passing an array—or any object, for that matter, as you saw in Chapter 7—as an argument to a method does not initially appear to work in the way as passing a simple variable. If you understand how arrays are represented inside the computer, Java's handling of arrays as arguments makes sense. If you don't understand the internal representation, Java's approach seems completely baffling.

In Chapter 7, you had the opportunity to learn a little bit about the way memory works. In particular, you learned that objects are stored in a region of memory called the *heap* and that each object is identified by its *address* in memory. In Java, all arrays are represented internally as objects and are stored in exactly the same way. The internal representation of an array value therefore consists of some standard information common to all objects, followed by the memory needed to store the elements of the array in consecutive locations within the heap.

To get a sense of how this works, consider what happens when you issue the local variable declaration

```
double[] scores = new double[N_JUDGES];
```

where **N_JUDGES** is defined to be the constant 5. Although you can usually think of this declaration pattern as a single operation, it actually consists of two distinct parts. The declaration to the left of the equal sign introduces a variable named `scores`, which, like all local variables, is stored on the stack. The stack, however, does not include the space for the actual elements. The array of `double`s is created by the initializer that appears to the right of the equal sign. The expression

new double[N_JUDGES]

allocates an array object in the heap that contains information common to all objects, the length of the array (in this case, five), and enough space for five values of type `double`. The five values themselves consume 40 bytes of memory, which you can calculate as follows:

$$8 \text{ bytes/element} \times 5 \text{ elements} = 40 \text{ bytes}$$

The `scores` variable itself is large enough to store only the address of the array object in the heap. The internal picture of memory therefore looks like the diagram shown in Figure 11-5.

The situation in the example of the `Student` array is even more convoluted. Figure 11-6 shows the layout of memory after executing the statements:

```
Student[] topStudents = new Student[5];
topStudents[0] = new Student("Hermione Granger", 314159);
```

This example involves three objects: the array itself, the result of the call to the `Student` constructor, and the string used to record Hermione's name. Each of these objects is stored on the heap, as shown in the diagram. The internal representation for the `String` object—which is diagrammed here as if it were a simple array of characters—is not entirely accurate, but the details of that representation lie beyond the scope of this text. The important idea conveyed by the diagram is that the memory allocated for the string is on the heap.

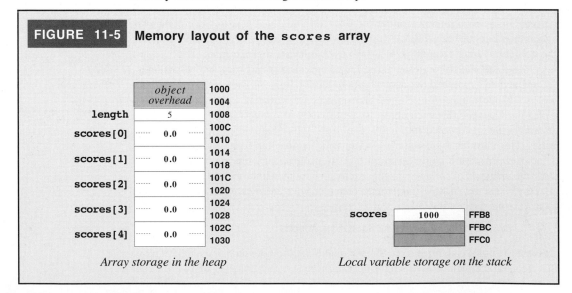

FIGURE 11-5 **Memory layout of the `scores` array**

Array storage in the heap

Local variable storage on the stack

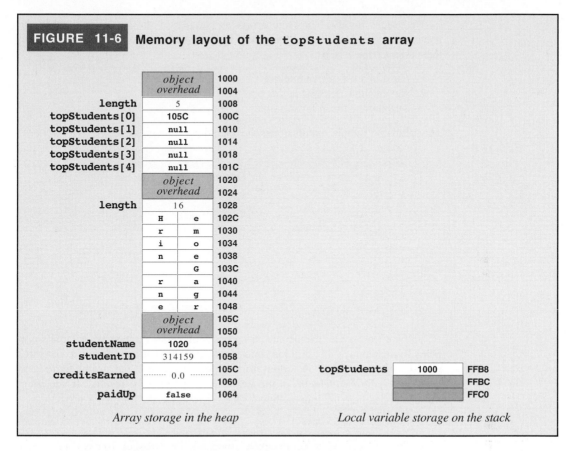

FIGURE 11-6 Memory layout of the `topStudents` array

	object overhead	1000
		1004
`length`	5	1008
`topStudents[0]`	105C	100C
`topStudents[1]`	null	1010
`topStudents[2]`	null	1014
`topStudents[3]`	null	1018
`topStudents[4]`	null	101C
	object overhead	1020
		1024
`length`	16	1028

H	e	102C
r	m	1030
i	o	1034
n	e	1038
	G	103C
r	a	1040
n	g	1044
e	r	1048

	object overhead	105C
		1050
`studentName`	1020	1054
`studentID`	314159	1058
		105C
`creditsEarned`	0.0	1060
`paidUp`	false	1064

`topStudents`	1000	FFB8
		FFBC
		FFC0

Array storage in the heap   *Local variable storage on the stack*

These memory diagrams contain far more information than necessary if all you are concerned with is having a mental image of the list of values in an array. For that level of abstraction, a simple box diagram is sufficient. The more accurate reductionistic model, however, is useful in understanding how array values are assigned or passed as parameters, as discussed in the section that follows.

11.3 Passing arrays as parameters

As you know from Chapter 5, the key to writing a large program is breaking it down into methods, each of which is small enough for you to comprehend as a unit. The individual methods communicate by passing parameters from one method to another. If a large program involves arrays, decomposing that program will often require you to define methods that pass entire arrays as parameters. In Java, the operation of passing an array as a parameter is closely tied to the internal representation of arrays in memory and can therefore seem mysterious. Now that you have some idea of that internal representation, you are ready to learn how array parameters work and how to use them effectively.

The issues involved in using arrays as parameters are best illustrated in the context of a simple example. Suppose that you have been asked to write a program that performs these steps:

1. Read in a list of five integers
2. Reverse the elements in that list
3. Display the list in reverse order

The following sample run illustrates the operation of the program:

```
○ ○ ○                    ReverseIntArray
This program reverses an integer array.
 ? 10
 ? 20
 ? 30
 ? 40
 ? 50
50
40
30
20
10
```

To give you some insight into the process of passing arrays as parameters, it helps to decompose this program into three methods that correspond to the three phases of the program's operation: reading the input values and storing them in an array, reversing the elements of the array, and displaying the results. If you adopt this decomposition, the **run** method for the program has the following structure:

```java
public void run() {
    int[] array = new int[N_VALUES];
    println("This program reverses an integer array.");
    readArray(array);
    reverseArray(array);
    printArray(array);
}
```

Although this decomposition makes intuitive sense, it will work correctly only if Java allows methods to change the values of array elements that are passed to those methods as arguments. If you pass a primitive value like an integer, Java copies the value, which means that it is impossible for a method to change it. As you learned in Chapter 7, however, passing an object as parameter to a method means that only the reference is copied, so the method effectively shares the object with the caller. The important question that arises in the suggested decomposition of the **ReverseArray** program is therefore whether arrays are treated as if they are primitive values or as if they are objects. The answer is that Java defines all arrays as objects, which in turn means that the elements of an array are shared between the calling method and the method being called.

Before going a bit more deeply into the details of how Java treats array parameters, it helps to expand a few of the methods in the proposed decomposition of the `ReverseArray` program. The simplest method is `printArray`, which is implemented like this:

```
private void printArray(int[] array) {
   for (int i = 0; i < array.length; i++) {
      println(array[i]);
   }
}
```

The declaration of the array parameter looks exactly like the definition of an array variable, but without the expression that specifies the initial value. That value is supplied by the caller, so the only thing the method needs to know is the fact that the parameter is an array of integers. The body of the `printArray` method uses a `for` loop to cycle through each element of the array and then calls `println` to display that value.

The only new feature in this implementation is the expression used as the upper bound of the `for` loop, which is written as

`array.length`

Every array in Java has a `length` field, which tells you how many elements the array contains. The fact that the length of the array is represented as if it were a field within an object and not as a method will almost certainly confuse you at some point, particularly if you try to make logical connections between arrays and other Java classes. For example, if you observe that arrays are conceptually sequences of objects in much the same way that strings are sequences of characters, it will seem odd that arrays use a `length` *field* but the `String` class uses a `length` *method*.

In the case of `printArray`, it doesn't matter how Java implements the process of passing an array to a method. If Java were to copy the entire array, the result would be just what you expected because `printArray` is merely looking up the values in the array without attempting to change them. The situation is different for `readArray`, which has to assign new values to the elements. The code, however, is very closely parallel to that of `printArray`:

```
private void readArray(int[] array) {
   for (int i = 0; i < array.length; i++) {
      array[i] = readInt(" ? ");
   }
}
```

Here, correct execution of the `readArray` method depends on being able to store new values in the array elements. If you think back to the diagram in Figure 11-5, you will see that the value being passed as the parameter `array` is merely the address of the array in the heap and does not contain the array elements themselves. As is true for any object passed as a parameter, this address gets copied into the corresponding parameter variable inside `readArray`, but continues to refer to the same object in the heap.

The one piece of the `ReverseArray` program that you have not yet seen is the `reverseArray` method itself. The basic algorithm is simple: to reverse an array, you need to exchange the first element with the last one, the second element with

> **COMMON PITFALLS**
>
> It is easy to forget that you use a different syntax to determine the length of an array than you use to find the length of a string. In Java, every array object has a `length` field that you select and not a method that you call.

the next-to-last one, and so on until all the elements have been exchanged. Because arrays are numbered beginning at 0, the last element in an array of **n** items is at index **n – 1**, the next-to-last element is at index **n – 2**, and so forth. In fact, given any integer index **i**, the array element that occurs **i** elements from the end is always at index position

```
n - i - 1
```

Thus, in order to reverse the elements of **array**, all you need to do is swap the values in **array[i]** and **array[n – i – 1]** for each index value **i** from the beginning of the array up to the center, which falls at index position **n / 2**. As soon as you reach the center, the elements in the second half of the array will already have their correct values because each cycle of the **for** loop correctly repositions two array elements—one in each half. In pseudocode, the implementation of **reverseArray** is therefore

```
private void reverseArray(int[] array) {
    for (int i = 0; i < array.length / 2; i++) {
        Swap the values in array[i] and array[n - i - 1]
    }
}
```

The operation of swapping two values in an array is useful even beyond the bounds of this example. For this reason, it makes sense to define that operation as a separate method and to replace the remaining pseudocode in **reverseArray** with a single method call.

Although it is tempting to try, the method call that exchanges the two elements cannot possibly be written as

```
swapElements(array[i], array[n - i - 1]);
```

In this call, the arguments to **swapElements** are individual array elements. Array elements act like simple variables and are therefore copied to the corresponding formal parameters. The **swapElements** method could interchange the local copies of these values but could not make permanent assignments to the calling arguments.

To avoid this problem, you can simply pass the entire array to the method that performs the swap operation, along with the two indices that indicate the positions that should be exchanged. For example, the call

```
swapElements(array, i, n - i - 1);
```

exchanges the elements at index positions **i** and **n – i – 1** of **array**, which is precisely what you need to replace the pseudocode in **reverseArray**.

Implementing **swapElements** is a little more complicated than it first appears. You cannot simply assign one element to another because the original value of the destination would then be lost. The easiest way to handle the problem is to use a local variable to hold one of the values temporarily. If you hold onto the value of one of the elements, you are then free to assign the other value directly, after which you can copy the first value from the temporary variable.

Suppose you want to exchange the values in **array** at positions 0 and 4. The strategy requires three separate steps.

1. Store the value in **array[0]** in the temporary variable, as illustrated in the following diagram:

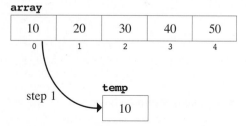

2. Copy the value from **array[4]** into **array[0]**, leaving the following configuration:

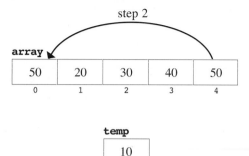

Because the old value of **array[0]** has previously been stored in **temp**, no information is lost.

3. Assign the value in **temp** to **array[4]**, as shown in this diagram:

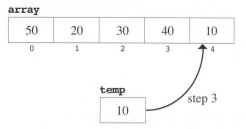

This three-step strategy is used as the basis for the following implementation of **swapElements**:

```
private void swapElements(int[] array, int p1, int p2) {
    int temp = array[p1];
    array[p1] = array[p2];
    array[p2] = temp;
}
```

This method fills in the last missing piece of the **ReverseArray** program, which appears in its complete form in Figure 11-7.

FIGURE 11-7   **Program to reverse an integer array**

```
import acm.program.*;

/**
 * This program reads in an array of five integers and then displays
 * those elements in reverse order.
 */
public class ReverseIntArray extends ConsoleProgram {

    public void run() {
        int[] array = new int[N_VALUES];
        println("This program reverses an integer array.");
        readArray(array);
        reverseArray(array);
        printArray(array);
    }

/* Reads the data into the array */
    private void readArray(int[] array) {
        for (int i = 0; i < array.length; i++) {
            array[i] = readInt(" ? ");
        }
    }

/* Prints the data from the array, one element per line */
    private void printArray(int[] array) {
        for (int i = 0; i < array.length; i++) {
            println(array[i]);
        }
    }

/* Reverses the data in the array */
    private void reverseArray(int[] array) {
        for (int i = 0; i < array.length / 2; i++) {
            swapElements(array, i, array.length - i - 1);
        }
    }

/* Exchanges two elements in an array */
    private void swapElements(int[] array, int p1, int p2) {
        int temp = array[p1];
        array[p1] = array[p2];
        array[p2] = temp;
    }

/* Private constants */
    private static final int N_VALUES = 5;
}
```

11.4 Using arrays for tabulation

The data structure of a program is typically designed to reflect the organization of data in the real-world domain of the application. If you are writing a program to solve a problem that involves a list of values, the idea of using an array to represent that list makes intuitive sense. For example, in the **GymnasticsJudge** program shown in Figure 11-1, the problem involves a list of scores—one for each of five judges. Because the individual scores form a list in the conceptual domain of the application, it is not surprising that you would use an array to represent the data in the program. The array elements have a direct correspondence to the individual data items in the list. Thus, **scores[0]** corresponds to the score for judge #0, **scores[1]** to the score for judge #1, and so on.

In general, whenever an application involves data that can be represented in the form of a list like

$$a_0, a_1, a_2, a_3, a_4, \ldots , a_{N-1}$$

an array is the natural choice for the underlying representation. It is also quite common for programmers to refer to the index of an array element as a **subscript,** reflecting the fact that arrays are used to hold data that would typically be written with subscripts in mathematics.

There are, however, important uses of arrays in which the relationship between the data in the application domain and the data in the program takes a different form. Instead of storing the data values in successive elements of an array, for some applications it makes more sense to use the data to generate array indices. Those indices are then used to select elements in an array that records some statistical property of the data as a whole.

Understanding how this approach works and appreciating how it differs from more traditional uses of arrays requires looking at a concrete example. Suppose you want to write a program that reads lines of text from the user and keeps track of how often each of the 26 letters appears. When the user types a blank line to signal the end of the input, the program should display a table indicating how many times each letter appears in the input data.

In order to generate this kind of letter-frequency table, the program has to search each line of text character by character. Every time a letter appears, the program must update a running count that keeps track of how often that letter has appeared so far in the input. The interesting part of the problem lies in designing the data structure necessary to maintain a count for each of the 26 letters.

It is possible to solve this problem without arrays by defining 26 separate variables—**nA, nB, nC,** and so forth up to **nZ**—and then using a **switch** statement to check all 26 cases:

```
switch (Character.toUpperCase(ch)) {
   case 'A': nA++; break;
   case 'B': nB++; break;
   case 'C': nC++; break;
   . . .
   case 'Z': nZ++; break;
}
```

This process results in a long, repetitive program. A better approach is to combine the 26 individual variables into an array and then use the character code to select the appropriate element within the array. Each element contains an integer representing the current count of the letter that corresponds to that index in the array. If you call the array `letterCounts`, you can declare it by writing

```
int[] letterCounts = new int[26];
```

This declaration allocates space for an integer array with 26 elements, as shown in this diagram:

letterCounts

0	1	2	3	4	5	6	7	8	9	10	11	12	13	14	15	16	17	18	19	20	21	22	23	24	25

Each time a letter character appears in the input, you need to increment the corresponding element in `letterCounts`. Finding the element to increment is simply a matter of converting the character into an integer in the range 0 to 25 by using character arithmetic as discussed in Chapter 8. The code for the `CountLetterFrequencies` program appears in Figure 11-8.

11.5 Initialization of arrays

Like any other variable, array variables can be declared as either local variables or instance variables. In either case, an array can also be given an initial set of values using a very convenient syntax, in which the equal sign specifying the initial value is followed by a list of the initial values for each element, enclosed in curly braces. For example, the declaration

```
int[] digits = { 0, 1, 2, 3, 4, 5, 6, 7, 8, 9 };
```

introduces a local variable called `digits` in which each of the 10 elements is initialized to its own index number.

As a second example, imagine you're writing a program that requires an array containing the names of all U.S. cities with populations of over 1,000,000. Taking data from the 2000 census, you could declare that array as a named constant using the following code:

```
private static final String[] US_CITIES_OVER_ONE_MILLION = {
    "New York",
    "Los Angeles",
    "Chicago",
    "Houston",
    "Philadelphia",
    "Phoenix",
    "San Diego",
    "San Antonio",
    "Dallas",
};
```

FIGURE 11-8   Program to produce a letter-frequency table

```
import acm.program.*;

/**
 * This program creates a table of the letter frequencies in a
 * paragraph of input text terminated by a blank line.
 */
public class CountLetterFrequencies extends ConsoleProgram {

    public void run() {
        println("This program counts letter frequencies.");
        println("Enter a blank line to indicate the end of the text.");
        initFrequencyTable();
        while (true) {
            String line = readLine();
            if (line.length() == 0) break;
            countLetterFrequencies(line);
        }
        printFrequencyTable();
    }

/* Initializes the frequency table to contain zeros */
    private void initFrequencyTable() {
        frequencyTable = new int[26];
        for (int i = 0; i < 26; i++) {
            frequencyTable[i] = 0;
        }
    }

/* Counts the letter frequencies in a line of text */
    private void countLetterFrequencies(String line) {
        for (int i = 0; i < line.length(); i++) {
            char ch = line.charAt(i);
            if (Character.isLetter(ch)) {
                int index = Character.toUpperCase(ch) - 'A';
                frequencyTable[index]++;
            }
        }
    }

/* Displays the frequency table */
    private void printFrequencyTable() {
        for (char ch = 'A'; ch <= 'Z'; ch++) {
            int index = ch - 'A';
            println(ch + ": " + frequencyTable[index]);
        }
    }

/* Private instance variables */
    private int[] frequencyTable;

}
```

Note that the last initializer for the `US_CITIES_OVER_ONE_MILLION` array is followed by a comma. This comma is optional, but it is often makes sense to include it. Doing so allows you to add new cities at the end without having to change the existing entries. For example, if metropolitan growth rates continue on their current trajectory, San Jose, California, will join this list in 2010. To add it to the end of the list, all you would need to do is add the line

```
"San Jose",
```

to the initializer list. You would not need to go back and add a comma to the end of the preceding entry.

■ 11.6 Multidimensional arrays

In Java, the elements of an array can be of any type. In particular, the elements of an array can themselves be arrays. Arrays of arrays are called **multidimensional arrays.** The most common form of multidimensional array is the two-dimensional array, which is most often used to represent data in which the individual entries form a rectangular structure marked off into rows and columns. This type of two-dimensional structure is called a **matrix.** Arrays of three or more dimensions are also legal in Java but occur much less frequently.

As an example of a two-dimensional array, suppose you wanted to represent a game of tic-tac-toe as part of a program. As you probably know, tic-tac-toe is played on a board consisting of three rows and three columns, as follows:

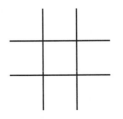

Players take turns placing the letters *X* and *O* in the empty squares, trying to line up three identical symbols horizontally, vertically, or diagonally.

To represent the tic-tac-toe board, the most sensible strategy is to use a two-dimensional array with three rows and three columns. Although you could also define an enumeration type to represent the three possible contents of each square—empty, *X*, and *O*—it is probably simpler in this case to use **char** as the element type and to represent the three legal states for each square using the characters `' '`, `'X'`, and `'O'`. The declaration for the tic-tac-toe board would then be written as

```
char[][] board = new char[3][3];
```

Given this declaration, you could then refer to the characters representing the individual squares on the board by supplying two separate indices, one specifying the row number and another specifying the column number. In this representation, each number varies over the range 0 to 2, and the individual positions in the board have the following names:

board[0][0]	board[0][1]	board[0][2]
board[1][0]	board[1][1]	board[1][2]
board[2][0]	board[2][1]	board[2][2]

Internally, Java represents the variable **board** as an array of three elements, each of which is an array of three characters. The memory allocated to **board** consists of nine characters arranged in the following form:

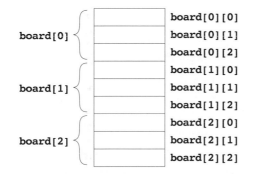

In the two-dimensional diagram of the **board** array, the first index is assumed to indicate the row number. This choice, however, is arbitrary because the two-dimensional geometry of the matrix is entirely conceptual; in memory, these values form a one-dimensional list. If you wanted the first index to indicate the column and the second to indicate the row, the only methods you would need to change would be those that depend on the conceptual geometry, such as a method that displays the current state of the board. In terms of the internal arrangement, however, it is always true that if you look at how the elements are arranged in memory, the first index value varies less rapidly than the second, and so on. Thus all the elements of **board[0]** appear in memory before any elements of **board[1]**.

Passing multidimensional arrays to methods

Multidimensional arrays are passed between methods just as single-dimensional arrays are. The parameter declaration in the method header looks like the original declaration of the variable and includes the index information. For example, the following method displays the current state of the **board** array:

```
        private void displayBoard(char[][] board) {
            for (int row = 0; row < 2; row++) {
                if (row > 0) println("-----+-----+-----");
                println("     |     |");
                print("  ");
                for (int col = 0; col < 2; col++) {
                    if (col > 0) print("  |  ");
                    print(board[row][col]);
                }
                println();
                println("     |     |");
            }
        }
```

Much of the code in **DisplayBoard** is used to format the output so that the board appears in an easy-to-read form.

Initializing multidimensional arrays

You can use static initialization with multidimensional arrays just as with single-dimensional arrays. To emphasize the overall structure, the values used to initialize each internal array are usually enclosed in an additional set of curly braces. For example, the declaration

```
        static double identityMatrix[3][3] = {
            { 1.0, 0.0, 0.0 },
            { 0.0, 1.0, 0.0 },
            { 0.0, 0.0, 1.0 }
        };
```

declares a 3x3 matrix of floating-point numbers and initializes it to contain the following values:

1.0	0.0	0.0
0.0	1.0	0.0
0.0	0.0	1.0

This particular matrix comes up frequently in mathematical applications and is called the **identity matrix.**

11.7 Image processing

In modern computing, one of the most important applications of two-dimensional arrays occurs in the field of computer graphics. As you learned in Chapter 2, graphical images are composed of individual pixels; Figure 2-10 offers a magnified view of the screen that shows how the pixels create the image as a whole. The connection with this chapter is that the pixels are arranged so that they form a two-dimensional array.

Representation of images

In Java, an image is a rectangular array in which the image as a whole is a sequence of rows, and each row is a sequence of individual pixel values. The value of each element in the array indicates the color that should appear in the corresponding pixel position on the screen. From Chapter 9, you know that you can specify a color in Java by indicating the intensity of each of the primary colors. Each of those intensities ranges from 0 to 255 and therefore fits in an eight-bit byte. The color as a whole is stored in a 32-bit integer that contains the red, green, and blue intensity values along with a measure of the transparency of the color, represented by the Greek letter alpha (α). For the opaque colors used in most images, the value of α is always 255, which is **11111111** in binary or **FF** in hexadecimal.

As an example, the following diagram shows the four bytes that form the color **PINK**, which Java defines using 255, 175, and 175 as the red, green, and blue components. Translating those values to their binary form gives you the following:

α	red	green	blue
1 1 1 1 1 1 1 1	1 1 1 1 1 1 1 1	1 0 1 0 1 1 1 1	1 0 1 0 1 1 1 1

The fact that Java packs all the information about a color into a 32-bit integer means that you can store an image as a two-dimensional array of type **int**. At the outer level, each element of the array is an entire row of the image. In keeping with Java's coordinate system, the rows of an image are numbered from 0 starting at the top of the image. Each row is an array of type **int** representing the value of each pixel as you move from left to right across the image.

Using the **GImage** class to manipulate images

The **GImage** class in the **acm.graphics** package exports several methods that make it easy to perform basic image processing. Given a **GImage** object, you can obtain the two-dimensional array of pixel values by calling **getPixelArray**. Thus, if the variable **image** contains a **GImage**, you can retrieve its pixel array by calling

```
int[][] pixelArray = image.getPixelArray();
```

The height of the image is equal to the number of rows in the pixel array. The width is the number of elements in any of the rows, each of which has the same length in a rectangular image. Thus, you can initialize variables to hold the height and width of the pixel array like this:

```
int height = pixelArray.length;
int width = pixelArray[0].length;
```

The **GImage** class also includes a constructor that creates a new **GImage** object from a two-dimensional array.

These new capabilities in the **GImage** class make it possible for you to write programs to manipulate images, in much the same way that a commercial system like Adobe Photoshop™ does. The general strategy consists of the following three steps:

1. Use `getPixelArray` to obtain the array of pixel values.
2. Perform the desired transformation by manipulating the values in the array.
3. Call the `GImage` constructor to create a new object from the modified image.

The following method definition uses this pattern to flip an image vertically:

```
private GImage flipVertical(GImage image) {
    int[][] array = image.getPixelArray();
    int height = array.length;
    for (int p1 = 0; p1 < height / 2; p1++) {
        int p2 = height - p1 - 1;
        int[] temp = array[p1];
        array[p1] = array[p2];
        array[p2] = temp;
    }
    return new GImage(array);
}
```

In this example, you don't actually have to look at the individual pixels. All you have to do is reverse the order of the rows using precisely the same strategy as in the **reverseArray** method in Figure 11-7.

The **flipVertical** method would be quite useful in creating a better solution to exercise 16 in Chapter 9. In that exercise, your job was to write a program that simulates using a lens to create an image. Instead of requiring two image files—one for the original and one for its inverted form—you can now use a image file only for the original object and then call **flipVertical** to create the inverted image.

Bit manipulation

Most image manipulation operations, however, are not as simple as **flipVertical**. In most cases, you have to take apart the integers that represent the individual pixels so that you can obtain their red, green, and blue components. To do so, you will need the low-level operators that Java provides for manipulating the bits of a word in memory. These operators, which are listed in Figure 11-9, are called **bitwise operators.** They take values of any scalar type and interpret them as sequences of bits that correspond to their underlying representation at the hardware level.

FIGURE 11-9   **Bitwise operators in Java**

x & y	Logical AND. The result has a **1** bit in positions where both **x** and **y** have **1** bits.
x | y	Logical OR. The result has a **1** bit in positions where either **x** or **y** has a **1** bit.
x ^ y	Exclusive OR. The result has **1** bits in positions where the bits in **x** and **y** differ.
~x	Logical NOT. The result has a **1** bit where **x** has a **0** bit, and vice versa.
x << n	Left shift. Shift the bits in **x** left **n** bit positions, filling on the right with zeros.
x >> n	Right shift (arithmetic). Shift the bits right **n** bit positions, leaving the first bit unchanged.
x >>> n	Right shift (logical). Shift the bits right **n** bit positions, filling on the left with zeros.

To understand the behavior of the bitwise operators, it helps to consider some specific examples. Just for fun, let's imagine that the variables **x** and **y** have been declared and initialized as follows:

```
int x = 0xACCEDED;
int y = 0xDEFACED;
```

where the initial values are entirely meaningless as bit patterns but just happen to be two of the longest English words you can write using only the letters **A** through **F**. If you translate the hexadecimal digits into their underlying bit patterns, you will discover that these variables look like this inside the machine:

| x | 0 0 0 0 1 0 1 0 | 1 1 0 0 1 1 0 0 | 1 1 1 0 1 1 0 1 | 1 1 1 0 1 1 0 1 |

| y | 0 0 0 0 1 1 0 1 | 1 1 1 0 1 1 1 1 | 1 0 1 0 1 1 0 0 | 1 1 1 0 1 1 0 1 |

The **&**, **|**, and **^** operators apply the logical operation specified in Figure 11-8 to each bit position in their operands. The **&** operator, for example, produces a result that has a **1** bit only in positions in which both operands have **1** bits. For example, if you evaluated the expression **x & y**, Java would calculate the result as follows:

| x | 0 0 0 0 1 0 1 0 | 1 1 0 0 1 1 0 0 | 1 1 1 0 1 1 0 1 | 1 1 1 0 1 1 0 1 |

| y | 0 0 0 0 1 1 0 1 | 1 1 1 0 1 1 1 1 | 1 0 1 0 1 1 0 0 | 1 1 1 0 1 1 0 1 |

| x & y | 0 0 0 0 1 0 0 0 | 1 1 0 0 1 1 0 0 | 1 0 1 0 1 1 0 0 | 1 1 1 0 1 1 0 1 |

The computation for the **|** operator is similar, except that the result contains a **1** bit in those positions in which either or both of the operands have **1** bits:

| x | 0 0 0 0 1 0 1 0 | 1 1 0 0 1 1 0 0 | 1 1 1 0 1 1 0 1 | 1 1 1 0 1 1 0 1 |

| y | 0 0 0 0 1 1 0 1 | 1 1 1 0 1 1 1 1 | 1 0 1 0 1 1 0 0 | 1 1 1 0 1 1 0 1 |

| x | y | 0 0 0 0 1 1 1 1 | 1 1 1 0 1 1 1 1 | 1 1 1 0 1 1 0 1 | 1 1 1 0 1 1 0 1 |

The **^** operator produces a result that contains a **1** bit only in those positions in which the bits in the two operands differ:

| x | 0 0 0 0 1 0 1 0 | 1 1 0 0 1 1 0 0 | 1 1 1 0 1 1 0 1 | 1 1 1 0 1 1 0 1 |

| y | 0 0 0 0 1 1 0 1 | 1 1 1 0 1 1 1 1 | 1 0 1 0 1 1 0 0 | 1 1 1 0 1 1 0 1 |

| x ^ y | 0 0 0 0 0 1 1 1 | 0 0 1 0 0 0 1 1 | 0 1 0 0 0 0 0 1 | 0 0 0 0 0 0 0 0 |

The **~** operator takes only one operand and reverses the state of each of its bits. Thus, if you apply the **~** operator to the bit pattern in **x**, the result looks like this:

x	0 0 0 0 1 0 1 0	1 1 0 0 1 1 0 0	1 1 1 0 1 1 0 1	1 1 1 0 1 1 0 1

~x	1 1 1 1 0 1 0 1	0 0 1 1 0 0 1 1	0 0 0 1 0 0 1 0	0 0 0 1 0 0 1 0

In programming, applying the **~** operation is called **taking the complement** of its operand.

The **<<** operator is written in the form

value **<<** *number of bits*

This operator shifts the bits in the value specified on the left by the number of bit positions indicated to the right. Thus, the expression **x << 1** produces a new value in which every bit in the value of **x** is shifted one position to the left, as follows:

x	0 0 0 0 1 0 1 0	1 1 0 0 1 1 0 0	1 1 1 0 1 1 0 1	1 1 1 0 1 1 0 1

x << 1	0 0 0 1 0 1 0 1	1 0 0 1 1 0 0 1	1 1 0 1 1 0 1 1	1 1 0 1 1 0 1 0

The bits shifted in at the right end are always **0**.

Shifting in the rightward direction turns out to be more complicated. In Java, the right-shift operator comes in two forms. The **>>>** operator performs a **logical shift** in which the new bits that appear on the end are always **0**. The **>>** operator performs what computer scientists call an **arithmetic shift** in which the bit at the extreme left end of the word never changes. This bit is called the **high-order bit,** but is also referred to as the **sign bit** because it marks a negative number.

The distinction between the two forms of right shift are impossible to illustrate with the current value of **x** because it has a **0** in its high-order bit. Shifting a bit pattern that begins with a **0** gives you the same result no matter which of the two right-shift operators you use. The statement

```
x = Color.PINK.getRGB();
```

assigns a new value to **x** which is the bit pattern for a pink pixel, which, as you saw earlier in the chapter, has the following binary representation:

1 1 1 1 1 1 1 1	1 1 1 1 1 1 1 1	1 0 1 0 1 1 1 1	1 0 1 0 1 1 1 1

Assigning this new value to **x** makes it easy to illustrate the difference between the **>>** and **>>>** operators, as shown in the following diagram:

x	1 1 1 1 1 1 1 1	1 1 1 1 1 1 1 1	1 0 1 0 1 1 1 1	1 0 1 0 1 1 1 1

x >> 8	1 1 1 1 1 1 1 1	1 1 1 1 1 1 1 1	1 1 1 1 1 1 1 1	1 0 1 0 1 1 1 1
x >>> 8	0 0 0 0 0 0 0 0	1 1 1 1 1 1 1 1	1 1 1 1 1 1 1 1	1 0 1 0 1 1 1 1

Both operators shift the bits in the original word eight positions to the right, which has the effect of moving them to the next byte position. The **>>** operator filled the gap with **1** bits because the high-order bit was a **1** in the original word. The **>>** operator filled that gap with **0** bits, as it always does.

Using bit operations to isolate components of a pixel

The examples in the preceding section are likely to seem arcane because they are not immediately relevant to any practical application. The point of introducing Java's bit-manipulation operators is not to sow confusion but rather to give the tools you need to manipulate images. If you want to work with the individual components of a color, you need to have a way to take apart the components of a pixel value stored in an integer word. As it turns out, the bit-manipulation operators are just the tools you need.

At the end of the preceding section, the variable **x** was assigned the pixel value for the color **PINK**, which looks like this in binary form:

| 1 1 1 1 1 1 1 1 | 1 1 1 1 1 1 1 1 | 1 0 1 0 1 1 1 1 | 1 0 1 0 1 1 1 1 |

From this starting point, how would you go about determining the values of the red, green, and blue components?

Isolating the blue component turns out to be the easiest. All you have to do is compute the value of the expression **x & 0xFF**, like this:

| x | 1 1 1 1 1 1 1 1 | 1 1 1 1 1 1 1 1 | 1 0 1 0 1 1 1 1 | 1 0 1 0 1 1 1 1 |
| 0xFF | 0 0 0 0 0 0 0 0 | 0 0 0 0 0 0 0 0 | 0 0 0 0 0 0 0 0 | 1 1 1 1 1 1 1 1 |

| | 0 0 0 0 0 0 0 0 | 0 0 0 0 0 0 0 0 | 0 0 0 0 0 0 0 0 | 1 0 1 0 1 1 1 1 |

The result contains a **1** bit only in those places in which both operands have a **1** bit. Another way to look at this expression, however, is to notice that the only bits that can possibly be **1**s in the result are the ones that are **1**s in the constant **0xFF**. For those bits, the result is determined by the value of **x**. The effect therefore is that the **1** bits in **0xFF** select the bits from **x** that you want in the result. In computer science, this operation is called **masking.**

You can use masking to isolate the red and green components as well, but you have to shift the result to the right end of the word. For example, you can determine the red component by shifting the value of **x** by 16 bits and then once again using **0xFF** as a mask. This operation is illustrated in the following diagram:

| x >> 16 | 1 1 1 1 1 1 1 1 | 1 1 1 1 1 1 1 1 | 1 1 1 1 1 1 1 1 | 1 1 1 1 1 1 1 1 |
| 0xFF | 0 0 0 0 0 0 0 0 | 0 0 0 0 0 0 0 0 | 0 0 0 0 0 0 0 0 | 1 1 1 1 1 1 1 1 |

| | 0 0 0 0 0 0 0 0 | 0 0 0 0 0 0 0 0 | 0 0 0 0 0 0 0 0 | 1 1 1 1 1 1 1 1 |

As these diagrams indicate, you can compute the four components of a pixel value stored in the variable **x** using the following declarations:

```
int alpha = (x >> 24) & 0xFF;
int red = (x >> 16) & 0xFF;
int green = (x >> 8) & 0xFF;
int blue = x & 0xFF;
```

When you need to convert in the other direction—from individual components to a complete pixel value—you can use the | operator. In the typical case in which the transparency value is **0xFF**, you can create a complete pixel value from the variables **red**, **green**, and **blue** like this:

```
int pixel = (0xFF << 24) | (red << 16) | (green << 8) | blue;
```

Creating a grayscale image

One important application that illustrates the process of manipulating individual pixel values is the process of converting an image from color to **grayscale**, a format in which all the pixels are either black, white, or some intermediate shade of gray. For example, the pictures in this book were created as color images but need to be converted to grayscale before they can be printed on the page. That conversion is carried out automatically by the software at the publishing house, just as it is by a black-and-white printer if you send it a color image.

For the most part, the implementation of a **createGrayscaleImage** method follows the standard pattern used for image manipulation programs in general. You begin by retrieving the pixel array from the original image and then go through it modifying the individual pixel values. At the end, you create a new image from the modified pixel array. In this example, your goal is to replace each pixel with a new shade of gray that approximates the apparent brightness of that color. In computer graphics, that apparent brightness is called **luminosity.** If you had a function to compute the luminosity of a pixel given its red, green, and blue components, you could write the rest of the **createGrayscaleImage** method like this:

```
private GImage createGrayscaleImage(GImage image) {
    int[][] array = image.getPixelArray();
    int height = array.length;
    int width = array[0].length;
    for (int i = 0; i < height; i++) {
        for (int j = 0; j < width; j++) {
            int pixel = array[i][j];
            int red = (pixel >> 16) & 0xFF;
            int green = (pixel >> 8) & 0xFF;
            int blue = pixel & 0xFF;
            int xx = computeLuminosity(red, green, blue);
            pixel = (0xFF << 24) | (xx << 16) | (xx << 8) | xx;
            array[i][j] = pixel;
        }
    }
    return new GImage(array);
}
```

Although you can do a rough job of calculating luminosity simply by averaging the red, green, and blue components of a pixel, you can in fact do somewhat better than that. The goal of a grayscale conversion is to produce a shade of gray that approximates the brightness of each pixel to the eye. As it turns out, luminosity does not depend on the color components equally and is controlled much more strongly by how much green is in the pixel than by how much red or blue appears. Red and blue, after all, tend to make an image appear darker, while green tends to lighten things up. The formula for luminosity adopted by the standards committee responsible for television signals in the United States looks like this:

$$luminosity = 0.299 \times red + 0.587 \times green + 0.114 \times blue$$

You can easily code this calculation in Java using the following function:

```
private int computeLuminosity(int r, int g, int b) {
   return GMath.round(0.299 * r + 0.587 * g + 0.114 * b);
}
```

Smoothing an image through averaging

Digital image manipulation can often improve the quality of an image substantially, particularly if the original is of low resolution. Many of the images that come from space probes are deliberately taken at fairly low resolution to minimize the amount of data that needs to be transmitted back to earth. For example, instead of sending 32 bits per pixel for a full-color image, a space probe might choose instead to send four bits of grayscale, thereby reducing the transmission time by a factor of eight.

The Cassini probe that recently visited Saturn did precisely that. The top image in Figure 11-10 shows a picture taken by Cassini's wide-angle camera on January 23, 2005, at a distance of approximately 2.8 million kilometers from the planet. This image is blotchy because the image uses only 16 gray levels, which gives rise to the rough contours you see as you move across the planet. Such imperfections can easily be removed by digital filtering, as shown in the bottom image, in which the rough contours have disappeared.

Although the smoothing techniques that generate the bottom image involve mathematics beyond the scope of this book, you can take a step in that direction by writing a simple digital filter that averages the luminosity of each pixel with that of its neighbors directly above, below, to the left, and to the right. The resulting image has fewer rough edges because the pixel values are smoothed in the neighborhood of any discontinuity.

The code for the `applyAveragingFilter` method appears in Figure 11-11. The only wrinkle in the code is that the edges of the image must be treated differently to avoid selecting elements outside the bounds of the pixel array.

Hiding complexity

In the last few sections, you have learned a great deal about the details of bit manipulation—almost certainly more than you ever wanted to know. Now that you have done so, it makes sense to find a way to hide those details so that you never have to think about them again. The usual approach for doing so is to define methods that encapsulate the details inside their implementations, in keeping with the principle of information hiding introduced in Chapter 5. Defining methods to hide the details of bit manipulation seems like a good place to start.

FIGURE 11-10 An image of Saturn taken by the Cassini space probe

The original NASA image using 16-bit grayscale

The same image after applying a digital filter

Source: NASA Cassini web site

FIGURE 11-11   Code for the `applyAveragingFilter` method

```java
/*
 * Creates a new image by applying an averaging filter to the original.
 * Each pixel in the original image is replaced by a grayscale pixel with the
 * average luminosity of the current pixel and its four immediate neighbors.
 */
   private GImage applyAveragingFilter(GImage image) {
      int[][] array = image.getPixelArray();
      int height = array.length;
      int width = array[0].length;
      for (int i = 0; i < height; i++) {
         for (int j = 0; j < width; j++) {
            int xx = averageNeighborLuminosity(array, i, j);
            array[i][j] = (0xFF << 24) | (xx << 16) | (xx << 8) | xx;
         }
      }
      return new GImage(array);
   }

/*
 * Computes the average luminosity of the pixel at array[i][j] and its four
 * immediate neighbors (up, down, left, and right).
 */
   private int averageNeighborLuminosity(int[][] array, int i, int j) {
      int sum = getLuminosity(array, i, j);
      int count = 1;
      if (i > 0) {
         sum += getLuminosity(array, i - 1, j);
         count++;
      }
      if (i < array.length - 1) {
         sum += getLuminosity(array, i + 1, j);
         count++;
      }
      if (j > 0) {
         sum += getLuminosity(array, i, j - 1);
         count++;
      }
      if (j < array[0].length - 1) {
         sum += getLuminosity(array, i, j + 1);
         count++;
      }
      return GMath.round((double) sum / count);
   }

/* Determines the luminosity of the pixel at array[i][j] */
   private int getLuminosity(int[][] array, int i, int j) {
      int pixel = array[i][j];
      int red = (pixel >> 16) & 0xFF;
      int green = (pixel >> 8) & 0xFF;
      int blue = pixel & 0xFF;
      return GMath.round(0.299 * red + 0.587 * green + 0.114 * blue);
   }
```

When you design a method, it is important that your design take into account the interests of the client. In an image-manipulation program, the client is not interested in the details of shifting and masking going on at the lowest levels of the code. Instead, what the client presumably wants is the ability to get the red, green, and blue components from a pixel value and to put the same values back together to form a pixel. If those are indeed the operations that clients are likely to want, you might think about creating the following general methods to hide the complexity involved in bit manipulation:

```
public static int getRed(int pixel) {
    return (pixel >> 16) & 0xFF;
}

public static int getGreen(int pixel) {
    return (pixel >> 8) & 0xFF;
}

public static int getBlue(int pixel) {
    return pixel & 0xFF;
}

public static int createRGBPixel(int r, int g, int b) {
    return (0xFF << 24) | (r << 16) | (g << 8) | b;
}
```

These methods are declared as **public** because they are likely to serve the needs of external clients even more than they serve the person who wrote the code. After all, the author of these methods had to figure everything out in order to write the implementations. Clients who use these methods never have to learn these details at all. The methods are declared as **static** because they don't depend on any instance variables in their class. Any client can call these methods without having to create an object of the class in which the methods are defined.

These definitions actually exist as part of the **GImage** class, which means you can use them by writing calls like

```
int red = GImage.getRed(pixel);
```

instead of the much less readable

```
int red = (pixel >> 16) & 0xFF;
```

The point of introducing the implementation is to let you know what's going on behind the scenes.

▉▉ 11.8 The **ArrayList** class

Although arrays remain important as a programming concept, object-oriented languages often include library classes that reduce the need for arrays in and of themselves. Java is no exception to that rule. The **java.util** package includes a number of classes that together make up the Java Collections Framework, which is described in Chapter 13. Partly because it serves as a preview of coming attractions and partly because it provides you with a useful tool, this section introduces the **ArrayList** class, which is one of the most widely used classes in the framework.

The **ArrayList** class offers counterparts for the traditional operations on arrays, but also includes several new operations that can make **ArrayList**s easier to use. In particular, an **ArrayList** allows you to add new elements to the end of a list or even insert them between existing elements. By contrast, you can't change the size of an existing array without allocating a new array and then copying all the elements from the old array into the new one.

Several of the most common methods available for the **ArrayList** class appear in Figure 11-12. The method headers, however, look somewhat different from those you have seen before. Several of these methods include the notation **<T>** in the place where you would normally expect a type name. For example, the first method in Figure 11-12 has the following method header

```
public void add(<T> element)
```

From the description, you know that this method adds a new element to the end of the **ArrayList**, but the method header offers no help in answering the question of what type the **element** parameter must have. The answer is that the type of the parameter depends on the type of the **ArrayList**, which is established when you declare it. If the declaration specifies that the **ArrayList** contains string values, then the type of element represented by the **<T>** syntax would be **String**. If, on the

---

| FIGURE 11-12 | Important methods in the ArrayList class |

boolean add(<T> element)
Adds a new element to the end of the **ArrayList**; the return value is always **true**.
void add(int index, <T> element)
Inserts a new element into the **ArrayList** before the position specified by **index**.
<T> remove(int index)
Removes the element at the specified position and returns that value.
boolean remove(<T> element)
Removes the first instance of the specified element, if any; the value is **true** if a match is found.
void clear()
Removes all elements from the **ArrayList**.
int size()
Returns the number of elements in the **ArrayList**.
<T> get(int index)
Returns the object at the specified index.
<T> set(int index, <T> value)
Sets the element at the specified index to the new value and returns the old value.
int indexOf(<T> value)
Returns the index of the first occurrence of the specified value, or -1 if it does not appear.
boolean contains(<T> value)
Returns **true** if the **ArrayList** contains the specified value.
boolean isEmpty()
Returns **true** if the **ArrayList** contains no elements.

other hand, the declaration specifies that the `ArrayList` contains `GPoint` values, then the `<T>` syntax would represent `GPoint` everywhere it appears.

The ability to define classes that can specify the type of object they contain is almost certainly the most important new feature in Java 5.0. In these classes, the designation `<T>` is a type parameter. Classes like `ArrayList` that use this feature are called **generic classes** in Java (or often simply **generics**), although classes of this sort are also referred to as **templates** or **parameterized classes** in the more general context of computer science as a whole. As long as you limit yourself to *using* generic classes, they will help you enormously to write code that is easier to read and maintain. The process of *implementing* generic classes, on the other hand, is fraught with pitfalls. This book covers the use of generics, deferring the problem of creating them to a more advanced course.

In Java 5.0, you specify the type of value stored in an `ArrayList` by writing the name of that class in angle brackets following the name of the `ArrayList` class wherever it appears. For example, you can construct an empty `ArrayList` of strings by writing the declaration

```
ArrayList<String> stringList = new ArrayList<String>();
```

Once you have done so, the Java compiler now knows that the `ArrayList` object stored in the variable `stringList` is restricted so that it can contain only strings. Moreover, when you apply any of the methods in Figure 11-12 to the `stringList` variable, the compiler will check to make sure that the arguments designated as being of type `<T>` are actually of type `String`. If you instead created an `ArrayList` class using the declaration

```
ArrayList<GPoint> vertices = new ArrayList<GPoint>();
```

the compiler would make sure that the `ArrayList` methods checked to make sure that those arguments were of type `GPoint`.

The type parameter used for `ArrayList` must be a Java class, and may not be a primitive type. It is therefore illegal, for example, to write a declaration of the form

```
ArrayList<int> intList = new ArrayList<int>();
```

What you can do instead is to use the wrapper classes defined in Chapter 7 for each of the primitive types. You can therefore achieve the effect of the preceding illegal declaration by rewriting it as

```
ArrayList<Integer> intList = new ArrayList<Integer>();
```

The value of making this sort of definition is enhanced substantially by the fact that Java 5.0 automatically converts values back and forth between a primitive type and its corresponding wrapper class using the technique of boxing and unboxing, which was also introduced in Chapter 7. The effect of Java's strategy is that you can write statements like

```
intList.add(17);
```

or

```
        int firstValue = intList.get(0);
```

without writing any type casts. The value stored inside the **IntList** is an **Integer**, but that value is freely converted to an **int** in both directions.

As the discussion in Chapter 7 makes clear, Java's strategy of boxing and unboxing has certain pitfalls. In practice, you can avoid these problems by limiting the ways in which you use methods that return objects that are members of the wrapper classes, such as the **get** method in the preceding statement. If you always assign that value to a variable of the appropriate primitive type and never use it in any other expression, you force the conversion to occur before any of the dangers can arise.

But what can you do if you don't have Java 5.0 available? The **ArrayList** class is still useful, although you no longer have the option of specifying the element type. In versions of Java prior to 5.0, the **ArrayList** class is defined to hold values of type **Object**. Because **Object** is the ultimate superclass of every Java object, you can put objects of any type into an **ArrayList**. In most cases, you need to use a type cast when you select an object from an **ArrayList** using the **get** method, but the increase in the complexity of the code is minor. Similarly, having to code the boxing and unboxing of primitive types on your own is a bit messy, but not conceptually difficult. The important thing that you lose by not having the generic capabilities of Java 5.0 is the ability to have the compiler check that you are using each **ArrayList** to store only values whose types match the **ArrayList** declaration. Parameterized types help to enforce the regimen of **strong typing** in which the compiler can detect any mismatches in type.

When you use an **ArrayList** in place of an array, the overall structure of the code tends to remain much the same, at least from a holistic perspective. The high-level operations of declaring the array object, initializing its elements, and selecting elements by supplying their index numbers do not change as the model changes.

At the reductionistic level, however, the code changes markedly, particularly in terms of the syntax. The most important difference is that the **ArrayList** is a Java class, which means that each of its operations is invoked as a method call. The brackets used in the array notation go away. Thus, whenever you want to retrieve the value of an **ArrayList** at a particular index position, you need to call the **get** method in place of using indexing. Similarly, you cannot use an assignment statement to change the value of an **ArrayList** element as you can with an array; you have to call the **set** method instead. The other changes are mostly minor changes in name. In particular, it is easy to forget that the method used to return the length of an **ArrayList** is called **size** and not **length**.

These differences in syntactic style that come from using **ArrayList**s are illustrated by the programs in Figures 11-13 and 11-14. Both of these programs update the **ReverseIntArray** program from Figure 11-3 but use an **ArrayList** rather than an array to store the individual elements. Figure 11-13 shows how to implement the program using Java's generic mechanism to specify that the list is actually the parameterized class **ArrayList<Integer>**. Figure 11-14 shows how the same program appears without the Java 5.0 features.

FIGURE 11-13   **Program to reverse an ArrayList of integers (Java 5.0 style)**

```java
import acm.program.*;
import java.util.*;

/**
 * This program reads in a list of integers and then displays that list in
 * reverse order. This version uses an ArrayList<Integer> to hold the values.
 */
public class ReverseArrayList extends ConsoleProgram {

   public void run() {
      println("This program reverses the elements in an ArrayList.");
      println("Use " + SENTINEL + " to signal the end of the list.");
      ArrayList<Integer> list = readArrayList();
      reverseArrayList(list);
      printArrayList(list);
   }

/* Reads the data into the list */
   private ArrayList<Integer> readArrayList() {
      ArrayList<Integer> list = new ArrayList<Integer>();
      while (true) {
         int value = readInt(" ? ");
         if (value == SENTINEL) break;
         list.add(value);
      }
      return list;
   }

/* Prints the data from the list, one element per line */
   private void printArrayList(ArrayList list) {
      for (int i = 0; i < list.size(); i++) {
         int value = (Integer) list.get(i);
         println(value);
      }
   }

/* Reverses the data in an ArrayList */
   private void reverseArrayList(ArrayList list) {
      for (int i = 0; i < list.size() / 2; i++) {
         swapElements(list, i, list.size() - i - 1);
      }
   }

/* Exchanges two elements in an ArrayList */
   private void swapElements(ArrayList list, int p1, int p2) {
      int temp = list.get(p1);
      list.set(p1, list.get(p2));
      list.set(p2, temp);
   }

/* Private constants */
   private static final int SENTINEL = 0;
}
```

FIGURE 11-14   **Program to reverse an ArrayList of integers (prior to Java 5.0)**

```java
import acm.program.*;
import java.util.*;

/**
 * This program also reverses a list of integers.  This version uses ArrayList as
 * it existed before Java 5.0 and must therefore do its own boxing and unboxing.
 */
public class ReverseArrayList extends ConsoleProgram {

    public void run() {
        println("This program reverses the elements in an ArrayList.");
        println("Use " + SENTINEL + " to signal the end of the list.");
        ArrayList list = readArrayList();
        reverseArrayList(list);
        printArrayList(list);
    }

/* Reads the data into the list */
    private ArrayList readArrayList() {
        ArrayList list = new ArrayList();
        while (true) {
            int value = readInt(" ? ");
            if (value == SENTINEL) break;
            list.add(new Integer(value));
        }
        return list;
    }

/* Prints the data from the list, one element per line */
    private void printArrayList(ArrayList list) {
        for (int i = 0; i < list.size(); i++) {
            Integer valueAsInteger = (Integer) list.get(i);
            println(valueAsInteger.intValue());
        }
    }

/* Reverses the data in an ArrayList */
    private void reverseArrayList(ArrayList list) {
        for (int i = 0; i < list.size() / 2; i++) {
            swapElements(list, i, list.size() - i - 1);
        }
    }

/* Exchanges two elements in an ArrayList */
    private void swapElements(ArrayList list, int p1, int p2) {
        Object temp = list.get(p1);
        list.set(p1, list.get(p2));
        list.set(p2, temp);
    }

/* Private constants */
    private static final int SENTINEL = 0;
}
```

The programs in Figure 11-13 and 11-14 improve on the original implementation by using a sentinel to indicate the end of the input instead of predefining a fixed number of items. This change is possible because the **ArrayList** can grow dynamically. As the user enters each new value, the code for **readArrayList** simply appends it to the end of the **ArrayList**. Any internal operations needed to allocate memory for the new object are completely hidden inside the **ArrayList** implementation.

Summary

In this chapter, you have learned about two strategies that Java provides for representing lists of data: a language-level facility called the *array* and a class in the **java.util** package called **ArrayList**. These two strategies are similar in many respects, but have different properties that make each strategy appropriate for particular applications. Arrays are built into Java and are supported by the syntax of the language. The **ArrayList** class is more powerful and is more closely integrated into Java's class hierarchy, although the syntax for using an **ArrayList** is slightly more cumbersome.

The most important points in this chapter include the following:

- Like most programming languages, Java uses arrays to represent collections of data that are both *ordered* and *homogeneous*.
- The individual values in an array are called *elements* and are identified by a numeric *index*. In Java, all arrays begin with index number 0.
- The number of elements in an array is called its *length*. In Java, you can determine the length of an array by selecting its **length** field.
- The process of creating an array variable consists of two steps: declaring the array variable and allocating space for the elements. In most applications, it is easiest to combine these operations into a single declaration line using the paradigmatic form

    type[] *name* = **new** *type*[*length*];

    which creates an array variable called *name* with *length* elements, each of which is an instance of *type*.
- The process of referring to an individual element in an array is called *selection* and is indicated by writing an expression in square brackets after the name of the array.
- The **++** and **--** operators may be written in either a *prefix* form, in which they precede their operand, or a *postfix* form, in which they follow it. Both forms have the same effect on the variable, which is incremented or decremented depending on which operator you use. The difference is that the postfix form of these operators returns the original value of the variable to the surrounding expression context.
- A Java array is an object, which means that passing an array as an argument to a method copies a *reference* to the array into the corresponding formal parameter. Because this reference refers to the same object as the caller, any

changes made to elements of the array within the method will persist after the method returns.

- You can specify the initial values in an array by using an initializer that consists of the elements enclosed in curly braces.

- Arrays can be declared with more than one index, in which case they are called *multidimensional arrays*. In Java, multidimensional arrays are treated as arrays of arrays. The first index selects an element of the outermost array, the second index selects an element from that subarray, and so on.

- Image data can easily be represented as a two-dimensional array of *pixel values,* which combine the red, green, blue, and transparency components of a color into a 32-bit integer word.

- You can retrieve the individual components of a pixel value by using Java's bit-manipulation operators (`&`, `|`, `^`, `~`, `<<`, `>>`, and`>>>`).

- The `ArrayList` class in `java.util` implements all the basic array operations but also extends them with several particularly useful capabilities, most notably the ability to extend the size of the list dynamically.

- In Java 5.0, you can specify the type of element in an `ArrayList` by writing its class name in angle brackets, as in `ArrayList<String>`. If you don't have Java 5.0, you can achieve the same effect by using type casts and the wrapper classes.

Review questions

1. What are the two characteristic properties of an array?

2. Define the following terms: *element, index, element type, array length,* and *selection.*

3. Write declarations that create the following array variables:

   a) An array **doubleArray** consisting of 100 values of type **double**

   b) An array **inUse** consisting of 16 values of type **boolean**

   c) An array **lines** consisting of 50 strings

4. Write the variable declaration and **for** loop necessary to create and initialize the following integer array:

   squares

0	1	4	9	16	25	36	49	64	81	100
0	1	2	3	4	5	6	7	8	9	10

5. How do you determine the length of an array?

6. What are the two approaches described in this chapter for representing an array in which the conventional, real-world index values begin at 1 instead of at 0? What are the tradeoffs between these two approaches?

7. The section entitled "Changing the index range" includes an example that uses the following line of code:

```
       scores[i] = readDouble("Score for judge " + (i + 1) + ": ");
```

Are the parentheses around the expression **i + 1** necessary? Why or why not?

8. What is the difference between the prefix and postfix forms of the **++** operator?

9. True or false: Arrays are represented in memory in the way that primitive values are.

10. What is the role of the variable **temp** in the **swapElements** method?

11. How would you declare and initialize an array variable **powersOfTwo** that contains the first eight powers of two (1, 2, 4, 8, 16, 32, 64, and 128) so that the entire initialization process appears in the declaration line?

12. What is a multidimensional array?

13. Draw a simple diagram that shows how the color components of a pixel are arranged in a 32-bit integer word.

14. Suppose that the variables **p** and **q** have been initialized as follows (where the hexadecimal digits that look as if they might be the letter **O** are the digit **0**):

```
    int p = 0xCOFFEE;
    int q = 0xDOODAD;
```

What are the values of the expressions **p & q**, **p | q**, **p ^ q**, and **~p**?

15. One clever student in your programming class just claimed that you can swap the values in the integer variables **x** and **y** without using a temporary variable. All you need to do is perform the following assignments:

```
    x = x ^ y;
    y = x ^ y;
    x = x ^ y;
```

Is she right?

16. What is the difference between the operators **>>** and **>>>**?

17. Write a single Java expression that uses the bit-manipulation operators to isolate the green component of the Java color **ORANGE**.

18. What are some of the advantages of using the **ArrayList** class as opposed to Java arrays?

19. Describe the effect of each of the following **ArrayList** methods: **size**, **add**, **set**, **get**, and **remove**.

20. Is it legal to create an **ArrayList<boolean>**?

Programming exercises

1. Because individual contest judges may have some bias, it is common practice to throw out the highest and lowest score before computing the average. Write a program that reads in scores from a panel of seven judges and then computes

the average of the five scores that remain after discarding the highest and lowest.

2. In statistics, a collection of data values is usually referred to as a **distribution.** A primary purpose of statistical analysis is to find ways to compress the complete set of data into summary statistics that express properties of the distribution as a whole. The most common statistical measure is the **mean,** which is simply the traditional average. The mean of a distribution is usually represented by the Greek letter μ.

   Write a method **mean(array)** that returns the mean of an array of type **double**. Test your method by incorporating it into the **GymnasticsJudge** program in Figure 11-1.

3. Another common statistical measure is the **standard deviation,** which provides an indication of how much the individual values in the distribution differ from the mean. To calculate the standard deviation whose elements are $x_1, x_2, \ldots,$ x_n you need to perform the following steps:

   a) Calculate the mean of the distribution as in exercise 2.
   b) Go through the individual data items in the distribution and calculate the square of the difference between each data value and the mean. Add all these values to a running total.
   c) Take the total from step b and divide it by the number of data items.
   d) Calculate the square root of the resulting quantity, which represents the standard deviation.

   In mathematical form, the standard deviation (σ) is given by the following formula:

   $$\sigma = \sqrt{\frac{\sum_{i=1}^{n}(\mu - x_i)^2}{n}}$$

   where μ signifies the mean. The Greek letter sigma (Σ) represents a summation of the quantity that follows, which in this case is the square of the difference between the mean and each individual data point. (Note: Statisticians use this formula to compute the standard deviation of a complete data distribution; to calculate the standard deviation based instead on a sample, the formula should divide by $n-1$ instead.)

   Write a method **stdev(array)** that takes an array of **double**s and returns the standard deviation of the data distribution contained in the array.

4. A **magic square** is a two-dimensional array of integers in which the rows, columns, and diagonals all add up to the same value. One of the most famous magic squares appears in the engraving *Melencolia I* by Albrecht Dürer shown in Figure 11-15, in which a 4×4 magic square appears in the upper right, just under the bell. In Dürer's square, all four rows, all four columns, and both

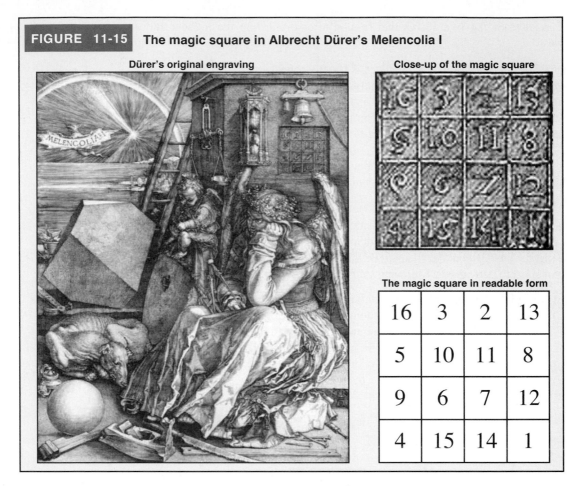

FIGURE 11-15 The magic square in Albrecht Dürer's Melencolia I

Dürer's original engraving

Close-up of the magic square

The magic square in readable form

16	3	2	13
5	10	11	8
9	6	7	12
4	15	14	1

diagonals add up to 34. Moreover, Dürer arranged the square so that the center columns on the bottom row show 1514, the year he produced the engraving.

A more familiar example is the following 3×3 magic square in which each of the rows, columns, and diagonals add up to 15, as shown:

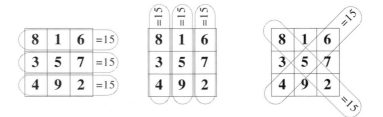

Implement a method **isMagicSquare** that tests to see whether an N×N array contains a magic square.

5. In the last several years, a new logic puzzle called *Sudoku* has become quite popular throughout the world. In Sudoku, you start with a 9×9 grid of numbers in which some of the cells have been filled in with digits between 1 and 9. Your job in the puzzle is to fill in each of the empty spaces with a digit between 1 and 9 so that each digit appears exactly once in each row, each column, and each of the smaller 3×3 squares. Each Sudoku puzzle is carefully constructed so that there is only one solution. For example, given the puzzle shown on the left of the following diagram, the unique solution is shown on the right:

		2	4		5	8		
	4	1	8				2	
6				7			3	9
2				3			9	6
		9	6		7	1		
1	7			5				3
9	6			8				1
		2			9	5	6	
		8	3		6	9		

3	9	2	4	6	5	8	1	7
7	4	1	8	9	3	6	2	5
6	8	5	2	7	1	4	3	9
2	5	4	1	3	8	7	9	6
8	3	9	6	2	7	1	5	4
1	7	6	9	5	4	2	8	3
9	6	7	5	8	2	3	4	1
4	2	3	7	1	9	5	6	8
5	1	8	3	4	6	9	7	2

Although the algorithmic strategies necessary to generate or solve Sudoku puzzles are beyond the scope of this book, you can easily write a method that checks to see whether a proposed solution follows the Sudoku rules against duplicating values in a row, column, or outlined 3×3 square. Write a method

```
private boolean checkSudokuSolution(int[][] grid)
```

that performs this check and returns **true** if the grid is a valid solution.

6. In the third century B.C.E., the Greek astronomer Eratosthenes developed an algorithm for finding all the prime numbers up to some upper limit *N*. To apply the algorithm, you start by writing down a list of the integers between 2 and *N*. For example, if *N* were 20, you would begin by writing the following list:

2   3   4   5   6   7   8   9   10   11   12   13   14   15   16   17   18   19   20

You then circle the first number in the list, indicating that you have found a prime. Whenever you mark a number as a prime, you go through the rest of the list and cross off every multiple of that number, since none of those multiples can itself be prime. Thus, after executing the first cycle of the algorithm, you will have circled the number 2 and crossed off every multiple of 2, as follows:

②   3   4̸   5   6̸   7   8̸   9   1̸0̸   11   1̸2̸   13   1̸4̸   15   1̸6̸   17   1̸8̸   19   2̸0̸

To complete the algorithm, you simply repeat the process by circling the first number in the list that is neither crossed off nor circled, and then crossing off its multiples. In this example, you would circle 3 as a prime and cross off all multiples of 3 in the rest of the list, which would result in the following state:

2 3 ⨉ 5 ⨉ 7 ⨉ ⨉ ⨉ 11 ⨉ 13 ⨉ ⨉ ⨉ 17 ⨉ 19 ⨉

Eventually, every number in the list will either be circled or crossed out, as shown in this diagram:

2 3 ⨉ 5 ⨉ 7 ⨉ ⨉ ⨉ 11 ⨉ 13 ⨉ ⨉ ⨉ 17 ⨉ 19 ⨉

The circled numbers are the primes; the crossed-out numbers are composites. This algorithm is called the **sieve of Eratosthenes.**

Write a `ConsoleProgram` program that uses the sieve of Eratosthenes to generate a list of the primes between 2 and 1000.

7. When statisticians seek to depict the behavior of some quantity that varies over time—the average world temperature in a year, the monthly unemployment birthrate, the daily close of a stock market index, or any similar data value—one of the most useful presentation formats is the **line graph,** in which you plot the data values on an *x/y* grid and then connect every pair of adjacent points with a straight line. In such graphs, the *x* axis indicates time and the *y* axis gives the value of the indicator. For instance, the following sample run shows a line graph in which the data points represent the monthly average stock price of Google, Inc. from the date of its initial public offering in August 2004:

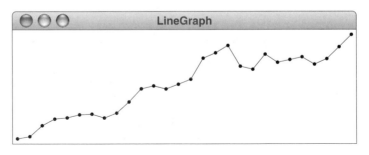

Write a `GraphicsProgram` called `LineGraph` that produces such a graph. Your program should include a `drawLineGraph` method that takes an array of doubles and plots it on the canvas. The implementation of `drawLineGraph` should adjust the *x* and *y* scales so that the data points in the array fill the space inside the window except for a small margin along each edge, as shown in the sample run. Calculating the scale along the *x* axis is simple: the distance between each data point is simply the available horizontal space (after taking away the margins) divided by the number of data points. Scaling the graph along the *y* axis requires a bit more work. To make sure that all points are visible in the window, you have to determine the minimum and maximum values in the array. The minimum value appears at the bottom margin, and the maximum value appears at the top. Each of the other values must be scaled proportionally so that it appears at the appropriate position between the minimum and maximum values.

8. In May of 1844, Samuel F. B. Morse sent the message "What hath God wrought!" by telegraph from Washington to Baltimore, heralding the beginning of the age of electronic communication. To make it possible to communicate information using only the presence or absence of a single tone, Morse designed a coding system in which letters and other symbols are represented as coded sequences of short and long tones, traditionally called *dots* and *dashes*. In Morse code, the 26 letters of the alphabet are represented by the following codes:

A	.−	J	.−−−	S	...
B	−...	K	−.−	T	−
C	−.−.	L	.−..	U	..−
D	−..	M	−−	V	...−
E	.	N	−.	W	.−−
F	..−.	O	−−−	X	−..−
G	−−.	P	.−−.	Y	−.−−
H	....	Q	−−.−	Z	−−..
I	..	R	.−.		

You can easily store these codes in a program by declaring an array with 26 elements and storing the sequence of characters corresponding to each letter in the appropriate array entry.

Write a **ConsoleProgram** that reads in a string from the user and translates each letter in the string to its equivalent in Morse code, using periods to represent dots and hyphens to represent dashes. Separate the words in the output by calling **println** whenever you encounter a space in the input, but ignore all other punctuation characters. Your program should be able to generate the following sample run:

```
●●●                    MorseCode
This program translates a line into Morse code.
Enter English text: What hath God wrought
.-- .... .- -
.... .- - ....
--. --- -..
.-- .-. --- ..- --. .... -
```

You might find it interesting to know that the introduction of the telegraph in the 19th century prompted social changes that are remarkably similar to those that accompanied the growth of the Internet in the 1990s. In a fascinating book entitled *The Victorian Internet* published in 1998, British journalist Tom Standage describes how the telegraph gave rise to entirely new business models (including novel opportunities for crime), on-line romances, a resurgence of interest in cryptography, and an unshakable faith among its promoters that the new technology would revolutionize the world.

9. Rewrite the Morse Code program from the preceding exercise so that it displays its results graphically and uses a **JTextField** to read the message from the user. The following sample run shows a portion of the message sent by the Titanic as it sunk on April 15, 1912:

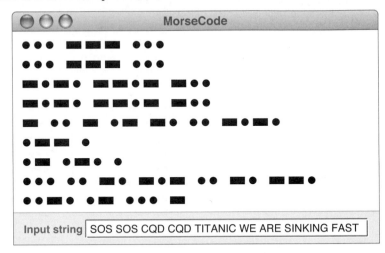

The **CQD** that appears in the message was an alternate form of distress call, which was eventually completely superseded by the more familiar **SOS**.

10. Write an interactive **GraphicsProgram** that plays the game of Nim against the computer. In its simplest version, two players start with a pile of 11 coins on the table between them. The players then take turns removing one, two, or three coins from the pile. The player who is forced to take the last coin loses.

Your program should begin by displaying the 11 coins so that they are centered in the window, like this:

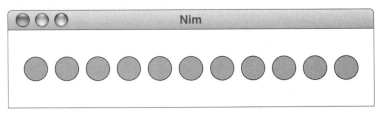

If you press the mouse down on any of the last three coins in the row, that coin and all the coins to its right should turn red. Thus, if you press the mouse on the third coin from the end, the display should look like this:

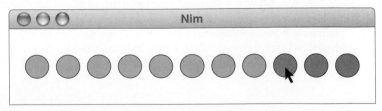

Pressing the mouse anywhere else in the window—even if it is on one of the coins further to the left—should simply be ignored.

When you release the mouse, the red coins should disappear, and the computer should make its move. The computer signals its move by coloring one, two, or three of the coins yellow, pausing for a second, and then removing them. Thus, after you have taken the red coins in the preceding diagram, the computer might choose to take the next three, as follows:

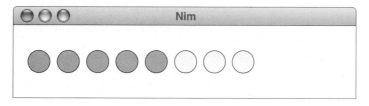

Part of the problem is to design the computer player so that it plays as well as possible. For example, if you think about the position after the yellow coins are removed, you can quickly convince yourself that the computer will always win if it makes the right play. How might you generalize that strategy over the whole of the game?

11. The bitwise operators in Figure 11-9 can seem difficult to understand, mostly because they are not as familiar as the operators from traditional arithmetic. One way to make it easier to visualize the effect of these operators is to devise an application that illustrates the action of those operators on the screen.

Write an interactive program called **BitwiseOperatorDemo** that displays three rows of eight buttons each, along with a **JComboBox** whose elements are the operators **&**, **|**, and **^**. The initial state of the display should look like this:

The idea behind the program is that applying the operator shown in the **JComboBox** to the top two rows of buttons should produce the bit pattern in the bottom row. The initial state of the demo shows only that applying the **&** operator to **0** bits produces **0** bits, which is true but perhaps not all that interesting.

The interactive aspect of the program is that it should be possible to change both the operator and the state of the bits in the upper two rows of buttons and see immediately what happens to the result. Clicking one of the buttons containing a **0** should change that button to a **1** and update the bottom row of buttons accordingly. For example, if you click the right-hand buttons in each of the input lines (clicking only one of the bits doesn't change the result given that the operator is **&**), the display will change as follows:

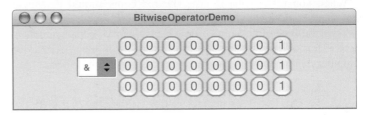

If you change the operator in the **JComboBox** to one of the other operators, the program should apply that bitwise operator instead. The ability to change the operator and the individual bits allows you to set up any configuration for these three operators that you like. The following sample run, for example, shows the effect of the **^** operator on input patterns that contain every possible pair of bits:

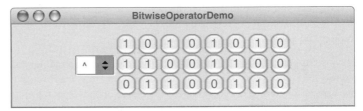

12. Write a method **flipHorizontal** that works similarly to the **flipVertical** method presented in the chapter except that it reverses the picture in the horizontal dimension. Thus, if you had a **GImage** containing the image on the left (of Jan Vermeer's *The Milkmaid*, c. 1659), calling **flipVertical** on that image would return a new **GImage** as shown on the right:

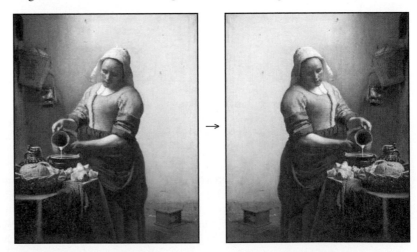

13. Write a method **rotateLeft** that takes a **GImage** and produces a new **GImage** in which the original has been rotated 90 degrees to the left. For example, if you started with the image of a candle used in exercise 9.16, calling **rotateLeft** should transform the image as follows:

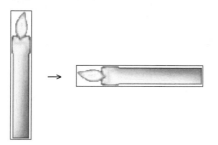

14. In the film version of Dan Brown's bestseller *The Da Vinci Code,* the British art historian Sir Leigh Teabing (played by Sir Ian McKellen) uses a computer to rearrange parts of Leonardo da Vinci's *The Last Supper* to reveal purported hidden meanings. Although selecting irregular areas from an image is beyond the scope of this book, the operation Teabing performs is similar to the rectangular clipping operation available in all image manipulation tools.

Write a **GraphicsProgram** that displays an image on the screen (the image name can be specified as a constant) and then allows the user to select a region from that image by dragging the mouse. As long as the mouse button remains down, the program should draw the outline of the clipping rectangle. As soon as the user releases the mouse button, the program should remove the original image and replace it with a new one constructed from the interior of the rectangle on the screen. For example, suppose that the picture just before the user releases the mouse looks like this:

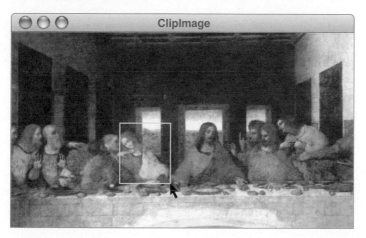

If the user then releases the mouse, your program should extract the pixels from inside the rectangle and display the smaller image in the upper left corner of the window, as follows:

15. Write a method **makeColorNegative** that creates a negative image of a **GImage**. In a color negative, each color component of the new image should become the opposite of its original on the 0 to 255 scale. Thus, a component value of 0 becomes 255, and a value of 200 becomes 55. For example, if you had a **GImage** containing the image on the left (of Vincent Van Gogh's *Starry Night,* 1889), calling **makeColorNegative** would return a **GImage** like that shown on the right:

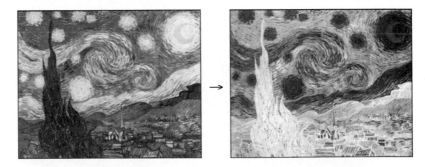

CHAPTER 12
Searching and Sorting

"I weep for you," the Walrus said:
"I deeply sympathize."
With sobs and tears he sorted out
Those of the largest size.
    —Lewis Carroll, *Through the Looking Glass*, 1872

C. A. R. Hoare

Sir Charles Antony Richard (Tony) Hoare is Professor Emeritus of Computer Science at Oxford University and a senior researcher at Microsoft's Research Laboratory in Cambridge, England. After completing a degree in philosophy at Oxford in 1956, Hoare became fascinated by the emerging world of computer science, which he turned to for graduate study. During his graduate-school years, Hoare developed a highly efficient sorting algorithm called Quicksort, which remains in active use today. He also led the effort during the 1960s to create the first commercial compiler for Algol 60, a programming language that served as an important model for subsequent languages, including Java. Professor Hoare received the ACM Turing Award in 1980.

In Chapter 11, you had the opportunity to learn about most of the fundamental array operations and to see how arrays are used in a variety of applications. There are, however, two important array operations Chapter 11 omits so that they can be covered more thoroughly in a chapter of their own. These operations are:

- **Searching,** which is the process of finding a particular element in an array
- **Sorting,** which is the process of rearranging the elements in an array so that they are stored in a well-defined order

Because searching and sorting are closely related to arrays, this chapter is in a sense a continuation of the array discussion. This chapter, however, has another central theme that links it not just to Chapter 11 but also to the discussion of algorithmic methods in Chapter 5. Because there are many different strategies for searching and sorting—with vastly different levels of efficiency—these operations raise interesting algorithmic issues.

12.1 Searching

As noted in the introduction to this chapter, the searching problem consists of finding an element in an array. The simplest strategy—although not necessarily the most efficient one—is captured in the following advice that the King of Hearts gives the White Rabbit in Lewis Carroll's *Alice's Adventures in Wonderland:*

>   *Begin at the beginning, and go on till you come to the end: then stop.*

Turning that informal statement into an algorithm for searching is not at all difficult. The only modification that you need to make is that the algorithm should also stop if it finds the element it is searching for. Thus, you might express a more complete account of Lewis Carroll's searching algorithm as follows:

>   *Begin at the beginning, and go on till you either find the element you're looking for or come to the end. If you find the element, you can report its position; if you reach the end, that means the element does not appear.*

Because the process starts at the beginning and proceeds in a straight line through the elements of the array, this algorithm is called **linear search.**

Searching in an integer array

Turning this informal description into a Java method requires adding some details to the specification of precisely what that method should do. For concreteness, suppose that you have been asked to write a method `linearSearch` that looks for the integer `key` in an array of integers. The header line for such a method would look like this:

```
private int linearSearch(int key, int[] array)
```

The result of the method is the first index at which the key appears as an element of the array, or -1 if the key does not exist in the array.

The implementation of `linearSearch` is really nothing more than a translation of Lewis Carroll's approach:

```
private int linearSearch(int key, int[] array) {
   for (int i = 0; i < array.length; i++) {
      if (key == array[i]) return i;
   }
   return -1;
}
```

The **for** loop begins at the beginning and continues until it comes to the end of the array. The method returns whenever it finds the key along the way or, failing that, at the end of the entire loop.

Searching a table

As a prelude to a discussion of different algorithms for searching, this section introduces a more sophisticated searching application that will make it easier to describe the issues that arise. Suppose that you want to represent in a program the mileage table shown in Figure 12-1. The individual entries in the table form a two-dimensional array with 12 rows and 12 columns. Each entry in the matrix is an integer that indicates the number of miles between the cities corresponding to that row and column. The code necessary to initialize a two-dimensional array called

FIGURE 12-1 Mileage table for U.S. cities

	Atlanta	Boston	Chicago	Denver	Detroit	Houston	Los Angeles	Miami	New York	Philadelphia	San Francisco	Seattle
Atlanta		1108	708	1430	732	791	2191	663	854	748	2483	2625
Boston	1108		994	1998	799	1830	3017	1520	222	315	3128	3016
Chicago	708	994		1021	279	1091	2048	1397	809	785	2173	2052
Denver	1430	1998	1021		1283	1034	1031	2107	1794	1739	1255	1341
Detroit	732	799	279	1283		1276	2288	1385	649	609	2399	2327
Houston	791	1830	1091	1034	1276		1541	1190	1610	1511	1911	2369
Los Angeles	2191	3017	2048	1031	2288	1541		2716	2794	2703	387	1134
Miami	663	1520	1397	2107	1385	1190	2716		1334	1230	3093	3303
New York	854	222	809	1794	649	1610	2794	1334		101	2930	2841
Philadelphia	748	315	785	1739	609	1511	2703	1230	101		2902	2816
San Francisco	2483	3128	2173	1255	2399	1911	387	3093	2930	2902		810
Seattle	2625	3016	2052	1341	2327	2369	1134	3303	2841	2816	810	

Source: Rand McNally

mileageTable appears in Figure 12-2, which also includes the code to initialize an array of the city names used in the table.

Now that you have the data, the next question to consider is how to write a program that reads in the names of two cities and displays the distance between them, as illustrated by the following sample run:

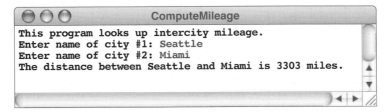

The code for this program appears in Figure 12-3.

FIGURE 12-2   Code to initialize a mileage table along with a table of city names

```
/* Initializes the mileage table */
    private int[][] mileageTable = {
        {    0, 1108,  708, 1430,  732,  791, 2191,  663,  854,  748, 2483, 2625},
        {1108,    0,  994, 1998,  799, 1830, 3017, 1520,  222,  315, 3128, 3016},
        { 708,  994,    0, 1021,  279, 1091, 2048, 1397,  809,  785, 2173, 2052},
        {1430, 1998, 1021,    0, 1283, 1034, 1031, 2107, 1794, 1739, 1255, 1341},
        { 732,  799,  279, 1283,    0, 1276, 2288, 1385,  649,  609, 2399, 2327},
        { 791, 1830, 1091, 1034, 1276,    0, 1541, 1190, 1610, 1511, 1911, 2369},
        {2191, 3017, 2048, 1031, 2288, 1541,    0, 2716, 2794, 2703,  387, 1134},
        { 663, 1520, 1397, 2107, 1385, 1190, 2716,    0, 1334, 1230, 3093, 3303},
        { 854,  222,  809, 1794,  649, 1610, 2794, 1334,    0,  101, 2930, 2841},
        { 748,  315,  785, 1739,  609, 1511, 2703, 1230,  101,    0, 2902, 2816},
        {2483, 3128, 2173, 1255, 2399, 1911,  387, 3093, 2930, 2902,    0,  810},
        {2625, 3016, 2052, 1341, 2327, 2369, 1134, 3303, 2841, 2816,  810,    0},
    };

/* Initializes an array of city names corresponding to the entries in the table */
    private String[] cityNames = {
        "Atlanta",
        "Boston",
        "Chicago",
        "Denver",
        "Detroit",
        "Houston",
        "Los Angeles",
        "Miami",
        "New York",
        "Philadelphia",
        "San Francisco",
        "Seattle",
    };
```

FIGURE 12-3   Code to calculate the distance between cities

```
import acm.program.*;

/**
 * This program uses a table of mileage data to calculate the distance
 * between cities in the United States.
 */
public class ComputeMileage extends ConsoleProgram {

   public void run() {
      println("This program looks up intercity mileage.");
      int city1 = getCity("Enter name of city #1: ");
      int city2 = getCity("Enter name of city #2: ");
      println("The distance between " + cityNames[city1]
            + " and " + cityNames[city2] + " is "
            + mileageTable[city1][city2] + " miles.");
   }

/*
 * Prompts the user for a city name, reads in a string, and returns the
 * index corresponding to that city, if it exists.  If the city name is
 * undefined, the user is given a chance to retry.
 */
   private int getCity(String prompt) {
      while (true) {
         String name = readLine(prompt);
         int index = linearSearch(name, cityNames);
         if (index != -1) return index;
         println("Unknown city name -- try again.");
      }
   }

/*
 * Finds the first instance of the specified key in the array
 * and returns its index.  If the key does not appear in the array,
 * linearSearch returns -1.
 */
   private int linearSearch(String key, String[] array) {
      for (int i = 0; i < array.length; i++) {
         if (key.equals(array[i])) return i;
      }
      return -1;
   }

/* Include the definitions of mileageTable and cityNames from the text */

};
```

The linear-search algorithm used in **linearSearch** starts at the beginning of the array and goes straight down the line of elements until it finds a match or reaches the end of the array. For an array of 12 city names, looking at every element takes very little time. But what if the array instead had thousands or even millions of elements? At some point, if the array became large enough, you would begin to notice a delay as the computer searched through every value. But is searching every value really necessary? It's worth stopping to think for a moment about this question.

Suppose that someone asked *you* to find the distance between Seattle and Miami in the mileage table. To find the entry for Seattle, would you start at the top of the page and work your way down? Probably not. Because the list of cities is in alphabetic order, you know that Seattle must come somewhere near the end of the list. Similarly, Miami is likely to appear near the middle. The odds are good that your eyes would find these values very quickly without ever looking at most of the names on the list.

Binary search

To take advantage of the fact that the `cityNames` array is in alphabetic order, you need to use a different algorithm. To illustrate the process as concretely as possible, let's suppose that you are looking for Miami in an array with the following values:

cityNames

0	Atlanta
1	Boston
2	Chicago
3	Denver
4	Detroit
5	Houston
6	Los Angeles
7	Miami
8	New York
9	Philadelphia
10	San Francisco
11	Seattle

Instead of starting at the top of the array as in linear search, what happens if you start by picking an element somewhere near the center? You can compute the index of the center element by averaging the endpoints of the index range like this:

$$\frac{0 + 11}{2}$$

When evaluated using integer arithmetic, this expression has the value 5.

The city name stored in `cityArray[5]` is Houston. Given that you're looking for Miami, what do you know at this point? You haven't found Miami yet, so you have to keep looking. On the other hand, you know that Miami must come after

Houston because the array is in alphabetic order. Thus, you can immediately eliminate all the city names in index positions 0 through 5, as follows:

cityNames

0	~~Atlanta~~
1	~~Boston~~
2	~~Chicago~~
3	~~Denver~~
4	~~Detroit~~
5	~~Houston~~
6	Los Angeles
7	Miami
8	New York
9	Philadelphia
10	San Francisco
11	Seattle

In one step, you've managed to cross out half the possibilities. The really good news, however, is that you can now do the same thing all over again. You know that Miami—if it exists in the list at all—must lie between positions 6 and 11 of **cityNames**. If you compute the center of that range using integer arithmetic, you get the index value 8. Miami comes earlier in the alphabet than New York does, so you can now cross off four more positions.

cityNames

0	~~Atlanta~~
1	~~Boston~~
2	~~Chicago~~
3	~~Denver~~
4	~~Detroit~~
5	~~Houston~~
6	Los Angeles
7	Miami
8	~~New York~~
9	~~Philadelphia~~
10	~~San Francisco~~
11	~~Seattle~~

On the next cycle, you look at the element in position 6, which is the result of averaging 6 and 7 using integer arithmetic. Miami comes after Los Angeles, so you can cross off that value as well. On the fourth cycle, you have only a single element to check, which is indeed the entry for Miami at index position 7.

This algorithm—looking at the center element in a sorted array and then determining which half to search on that basis—is called **binary search.** To implement the algorithm, all you need to do is keep track of two indices that mark the endpoints of the index range within which the search is limited. In the method, these indices are stored in the variables **lh** and **rh**, which represent the left-hand (lower) index and right-hand (upper) index, respectively. Initially, these index bounds cover the entire array, but move closer together as possibilities are eliminated. If the index values ever cross, the key value does not exist in the array.

The code for the method **binarySearch** appears in Figure 12-4.

The relative efficiency of the search algorithms

The discussion in the previous section suggests that the binary search algorithm is more efficient than the linear search algorithm. Even so, it is hard to appreciate just how much better binary search is without being able to compare the performance of the two algorithms using some quantitative measure. For searching, a convenient measure that provides a good indication of algorithmic performance is the number of times **equals** or **compareTo** is called to compare the key against some element in the array.

FIGURE 12-4 **Implementation of the binary search algorithm for string arrays**

```
/*
 * Finds an instance of the specified key in the array, which must be sorted
 * in lexicographic order.  If the key exists, the method returns an index at
 * which that key appears, but this index will not necessarily be the first
 * if the same key appears multiply.  If the key does not appear in the array,
 * binarySearch returns -1.
 */

  private int binarySearch(String key, String[] array) {
      int lh = 0;
      int rh = array.length - 1;
      while (lh <= rh) {
          int mid = (lh + rh) / 2;
          int cmp = key.compareTo(array[mid]);
          if (cmp == 0) return mid;
          if (cmp < 0) {
              rh = mid - 1;
          } else {
              lh = mid + 1;
          }
      }
      return -1;
  }
```

Suppose that you execute the linear search algorithm on an array containing N elements. How many times will the method call **equals**? The answer depends of course on where the key value shows up in the list. In the worst case—which occurs when the key is in the last position or does not appear at all—**linearSearch** will call **equals** N times, once for each element in the array.

What about the binary search algorithm used in **binarySearch**? After the first call to **compareTo**, the algorithm can immediately eliminate half of the array elements, leaving only $N/2$ elements to search. After the second call, it can rule out half of those elements, leaving $N/4$ elements. Each time, the number of possibilities is halved. Eventually, after you divide an integer N in half enough times, you will end up with 1, at which point there is only a single comparison left to be made. The number of steps required to reach this point is the number of times you can divide N by 2 before you get 1, which is represented by k in the following formula:

$$\underbrace{N \ / \ 2 \ / \ 2 \ / \ \ldots \ / \ 2 \ / \ 2}_{k \text{ times}} = 1$$

Multiplying by all those 2s gives the equivalent equation

$$N = 2^k$$

If you remember logarithms from high-school algebra, you can express the value of k as

$$k = \log_2 N$$

Thus, to search an array of N elements requires N comparisons if you use linear search and $\log_2 N$ comparisons if you use binary search.

Expressing the relative efficiency of these algorithms in mathematical form is useful as a means of making quantitative predictions about efficiency. For most people, however, such formulas do not convey a real sense of how these algorithms compare. For that, you need to look at some numbers. The following table shows the closest integer to $\log_2 N$ for various values of N.

N	$\log_2 N$
10	3
100	7
1000	10
1,000,000	20
1,000,000,000	30

Reflecting on what the values in this table mean, you can see that, for small arrays, both strategies work reasonably well. On the other hand, if you have an array with 1,000,000,000 elements, linear search requires 1,000,000,000 comparisons to search that array in the worst case, whereas the binary search algorithm gets the job done using at most 30 comparisons. Clearly, this reduction in the number of required comparisons represents an overwhelming increase in algorithmic efficiency.

At the same time, the binary search algorithm has two weaknesses with respect to linear search. The first is that the binary search algorithm requires that the array elements be sorted. If they are not, you may have to use linear searching instead. Alternatively, you can ensure that the array elements are in the correct order by sorting the array yourself. Sorting an array is a slightly more challenging problem than searching one and is the subject of the remainder of this chapter.

The second way in which the linear search algorithm wins out over binary search is that it is much simpler to code. Writing the binary search algorithm requires a certain amount of care to ensure that you get all the special cases right. By contrast, the **`for`** loop in the typical linear search implementation is so simple that you can write it down without giving the details a lot of thought. If you are writing a program that has to search only relatively small arrays, there is no point in incurring the additional complexity of binary search, despite its greater efficiency. It is only when arrays become large that the advantages of binary search outweigh its complexity.

12.2 Sorting

In most commercial applications, computers are used for extremely simple operations such as adding a sequence of numbers or calculating an average—precisely the kind of problem you learned to solve in the earlier chapters. However, several important operations required for commercial programming are more sophisticated. The most important example is **sorting,** which is the process of arranging a list of values (usually represented as an array) into some well-defined order. Examples of sorting include arranging a list of numbers from lowest to highest based on their numeric value or alphabetizing a list of names. These two operations turn out to be quite similar. Despite differences in detail (one uses numbers and the other uses strings), the problem to be solved is precisely the same: given a list and a mechanism for comparing two elements in that list, how can you rearrange the elements of the list so that the elements are properly ordered?

Sorting an integer array

Let's consider, for example, the problem of sorting an array of integers. Suppose that you have been presented with an array of integers in some random order, such as the following:

31	41	59	26	53	58	97	93
0	1	2	3	4	5	6	7

What you need to do at this point is define a new method, which you could call **`sort`**, that would rearrange the elements of this array so that they run from lowest to highest, as follows:

26	31	41	53	58	59	93	97
0	1	2	3	4	5	6	7

The header line for the **sort** method presumably looks like this:

```
private void sort(int[] array)
```

Writing the corresponding implementation, however, is trickier than it might seem, particularly if you are interested in finding an efficient strategy for sorting the data. As is the case with many problems in computer science, there are many different algorithms you can use. In an advanced computer science course, you might well spend several weeks or even months studying various different algorithms for sorting, each of which has particular advantages or disadvantages. At this point in your study of computer science, however, it is best to begin with one algorithm for sorting that you can understand in detail.

The selection sort algorithm

Of the many possible sorting algorithms, one of the easiest to explain is the **selection sort** algorithm. When you apply the selection sort algorithm, you put the array into its final order one element at a time. In the first step, you find the smallest element in the entire list and put it where it belongs—at the beginning. In the second step, you find the smallest remaining element and put it in the second position. If you continue this process for the entire array, the final result is in sorted order.

To get a sense of the selection sort approach, watch what happens if you start with the following array of numbers:

31	41	59	26	53	58	97	93
0	1	2	3	4	5	6	7

Because the smallest element is the value 26 in position 3, you move this element into position 0. As with the **ReverseIntArray** program from Chapter 11, you don't want to lose track of the value that was originally in position 0, so the easiest thing to do is exchange the values in positions 0 and 3. Doing so leaves the array in the following state:

correctly positioned

26	41	59	31	53	58	97	93
0	1	2	3	4	5	6	7

After the exchange, position 0 is correctly filled with the smallest value.

From this point, you can proceed with the rest of the list. The next step is to use the same strategy to correctly fill the second position in the array. The smallest value (except for the value 26 already placed correctly) is the 31, which is now in position 3. If you exchange this value with the one at index position 1, you reach the following state, with the correct values in the first two elements:

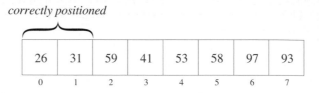

correctly positioned

On the next cycle, you switch the next smallest value (41) into position 2:

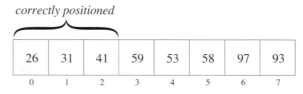

correctly positioned

If you continue on in this way, you can correctly fill up index positions 3, 4, and so on until the array is completely sorted.

To keep track of which element you are trying to fill at each step in the algorithm, you can imagine that you use your left hand to point to each of the index positions in turn. For each left-hand position, you then use your right hand to identify the smallest element remaining in the rest of the array. Once you find it, you can just take the values to which your hands point and exchange them. In the implementation, your left and right hands are replaced by variables—**lh** and **rh**— that hold the index number of the appropriate element in the array.

You can turn this intuitive outline into pseudocode as follows:

```
for (each index position lh in the array) {
        Let rh be the index of the smallest value between lh and the end of the list
        Swap the elements at index positions lh and rh
}
```

Replacing the pseudocode with the correct Java statements is straightforward, mostly because two of the operations are familiar: the **for** loop control line is a standard idiom, and you can accomplish the swap operation at the end of the loop by calling the **swapElements** method defined as part of the **ReverseIntArray** program in Figure 11-3. The one remaining step is the one that finds the smallest value. Following the discipline of stepwise refinement, you can define a new method to perform this operation and complete the coding of the **sort** method as follows:

```
private void sort(int[] array) {
   for (int lh = 0; lh < array.length; lh++) {
      int rh = findSmallest(array, lh, array.length);
      swapElements(array, lh, rh);
   }
}
```

The **findSmallest** method takes three arguments: the array and two index numbers indicating the range within the array in which to find the smallest value. For consistency with other methods in Java that use two indices to specify a range (such as the **substring** method in the **String** class), the **findSmallest** method looks for the smallest element starting at index position **p1** and continuing up to just before index position **p2**. The method returns the index—not the value—of the smallest element of the array between the specified index positions.

The simplest implementation strategy for **findSmallest** is to go through the list, keeping track at each loop cycle of the index of smallest value so far. When you reach the end of the selected range, that value will be the smallest value in the range as a whole. This suggests the following code, in which the variable **smallestIndex** keeps track of the index position of the smallest value up to this point:

```java
private int findSmallest(int[] array, int p1, int p2) {
    int smallestIndex = p1;
    for (int i = p1 + 1; i <= p2; i++) {
        if (array[i] < array[smallestIndex]) smallestIndex = i;
    }
    return smallestIndex;
}
```

At the beginning of the scan, the first value you consider is automatically the smallest value so far. Thus, you can initialize **smallestIndex** to the starting index position, which is given by the parameter **p1**. As you look at each position in turn, you have to see if the current value is smaller than your previous candidate for the smallest value. If it is, the old value can no longer be the smallest in the entire list, and you need to correct the value of **smallestIndex** to indicate the new position, which will retain its value until you find an even smaller value.

The method **swapElements** has precisely the same implementation as it did in the **ReverseIntArray** implementation from Chapter 11. The method you want in this application has exactly the same effect and there is no reason to rewrite it. Whenever you write a method that implements some generally useful operation, it is wise to keep that method around so that it is available for future use. Successful programmers always try to reuse existing code as much as possible because doing so saves the trouble of writing and debugging those parts of the program from scratch.

Copying the code for **swapElements** completes the code for the entire selection sort algorithm. The code for the **sort** method appears in Figure 12-5.

Evaluating the efficiency of selection sort

The selection sort algorithm has several positive qualities. For one thing, it is relatively easy to understand. For another, it gets the job done. There are, however, sorting algorithms that are far more efficient. Unfortunately, the best ones require techniques beyond your current level of programming knowledge. At the same time, you certainly have enough background to evaluate how efficient the selection sort algorithm is, even if you are not yet in a position to improve it.

| FIGURE 12-5 | **Implementation of the selection sort algorithm** |

```
/**
 * Sorts an integer array into increasing order.  The implementation uses
 * an algorithm called selection sort, which can be described informally
 * in English as follows:
 *
 *   With your left hand, point at each element in the array in turn, starting
 *   at index 0.  At each step in the cycle:
 *
 *     1. Find the smallest element in the range between your left hand and the
 *        end of the array, and point at that element with your right hand.
 *
 *     2. Move that element into its correct index position by switching the
 *        elements indicated by your left and right hands.
 */
    private void sort(int[] array) {
        for (int lh = 0; lh < array.length; lh++) {
            int rh = findSmallest(array, lh, array.length);
            swapElements(array, lh, rh);
        }
    }

/* Returns the index of the smallest array element between p1 and p2 - 1 */
    private int findSmallest(int[] array, int p1, int p2) {
        int smallestIndex = p1;
        for (int i = p1 + 1; i < p2; i++) {
            if (array[i] < array[smallestIndex]) smallestIndex = i;
        }
        return smallestIndex;
    }

/* Exchanges the elements in an array at index positions p1 and p2. */
    private void swapElements(int[] array, int p1, int p2) {
        int temp = array[p1];
        array[p1] = array[p2];
        array[p2] = temp;
    }
}
```

One interesting question is how long it takes to execute selection sort on a given set of input data. There are two ways you can approach this question:

1. You can run the program and measure how long it takes. Because programs run very quickly on modern computers and often finish their work in a fraction of a second, you might not be able to measure the elapsed time with a stopwatch, but you can accomplish the same result by using the computer's internal clock.
2. You can think more generally about the operation of the program and try to develop a qualitative sense of how it behaves.

Measuring the running time of a program

To determine how long it takes to run a program, the most common approach is to use the **System** class in the **java.lang** package to keep track of the total time required. The **System** class exports a static method called **currentTimeMillis** that returns the current time. The result is expressed as a **long** that records the number of milliseconds between the current setting of the system clock and midnight on January 1, 1970, which is defined as the base for time calculations. Thus, it is possible to obtain a rough assessment of the time required to perform a calculation as follows:

```
long start = System.currentTimeMillis();
. . . Perform some calculation . . .
long elapsed = System.currentTimeMillis() - start;
```

This code, however, requires several cautionary notes:

- Short computations can often be completed in less than a millisecond, which means that the elapsed time given by comparing two calls to **currentTimeMillis** may in some cases return 0. Worse yet, the definition of **currentTimeMillis** does not guarantee that the result is accurate at the millisecond level, because the internal clock in some systems does not provide that level of accuracy.
- The **currentTimeMillis** method returns the total elapsed time, which is not always a good measure of how much actual processing time has been dedicated to the algorithm you are seeking to measure. The Java runtime system introduces a certain amount of overhead, and there is no reliable way in Java to factor out this additional overhead time from the calculation. These variations, moreover, can be quite large in Java. If, for example, the Java runtime environment discovers that it needs to reclaim memory space in the middle of a process that you're timing, that experiment may take several times as long as it usually would.
- The time required to perform some calculation may be data dependent. Depending on the algorithm, the number of steps required to perform a calculation may depend on the input data. To get a reasonable assessment of typical performance, one must therefore repeat the experiment with different data values.

You can, however, take steps to minimize the effect of these problems. If you are trying to measure the time of a computation that is so short that the precision of the system clock matters, you can simply repeat the computation many times, measure the total elapsed time, and then divide the total time by the number of repetitions. For example, if you sort the same array 1000 times and measure the elapsed time from the beginning to the end of that process, the running time for a single sorting step is presumably approximately one thousandth of the total elapsed time. Similarly, to minimize the effect of any overhead costs that occur in some runs and not others, you can perform the same experiment many times and average the results after discarding any values that are wildly out of line. Finally, given the inherent lack of accuracy in the measurement process, it is important not to estimate the running time of an algorithm with any greater precision than you are entitled to claim. It would, for example, be statistically inappropriate to report seven digits of accuracy on a timing experiment if you have confidence in only two.

These principles are illustrated by the data shown in Figure 12-6. This table shows the results of a timing experiment in which **sort** is called repeatedly on arrays of various sizes. For each number of elements, the entries in the table show the measured time in milliseconds to sort that many integers in each of ten independent trials. The last two columns show the mean and standard deviation over those trials, conventionally indicated by the Greek letters *mu* (μ) and *sigma* (σ), respectively. (These measures are explained on page 451.) As you can see, there is a reasonable amount of variation in each of the rows, indicating that the timing process is not as accurate as one might hope. It is also significantly out of line in the four shaded entries in the table. In the various trials for sorting 50 integers, for example, most of the values come out somewhere in the neighborhood of 40 microseconds, with a good deal of variation on each side. Trial 7, however, shows a running time of 140 microseconds, which is almost three standard deviations away from the mean. The other shaded items are also off by a statistically significant amount. To ensure that these timing measurements—which probably reflect the cost of Java's overhead rather than actual computation time—do not distort the timing data, it is probably best to remove them from the computation.

The following table summarizes the data from Figure 12-6 after removing the outliers, using a form that emphasizes the inherent uncertainty in the measurement:

N	*running time*	
10	0.0024	± 0.0006
20	0.007	± 0.0007
30	0.014	± 0.0003
40	0.025	± 0.003
50	0.039	± 0.005
100	0.16	± 0.03
500	3.7	± 0.5
1000	14.3	± 3.4
5000	346.0	± 68.0
10000	1326.0	± 21.0

The error range shown in each entry corresponds to two standard deviations in each direction from the mean. If the data were normally distributed, using two standard deviations as the error bar would ensure that the actual value of the mean occurs within the specified range roughly 95 percent of the time.

The table reveals some interesting results. For small values of *N*, selection sort runs reasonably quickly. As *N* gets larger, however, the selection sorting algorithm slows down precipitously. If the array contains 100 values, for example, **sort** can sort the array in a little more than a tenth of a millisecond. By the time you reach 10,000 items, selection sort takes over a second to run. Commercial applications

FIGURE 12-6	Sort timings for the selection sort algorithm

	Trial 1	Trial 2	Trial 3	Trial 4	Trial 5	Trial 6	Trial 7	Trial 8	Trial 9	Trial 10	μ	σ
N = 10	.0021	.0025	.0022	.0026	.0020	.0030	.0022	.0023	.0022	.0025	.0024	.00029
20	.006	.007	.008	.007	.007	.011	.007	.007	.007	.007	.007	.00139
30	.014	.014	.014	.015	.014	.014	.014	.014	.014	.014	.014	.00013
40	.028	.024	.025	.026	.023	.025	.025	.026	.025	.027	.025	.0014
50	.039	.037	.036	.041	.042	.039	.140	.039	.034	.038	.049	.0323
100	.187	.152	.168	.176	.146	.146	.165	.146	.178	.154	.162	.0151
500	3.94	3.63	4.06	3.76	4.11	3.51	3.48	3.64	3.31	3.45	3.69	0.272
1000	13.40	12.90	13.80	17.60	12.90	14.10	12.70	81.60	16.00	15.50	21.05	21.33
5000	322.5	355.9	391.7	321.6	388.3	321.3	321.3	398.7	322.1	321.3	346.4	33.83
10000	1319.	1388.	1327.	1318.	1331.	1336.	1318.	1335.	1325.	1319.	1332.	20.96

often require sorting 100,000 or 1,000,000 values or more. With arrays on that scale, selection sort becomes prohibitively slow.

Analyzing the selection sort algorithm

To understand why these timing numbers come out as they do, it is important to think about how the algorithm works. Let's consider the timing data for selection sort as summarized in the preceding section. When N is 50, the algorithm requires 0.039 milliseconds to run. When N doubles to 100, however, the algorithm requires 0.16 milliseconds, which is approximately four times as long. The rest of the table shows the same progression. Whenever you double the number of data items—from 500 to 1000 or from 5000 to 10,000, for example—the time required goes up by a factor of approximately four. Algorithms of this sort are said to be **quadratic,** because their running time grows as the square of the size of the input.

The fact that selection sort is a quadratic algorithm is not surprising if you think about how it works. In sorting a list of eight numbers, the selection sort implementation of the **sort** method executes the outer **for** loop eight times. The first cycle finds the smallest value out of a group of eight numbers, the next cycle finds the smallest value out of the remaining seven numbers, and so on. The number of operations the program executes is proportional to the number of values it must check, which in this specific case is

$$8 + 7 + 6 + 5 + 4 + 3 + 2 + 1$$

More generally, given N elements, the time required to execute the selection sort algorithm is proportional to the following sum:

$$N + N-1 + N-2 + \ldots + 3 + 2 + 1$$

The sum of the first N integers can be expressed more compactly by applying the following mathematical formula

$$N + N\text{–}1 + N\text{–}2 + \ldots + 3 + 2 + 1 = \frac{N^2 + N}{2}$$

The quadratic behavior comes from the appearance of the N^2 term.

The fact that selection sort is quadratic in its performance does not mean that all sorting algorithms perform with this level of efficiency. Many sorting algorithms are much, much faster. The best algorithms for sorting depend on the use of an algorithmic concept called **recursion,** which is introduced briefly in Chapter 14. There is, however, a sorting algorithm with certain historical interest that will serve as an effective demonstration of the relationship between algorithms and efficiency, even though it has shortcomings in practice.

The radix sort algorithm

As Chapter 1 observes in its brief tour of computing history, mechanical calculators have been used for hundreds of years. Although such machines have less flexibility than modern computers, they can nonetheless perform useful tasks. The United States used began using tabulating machines during the 1890 census. Individual responses to the census questionnaires were punched into cards and tabulated by a machine invented by Herman Hollerith that could count the number of times a particular punched hole appeared. Such devices opened up the field of data processing and led to the creation of companies, such as IBM, that built large and successful businesses based on machines that could tabulate information mechanically.

The cards that were used for data processing through the 1970s (and which still survive in voting machines and a few other applications) look something like this:

The standard punched card is divided up into 80 columns of data. Numeric values are represented on the card in the form of rectangular holes covering the appropriate digit. Thus, the card in the preceding diagram contains the number 42 in columns 1 and 2.

In the 1940s, IBM introduced a electromechanical device called a **sorter.** The sorter was a large machine with a hopper on one end into which the operator would load a stack of punched cards. When the machine was activated, it would take cards from the hopper one at a time and distribute them among a set of numbered output areas—which I'll call **buckets**—depending on what value was punched in a particular column on the card. If the sorter, for example, were set to look at column 1, the card shown in the diagram above would be sent to bucket #4, because column 1 is punched in digit position 4. If the card were sorted according to the digit in column 2 instead, the card would end up in bucket #2.

You could clearly use such a sorter to arrange cards containing one-digit numbers into ascending order. You would just take the entire stack of cards and run it through the sorter. If you then picked up the cards from bucket #0, followed by the cards in bucket #1, followed by the cards in bucket #2, and so on up to bucket #9, the values on the cards would be in sorted order. Suppose, however, that the numbers you were sorting contained more than one digit. How could you use the sorter to put these cards in order by the entire multidigit numeric field?

The fundamental insight that made the IBM sorter so useful—and the key to the radix sort algorithm—is that a set of multidigit numbers can be sorted by making several passes through the sorter, one for each column in the number. The trick is that the sorting operation must start with the last digit of the number and then proceed toward the first. For example, to sort a set of cards containing two-digit numbers in columns 1 and 2, you would first sort the cards using the digits in column 2, collect the individual buckets of cards together, and then sort again using the digits in column 1.

This process is best illustrated by example. Suppose that the data on the cards consists of the following 15 values:

$$42, 25, 37, 58, 95, 25, 73, 30, 54, 21, 17, 45, 34, 43, 98$$

The first pass through the sorter arranges the values into ten buckets based on the second digit, which results in the following configuration:

0	1	2	3	4	5	6	7	8	9
					45				
					25				
			43	34	95		17	98	
30	21	42	73	54	25		37	58	

You then pick up the cards from each bucket in turn, being careful to preserve the order of cards within each bucket. This process leaves the cards in the following sequence:

$$30, 21, 42, 73, 43, 54, 34, 25, 95, 25, 45, 37, 17, 58, 98$$

You then send this new stack of cards through the sorter, this time dividing up the cards according to the first digit of the number, which is punched in column 1. This process results in the following buckets:

		25	37	45					
		25	34	43	58				98
	17	21	30	42	54		73		95
0	1	2	3	4	5	6	7	8	9

If you then collect these cards from the buckets in order, the sequence is

$$17, 21, 25, 25, 30, 34, 37, 42, 43, 45, 54, 58, 73, 95, 98$$

which is correctly sorted from smallest to largest.

The same strategy works for numbers of any length as long as you start with the last digit position and proceed toward the first. The algorithm works because the cards that end up in each bucket are in the same relative order as they were in the original stack. Thus, when the final step sorts the numbers according to their first digit, the values end up sorted within each bucket just as they were at the end of the preceding step, when they were put in order by the next most significant digit.

This algorithm is called **radix sort** because each step in the process sorts the data into the number of buckets specified by the base, or **radix,** in which the data values are expressed. The IBM sorter worked with numbers in their decimal (base 10) form and therefore distributed the data among 10 buckets.

Coding the radix sort algorithm is more difficult than coding selection sort, but it is not too hard if you choose a good decomposition. Using radix sort, the **sort** method itself has the following pseudocode form:

```
private void sort(int[] array, int n) {
    for (each digit position starting at the right) {
        Fill up the individual buckets with values from array
        Reassemble array by taking the contents from each bucket in turn
    }
}
```

You will have a chance to complete this implementation in exercise 10.

The running time for radix sort is proportional to the number of values multiplied by the maximum number of digits, which is far smaller than the quadratic time required for selection sort. Because the number of digits is proportional to the logarithm of the maximum number size, the complexity of radix sort is proportional to $N \log N$, which represents a huge increase in efficiency. You can get a sense of how much better by looking at the values of these functions for different values of N, as follows:

N	N^2	$N \log N$
10	100	33
100	10,000	664
1000	1,000,000	9965
10,000	100,000,000	132,877

The numbers in both columns grow as N becomes larger, but the N^2 column grows much faster than the $N \log N$ column. Sorting algorithms based on an $N \log N$ algorithm are therefore useful over a much larger range of array sizes.

The process of applying mathematical techniques to predict algorithmic efficiency is called **analysis of algorithms,** which is described briefly in the following section. If you continue with your study of computer science, you will learn how to analyze the performance of algorithms in much more detail. This knowledge will prove to be a powerful tool for evaluating which algorithm is best suited for a particular application.

12.3 Assessing algorithmic efficiency

The problem with conducting a detailed timing analysis such as the one for selection sort earlier in this chapter is that you often end up with too much information. Although it is occasionally useful to have a formula for predicting exactly how long a program will take, you can usually get away with more qualitative measures. The reason that selection sort is impractical for large values of N has little to do with the precise timing characteristics of a particular implementation running on a specific machine. The problem is much simpler and more fundamental. At its essence, the problem with selection sort is that doubling the size of the input array increases the running time of the selection sort algorithm by a factor of four, which means that the running time grows more quickly than the number of elements in the array.

The most valuable qualitative insights you can obtain about algorithmic efficiency are usually those that help you understand how the performance of an algorithm responds to changes in problem size. Problem size is usually easy to quantify. For algorithms that operate on numbers, it generally makes sense to let the numbers themselves represent the problem size. For most algorithms that operate on arrays, you can use the number of elements in the array. When evaluating algorithmic efficiency, computer scientists traditionally use the letter N to indicate the size of the problem, no matter how it is calculated. The relationship between N and the performance of an algorithm as N grows large is called the **computational complexity** of that algorithm. In general, the most important measure of performance is execution time, although it is also possible to apply complexity analysis to other concerns, such as the amount of memory space required. Unless otherwise stated, all assessments of complexity used in this text refer to execution time.

Big-O notation

Computer scientists use a special notation to denote the computational complexity of algorithms. Called **big-O notation,** it was introduced by the German mathematician Paul Bachmann in 1892—long before the development of computers. The notation itself is very simple and consists of the letter O, followed by a formula enclosed in parentheses. When it is used to specify computational complexity, the formula is usually a simple function involving the problem size N. For example, in this chapter you will soon encounter the big-O expression

$$O(N^2)$$

which is read aloud as "big-oh of N squared."

Big-O notation is used to specify qualitative approximations and is therefore ideal for expressing the computational complexity of an algorithm. Coming as it does from mathematics, big-O notation has a precise definition, but understanding the details of that definition is not really important at this point. For now, it is far more important for you—no matter whether you think of yourself as a programmer or a computer scientist—to understand what big-O means from a more intuitive point of view.

Standard simplifications of big-O

When you use big-O notation to estimate the computational complexity of an algorithm, the goal is to provide a *qualitative* insight as to how changes in *N* affect the algorithmic performance as *N* becomes large. Because big-O notation is not intended to be a quantitative measure, it is not only appropriate but desirable to reduce the formula inside the parentheses so that it captures the qualitative behavior of the algorithm in the simplest possible form. The most common simplifications that you can make when using big-O notation are as follows:

1. *Eliminate any term whose contribution to the total ceases to be significant as N becomes large.* When a formula involves several terms added together, one of those terms often grows much faster than the others and ends up dominating the entire expression as *N* becomes large. For large values of *N,* this term alone controls the running time of the algorithm, and you can ignore the other terms in the formula entirely.

2. *Eliminate any constant factors.* When you calculate computational complexity, your main concern is how running time changes as a function of the problem size *N.* Constant factors have no effect on the overall pattern. If you bought a machine that was twice as fast as your old one, any algorithm that you executed on your machine would run twice as fast as before for every value of *N.* The growth pattern, however, would remain exactly the same. Thus, you can ignore constant factors when you use big-O notation.

The computational complexity of selection sort

You can apply the simplification rules from the preceding section to derive a big-O expression for the computational complexity of selection sort. From the analysis in the section on "Analyzing the selection sort algorithm" earlier in the chapter, you know that the running time of the selection sort algorithm for an array of *N* elements is proportional to

$$\frac{N^2 + N}{2}$$

Although it would be mathematically correct to use this formula directly in the big-O expression

$$O\left(\frac{N^2 + N}{2}\right)$$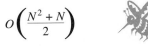

you would never do so in practice because the formula inside the parentheses is not expressed in the simplest form.

The first step toward simplifying this relationship is to recognize that the formula is actually the sum of two terms, as follows:

$$\frac{N^2}{2} + \frac{N}{2}$$

You then need to consider the contribution of each of these terms to the total formula as N increases in size, which is illustrated by the following table:

N	$\dfrac{N^2}{2}$	$\dfrac{N}{2}$	$\dfrac{N^2 + N}{2}$
10	50	5	55
100	5000	50	5050
1000	500,000	500	500,500
10,000	50,000,000	5000	50,005,000
100,000	5,000,000,000	50,000	5,000,050,000

As N increases, the term involving N^2 quickly dominates the term involving N. As a result, the simplification rule allows you to eliminate the smaller term from the expression. Even so, you would not write the computational complexity of selection sort as

$$O\!\left(\frac{N^2}{2}\right)$$

because you can eliminate the constant factor. The simplest expression you can use to indicate the complexity of selection sort is

$$O(N^2)$$

This expression captures the essence of the performance of selection sort. As the size of the problem increases, the running time tends to grow by the square of that increase. Thus, if you double the size of the array, the running time goes up by a factor of four. If you instead multiply the number of input values by 10, the running time explodes by a factor of 100. Algorithms like selection sort that exhibit $O(N^2)$ performance are said to run in **quadratic time.**

Predicting computational complexity from code structure

How would you determine the computational complexity of the method

```
double sumArray(double[] array) {
   double total = 0;
   for (int i = 0; i < array.length; i++) {
      total += array[i];
   }
   return total;
}
```

which computes the sum of the elements in an array? When you call this method, some parts of the code are executed only once, such as the declaration that initializes **total** to 0. This initialization step takes a certain amount of time, but that time is constant in the sense that it doesn't depend on the size of the array. Code whose execution time does not depend on the problem size is said to run in **constant time,** which is expressed in big-O notation as $O(1)$. Some students, however, find the designation $O(1)$ confusing, because the expression inside the parentheses does not depend on N. In fact, this lack of any dependency on N is the whole point of the $O(1)$ notation. As you increase the size of the problem, the time required to execute code whose running time is $O(1)$ increases in exactly the same way that 1 increases; in other words, the running time of the code does not increase at all.

There are, however, other parts of the **sumArray** method that are executed exactly N times, once for each cycle of the **for** loop. These components include the expression **i++** in the **for** loop and the statement

```
total += array[i];
```

which constitutes the loop body. Although any single execution of this part of the computation takes a fixed amount of time, the fact that these statements are executed N times means their total execution time is proportional to the array size. The computational complexity of this part of the **sumArray** method is $O(N)$, which is commonly called **linear time.**

The total running time for **sumArray** is therefore the sum of the times required for the constant parts and the linear parts of the algorithm. As the size of the problem increases, however, the constant term becomes less and less relevant. By exploiting the simplification rule that allows you to ignore terms that become insignificant as N gets large, you can assert that the **sumArray** method as a whole runs in $O(N)$ time.

You could, however, predict this result just by looking at the loop structure of the code. For the most part, the individual expressions and statements—unless they involve method calls that must be accounted separately—run in constant time. What matters in terms of computational complexity is how often those statements are executed. For many programs, you can determine the computational complexity simply by finding the piece of the code that is executed most often and determining how many times it runs as a method of N. In the case of the **sumArray** method, the body of the loop is executed N times. Because no part of the code is executed more often than this, you can predict that the computational complexity will be $O(N)$.

You can use a similar strategy to analyze the performance of the selection sort method in Figure 12-5. The most frequently executed part of the code is the comparison in the statement

```
if (array[i] < array[smallestIndex]) smallestIndex = i;
```

in the **findSmallest** method. That statement is nested inside two **for** loops, one in the **findSmallest** method itself and one in the **sort** method that calls it. As you saw in the section entitled "Analyzing the selection sort algorithm" earlier in the chapter, this statement is executed $O(N^2)$ times.

Worst-case versus average-case complexity

In some cases, the running time of an algorithm depends not only on the size of the problem but also on the specific characteristics of the data. For example, consider the method

```
private int linearSearch(int key, int[] array) {
   for (int i = 0; i < array.length; i++) {
      if (key == array[i]) return i;
   }
   return -1;
}
```

introduced near the beginning of this chapter. Because the **for** loop in the implementation executes N times, you expect the performance of **linearSearch** to be $O(N)$.

On the other hand, some calls to **linearSearch** can be executed very quickly. Suppose, for example, that the key element you are searching for happens to be in the first position in the array. In that case, the body of the **for** loop will run only once. If you're lucky enough to search for a value that always occurs at the beginning of the array, **linearSearch** will run in constant time.

When you analyze the computational complexity of a program, you're usually not interested in the minimum possible time. In general, computer scientists tend to be concerned about the following two types of complexity analysis:

- *Worst-case complexity.* The most common type of complexity analysis consists of determining the performance of an algorithm in the worst possible case. Such an analysis is useful because it allows you to set an upper bound on the computational complexity. If you analyze for the worst case, you can guarantee that the performance of the algorithm will be at least as good as your analysis indicates. You might sometimes get lucky, but you can be confident that the performance will not get any worse.

- *Average-case complexity.* From a practical point of view, it is often useful to consider how well an algorithm performs if you average its behavior over all possible sets of input data. Particularly if you have no reason to assume that the specific input to your problem is in any way atypical, the average-case analysis provides the best statistical estimate of actual performance. The problem, however, is that average-case analysis is usually much more difficult to carry out and typically requires considerable mathematical sophistication.

The worst case for the **linearSearch** method occurs when the key is not in the array at all. When the key is not there, the method must complete all N cycles of the **for** loop, which means that its performance is $O(N)$. If the key is known to be in the array, the **for** loop will be executed about half as many times on average, which implies that average-case performance is also $O(N)$. As you will discover in the section on "The Quicksort algorithm" later in this chapter, the average-case and worst-case performances of an algorithm sometimes differ in qualitative ways, which means that in practice it is often important to take both performance characteristics into consideration.

▰▰▰ 12.4 Using data files

As the preceding section makes clear, the running time of a program can vary substantially depending on the size of the problem it is trying to solve. Even though an algorithm like linear search is fine for small arrays, it becomes less practical as the number of elements in the array increases. The fact that particular algorithms may be substantially more or less efficient with large arrays brings up an important practical question: if you want to test a program with large arrays, how do you go about reading data into those arrays? In the simple programming examples in the early chapters of this book, it was easy enough to type in the data values that the application needed. Requesting input from the user becomes less feasible as the volume of data grows. Entering values by hand into a program that adds two numbers is easy enough; filling up an array of 10,000 elements by hand is a different situation altogether.

The rest of this chapter is devoted to the question of reading data from a file and, to a lesser extent, the symmetric process of writing data into a new file. The point of this discussion is not to offer a complete description of the file operations available in Java, but instead to give you the tools you need to write application programs that work with larger amounts of data.

The concept of a file

Programs use variables to store information: input data, calculated results, and any intermediate values generated along the way. The information in variables, however, is ephemeral. When the program stops running, the values of those variables are lost. For many applications, it is important to be able to store data in some more permanent fashion.

Whenever you want to store information on the computer for longer than the running time of a program, the usual approach is to collect the data into a logically cohesive whole and store it on a permanent storage medium as a *file,* a concept that was introduced in Chapter 1. Ordinarily, a file is stored on a hard disk inside the machine, but it can also be stored on removable medium, such as a CD or flash memory drive. In either case, the basic principles and modes of operation remain the same. The important point is that the permanent data objects you store on the computer—documents, games, executable programs, source code, and the like—are all stored in the form of files.

On most systems, files come in a variety of types. For example, in the programming domain, you work with source files, object files, and executable files, each of which has a distinct representation. When you use a file to store data for use by a program, that file usually consists of text and is therefore called a **text file.**

You can think of a text file as a sequence of characters stored in a permanent medium and identified by a file name. The name of the file and the characters it contains have the same relationship as the name of a variable and its contents.

As an example, let's suppose that you want to collect a set of your favorite quotations from Shakespeare and have decided to store each quotation in a separate file. You might begin your collection with the following quotation from *Hamlet:*

`Hamlet.txt`

```
To be, or not to be: that is the question.
Whether 'tis nobler in the mind to suffer
The slings and arrows of outrageous fortune,
Or to take arms against a sea of troubles,
And by opposing end them?
```

The diagram shows the name of the file—in this case `Hamlet.txt`—as being external to the file, just as diagrams of variables show the name on the outside and the value on the inside.

For your second quotation, you might choose the following lines from Juliet's balcony scene in *Romeo and Juliet:*

`Juliet.txt`

```
What's in a name?
That which we call a rose
By any other name would smell as sweet.
```

Your computer can keep the data for the two files separate because the files have different names.

When you look at a file, it often makes sense to regard it as a two-dimensional structure—a sequence of lines composed of individual characters. Internally, however, text files are represented as a continuous sequence of characters. In addition to the printing characters you can see, files also contain a special character or character sequence that marks the end of each line. Unfortunately, different operating systems use different character sequences for this purpose. The good news, however, is that Java's input and output operations hide the differences among the different operating systems and make it much easier to view a text file as a sequence of lines.

In many ways, a text file is similar to a string. Both are ordered sequences of characters. The two critical differences are that

- *The information stored in a file is permanent.* The value of a string variable persists only as long as the variable does. Local variables disappear when the method returns, and instance variables disappear when the object goes away, which typically does not occur until the program exits. Information stored in a file exists until the file is deleted.
- *Files are usually read sequentially.* When you read data from a file, you usually start at the beginning and read the characters in order. Once a character has been read, you go on to the next character until you reach the end of the file.

Reading text files in Java

If you want to read a text file as part of a Java program, you begin by constructing an object that is ultimately an instance of the `Reader` class in the `java.io` package. This process is called **opening** the file. As with most of Java's library classes, the `Reader` class is part of a more elaborate hierarchy that offers a variety of classes for different purposes. Part of the process of opening a file includes choosing the particular subclass of `Reader` that you want.

In reading from a text file, one of the classes you need to use is `FileReader`, which creates a `Reader` by looking up the specified name in the file system. For example, if you were to execute the declaration

```
FileReader rd = new FileReader("Hamlet.txt");
```

the implementation of the `FileReader` class would ask the file system to open the file named `Hamlet.txt` and then return a `FileReader` object that you could use to read data from that file. If all you had was a `FileReader` object, however, you wouldn't be able to read the contents of `Hamlet.txt` as conveniently as you might like. The `FileReader` class offers a low-level set of methods that supports reading characters from the file one at a time, but does not allow you to read data in larger units. In particular, a `FileReader` does not make it easy to read entire lines at once, which is often the most useful operation. For that, you need to turn your `FileReader` into a `BufferedReader`.

The constructor for the `BufferedReader` class takes any kind of reader and creates a new reader with additional capabilities. The new reader and the old one, however, still read data from the same source. Although you can declare separate variables for the `FileReader` and `BufferedReader`, you don't in fact need the `FileReader` value except to create the `BufferedReader`. It is therefore common practice to call both constructors in the same declaration, as follows:

```
BufferedReader rd
    = new BufferedReader(new FileReader("Hamlet.txt"))
```

Once you have declared and initialized the variable `rd`, you can call methods on that `BufferedReader` to read data from the file. You can read a single character from the file by calling `read`, just as you could with the underlying `FileReader` object. More importantly, the fact that you have a `BufferedReader` allows you to call `readLine`, which reads the entire next line as a string.

To get a better sense of how to use the `readLine` method, imagine for a moment that you are trying to read the file `Antony.txt`, which contains the following famous excerpt from Marc Antony's funeral oration in *Julius Caesar:*

```
Antony.txt
Friends, Romans, countrymen,
Lend me your ears;
I come to bury Caesar,
Not to praise him.
```

You can open the file by writing the declaration

```
BufferedReader rd
  = new BufferedReader(new FileReader("Antony.txt"));
```

which has the effect of establishing a link between the file and the value of the variable **rd**. To keep track of how far it has progressed in reading the file, the reader maintains an internal file pointer that marks the next character to be read. In the diagrams that follow, the position of the file pointer is indicated using a vertical bar, even though that information is stored entirely inside the reader and is not reflected at all in the actual file. When you open a file, the file pointer begins at the first character of the file, like this:

```
|Friends, Romans, countrymen,
 Lend me your ears;
 I come to bury Caesar,
 Not to praise him.
```

If you then read a line by calling

```
line = rd.readLine();
```

the string variable **line** will be set to the string

```
"Friends, Romans, countrymen,"
```

and the file pointer will advance past the entire first line to the beginning of the second:

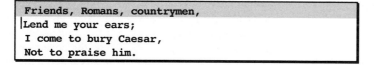

```
 Friends, Romans, countrymen,
|Lend me your ears;
 I come to bury Caesar,
 Not to praise him.
```

Calling

```
line = rd.readLine();
```

a second time will reset the value of **line** to the string

```
"Lend me your ears;"
```

and the file pointer will move to the beginning of the third line, as follows:

```
 Friends, Romans, countrymen,
 Lend me your ears;
|I come to bury Caesar,
 Not to praise him.
```

Eventually, after you have read all four lines of the file, the call to **readLine** will return the sentinel value **null** to indicate that there are no more lines in the file. At that point, you should close the reader by calling

```
        rd.close();
```

This call breaks the connection between the reader and the file system.

Exception handling

Opening a file is an example of an operation that can sometimes fail. For example, if you request the name of an input file from the user, and the user types the name incorrectly, the **FileReader** constructor will be unable to find the file you requested. To signal a failure of this sort, the methods in Java's libraries respond by **throwing an exception,** which is the phrase Java uses to describe the process of reporting an exceptional condition outside the normal program flow. When a Java method throws an exception, the Java runtime system stops executing code at that point and looks to see whether any of the methods on the control stack—starting with the current method and then proceeding backwards through the stack to the method that called the current one, the method that called that one, and so on—until it finds a method that expresses an intention to "catch" such an exception if one is "thrown." If an exception is never caught, the program simply stops running, and the Java runtime system reports the uncaught exception to the user.

Many of the exceptions that occur in Java, such as dividing by 0 and the like, are called **runtime exceptions** and can occur at any point in the code. When you write programs, you don't need to declare an interest in runtime exceptions. If your code doesn't catch them, the exception will simply propagate backwards on the control stack as described in the preceding paragraph.

The situation, however, is different with exception classes that are outside the runtime exception hierarchy. The designers of Java decided that they would *force* clients of the **java.io** package to check for situations like nonexistent input files by requiring clients to catch the exceptions that the methods in the package throw. Thus, the code to open and read a file in Java is not complete unless it explicitly catches exceptions in the **IOException** class. To do so, the code that works with data files must appear inside a **try** statement, which has the general form shown in the syntax box on the left. In the context of file-processing applications, the template looks more like this:

Simplified syntax for the try statement

```
try {
      Code in which an exception might occur
} catch (type identifier) {
      Code to respond to the exception
}
```
where:
    type is the type of the exception
    identifier is the name of a variable that
        holds the exception information

```
try {
      Code to open and read the file
} catch (IOException ex) {
      Code to respond to exceptions that occur
}
```

As an example of how you can use exception handling to check for errors in opening a file, it is convenient to write a general method for use with console programs that allows the user to select a file by entering its name in response to a prompt. If the file exists, the method returns a **BufferedReader** that can read the contents of the file. If not, the method displays a message indicating that it can't find the specified file and then gives the user another chance to enter the file name. The implementation for that method looks like this:

```
private BufferedReader openFileReader(String prompt) {
   BufferedReader rd = null;
   while (rd == null) {
      try {
         String name = readLine(prompt);
         rd = new BufferedReader(new FileReader(name));
      } catch (IOException ex) {
         println("Can't open that file.");
      }
   }
   return rd;
}
```

The **try** statement allows the program to detect whether an **IOException** appears anywhere within the execution of the body, even if that exception occurs in one of the library methods that **openFileReader** calls. In the case of a missing file, that exception is thrown by the constructor for the **FileReader** class, but is caught by the **catch** block in the **try** statement. When that exception occurs, the program executes the **println** statement to report the error to the user. Moreover, because the assignment to the **rd** variable was never completed, it still has the value **null**, which causes the **while** loop to request another file name.

In a context such as the one in **openFileReader**, it is relatively easy to determine what to do when the exception occurs. In that case, the cause of the exception was almost certainly that the user incorrectly entered the name of the file. The problem of responding to an **IOException** is more difficult when the exception occurs on a call such as **readLine** or **close**. In these cases—which are fortunately extremely rare—the likely cause is a real error in the file system. Given that there is nothing your program can do to try to fix such an error, the easiest strategy is to abandon any attempt at responding to the exception and let the exception handler report that an unrecoverable error has occurred. The usual way to do so is to throw a runtime exception that will propagate back to the operating system. The **acm.util** package defines a runtime exception subclass called **ErrorException**, which is designed expressly for this purpose. You can throw an error exception either by supplying a message, as in

```
throw new ErrorException("Division by zero");
```

or by forwarding along some other exception that has already occurred. The file manipulation programs in this chapter adopt the second strategy by embedding the code to read a file in the following context:

```
try {
   Code to open and read the file
} catch (IOException ex) {
   throw new ErrorException(ex);
}
```

A program to reverse a file

The **ReverseFile** program in Figure 12-7, which reads a data file and then displays the lines of that file in reverse order, gives you a chance to see how the various techniques described in the earlier sections fit together to form a complete application. The program begins by asking the user for the name of a file, making use of the **openFileReader** method introduced in the preceding section. Once the user has successfully entered the name of an existing file, the program reads the entire file into an array and then prints out the lines of that array in reverse order.

You could use the **ReverseFile** program to reverse the lines in the following file, which lists a few of the ingredients in the witches' brew from *Macbeth* (some of which might give even Professor Snape at Hogwarts a moment's pause):

WitchesBrew.txt

```
In the cauldron boil and bake;
Eye of newt and toe of frog,
Wool of bat and tongue of dog,
Adder's fork and blind-worm's sting,
Lizard's leg and howlet's wing,
For a charm of powerful trouble,
Like a hell-broth boil and bubble.
Double, double, toil and trouble;
Fire burn and cauldron bubble.
```

Were you to run this program—and eventually get the name of the file right after mistyping it the first time around—you would see the following output, which makes almost as much sense as the original:

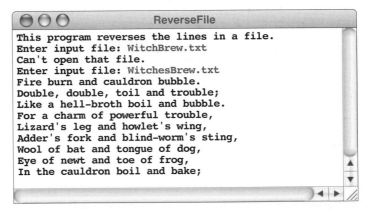

Selecting files interactively

Although being able to enter a file name in a console window might have seemed sufficient a couple of decades ago, few modern applications force the user to enter a file name by hand. What you do instead is use a **file dialog,** which is an interactive dialog window that lets you navigate through directories and select a file by using the mouse. The Java libraries include classes that allow you to do exactly that.

FIGURE 12-7 Program to print the lines of a file in reverse order

```java
import acm.program.*;
import acm.util.*;
import java.io.*;
import java.util.*;

/** This program reverses the lines in a file */
public class ReverseFile extends ConsoleProgram {

    public void run() {
        println("This program reverses the lines in a file.");
        BufferedReader rd = openFileReader("Enter input file: ");
        String[] lines = readLineArray(rd);
        for (int i = lines.length - 1; i >= 0; i--) {
            println(lines[i]);
        }
    }

/*
 * Reads all available lines from the specified reader and returns an array
 * containing those lines.  This method closes the reader at the end of the file.
 *
 * Implementation note:
 *   This implementation uses an ArrayList internally to read the lines of the
 *   file because doing so allows the list to expand dynamically.  However,
 *   because the definition of the method indicates that the method returns an
 *   array rather than an ArrayList, the implementation copies the ArrayList
 *   to an array after all the lines have been read.
 *
 * @param rd A BufferedReader for the input file
 * @return A string array containing the lines read from the reader
 */
    private String[] readLineArray(BufferedReader rd) {
        ArrayList<String> lineList = new ArrayList<String>();
        try {
            while (true) {
                String line = rd.readLine();
                if (line == null) break;
                lineList.add(line);
            }
            rd.close();
        } catch (IOException ex) {
            throw new ErrorException(ex);
        }
        String[] result = new String[lineList.size()];
        for (int i = 0; i < result.length; i++) {
            result[i] = lineList.get(i);
        }
        return result;
    }

/* Include the definition of openFileReader from the text */

}
```

Whenever you want to create a file dialog, you need to create an instance of the **JFileChooser** class, which is part of the **javax.swing** package. The most common version of the **JFileChooser** constructor takes no arguments, so the code you need to create one looks like this:

```
JFileChooser chooser = new JFileChooser();
```

At this point, you have created the chooser object, although nothing appears on the screen as yet. When you need to request an input file name from the user, you call the **showOpenDialog** method. That method takes an argument, which must be a component displayed on the screen. If you are calling this method from a **Program** subclass, the simplest option is to use the **Program** object itself, which you can indicate with the keyword **this**. The **showOpenDialog** method also returns a result that you need to save in a variable of type **int**. A typical call to **showOpenDialog** therefore looks like this:

```
int result = chooser.showOpenDialog(this);
```

As soon as you make this call, a dialog window pops up on the screen, looking like the one shown in Figure 12-8. That dialog allows you to move around in the file system and eventually select a file. In this example, the user has highlighted the file **Hamlet.txt**. If the user clicks the **Open** button, the idea is that your program should open the **Hamlet.txt** file. On the other hand, if the user clicks the **Cancel** button, your program should *not* open the selected file.

FIGURE 12-8   **Example of a JFileChooser dialog box**

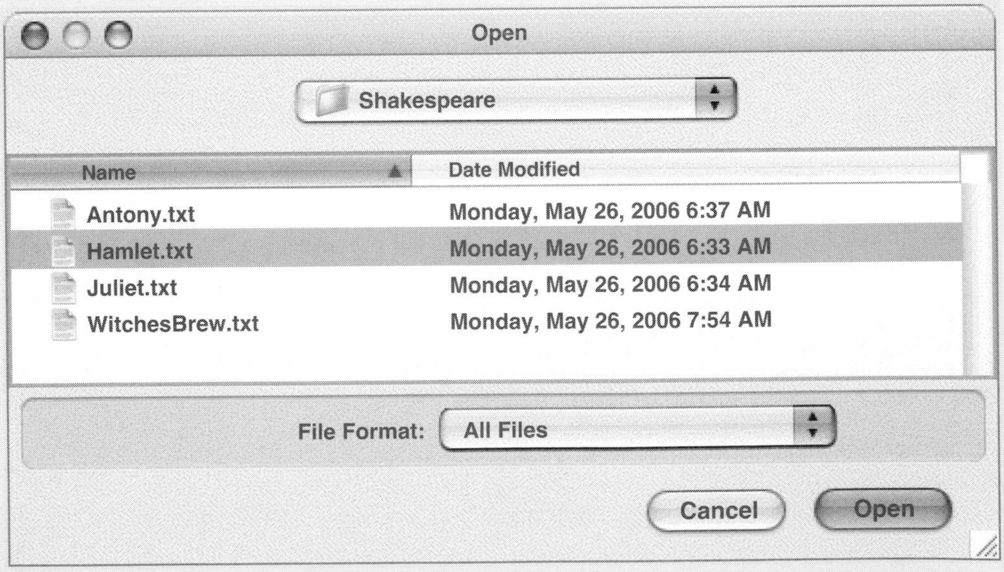

The way you tell what button was clicked is by checking the result of the **showOpenDialog** call. If the user clicks **Open**, the **showOpenDialog** method returns the constant **JFileChooser.APPROVE_OPTION**; if the user clicks **Cancel**, the method returns **JFileChooser.CANCEL_OPTION** instead. Your program should therefore check to make sure **result** is equal to **JFileChooser.APPROVE_OPTION** before opening the file.

In order to find out what file to open, you need to ask the **JFileChooser** dialog for that information. You do so by calling the **getSelectedFile** method, which returns the file selected by the user. The result of **getSelectedFile** is not simply the name of the file but is instead a **File** object, as defined in the **java.io** package. The advantage of using a **File** object rather than the name is that the **File** object includes the directory information, which makes it possible for Java to open the file no matter where it appears in the file system. Fortunately, the **FileReader** constructor can accept a **File** as well as a **String**.

If you want to put all this together, you can replace the call to **openFileReader** in Figure 12-7 with a call to the following method, which opens an input file using a file chooser.

```
private BufferedReader openFileReaderUsingChooser() {
   BufferedReader rd = null;
   JFileChooser chooser = new JFileChooser();
   int result = chooser.showOpenDialog(this);
   if (result == JFileChooser.APPROVE_OPTION) {
      try {
         File file = chooser.getSelectedFile();
         rd = new BufferedReader(new FileReader(file));
      } catch (IOException ex) {
         println("Can't open that file.");
      }
   }
   return rd;
}
```

As before, the method returns an open **BufferedReader** associated with the selected file, but only if the user clicks **Open**. If the user clicks **Cancel**, the **openFileReader** method returns **null**, which means that you also need to change the **run** method to check for that case.

Using the Scanner class

While the **readLine** method is useful for reading entire lines from a file, it doesn't really address the problem of reading other kinds of data. How, for example, would you go about reading an array of integers from a file containing a list of floating-point numbers, one value per line? One strategy that works perfectly well is to use the **Double.parseDouble** method introduced in Chapter 7 to convert each line to a **double**. Indeed, that strategy is pretty much the only one you can use if you are working with a version of Java prior to Java 5.0. To simplify the problem of reading data values of any of Java's primitive types, the designers of Java 5.0 introduced a new class called **Scanner** that simplifies these operations considerably.

Like many classes in Java 5.0, the `Scanner` class in the `java.util` package exports a large number of methods—over 70 if you count the constructors—that make it difficult to understand if you try to master the class as a whole. If, however, you work only with a subset of those methods, the `Scanner` class turns out to be easy to use. Figure 12-9 highlights ten methods that will serve you well in most applications.

The basic paradigm for using the `Scanner` class is to create an instance that reads data from a particular source, which is usually a `Reader` of some kind. You can then call the various methods beginning with `next` to read data values of specific types. For example, if you want to read a `double` value from the `Scanner`, you can call the `nextDouble` method. That method will skip over any whitespace characters and then try to read the next token as a `double`. If it succeeds, you get the `double` as the return value of the method. If it fails—presumably because the file does not contain a valid double-precision number at that point in the input—the `Scanner` throws an `InputMismatchException`. Unlike the exceptions in the `java.io` package, `InputMismatchException` is a subclass of `RuntimeException`, which means that you aren't forced to catch it. If such an exception occurs and you haven't taken any steps to catch it, the program will simply stop running because of an uncaught exception error. One of the tremendous advantages of using the

---

FIGURE 12-9 **Selected methods in the `Scanner` class**

Constructor

`new Scanner(Reader rd)`
Creates a new `Scanner` that reads values from the reader.

Methods to read the next value of the most common types

`String next()`
Returns the next token separated by whitespace.

`int nextInt()`
Reads an `int` if one appears next in the token stream; if not, the scanner throws an exception.

`double nextDouble()`
Reads a `double` if one appears next in the token stream; if not, the scanner throws an exception.

`boolean nextBoolean()`
Reads a `boolean` if the next token is `true` or `false`; if not, the scanner throws an exception.

Methods to test whether tokens of a particular type exist

`boolean hasNext()`
Returns `true` if there are any more tokens to be read.

`boolean hasNextInt()`
Reads `true` if it is possible to read an `int` at this point in the token stream.

`boolean hasNextDouble()`
Reads `true` if it is possible to read a `double` at this point in the token stream.

`boolean hasNextBoolean()`
Reads `true` if it is possible to read a `boolean` at this point in the token stream.

Methods to close the scanner stream

`void close()`
Closes the scanner and the underlying reader.

Scanner class is that it eliminates the need to take account of any **IOException**s that occur, because this exception is automatically caught inside the **Scanner**.

To get a sense of how you might use the **Scanner** in a simple way, the following method takes a **Reader** that has been opened so that it is reading from a file containing a list of floating-point values, one per line:

```
private double[] readDoubleArray(Reader rd) {
   ArrayList<Double> doubleList = new ArrayList<Double>();
   Scanner scanner = new Scanner(rd);
   while (scanner.hasNextDouble()) {
      doubleList.add(scanner.nextDouble());
   }
   double[] result = new double[doubleList.size()];
   for (int i = 0; i < result.length; i++) {
      result[i] = doubleList.get(i);
   }
   scanner.close();
   return result;
}
```

The method returns an array of **double**s that appear in the file. This method will come in handy if you need to write programs that work with numeric arrays.

Using files for output

As the final comment in the discussion of files, it is important to note that files can also be used to write data to the file system. In many respects, writing data is easier than reading data because you can use the **println** method, which works exactly the way you've been using it all along. The only difference is that you need to supply a receiver, which must be a **PrintWriter**.

Creating a **PrintWriter** from a file name is in many ways symmetrical to creating a **BufferedReader** for input. You first create a **FileWriter** and then use it to create a **PrintWriter**. This technique is illustrated by the following **run** method, which creates a file **Hello.txt** containing the message **"hello, world"**:

```
public void run() {
   try {
      PrintWriter wr
         = new PrintWriter(new FileWriter("Hello.txt"));
      wr.println("hello, world");
      wr.close();
   } catch (IOException ex) {
      throw new ErrorException(ex);
   }
}
```

As you can see from the code, writing a file also requires you to catch **IOException**.

You can use the **JFileChooser** class to choose a file for writing. The only difference is that you call **showSaveDialog** instead of **showOpenDialog**.

Summary

In this chapter, you have had the opportunity to learn about two of the most important operations on arrays—*searching* and *sorting*—each of which is an interesting algorithmic problem in its own right. The important points covered in this chapter include:

- The *linear search algorithm* operates by looking at each element of an array in sequential order until the desired element is found.

- The *binary search algorithm* is much more efficient than linear search but requires that the elements of the array be in sorted order. The efficiency advantage of the binary search algorithm lies in the fact that you can discard half of the potential array elements in every cycle.

- Despite the theoretical improvement in efficiency that binary search offers, linear search is substantially easier to code and is therefore the better choice when the size of the array is small.

- Sorting algorithms vary considerably in their efficiency. For arrays containing a small number of elements, simple algorithms such as *selection sort* are perfectly adequate. For larger arrays, however, such algorithms cease to be cost-effective.

- Many algorithmic problems can be characterized by an integer *N* that represents the size of the problem. For algorithms that operate on arrays, it usually makes sense to define the problem size as the number of elements.

- The most useful qualitative measure of efficiency is *computational complexity,* which expresses the relationship between problem size and algorithmic performance as the problem size becomes large.

- *Big-O notation* provides an intuitive way of expressing computational complexity because it allows you to highlight the most important aspects of the complexity relationship in the simplest possible form.

- When you use big-O notation, you can simplify the formula by eliminating any term in the formula that becomes insignificant as *N* becomes large, along with any constant factors.

- You can often predict the computational complexity of a program by looking at the nesting structure of the loops it contains.

- A convenient strategy for reading a data file consists of opening that file to obtain a **BufferedReader** object and then calling the **readLine** method to read each line from the file as a string. The **readLine** method returns **null** at the end of the file.

- You can write data to a file by creating a **PrintWriter** object and then calling the **println** method to write each line of data to the file.

- Code that uses **java.io** to read or write data files must include a **try** statement to catch **IOException**s that occur during file processing.

- The **JFileChooser** class makes it easy for applications to let the user choose a file through an interactive dialog box.

- You can use the **Scanner** class in Java 5.0 to read numeric data from a reader.

Review questions

1. Define the terms *searching* and *sorting*.

2. What changes would you have to make to the **linearSearch** method so that it finds a matching value in an array of values of type **double**? Could you include both versions of **linearSearch** in the same program?

3. Describe the linear search and binary search algorithms in simple English.

4. True or false: If the number of data items is large enough, the binary search algorithm can be millions of times faster than the linear search algorithm.

5. What condition must be true before the binary search algorithm can be applied?

6. Describe the steps that are involved in the selection sort algorithm.

7. The **for** loop control line in the selection sort implementation of **sort** was written as

        for (int lh = 0; lh < array.length; lh++)

    Would the method still work if you changed this line to

        for (int lh = 0; lh < array.length - 1; lh++)

8. What method can you call to determine the current time in milliseconds?

9. What does it mean to say that an algorithm is quadratic?

10. When you apply the radix sort algorithm, do you perform the first sorting pass on the most significant digit or the least significant digit? Why?

11. What is the closed-form expression that computes the sum of the series

$$N + N{-}1 + N{-}2 + \ldots + 3 + 2 + 1$$

12. In your own words, define the concept of computational complexity.

13. What are the two rules presented in this chapter for simplifying big-O notation?

14. Is it technically correct to say that selection sort runs in

$$O\left(\frac{N^2 + N}{2}\right)$$

    time? What, if anything, is wrong with doing so?

15. Is it technically correct to say that selection sort runs in $O(N^3)$ time? Again, what, if anything, is wrong with doing so?

16. Explain the difference between worst-case and average-case complexity. In general, which of these measures is harder to compute?

17. In terms of big-O notation, what is the average-case computational complexity of each of the following algorithms: linear search, binary search, selection sort, and merge sort?

18. Use big-O notation to express the computational complexity of each of the following methods as a function of the argument **n**:

a)
```java
private int Mystery1(int n) {
    int sum = 0;
    for (int i = 0; i < n; i++) {
        for (int j = 0; j < i; j++) {
            sum += i * j;
        }
    }
    return sum;
}
```

b)
```java
private int Mystery2(int n) {
    int count = 0;
    while (n > 0) {
        n /= 2;
        count++;
    }
    return count;
}
```

c)
```java
private int Mystery3(int n) {
    int sum = 0;
    for (int i = 0; i < 10; i++) {
        for (int j = 0; j < i; j++) {
            sum += j * n;
        }
    }
    return sum;
}
```

19. What method does the code in this chapter use in the **BufferedReader** class that does not exist in the more primitive **FileReader** class?

20. What is an exception?

21. Exception processing usually involves two different methods: one method detects the exceptional condition and sends a signal that it occurred, while the other responds to that signal. What evocative verbs does Java use to describe the actions taken by each of those methods?

22. Several of the programs in this chapter call a method in the **BufferedReader** class that does not exist in the more primitive **FileReader** class. What is the name of that method?

Programming exercises

1. Write a program **GuessTheNumber** that plays a number-guessing game with its user, who is presumably an elementary-school child. The child thinks of a number and then answers a series of questions until the computer correctly guesses the number. The following sample run shows what happens when the number is 17:

```
○ ○ ○                 GuessTheNumber
Think of a number between 1 and 100.
Is it 50? no
Is it less than 50? yes
Is it 25? no
Is it less than 25? yes
Is it 12? no
Is it less than 12? no
Is it 18? no
Is it less than 18? yes
Is it 15? no
Is it less than 15? no
Is it 16? no
Is it less than 16? no
Is it 17? yes
I guessed the number!
```

2. Write a predicate method **isSorted(array)** that takes an integer array and returns **true** if the array is sorted in nondecreasing order.

3. Rewrite the selection sort implementation so that the **sort** method can also take an **ArrayList<Integer>** as well as an array of **int**s. The **ArrayList** version of the method should use only **ArrayList** operations and should not merely convert the **ArrayList** to an array, sort it, and then convert it back.

4. Modify the code for the selection sort algorithm to produce a method called **alphabetize** that sorts an array of strings into lexicographic order.

5. In the exercises for Chapter 11, you had the chance to write two programs to compute common statistical measures: the mean and the standard deviation. Another important statistical measure is the **median,** the data value that occupies the central element position in a distribution whose values have been sorted from lowest to highest. If the distribution contains an even number of values and therefore has no central element, the standard convention is to average the two values that fall closest to the midpoint.

   Write a method **median(array)** that returns the median of an array of **double**s. Your implementation may not assume that the array is sorted, nor may it change the array in any way, although it may create a copy of the array.

6. Besides the mean and the median, the third statistical measure designed to indicate the most representative element of a distribution is the **mode,** the value that occurs most often in an array. For example, in the array

65	84	95	75	82	79	82	72	84	94	86	90	84
0	1	2	3	4	5	6	7	8	9	10	11	12

   the mode is the value 84, because it appears three times. The only other value that occurs more than once is 82, which only appears twice.

   Write a method **mode(array)** that returns the mode of an array of **double**s. If there are several values that occur equally often and outnumber any of the other values (such distributions are called **multimodal**), your method may return any of those values as the mode. As in exercise 5, your implementation may not assume that the array is sorted or change the order of its elements.

7. Many algorithmic problems are related to sorting in their solution structure. For example, you can shuffle an array by "sorting" it according to a random key value. One way to do this is to begin with the selection sort algorithm and then replace the step that finds the position of smallest value with one that selects a random position. The result is a shuffling algorithm in which each possible output configuration is equally likely.

   Write a program **Shuffle** that displays the integers between 1 and 52 in a randomly sorted order.

8. One of the most famous algorithmic problems taught at the introductory level is the Dutch National Flag problem, first proposed by Edsger Dijkstra. Suppose that you have an array with *N* elements, each of which is a character—`'R'`, `'W'`, or `'B'`—representing one of the colors in the Dutch flag. Initially, these values might be jumbled in the array, as shown in the following configuration:

R	B	W	W	B	B	R	W	W	R	R	W	R	B	R
0	1	2	3	4	5	6	7	8	9	10	11	12	13	14

Your job is to rearrange these characters so that they appear in the same order as they do in the Dutch flag: all the reds, followed by all the whites, followed by all the blues.

Try to infer the algorithm by studying the following sample run of a program to solve this problem, which displays the sequence of the colors each time it interchanges two positions:

```
DutchNationalFlag
Initial state:
R B W W B B R W W R R W R B W
After swapping positions 1 and 14:
R W W W B B R W W R R W R B B
After swapping positions 4 and 13:
R W W W B B R W W R R W R B B
After swapping positions 4 and 12:
R W W W R B R W W R R W B B B
After swapping positions 1 and 4:
R R W W W B R W W R R W B B B
After swapping positions 5 and 11:
R R W W W W R W W R R B B B B
After swapping positions 2 and 6:
R R R W W W W W W R R B B B B
After swapping positions 3 and 9:
R R R R W W W W W R W R B B B B
After swapping positions 4 and 10:
R R R R W W W W W W B B B B
```

Write a program that implements the algorithm on a randomly constructed initial state.

9. There are several other sorting algorithms besides selection sort that make
    sense at your level of programming knowledge. One of those algorithms,
    which has some utility in practical applications because it runs quickly on
    arrays that are almost sorted, is called **insertion sort.**

    The insertion sort algorithm operates as follows. You go through each
    element in the array in turn, as with the selection sort algorithm. At each step
    in the process, however, your goal is not to find the smallest value remaining
    value and switch it into its correct position, but rather to ensure that the values
    you've covered so far in the array are correctly ordered with respect to one
    another. Although those values may shift as more elements are processed, they
    form an ordered sequence in and of themselves.

    For example, if you consider again the data used in the selection sort
    discussion, the first cycle of the insertion sort algorithm requires no work
    because an array of one element is always sorted:

    in order

31	41	59	26	53	58	97	93
0	1	2	3	4	5	6	7

    The next two cycles of the main loop also require no rearrangement of the
    array, because the sequence 31-41-59 forms an ordered subarray.

    The first significant operation occurs on the next cycle, when you need to fit
    26 into this sequence. To find where 26 should go, you need to move backward
    through the earlier elements, which you know are in order with respect to each
    other, looking for the position where 26 belongs. At each step, you need to
    shift the other elements over one position to make room for the 26, which
    winds up in position 0. Thus, the configuration after the fourth cycle is

    in order

    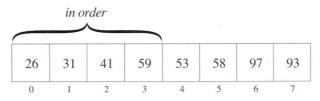

26	31	41	59	53	58	97	93
0	1	2	3	4	5	6	7

    On each subsequent step, you again insert the next element into its proper
    position in the initial subarray, which is always sorted at the end of each step.

    Reimplement the **sort** method using the insertion sort algorithm.

10. Complete the implementation of the radix sort algorithm that will sort an array
    of nonnegative integers up to ten digits in length. A pseudocode version of the
    algorithm appears on page 480.

11. Write a program **WordCount** that reads a file and reports how many lines,
    words, and characters appear in it. For this exercise, your program should not
    counting end-of-line characters at all, and should assume that a word consists of
    a consecutive sequence of any characters except whitespace characters. For
    example, if the file **Lear.txt** contains the following passage from *King Lear,*

```
Lear.txt
┌──────────────────────────────────────────────────────┐
│ Poor naked wretches, wheresoe'er you are,             │
│ That bide the pelting of this pitiless storm,         │
│ How shall your houseless heads and unfed sides,       │
│ Your loop'd and window'd raggedness, defend you       │
│ From seasons such as these?  O, I have ta'en          │
│ Too little care of this!                              │
└──────────────────────────────────────────────────────┘
```

your program should be able to generate the following sample run:

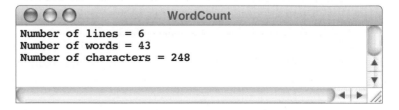

```
● ● ●                    WordCount
Number of lines = 6
Number of words = 43
Number of characters = 248
```

12. Some files use tab characters to align data into columns. Doing so, however, can cause problems for certain applications that are unable to work directly with tabs. For these applications, it is useful to have access to a program that replaces tabs in an input file with the number of spaces required to reach the next tab stop. In programming, tab stops are usually set every eight spaces. For example, suppose that the input file contains a line of the form

```
┌──────────────────────────────────────────────────────┐
│ abc————┤nopqr——┤xyz                                   │
└──────────────────────────────────────────────────────┘
```

where the ——┤ symbol represents the space taken up by a tab, which differs depending on its position in the line. If the tab stops are set every eight spaces, the first tab character must be replaced by five spaces and the second one by three.

Write a program **Untabify** that uses a **JFileChooser** from the user and updates the file so that all the tabs are replaced by enough spaces to reach the next tab stop. To replace a file, the easiest thing to do is read the entire file into memory, close it, modify the stored version of the file, reopen the same file for output, and write the modified text.

13. On occasion, publishers find it useful to evaluate layouts and stylistic designs without being distracted by the actual words. To do so, they sometimes typeset sample pages in such a way that all of the original letters are replaced by random letters. The resulting text has the spacing and punctuation of the original, but no longer conveys any meaning that might get in the way of the design. The publishing term for text that has been replaced in this way is **greek.**

Write a program **Greek** that reads characters from an input file and displays them on the console after making the appropriate random substitutions. Any uppercase character in the input should be replaced by a random uppercase character and every lowercase character by a random lowercase one.

Nonalphabetic characters are displayed without change. As an example, suppose that the input file contains the following conversation between Cassius and Casca in Act I of *Julius Caesar:*

CassiusCasca.txt

```
CASSIUS. Did Cicero say anything?
CASCA. Ay, he spoke Greek.
CASSIUS. To what effect?
CASCA. Nay, an I tell you that, I'll ne'er look
you i' the face again; but those that understood
him smiled at one another and shook their heads;
but for mine own part, it was Greek to me.
```

your program should generate output that looks something like this:

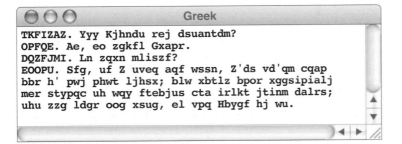

```
TKFIZAZ. Yyy Kjhndu rej dsuantdm?
OPFQE. Ae, eo zgkfl Gxapr.
DQZFJMI. Ln zqxn mliszf?
EOOPU. Sfg, uf Z uveq aqf wssn, Z'ds vd'qm cqap
bbr h' pwj phwt ljhsx; blw xbtlz bpor xggsipialj
mer stypqc uh wqy ftebjus cta irlkt jtinm dalrs;
uhu zzg ldgr oog xsug, el vpq Hbygf hj wu.
```

14. The first crossword puzzle published in the United States was designed by Arthur Wynne and appeared on December 21, 1913, in *The New York World*. The solution grid for the puzzle looked like this:

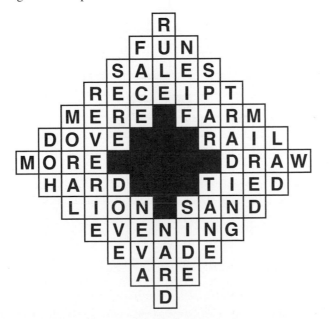

You could easily store this solution in a data file by using spaces for the squares that are entirely missing around the edges and the @ character for the black squares in the interior. The file form of this puzzle would then look like this:

FirstCrossword.txt

```
        R
       FUN
      SALES
     RECEIPT
    MERE@FARM
   DOVE@@@RAIL
  MORE@@@@@DRAW
   HARD@@@TIED
    LION@SAND
     EVENING
      EVADE
       ARE
        D
```

Write a **GraphicsProgram** that reads a data file in this format and draws the blank crossword grid for the puzzle. The positions that are indicated by spaces in the file should not appear at all, the positions indicated by the @ character should appear in the grid as filled squares, and the positions marked with a letter should appear in the grid as an outlined square. If the square is at the beginning of a word running across, down, or both, the square should also contain a number that is assigned sequentially through the puzzle. Given this grid, for example, the output of the graphics program should look like this:

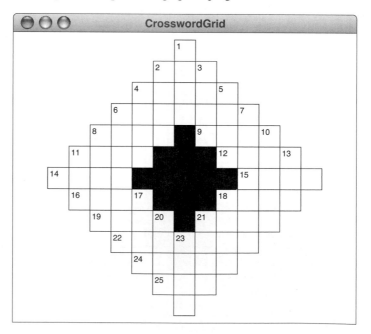

CHAPTER 13

Collection Classes

I think this is the most extraordinary collection of talent, of human knowledge, that has ever been gathered at the White House—with the possible exception of when Thomas Jefferson dined alone.
— John F. Kennedy, dinner for Nobel laureates, 1962

Joshua Bloch

Joshua Bloch first got excited about programming in 1975, when he had the chance to use a timeshared PDP-10 computer. Three years later, he entered Columbia University, where he majored in computer science, and then went on to get a Ph.D. at Carnegie Mellon. After completing his Ph.D., Bloch went to work for Transarc, a startup company founded by his dissertation advisor. In 1994, he moved to California to join the Java development team at Sun Microsystems. While there, Bloch designed and implemented the Java Collection Framework described in this chapter. In 2004, Bloch left Sun to join Google, where he holds the positions of Principal Engineer and Chief Java Architect. Josh Bloch and his colleague Neal Gafter recently wrote a wonderful collection of Java pitfalls entitled *Java Puzzlers,* which is also published by Addison-Wesley.

Although using tools like the ACM Java libraries or the many useful classes in the standard Java packages can simplify the programming process considerably, becoming an effective programmer does not require you to memorize the contents of every available library package. Most experienced programmers know well only those packages and classes that they use often. If you use a class once a year or so, it makes much more sense to look up its documentation when you actually need it than it does to try to keep all the details in your head. What is important is that you know how to find that information and how to understand it once you do.

Typically, the best resource for finding detailed information about a Java package is its web-based documentation, which usually exists as a set of **javadoc** pages. As you know from Chapter 6, the **javadoc** entries for a package describe each of its classes and, for each class, the public entries that you might want to use as a client. The fact that **javadoc** is web-based makes it particularly easy to navigate. If a method in one class relies on a definition from some other class, you can jump immediately to the documentation you need just by following the link.

Understanding the documentation once you find it, however, takes a certain amount of practice. As a new programmer, you can easily find yourself just as overwhelmed by the documentation as by the classes they describe. The fact that there is so much information out there creates a problem of **information overload,** in which the information you need is there, but you can't easily find it in the vast sea of details. To avoid becoming hopelessly lost, you must find ways to fit the many pieces of information into a conceptual structure that allows you to navigate all that complexity.

Most Java packages have an underlying conceptual model that helps to bring some order to the chaos. If you dive right in without bothering to understand that model, you are much less likely to succeed. Taking the time to appreciate what binds the different classes in a package together and makes them work as an integrated system is usually well worth the time.

The purpose of this chapter is to introduce you to a particularly important part of the standard Java library called the **Java Collections Framework,** which is an integrated set of classes that make it easy to manipulate collections of data in useful ways. Although some of the classes—most notably **ArrayList** and **HashMap**—are likely to become part of your everyday set of tools, the point of this chapter is to look at the Java Collections Framework, not as a set of individual classes, but as an integrated whole. By thinking about the overarching model, you will not only gain a better sense of how to use those classes, but also begin to appreciate how to design good packages of your own.

13.1 The `ArrayList` class revisited

You have already seen the **ArrayList** class, which is surely the most commonly used class in the Java Collections Framework. As you know from the discussion in Chapter 11, the **ArrayList** class provides the basic operations that can be applied to arrays but extends the standard behavior of arrays by making it possible to add and remove elements dynamically.

The power of dynamic allocation

The ability to add new elements makes the **ArrayList** class far more useful than the built-in array mechanism on which it is based. As an example, the following code, which is taken from the implementation of the **readLineArray** method in Figure 12-7, creates an **ArrayList** called **lineList** and fills it with the lines of the file associated with the **BufferedReader** stored in the variable **rd**:

```
ArrayList<String> lineList = new ArrayList<String>();
try {
   while (true) {
      String line = rd.readLine();
      if (line == null) break;
      lineList.add(line);
   }
   rd.close();
} catch (IOException ex) {
   throw new ErrorException(ex);
}
```

Although the **try** statement required to catch exceptions makes this example a little difficult to read, the rest of the code is straightforward. The first statement creates a new **ArrayList** of strings that is initially empty. The **while** loop inside the **try** statement then calls **readLine** on the reader to obtain the next line of the file. As long as the line that comes back from **readLine** is not the **null** sentinel, the code adds the line to the end of **lineList**.

The fact that the **ArrayList** class can make room for each new line as it appears represents a substantial simplification of the program, at least when compared to an implementation that relies on arrays alone. Any implementation that relies only on arrays, however, must somehow address the problem of knowing how big to make the array. If you knew in advance how many lines were in the file, you could allocate an array of the correct size. In the absence of that information, it is harder to see how such a strategy might work.

The solution to this problem lies in the fact that Java implements **dynamic allocation,** which means that a program can allocate new objects in the heap as the program runs. The basic idea is to allocate an array using some default size and then expand the array whenever it runs out of space. The revised implementation of **readLineArray** shown in Figure 13-1 offers one implementation of that approach. In that implementation, the code allocates an array containing **INITIAL_CAPACITY** elements at the beginning and then doubles the size of the array whenever it runs out of room. Because it is impossible to change the size of an existing array object, the **readLineArray** implementation has to allocate a new array that is twice the size of the old one, copy all the values from the old array to the new one, and finally replace the old array with the new one. In the code in Figure 13-1, this work is carried out by the method **doubleArraySize**.

The code for Java's **ArrayList** class uses a similar strategy that differs only in a few minor details. Those details, however, are not important to you as a client of the **ArrayList** class. For you, it is not important *how* the **ArrayList** class makes additional space available. What is important is that it does so.

| FIGURE 13-1 | Implementation of `readLineArray` that uses only array operations |

```
/*
 * Reads all available lines from the specified reader and returns an array
 * containing those lines.  This method closes the reader at the end of the file.
 *
 * Implementation note:
 *   This version of the implementation uses arrays rather than array lists
 *   to read the lines.  Because you cannot add new elements to an array in
 *   the way you can with an ArrayList, this implementation reallocates the
 *   array whenever it runs out of space by doubling the available capacity.
 *   As in the original version, this method uses a second pass to copy the
 *   contents of lineArray into a new array with the right number of elements.
 *
 * @param rd A BufferedReader for the input file
 * @return A string array containing the lines read from the reader
 */
   private String[] readLineArray(BufferedReader rd) {
      String[] lineArray = new String[INITIAL_CAPACITY];
      int nLines = 0;
      try {
         while (true) {
            String line = rd.readLine();
            if (line == null) break;
            if (nLines + 1>= lineArray.length) {
               lineArray = doubleArrayCapacity(lineArray);
            }
            lineArray[nLines++] = line;
         }
         rd.close();
      } catch (IOException ex) {
         throw new ErrorException(ex);
      }
      String[] result = new String[nLines];
      for (int i = 0; i < nLines; i++) {
         result[i] = lineArray[i];
      }
      return result;
   }

/*
 * Creates a string array with twice as many elements as the old array and
 * then copies the existing elements from the old array to the new one.
 */
   private String[] doubleArrayCapacity(String[] oldArray) {
      String[] newArray = new String[2 * oldArray.length];
      for (int i = 0; i < oldArray.length; i++) {
         newArray[i] = oldArray[i];
      }
      return newArray;
   }

/* Private constants */
   private static final int INITIAL_CAPACITY = 10;
```

One important observation that will help you understand the code in Figure 13-1 is that the implementation keeps track of two different measures of how many elements the array contains. From the client's perspective, the only important measure is the number of lines read from the file, which is called the **effective size.** The revised implementation of `readLineArray` uses the variable `nLines` to keep track of the effective size. The other measure is the space reserved for new elements, including those that do not yet exist. This measure is called the **capacity** of the array. The program must ensure that the effective size never exceeds the capacity. If adding a new element would extend the array beyond its current capacity, the implementation has to make room by making the array larger.

Separating behavior from representation

The point of presenting the implementation details in the preceding section is not to teach you how you can avoid using the `ArrayList` class in your code, but rather to increase your appreciation for the flexibility the `ArrayList` class provides. Most programmers do not want to be bothered with the details of the internal representation. The `ArrayList` class is a wonderful tool that keeps those details at a comfortable distance, leaving programmers free to concentrate on the inherent complexity of the problems they are trying to solve.

In at least one respect, using the `ArrayList` class at all exposes clients to the underlying representation. As the name suggests, the `ArrayList` class is built on top of Java's array model. For many clients, however, even that fact is not essential. What matters to clients is being able to call the methods that the `ArrayList` class exports, which are the ones listed in Figure 11-12. If some other class exports the same methods, and if those methods have the same effect, clients should be able to use that class just as easily.

In object-oriented programming languages like Java, the essential characteristic of any class is its *behavior,* particularly in terms of what methods the class exports and what effect those methods have on the visible state of an object. While clients rely on the implementation to ensure that each method behaves as intended, the details of that implementation are of no concern. Similarly, the implementation should be free to change the underlying representation of a class as long as the behavior clients see remains the same. For example, if it were possible to achieve the behavior of an `ArrayList` without using an array at all, implementing such a strategy would presumably have no effect on clients.

In Java, however, defining a class imposes restrictions on the underlying representation. Whenever you define a new class, that class inherits not only the *behavior* of its superclass but its *implementation* and *representation* as well. To provide more effective separation of behavior from the details of representation, Java uses a structure called an **interface,** which specifies the methods a class must implement without constraining the strategy it uses to do so.

You have been working with interfaces ever since Chapter 9, which introduced the interfaces `GFillable`, `GScalable`, and `GResizable` to describe classes that share particular behavioral characteristics. Any class that declared itself as `GFillable`, for example, was obligated to implement the methods `setFilled`,

isFilled, **setFillColor**, and **getFillColor**, thereby allowing clients to rely on that behavior. The implementation of those methods, however, was left to each individual class.

In general, using interfaces provides greater flexibility and imposes fewer constraints than inheriting behavior through class extension. In particular, interfaces make it possible to specify behavior that does not conform to the class hierarchy, in which each class has exactly one superclass. By contrast, a single class can implement many different interfaces. By doing so, it can share behavior with other classes without having to rely on subclassing and inheritance.

In many cases, it is impossible to achieve the effect of interfaces using class extension alone. As an example, consider just the **GFillable** and **GResizable** interfaces from the **acm.graphics** package. It would certainly be possible to achieve the effect of either of these interfaces by creating an abstract class that individual shape classes could then extend. Thus, you might create an abstract class called **FillableShape** and have **GRect**, **GOval**, **GArc**, and **GPolygon** all extend that class. Alternatively, you could define an abstract class called **ResizableShape** and have **GRect**, **GOval**, and **GImage** extend that class. The problem comes if you try to implement both of these hierarchies together. If every resizable shape were also fillable, you could make **ResizableShape** a subclass of **FillableShape**. As it happens, that strategy wouldn't work because **GArc** is fillable but not resizable, while **GImage** is resizable but not fillable. This asymmetry means that neither of the **FillableShape** or **ResizableShape** classes can be a subclass of the other.

Java's interface mechanism eliminates the problem by allowing classes to implement more than one interface. The **ArrayList** class, for example, implements a general interface called **List** that specifies the methods that define the behavior of an **ArrayList** without constraining its representation. The advantages of this strategy will become more clear in the general discussion of the Java Collections Framework in section 13.3.

▆▆▆▆ **13.2 The** HashMap **class**

Before moving on to describe the Java Collections Framework as an integrated whole, it makes sense to introduce another class called **HashMap** that turns out to be quite useful in many applications. The **HashMap** class implements the abstract idea of a **map,** which is an associative relationship between *keys* and *values*. A **key** is an object that never appears more than once in a map and can therefore be used to identify a **value,** which is the object associated with a particular key. The same value can appear several times in a map; each key, however, must be unique. In much the same way that an **ArrayList** is a particular implementation of **List**, a **HashMap** is a particular implementation of the more general **Map** interface.

There are many real world analogues of the map concept. Of these, the most familiar is a dictionary in which each word is associated with a corresponding definition. In the dictionary context, the word represents the key, and the definition represents the value. A typical university database uses a similar strategy to keep track of student information. In this case, the key is an ID number that uniquely identifies each student. The corresponding value might then be an instance of a

Student class similar to the one defined in Chapter 6, presumably with a few more data fields to keep track of more detailed information.

A simple example of a map

In 1963, the Post Office (now the United States Postal Service) introduced a set of two-letter codes for the individual states, districts, and territories of the United States. Those codes (omitting those for the smaller island territories) appear in Figure 13-2. Although you might also want to translate in the opposite direction as well, this section considers only the problem of translating two-letter codes into state names. Thus, if you were to represent the data from Figure 13-2 as a map, the keys would be the two-letter codes and the values would be the corresponding names of the states.

The purpose of a map is to implement the association between keys and values in a way that makes it easy to add new key/value pairs or to find the value for an existing key. For example, if you initialize a map with the data from Figure 13-2, you can then ask the map for the value associated with the code **HI**. Assuming that you have initialized the map correctly, it will report back that **HI** corresponds to the state of Hawaii.

You could easily use the **HashMap** class to represent the table of two-letter postal code from Figure 13-2. The first step is to create an empty map to which you can add the individual data entries. As you learned in the discussion of the **ArrayList** in Chapter 11, Java 5.0 allows you to specify what types a collection contains by indicating the types in angle brackets. A **Map** requires you to specify two type parameters. The first is the class used for the key, and the second is the class used for the value. In the case of the map of the two-letter state codes, both of these classes are **String**. The declaration necessary to create an empty map is therefore

```
Map<String,String> stateMap = new HashMap<String,String>();
```

FIGURE 13-2   **Two-letter state codes for the United States**

AK	Alaska	**IA**	Iowa	**MT**	Montana	**PR**	Puerto Rico
AL	Alabama	**IL**	Illinois	**NC**	North Carolina	**RI**	Rhode Island
AR	Arkansas	**IN**	Indiana	**ND**	North Dakota	**SC**	South Carolina
AZ	Arizona	**KS**	Kansas	**NE**	Nebraska	**SD**	South Dakota
CA	California	**KY**	Kentucky	**NH**	New Hampshire	**TN**	Tennessee
CO	Colorado	**LA**	Louisiana	**NJ**	New Jersey	**TX**	Texas
CT	Connecticut	**MA**	Massachusetts	**NM**	New Mexico	**UT**	Utah
DC	District of Columbia	**MD**	Maryland	**NV**	Nevada	**VA**	Virginia
DE	Delaware	**ME**	Maine	**NY**	New York	**VT**	Vermont
FL	Florida	**MI**	Michigan	**OH**	Ohio	**WA**	Washington
GA	Georgia	**MN**	Minnesota	**OK**	Oklahoma	**WI**	Wisconsin
HI	Hawaii	**MO**	Missouri	**OR**	Oregon	**WV**	West Virginia
ID	Idaho	**MS**	Mississippi	**PA**	Pennsylvania	**WY**	Wyoming

This declaration uses the **HashMap** constructor to create an empty **HashMap** object that maps strings into strings. The **stateMap** variable, however, has the more general type **Map<String,String>**. As you will see later in this chapter, there are advantages to using the more general interface type for declarations, even though you need to construct initial values of a particular class.

You add new associations to a map by calling the **put** method with the key and value. Thus, to initialize the variable **stateMap** to contain the necessary key/value pairs, you would begin by writing

```
stateMap.put("AK", "Alaska");
```

and end some fifty lines later with the statement

```
stateMap.put("WY", "Wyoming");
```

The corresponding operation to retrieve the value associated with a key is called **get**. If you call

```
stateMap.get("NV");
```

the method returns the string **"Nevada"**. If you supply a key that doesn't exist in the map, calling **get** returns the value **null**.

This simple overview of the **get** and **put** methods is all you really need to use the **HashMap** class as a tool. Much of the value of classes like **HashMap** comes from the fact that you don't need to know how it implements the association between keys and values. What's important to you as a client is that it works.

If, however, you are thinking about pursuing further study in computer science, having some curiosity about the underlying implementation would be a promising sign. You might, for example, be interested to know how efficient the **get** and **put** methods are, so that you have some sense of how you long it might take to look up a value for a specific key. As it turns out, the implementation strategy used in the **HashMap** class is blindingly efficient, to the point that the implementation can guarantee that the average running time for the **get** and **put** methods is independent of the number of keys in the map. If you express that same idea using the big-O notation from Chapter 12, the **get** and **put** methods are both $O(1)$, which is the best that you could ever hope to achieve.

Before looking at the clever insight that makes the **HashMap** class so efficient, it helps to think more deeply about the specific problem of translating two-letter state codes into the corresponding names. How could you make the problem of looking up these codes as efficient as possible?

Exploring possible implementation strategies

One way to get a feel for algorithmic problems of this sort is to experiment with implementation strategies and see whether anything occurs to you that might speed things up. If your only concern is translating two-letter state codes into state names, you might begin by putting the data in two arrays so that the index number of a specific two-letter code in one array matches the index of the corresponding name in the other. You can initialize the arrays automatically by listing their elements. For example, the following statement initializes a constant array of two-letter codes:

```
private static final String[] STATE_CODES = {
    "AK", "AL", "AZ", "AR", "CA", "CO", "CT", "DE", "DC",
    "FL", "GA", "HI", "ID", "IL", "IN", "IA", "KS", "KY",
    "LA", "ME", "MD", "MA", "MI", "MN", "MS", "MO", "MT",
    "NE", "NV", "NH", "NJ", "NM", "NY", "NC", "ND", "OH",
    "OK", "OR", "PA", "PR", "RI", "SC", "SD", "TN", "TX",
    "UT", "VT", "VA", "WA", "WV", "WI", "WY"
};
```

You can create an array called **STATE_NAMES** in exactly the same way, as follows:

```
private static final String[] STATE_NAMES = {
    "Alaska", "Alabama", "Arkansas", "Arizona", "California",
    "Colorado", "Connecticut", "District of Columbia",
    "Delaware", "Florida", "Georgia", "Hawaii", "Iowa",
    "Idaho", "Illinois", "Indiana", "Kansas", "Kentucky",
    "Louisiana", "Massachusetts", "Maryland", "Maine",
    "Michigan", "Minnesota", "Missouri", "Mississippi",
    "Montana", "North Carolina", "North Dakota", "Nebraska",
    "New Hampshire", "New Jersey", "New Mexico", "Nevada",
    "New York", "Ohio", "Oklahoma", "Oregon", "Pennsylvania",
    "Puerto Rico", "Rhode Island", "South Carolina",
    "South Dakota", "Tennessee", "Texas", "Utah", "Virginia",
    "Vermont", "Washington", "Wisconsin", "West Virginia",
    "Wyoming"
};
```

Once you have declared these arrays, you can write a method **getStateName** that takes a two-letter code and returns the corresponding state name, like this:

```
private String getStateName(String code) {
    int index = linearSearch(code, STATE_CODES);
    if (index == -1) {
        return null;
    } else {
        return STATE_NAMES[index];
    }
}
```

This code uses the **linearSearch** method from Chapter 12 to find the specified code in the **STATE_CODES** array. If it is there, the **getStateName** method simply returns the element at the corresponding position in **STATE_NAMES**. Since the states appear in the same order in each array, that element will contain the name of the state that corresponds to the code that **linearSearch** found. If the specified code does not appear in the array, the **getStateName** method returns **null**. Arrays in which related items appear at the same index position are called **parallel arrays.**

The computational complexity of this implementation is identical to that of the **linearSearch** method, which does all the real work. As discussed in Chapter 12, the linear search method must look at every element in the array in the worst case, which makes it $O(N)$.

You can improve the performance somewhat by taking advantage of the fact that the **STATE_CODES** array is sorted alphabetically, which allows you to use the binary search algorithm instead. Replacing the call to **linearSearch** with an identical call to **binarySearch** reduces the computational complexity to $O(\log N)$. Although that level of efficiency is good enough to be practical even for very large arrays, it still falls short of the $O(1)$ performance that **HashMap** claims to provide. How is possible to outperform binary search?

If you think for a few minutes about the specific example of translating two-letter codes into state names, you might come up with the answer. Give it a try before reading on to the next section.

Achieving O(1) performance

In the case of the specific problem, you can achieve the desired $O(1)$ performance by taking advantage of the fact that the United States Postal Codes for the states are exactly two letters long. All you need to do is store the names of the states in a two-dimensional array in which the indices are computed directly from the characters in the two-letter state code.

The first step toward implementing this strategy is to create a two-dimensional array to hold the state names. You can do so by writing the declaration

```
private String[][] stateMap = new String[26][26];
```

which creates a 26 × 26 array in which each of the values is initially **null**.

You can then use the following method to insert codes for the individual states:

```
private void putStateName(String code, String name) {
   char c1 = code.charAt(0);
   char c2 = code.charAt(1);
   stateMap[c1 - 'A'][c2 - 'A'] = name;
}
```

This method assigns the name of the state to the row indicated by the first letter in its two-letter code and to the column indicated by the second letter. If you adopt this approach, you can initialize the **stateMap** array using a sequence of calls to **putStateName** that begins like this:

```
putStateName("AK", "Alaska");
putStateName("AL", "Alabama");
```

Given this design, the **getStateName** method looks like this:

```
private String getStateName(String code) {
   char c1 = code.charAt(0);
   char c2 = code.charAt(1);
   return stateMap[c1 - 'A'][c2 - 'A'];
}
```

All the method does is divide the two-letter code into characters and then look up the element in the corresponding position in the two-dimensional **stateMap** array. If that element of the array corresponds to the code for a state, then it must have been initialized by one of the calls to **putStateName**. If not, that element must contain the **null** value it was given when it was initialized. In either case, the value is precisely what you want to return as the value of **getStateName**. Selecting an element in an array takes $O(1)$ time.

The idea of hashing

Although the **HashMap** class does not use precisely the approach described in the preceding section, there are certain similarities. Using a two-dimensional array representation for the map between two-letter codes and state names achieves the $O(1)$ performance target because **getStateName** knows exactly where to look. If a two-letter state code is in the **HashMap**, it must be in the row and column specified by the two characters in that code. Knowing where to look eliminates the need for searching, which is what slows the process down.

To get a sense of how you might satisfy this goal of knowing where to look in the more general context of a map, it helps to think for a moment about the dictionary analogy. If you were trying to find a word in a dictionary, you could start at the first entry, go on to the second, and then the third, until you found the word. This strategy, of course, is just the linear search algorithm, which requires $O(N)$ time. Alternatively, you could use the binary search algorithm and open the dictionary exactly at the middle. By comparing the first entry on the page to the word you're searching for, you could easily determine whether your word appears in the first or second half. By applying this algorithm repeatedly to smaller and smaller parts of the dictionary, you could find your word much faster than you did using the linear search technique. On the other hand, you probably don't use either of these strategies with a real dictionary. Most dictionaries have thumb tabs along the side that indicate where the entries for each letter appear. You look for words starting with *A* in the *A* section, words starting with *B* in the *B* section, and so on.

Hash codes

The **HashMap** class uses a strategy that is different in its specifics but comparable in its conception. The **HashMap** implementation also uses the value of the key to compute where it should look. To do so, it begins by transforming the key into an integer called its **hash code.** Every Java object has a hash code, even though you won't ordinarily have any idea what it is. For example, the hash code for the string **"AK"** at the beginning of the list of state abbreviations happens to be 2090. The hash code for **"WY"** at the end of the list is 2786. Knowing why each of these strings has the hash code it does will not help you at all in writing programs. The only critical point to remember about hash codes is that every Java object has one.

The **HashMap** class uses the hash code for the key to determine where it should look for that value. Given that the string **"AK"** has 2090 as its hash code, the **HashMap** implementation looks for **"AK"** in the place reserved for hash code 2090. When it has to look for the key **"WY"**, it looks instead in the place reserved for hash code 2786. One possible strategy for finding those keys is outlined later in this chapter, but the fundamental idea should nonetheless be clear even before you understand all the details. Because the hash code tells the **HashMap** implementation exactly where to look for a particular key, it can usually find that key without having the undertake a search process that can only slow things down.

Usually, but not always. From time to time, the **HashMap** implementation does indeed have to search for a key. The reason that this search does not compromise the $O(1)$ performance goal is that the implementation does not have to search very far. Moreover, as you will discover in the more detailed discussion of the implementation later in this chapter, a **HashMap** can adjust its internal representation dynamically to reduce the need for searching if the **HashMap** starts to get too full.

Duplication of hash codes

Even though every Java object has a hash code, it is important to recognize that different objects will sometimes have the *same* hash code. There are, after all, many more possible objects than there are 32-bit integers to serve as their hash codes. For example, the number of strings that contain exactly seven lowercase letters is 26^7, which works out to 8,031,810,176. The number of possible hash codes, however, is 2^{32}, which is only 4,294,976,296. Because there are more seven-letter combinations than there are integers, at least some of the seven-letter strings must have the same hash code.

In mathematics, the observation that you must end up with duplicates whenever you try to map a larger set onto a smaller one is called the **pigeonhole principle.** The name comes from the idea of filing letters into pigeonholes in a desk. If you have more letters than you have pigeonholes, you must end up with more than one letter in some pigeonhole.

Given that the number of possible hash codes is so large, running across two objects that share the same hash code does not happen very often. For example, if you look at all the English words containing ten or fewer letters, Java's **hashCode** method produces only two word pairs that share the same hash code: *buzzards* has the same hash code as *righto,* as do the words *hierarch* and *crinolines*. While the likelihood of finding matching hash codes is small, the pigeonhole principle dictates that it must be possible. The code for **HashMap** must take that possibility into account and come up with a way to proceed when two objects have the same hash value.

The research literature in computer science is full of strategies for resolving this dilemma. The most straightforward is simply to maintain a list of all the objects you encounter whose hash codes cause them to share the same space in the **HashMap**; a simple implementation that uses that strategy appears in the following section. As long as duplications are rare, those lists will typically have just one entry. As a result, finding an item in a **HashMap** will usually require looking only at the one entry that exists. From time to time, however, a list may end up with multiple items, but the average time required to find a value will still be $O(1)$.

A simple implementation of a map class

Although the complete implementation of Java's **HashMap** class is beyond the scope of this book, understanding the issues in the last few sections is much easier if you can see a simplified version, such as the code for **SimpleStringMap** in Figure 13-3.

> ### FIGURE 13-3   Implementation of the `SimpleStringMap` class
>
> ```java
> /** This class implements a simplified version of a Map class for strings. */
> public class SimpleStringMap {
>
> /** Creates a new SimpleStringMap with no key/value pairs */
>    public SimpleStringMap() {
>       bucketArray = new HashEntry[N_BUCKETS];
>    }
>
> /**
>  * Sets the value associated with key.  Any previous value for key is lost.
>  * @param key The key used to refer to this value
>  * @param value The new value to be associated with key
>  */
>    public void put(String key, String value) {
>       int bucket = Math.abs(key.hashCode()) % N_BUCKETS;
>       HashEntry entry = findEntry(bucketArray[bucket], key);
>       if (entry == null) {
>          entry = new HashEntry(key, value);
>          entry.setLink(bucketArray[bucket]);
>          bucketArray[bucket] = entry;
>       } else {
>          entry.setValue(value);
>       }
>    }
>
> /**
>  * Retrieves the value associated with key, or null if no such value exists.
>  * @param key The key used to look up the value
>  * @return The value associated with key, or null if no such value exists
>  */
>    public String get(String key) {
>       int bucket = Math.abs(key.hashCode()) % N_BUCKETS;
>       HashEntry entry = findEntry(bucketArray[bucket], key);
>       if (entry == null) {
>          return null;
>       } else {
>          return entry.getValue();
>       }
>    }
>
> /*
>  * Scans the entry chain looking for an entry that matches the specified key.
>  * If no such entry exists, findEntry returns null.
>  */
>    private HashEntry findEntry(HashEntry entry, String key) {
>       while (entry != null) {
>          if (entry.getKey().equals(key)) return entry;
>          entry = entry.getLink();
>       }
>       return null;
>    }
> ```
> ☞

| FIGURE 13-3 | Implementation of the `SimpleStringMap` class (continued) |

```
/* Private constants */
   private static final int N_BUCKETS = 7;

/* Private instance variables */
   private HashEntry[] bucketArray;

}


/* Package-private class: HashEntry */
/*
 * This class represents a pair of a key and a value, along with a reference
 * to the next HashEntry in the chain.  The methods exported by the class
 * consist only of getters and setters.
 */
class HashEntry {

/* Creates a new HashEntry for the specified key/value pair */
   public HashEntry(String key, String value) {
      entryKey = key;
      entryValue = value;
   }

/* Returns the key component of a HashEntry */
   public String getKey() {
      return entryKey;
   }

/* Returns the value component of a HashEntry */
   public String getValue() {
      return entryValue;
   }

/* Sets the value component of a HashEntry to a new value */
   public void setValue(String value) {
      entryValue = value;
   }

/* Returns the next link in the entry chain */
   public HashEntry getLink() {
      return entryLink;
   }

/* Sets the link to the next entry in the chain */
   public void setLink(HashEntry nextEntry) {
      entryLink = nextEntry;
   }

/* Private instance variables */
   private String entryKey;     /* The key component for this HashEntry   */
   private String entryValue;   /* The value component for this HashEntry */
   private HashEntry entryLink; /* A reference to the next entry in the chain */

}
```

The **SimpleStringMap** class in Figure 13-3 implements only the **get** and **put** operations and ignores the more sophisticated methods that are part of the **Map** interface in the Java Collections Framework. The **SimpleStringMap** class, moreover, always uses strings for both its keys and its values, which means that it need not incur the complexity involved in using parameterized types.

The basic strategy used by the **SimpleStringMap** implementation is to store each key/value pair in a list determined by the hash code of the key. Each of those lists is traditionally called a **bucket.** The number of buckets is determined by the constant **N_BUCKETS**, which is defined in this implementation as having the value 7, even though such a value would be unreasonably small in practice. Using a small value for **N_BUCKETS**, however, makes it much easier to diagram the internal structure of the data.

When you call **get** or **put**, the first thing that method does is to determine which bucket corresponds to the specified key. Although the index of the bucket is determined by the hash code, the number of possible hash codes is inevitably larger than the number of buckets. To transform the result of the **hashCode** method into a bucket number, the simplest approach is to divide the hash code by **N_BUCKETS** and take the remainder. As you can see from the first line of the **get** and **put** methods, you need to use the absolute value of the hash code to ensure that the **%** operator is not applied to a negative number.

Colloquially, computer scientists say that a key **hashes to a bucket** if this transformation of the hash code for the key returns the index of the bucket. The situation of having two or more keys hash to the same bucket—which is much more common than finding two keys with the same hash code—is called a **collision.**

The instance variable **bucketArray** is an array of **HashEntry** objects. Each **HashEntry** object contains both a key and a value, along with a reference to the next entry that hashes to that bucket. Each time you call **put** with a new key, the implementation adds a new **HashEntry** to the chain. The following diagram shows the state of the bucket chains after you add entries for the keys **"AK"**, **"AL"**, **"AR"**, **"AZ"**, and **"CA"**, which hash to the buckets shown in the diagram:

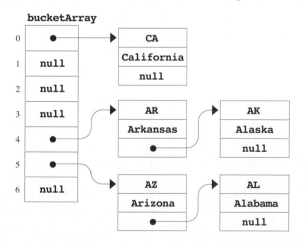

The bucket chains in this diagram are connected by the links in each **HashEntry** object in precisely the way that the Beacons of Gondor were linked in section 7.4. Each chain is an example of an important programming structure called a linked list, which will come up again in the section 13.3.

Implementing hashCode methods

For the most part, you won't have much occasion to look deeply into the details of how classes implement their **hashCode** methods. On the whole, being protected from such details is a wonderful thing, given that **hashCode** methods tend to be rather cryptic. As an example, the **hashCode** method for Java's **String** class—strings that are shorter than 16 characters—is functionally equivalent to the following method:

```
public int hashCode() {
    int hash = 0;
    for (i = 0; i < length(); i++) {
        hash = 37 * hash + charAt(i);
    }
    return hash;
}
```

Although you can certainly work through the statements in this method and figure out what each one does, understanding *why* the code is written this way is a bit more challenging.

In many respects, the task of writing an effective **hashCode** method is similar to the problem of writing an effective random number generator, which was discussed in Chapter 6. Creating a random number generator that works well depends on mathematics that lie beyond the scope of this book. Writing a good **hashCode** method relies on much the same mathematical principles. On the whole, it makes sense to leave the job of writing **hashCode** methods to the experts, just as it would be foolhardy to try making a random number generator on your own.

Unfortunately, even though you can generally avoid writing random number generators, you will have to write a **hashCode** method from time to time. If you implement a class that someone might reasonably want to use as a key, you have a certain obligation to implement a **hashCode** method for that class. When you do, it is important to keep the following criteria for an effective **hashCode** method in mind:

1. The **hashCode** method must always return the same code if it is called on the same object. This requirement is part of the essential character of the hashing strategy. The **HashMap** code knows where to look for a particular key because its hash code determines where it goes. If that code is subject to change, the **hashMap** implementation might put it in one place and then look for it in another.

2. The implementation of **hashCode** must be consistent with the implementation of the **equals** method, because the hashing mechanism uses the **equals** method internally to compare keys. This condition is stronger than the first one, which says only that the hash code for a specific object should not

change arbitrarily. This new requirement strengthens the first one by insisting that any two objects that are considered equal by the **equals** method must have the same hash code.

3. The **hashCode** method should avoid returning hash codes that lead to collisions. For example, it would not be ideal for the **String** class to use the internal code of the first character as its hash code. If it did, every string beginning with the same character would collide in the **hashMap**, which would dramatically reduce performance.

4. The **hashCode** method should be relatively simple to compute. If you write a **hashCode** method that takes a long time to evaluate, you give up the primary advantage of hashing, which is that the basic algorithm runs very quickly.

If you do find yourself implementing **hashCode** methods, you can adopt a simple strategy that helps you meet these criteria. In most cases, classes that you define include instance variables that specify the value of the object. To compute a hash code for the object as a whole, you can compute the hash code for each of its identifying components and then combine those pieces in some way that does not increase the odds of a collision. The bitwise operator ^ introduced in Chapter 11 is particularly useful in this context. Unlike the **&** and | operators, the ^ operator does not reduce the information content of its operands. Thus, if you take the hash codes of the components of an object and combine them with the ^ operator, you can write a **hashCode** method that usually works well.

As an example, the code in Figure 13-4 adds two useful methods to the **Rational** class that was introduced in Chapter 6. The **equals** method allows you to determine whether two **Rational** numbers are equal, and the **hashCode** method allows you to use **Rational** objects as keys in a **hashMap**. The implementation of **hashCode** adopts the strategy outlined in the preceding paragraph. It begins by computing the hash codes for the instance variables **num** and **den** and then combines those values using the ^ operator. What works even better in practice is to multiply one of those values by a small prime number, as shown in Figure 13-4.

The code in Figure 13-4 also makes it possible to emphasize a tremendously important point about class design in Java. The **equals** method is useful enough that you might have expected it to be part of the initial implementation of the **Rational** class in Chapter 6. There is nothing about the **equals** method itself that would make it at all hard to implement given the knowledge you had at that point. The problem is that overriding the **equals** method without also overriding the **hashCode** method is an example of poor programming practice. If you made this mistake in defining a class, you would not be able to use that class as a key in a **hashMap**. The original definition of the **Rational** class excluded **equals** because you were unprepared at that time to write the associated **hashCode** method.

> **COMMON PITFALLS**
>
> Never override the definition of the **equals** method unless you also override **hashCode**. Overriding one of these methods but not the other almost always violates the design criteria for **hashCode** and makes it impossible to use that class as a **HashMap** key.

Adjusting the number of buckets

Although the characteristics of the **hashCode** method are also a factor, it is clear that the likelihood of collision in a **HashMap** also depends on the number of buckets. If the number of buckets is small, collisions naturally occur more frequently. Collisions reduce the efficiency of a **HashMap** because they force the **get** and **put**

FIGURE 13-4 **Implementation of `equals` and `hashCode` for the `Rational` class**

```
/**
 * Returns true if this rational number is equal to the specified
 * object.  Because the implementation for the Rational class always
 * reduces fractions to lowest terms, all this method needs to do is
 * make sure that both the numerators and denominators match.
 * @param obj The value to which this object is being compared
 * @return A boolean value indicating whether this number is equal to obj
 */
   public boolean equals(Object obj) {
      if (obj instanceof Rational) {
         Rational r = (Rational) obj;
         return this.num == r.num && this.den == r.den;
      } else {
         return false;
      }
   }

/**
 * Returns a hash code for this Rational object.  That hash code is
 * derived from the hash codes for its two components.  This design
 * decision ensures that two Rational objects that are equal will have
 * the same hash code.
 * @return An integer hash code for this object
 */
   public int hashCode() {
      return new Integer(num).hashCode() ^ (37 * new Integer(den).hashCode());
   }
```

---

methods to search through longer chains. As the buckets in `HashMap` fill up, the number of collisions rises and the performance of the `HashMap` ceases to be $O(1)$.

The best strategy for maintaining high performance in a `HashMap` is to increase the number of buckets dynamically whenever the existing buckets begin to fill up. For example, you can design the implementation so that it allocates a larger bucket array whenever the ratio of the number of keys to the number of buckets passes a certain threshold. Unfortunately, if you increase the number of buckets, all the bucket numbers change, which means that the code to expand the bucket array must also reenter all the keys from the old `HashMap` into the new one. This process is called **rehashing**. Although rehashing can be time-consuming, it is performed infrequently and therefore has minimal impact on the average running time of an application. You will have a chance to implement a rehashing algorithm for the `SimpleStringMap` class in exercise 4.

13.3 The Java Collections Framework

Although there is more to learn about the `HashMap` class, it makes sense to describe those additional features in the context of the Java Collections Framework as a whole, where the presentation will fit more closely with similar features in other classes. Although **ArrayList** and **HashMap** are important classes in their own right, the real power of the Java Collections Framework is that it allows you to think about collections more abstractly.

The structure of the Java Collections Framework

The principal classes and interfaces that make up the Java Collections Framework appear in Figure 13-5. The boxes in the diagram correspond to three different

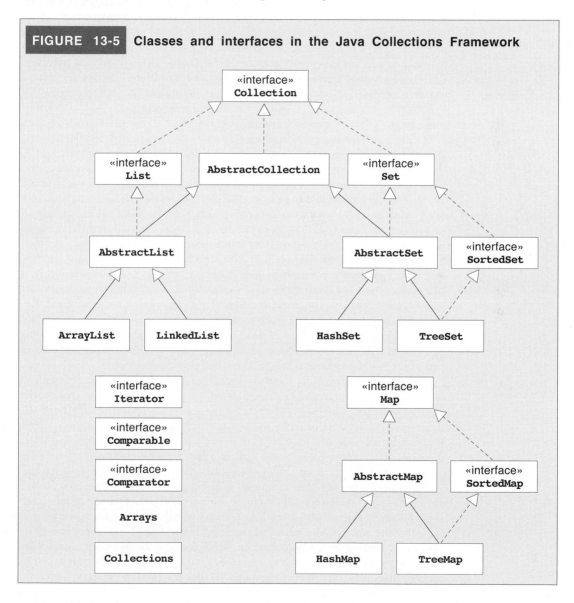

FIGURE 13-5   **Classes and interfaces in the Java Collections Framework**

structures available in Java. The boxes that contain a name in the standard font used for Java code represent class definitions. The boxes whose names appear in italics represent abstract classes, which cannot be constructed on their own but can nonetheless pass on data structures and methods to their subclasses through inheritance. Previous diagrams have included both concrete and abstract classes, so those portions of the diagram should seem familiar. What's new in Figure 13-5 are the boxes that represent interfaces, which are marked with a tag labeled «interface». Instead of the solid lines used to mark the relationship between each class and its superclass, the link between a class and an interface appears as a dashed line.

Interface relationships are not tied to the structure of the class hierarchy. Although every class has exactly one superclass from which it inherits behavior, a single class can implement any number of interfaces. Those interfaces, however, form a hierarchy of their own as shown in Figure 13-5. If one interface extends an existing interface, the new interface becomes a subinterface of the original, in exactly the same way that subclasses extend superclasses. Any class that implements the subinterface automatically implements the original interface as well.

To illustrate how these relationships play out in the Java Collections Framework, it helps to chart the inheritance relationships for one of the concrete classes, such as the `ArrayList` class at the left edge of the figure. In terms of the class hierarchy, the `ArrayList` class is a subclass of the class `AbstractList`, which is in turn a subclass of `AbstractCollection`. The solid lines in this inheritance hierarchy show that every `ArrayList` object is also both an `AbstractList` and an `AbstractCollection`. The `ArrayList` class, moreover, inherits the methods defined in its superclasses and need not implement them on its own.

If you instead follow the dotted lines that trace the interface structure, you see that an `ArrayList` implements both the `List` and the `Collection` interfaces. It implements the `List` interface because its superclass does. You can establish that `ArrayList` implements `Collection` in either of two ways. On the one hand, any class that implements the `List` interface also implements the `Collection` interface because `List` is a subinterface of `Collection`. On the other, you know that the `AbstractList` class inherits the structure and behavior of its `AbstractCollection` superclass, which implements the `Collection` interface directly.

Although this text has not focused a great deal of attention on class diagrams, it is worth noting that the symbols these diagrams use are consistent with those in the **Unified Modeling Language,** which is almost always abbreviated to **UML.** UML diagrams have been endorsed by the International Standards Organization, which means that such diagrams have broad acceptance throughout the world. Full UML diagrams, however, are much more expressive than the limited examples used in the book and allow you to express many other relationships beyond simple inheritance.

The other interesting feature to observe in Figure 13-5 is that the classes in the Java Collection Framework fall into three distinct clusters. At the top of the figure is the hierarchy that includes everything that implements the `Collection` interface, including the now familiar `ArrayList` class. In the lower right corner is a set of classes that implement the `Map` interface, which includes the `HashMap` class. In the lower left is a set of classes and interfaces that fall outside the hierarchy. The sections that follow offer more insight into the different parts of the framework.

The `Collection` hierarchy

The largest set of classes in the Java Collections Framework is the one that descends from the `Collection` interface at the top of Figure 13-5. Each of the classes in that collection serves as a container for a particular class of object. In Java 5.0, you specify the type of object a collection contains by indicating the name of a class in angle brackets, as in `ArrayList<Integer>`. That same pattern applies to each of the classes in the `Collection` hierarchy, so you could specify the type for a linked list of strings by writing `LinkedList<String>`. As you saw in Chapter 11, the value type is designated as `<T>` in generic descriptions of methods. Older versions of Java do not permit the type parameter and simply use `Object` instead.

Since `ArrayList` implements the `Collection` interface, it must implement all the methods in that interface. The most important methods in the `Collection` interface appear in Figure 13-6. Most of these methods are familiar from the discussion of the `ArrayList` class in Chapter 11. The only new method in Figure 13-6 is `iterator`, which applies equally well to the `ArrayList` class even though it did not make sense to introduce it earlier. The `iterator` method and the `Iterator` interface on which it depends are discussed in the section on "Iterators" later in this chapter.

There are, however, several methods in the `ArrayList` class that are missing from the `Collection` interface described in Figure 13-6, such as the `get` and `set` methods and the version of the `add` method that lets you add a value at a specific position. The reason these methods are not part of the `Collection` interface is that they don't make sense at this level of the abstraction. Being able to add a new value at a particular index position depends on the collection having index positions in the first place. The `Collection` interface offers no such guarantee. The idea of index positions appears at the level of the `List` interface, which describes the operations on ordered collections. The more general `Collection` interface must also serve the needs of unordered collections, which are called **sets** in the Java framework.

FIGURE 13-6   Useful methods specified by the `Collection` interface

`boolean add(<T> value)`
Adds the specified value to the collection. The method returns **true** if the collection changes.
`boolean remove(<T> element)`
Removes the first instance of the specified element, if any; the value is **true** if a match is found.
`void clear()`
Removes all values from the collection.
`int size()`
Returns the number of values in the collection.
`boolean contains(<T> value)`
Returns **true** if the collection contains the specified value.
`boolean isEmpty()`
Returns **true** if the collection contains no elements.
`Iterator iterator()`
Returns an iterator that allows clients to step through the values in the collection.

In all likelihood, you have already encountered sets at some point in your study of mathematics. Informally, sets are unordered collections of objects in which each object can appear at most once. The methods in the **Collection** interface are just as well suited to sets as they are to lists, although the meaning of those operations might change depending on the domain. If you apply the **add** method to a list, the value is inserted at the end. Because sets are unordered, the phrase "at the end" has no meaning for sets, but it is still possible to add a new element. If you add the same value to a list twice in succession, both copies will be added to the end of the list. In the context of a set, calling **add** with a value that already occurs in the set has no effect, since each value can appear only once. This difference in behavior explains why it makes sense for the **add** method to return a value. In the case of a list, the **add** method always returns **true**, which renders the result somewhat useless. In the case of a set, you can use the result of the **add** method to determine whether the set already contained that value.

Separating behavior and representation

The first division in the **Collection** hierarchy is between lists and sets, as discussed in the preceding paragraph. That division is primarily a matter of behavior. Lists and sets behave differently. The elements of a list are ordered, while the elements of set are unordered. As a result, it is meaningful to talk about index positions in a list, but meaningless in a set.

The next level of division in the hierarchy, however, is one of representation. In the Java Collections Framework, the **AbstractList** class and the **AbstractSet** class each divide into two concrete subclasses. The **ArrayList** and **LinkedList** classes offer two different implementations of the **List** interface, while the **HashSet** and **TreeSet** classes offer different implementations of the **Set** interface. In terms of the methods these classes implement and the effects those methods have, the **ArrayList** and **LinkedList** classes are functionally identical. And although there are a few behavioral differences—most notably the fact that **TreeMap** implements the **SortedSet** interface while **HashMap** does not—the two implementations of the **Map** interface are functionally quite similar as well.

The differences between these pairs of classes lie primarily in their implementations and, more specifically, in the representation strategy each class uses to store the values in the collection. The **ArrayList** implementation, for example, stores the elements in an internal array. The **LinkedList** implementation, by contrast, uses reference links to thread the objects together in the style used in the **SimpleStringMap** implementation from Figure 13-3. As you might guess from the name, the **HashSet** implementation uses hash codes to determine membership in a set. The **TreeSet** implementation uses a different data structure called a *binary tree* to store the elements. Binary trees are beyond the scope of this book, but you will certainly encounter them if you continue your study of computer science.

The fact that these pairs of classes differ only in terms of their implementation raises an interesting question. Given that clients are largely unconcerned about implementation details, it seems inappropriate to provide multiple implementations of the same basic model. Why not simply choose one of the list implementations, call it `List`, and let clients rely on that? Doing so would banish the distinction between the `ArrayList` and `LinkedList` classes and reduce the complexity of the collections framework.

The reason for allowing the client to choose a particular implementation is that `ArrayList` and `LinkedList` have different performance characteristics even though they share the same abstract behavior. Adding a new value at the front of an `ArrayList` requires $O(N)$ time. Adding an element at the front of a linked list can be done in $O(1)$ time. Conversely, selecting an element at index position k reverses these performance measures. In an `ArrayList`, selecting an element is always a constant time operation. The `LinkedList` implementation, however, has to follow the links in all the preceding elements to find the one at position k, which means that this operation has $O(N)$ performance in the worst case. Depending on which type of operation predominates in your application, you might well want to choose one or the other list representation to optimize the behavior of your program.

One of the strengths of the Java Collections Framework is that it does not force you to choose a particular representation except in the call to a constructor. If, for example, you want to write an `alphabetize` method that takes a list of strings as an argument, it is better to write the method header as

```
public void alphabetize(List<String>)
```

than it would be to specify the argument as either an `ArrayList` or a `LinkedList`. Because both of these classes implement the `List` interface, declaring the parameter as a `List` means that it can accommodate either of the concrete list classes.

The ability to generalize the `ArrayList` and `LinkedList` classes into a common framework depends entirely on the ability to define interfaces in Java. Although the `ArrayList` and `LinkedList` classes do share some methods that they inherit from `AbstractList`, the underlying representation for these two classes is quite different, and it would be hard to unify them under the standard inheritance model. It is, however, easy to use common names for the public methods and insist that each class implement the same conceptual model.

Iterators

Before you can appreciate the difference between the `HashSet` and `TreeSet` classes, you need to understand how the Java Collection Framework approaches the concept of iteration. You have been using iteration in the form of `while` and `for` loops ever since Chapter 4. Iterating through the elements in a collection, one element at a time, is a similar operation.

In the case of an ordered collection such as an `ArrayList`, you can already cycle through the elements using a `for` loop. For example, if the variable `nameList` is declared as a `ListArray<String>`, you can print the elements one per line using the following code:

```
for (int i = 0; i < nameList.size(); i++) {
   String name = nameList.get(i);
   println(name);
}
```

Using a **for** loop is at least possible when you work with an **ArrayList** because the elements have index numbers. If you were working with a **Set** object instead, this strategy would not be effective because you cannot ask for the ith element in a set.

To make it possible to iterate through the values in any collection—ordered or unordered—the Java Collections Framework includes an interface called **Iterator** that specifies two essential methods:

1. A predicate method called **hasNext** that returns **true** if the collection has values that the iterator has not yet supplied.
2. A method called **next** that returns the next element from the collection.

Like the classes and interfaces in the **Collection** hierarchy, the **Iterator** class is a parameterized type in Java 5.0, which means that you include the element type in angle brackets. Thus, if you have a collection that contains strings, you can iterate through the elements of that collection using an **Iterator<String>**.

The following code example shows how you would use the **Iterator** facility to duplicate the effect of the **for** loop presented earlier in this section:

```
Iterator<String> iterator = nameList.iterator();
while (iterator.hasNext()) {
   println(iterator.next());
}
```

This loop has the same effect as the earlier one but no longer depends on index numbers. As a result, it works for sets as well.

> **Extended syntax for the `for` statement**
>
> ```
> for (type variable : collection) {
>    statements
> }
> ```
>
> where:
>   *type* is the element type of the collection
>   *variable* is a variable that takes on each
>   of the values
>   *collection* is the collection object over
>   which the iteration is performed
>   *statements* are the statements to be
>   repeated

Iterators in Java turn out to be so useful that Java 5.0 includes new language features to support them. For any collection class that implements the **iterator** method, Java 5.0 makes it possible to indicate iteration over that collection by using a new version of the **for** statement shown in the syntax box on the left. The new syntax of the **for** statement allows you, for example, to streamline the code for printing each element in **nameList** as follows:

```
for (String name : nameList) {
   println(name);
}
```

When written in this form, the iterator does not appear explicitly, even though it is used in the implementation.

Because the elements of any list are ordered, the iterator for an **ArrayList** returns the elements in the order in which they appear in the list. In the case of an unordered list, there is no immediately apparent reason to choose one order over another. The iterator presumably has to choose some order internally so that it can avoid skipping over elements or returning others twice, but that order need not match anything that the client might understand.

To illustrate the flexibility that set classes have in determining iteration order, it helps to go back to the example of translating two-letter state codes presented earlier in the chapter. In the version of the implementation based on a **HashMap**, the variable **stateMap** is declared as a **Map<String,String>** and then initialized using a long sequence of calls to the **put** method, all of which look like this, with the appropriate substitution of the two-letter code and the state name:

```
stateMap.put("AK", "Alaska");
```

Although you can use the iterator facility to display a table of two-letter codes and state names, such a table will be useful only if the lines of that table are arranged alphabetically so that you can find a particular entry. Before you write the code to create that table, you need to know whether iterating over the keys in a **HashMap** will produce the keys in that order.

You can investigate this question by writing a simple test program. Although the **Map** classes do not themselves supply an iterator, the keys contained in a map form a set. Each key appears at most once in the **HashMap**, and there is no obvious ordering relationship among the keys. The **Map** interface specifies a method called **keySet**, which returns the set of keys. You can then use that set to create an iterator.

The following method displays the keys in the specified map, packing several state codes onto the same output line:

```
private void listKeys(Map<String,String> map, int nPerLine) {
   String className = map.getClass().getName();
   int lastDot = className.lastIndexOf(".");
   String shortName = className.substring(lastDot + 1);
   println("Using " + shortName + ", the keys are:");
   Iterator<String> iterator = map.keySet().iterator();
   for (int i = 1; iterator.hasNext(); i++) {
      print(" " + iterator.next());
      if (i % nPerLine == 0) println();
   }
}
```

For example, if you initialize **stateMap** to be a **HashMap** containing the two-letter state codes from Figure 13-2, calling

```
listKeys(stateMap, 13);
```

produces the following output:

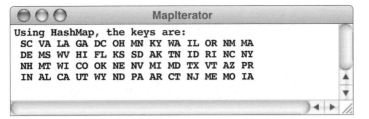

If there is any logic behind the ordering of these keys, that logic is not at all apparent to anyone looking at the sample run. Because sets are unordered, the implementation is free to use any strategy that is convenient for the implementation. In the case of a **HashMap**, the easiest way to cycle through the keys is to step through each of the buckets and then to cycle though the keys in the bucket, one key at a time. The order of keys then depends on how they are assigned to buckets, which in turn depends on their hash codes.

The situation changes if you substitute a **TreeMap** for the **HashMap**. If you run the same method after making this change, the output will look like this instead:

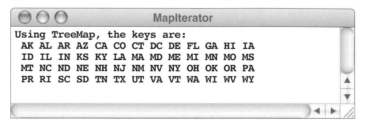

In this example, the keys came out in alphabetical order, which is certain to make a table of codes more usable. The reason for this difference is that the **TreeMap** class implements the **SortedMap** interface, which ensures that iteration will proceed in a natural order.

The only remaining question is what defines a natural order. For many types, the answer is clear. The various types of numbers can be sorted numerically. Strings and characters can be sorted alphabetically. But what about a class like **GObject**? Is there any useful way to define a natural order that establishes whether a red rectangle should come before or after a green oval? Probably not. The **SortedMap** and **SortedSet** interfaces are therefore appropriate only for classes that have something akin to a natural order.

In Java, classes that support a concept of ordering do so by implementing the **Comparable** interface. Classes that implement **Comparable** must define a method

```
public int compareTo(Object obj)
```

that compares the current object to **obj** and returns an integer that expresses their relative order. If the current object comes before **obj**, the **compareTo** method must return a negative integer. If the current object comes after **obj**, **compareTo** must return a positive integer. If the two objects are equal, **compareTo** must return 0. The **String** class implements this method, as do the wrapper classes for all the numeric types. The **compareTo** method defines an ordering relationship among objects, which is called the **default ordering** for that class.

The **Arrays** and **Collections** method libraries

Although they sound as if they would be critical links in the collection class hierarchy, the classes named **Arrays** and **Collections**—not to be confused with the interface named **Collection**—fill a rather different role in the Java Collections Framework. Each of these classes exports only static methods that serve as general tools. The **Arrays** class exports methods that work for any array type; the **Collections** class exports a similar set of methods that work for any collection. This section describes the most useful methods in the **Collections** class; you can easily master the similar methods in the **Arrays** class on your own.

Figure 13-7 lists several of the most important static methods exported by the `Collections` class. As you can see, the list starts off with the two algorithmic methods—searching and sorting—that form the entire focus of Chapter 12. The fact that the `Collections` class exports these operations as utility methods applicable to any list means that you don't have to write these methods on your own. If, for example, you needed to sort an `ArrayList<Integer>` called `examScores`, all you would need to do is call

```
Collections.sort(examScores);
```

Done! The advantage of using a package is that someone has already finished the hard work of implementing and testing the algorithm; it is extremely convenient to rely on such methods when you can.

The `sort` and `binarySearch` methods ordinarily use the default ordering imposed by the `compareTo` method of its element type. The `Collections` class, however, also offers these methods in a second form in which you can supply the comparison method yourself. To do so, you need to provide an object that implements the `Comparator` interface, which is not the same as the `Comparable` interface, despite some similarities. The `Comparator` interface specifies the method

```
public int compare(<T> v1, <T> v2)
```

where `<T>` indicates the type parameter used with the `Comparator` interface. Like the `compareTo` method in the `Comparable` interface, the `compare` method must

---

FIGURE 13-7	Useful methods exported by the `Collections` class

`static void binarySearch(List list, Object key)`
　Uses binary search to find an object in a sorted list using its default ordering.

`static void sort(List list)`
　Sorts the list into ascending order using its default ordering.

`static void binarySearch(List list, Object key, Comparator cmp)`
　Uses binary search to find an object in a sorted list using `cmp` as a comparator function.

`static void sort(List list, Comparator cmp)`
　Sorts the list into ascending order using `cmp` as a comparator function.

`static Object min(List list)`
　Returns the minimum element in a list as an object.

`static Object max(List list)`
　Returns the maximum element in a list as an object.

`static void reverse(List list)`
　Reverses the order of the elements in a list.

`static void shuffle(List list)`
　Randomly shuffles the elements in the list.

`static void swap(List list, int i, int j)`
　Exchanges the elements at index positions `i` and `j`.

`static void rotate(List list, int n)`
　Moves the last `n` elements to the beginning of the list (or the first `n` to the end if `n` is negative).

`static boolean replaceAll(List list, Object oldValue, Object newValue)`
　Replaces every instance of `oldValue` with `newValue`. Returns `true` if any changes were made.

return a value whose sign indicates the ordering relationship between **v1** and **v2**. The primary difference between these interfaces is that **Comparable** describes the ordering that a class uses for its own elements, while **Comparator** describes an order that can be applied to objects of some other class.

You can use these extended versions of **binarySearch** and **sort** to change the ordering rules from the default order imposed by the element type. The **SortIgnoringCase** program in Figure 13-8 sorts the lines of an input file, ignoring differences in case. The default order for strings considers case to be significant, so that, for example, the film title *THX 1138* comes before *Tarzan* because the uppercase letters come before the lowercase letters in lexicographic order.

▆▆ **13.4 Principles of object-oriented design**

Although the tools that well-designed object-oriented packages provide are certainly interesting in their own right, one of the reasons that it is valuable to study such packages is that doing so provides you with models for your own designs. At every level—methods that perform specific functions, classes that offer a suite of those methods, or packages that combine a set of classes—you need to think carefully about design. If you are programming entirely for your own amusement, design issues are likely to seem unimportant. That situation, however, rarely applies in the computing industry. Programs are developed cooperatively. In any large project, programmers working on different parts of the implementation must agree to share a common set of stylistic conventions and to coordinate the ways in which their independent pieces fit together. In the absence of cooperative agreements, the programming process would descend—as it all too often does—into chaos. The important question, therefore, is how one should design methods, classes, and packages for *other* programmers to use. What are the principles that underlie well-chosen designs?

Developing a solid understanding of these principles requires you to understand that clients and implementors look at the facilities provided by a method, class, or package from different perspectives. Clients want to know what operations are available and are unconcerned about the details of the implementation. For implementors, the details of how those operations work are fundamental issues.

It is, however, essential for implementors to keep the needs of clients in mind. If you are trying to design effective resources for others, you need to balance several competing factors. The criteria that follow are described at the level of a package, but these same considerations also apply at the lower levels of classes and methods. The packages you design must be

- *Unified*. Each package should define a consistent abstraction with a clear unifying theme. If a class does not fit within that theme, it should not be part of the package.
- *Simple*. The package design should simplify things for the client. To the extent that the underlying implementation is itself complex, the package must seek to hide that complexity.

FIGURE 13-8   **Program to sort a file ignoring the uppercase/lowercase distinction**

```
import acm.program.*;
import acm.util.*;
import java.io.*;
import java.util.*;

/** This program sorts the lines of a file ignoring the case of letters */
public class SortIgnoringCase extends ConsoleProgram implements Comparator<String> {

   public void run() {
      println("This program sorts a file without regard to case.");
      BufferedReader rd = openFileReader("Enter input file: ")
      List<String> lines = readLineList(rd);
      Collections.sort(lines, this);
      Iterator<String> iterator = lines.iterator();
      while (iterator.hasNext()) {
         println(iterator.next());
      }
   }

/*
 * Implements a string comparison method that ignores case.
 * This method implements the Comparator<String> interface.
 */
   public int compare(String s1, String s2) {
      return s1.toUpperCase().compareTo(s2.toUpperCase());
   }

/*
 * Reads all available lines from the specified reader and returns a List<String>
 * containing those lines.  This method closes the reader at the end of the file.
 */
   private List<String> readLineList(BufferedReader rd) {
      List<String> lineList = new ArrayList<String>();
      try {
         while (true) {
            String line = rd.readLine();
            if (line == null) break;
            lineList.add(line);
         }
         rd.close();
      } catch (IOException ex) {
         throw new ErrorException(ex);
      }
      return lineList;
   }

/* Include the code for openFileReader from Chapter 12. */

}
```

- *Sufficient*. For clients to adopt a package, it must provide classes and methods that meet their needs. If some critical operation is missing from a package, clients may decide to abandon it and develop their own tools. As important as simplicity is, the designer must avoid simplifying a package to the point that it becomes useless.
- *Flexible*. A well-designed package should be general enough to meet the needs of many different clients. A package that offers narrowly defined operations for one client is not nearly as useful as one that can be used in many different situations.
- *Stable*. The methods defined in a class exported as part of a package should continue to have precisely the same structure and effect, even as the package evolves. Making changes in the behavior of a class forces clients to change their programs, which reduces its utility.

The sections that follow discuss each of these criteria in more detail.

The importance of a unifying theme

> *Unity gives strength.*
> — Aesop, *The Bundle of Sticks,* 6th century BCE

A central feature of a well-designed package or class is that it presents a unified, consistent abstraction. In part, this criterion implies that the classes within a package and the methods within a class should be chosen so that they reflect a coherent theme. For example, the **acm.program** package offers a set of classes that make it easy to construct programs, all of which are subclasses of the **Program** class that forms the foundation for the package. In much the same way, the classes in the **acm.graphics** package combine in consistent ways to support arranging graphical objects on a canvas. Each method exported by these classes fits the model of the package as a whole.

The principle of a unifying theme also influences the design of the methods within a class. The methods within a class should behave in as consistent a way as possible. Differences in the ways its methods operate make using a class much harder for the client. For example, all the methods in the **acm.graphics** package use coordinates specified in pixels and angles specified in degrees. If the implementor of some class had decided to toss in a method that required a different unit of measurement, clients would have to remember what units to use in every case, because the consistency would be lost.

Simplicity and the principle of information hiding

> *Embrace simplicity.*
> — Lao-tzu, *The Way of Lao-tzu,* c. 550 BCE

Because a primary goal of object-oriented design is to reduce the complexity of the programming process, it makes sense that simplicity is a desirable design criterion. In general, packages and classes should be easy to use. The underlying implementation may perform extremely intricate operations, but the client should nonetheless be able to think about those operations in a simple, abstract way.

As described in the section on **javadoc** in Chapter 6, the documentation that you need to use Java packages and classes is usually presented on the web. If, for example, you want to know how to use the **Math** class, you can go to the web page that contains its **javadoc** description. If that documentation is well-designed, it tells you precisely the information that you need to know as a client, but no more. For clients, getting too much information can be as bad as getting too little, because additional detail is likely to make the class more difficult to understand. Often, the true value of a design lies not in the information it *reveals* but rather in the information it *hides*.

When you design a class (or even a single method), you should try to protect the client from as many of the details of the implementation as possible. In that respect, it is perhaps best to think of a class not as a communication channel between the client and the implementation, but instead as a wall that divides them.

client   *implementation*

Like the wall that separated the lovers Pyramus and Thisbe in Greek mythology, the wall that separates the client and the implementation contains a small chink that allows the two sides to communicate. The main purpose of the wall, however, is to keep the two sides apart.

Because the wall shown in this diagram forms a border between the conceptual abstractions on each side, that wall is often called an **abstraction boundary.** Ideally, all the complexity involved in the realization of a class lies on the implementation side of the wall. The design is successful if it keeps that complexity away from the client side. As noted in Chapter 5, keeping details confined to the implementation domain is part of a more general process of *information hiding*.

The principle of information hiding has important practical implications for class design. When you write a class, you should be sure you don't reveal details of the implementation in the comments that become part of the **javadoc** description. Especially if you are focusing most of your attention on the implementation, you may be tempted to document in your public commentary all the clever ideas you used to write the implementation. Resist that temptation. The place for that kind of documentation is in the internal comments that are read by other programmers. The public documentation is written for the benefit of the client and should contain only what the client needs to know.

Similarly, you should design the methods in a class so that they are as simple as possible. If you can reduce the number of arguments or find a way to eliminate confusing special cases, it will be easier for the client to understand how to use your methods. Moreover, it is usually good practice to limit the total number of methods exported by a class, so that the client does not become overwhelmed by choices and unable to make sense of the whole.

Meeting the needs of your clients

Everything should be as simple as possible, but no simpler.

— attributed to Albert Einstein

Simplicity, however, is only part of the story. You can easily make a class simple just by throwing away any parts of it that are hard or complicated. In doing so, there is a good chance that you will also make the class useless. Sometimes clients need to perform tasks that have inherent complexity. Denying your clients the tools they require just to make the class simpler is not an effective strategy. Your class must provide sufficient functionality to serve the clients' needs. Learning to strike the right balance between simplicity and completeness in class design is one of the fundamental challenges in programming.

In many cases, the clients of a class are concerned not only with whether a particular method is available but also with the efficiency of the underlying implementation. For example, if a programmer is developing a system for air-traffic control and needs to call methods provided by a class, those methods must return the correct answer quickly. Late answers may be just as devastating as wrong answers.

For the most part, efficiency is a concern for the implementation rather than the abstract design. Even so, you will often find it valuable to consider implementation strategies while you are designing the class itself. Suppose, for example, that you are faced with a choice of two designs. If you determine that one of them would be much easier to implement efficiently, it makes sense—assuming that there are no compelling reasons to the contrary—to choose that design.

The advantages of flexibility

Give us the tools and we will finish the job.

— Winston Churchill, radio address, 1941

A class that is perfectly adapted to a particular client's needs may not be useful to others. A good class abstraction serves the needs of many different clients. To do so, it must be general enough to solve a wide range of problems and not be limited to one highly specific purpose. By maximizing flexibility for your clients, you will expand the potential audience for the classes you create.

The desire to ensure that a class remains general has an important practical implication. When you are writing a program, you will often discover that you need a particular tool. If you decide that the tool is important enough to go into a publicly available package, you then need to change your mode of thought. When you design the public version of the class, you have to forget about the application that caused you to want the tool in the first place and instead design such a tool for the most general possible audience.

In Java, interfaces offer one of the best strategies for making your designs flexible. As you saw in this chapter, defining interfaces for **List**, **Set**, and **Map** make it possible to specify the behavior of those abstract ideas without constraining the actual representation.

The value of stability

People change and forget to tell each other. Too bad—causes so many mistakes.
— Lillian Hellman, *Toys in the Attic*, 1959

Packages and classes that end up gaining popularity with clients typically have another property that makes them particularly useful to clients: they tend to remain stable over long periods of time. Stable classes—and particularly stable interfaces—simplify the problem of maintaining large programming systems by establishing clear boundaries of responsibility. As long as the client can count on the fundamental aspects of a class remaining constant, both implementors and clients are free to make changes on their own side of the abstraction boundary.

For example, suppose that you are the implementor of the **Math** class. In the course of your work, you discover a clever new algorithm for calculating the **sqrt** method that cuts in half the time required to calculate a square root. If you can say to your clients that you have a new implementation of **sqrt** that works just as it did before, only faster, they will probably be pleased. If, on the other hand, you were to say that the name of the method had changed or that its use involved certain new restrictions, your clients would be justifiably annoyed. To use your "improved" implementation of square root, they would be forced to change their programs. Changing programs is a time-consuming, error-prone activity, and many clients would happily give up the extra efficiency for the convenience of being able to leave their programs alone. Keeping things stable—at least to the point that existing clients are not forced to revise their code—makes everyone's life easier.

Summary

This chapter has focused on two related topics. On the one hand, it has given you the opportunity to learn about the Java Collections Framework and the classes it contains, most notably **ArrayList** and **HashMap**. On the other, it has also used that framework as a paradigmatic example of object-oriented design. The important points in this chapter include:

- One of the most important advantages of the **ArrayList** class over Java's built-in array model is that **ArrayList** uses dynamic allocation to expand its internal array as necessary.

- You can implement the dynamic allocation strategy used in the **ArrayList** class by allocating more array elements than you need and keeping track of both the *capacity* of the array, which is the number of elements you have allocated, and the *effective size* of the array, which is the number of elements that are actually in use. Whenever the effective size threatens to exceed the capacity, you have to increase the capacity by allocating a larger array.

- Java achieves flexibility primarily through the use of *interfaces,* which make it possible to specify the behavior of a class without constraining its underlying representation. In the Java Collections Framework, each of the concrete classes implements a more general interface that makes it easier to focus on the abstract behavior of the class.

- The **HashMap** class is the most widely used implementation of the general concept of a map, which specifies associations between a key and a value. The fundamental operations on the **HashMap** class are **put** and **get**, which allow clients to associate a key with a value or retrieve the value associated with a specified key.

- The **HashMap** class uses an algorithm called *hashing* to speed up the process of finding a particular key. This algorithm depends on the fact that every Java class includes a method called **hashCode** that returns an integer indicating exactly where the **HashMap** implementation should look for a particular key. As long as the **HashMap** class is allowed to increase the size of its internal data structures when it runs out of space, the **put** and **get** methods each run in $O(1)$ time.

- If you find that you have to implement a **hashCode** method for your own classes, a useful strategy is to compute the hash code of an object by computing the hash codes of its components, multiplying one of the codes by a small prime number, and then combining those values using the ^ operator.

- If you override the **equals** method for one of your classes, you must also override its **hashCode** method.

- The Java Collection Framework offers more than one concrete representation for each abstract behavioral description specified by an interface. For example, both **ArrayList** and **LinkedList** implement the **List** interface, and both **HashMap** and **TreeMap** implement the **Map** interface. Clients can choose the representation that best supports the performance needs of a specific application.

- The Java collection framework includes a useful interface called **Iterator** that steps through the elements of a collection one at a time. This facility is so useful that Java 5.0 introduced a new syntax for the **for** statement to simplify the format of **Iterator**-based loops.

- The **Arrays** and **Collections** classes contain a set of static utility methods that operate on arrays and collections, respectively. These methods include both **sort** and **binarySearch**.

- Effective design is important at all levels of the programming process. When you are designing packages and classes, you should seek to make them *unified, simple, sufficient, flexible,* and *stable*.

Review questions

1. Describe in general terms the strategy used in this chapter to implement the dynamic behavior of an **ArrayList** using only arrays.

2. What is the difference between capacity and effective size?

3. What makes Java interfaces more flexible than abstract classes?

4. What are the two fundamental operations that define a map?

5. True or false: The same value can appear more than once in a map.

6. What is the result type of the **hashCode** method?

7. State the pigeonhole principle.

8. What is meant by the term *collision* in the context of a **HashMap**?

9. What strategy does **SimpleStringMap** use to resolve the collision problem?

10. The **GPoint** class in the **acm.graphics** library uses two private instance variables to store the coordinates of the point, which are declared like this:

    ```
    private double xc;
    private double yc;
    ```

    Write a **hashCode** method that would be suitable for this class.

11. The discussion of the **hashCode** method in this chapter emphasizes that there is a method in the **Object** class which you should never override without also overriding **hashMap**. What is that method?

12. How does the diagram in Figure 13-5 tell you that a **TreeSet** implements the **Collection** interface?

13. What is an iterator?

14. Describe the special syntax introduced in Java 5.0 to specify iteration over a collection.

15. What changes do you need to make in your use of the Java Collections Framework if you don't have Java 5.0?

16. What is the distinction between the interfaces **Comparable** and **Comparator**?

17. Describe briefly the differences in role between the **Collection** interface and the **Collections** class.

18. How would you write a **compare** method that would allow you to sort an **ArrayList<String>** so that the strings appeared in increasing order of length?

19. What are the five criteria this chapter suggests for well-designed packages, classes, and methods?

Programming exercises

1. Reimplement the **SimpleStringMap** class from Figure 13-3 so that it uses two parallel arrays to store the keys and the corresponding values. As in the **readFile** method in Figure 13-1, your implementation should be able to expand these arrays when needed.

2. Modify your solution to the preceding exercise so that the **put** method always keeps the keys in sorted order in the internal array. Maintaining the sorted array makes it possible to use binary search with both the **put** and **get** methods. Using this strategy, moreover, would allow your implementation to satisfy the constraints of the **SortedMap** interface, although a full implementation of that interface is beyond the scope of this exercise.

3. Extend the implementation of the **SimpleStringMap** class so that it also exports a method

   public void delete(String key);

   that deletes the entry containing the specified key from the map. Given the implementation used in Figure 13-3, implementing this method is somewhat trickier than it might at first appear.

4. Extend the implementation of the **SimpleStringMap** class so that the array of buckets can expand dynamically. Your implementation should keep track of the number of items in the map and perform a rehashing operation whenever the number of items becomes larger than half the number of buckets.

5. Although the bucket-chaining approach used in the text is extremely effective in practice, many other strategies exist for resolving collisions in a **HashMap**. In the early days of computing—when memories were small enough that the cost of introducing extra pointers was taken seriously—hash maps often used a more memory-efficient strategy called **open addressing,** in which the key/value pairs are stored directly in an array, like this:

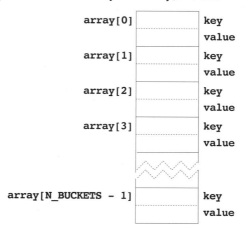

For example, if a key hashes to bucket #3, the open-addressing implementation of a hash table tries to put that key and its value directly into the entry at **array[3]**.

The problem with this approach is that **array[3]** may already be assigned to another key that hashes to the same bucket. The simplest approach to dealing with collisions of this sort is to store each new key in the first free cell at or after its expected hash position. Thus, if a key hashes to bucket #3, the **get** and **put** methods first try to find or insert that key in **array[3]**. If that entry is filled with a different key, however, these methods move on to try **array[4]**, continuing the process until they find an empty entry or an entry with a matching key. If the index advances past the end of the array, it should wrap back to the beginning. This strategy is called **linear probing.**

Reimplement the **SimpleStringMap** class so that it uses open addressing with linear probing. Make sure your method generates an error if the client tries to enter a new key into a table that is already full. For an additional challenge, extend your implementation so that it supports the **delete** method from exercise 3 or expands dynamically as in exercise 4.

6. Suppose that you have a data file called **EnglishWords.txt** that contains all valid English words, one per line. If you wanted to use this list of words in an application, it would be useful to have a few methods for working with the complete list of words. That word list is like a traditional dictionary, except for the fact that it doesn't contain definitions. In computer science, a dictionary of words without their definitions is sometimes called a **lexicon.**

Define a **Lexicon** class that exports the constructor and methods shown in Figure 13-9. Once you have implemented this class, you could use it in the following **run** method to generate a list of all legal two-letter words (which is of enormous importance to Scrabble players):

```
public void run() {
    Lexicon legalWords = new Lexicon("EnglishWords.txt");
    Iterator<String> iterator = legalWords.iterator();
    while (iterator.hasNext()) {
        String word = iterator.next();
        if (word.length() == 2) {
            println(word);
        }
    }
}
```

In writing this program, it is absolutely appropriate to use the **HashMap** class as part of the implementation. It would be poor programming practice to implement the same behavior from scratch.

7. In Chapter 8, one of the programming examples was a **PigLatin** translator, for which the complete code appears in Figure 8-6. As given in Chapter 8 (it turns out that there are regional dialects), the rules for forming the Pig Latin equivalent of an English word are:

FIGURE 13-9 Methods exported by the **Lexicon** class

new Lexicon(String filename)
    Creates a new **Lexicon** object initialized to contain all the words in the specified file.

boolean isWord(String word)
    Returns **true** if the specified word exists in the lexicon.

int getWordCount()
    Returns the number of words in the lexicon.

String getRandomWord()
    Returns a randomly chosen word from the lexicon.

Iterator<String> iterator()
    Returns an iterator that steps through the words in the lexicon (in no predictable order).

1. If the word begins with a consonant, you form its Pig Latin equivalent by moving the initial consonant string (that is, all the letters up to the first vowel) from the beginning of the word to the end and then adding the suffix *ay*.

2. If the word begins with a vowel, you simply add the suffix *way*.

There are a small number of words in English that continue to be English words when you translate them to Pig Latin. One such example is *trash,* which becomes *ashtray,* as illustrated in the following diagram:

Similarly, the English word *plunder* becomes the word *underplay*. And in the somewhat less interesting case involving words that begin with vowels, the word *any* becomes *anyway*.

Use the **Lexicon** class from exercise 6 to implement a **ConsoleProgram** that displays all such words.

8. The text notes in passing that there are exactly two pairs of English words containing no more than 10 letters for which the hash codes are the same: *buzzards* and *righto* are one such pair, *crinolines* and *hierarch* are the other. Write a Java program that verifies this claim.

9. In the discussion of the **Comparator** interface, the example used to provide background motivation for sorting without regard to case is a pair of movie titles, *THX 1138* and *Tarzan*. While the case of the letters is important in this specific example, a more significant problem in sorting titles is that the ordering needs to ignore the articles *a, an,* and *the* if they appear at the beginning of the title.

Write an interactive program that asks the user for a file that contains a list of film titles, with one title per line. Your program should read the entire file into a list, sort that list using **Collections.sort**, and then write the sorted lines back to the file. The **Comparator** that you supply to **Collections.sort** should ignore articles that appear at the beginning of titles as well as any case distinctions.

10. One of the important applications of hashing is to represent two-dimensional numeric arrays in which relatively few of the entries are nonzero. Such arrays are called **sparse matrices.** The advantage of using a **HashMap** instead of an array to store the elements is that the implementation doesn't actually have to assign array space to the zero elements. If an element is not in the **HashMap**, it is assumed to be zero.

Design and implement a class called **SparseMatrix** that uses **HashMap** to simulate a two-dimensional array of **double**s. Your class should export a constructor along with **get** and **put** methods to retrieve the value of an element or set an element to a new value, respectively. An important part of the problem consists of designing the argument structure for those methods.

CHAPTER 14

Looking Ahead

The best way to predict the future is to invent it.
— Alan Kay, Xerox Palo Alto Research Center, 1971

Anita Borg (1949–2003)

By rights, a chapter entitled "Looking Ahead" should be introduced with a picture of someone who will create the future of computer science. That future belongs to those who are currently studying computer science—that picture will be your picture. But the future is also shaped by those who have paved the way for the next generation. In her all-too-short life, Anita Borg worked tirelessly not only to advance the state of computer science as a research scientist, but also to broaden participation in the computing disciplines, particularly among women. She was the founder of the Systers online community for women in computer science, the Grace Hopper Celebration of Women in Computing, and the Institute for Women in Computing, which was rechristened as the Anita Borg Institute following her death from cancer in 2003. Her spirit, however, lives on in everyone who overcomes barriers to enter and succeed in this dynamic and exciting field that Anita loved so much.

After completing the first 13 chapters of this text, you have learned the fundamentals of Java programming along with many important concepts from computer science. Computer science is, however, a large and ever-expanding field, about which you still have much to learn. This chapter introduces four additional topics that you will surely encounter if you continue your study:

- *Recursion*
- *Concurrency*
- *Networking*
- *Programming patterns*

Because these topics are central to modern computer science, many schools introduce them in the first programming course. To make sure that this text meets the needs of a wide range of institutions, this chapter offers a brief overview of each topic. Even if you are not required to learn this material for a course, reading through this chapter will help if you continue in computer science. When you encounter these ideas in a more advanced course, they will not be entirely new, and you will be able to pick them up more quickly.

14.1 Recursion

Most algorithmic strategies used to solve programming problems have counterparts outside the domain of computing. When you perform a task repeatedly, you are using iteration. When you make a decision, you exercise conditional control. Because these operations are familiar, most people learn to use the control statements **for**, **while**, and **if** with relatively little trouble.

Before you can solve many sophisticated programming tasks, however, you will have to come to grips with a powerful problem-solving strategy that has few direct counterparts in the real world. That strategy, called **recursion,** is defined as any solution technique in which large problems are solved by reducing them to smaller problems *of the same form*. The italicized phrase is crucial to the definition, which otherwise describes the strategy of stepwise refinement introduced in Chapter 5. Both strategies involve decomposition. What makes recursion special is that the subproblems in a recursive solution have the same form as the original problem.

If you are like most new programmers, the idea of breaking a problem down into subproblems of the same form does not make much sense when you first hear it. Unlike repetition or conditional testing, recursion is not a concept that comes up in day-to-day life. Because it is unfamiliar, learning how to use recursion can be difficult. To do so, you must develop the intuition necessary to make recursion seem as natural as all the other control structures. For most students of programming, reaching that level of understanding takes considerable time and practice. Even so, learning to use recursion is definitely worth the effort. As a problem-solving tool, recursion is so powerful that it at times seems almost magical. In addition, using recursion often makes it possible to write complex programs in simple and profoundly elegant ways.

A simple illustration of recursion

To gain a better sense of what recursion is, imagine that you have been appointed as the funding coordinator for a large charitable organization that, like many such organizations, is long on volunteers and short on cash. Your job is to raise $1,000,000 in contributions so that the organization can meet its expenses.

If you know someone who is willing to write a check for the entire $1,000,000, your job is easy. On the other hand, you may not be lucky enough to have friends who are generous millionaires. In that case, you must raise the $1,000,000 in smaller amounts. If the average contribution to your organization is $100, you might choose a different tack: call 100,000 friends and ask each of them for $100. But then again, you probably don't have 100,000 friends. So what can you do?

As is often the case when you are faced with a task that exceeds your own capacity, the answer lies in delegating part of the work to others. Your organization has a reasonable supply of volunteers. If you could find 10 dedicated supporters in different parts of the country and appoint them as regional coordinators, each of those 10 people could then take responsibility for raising $100,000.

Raising $100,000 is simpler than raising $1,000,000, but it hardly qualifies as easy. What should your regional coordinators do? If they adopt the same strategy, they will in turn delegate parts of the job. If they each recruit 10 fundraising volunteers, those people will only have to raise $10,000. The delegation process can continue further until the volunteers are able raise the money they need all at once. Because the average contribution is $100, the last tier of volunteer fundraisers can probably each find a single donor who is willing to give that much, which eliminates the need for further delegation.

If you express this fundraising strategy in pseudocode, it has the following structure:

```
private void collectContributions(int n) {
    if (n <= 100) {
        Collect the money from a single donor.
    } else {
        Find 10 volunteers.
        Get each volunteer to collect n/10 dollars.
        Combine the money raised by the volunteers.
    }
}
```

The most important thing to notice about this pseudocode translation is that the line

> *Get each volunteer to collect **n**/10 dollars.*

is simply the original problem reproduced at a smaller scale. The basic character of the task—raise *n* dollars—remains exactly the same; the only difference is that *n* has a smaller value. Moreover, because the problem is the same, you can solve it by calling the original method. Thus, the preceding line of pseudocode would eventually be replaced by the following line:

```
collectContributions(n / 10);
```

It's important to note that the `collectContributions` method ends up calling itself if the contribution level is greater than $100. In the context of programming, having a method call itself is the defining characteristic of recursion.

The Factorial function

The `collectContributions` example is useful because it conveys the idea of recursion in an easily understood way. On the other hand, it gives little insight into how recursion is used in practice, mostly because the primitive operations it uses— finding ten volunteers and collecting money—are not easily represented in a Java program. To get a more practical sense of recursion, you need to look at problems that fit more easily into the programming domain.

It is easiest to illustrate recursion in the context of a simple mathematical function, such as the factorial method introduced in Chapter 5. The factorial of an integer n—denoted in mathematics as $n!$—is simply the product of the integers between 1 and n. As you discovered in Chapter 5, you can easily implement the factorial method using a **for** loop, as illustrated by the following implementation, which is taken from Figure 5-4:

```
private int factorial(int n) {
    int result = 1;
    for (int i = 1; i <= n; i++) {
        result *= i;
    }
    return result;
}
```

This implementation, however, does not take advantage of an important property of factorials. Each factorial is related to the factorial of the next smaller number in the following way:

$$n! = n \times (n - 1)!$$

Thus, 4! is 4 × 3!, 3! is 3 × 2!, and so on. To make sure that this process stops at some point, mathematicians define 0! to be 1. Thus, the conventional mathematical definition of the factorial method looks like this:

$$n! = \begin{cases} 1 & \text{if } n = 0 \\ n \times (n - 1)! & \text{otherwise} \end{cases}$$

This definition is recursive, because it defines the factorial of n in terms of the factorial of $n - 1$. The new problem, finding the factorial of $n - 1$, has the same form as the original problem, which is the defining characteristic of recursion. You can then use the same process to define the factorial of $n - 1$ in terms of the factorial of $n - 2$. Moreover, you can carry this process forward step by step until you try to find the factorial of 0, which mathematicians have defined to be equal to 1. At that point, the recursion stops, and you can go back through all the levels, multiplying each result by the next number in turn.

The most exciting aspect of this approach is that you can use it directly as a solution technique. Because Java allows methods to call themselves recursively, you can implement the **factorial** method in the following way, which is a direct translation of the mathematical definition:

```java
private int factorial(int n) {
   if (n == 0) {
      return 1;
   } else {
      return n * factorial(n - 1);
   }
}
```

If you work from the mathematical definition, writing the recursive implementation of **factorial** is straightforward. On the other hand, when you are learning about recursion for the first time, this implementation seems to leave something out. Even though it clearly reflects the mathematical definition, the recursive implementation makes it hard to identify where the actual computational steps occur. When you call **factorial**, you want the computer to give you the answer. In the recursive implementation, all you see is a formula that transforms one call to **factorial** into another one. Because the steps in that calculation are not explicit, the fact that the computer gets the right answer sometimes seems magical.

If you follow through the logic that the computer uses to evaluate any method call, however, it becomes clear that no magic is involved. When the computer evaluates a call to the recursive **factorial** method, it goes through the same process it uses to evaluate any other method call. To illustrate the process, let's suppose that you have executed the statement

```java
int fact = factorial(4);
```

as part of the **run** method. When the **run** method calls **factorial**, the Java runtime system creates a new frame and copies the argument value into the formal parameter **n**. The frame for **factorial** temporarily supersedes the frame for **run**, as shown in the following diagram:

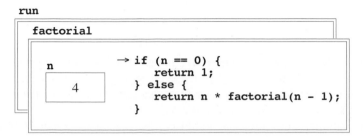

In the diagram, the code for the body of **factorial** is shown inside the frame to make it easier to keep track of the current position in the program, which is indicated by an arrow. In the current diagram, the arrow appears at the beginning of the code because all method calls start at the first statement of the method body.

The computer now proceeds to evaluate the body of the method, starting with the **if** statement. Because **n** is not equal to 0, control proceeds to the **else** clause, where the program must evaluate and return the value of the expression

> **n * factorial(n - 1)**

Evaluating this expression requires computing the value of **factorial(n - 1)**, which requires a recursive call. When that call returns, all the program has to do is to multiply the result by **n**. The current state of the computation can therefore be diagrammed as follows:

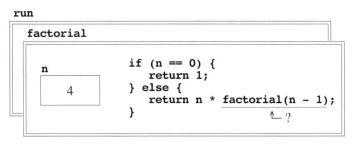

As soon as the call to **factorial(n - 1)** returns, the result is substituted for the underlined expression, which allows computation to proceed.

The next step in the computation is therefore to evaluate the call to **factorial(n - 1)**, which begins by evaluating the argument expression. Because the current value of **n** is 4, the argument expression **n - 1** has the value 3. The computer then creates a new frame for **factorial** in which the formal parameter is initialized to this value. Thus, the next frame looks like this:

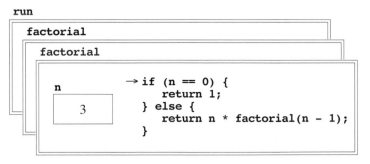

There are now two frames labeled **factorial**. In the most recent one, the computer is just starting to calculate **factorial(3)**. In the preceding frame, which the newly created frame hides, the **factorial** method is awaiting the result of the call to **factorial(n - 1)**.

The current computation, however, is always the one in the topmost frame. Once again, because **n** is not 0, control passes to the **else** clause of the **if** statement, where the computer must evaluate **factorial(n - 1)**. In this frame, however, **n** is equal to 3, so the required result is that computed by calling **factorial(2)**. As before, this process requires the creation of a new stack frame, as shown:

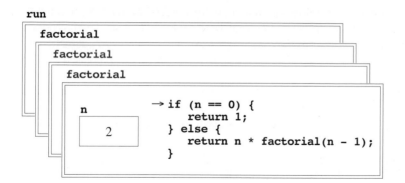

Following the same logic, the program must now call **factorial(1)**, which in turn calls **factorial(0)**, thereby creating two new stack frames. The resulting stack configuration looks like this:

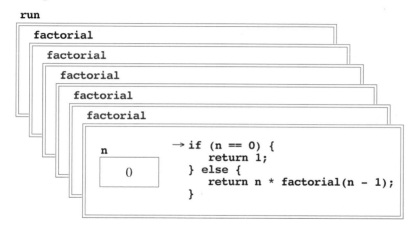

At this point, however, the situation changes. Because **n** is 0, the method will return the value 1 to its caller. The frame for the current call goes away, and the preceding frame becomes the top of the stack:

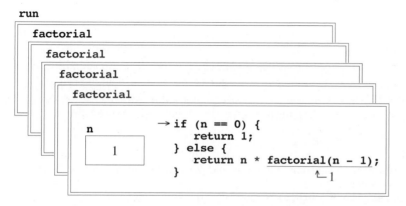

From here on, the computation consists of proceeding back through each of the recursive calls, using the value returned by **factorial** at one level to compute the result at the next level. In this frame, for example, the call to **factorial(n – 1)** is replaced by the value 1, so that the result at this level can be expressed as follows:

$$\texttt{return n * }\boxed{1}\texttt{);}$$

In this stack frame, because **n** has the value 1, the result of this call is simply 1. This result gets propagated back to its caller, just as in the preceding example.

After returning through several levels, the computation will reach the original factorial frame with the value 6, like this:

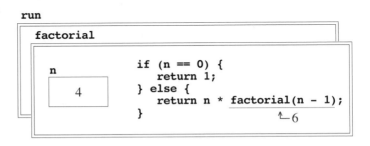

Because **n** is now 4, evaluating the **return** statement returns the value 24 to the **run** method.

The recursive leap of faith

The point of the long **factorial(4)** example in the preceding section is to show you that the computer treats recursive methods just like any other methods. When you are faced with a recursive method, you can—at least in theory—mimic the operation of the computer and figure out what it will do. By drawing all the frames and keeping track of all the variables, you can duplicate the operation of the computer and come up with the answer. If you do so, however, you will usually discover that the complexity of the process ends up making the problem much harder to understand.

When you think about a recursive program, you must be able to put these underlying details aside and focus instead on a single level of the operation. At that level, you are allowed to assume that any recursive call automatically gets the right answer as long as the arguments to that call are simpler than the original argument in some respect. For example, to compute **factorial(n)** with **n** equal to 4, the recursive implementation must compute the value of the expression

    n * factorial(n - 1)

By substituting the current value of **n** into the expression, you know that the result is

    4 * factorial(3)

Stop right there. You're finished! Computing `factorial(3)` is simpler than the original task of computing `factorial(4)`. Because it is simpler, you are allowed to assume that it works. You know that `factorial(3)` is $3 \times 2 \times 1$, or 6. The result of calling `factorial(4)` is therefore 4×6, or 24, which is the right answer.

Learning to assume that any simpler recursive call works is an essential programming strategy called the **recursive leap of faith.** Until you have had extensive experience working with recursive methods, the recursive leap of faith will not come easily. After all, when you write a program, the odds are good—even if you are an experienced programmer—that your program *won't* work the first time. Suspending your disbelief and assuming that it does work violates your own healthy skepticism about the likely correctness of your programs. Even so, mastering the concept of recursion requires you to conquer that psychological barrier. Looking more than one level down in a recursive method inevitably makes the problem harder to solve.

The recursive paradigm

Most of the recursive methods you are likely to encounter will have the same basic structure as the `factorial` method in the preceding section. The body of the typical recursive method has the following paradigmatic form:

```
if (test for a simple case) {
    Compute and return the simple solution without using recursion.
} else {
    Divide the problem into one or more subproblems that have the same form.
    Solve each of the problems by calling this method recursively.
    Return the solution from the results of the various subproblems.
}
```

The recursive `factorial` method fits this paradigm, as does the following method that raises an integer n to the kth power:

```
private int raiseIntToPower(int n, int k) {
    if (k == 0) {
        return 1;
    } else {
        return n * raiseIntToPower(n, k - 1);
    }
}
```

This implementation of `raiseIntToPower` relies on the mathematical property that

$$n^k = \begin{cases} 1 & \text{if } k = 0 \\ n \times n^{k-1} & \text{otherwise} \end{cases}$$

The problems of computing a factorial or raising a number to a power have natural recursive solutions because the problems meet the following conditions:

1. You can identify *simple cases* for which the answer is easily determined.
2. You can apply a *recursive decomposition* to break down more complicated instances of the problem into simpler problems of the same type, which you can then solve by applying the same solution technique.

When a recursive decomposition follows directly from a mathematical definition, as it does in the case of the methods `factorial` and `raiseIntToPower`, applying recursion is not particularly hard. The situation changes, however, when the problems themselves become more complicated and the recursive decomposition requires some cleverness to find. The next section solves a more complex problem in which the recursive decomposition is more difficult to see.

Graphical recursion

In the late 1970s, a researcher at IBM named Benoit Mandelbrot generated a great deal of excitement by publishing a book on **fractals,** which are geometrical structures in which the same pattern is repeated at many different scales. Although mathematicians have known about fractals for a long time, there was a resurgence of interest in the subject during the 1980s, partly because the development of computers made it possible to do so much more with fractals than had ever been possible before.

One of the earliest examples of fractal figures is called the **Koch fractal** after its inventor, Helge von Koch, although it is often referred to as a **snowflake fractal** because of the beautiful, six-sided symmetries it displays as the figure becomes more detailed. The simplest version of this fractal, which is called the snowflake fractal of order 0, is simply an equilateral triangle like this:

To obtain a snowflake fractal of the next higher order, you simply replace every line segment in the current snowflake with a set of lines that looks much like the original line except that the middle third has been replaced by a triangular bump protruding outward from the figure. Thus, the first step is to replace each line segment in the order-0 snowflake with a set of four shorter line segments arranged like this:

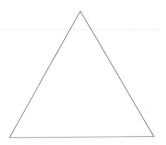

Applying this transformation to each of the three sides of the original triangle generates the order-1 snowflake, as follows:

If you then replace each line segment in this figure with a new line that again includes a triangular wedge, you create the following order-2 snowflake:

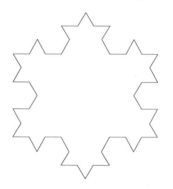

Replacing each of these line segments again produces the order-3 fractal shown in the following diagram, which has started to resemble a snowflake:

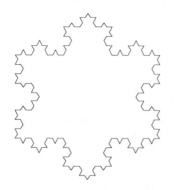

Writing a program to create a snowflake fractal is easy if you use the facilities from the **acm.graphics** package, particularly if you think about the problem from an object-oriented perspective rather than a procedural one. In this case, the goal is to create a graphical object that looks like the fractals in the diagrams, all of which are polygons. It therefore seems natural to define a **SnowflakeFractal** class as a subclass of **GPolygon**.

Suppose, for example, that you wanted to create the triangular order-0 fractal as a graphical object. The strategy is similar the one used to create the **GStar** class in Figure 9-16. The following class definition for **SnowflakeFractal0** defines a **GPolygon** subclass whose edge length is passed as a parameter to the constructor and whose reference point is at the center of the triangle:

```
public class SnowflakeFractal0 extends GPolygon {

    public SnowflakeFractal0(double edge) {
        addVertex(-edge / 2, edge / (2 * Math.sqrt(3)));
        addPolarEdge(edge, 0);
        addPolarEdge(edge, 120);
        addPolarEdge(edge, 240);
    }

}
```

As was true with the **GStar** class as well, the only complicated part of this implementation is figuring out the coordinates of the starting point, which is taken to be the corner at the bottom left of the triangle. The three calls to **addPolarEdge** add the edges of the triangle. The first edge runs horizontally across the bottom, and each of the next two edges is rotated 120 degrees counterclockwise from the preceding one.

If you then wanted to draw the order-1 fractal, all you would have to do is replace each call to **addPolarEdge** in the constructor with a call to a method that adds the fractal line with a triangular wedge. The new version of the class, which is now called **SnowflakeFractal0**, looks like this:

```
public class SnowflakeFractal1 extends GPolygon {

    public SnowflakeFractal1(double edge) {
        addVertex(-edge / 2, edge / (2 * Math.sqrt(3)));
        addFractalLine(edge, 0);
        addFractalLine(edge, 120);
        addFractalLine(edge, 240);
    }

    private void addFractalLine(double r, int theta) {
        addPolarEdge(r / 3, theta);
        addPolarEdge(r / 3, theta + 60);
        addPolarEdge(r / 3, theta - 60);
        addPolarEdge(r / 3, theta);
    }

}
```

So far, so good. You've created new classes for each fractal order, but that process does not offer a general solution to the problem. It would be far better if the **SnowflakeFractal** constructor took the order of the fractal as well as the edge length. It could then pass that order to the **addFractalLine** method to draw the three fractal lines of the desired order.

Adding an `order` parameter to `addFractalLine` makes it well suited to a recursive solution. The simple case occurs when `order` is 0, because an order-0 fractal line is simply a straight line. The recursive insight is that a fractal line of order k is composed of four fractal lines of order $k - 1$. You can use this insight to write a more general implementation of `SnowflakeFractal` that includes an `order` parameter. To do so, you will have to modify the `addFractalLine` method so that it calls itself recursively, except in the simple case where the `order` parameter is 0, in which case the edge is a straight line. Figure 14-1 shows the full implementation of the `SnowflakeFractal` class:

FIGURE 14-1   **GPolygon subclass that displays a snowflake fractal**

```java
import acm.graphics.*;

/**
 * Defines a new GObject class that appears as a snowflake fractal.  Because
 * the result is a GPolygon, you can fill the snowflake or move it as a unit.
 */
public class SnowflakeFractal extends GPolygon {

/**
 * Creates a new SnowflakeFractal centered at the origin with the
 * specified edge length and fractal order.
 * @param edge The length of an edge in the order-0 snowflake
 * @param order The order of this fractal
 */
   public SnowflakeFractal(double edge, int order) {
      addVertex(-edge / 2, -edge / (2 * Math.sqrt(3)));
      addFractalLine(edge, 0, order);
      addFractalLine(edge, -120, order);
      addFractalLine(edge, +120, order);
   }

/**
 * Adds a fractal line to the polygon with the specified radial
 * length, starting angle, and fractal order.
 * @param r The length of the line
 * @param theta The direction in which to draw the line (in degrees)
 * @param order The order of this fractal
 */
   private void addFractalLine(double r, int theta, int order) {
      if (order == 0) {
         addPolarEdge(r, theta);
      } else {
         addFractalLine(r / 3, theta, order - 1);
         addFractalLine(r / 3, theta + 60, order - 1);
         addFractalLine(r / 3, theta - 60, order - 1);
         addFractalLine(r / 3, theta, order - 1);
      }
   }
}
```

Thinking recursively

More than any other aspect of programming, learning to use recursion requires you to think about the programming process holistically. If you adopt the reductionistic approach of tracing through all the steps in a complex recursive decomposition, you end up having to manage a huge amount of detail—detail that is better left to the computer. The process of going through the steps in the calculation of `factorial(4)` earlier in this chapter takes several pages. In contrast, the holistic idea that

```
factorial(4) = 4 * factorial(3)
```

takes only a single line. The difference in the conceptual complexity of these two approaches to recursion is enormous. By maintaining a holistic perspective, you can reduce the complexity of most recursive programs to a point at which you can comprehend the solution. If, on the other hand, your uncertainty about the correctness of your solution forces you down the reductionistic path, the mass of details will almost certainly make it impossible for you to understand the high-level structure of the solution.

Thinking about recursive problems in the right way does not come easily. Learning to use recursion effectively requires practice and more practice. For many students, mastering the concept takes years. But because recursion will turn out to be one of the most powerful techniques in your programming repertoire, that time will be well spent.

14.2 Concurrency

At the beginning of this book, in an attempt to give you some insight into the rationale behind the development of Java, Figure 1-4 outlined several principles that Java's designers believe set it apart from other programming languages. One of those design principles was that Java should be "multithreaded, for high performance in applications that need to perform multiple concurrent activities." Up to now, however, the programs in this book have not made particular use of Java's ability to perform the "multiple concurrent activities" this principle describes. This section provides a brief introduction to concurrency and the features that Java offers to support it.

Processes and threads

Although hardware architecture is increasingly moving toward machines that contain more than one processor, it is still true that most computers have a single central processing unit that executes one program at a time. Since the early 1960s, computers have used a strategy called **multiprogramming** that simulates the concurrent execution by having the computer run one program for a while (usually measured in tens or hundreds of milliseconds) and then stop and run a completely independent program for a similar amount of time. Because the computer switches back and forth between these different programs, all of them appear to be moving forward, even though the computer executes only one at a time. Whenever the computer switches from one program to another, it has to save the execution state of the program it is suspending and restore the state of the one it is starting up. The conceptual entity that encompasses both a program and its state is called a **process.**

The idea of **multithreading** extends this idea to reflect the fact that a single program can also benefit from this kind of parallel operation. As part of a coordinated effort toward the completion of a task, a program might initiate several independent activities called **threads** (or sometimes **threads of control**) that appear to run simultaneously, just as programs do in a multiprogramming environment. The difference between threads and processes is largely one of scale. Processes typically describe the execution state of entire programs, while threads do the same for independent activities within the same program. Unlike processes, multiple threads can coexist within the same program and share access to the resources of that program.

The programs you have seen so far in this book have a single primary thread of control. That thread is created when the program is initialized; its only job is to execute the **run** method of the program. Other threads, however, have been active behind the scenes. In particular, Java creates a thread called the **event thread** that responds to user actions such as clicking a button or dragging the mouse. It is this thread that calls the event listeners and triggers the program's response. You can, however, create your own threads as well, as described in the following section.

A simple example of concurrency

Chapter 4 introduced a simple model for animating a program that has the following pseudocode form:

```
public void run() {
    Initialize the graphical objects in the display.
    while (you want to keep running the animation) {
        Update the properties of the objects that you wish to animate.
        pause(delay time);
    }
}
```

Because the animation takes place within the implementation of **run**, this model uses the primary program thread that is created specifically for the purpose of executing the **run** method. Because this model involves only a single thread of control, all the code that updates the objects from time step to time step must take place within this method. In many cases, it makes more sense to use independent threads of control to animate each object.

The code for the **AnimatedSquare** class in Figure 14-2 offers a simple example of this technique. The code in this example defines a **GRect** subclass whose size is set by a single parameter passed to the constructor. What makes this class different is that it implements the **Runnable** interface, which means that the object can serve as the context for a new thread of control. The **run** method specifies what happens when this thread is started in much the same way that it does for the **Program** class. In this case, the **run** method uses a standard animation loop to move the square in a direction that changes every 50 time steps.

FIGURE 14-2   The `AnimatedSquare` class

```
import acm.graphics.*;
import acm.util.*;
import java.awt.*;

/**
 * This class creates an animated square that has its own thread of control.
 * Once started, the square moves in a random direction every time step.
 * After N_STEPS time steps, the square picks a new random direction.
 */
public class AnimatedSquare extends GRect implements Runnable {

/* Creates a new AnimatedSquare of the specified size */
   public AnimatedSquare(double size) {
      super(size, size);
   }

/* Runs when this object is started to animate the square */
   public void run() {
      for (int t = 0; true; t++) {
         if (t % CHANGE_TIME == 0) {
            direction = rgen.nextDouble(0, 360);
         }
         movePolar(DELTA, direction);
         pause(PAUSE_TIME);
      }
   }

/* Private constants */
   private static final double DELTA = 2;      /* Pixels to move each cycle      */
   private static final int PAUSE_TIME = 20;   /* Length of time step            */
   private static final int CHANGE_TIME = 50;  /* Steps before changing direction */

/* Private instance variables */
   private RandomGenerator rgen = RandomGenerator.getInstance();
   private double direction;

}
```

Objects that implement the **Runnable** interface are called **runnable objects.** To activate a runnable object from some other part of the program, you first need to create a thread attached to it. For example, you can create an **AnimatedSquare** and its associated thread by executing the following code:

```
AnimatedSquare square = new AnimatedSquare(75);
Thread squareThread = new Thread(square);
```

If you then add the square to a **GraphicsProgram** canvas, you can make it move by calling **start** on its thread, like this:

```
squareThread.start();
```

What makes thread-style animation interesting is that you can use it to animate many different objects, each with its own thread. The code in Figure 14-3, for example, creates two **AnimatedSquare** objects, fills them both, sets the color of one to be red and the other to be green, and then adds them to the canvas so that they are each one-third of the distance from one of the edges. When the user clicks the mouse, the program starts both threads.

If all you are interested in doing is animating a graphical display, there is no obvious reason to prefer the strategy of using runnable objects over the more familiar strategy of performing that animation in the **run** method for the program itself. If anything, there are advantages to the style you have been using all along, most notably the fact that it is difficult to keep runnable objects in sync. Because each runnable object has a separate thread, those threads may run at different rates. Having the same code update all the objects involved in the animation ensures that all the updates happen together.

If you do decide to use separate threads to animate the individual objects in a graphical program, you may well want to explore some library packages that make

---

FIGURE 14-3   **Program to test the AnimatedSquare class**

```java
import acm.program.*;
import java.awt.*;

/**
 * This program tests the AnimatedSquare class by putting two squares
 * on the screen and having them move independently.
 */
public class TestAnimatedSquare extends GraphicsProgram {

    public void run() {
        double x1 = getWidth() / 3 - SQUARE_SIZE / 2;
        double x2 = 2 * getWidth() / 3 - SQUARE_SIZE / 2;
        double y = (getHeight() - SQUARE_SIZE) / 2;
        AnimatedSquare redSquare = new AnimatedSquare(SQUARE_SIZE);
        redSquare.setFilled(true);
        redSquare.setColor(Color.RED);
        add(redSquare, x1, y);
        AnimatedSquare greenSquare = new AnimatedSquare(SQUARE_SIZE);
        greenSquare.setFilled(true);
        greenSquare.setColor(Color.GREEN);
        add(greenSquare, x2, y);
        Thread redSquareThread = new Thread(redSquare);
        Thread greenSquareThread = new Thread(greenSquare);
        waitForClick();
        redSquareThread.start();
        greenSquareThread.start();
    }

/* Private constants */
    private static final double SQUARE_SIZE = 75;

}
```

it easier to control this style of animation. In particular, the `acm.util` package includes a class called `Animator` that extends the basic `Thread` class to support more flexible strategies for interactive control. For example, the `Animator` class makes it easy to create a control bar that uses buttons to start, stop, and single-step an animation. The details of the `Animator` class are beyond the scope of this book, but you can look at its **javadoc** page for more information.

There is, however, one important cautionary note that you need to keep in mind. It is sometimes tempting to consider putting an animation loop inside one of the listener methods. For example, if you wanted to have an object start moving when you click it, you might try putting a loop to do so inside the definition of the `mouseClicked` method. Although that strategy might seem to work at first, it creates serious problems because it occupies Java's event thread, rendering it unable to respond to other events. As a general rule, you should make sure that all your listener methods run to completion quickly.

The topic of concurrency is much larger than the simple overview you've gotten in this section. In particular, it is often important to ensure that two threads do not interfere with each other as they run, which can easily happen if one thread changes the value of a variable on which another thread relies. Ensuring that only one thread is able to work with particular data items in critical parts of the code is called the **mutual-exclusion problem.** The Java language and its libraries include many tools for helping to manage concurrency, although those tools are beyond the scope of this presentation.

> **COMMON PITFALLS**
>
> Listener methods are designed to run for very short periods of time to avoid tying up Java's event thread. You should therefore make sure that your listener methods complete their work quickly and never, for example, call the **pause** method.

14.3 Using the network

Another important factor that influenced the development of Java is the explosive growth of the Internet and the World-Wide Web during Java's early years. Partly because the applet mechanism made it possible to run Java programs in the context of a web page, Java quickly became one of the leading languages for web-based applications.

Java's support of web-based programming extends well beyond applets. The standard Java library packages include one called `java.net` that allows programs to reach out to the network and gain access to its vast amount of information.

Although most of the facilities in the `java.net` package are beyond the scope of an introductory text, there are a few simple operations you can perform. The `openNetworkReader` method in Figure 14-4, for example, opens a `BufferedReader` on a network URL in much the same way that the `openFileReader` method from Chapter 10 opens an input file. You can use this method in a program to read the contents of a URL anywhere on the World-Wide Web. Such a method could become the core of a web-based application of your own. Who knows? You might create the next Google or YouTube.

14.4 Programming patterns

The final topic in this book is an extension of an idea that played an important role in the early chapters—the concept of a programming pattern. You have seen

---

FIGURE 14-4   Code for the `openNetworkReader` method

```
/**
 * This program prompts the user for a URL and returns a BufferedReader
 * that allows clients to read data from that URL.  If the URL does not
 * exist or cannot be read, the user is given another chance to enter
 * a valid URL.
 * @param prompt The string used to prompt the user for a URL
 * @return A BufferedReader opened so that it reads data from the specified URL
 */
   public BufferedReader openNetworkReader(String prompt) {
      BufferedReader rd = null;
      while (rd == null) {
         try {
            URL url = new URL(readLine(prompt));
            InputStream in = url.openStream();
            rd = new BufferedReader(new InputStreamReader(in));
         } catch (IOException ex) {
            println("Can't open that URL.");
         }
      }
      return rd;
   }
```

---

several examples of programming patterns at different points in the text, ranging from simple idioms such as the **x++** expression used to increment the value of **x** all the way up to much larger pseudocode templates such as the one for animation that was introduced in Chapter 4 and reprised in section 14.2. As programming languages and systems become ever more sophisticated, the programming patterns that one uses become larger in scale, to the point that the term now encompasses general solution strategies for solving a particular problem.

The use of design patterns has become far more prevalent since the publication of an extremely influential book entitled *Design Patterns: Elements of Reusable Object-Oriented Software* (Addison-Wesley, 1995) by a team consisting of Erich Gamma, Richard Helm, Ralph Johnson, and John Vlissides, popularly known as "The Gang of Four." Their book describes a wide array of patterns that solve many different programming problems. Those patterns range in scale from simple ones that can be implemented within a single method to much larger examples that require a hierarchy of classes and interfaces. Although much of *Design Patterns* focuses on programming problems that are probably too advanced for someone just finishing an introductory text, it is worth keeping this book in mind as you learn more about computer science and programming.

The model/view/controller pattern

To get a sense of how patterns work, it is useful to look at least one pattern in some detail. An obvious choice for such an example is a classic pattern called **model/view/controller,** which is widely used in user-interface design. This pattern was developed as part of the Smalltalk 80 system and therefore predates the *Design Patterns* book.

The basic idea behind the pattern is that it is important to separate those parts of the program that have to do with user interaction from the underlying structures that represent the overall state of the application. The **model** portion of the design maintains the state of the application but is entirely separate from any interaction with the user. The user interacts with the model by issuing commands to a **controller** and can see the results of any calculations through an independent part of the program called a **view.** The following diagram illustrates the relationship among these components:

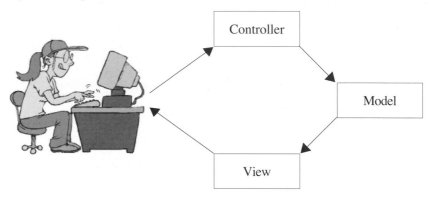

Using the model/view/controller pattern offers three significant advantages over adopting a less structured style:

1. The individual classes in the model/view/controller pattern are responsible for only one part of the overall task, which makes them simpler to understand individually. You can read the code for the model without getting bogged down in details about graphical objects and interactors.
2. The model/view/controller pattern makes it much easier for an application to have multiple views of the same model. Most modern word processors, for example, allow you to have more than one editing window open on the same file. Any change you make in one window automatically gets reflected in other windows that share the same model.
3. Programmers who have been trained in modern principles of object-oriented design are familiar with the model/view/controller pattern and can use that familiarity to streamline the coding process by taking advantage of their understanding of that idea.

An illustrative example: Graphing spreadsheet data

Spreadsheets offer a useful illustration of an application that supports multiple views. Suppose that you have an array of numbers corresponding to a single row of spreadsheet data. That array might contain the following values:

312	352	426	472
0	1	2	3

The values of those elements just happen to be the number of points accumulated by the houses at Hogwarts in the final chapter of *Harry Potter and the Sorcerer's Stone* (or *Harry Potter and the Philosopher's Stone* for English-speaking readers outside North America)—just before Professor Dumbledore makes some final adjustments. A spreadsheet program would give you the opportunity to graph those values in various ways. The following diagrams, for example, show that set of data graphed as a bar graph and as a pie chart:

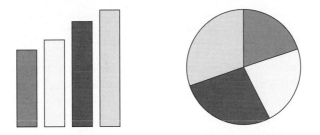

If you use a spreadsheet program, you can add both of these charts to your spreadsheet in such a way that updating the spreadsheet automatically updates both of the graphs. In this case, the spreadsheet acts as the model, and the two graphs represent views.

Rather than try to implement pieces of a spreadsheet, it is easier to embed these graphs in an interactive application of the sort described in Chapter 10. The control bar for the application contains a **JTextField** into which the user can enter four integers representing the number of house points for the four Hogwarts houses in alphabetical order: Gryffindor, Hufflepuff, Ravenclaw, and Slytherin. The control bar also contains a **JButton** to update the graphs. The initial configuration of the program therefore looks like this:

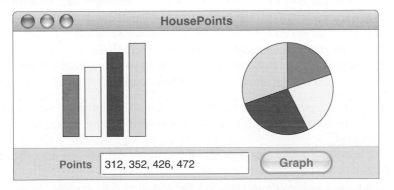

When you click the **Graph** button, the **HousePoints** program reads the numbers from the **JTextField** and updates both graphs. Thus, when Professor Dumbledore decides that he has "a few last-minute points to dish out," Gryffindor ends up with

170 additional points. If you change the first value in the **JTextField** and then click the **Graph** button, the display will change as follows:

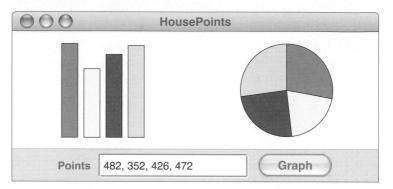

If you want to implement this program using the model/view/controller pattern, you need to define several classes beyond the **HousePoints** code itself. First, you need a **HousePointsModel** class that keeps track of the number of points for each house. The information for all the houses consists of an array of four integers. The **HousePointsModel** class should include methods such as

public void setHousePoints(int[] points)

which sets the internal data to the given array, and

public int[] getHousePoints()

which retrieves the stored data so that the views can determine what values to display. In addition, the model must keep track of the views that need to be notified when a user makes a change to the data. The **HousePointsModel** class should therefore export a method

public void addView(HousePointsView view)

that adds a new value to an internal list of views. Whenever the controller calls **setHousePoints**, each of these views will be notified of the change.

The **HousePointsView** class is an abstract class with two concrete subclasses for the two types of graphs: **BarGraphView** and **PieGraphView**. Each of these classes supports an **update** method that reconstructs the picture in accord with the current data from the model. The sequence of events that triggers the update looks like this:

1. The user enters new data in the **JTextField** at the bottom of the window and clicks the **Graph** button. These interactors represent the controller portion of the model.
2. The controller calls **setHousePoints** on the model, passing the new array of values as a parameter.
3. The model updates its internal storage and then calls **update** on each of its views, passing the model as a parameter.
4. Each view calls **getHousePoints** on the model to retrieve the new data.
5. Each view updates the display to correspond with the new values.

Figure 14-5 shows a possible implementation of the classes **HousePointsModel**, **HousePointsView**, and **LineGraphView**. The implementation of the main program and the **PieChartView** classes are left for you as an exercise.

FIGURE 14-5   Implementation of the program to graph house points

```
/*
 * This class keeps track of the data in the model but is not responsible
 * for the actual display, which is managed by the registered views.
 */
public class HousePointsModel {

/** Creates a new HousePointsModel with no views */
   public HousePointsModel() {
       housePoints = new int[0];
       views = new ArrayList();
   }

/** Adds a view to the list of views for this model */
   public void addView(HousePointsView view) {
       views.add(view);
   }

/** Sets the house points data to the contents of the integer array */
   public void setHousePoints(int[] points) {
       housePoints = new int[points.length];
       for (int i = 0; i < points.length; i++) {
           housePoints[i] = points[i];
       }
       notifyViews();
   }

/** Returns a copy of the internal house points data */
   public int[] getHousePoints() {
       int[] points = new int[housePoints.length];
       for (int i = 0; i < points.length; i++) {
           points[i] = housePoints[i];
       }
       return points;
   }

/* Calls update(this) on every view to reconstruct its display */
   private void notifyViews() {
       for (int i = 0; i < views.size(); i++) {
           HousePointsView view = (HousePointsView) views.get(i);
           view.update(this);
       }
   }

/* Private instance variables */
   private int[] housePoints;
   private ArrayList views;

}
```

FIGURE 14-5 **Implementation of the program to graph house points** (continued)

```java
import acm.graphics.*;
import java.awt.*;

/**
 * This abstract class defines the operations that any specific view class
 * must support.  Each HousePointsView is a GCompound that responds to update
 * messages from the model.
 */
public abstract class HousePointsView extends GCompound {

/** Creates a new HousePointsView with a given model and size */
    public HousePointsView(double width, double height) {
        background = new GRect(width, height);
        background.setFilled(true);
        background.setColor(Color.WHITE);
    }

/** Each subclass must define a method to create the graph */
    public abstract void createGraph(int[] data);

/** Updates the display image from the model */
    public void update(HousePointsModel model) {
        removeAll();
        add(background);
        createGraph(model.getHousePoints());
    }

/** Returns a color to use for the kth data value */
    public Color getColorForIndex(int k) {
        return COLORS[k % COLORS.length];
    }

/* Private constants */
    private static final Color[] COLORS = {
        Color.RED, Color.YELLOW, Color.BLUE, Color.GREEN,
        Color.PINK, Color.CYAN, Color.MAGENTA, Color.ORANGE
    };

/* Private instance variables */
    private GRect background;
}
```

☞

FIGURE 14-5 Implementation of the program to graph house points (continued)

```java
import acm.graphics.*;

/**
 * This class represents a concrete implementation of the
 * GraphView class that builds a bar chart.  The chart is
 * scaled so that the maximum value fills the vertical space.
 */
public class BarGraphView extends HousePointsView {

/** Creates a new BarGraphView */
    public BarGraphView(double width, double height) {
        super(width, height);
    }

/** Arranges the data as a set of bars */
    public void createGraph(int[] data) {
        int n = data.length;
        double max = maxIntArray(data);
        if (max == 0) return;
        double sep = (getWidth() - n * BAR_WIDTH) / (n + 1);
        for (int i = 0; i < n; i++) {
            double height = data[i] / max * getHeight();
            double x = i * (BAR_WIDTH + sep);
            double y = getHeight() - height;
            GRect bar = new GRect(x, y, BAR_WIDTH, height);
            bar.setFilled(true);
            bar.setFillColor(getColorForIndex(i));
            add(bar);
        }
    }

/* Returns the maximum value of an integer array (or 0 if empty) */
    private int maxIntArray(int[] array) {
        if (array.length == 0) return 0;
        int largest = array[0];
        for (int i = 1; i < array.length; i++) {
            largest = Math.max(largest, array[i]);
        }
        return largest;
    }

/* Private constants */
    private static final double BAR_WIDTH = 20;

}
```

Summary

This chapter offers short introductions to four interesting topics—recursion, concurrency, networking, and design patterns—that you are certain to come across if you continue studying computer science. The important points covered in this chapter include:

- Recursion is the process of solving a problem by breaking it down into subproblems of the same form. Many practical problems are particularly well suited to recursive solutions, which proves to be a powerful tool in those domains.
- The first steps in developing a recursive solution consist of (1) identifying *simple cases* for which the answer is easily determined and (2) finding a *recursive decomposition* that breaks the program down into simpler problems that you can solve by applying the same method.
- When you begin to adopt recursive techniques, it is important to learn to "think recursively." In particular, you need to have confidence that your methods will work correctly whenever they are applied to simpler subproblems. This confidence is called the *recursive leap of faith*.
- In modern computing applications, there are usually many different activities going on simultaneously. In computer science, this type of simultaneous process is usually called *concurrency*. Java includes extensive support for concurrency, particularly at the level of *threads*, which are concurrent processes that occur within the same program.
- Partly because Java was developed at a time of growing interest in the World-Wide Web, the language includes extensive support for network-based programming. Most of these facilities are in the **java.net** package.
- Programming patterns are becoming increasingly important as tools for creating applications, particularly since the publication of *Design Patterns* in 1995. If you continue your study of computer science, you will certainly have occasion to explore this area in more detail.
- One especially important pattern is called *model/view/controller,* which offers a useful structure for designing user interfaces.

Review questions

1. What is the fundamental characteristic of a recursive process?

2. What mathematical function does the following method compute:

```
private int mystery(int x) {
   if (x == 0) {
      return 1;
   } else {
      return 2 * mystery(x - 1);
   }
}
```

3. When you design a recursive solution, what two aspects of the problem do you have to identify?

4. What is meant by the *recursive leap of faith?* Why is this concept important to you as a programmer?

5. What is the difference between a thread and the more traditional notion of a process?

6. What package contains most of Java's library facilities for working with the World-Wide Web?

7. In terms of its significance for modern object-oriented programming, what is the Gang of Four?

8. What is the division of labor between the model and the view in the model/view/controller pattern?

Programming exercises

1. Exercise 9 in Chapter 4 introduced you to the Fibonacci series, in which the first two terms are 0 and 1 and every subsequent term is the sum of the two preceding terms. The series therefore begins with

$$
\begin{aligned}
F_0 &= 0 \\
F_1 &= 1 \\
F_2 &= 1 \quad (F_0 + F_1) \\
F_3 &= 2 \quad (F_1 + F_2) \\
F_4 &= 3 \quad (F_2 + F_3) \\
F_5 &= 5 \quad (F_3 + F_4) \\
F_6 &= 8 \quad (F_4 + F_5)
\end{aligned}
$$

and continues in the same fashion for all subsequent terms. Write a recursive implementation of the method `Fib(n)` that returns the nth Fibonacci number. Your implementation must depend only on the relationship between the terms in the sequence and may not use any iterative constructs such as `for` and `while`.

2. The year: 1777; the setting: General Washington's camp somewhere in the colonies. You have been assigned a dangerous reconnaissance mission: to evaluate the amount of ammunition available to the British for use with their large cannon that has been shelling the Revolutionary forces. Fortunately for you, the British (being neat and orderly) have stacked the cannonballs into a single pyramid-shaped stack with one cannonball at the top sitting on top of a square composed of four cannonballs sitting on top of a square composed of nine cannonballs, and so forth. Unfortunately, however, the British soldiers are also vigilant and manage to spot you after you have only had a chance to count the number of layers in the pyramid. Luckily, though, you do manage to scramble back to your own troops.

Even though computers will not be invented for at least 150 years, your mission in this problem is to write a recursive function **Cannonball** which takes as its argument the number of layers in the pyramid and returns the number of cannonballs therein. Your function must operate recursively and must not use any iterative constructs, such as **while** or **for**.

3. Exercise 10 in chapter 9 showed how you can use Pascal's triangle as a way to visualize the combinations function $C(n, k)$, which was itself introduced in Chapter 5. As you can see from the diagram of Pascal's triangle on page 342, every entry in the table is either along one of the diagonal edges, in which case it has the value 1, or inside the triangle, in which case the value is always the sum of the two entries above it, diagonally to the left and right.

    Use this insight into the structure of Pascal's triangle to write a recursive implementation of the **combinations** method that uses no loops, no multiplication, and no calls to **factorial**.

4. Exercise 6 in Chapter 8 defines a *palindrome* as a string that reads identically backward and forward, such as **"level"** or **"noon"**. For that exercise, you were asked to write a predicate method **isPalindrome(str)** that tests whether **str** is a palindrome. Although at the time, you would have used an iterative strategy to solve the problem, you can also write the **isPalindrome** method recursively. The recursive insight is that long palindromes must contain shorter palindromes in their interior. For example, the string **"level"** consists of the palindrome **"eve"** with the one-character string **"l"** at each end. Use this insight to write a recursive implementation of **isPalindrome**.

5. In almost any computer science course that covers recursion, you will learn about a nineteenth-century puzzle that stands as the archetypal recursive problem. This puzzle, which goes by the name *Tower of Hanoi,* consists of three towers, one of which contains a set of disks—usually eight in commercial versions of the puzzle—arranged in decreasing order of size as you move from the base of the tower to its top, as illustrated in the following diagram:

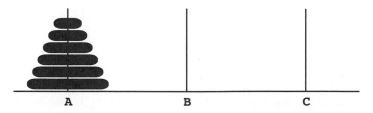

The goal of the puzzle is to move the entire set of disks from Tower A to Tower B, following these rules:

    a) You can only move one disk at a time.
    b) You can never place a larger disk on top of a smaller one.

Write a program to display the individual steps required to transfer a tower of N disks from Tower A to Tower B. For example, your program should generate the following output when N is 3:

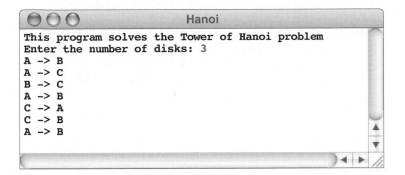

The key to solving this problem is to find a decomposition of the problem that allows you to transform the original Tower of Hanoi problem into a simpler problem of the same form.

6. One of the reasons that fractals have generated so much interest is that they turn out to be useful in some surprising practical contexts. For example, the most successful techniques for drawing computer images of mountains and certain other landscape features involve using fractal geometry.

    As a simple example of where this issue comes up, consider the problem of connecting two points **A** and **B** with a fractal that looks like a coastline on a map. The simplest possible strategy would be to draw a straight line between the two points:

A ——————————————————————— B

This is the order-0 coastline, which represents the base case of the recursion.

Of course, a real coastline will have small peninsulas or inlets somewhere along its length, so you would expect a realistic drawing of a coastline to jut in or out occasionally. As a first approximation, you could replace the straight line with precisely the same fractal line used to create the snowflake fractal in the program described in the section on "Graphical recursion" earlier in the chapter, as follows:

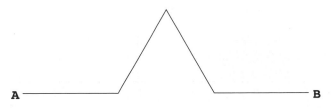

This process produces the order-1 coastline. However, in order to give the feeling of a traditional coastline, it is important for the triangular wedge in this line sometimes to point up and sometimes down, with equal probability.

If you then replace each of the straight line segments in the order-1 fractal with a fractal line in a random direction, you get an order-2 coastline, which might look like this:

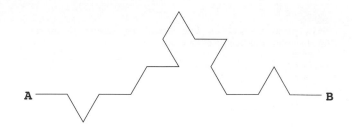

Continuing this process eventually results in a drawing that conveys a remarkably realistic sense, as in this order-5 coastline:

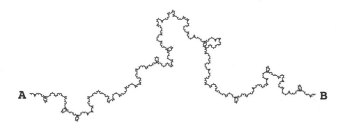

Although this coastline seems similar in many respects to the snowflake fractal from the text, the fact that it is not closed makes it impossible to use a **GPolygon** as a subclass for the figure as a whole.

7. Modify the **AnimatedSquare** class in Figure 14-2 so that the red square continues to move in the random way it does in the original example, but the green square always moves at the same speed directly toward the current position of the red square. To do so, you will need to enhance the definition of **AnimatedSquare** so that the two squares can communicate.

8. Complete the implementation of the **HousePoints** application in Figure 14-5 by implementing the main program and the **PieChartView** class.

9. Go to your library or bookstore and look at a copy of *Design Patterns* by Erich Gamma, Richard Helm, Ralph Johnson, and John Vlissides. Look through the various patterns and find one that appears as if it might be useful. Write a simple application that illustrates the use of that pattern.

INDEX

- Revision type casting
- go over moving graphics
- deliver string
- For Karel: remember to repeat the operation inside while loop
    once more outside loop.
    ```
    while (condition) {
        method ();
    }
    method ();
    ```
- Standard format for animation code:
    ```
    while (condition ()) {
        updateGraphics ();
        performChecks ();
        pause (PAUSE_TIME);
    }
    ```
- Type casting
```
double y = 5.9;
  int x = (int) y;   // x = 5

    x = 7;
    y = x        // y = 7.0
    x = y        // error : correct x = (int) y
```

- Import:
    ```
    acm. program. *      Console (always).
    acm. graphics. *     Graphics
    acm. util. *         RandomGen. and Tokenizers
    java. awt. event. *  Mouse events.
    ```